Prophecy
in
Early Christianity
AND THE
Ancient Mediterranean World

DAVID E. AUNE

WILLIAM B. EERDMANS PUBLISHING COMPANY
Grand Rapids, Michigan

Copyright © 1983 by William B. Eerdmans Publishing Company
255 Jefferson Ave. SE, Grand Rapids, MI 49503

Library of Congress Cataloging in Publication Data

Aune, David E., 1939-
Prophecy in early Christianity and the ancient Mediterranean world.

Bibliography: p. 445.
Includes indexes.
1. Prophecy (Christianity) — History of doctrines — Early church, ca. 30-600.
2. Prophecy — History.
I. Title.
BR115.P8A96 1983   200.1'5   83-8966
ISBN 0-8028-3584-8

CONTENTS

Chapter 3 The Form and Function of Greco-Roman Oracles   49

Chapter 4 Ancient Israelite Prophecy   81

Chapter 11 The Form and Content of Early Christian Prophecy: Part II   291

PREFACE

This study is written from the perspective that early Christianity must be understood within the setting of the ancient Mediterranean world, without unduly emphasizing the Israelite-Jewish heritage of early Christians nor neglecting the dominant Greco-Roman culture within which both Judaism and early Christianity grew and changed. There is an enormous amount of secondary literature on various aspects of the subjects covered in this book, and I must confess that I have not mastered that literature. Since the bulk of the manuscript (apart from the first and last chapters) was completed in June of 1979, many important studies have appeared. I have been able to utilize some of them, but not all. (Professor M. Eugene Boring's recent book *Sayings of the Risen Jesus: Christian Prophecy in the Synoptic Tradition* [New York, 1982], for example, is a book I know about but have not yet seen.)

Most of the basic research for the book was done in the fall of 1977 during a subsidized leave of absence from Saint Xavier College. Those portions of Chapters 2 and 3 that relate to Plutarch are largely based on research carried out during the summer of 1976 with the aid of a stipend from the National Endowment for the Humanities. The final chapter was written during the fall of 1982 at the University of Trondheim (Norway), where I am now completing a year as a Fulbright guest professor in the Department of Religious Studies and the Department of Classics, and I want to express my appreciation particularly to Professor Peder Borgen (Religious Studies) and his colleagues and to Professor Øivind Andersen (Classics) for their friendship and scholarly advice. Portions of the final chapter were presented as lectures at the University of Edinburgh (New College), where Douglas Templeton and his colleagues made my visit very pleasant, and at the University of Lund, where Professor Birger Gerhardsson and Docent Rene Kieffer were gracious hosts. Portions of Chapter 8 relating to the Apocalypse of John were presented in lectures at King's College, the University of Aberdeen (where my hosts were Professor I. Howard Marshall and Professor Robin Barbour), at the University of Århus (where Dosent Poul Nepper-Christensen and his colleagues were helpful in every way), at the Theological Faculty of the University of Oslo, where Dean Nils Bloch-Hoell arranged a very pleasant morning, and at Baptistenes Teologiske Seminar (the Baptist Theological Seminary) in Oslo, where Rektor Nils Engelsen and his faculty extended every courtesy.

In addition, a number of scholars have given me the benefit of their advice and criticism by reading and making suggestions of various portions of the manuscript. These include Professors Arthur W. H. Adkins (University of Chicago), Hans Dieter Betz (University of Chicago), M. Eugene Boring (Philips University), Charles Carlston

(Andover Newton Theological Seminary), Gerald F. Hawthorne (Wheaton College), Jackson Hershbel (University of Minnesota), and Dr. Howard Teeple (Chicago State University and the Religion and Ethics Institute). Their innocent involvement means that they must not share the blame for the book's deficiencies.

Abbreviations for journals and ancient literature follow the style of the *Journal of Biblical Literature*, 95 (1976), 331-46. Abbreviations of Greek literature follow Liddell-Scott-Jones, *Greek-English Lexicon*, pp. xvi-xxxviii for the most part, though some of their very short abbreviations have been lengthened. Abbreviations of treatises in Plutarch's *Moralia* follow the system in H. D. Betz (ed.), *Plutarch's Theological Writings and Early Christian Literature* (Leiden, 1975). In the index of passages all references to ancient literature are written out in full.

Finally, I want to dedicate this book to my four children, Karl Erik, Kristofer, Kurt, and Karen, without whom life would not nearly be so enjoyable and adventuresome. However, they have paid dearly for this honor. They have allowed their mother and me to take them to Norway, where they had to learn a new language within a very few weeks. They have helped to compile the enormous index which concludes the book. And finally, they have promised that I never need play Monopoly with them again.

Trondheim, Norway
May 1983

D. E. AUNE

1 | THE STUDY OF EARLY CHRISTIAN PROPHECY

I. INTRODUCTION

During the last ten years NT scholars have exhibited a renewed interest in the neglected subject of early Christian prophecy.[1] Most of the research has had an appropriately narrow focus on very specific problems and issues. Some of these studies have advanced our knowledge of early Christian prophecy to the point where a new synthesis of the present state of research is appropriate. The purpose of this book is not only to present a reconstruction of the phenomenon of early Christian prophecy informed by recent research, but also to suggest new frameworks within which to understand the subject better. Since 1947 at least five important general treatments of NT or (more broadly conceived) early Christian prophecy have appeared, each produced by a reputable scholar. These discussions have served the useful task of interacting with the contemporary studies on the subject within the framework of an overall conception of Christian prophecy distinctive to each author. A general synthetic presentation of early Christian prophecy makes it necessary to develop a conception of the subject as a whole, a conception which inevitably influences the manner in which various constituent features of the phenomenon are understood. In this introductory chapter, I propose first to review and critique each of the five general presentations of early Christian prophecy written since 1947, then I will isolate the more important issues and problems which will be dealt with in the remaining chapters of the book.

II. PREVIOUS SURVEYS OF EARLY CHRISTIAN PROPHECY

When H. A. Guy published a revision of his thesis entitled *New Testament Prophecy: Its Origin and Significance* in 1947, he described the book as a contribution toward a "somewhat neglected" subject. In this relatively slim volume the author devotes a very modest section to "Prophetism in the First Century Church" (pp. 90-118). In successive chapters the author deals with "Hebrew Prophetism," "John the Baptist," "The Prophetic Consciousness of Jesus," "Prophetism in the First-Century Church," "Prophetism in Contemporary Religion," and "Prophetism — Hebrew, Greek, and Christian." The focus of the book is not so much NT prophecy as it is the superior and ultimate form of prophecy represented by Jesus of Nazareth. In effect the book is a statement of faith in which theologically laden concerns and presuppositions are lightly seasoned with a mild strain of historical criticism. Indicative of the author's approach is the last sentence in the chapter on Hebrew prophetism where he suggests that "the highest level is not yet reached."[2] At the conclusion of the book, in a discussion of reasons for the decline of NT prophecy, Guy intimates that Christian prophecy died out because the pinnacle reached by Jesus could never again be attained: "There are hints in the Gospels that Jesus himself regarded the prophetic order as closed, because he saw himself as its culmination."[3]

The book is unevenly written and argued. While arguments for some views are discussed *ad nauseam,* other questionable views are assumed rather than argued. The discussion of Hebrew prophetism focuses on an issue dear to the heart of many biblical theologians — the uniqueness of Israelite religion as exhibited in the OT. For Guy this resolves into an original, preconquest Israelite prophetic tradition of the lonely seer (who receives visual and auditory messages from Yahweh and possesses second sight and hearing) that is nearly corrupted by the nasty Canaanite prophetic tradition of ecstatic possession practiced by wandering bands of *nebi'im.* The classical prophets, of course, were the true successors of the early seers of Israel, and did not derive from the primitive, ecstatic *nebi'im.* Guy confidently schematized this development (dependent, to be sure, on the conclusions of an earlier generation of OT scholarship):

> If we bear in mind the distinction of the stages in the evolution of Hebrew prophetism, it would appear that the manifestations of the prophetic spirit among the Hebrews before the entry into Canaan are more akin to the gift of the seers and that the ecstatic possession of the *nebi'im* represents a retrograde step, when the Hebrews came into contact with Canaanite life and religion. In one sense it may be said that the Hebrews borrowed prophetism from the Canaanites, but in a deeper sense prophetism was native to Israel and, as we shall see, the genuine Hebrew type finally triumphed over that which owed its distinctive characteristics to foreign influence.[4]

This statement is revealing both for its naive use of the adjective "genuine" (for which the author frequently substitutes "true"), and for its assumption that syncretistic elements are woven into a people's experience in such a manner that various "foreign" strands can be disentangled from the braid with relative ease.

In an extensive treatment of John the Baptist, Guy presents a very detailed and critical discussion of research up to World War II, and concludes that "John is rightly regarded as the successor of the Old Testament prophets and the last of their line."[5] In the structural center of the book, the chapter on "The Prophetic Consciousness of Jesus," the author begins with a lengthy discussion of the prophetic characteristics found in the portrait of Jesus in the gospels. These include: (1) Certain outward features of Jesus' ministry which recall characteristics of OT prophets, such as his authority, his use of "I say to you" as an equivalent to the messenger formula "thus says the Lord," and certain symbolic actions such as the Last Supper, the cursing of the fig tree, the feeding of the multitude, and the entry into Jerusalem. (2) Jesus' teaching is prophetic in both form and content, i.e. he spoke in parables, in short sayings, and in poetic form, and he bore a prophetic message to his nation. (3) The insight and emphases of great prophets are found in Jesus, such as his discernment of human character, his prophetic insight into contemporary political, social, and international conditions, and his predictions in which the historical perspective is foreshortened. Guy then concludes, after discussing the applications of the title "prophet" to Jesus in the gospels:

> There is thus abundant evidence to show that Jesus was popularly regarded as a great prophet and that he himself accepted this designation. The passages which have been quoted do not bear out the contention of R. Bultmann, that Jesus was characterized as a prophet on the basis of his eschatological purpose alone. It was rather the whole impression of his purpose, work and person which gave him the right to this title.[6]

Here the chief difficulty with Guy's presentation lies in his mode of argumentation. The "prophetic" status of Jesus is argued on the basis of how twentieth-century biblical scholars read the OT, rather than on the conceptions of "prophet" which were current in late Second Temple Judaism.

In discussing prophetism in the first-century church, the author moves quickly and superficially through Acts and the Corinthian situation, which he characterizes by concluding that there is no suggestion that Christian prophets held official positions or formed a separate category of church leaders (except possibly at Antioch, Acts 13:1). Christians at Corinth were "infected with the atmosphere of their environment."[7] In characterizing the Christian prophetic movement Guy comes to three conclusions: (1) "The solitary prophet is a rare, almost unknown figure,"[8] since the Christian community is the dwelling place of the Spirit and spiritual gifts are exercised in the community. (2) According to Paul prophecy is valuable for edification, exhortation, and consolation. (3) There was a close association between Christian prophetism and apocalyptic expectation. The last point is a rather significant one, since many German and American NT scholars tend to place prophecy and apocalyptic farther apart.

Finally, in two concluding chapters Guy considers prophetism in contemporary religion by surveying early Judaism, Roman religion, Greek religion, and the mystery religions. He concludes:

> The parallel between these movements in contemporary religion and the spirit which manifested itself in early Christianity is by no means complete. Ultimately no place can be found in the heathen *Weltanschauung* for the New Testament apostle and the Christian prophet who speaks with the authentic accent. Above all, there is no contemporary figure which approaches that of "Jesus, the prophet, from Nazareth of Galilee."[9]

Thus the author concludes with the theme that dominates the book, the prophetic status of Jesus:

> In his words and his works, as portrayed in the Gospels, Jesus appears as a true prophet. He shared many of the characteristics of the Old Testament prophets and seers, but transcended them all.[10]

Guy has been concerned throughout his book with several main issues. One such issue is the prophetic status of Jesus as the culmination of classical Hebrew prophecy, based on the tradition of the independent seers of ancient Israel rather than on the ecstatic associations of Canaanite-influenced *nebi'im*. Like the errant *nebi'im*, all the prophetic types of the Greco-Roman world cannot be compared to the prophetic status of Jesus. With Fascher, Guy accepts the notion that early Christian prophecy is morally oriented and functions to exhort, comfort, and edify. Here he accepts Paul's assessment, though Paul may be describing how prophecy ought to function rather than how it does function. Early Christian prophets and prophecy itself receive minimal treatment by Guy, perhaps suggesting that the book itself is inappropriately titled.

Twelve years after the appearance of H. A. Guy's book, the fascicle of the *Theologisches Wörterbuch zum Neuen Testament* containing the lengthy article on "*prophētēs,* etc.," appeared. The English version, translated in volume VI of the *Theological Dictionary of the New Testament,* appeared in 1968, pp. 781–861. As in all articles in *TDNT,* this one is oriented around a word-group regarded as a "concept," i.e. that of *prophētēs* and related terms. In this article the pagan Greek evidence is discussed by H. Krämer, the OT data by R. Rendtorff, the early Jewish material by R. Meyer, and the NT and early Christian sources by G. Friedrich in what must be regarded as the focal section. For the most part Krämer's discussion is very informative, and summarizes a great deal of useful information from both primary and secondary sources. He is, of course, bound to the usage of *prophētēs,* which proves a considerable limitation when he must jump from the Greek oracle prophet of the fifth century B.C. to Alexander of Abonuteichos in the second century A.D. He errs in portraying the Delphic Pythia as "stirred to mantic frenzy,"[11] for even though there is little evidence for such a view it is very widely held.[12] Krämer is properly cautious about describing the function and relationship between the Delphic Pythia and the prophets of Delphi. Although Krämer claims that Alexander of Abonuteichos' production of spontaneous or unsolicited oracles is an innovation, a number of Delphic oracles are preserved which appear to have been unsolicited.[13] He never deals with the problem of the authenticity of Greek oracles, nor with the problem of their literary use, form, and modifications which were introduced in successive literary settings. A theological dimension is injected into the discussion only toward the conclusion, when the author makes some loaded statements, such as "The oracle prophets and prophetesses of Greece are chosen for their ministry by men and not by the god,"[14] or the fact that the oracle prophet responds only when consulted, or that inspiration is "induced by human initiative."[15] His claim that the *prophētēs* word-group is "marked both by solemnity and also by lack of content"[16] is semantic nonsense.

The portion of the article by Rendtorff[17] on the use of *nabi'im* is on the whole excellent; the author surveys his subject with obvious expertise, yet exposes the critical issues upon which scholars have not enough solid evidence to make confident judgments. The article on *prophētēs* in early Judaism by R. Meyer has become something of a classic.[18] Dealing essentially with the Second Temple period, Meyer discusses the "problem" of contemporary prophecy in terms of the nonrabbinic and rabbinic literary witnesses. Meyer uses the entire article to argue against the common opinion that the Spirit of prophecy ceased activity with the last of the OT prophets, Haggai, Zechariah, and Malachi, only to become active again at the beginning of early Christianity. Meyer first considers the proof texts commonly used to support this view (Zech. 13:26; Ps. 74:9; 1 Macc. 4:46; 9:27; 14:41; etc.) and shows how they cannot be used legitimately for this purpose. He notes the tendency of the rabbis to restrict prophecy to a past era and to regard themselves as successors of the prophets, whom they regard as essentially interpreters of Torah. Meyer then turns to discuss the historical evidence for manifestations of prophecy during the Hellenistic and Roman periods, and finds a wealth of information regarding a great variety of prophetic figures, messianic prophets, the notion of a prophetic priesthood, the conception of a ruler with threefold powers (including prophecy), etc. Meyer leaves little doubt in the mind of the reader that prophetic phenomena, though characterized by a bewildering variety of manifestations, flourished during the late Second Temple period.

The focal article is, of course, G. Friedrich's discussion of prophets and prophecy in the NT, which has become a standard treatment of the subject.[19] Characteristically, Friedrich provides the reader with a succinct yet informed discussion of the subject with appropriate references to primary and secondary literature. Friedrich's concerns, however, are not limited to a discussion of prophets and prophecy as historical and literary phenomena; he provides a distinctive theological framework within which he evaluates the evidence. He defines a Christian prophet as "essentially a proclaimer of God's Word,"[20] a definition which he expands:

> Primitive Christian prophecy is the inspired speech of charismatic preachers through whom God's plan of salvation for the world and the community and His will for the life of individual Christians are made known.[21]

He goes on to observe that Christian prophets are gifted leaders of the congregation (Rom. 12:6; 1 Cor. 12:10, 28-29; Eph. 2:20; 3:5; 4:11; Rev. 10:7; 11:18; 16:6; 18:20, 24; 22:9). Basically, however, Friedrich holds that prophecy is not restricted to just a few individuals, for "all are filled with the prophetic spirit."[22] Friedrich compares the NT prophet with his OT counterpart, and concludes that the former does not enjoy the kind of unlimited authority possessed by the latter. The Christian prophet "does not stand above the community; like all the rest he is a member of it."[23] Closest to Jewish prophecy is the prophet of the Apocalypse, for there can be no testing of his sayings, which are attested by none other than God himself. "Criticism of what he says is impossible."[24] Friedrich strays into an impossible set of choices when he suggests that "It is not always possible to make a sharp distinction between ecstasy, inspiration by Spirit-possession, and prophetic revelation."[25] This is the closest he, or the other authors we are considering, comes to articulating a typology of possession; this one, however, makes little sense and is developed in a significant manner by Friedrich.

Friedrich contrasts the Pauline evidence for Christian prophets to that of the Apocalypse. In the Pauline congregations the prophet "is not characterized by visions and auditions which transport him out of the world."[26] John, by contrast, is more an apocalyptic seer than a primitive Christian prophet. Friedrich summarizes a basic distinction between the prophets depicted in the Pauline letters and those of the Apocalypse of John:

> For the prophets of the Pauline Epistles exhortation is paramount and predictions are mentioned only incidentally; in Rev. prediction is central and the exhortations are more or less on the margin.[27]

He characterizes the Pauline prophet as one who is completely in control of his senses and the exercise of his prophetic gifts. "The responsible personhood of the prophet remains intact even though the whole man with his understanding and will stands under the operation of the Spirit."[28]

Friedrich has presented a very structured and comprehensive portrait of prophets and prophecy in early Christianity, though a number of the issues on which he focuses need further comment. Friedrich does not separate statements describing the phenomena of Christian prophecy reflected in the primary sources (presumably with some historical value) from statements about prophecy made by Paul and others. The Pauline letters in particular contain many prescriptive statements relating to the practice and function of prophets and prophecy that, while they certainly reflect Paul's opinions and indicate the major contours of his ideology of Christian prophecy, must be used only with caution in reconstructing the historical reality. The notion that early Christianity was conscious of the Spirit dwelling in the midst of the community so that the gift of prophecy, strictly speaking, was not and could not be monopolized by particular individuals, is a theological rather than a historical statement. Further, Friedrich's views on the similarities between John the Apocalyptist and OT prophets on the one hand and the contrast between John and early Christian prophets on the other is a view which cannot be substantiated, though it has become influential.[29]

The next major contribution to the general understanding of NT prophecy was the monograph-length article by É. Cothenet, "Prophétisme dans le Nouveau Testament," which appeared in *Dictionnaire de la Bible, Supplement,* vol. 8 (1972), cols. 1222-1337, but which was doubtless completed several years earlier. This article, which is "genre-bound" in the sense that it provides an extensive and generally objective overview of the subject representing the current state of scholarship, is nevertheless a first-rate achievement. The author discusses, in order, the following topics: (1) prophetic survivals in early Judaism, (2) John the Baptist, (3) prophets of the first Christian community, (4) Christian prophets according to the major Pauline letters, (5) apostles and prophets in the captivity letters, (6) the struggle against false prophets, (7) the Spirit of prophecy in the Johannine corpus, and (8) the decline of prophecy. In every section of the discussion Cothenet's bibliography is up-to-date (ca. 1968), and he very often enters into dialogue with major scholarly contributions to the subject.

The author provides a thorough discussion of prophetic survivals in early Judaism (following Meyer), though he suggests that the later consciousness of the Christian church as having received the Spirit and a corresponding new knowledge of God is unique and without parallel.[30] Cothenet's discussion of John the Baptist is exceptionally long and detailed,[31] a fact perhaps accounted for by the absence of an article on "Jean-Baptiste" elsewhere in the *DBSupp.* John's costume, ascetic life, and station in the desert are all self-consciously prophetic, and he warned his contemporaries of an imminent eschatological catastrophe. "John's preaching," claims Cothenet, "is nourished by exhortations of the prophets more than by the visions of the apocalyptists."[32] Surprisingly, the author does not follow this up by a treatment of Jesus' prophetic role, though aspects of this subject are treated under discussions of each of the gospels. In discussing the prophets of the first Christian community, Cothenet carefully describes the theories of Bultmann and Käsemann that prophets produced sayings of the risen Lord that later became assimilated to the traditional sayings of the earthly Jesus. He carefully discusses the phenomena of prophets and prophecy in Matthew,[33] then Luke and Acts.[34] Cothenet suggests that the prophetic features of the Lukan infancy stories can be used to reconstruct the liturgical life of the first Christian community.[35] The Roman Catholic theological orientation of the author is evident in the conclusion to this section: Jesus is the prophet par excellence, and Christian prophecy is connected to the promise of Christ to send the Holy Spirit to his disciples. Of these, the Twelve hold first place. Prophetism needs to take account of the apostolic tradition. Bultmann errs by regarding the Twelve as an abstraction (in contrast to Gerhardsson), and Käsemann's theory of sentences of holy law is dubious.[36] In Cothenet's words:

> The role of the prophet in the community cannot be considered without taking account, on the one hand, of the active presence of those whom Jesus had called as a point of departure for eschatological Israel and, on the other hand, of the

importance of the tradition in the community which proclaims that its savior is Jesus of Nazareth.[37]

In considering Christian prophets in the major Pauline letters, the author places a great deal of emphasis on the "traditional list" produced by Paul in 1 Cor. 12; he is very receptive to the threefold charismatic offices proposed by Harnack as complimentary to the local hierarchical structure of bishop, elder, and deacon. Cothenet enters into debate at this point only with H. Küng, who wants to place the more original charismatic order in opposition to the hierarchical order.[38] The function of prophecy in the major Pauline letters, concludes Cothenet, is edification,[39] exhortation, and consolation.[40] After a survey of prophecy in the captivity letters and the struggle against false prophets in the Pastorals and the Catholic letters, where the main theme is the close relationship between charisma and hierarchy, the author turns to the Johannine corpus,[41] i.e. the letters and the Apocalypse of John (excluding the Gospel, considered only in terms of the prophetic role of the Paraclete). In discussing the Apocalypse Cothenet shares the basic perspective of Bornkamm and Satake:

> One can deduce nothing from the Apocalypse concerning the concrete activity of the prophets and, as Bornkamm has seen, the Apocalypse reflects the archaic situation of a minuscule group of Christians.[42]

The Apocalypse, particularly toward the end, suggests the liturgical function of prophecy, a factor which Cothenet frequently emphasizes. He concludes his discussion of the Apocalypse with this observation:

> Proceeding from the witness of Jesus, raised by the Spirit of God, the prophetic mission of the Church in the course of the centuries is connected to the witness of those who have been constituted "apostles and prophets" and form the sure foundation of the new Jerusalem (Apoc. 21:14; cf. Eph. 2:20).[43]

The article concludes with a brief discussion of the decline of Christian prophecy in which some of the writings grouped in the Apostolic Fathers are briefly considered. Several reasons for the decline are suggested; in harmony with the leitmotiv throughout the article on the prophetic role in transmitting authentic apostolic tradition, Cothenet proposes that the prophetic gift belonged to the period of foundation, while the construction of the edifice itself belonged to a different type of gifted individual. Yet prophecy has not really ceased, for it is the continuing task of the church to preach in spite of the opposition of the audience.

One of the more significant contributions to our subject in recent years has been T. M. Crone's *Early Christian Prophecy: A Study of Its Origin and Function,* a book which has unfortunately had very limited distribution and is difficult to obtain. Methodologically the book is superior to all the other general presentations we are reviewing, a feature to which we shall refer more than once below. Although very well written, the book occasionally lapses into "dissertationese," a characteristic reflecting its origin as a doctoral dissertation at a Roman Catholic faculty of a German university by an American priest. Recognizing the importance of setting early Christian prophecy in its appropriate history-of-religions setting, Crone devotes half the book to a consideration of "Prophecy in the Contemporary World of Early Christianity,"[44] in which he includes such topics as prophecy in Greek religion,[45] Judaism,[46] John the Baptist, and Jesus.[47] The author's discussion of Greek religion is helpful in that he isolates two important prophetic types, oracle prophets (the only figures commonly labeled *prophētai*), and the Hellenistic wandering preacher. In his treatment of Judaism Crone does not fall into the common error of homogenizing the variety within late Second Temple Judaism, particularly in the matter of the later rabbinic view that prophecy had ceased. The self-designation "prophet" was frequently used, claims Crone, by prophetic figures in the Jewish freedom movement. To his credit the author has a balanced discussion of Jewish apocalyptic in which he sees both continuity and discontinuity with classical Hebrew prophecy. He nevertheless sees a lack of "prophetic consciousness" (i.e. few references to the Spirit) on the part of the apocalyptists. Further, the apocalyptists prepared for revelations, which were regularly received in dreams or visions or through past writings, while classical prophets received revelations spontaneously. Some sections of apocalyptic literature, he claims, could justly be designated prophetic, e.g. 1 Enoch 94:6ff.; Syr. Bar. 13:1ff.; 54:21. Josephus regards prophecy as a kind of ecstatic possession, as does Philo, though the latter makes greater use of more typical Greek terminology for possession phenomena; for both, prophets are largely figures of the past.

According to Crone, John the Baptist is a prophetic type very similar to Jesus ben Hananiah mentioned by Josephus (*Bell.* vi.301), since both are "examples of first century Jewish prophets who preached an imminent eschatological judgment."[48] Jesus of Nazareth too was a popular preacher who, like John, included an eschatological call to repentance.

In discussing NT prophecy specifically Crone devotes separate discussions to evaluating the evidence found in such major witnesses as Acts, Paul, the synoptic gospels, the Apocalypse, and the Didache. Prophecy in Acts

> was considered a standard manifestation of the reception of the Spirit. Prophets existed in Palestine and Syria; and their functions included the prediction of the future, exhortatory preaching, prayer, and the direction of the community.[49]

In Paul prophecy was a "form of preaching whose purpose was exhortation, admonishment, judgement, and instruction,"[50] primarily exercised in Christian worship. Prophets had control over their gift, though at Corinth competition between ecstatic prophets caused confusion. Every prophetic utterance was not accepted as genuinely inspired but was subject to judgment.

In discussing prophetic sayings purportedly found in the synoptic gospels Crone concludes that it is probable that Christian prophets are responsible for some sayings attributed to Jesus. However, he judges that "no attempt to single out these prophetic sayings has proved successful."[51]

In the Apocalypse Crone sees two prophetic traditions, one with strong connections to Jewish apocalypticism, represented by the author (who is equal in status with a number of other prophets in his area), and the other exemplified by "Jezebel," who represents a Hellenizing influence in the community. "Both, however, claimed inspiration."[52] Prophets probably constituted a distinguishable group in the communities reflected in the Apocalypse. In the Didache prophets were full-time specialists, most of whom were wandering preachers, but some of whom had settled in local communities. They were preachers who led worship and were especially concerned with the needs of the poor.

Crone concludes his study with a short but carefully formulated discussion of the origins, development, and functions of early Christian (i.e. NT) prophecy. Prophecy in the Palestinian church is influenced by the eschatological prophecy of the Jewish freedom movement:

That such a prophecy existed in the early Church is indicated indirectly by the traditional apocalyptic warnings against false messiahs and false prophets. These references are best understood against the background of the prophetic and messianic claims of the Zealots. And the implication is that they offered competition to the Christian claim. The Christian prophets would have found their counterparts in the prophetic preachers of these false messianic claims.[53]

Even John the Apocalyptist stands in this tradition. The phenomenon of the wandering Christian prophet is first met in the Didache and Matthew (10:41), and has a counterpart in the religious teacher or wandering preacher of popular Hellenistic religion. Further, in the Gentile Christian communities prophecy was not only influenced by Hellenism, it also contributed to the Hellenization of the Church. The one comprehensive function of early Christian prophecy was preaching, particularly exhortation or admonition in its enthusiastic or ecstatic form, teaching, foretelling the future, and second sight. The common setting for this activity was the liturgy. Prophecy was a function rather than an office.

Crone's primary contribution to the study of early Christian prophecy is the case he makes for the typological similarity between prophets in the Jewish liberation movement and some early Christian prophets with an apocalyptic orientation on the one hand, and the similarity between Hellenistic wandering preachers and other types of early Christian prophets, most notably those described in the Didache, on the other. Indeed, his conception of the early Christian prophet is a blend of the eschatological orientation and inspired prophetic consciousness of the prophets of the Jewish liberation movement combined with the hortatory and admonitory emphases and even peripatetic life-style of the wandering Hellenistic moral philosophers. Aside from this the author synthesizes an enormous number of relevant secondary studies, nimbly picking his way through competing views and carefully interpreting primary texts. To his credit Crone does not readily transmit received opinion without a thorough sifting and evaluation of the evidence. Further, he does not attempt to force an artificial differentiation between Hellenistic and early Christian prophecy using the issue of possession phenomena as a criterion. His study is a model of historical investigation with theological tendencies for the most part remarkably absent.

The most recent general treatment of early Christian prophecy is D. Hill's *New Testament Prophecy* (1979). The author's purpose is the presentation of a fresh review of the evidence and recent scholarly research since the publication of H. A. Guy's book in 1947. Hill begins with a chapter devoted to "Matters of Definition and Background," where he proposes that the "functional" approach is best suited to the study of early Christian prophecy. First Hill focuses on those who are explicitly designated prophets in early Christian literature, and forms his definition on that basis:

> Then the group so labelled as "prophets" should be used as a kind of sample-group for the purpose of formulating a working-definition. This core-group will include the prophets mentioned in Acts and the Pauline letters, the book of Revelation, perhaps Mark 13 and parallels and Matthew 7, the Didache, and the Shepherd of Hermas (depending on the dating of these last-mentioned documents): this group has sufficient variety to keep the definition from being too narrow, yet has sufficient in common (in terms of function) to keep the definition from becoming so broad and vague as to be meaningless.[54]

He formulates a definition of the Christian prophet on the basis of the functions which these sources have in common:

> A Christian prophet is a Christian who functions within the Church, occasionally or regularly, as a divinely called and divinely inspired speaker who receives intelligible and authoritative revelations or messages which he is impelled to deliver publicly, in oral or written form, to Christian individuals and/or the Christian community.[55]

Whoever fits this definition, proposes Hill, is a prophet, whether or not they are so designated in the sources. This definition makes it clear that by "functional" Hill simply means "characteristic activities" of Christian prophets. Most of the definition, however, has a substantive character; when he describes the Christian prophet as "divinely called and divinely inspired," he is describing what a prophet *is*. Transposed to a more functional formulation, the Christian prophet might be described as one who *claims* to be divinely called and divinely inspired. This definition will make it very difficult for Hill to distinguish among a prophet, an apostle, a preacher, and a teacher later on in his study, for he later observes that "the prophet is not the only leader in the Church whose speech is inspired by the Spirit,"[56] and that "it cannot be assumed that all inspired speech in the early Christian community emanated from prophets: were not 'teachers' and 'evangelists' also inspired by the Spirit?"[57] These statements suggest that Hill is not trying to use history-of-religion categories to describe the role of the NT prophet.

A number of other features of Hill's definition require discussion. The phrase "within the Church" appears unnecessary if it indicates the scene for the prophetic performance, for that is explicitly stated in the latter portion of the definition. The notion of the "divine call" of the prophet is widely held but cannot be substantiated from the sources, unless it is assumed that a "commission" is implied in the reception of a divinely inspired message which the prophet is impelled to deliver. Even the notion of divine compulsion, while characteristic of some prophets, cannot be demonstrated for all. The way in which Hill substantively describes the prophet as "divinely inspired" and "divinely called" suggests that he is not providing a phenomenological description of the Christian prophet (in which "truth" is bracketed out), but rather is presenting us with a theological definition in which he commits himself to the reality of the prophetic claim. This accounts for Hill's subsequent use of the loaded phrases "genuine prophet"[58] and "true prophet,"[59] a theological stance which we noted above in the work of H. A. Guy. All this suggests that Hill is caught up, like Guy before him, in a methodological muddle. He has not decided if he is presenting a history of early Christian prophetism or a theologically normative study in which the NT evidence is regarded prescriptively. This basically theological orientation is doubtless the reason why the author insists on staying within the canonical framework in treating NT prophecy.

In the second half of the same chapter Hill surveys prophecy in the Hebrew-Jewish tradition,[60] where he touches upon OT prophecy, intertestamental literature, Josephus, Philo, rabbinic literature, the Dead Sea Scrolls, and John the Baptist. Greco-Roman sources are lightly touched upon and written off as less than useful in understanding NT prophecy. Unlike Crone, Hill's discussion of the various Jewish sources is riddled with many commonly held but erroneous views of the previous generation of scholars. He holds the peculiar view that "the message of the divinely commissioned prophet was self-authenticating and unchallengeable."[61] Here he is presumably accepting Jeremiah's views of truth, not recognizing that historically others were making the identical claim; the attempt to distinguish the true from the false prophet in Israel is a theological problem which permeates the OT. Hill makes another dubious claim:

> There can be no doubt that long before the turn of the eras, the Jews believed that prophecy as such had ceased in Israel and that the prophetic Spirit had withdrawn.[62]

He suggests (like Guy) that John the Baptist is more truly a successor of the OT prophets than the Teacher of Righteousness or his disciples.[63] That too of course is a theological evaluation rather than a historical judgment.

Hill's discussion of "Jesus: 'A Prophet Mighty in Deed and Word' " is very well done, in spite of the inadequate conceptual framework within which it is treated; he includes a thorough discussion of evidence suggesting that Jesus was designated a prophet by some of his contemporaries, by some phases of earliest Christianity, and by the canonical evangelists. In discussing the prophetic characteristics of Jesus' ministry (an almost obligatory section in all such treatments of Jesus' prophetic role), Hill proposes seven such characteristics: (1) the poetic form of some of his teaching, (2) his visions, auditions, and ecstatic-prophetic experiences, (3) his gift of insight into the thoughts of those about him, (4) his prophetic foresight, (5) his symbolic actions, (6) the phrase "Amen, I say to you" as an equivalent to the prophetic messenger formula "Thus says the Lord," and (7) his consciousness of a commission, i.e. of having been sent by God. In spite of all these apparent similarities Hill concludes that the prophetic designation for Jesus is ultimately inadequate:

> But this "prophet" was unique in the sense that his proclamation and activity were confronting men and women with the present saving action of God in the midst of history, and that his commitment and obedience to God made him the channel of that gracious and saving action.[64]

This is the familiar christological characteristic of NT theologians in which a review of the various christological titles applied to Jesus in the NT is followed by the claim that these titles have been superseded by one whose person eludes all attempts at historical categorization and who breaks through the constrictions inherent in historical conceptualizations. This is theology, not history. In an evaluation of Hill's use of arguments to show that Jesus is a prophet (even though he ultimately transcends that category), it must be said that he does not try to give a *functional* description of Jesus' prophetic role. He does not do this, it appears, because he has not discussed Hebrew-Jewish prophetism in functional terms. Why he does not do so is a mystery. Even though he follows the traditional mode of comparing John the Baptist and Jesus with the classical Israelite prophet, he does not articulate the basis of comparison. Presumably, if "prophet" were an appropriate first-century category for John the Baptist and/or Jesus, it would be the conception widely held at that time rather than one which modern biblical scholars derive from their study of Israelite prophets.

Since the Revelation of John explicitly claims to be prophecy, Hill next turns to that document. In assessing whether the categories "prophecy" or "apocalyptic" are more suitable to the Apocalypse, Hill concludes that while some of John's style and imagery are dependent upon apocalyptic tradition, "in his interpretation of history and the sensitivity to the actualities of his situation the writer stands in the tradition of prophetic faith and proclamation."[65] It is hardly necessary to underscore the subjectivity of this comparison. Hill then turns to consider the form of prophecy in Revelation in terms of vocabulary, phrases, and extended formal elements. These formal elements include: (1) speech in the first person of the deity, (2) call narratives, (3) sentences of holy law, and (4) patterns of instruction and repentance preaching (*Busspredigt*), drawing on the work of U. B. Müller for the latter. This section is significant, for it is one of the very few attempts to provide a formal description of early Christian prophetic speech. After a discussion of the content of prophecy Hill suggests that the prophet is somehow inseparable from the body of believers who themselves have a prophetic character. John's prophetic authority, however, is greater than the authority of the group of prophets which he leads.

In discussing prophets and prophecy in Acts Hill adduces various passages which suggest that since all believers had received the prophetic Spirit and could prophesy, Luke understands prophetic activity as the proclamation among Jews and Gentiles of the good news of God's grace and action in Christ.[66] Those who are called "prophets" are not so designated because of their exclusive exercise of the prophetic gift, but because of their more regular and frequent exercise of it than others. Hill concludes, following E. E. Ellis, that in Acts the cognates *paraklēsis* and *parakaleō* are used in a distinctive way of early Christian prophetic speech. In short, "the prophetic ministry has the characteristics of pastoral preaching."[67] The element of prediction, characteristic of the prophet Agabus, is not the main function of Christian prophets in the view of the author of Acts.

Some of the earliest and most important evidence for early Christian prophecy is preserved in the letters of Paul. In treating Paul, Hill deals with the problem of whether he can appropriately be categorized as a prophet,[68] as well as with the evidence he transmits for the phenomenon of Christian prophecy. On the problem of whether to label Paul a prophet, Hill focuses on the functional definition developed in the first chapter. Paul is a prophet on that basis, though he never designates himself such, since he "received revelations and . . . felt himself under divine constraint to proclaim in word and letter, what he had been given."[69] Yet Paul does not call himself a prophet, possibly because the NT apostle is more fully a functional equivalent of the OT prophet:

> We may make Old Testament prophets completely definitive for our understand-
> ing of what is meant by "prophet" in the New Testament: in which case we
> may have to say that the apostles are the real successors of these prophets — as
> divinely authoritative messengers — and that the New Testament prophets are
> inferior or secondary bearers of revelation and not genuine "prophets."[70]

If Paul is made the paradigm for NT prophets because of close similarities with OT prophets, reasons Hill, there is a danger that only he and John the Apocalyptist could be regarded as genuine prophets. Paul, however, is primarily an apostle, though he exhibits characteristic features of the evangelist, teacher, preacher, and prophet.

Paul's views on prophecy in 1 Cor. 14 are in tension with the views of the Corinthians. The conflict, claims Hill, is basically between pagan prophetic traditions and OT-Jewish prophetic traditions:

> Presumably Paul derived his view of the phenomenon [of prophecy] from Old
> Testament/Jewish models and possibly from contact with prophets influenced
> by such models (like those in Acts), whereas the Corinthians' understanding
> seems to reflect the Greek ecstatic model: those who practised according to it
> were employed in the mystery cults and their activities were described . . . by
> terms like *mainomai, mantis, enthousiasmos,* etc., terms which are not used of New
> Testament prophets.[71]

Paul's limitation of public performances by prophets to two or three individuals suggests that their speeches were longer than the short, ejaculatory words of revelation uttered without connection which presumably characterized their usual prophecies. "We may therefore reasonably infer," he observes, "that prophetic *paraklēsis* is expressed in sustained utterance."[72] In discussing Paul's notion of the function of prophecy, Hill fixes on the designation "pastoral preaching,"[73] a characterization justified by Paul's use of such terms as "upbuild" (*oikodomē, oikodomein*), "learn" (*manthanō*), "instruct" (*katēchein*) in 1 Cor. 14. *Paraklēsis* stands at the center of the prophetic task:

> It is exhortatory preaching; it constantly refers back to the work of salvation as its presupposition and basis; its locus is normally in the worshipping congregation and it contributes to the guidance, correction, encouragement — in short, the *oikodomē* of the community.[74]

This parenetic function of prophecy is in continuity with the Deuteronomistic conception of prophecy:

> It is this kind of understanding of the prophetic role that is carried forward when the New Testament attributes to prophets the task, not only of kerygmatic proclamation but of warning, instructing and correcting the congregation and individuals on the fringe, of guiding Christians towards conduct more worthy of the Gospel by the communication of the *paraklēsis* that upbuilds.[75]

Hill then makes a summary statement in which he distinguishes Paul from other Christian prophets: "It is exceedingly doubtful that all Christian teachers and prophets were gifted with an authority and an inspiration like Paul's."[76] His judgment is based of course on what Paul himself claims without considering the legitimacy of counterclaims. According to 1 Cor. 14:29, claims Hill, prophetic utterances were judged and evaluated by other prophets; if this is so, he continues:

> then it is implied that utterances of New Testament prophets (at least those in Corinth) are not always accorded the unchallengeable authority which the "Thus says the Lord" of the Old Testament prophets possessed.[77]

In short, Paul is more a prophet of the OT type than are those prophets he attempts to regulate in Corinth.

Hill's discussion of the evidence from 1 Cor. 12-14 is very carefully done and attuned to the most recent scholarship throughout. Yet the discussion is so theologically oriented that little or no concern is in evidence for understanding Christian prophecy as a religious phenomenon in the history of early Christianity. Paul's discussion in 1 Corinthians is oriented toward persuading Christians to accept his view of prophecy and glossolalia, i.e. what their view and practice *ought* to be. Paul, therefore, is articulating an ideology of Christian prophecy. We cannot be sure that what he recommends was actually practiced anywhere in the Christian world. The Corinthians, like Paul, were Christians. Their use of prophecy and glossolalia, so far as the historian of religions is concerned, is no less significant or interesting than the views of Paul himself. In making Paul's conception of Christian prophecy the norm Hill abandons the perspective of historical criticism and adopts the normative framework of a NT theologian.

Following H. A. Guy, Hill suggests that Hebrews is an example of written pastoral preaching composed by a Christian prophet. He doubts, however, whether the homilies of the Fourth Gospel had a similar prophetic origin. Following R. A.

Edwards' cautious approach to Q, Hill doubts that the prophetic material in Q can confidently be attributed to the creativity of Christian prophets. In the Matthean community, on the other hand, it is probable that Christian prophets were active in a ministry of preaching, warning, revelation, and teaching. Following P. Minear, he emphasizes the prophetic elements in the Lukan redaction, suggesting that the distinctive Lukan emphasis on the suffering and death of Jesus as a prophet may have been forged as an example to those Christians who, in Luke's view, would continue the prophetic ministry of Jesus and could themselves expect a similar treatment from the world.

Turning to the thorny problem of "Christian Prophets and the Sayings of Jesus," Hill tackles an issue which has been frequently debated in recent years. The central problem is whether Christian prophets, speaking in the name of the exalted Jesus, produced prophetic sayings which ultimately came to be included in the tradition of the sayings of the earthly Jesus. While prophets and teachers may have been active in adapting the sayings of Jesus to the post-Easter situation, Hill doubts that sayings were created out of nothing. He argues that sayings of Jesus in the Apocalypse could well have been elaborations of actual Jesus traditions. Further, John's unique prophetic status does not allow the generalization that because he spoke in the name of the risen Lord, all Christian prophets did the same. He argues further that E. Käsemann's sentences of holy law cannot be shown to have had a prophetic origin. He concludes that while some sayings in gospel tradition might conceivably have originated with Christian prophets, the methodological difficulty in identifying such sayings is enormous.

In the last significant chapter of the book Hill deals with the problem of the decline of prophecy. It is here, significantly, that he surveys some of the material found in the Didache, the Shepherd of Hermas, Ignatius, and Montanism. He makes a very important statement:

> Consequently, when the era of the prophets closed, with the condemnation of Montanist enthusiasm and ecstasy, the increasing hellenisation of the Church—with its emphasis on the spirituality and rationality of the faith—created the tendency to rely more and more on rational and didactic forms of spiritual utterance: therefore the place of the prophets, as witnesses to the living truth, was taken by the "teachers" of both the free and the official Church, that is, by catechists, preachers, scholars and theologians (e.g. Clement of Alexandria), men who were the first conscious champions of an individualist and personal spirituality in the Church, but whose authority was based not on any revelation directly received but on the exposition of existing traditions, and very particularly of the Scriptures, at first those of the Old Covenant, but later those of the New and of the apostles.[78]

In addition to this major reason for the decline of prophecy, Hill agrees with Friedrich and Käsemann that the increasing authority of an official ministry in an institutionalized church resulted in the decline of prophecy. He also agrees with H. von Campenhausen that the increased inability of prophets to transmit properly the apostolic truth resulted in others taking over that function. Finally, he cites the presence of false prophets as ultimately serving to undermine the position and authority of genuine prophets.

Hill has contributed a very important study on NT prophecy to the world of scholarship, yet one which is more significant for its individual discussions of particular problems than for the subject generally.

III. MAJOR ISSUES IN THE STUDY OF EARLY CHRISTIAN PROPHECY

In our review of the five general presentations of early Christian prophecy by H. A. Guy, G. Friedrich (et al.), E. Cothenet, T. Crone, and D. Hill, our primary objective was to summarize the contribution to the subject of each scholar, characterize their basic stance, and give some indication of the particular approach of each study to the subject of early Christian prophecy together with some of the more distinctive features of their contributions. Several major issues in the study of early Christian prophecy have emerged from our discussion, and they may be presented at this point. It is these issues which will become the focus of the chapters to follow.

A. THE PROBLEM OF METHOD

From the five general studies on early Christian prophecy which we have considered above, it is clear that the problem of methodology is an issue of primary importance. It is not necessary of course for scholars pedantically to preface their studies with elaborate descriptions of the precise methods which they intend to employ in research. On the other hand, unless a study of early Christian prophecy is based on a definite set of objectives, facilitated by the utilization of appropriate methods, the results will inevitably be disappointing. At various points in our review above we have objected to the indiscriminate blending of a theological (i.e. normative) approach to the subject, together with a historical (i.e. descriptive) approach. Since the First World War, NT scholars have been profoundly influenced by the theological tendency subsequently labeled Neoorthodoxy. The resultant "biblical theology movement" has been described in terms of its rise and supposed fall by B. Childs in *Biblical Theology in Crisis* (1970). There he proposed that the canon be regarded as the most appropriate setting for a renewed biblical theology, since traditional historical criticism had shown itself unable to deal with the normative claims of scripture. While it is not my intention to criticize or reject the theological approach to the Bible as either inappropriate or illegitimate, I do wish to emphasize that different methodologies can be successfully employed in studying the biblical text for different interpretive and critical goals. The purpose of the present study is to understand prophets and prophecy as historical phenomena in the history of early Christianity. To that end the literary heritage of early Christianity will be examined for evidence pertinent to the reconstruction of the history and character of early Christian prophecy.

Since the time of G. L. Bauer's *Biblische Theologie des Neuen Testaments* (4 vols., 1800-1802), NT scholars have often treated books and groups of related books in the NT separately, investigating, for example, the Christology of Johannine literature, Paul, and so forth. This tendency, emphasized in biblical theology, also characterizes each of the five general presentations of early Christian prophecy which we reviewed above. This approach can be based on the supposition that the NT does not possess the kind of theological and conceptual unity which the proof-texting method once imposed on it.[79] It can also be based on the notion that each NT author is so separated in time, space, and perspective from other authors that a more synthetic presentation is not really viable. However, to use that approach in an attempt at a historical reconstruction of early Christian prophecy amounts to a presentation of the evidence organized in terms of the sources used; this procedure is rarely used by historians and serves to impede rather than facilitate the synthetic conceptualization of the evidence.

There is also an important methodological issue implicit in the limitation of the presentations reviewed above to the canonical NT. In view of the general critical consensus that some NT documents must be dated well into the second century and some noncanonical literature (e.g. the Didache, the Shepherd of Hermas) may reach in part or in whole into the latter part of the first century, the historical study of early Christian prophecy cannot reasonably be limited to the canonical NT. Even Christian literature which can be dated well into the second century with some confidence can preserve earlier traditions and may be of considerable value in tracing the trajectories of tendencies observable in earlier literature. With the exception of T. Crone, all the general studies reviewed above have consciously limited their scope of investigation to the NT, though passing attention is sometimes given to other early Christian sources.

In the following chapters the attempt will be made to synthesize the evidence for the historical and social phenomenon of prophecy in early Christianity. This procedure is inherently problematic, for the sources are so fragmentary and scattered with regard to both time and place that the evidence will be skewed. Further, the literature under investigation from early Christianity will certainly begin with the earliest Christian literature, but it will attempt to discuss all Christian prophetic phenomena up to and including Montanism in the late second century A.D.

B. THE BACKGROUND OF EARLY CHRISTIAN PROPHECY

Early Christianity emerged as a religion separate from Judaism in a gradual and extended process which began near the middle of the first century and continued well into the second. Beginning as a Jewish sectarian movement, Christianity soon began attracting numbers of Gentiles so that by the end of the first century the movement was largely non-Jewish. From the Jewish perspective Christianity had become intolerably paganized. Thus early Christianity began its existence in Jewish Palestine and was heir to centuries of Israelite-Jewish tradition, central to which were the scriptures. Nevertheless it matured in a Greco-Roman environment and was profoundly altered by western culture and traditions. The adherents of the German history-of-religions school early in the twentieth century regarded Christianity as a syncretistic religion in which various features from eastern and western religions and cultures had combined in a unique way to form a new and viable faith. From this perspective knowledge of the Semitic-Jewish heritage of Christianity was no less important than a knowledge of Greco-Roman traditions. The biblical theology movement, particularly encouraged by the discovery of the Dead Sea Scrolls in 1947, began to place a more exclusive emphasis on the explanatory value of the Israelite-Jewish heritage of early Christianity with the result that the earlier assumption of the explanatory value of Greco-Roman religion and culture for understanding Christianity began to be treated with a sort of benign neglect. This trend was encouraged by educational changes during the first half of the twentieth century that increasingly neglected the study of classical languages and literatures. Seminaries and graduate programs emphasizing biblical studies, on the other hand, propagated Biblical Greek and Hebrew and unwittingly encouraged a narrowing focus on Israelite-Jewish-Christian tradition with scant attention to the wider world within which Christianity developed into a potent religious and social force.

In the period following World War Two it was common for biblical scholars to make a distinction between Palestinian Judaism and Hellenistic (or Diaspora) Judaism.

That distinction, while axiomatic for the German history-of-religions school, has increasingly come to be regarded as invalid. There has been in fact growing recognition of the extent to which Palestinian Judaism had undergone profound Hellenization (to various extents and in various segments of Palestinian society) already by the second century B.C. The appropriate cultural and religious setting within which early Christianity must be interpreted then is neither exclusively Israelite-Jewish tradition and culture nor Greco-Roman tradition and culture, but both.

With the exception of T. Crone, all the scholars whose works we surveyed above regard the contribution of Greco-Roman prophetic and oracular traditions as being of little value in understanding the phenomenon of early Christian prophecy. Even prophetic phenomena in early Judaism, such as that connected with the liberation movements, is taken seriously only by Crone. More often than not neglect of the Greco-Roman material is based on the implicit notion that whatever is distinctively Greco-Roman is somehow a corruption of the Christian faith, while continuities with Israelite-Jewish tradition indicate a faithfulness to biblical (and hence normative) tradition. That this construct is theologically rather than historically grounded is patent in the fact that Judaism had experienced acute Hellenization (with desultory nativistic reactions) during the three centuries prior to the appearance of Jesus and the birth of the Christian religion. It is clear not only that Greco-Roman revelatory traditions and procedures *could* have influenced early Christianity, but that they *did* have a widespread and profound effect. Hill, for instance, while admitting that the Corinthians had been influenced by the "Greek ecstatic model,"[80] is far more interested in the normative significance of Paul's views than in the reported practice of the Corinthians. Yet on closer examination the Corinthians were Christians like Paul, and a discussion of early Christian prophecy, historically considered, would be incomplete without a careful and serious consideration of the prophetic traditions which characterized the Corinthians. J. Reiling's investigation of Hermas *Mand.* 11 has made it abundantly clear that Hellenistic magical divination had made significant inroads into the Christian communities in and around Rome from the last decade of the first century to the middle of the second. The present study will attempt to show that the influence of Hellenistic revelatory traditions was even more influential on early Christianity than has previously been recognized.

Not only is it essential then that the Israelite-Jewish prophetic and revelatory traditions be considered in order to understand fully the phenomenon of early Christian prophecy, but the Greco-Roman oracular and prophetic traditions must also be made part of the picture. In treating these two linguistic and cultural traditions as backgrounds for understanding early Christianity, however, there are several perils to be avoided. There is the ever-present danger of seizing upon ostensible "parallels," all the while wrenching them from their structural context and isolating them from their original cultural-religious setting. What must be compared are not isolated features but features considered within their structural framework. That means that both the Israelite-Jewish and the Greco-Roman revelatory traditions must be treated with integrity. Potential parallels for illuminating one or another aspect of early Christian prophecy must be seen as part of a structure and not as an isolated tidbit. In this book, therefore, I have devoted four chapters to the consideration of various aspects of ancient Mediterranean revelatory and prophetic traditions. In every instance the evidence has been presented as significant in and of itself and not only in the ways in which it might be related to similar phenomena in early Christianity.

C. THE FORM OF PROPHETIC SPEECH

Except for a few instances all five general studies on early Christian prophecy ignore the problem of the genre and forms of prophetic speech. Virtually every issue associated with early Christian prophets and prophecy is discussed in detail by one or another author with the exception of this one. Hill, in his excellent discussion of prophecy in the Apocalypse of John, does devote considerable attention to the problem of forms in that document. In dependence upon E. Käsemann, M. E. Boring, and U. B. Müller, Hill presents some important material which is of direct relevance for understanding the locution of early Christian prophecy. The one recent contribution to the study of early Christian prophecy which focuses on form-critical questions is the ambitious study by U. B. Müller, *Prophetie und Predigt im Neuen Testament: Formgeschichtliche Untersuchungen zur urchristlichen Prophetie* (Prophecy and preaching in the New Testament: Form-critical investigations of early Christian prophecy). This is a very important study and we shall have frequent occasion to refer to it in the relevant chapters which follow. An earlier study which has had a significant impact on NT scholarship is E. Käsemann's proposal regarding sentences of holy law, a form which he attributes to early Christian prophets and which is readily identifiable through a number of recurring formal features. Yet a third study in which form-critical issues are dealt with desultorily is J. Reiling's important study *Hermas and Christian Prophecy,* in which he identifies some prophetic utterances embedded in the Shepherd of Hermas.

In the present study the contributions to the study of the form and genre of Christian prophetic speech have been considered and every utterance which appears to owe its origin to prophetic speech has been analyzed in terms of formal elements, recurring features, and similarities to other forms in Israelite-Jewish and Greco-Roman prophetic tradition. Every attempt has been made to treat the material in its own terms rather than impose foreign categories upon it, a frequent tendency in form-critical analysis. Form-critical analyses of OT prophetic speech are so numerous that they are difficult even to survey, so that the major problem in this area is to synthesize an enormous amount of scholarly research for the purpose of understanding the basic forms of ancient Israelite prophetic speech. For Judaism the situation is quite different. Few analyses of the forms of early Jewish prophetic speech exist, though admittedly there is little material upon which to draw. One of the assumptions of this study is that prophetic utterances are frequently embedded in apocalyptic literary settings so that the problems involved in identification and analysis are compounded. One major problem of the present study was the almost complete lack of scholarly research on the genre and forms of Greek oracles and oracular speeches. Chapter 3 is devoted to this subject, an effort which was necessary if any significant comparison was to be made between Greek oracles and early Christian oracles. After this analysis had been completed, the excellent discussion of J. Fontenrose on *The Delphic Oracle* appeared (1978). Although Fontenrose's analysis is limited to the Delphic oracles (both genuine and spurious), there are many similarities between his analyses and my own. The major difficulty in analyzing Christian prophetic speech formally is the problem of identification. Criteria for identification of prophetic utterances are stated at the beginning of Chapter 10. Some will suggest that I have not included all the relevant material, while others will take me to task for having included too much. The results must speak for themselves. One guiding principle in the analysis is that spurious oracles and prophetic speeches constitute perhaps better examples of generic and formal expectations than do some legitimate oracles, for they were closely formulated in order to be accepted as genuine.

D. THE FUNCTIONS OF PROPHETIC SPEECH

The most obvious meaning of "function" is "characteristic activity." The early Christian prophet may be defined in broadly functional terms, as Hill attempts to do, by describing him as one who delivers what he claims are divinely inspired messages in oral or written form to Christian individuals or groups, often within a cultic setting. This kind of "functional" definition, however, reveals very little about the nature of Christian prophets and prophecy, and does not in fact take us very far. All the studies which we reviewed above emphasize (by tying together the evidence from Acts and the Pauline letters) that Christian prophecy functions to edify, exhort, and console Christians. Further, Christian prophets are regarded as proclaimers of God's plan both for the world and for those in it, and to that extent they occasionally predict future events and exhibit a kind of second sight regarding those with whom they come into contact. David Hill has carried this further with his characterization of early Christian prophets as "pastoral preachers." Yet after we have listed the various characteristic activities of Christian prophets, we are still left with a great many unanswered questions. Why was the phenomenon of prophecy so widespread in early Christianity? What is the relationship between the specialized roles, variously labeled "evangelist," "teacher," "preacher," "apostle," and "prophet" in early Christian literature? Why did Christian prophets, if the summary of their activities above is essentially correct, focus so much of their efforts on exhortation, encouragement, admonition, and consolation?

One very important set of questions, and one with which none of the five general presentations deals, pertains to the *social* function of Christian prophets. Indeed, each of the questions which were just enumerated is basically sociological in orientation. The sociological study of early Christianity has recently become a subject of central concern for many NT scholars. While important contributions have been made in assessing the social function of the ancient Israelite prophet, few NT scholars have focused attention on the social role and function of the early Christian prophet. Correspondingly, few studies have addressed the social functions of the oracle prophets and free-lance mantics of Greco-Roman antiquity. While this present study has attempted to emphasize the social functions of the prophetic figures of Israelite-Jewish, Greco-Roman, and early Christian tradition, the current state of research has necessarily limited this task. The social function of early Christian prophets and prophecy, however, cannot be adequately assessed without due consideration of the problem of altered states of consciousness, an issue to which we now turn.

E. ANCIENT PROPHECY AND THE PROBLEM OF ALTERED STATES OF CONSCIOUSNESS

The phrase "altered states of consciousness" is used by contemporary anthropologists to describe a wide range of psychosocial phenomena. Our focus here will be on the notions "possession" and "trance," two terms which are often used interchangeably. However, following E. Bourguignon, we shall use two terms to describe in terms of a cultural classification two primary, institutionally patterned forms of altered conscious states, namely, *possession trance* and *vision trance*.[81] Both states exhibit behavioral modifications, but the former is a category which deals with possession by spirits, while the latter typically involves visions, hallucinations, adventures, or experiences of the soul during temporary absences from the body, and so forth. Since the early Christian prophet is one who mediates an oral or written message received from supernatural sources, the notions of "possession trance" and "vision trance" include the major ways in which such messages were thought to be received. Earlier in this century possession phenomena were closely linked to abnormal psychology. Small wonder that OT and NT scholars found it infelicitous to describe the prophetic experience in such apparently jaded terms. Recent research on altered states of consciousness, however, has moved from the psychobiological perspective exclusively to considering possession phenomena in terms of categories of cultural interpretation. According to Bourguignon, for example, "possession is an idea, a concept, a belief, which serves to interpret behavior."[82]

One biblical scholar in recent years who has dealt most directly and forthrightly with possession phenomena in connection with OT prophecy is R. Wilson. In *Prophecy and Society in Ancient Israel,* after considering the various terms given by anthropologists to prophetic figures in various cultures (e.g. prophet, shaman, witch, sorcerer, medium, diviner, priest, mystic), Wilson selects the term "intermediary" for its utility and neutrality. Societies attribute the distinctive behavior of some intermediaries to spirit possession (often designated "ecstasy" in religious contexts), or to nonpossession theories (i.e. the individual's soul is thought to leave the body and journey to a different world). Following I. M. Lewis, Wilson employs the categories "central intermediary" and "peripheral intermediary." The former play a role in the central cult and are regarded as official links to the supernatural world, while the latter are not. Both types of intermediary exhibit stereotypical patterns of speech and behavior, suggesting that such patterns are culturally "learned." Further, both kinds function within a support group which either tolerates or encourages them. Peripheral mediation has several social functions: (1) the attainment of social status, (2) a means of bringing about social change, and (3) a means of maintaining social stability. Central intermediaries, on the other hand, are "primarily responsible for maintaining their societies and for promoting community welfare."[83] This is accomplished by their mediation in providing divine legitimation for the existing social order and by their functions in easing social tensions. Wilson's purpose, of course, is to formulate a typology of the institutional frameworks within which intermediaries function in order to be able to pose appropriate questions in analyzing the social function of ancient Near Eastern, and more particularly ancient Israelite, prophecy.

The historian of early Christianity can certainly derive benefit from both the modern anthropological studies on altered states of consciousness and the theoretical application of such studies to the phenomenon of ancient Israelite prophecy. Yet there are several barriers which hinder our investigation. First, the evidence for early Christian prophetic activity is very meager in comparison with that for ancient Israelite prophecy. Second, though the time period during which early Christian prophecy flourished was far more restricted than for its ancient Israelite counterpart, the first century of early Christian experience was not limited to a single, relatively stable and unified nation and culture. Rather, early Christianity flourished throughout the Mediterranean world, which was characterized by a mélange of nativistic traditions, aspirations, and languages, held together in an unsteady state by Roman political and military authority. It is therefore far from certain that the institutional complexion of early Christian congregations maintained any kind of consistent structure from one end of the Mediterranean world to the other.

With the exception of T. Crone the five studies we have surveyed tend to use the term "ecstasy" for what they regard as an infelicitous form of prophetic inspiration. Frequently the so-called "ecstatic Greek model" of prophecy is opposed to the Israelite-Jewish model which is thought to be characterized, if not by complete rationality, at least by a greater degree of restraint and decorum. H. Bacht has discussed the characteristics of Greco-Roman prophetic inspiration in comparison with early Christian prophecy, with the latter appearing far superior to the former. He proposes five characteristic elements of Greco-Roman prophetic inspiration,[84] some of which we have found in the work of H. Krämer: (1) a state of divine possession, (2) mantic frenzy (madness), (3) dependence on artificial means for inducing the prophetic experience, (4) the initiative for prophetic inspiration is taken by man, frequently through the use of magic, and (5) the content of inspired speech is only occasionally of religious or moral value.

Let us consider each of these points seriatim. The first is certainly valid, though there appear to be different behavioral features associated with the phenomenon of divine possession in various social settings in the Greco-Roman world. Further, the supposition of divine possession (here I understand both "possession trance" and "vision trance" in the sense adopted above) underlies all ancient oracular speech, whether Greco-Roman, Jewish, or early Christian. Second, "mantic frenzy" is sometimes associated with inspired divination, but often it is not. In the Greek world it appears to be more characteristic of situations of "peripheral mediation" than of situations concerning intermediaries in central cults. The presence of abnormal behavior of the type associated with possession trance and possession cannot be inferred from the root meanings of such terms as *mania, enthysiasmos, entheos, katochē,* or the like, where no explicit description of such behavior accompanies these terms.[85] The ritual possession characteristic of some of the mystery cults was not the same phenomenon as divine possession enabling individuals to utter divine oracles, though the two were frequently confused in antiquity. There is some evidence that means were used to induce prophetic experience, yet in local consultation oracles the means was not intended to induce possession trance or vision trance so much as to put the intermediary into direct contact with the oracular potencies of the site. Bacht, with many other scholars, speaks confidently about the terms "magic" and "magical" as if they can be clearly differentiated from a more religious approach to prophecy and revelation. Magic and religion can be differentiated only in sociological terms, i.e.

> magic is defined as that form of religious deviance whereby individual or social goals are sought by means alternate to those normally sanctioned by the dominant religious institution.[86]

Finally, while it is true that pagan oracles are only occasionally concerned with religious or moral values, that means only that divine revelation played a different social function in the Greco-Roman world generally than it did for the Jew or the Christian. Oracle prophets in the Greek world were personnel supported by and functioning in a central cult, functioning more to create stability and continuity with traditional values (which were assumed more often than not) than to introduce or legitimate innovations. Bacht's article, at bottom, is another theologically motivated attempt to make artificial distinctions between the biblical and the nonbiblical world of thought in order to focus on the theologically normative character of the former and the illegitimate nature of the latter.

F. SPECIAL ROLES PROPOSED FOR CHRISTIAN PROPHETS

Two very particular issues have received a great deal of emphasis in studies relating to early Christian prophecy in the last few years. One issue is the problem of the relationship between the prophetic utterances of Christian prophets and the transmission of the sayings of Jesus. Another is concerned with the Christian prophet as a charismatic exegete of the OT scriptures. If it can be demonstrated that Christian prophets, speaking in the name of the risen Jesus, made substantial contributions to the collection of sayings of the earthly Jesus, our knowledge of the transmission of gospel tradition will be immensely enriched. Chapter 9 will focus on this important issue. The problem of the relationship between the Christian prophet and the task of OT interpretation is one which has been formulated in the light of new knowledge produced by the discovery of the Dead Sea Scrolls. The Teacher of Righteousness, in the opinion of many, appears to have functioned as a consciously inspired interpreter of the OT; that has led some scholars to understand part of the role of the Christian prophet in an analogous manner. This problem is dealt with at some length in the Appendix.

2 | GRECO-ROMAN PROPHECY: ORACULAR PLACES AND PERSONS

I. INTRODUCTION

Oracles and divination played a regular and significant role in the lives of Greeks and Romans from earliest times down to the triumph of Christianity over competing pagan religions in the fourth century A.D.[1] For the most part the Greeks did not collect divine revelations in permanent and authoritative written form.[2] In the Greco-Roman view, in contrast to that of segments of early Judaism, divine revelation was not usually confined to a past era.[3] Rather, the science of divination was a regular and continual means for determining the will of the gods on almost every conceivable issue. Various collections of oracles were made nonetheless, not because oracular revelation was no longer available, but because the enigmatic nature of older oracles placed their complete fulfilment somewhat in doubt (making the role of interpreters necessary), and because of an increased respect for revelation in written form.[4]

Divination may be defined as the art or science of interpreting symbolic messages from the gods. Often these symbols are unpredictable or even trivial.[5] Oracles, on the other hand, are messages from the gods in human language, received as statements from a god, usually in response to inquiries. The term "oracle" is also used for the place where such messages are requested and received.[6] Important varieties of divination practiced in the Greco-Roman world include interpretation of: (1) the casting of lots (kleromancy), (2) the flight and behavior of birds (ornithomancy), (3) the condition and behavior of sacrificial animals, or their vital organs, before and after sacrifice (hepatoscopy, hieromancy, pyromancy), (4) various omens or sounds (cledonomancy), and (5) dreams (oneiromancy).[7] Both kleromancy and oneiromancy were commonly used to secure oracular responses from various divinities, a fact which underlines the close relationship between oracular divination and other forms of divination.[8]

The term which the Greeks most frequently used for the practitioner of divination was *mantis,* which is usually translated "diviner," "soothsayer," "seer," or, less appropriately, "prophet." Although more elementary forms of divination could be practiced by nearly everyone, the importance of decoding divine messages, which were ambiguous and had complex symbolism, led the ancients to rely on the interpretative expertise of the *mantis.*

Greco-Roman thinkers carefully distinguished between "technical divination" and "natural divination."[9] Technical divination is dependent on the knowledge, training, and skill of the *mantis* in observing and correctly interpreting signs, sacrifices, dreams, omens, prodigies, and the like, while natural divination is the direct inspiration of the *mantis* through trance, ecstasy, or vision.[10] Oracular divination may be placed, somewhat uneasily, in the second category.[11]

Oracular divination used a variety of methods for securing oracular responses from the gods on any number of specific issues about which the inquirer wished to receive divine advice. There were three major types of oracular technique, and normally one technique was dominant at a particular oracle sanctuary: (1) the lot oracle, (2) the dream or incubation oracle (which ordinarily involved healing), and (3) the inspired oracle. Although a great variety of techniques were used to secure oracles, there were only three primary contexts or modes within which oracular activity was regarded as possible and appropriate. One very common context for oracular activity took place within the precincts of a sacred place.[12] Another common mode of oracular activity was that of the oracularly endowed person, who could provide revelatory responses to inquirers wherever and whenever consulted. A third mode of oracular activity was the oracular dream, which, though used at local consultation oracles and by the free-lance *mantis,* was nevertheless available to everyone; in short, all persons were potential mantics.[13] Each of these three contexts for oracular activity will be discussed in the present chapter.

II. LOCAL CONSULTATION ORACLES

All ancient Greek consultation oracles either were located in sacred places which had venerable histories supported by a variety of foundation myths, or they were recent discoveries of holy places whose oracular powers had not been recognized earlier.[14] During the Hellenistic period (mid-fourth to mid-first centuries B.C.) the great oracle sanctuaries had experienced a slow but steady decline, reaching their lowest ebb at the beginning of the Roman period (mid-first century B.C.). Many of these oracles experienced a renaissance in the second and third centuries A.D., a period which many have erroneously regarded as one of social and cultural decline.[15] The decline of the great oracle centers may have been caused by the changed political situation of the Greek city-states. Embassies from various states were less frequently sent to Delphi, but whether that was because local leaders retained no genuine confidence in the revelations of Apollo cannot be affirmed with any certainty. When the old oracle shrines began to increase again in popularity, it was not delegations from various Greco-Roman cities who came to consult the gods, as in the classical period, but rather individuals with more private problems and concerns.

During the second century A.D., when local oracle sanctuaries were experiencing a renaissance, few of the once illustrious oracle centers still functioned. According to Plutarch the oracle of Apollo at Delphi, that of Zeus Ammon at the Oasis of Siwah in Libya, that of Mopsos and Amphilokos at Mallos in Cilicia, and that of Trophonios in Lebadeia were still operating at the beginning of the second century.[16] Lucian speaks of the oracles of Apollo at Claros and Branchidae (Didyma) as active,[17] and Pausanias mentions the lesser oracles of Nyx in Megara and Apollo Deiradiotes in Argos[18] (both Lucian and Pausanias wrote near the middle of the second century A.D.). Lucian also informs us of the foundation of a new oracle shrine of Glykon-Asklepios by Alexander of Abonuteichos, whom he regards as a charlatan.[19]

A. TYPES OF LOCAL CONSULTATION ORACLES

1. Lot Oracles.

The sacred lot was used for determining the will of God in ancient Israel (e.g. the Urim and Thummim used by priests) and early Christianity (Acts 1:26) as well as in Greco-Roman religions. Many of the oracle questions which have survived are phrased in such a way that the god is presented with an alternative to which he may respond only positively or negatively. Typical forms of such inquiries, which will be discussed in the next chapter, are: "Shall I, or shall I not, do such and such?" or, "Is it better and more beneficial that the people of city X found a colony at Y?" Such questions are obviously designed to require only a yes or no answer, a kind of response for which the lot was eminently suited. Although the oracle of Apollo at Delphi is most famous for the inspired oracular responses of the Pythia, a priestess of Apollo, the lot oracle was used more frequently to provide oracular responses to inquirers than was the inspired speech of the Pythia.[20] At Dodona, a very ancient oracle of Zeus, an unusual form of lot oracle was used. Oracle questions there were written on thin strips of lead (many of which have survived), which were then rolled up and marked with an identifying symbol and placed in a jar.[21] Although the exact mode of response is not known, it is probable that in another jar objects signifying a positive or negative response (such as white and black beans) were stored. The priestess may then have drawn the inquiry and the response simultaneously from both jars with her hands.[22]

An oracle which relied exclusively on the lot without the aid of cult functionaries was the oracle of Herakles in a cave near Bura.[23] Inquirers first prayed before the image and then cast four dice. The figures on the dice corresponded to explanations or responses on a tablet in the shrine. This form of divination has been designated *astragalomanteia,*[24] from the Greek word *astragaloi* meaning "knucklebones" (i.e. dice). These knucklebones had four flat sides with the numbers 1, 3, 6, and 4. One knucklebone might be cast five times or five knucklebones could be thrown at once; the object was to obtain a sequence of five numbers (totaling five to thirty, in 1024 possible combinations) that would correspond to one of a series of oracular inscriptions.[25] The following quotation is a translation of one such lot oracle found inscribed at Attalia in Pamphylia:

> 66633   24   From Pythian Apollo
> Wait and do nothing, but obey the oracles of Phoebus.
> Watch for another opportunity; for the present leave quietly.
> Shortly all your concerns will find fulfilment.[26]

The sequence of five numbers at the left indicates the results of five casts of one knucklebone (or one cast of five), the number in the middle indicates the total, and the inscription on the top right indicates the divine source of the oracular advice.

A different but related type of lot oracle is the *Sortes Astrampsychi,* papyrus fragments of a series of numbered oracle questions and answers.[27] The inquirer noted the number of the question selected, selected another number by lot, and through a fairly complicated process arrived at the number of a response which was supposed to provide an answer to his original inquiry.[28]

2. Incubation Oracles.

Dream oracles in the Greco-Roman world are referred to as incubation oracles when the inquirer was required to spend the night in the innermost sanctuary of a temple (the *abaton* or *adyton*) where a revelatory dream might be granted. The term *enkoimēsis*, translated "incubation," means "a sleeping in a temple" to seek oracular dreams and curing. Most incubation oracles were healing oracles, and most healing oracles were those of the god Asklepios; it has been estimated that there were more than two hundred such sanctuaries of Asklepios throughout the Greco-Roman world by the end of the third century A.D.[29] The procedure at incubation oracles generally involved a preparatory regimen of purificatory rites and sacrifices. The god, it was fervently hoped, would reveal himself or his will to the inquirer either by dream (*onar*) or, less commonly, through a vision (*hypar*). If Asklepios himself appeared to the patient it was thought that a cure would inevitably follow. Frequently the oracular dream contained instructions which the inquirer was expected to fulfil before he could expect healing. One of the more interesting documents from late antiquity is the diary of the rhetorician and chronic hypochondriac Aelius Aristides (A.D. 118-180), who recounted many of the oracular dreams which he experienced in various sanctuaries of Asklepios.[30]

While many healing oracles used incubation as a means of communicating divine prescriptions to the ill and infirm, incubation was also used at oracles of the dead. In archaic Greek belief the heroes who were worshiped as chthonic divinities were originally prominent mortals who had died or had somehow been swallowed up by the earth. Further, those who had died a violent death were thought to continue on as malevolent spirits unless and until some form of restitution had been paid to them. The tombs of these heroized dead, where their real or imagined remains resided, were holy places which were sometimes regarded as having oracular potency. Pausanias outlines the procedure used at the incubation oracle of the hero Amphiaraos near Thebes:

> One who has come to consult Amphiaraos is wont first to purify himself. The mode of purification is to sacrifice to the god, and they sacrifice not only to him but also to all those whose names are on the altar. And when all these things have been first done, they sacrifice a ram, and, spreading the skin under them, go to sleep and await enlightenment in a dream.[31]

Plutarch relates a story about an oracle of the dead (*psychomanteion*) in which a certain Elysios, suspecting foul play in the death of his only son, consulted such an oracle.[32] After the preliminary sacrificial ritual he fell asleep in the sanctuary. Elysios' deceased father appeared to him and pointed out someone who could satisfy his suspicions. The one indicated was none other than Elysios' dead son Euthynoüs, who told his father that he was the *daimon* of Euthynoüs. He gave his father a small tablet on which it was written that it was not good that Euthynoüs continue living, either for himself or for his parents. While the story is legendary, it clearly exemplifies the essential features involved in consulting an oracle of the dead.

In an intriguing epitaph of a Phrygian priestess, the deceased advertises her abilities as an oracular intermediary:

> If anyone wishes to learn the truth from me,
> let him come to the altar [tomb] and ask what he will,
> and he shall have his answer, at any time, night or day.[33]

Although the means of consultation is unspecified, the results are certainly guaranteed.

3. Inspired Oracles.

In contrast to the divinatory methods used at lot oracles and incubation oracles, at inspired oracles the oracular responses to questions posed by inquirers took the form of pronouncements made by a cult official. These oracular responses, examples of which we shall examine in the next chapter, are nearly always easily intelligible[34] and are formulated as the direct speech of the inspiring divinity. In former generations oracular inspiration was widely regarded as a non-Greek phenomenon which had invaded Greece from the north or east with the arrival of the worship of Dionysos.[35] More recently the phenomenon of oracular inspiration has come to be accepted as a thoroughly Greek phenomenon.[36] Many of the more characteristic features of inspired consultation oracles will be discussed in greater detail below, since this form of natural divination lends itself to comparison with similar phenomena in early Judaism and early Christianity.

B. LOCATION

The local oracle sanctuaries where inquiries were directed to such gods as Apollo (there were more than 30 Apolline oracles),[37] Zeus, and Dionysos, or such heroes as Amphilokos, Trophonios, and Amphiaraos, exhibit a number of common features. Oracles of the gods were believed to go back to remote antiquity.[38] The sacred precincts within which the oracle cult functioned had inherent oracular potencies which were institutionalized through the foundation of the cult. Oracles of heroes were located at those sites where their remains were thought buried or where they had descended into the underworld. Oracles of both gods and heroes, all of which have a chthonic character, were inseparably connected with the traditional sites of their cults.

Each local oracle shrine preserved legends explaining how the site had originally been discovered, how the cult had been instituted, or how the place had received its oracular potencies. Several such stories have been preserved that describe the recognition of the oracle of Zeus at Dodona.[39] In one story, an oak cutter named Hellos, when attempting to fell the oak at Dodona, was warned of his impending impiety by a talking dove perched in its branches.[40] In another story, Herodotus, who travelled to Dodona about the mid-fifth century B.C., asked the prophetic priestesses about the origin of their oracle. He was told that two black doves had flown from Thebes in Egypt, one to the oracle of Zeus Ammon in Libya and the other to the oracle of Zeus at Dodona. The dove at Dodona settled on an oak and commanded the natives to establish an oracular shrine there.[41]

The antiquity and discovery of Delphi was emphasized in several legends. According to one legend, prior to being taken over by Apollo the oracle belonged to Earth with the nymph Daphnis functioning as prophetess. Earth turned the oracle over to Themis, Themis to Phoebe, and finally Phoebe placed it in the care of Apollo.[42] Another Delphic legend told of a shepherd named Koretas who fell down at the site of the later oracle sanctuary and began to utter prophecies involuntarily.[43] The incubation oracle of Amphiaraos near Thebes was said to have begun after the hero and his horses were swallowed up by the earth at the site of the later oracle.[44]

Each oracle shrine appears to have had within its precincts some natural feature, such as a spring, grotto, or tree, to which much of the sanctity of the site was attributed. Springs or pools were closely associated with the functioning of the oracles of Apollo at Claros, Mopsos and Amphilokos at Mallos in Cilicia, Apollo at Branchidae, Apollo at Delphi, the healing oracle of Demeter at Patrae, the oracle of Apollo Thyrxeus in Lycia, and the oracle of Glykon-Asklepios at Abonuteichos, to name but a few.[45] Caverns or grottoes were associated with the oracles of Apollo at Delphi,

Trophonios at Lebadeia, Apollo at Claros, and Herakles Buraikos in Achaia.[46] The sacred oak was the distinctive feature of the oracle of Zeus at Dodona,[47] while the laurel became increasingly important at Delphi. The grotto at Delphi became identified as the source of an "inspiring vapor" (*pneuma enthousiastikon*), over which the Pythia sat on her tripod.[48]

C. ORACULAR PERSONNEL

Since local consultation oracles received their oracular potency from the sacred site, the cult officials could function only within the bounds of that sacred precinct. At Delphi there were three kinds of cult personnel: the Pythia, a priestess whose official title was *promantis* or *prophētis*;[49] two prophetic priests, appointed for life, who were probably identical with the two *prophētai* mentioned by Plutarch;[50] and a board of five *Hosioi* ("holy ones").[51] The Pythia was an oracular prophetess who sat upon a tripod (representing the throne of Apollo) where she delivered oracular responses inspired by Apollo.[52] In Plutarch's time (ca. A.D. 50-120) only one such Pythia was employed, whereas formerly (when business was more brisk) two such prophetesses were sent into the sanctuary alternately while a third was held in reserve.[53] In Plutarch's time the young girl chosen to be the Pythia was taken from the lower class of farmers and lacked formal education.[54] Precisely how the Pythia was selected is never explained, and there is no evidence that she was thought to possess exceptional clairvoyant gifts.[55]

The earliest cult personnel mentioned in connection with the oracle of Zeus at Dodona are *Selloi,* who are designated as *hypophētai,* i.e. "prophets" or "interpreters" of Zeus.[56] They functioned as interpreters or spokesmen for Zeus in that they probably gave oracular responses to inquirers by explaining the meaning of the sound produced by rustling leaves on the sacred oak. Since they are described as sleeping on the ground and avoiding washing their feet, practices with no Greek parallels, foreign influence has often been proposed.[57] Writing near the middle of the fifth century B.C., Herodotus does not mention the *Selloi,* but reports the existence of three *promanteis* ("prophetesses"), also called *Peliai* ("doves"), who deliver oracular responses from Zeus.[58]

Unlike Delphi and Dodona, the oracle of Clarian Apollo never employed female priestesses or prophetesses.[59] There a male *mantis* with the title *prophētēs* would receive an oracle from Apollo in response to an inquiry, and a poet (called a *thespiodos,* "oracle singer") kept on the premises would reproduce the prose oracle in poetic form and sing it to the inquirer.[60] Nikander of Colophon, who speaks of himself as "seated by the Clarian tripods of the far-darter,"[61] held the (probably hereditary) post of *prophētēs* at Colophon.[62] At the oracle of Apollo at Branchidae the highest cult official was the *prophētēs,*[63] who was chosen from a select group of families to hold office for one year.[64] However, as at Delphi (and perhaps in conscious imitation of that famous oracle), the medium for the oracular response of Apollo was a female *promantis.*[65] In addition to the prophet and *promantis* at Branchidae, another cult official mentioned in the inscriptions is the *grammateus,* or secretary, who was responsible for writing down the official version of the oracle.[66] The *prophētēs* and the *grammateus* are officials mentioned in connection with the oracle of Apollo at Coropaeos.[67] At the oracle of Dionysos at Amphikleia the male priest designated as the *promantis* uttered oracles in a state of inspiration,[68] while at the oracle of Apollo at Patara the *promantis* was a female.[69] At the oracle of Ptoan Apollo the oracle priest, called a *promantis* or *prophētēs*, gave the oracular responses himself.[70]

In this sampling of some of the cult officials at local consultation oracles, three of the more important titles for those responsible for receiving and transmitting oracles are *hypophētēs, prophētēs* (fem. *prophētis*), and *promantis*. The term *prophētēs*, which has been transliterated in English as "prophet," is of particular interest in view of its widespread use in early Judaism and early Christianity. The term *prophētēs*, like *hypophētēs*, simply means "spokesman," "announcer."[71] As titles for officials at local consultation oracles, however, all three terms take on the technical meaning of "one who speaks in place of or on behalf of the god," i.e. as a medium between god and man.[72] While the oracular responses of the *prophētēs* frequently were predictive, the prefix *pro-* in the title never indicates the future.[73] Further, while the term *mantis* is not synonymous with the terms *prophētēs, hypophētēs,* or *promantis* (not every *mantis* is a *prophētēs*, though every *prophētēs* is a *mantis*), the last three terms are essentially synonymous.[74]

D. RITUAL PROCEDURES IN SECURING ORACLES

Comparatively little is known about the procedures used at local oracle sanctuaries, though fragmentary data have survived. Both the inquirer and the oracle priest or priestess were expected to complete a prescribed regimen of ritual requirements before an oracle question could be posed and a response granted. This regimen usually involved specifically defined forms of purification, sacrifice, prayer, and the taking of auspices. In the Roman period cult officials instructed inquirers in appropriate modes of speech and behavior,[75] and ritual purification was applied to the area of personal morality.[76] Without these ritual prerequisites the inquirer would not be allowed to enter the sanctuary.

The ritual procedure for the inquirer prior to consulting the oracle of Trophonios in Lebadeia is given in a fairly complete form by Pausanias, who had consulted Trophonios himself.[77] Those who wished to consult Trophonios had to reside in a certain building for several days and abstain from hot baths, bathing only in the river Hercyna. Numerous sacrifices were made, not only to Trophonios himself, but also to the children of Trophonios, Apollo, Cronos, Zeus, Hera, Demeter, and Europa. Each sacrifice was inspected by a *mantis* who foretold (*prothespizei*) whether Trophonios would receive the inquirer graciously. The night before the consultation, the inquirer had to sacrifice a ram over a pit while calling upon Agamedes. This sacrifice also had to be interpreted auspiciously if the consultation was to occur. The inquirer was then taken to the river Hercyna by two thirteen-year-old boys called *Hermai,* who washed him and anointed him with oil. Then the priests took him to a spring to drink the water of forgetfulness, and to another spring to drink the water of memory, after which he had to look upon the image of Trophonios putatively fashioned by Daedalos. After prayers there the inquirer, dressed in a linen tunic tied with ribbons and wearing the local style of footwear, proceeded to the entrance of the chasm where the consultation took place. This very complicated and prolonged series of rites prepared the inquirer for a terrifying experience with Trophonios in the underground chasm. When the badly shaken consultant emerged from the chasm, the priests questioned him and made a record of his visionary experience. While these ritual procedures are more complicated than those at many other local consultation oracles, they vividly illustrate the kind of steps that a consultant might be called upon to take.

The ritual protocol for the oracle priest or priestess can be illustrated by that which was followed by Delphic officials. Since Apollo was believed to be absent from Delphi during the three winter months, the oracular activity of the Pythia was confined to nine months each year. In ancient times the Pythia could be consulted on only one day each year, the seventh day of the seventh Delphic month Bysios (the number seven was sacred to Apollo). During the sixth century B.C. monthly consultations, on the seventh day of each of the nine months, were introduced.[78] Most inquiries, however, appear to have been answered by the sacred lot, which was probably accessible to inquirers on most auspicious days.[79]

The ritual procedure for oracular consultations appears to have been as follows. On auspicious days a procession of cult officials would accompany the Pythia to the spring Kassotis, where she would take a ritual bath of purification. Proceeding back to the temple of Apollo, the goat which was to be sacrificed to Apollo was first sprinkled (or dashed) with cold water. If it trembled all over (a not unlikely prospect), then the god was believed to be present and the consultation could take place.[80] The Pythia then descended with the cult officials and the inquirers to a two-room complex below the temple of Apollo, she to the *adyton* ("inmost sanctuary") where she took her seat on the tripod of Apollo, and they to the waiting room outside.[81] In the *adyton* the Pythia drank from the spring Kassotis, whose waters were probably piped into the *adyton* for that purpose;[82] these waters were widely believed to cause her divine inspiration.[83] The chewing of laurel leaves by the Pythia is a ritual unmentioned until the second century A.D.[84] The vapors often mentioned as a source of the Pythia's inspiration were the invention of the ancients.

The ritual of drinking or chewing certain substances within the sacred precincts was the means whereby the oracle priest or priestess sought to absorb the oracular potencies of the site. At the oracle of Apollo Deiradiotes the prophetess drank the blood of a lamb just sacrificed before experiencing the inspiration of Apollo.[85] At Claros the prophet, after hearing only the name and number of the consultants, would descend into a cavern, the *adyton* of the sanctuary, where he drank water from a spring.[86] He then delivered a response in verse on the subject of whatever question the inquirers had in mind.[87] At Branchidae, too, the prophetess drank spring water before delivering oracular responses from the *adyton* where she was sequestered.[88]

A further requirement for oracle consultation was a fee, frequently computed in terms of sacrificial cakes and animals, which were the necessary preliminaries for consultation.[89] Further, Delphi was filled with votive offerings dedicated by grateful inquirers who chose to express their gratitude in concrete ways. Inquirers to the oracle of Amphilokos were each charged two obols,[90] a fee typical of other oracle sanctuaries. The oracle of Amphiaraos charged one-and-one-half drachmas (nine obols) for each consultation.[91] Alexander of Abonuteichos charged a drachma and two obols (eight obols), a high fee considering the average daily wage was four obols.[92]

E. MODES OF INQUIRY AND RESPONSE

The oracle questions submitted to the cult personnel at oracle sanctuaries were generally in oral form. The phenomenon of oracular clairvoyance, a knowledge of the content of the inquiry before it is expressed, is occasionally attributed not only to the *prophētēs* at Clarian Apollo but to other oracles also, as well as to the practitioners of magical divinations.[93] Written inquiry, a comparatively rare procedure, was characteristic of the oracle of Zeus at Dodona.[94] If written questions were submitted to the

Pythia, they must have been recorded on perishable material, for none has survived. However, there is no literary evidence that written inquiries were submitted to the Pythia. Other oracles that occasionally made use of written inquiries were the oracle of Apollo at Corope, the oracle of Amphilokos and Mopsos at Mallos in Cilicia, and the oracle of Alexander of Abonuteichos.[95] A number of oracle questions in Greek and Demotic were preserved on scraps of papyrus in Egypt, though the exact procedure involved in their use remains unclear.

At Delphi and at virtually every other oracle sanctuary, the oracle priest or priestess received oracular inspiration only in the *adyton* of the temple complex. At Delphi, as elsewhere, the oracular priest or priestess appears to have entered the *adyton* alone, and from there the oracular utterances were either heard by the inquirers in an outer room or were conveyed to them by a cultic official. The general view is that the ecstatic utterances of the Pythia were put into comprehensible language, sometimes even in verse, by one of the two priest-prophets attached to the sanctuary. However, there is little evidence indicating that the prophets had a direct hand in formulating the oracles originally delivered by the Pythia.[96] The title *prophētēs* could mean that this official *interpreted* the utterances of the Pythia to the inquirers, or it could simply mean that he *announced* the oracle that the Pythia had uttered. Some think that the Pythia merely transmitted the answer already formulated by the prophets to the inquirer.[97] The responses of the Pythia were probably oral, and there is no evidence that this response was reworded by the priest-prophets.[98] Some have suggested that the poets mentioned by several ancient authors as part of the sanctuary establishment at Delphi may have been identical with the prophets,[99] but there is no evidence to substantiate this proposal. At Claros the *prophētēs* would produce an oracular response from Apollo that a *thespiodos* ("oracle singer") would then put into meter and sing to the inquirer.[100] At Branchidae the *prophētēs* would receive the response from Apollo and communicate it directly to the inquirer, while the official version of the oracle was then recorded by the *grammateus*.[101] At the oracle of Ptoan Apollo a board of three recorded the oracles.[102] In all of these instances there is not the slightest suggestion that the inspired utterances of the Pythia or of any other *promantis* or *prophētēs* of which we have knowledge was incomprehensible until "interpreted" by other cult officials.[103] The evidence does suggest that it was often thought appropriate to polish the style of inspired oracular responses, even to the extent of putting them into verse or to improve on the verse. At Delphi it is clear that the oracular response of the Pythia in human language was less frequent than the positive or negative response of the lot oracle.

Early references to the oracle of Dodona seem to indicate that the oracle was somehow communicated by the sacred oak itself.[104] The rustling of its branches may have been interpreted as oracular by the *Selloi* or by the three priestesses who apparently succeeded them. The legend of the talking doves perched in the branches of the oak is another possible way of accounting for the mode of oracular response used at the oracle; the sounds of the doves may have been interpreted by cult officials as divine responses to oracular inquiries.[105] Many oracular responses attributed to the oracle at Dodona have been preserved in literature.[106] If these oracles are genuine, and some of them probably are, they would indicate that both oracular responses in human language and the lot oracle and other forms of divination were in use at Dodona as at Delphi. In a late reference to the function of the oracle at Dodona, the inquiry from a visitor found response in the stirring of the oak tree, followed by the interpretation of that response by a priestess who prefaced her oracle with the introductory formula "Thus says Zeus,"[107] though normally the oracles were introduced with the formula "He of Zeus in Dodona declares. . . ." At both Delphi and Dodona the relative infrequency of oracular responses in human language in comparison to the use of various forms of the lot oracle indicates the compatibility of both methods of divination as well as the comparatively greater value assigned to oracular responses in human language.

At the oracle of Glykon-Asklepios, founded by Alexander of Abonuteichos in the middle of the second century A.D., three distinctive modes of oracular response were used. One type was the autophonous oracle, an oracular response not given through a cult intermediary such as a *prophētēs* or *promantis,* but directly by the deity itself, or its iconic representation, to the inquirer. According to Lucian, Glykon-Asklepios, a tame snake which Alexander claimed was a theriomorphic incarnation of Asklepios, was fitted with a fake human head through which an assistant would utter oracles using a concealed speaking tube.[108] Elsewhere Lucian reports an autophonous oracle of the bearded Apollo.[109] A second form of oracular response used by Alexander was the nocturnal dream oracle. Alexander slept on inquiries inscribed and sealed in papyrus rolls, and he claimed to receive oracular responses to these questions in dreams.[110] This is a rare instance of incubation practiced by the *prophētēs* rather than by the inquirer. A third method used by Alexander was to receive written inquiries in sealed rolls and then to return them, ostensibly unopened, with the answer inscribed on the outside.[111] Through these and other means Alexander emphasized the clairvoyant powers of Glykon-Asklepios.

The famous oracle of Zeus Ammon at the Oasis of Siwah in Libya, while having more in common with Egyptian than Greek oracles,[112] was nevertheless immensely popular with Greeks, particularly Spartans, after 500 B.C.[113] At this oracle responses were not given in human language, but through various kinds of sounds or movements which were interpreted by the cult officials.[114] When the oracle was functioning, a bejewelled image of Ammon was carried about on a boat-shaped litter by eighty priests. The movements of the image were regarded as symbolic oracular responses which the *prophētēs* interpret for the inquirer.[115] It has been suggested that the movements of the image of Ammon toward the written inquiry, which was placed on the ground, indicated a positive response, while a movement away from the question indicated a negative response.[116] The sounds which seem to have been regarded as symbolic oracular messages may have been caused by silver cups suspended from the litter that would tinkle while the litter was in motion.[117]

F. ORACULAR INSPIRATION

With the exception of some of the philosophical schools, most ancient Greeks firmly believed that the oracular responses to their inquiries, whether conveyed through lot, sign, dream, or human language, were truly messages from the gods. This conviction was so deeply rooted in the Greek outlook that only rarely do we find attempts to test the validity of oracular responses; most such attempts were made by barbarians.[118] By the time of the Neoplatonist Hermias of Alexandria (fifth century A.D.), doubts about the validity of oracles had become common.[119] But while the gods may have sent the sign, dream, or oracular utterance, many ancients regarded the interpretations and interpreters of these messages with a certain degree of wariness and skepticism. The gods were infallible, but the *mantis* was not.

The Greeks believed that oracular responses in human speech were not only divinely inspired, but that they were the utterances of the gods themselves through human intermediaries. This conviction is borne out by the form of most oracles: they are frequently presented as the direct speech of the oracular divinity.[120] However, rather than use the theologically laden term "inspiration," we prefer to use the more descriptive terms "vision trance" and "possession trance" proposed in the Introduction. While both psycho-physiological states presuppose some form of behavior modification (i.e. an altered state of consciousness), "vision trance" is a state in which audio and/or visual experiences imperceptible to others are perceived by the intermediary, while "possession trance" is a state in which an alien spirit is regarded as having invaded the personality of the intermediary. When oracles are presented as the direct speech of the inspiring oracular divinity, the psycho-physiological state of possession trance is presupposed. One very popular ancient view of the origin of the oracular abilities of the Pythia was that a god or daimon took possession of her organs of speech to make oracular responses.[121] This kind of direct divine inspiration is normally thought to be clearly expressed in the terms *entheos* and *enthysiasmos,* and by the phrase *ek tou theou katochos,* all of which have been understood to mean "divine possession," or in our terms "possession trance." Despite the obvious etymological derivation of *entheos* and *enthysiasmos,*[122] it is not completely clear that the Greeks, when using such terms, always meant that a god invaded or took possession of a human personality (i.e. possession trance).[123] The world of the ancients was populated by multitudes of gods and daimones, and the normal way in which such supernatural beings were thought to exercise influence on human beings was *from without,* using a variety of physical and psychical means to affect people (i.e. vision trance).[124] Clear expressions of the belief that a god or daimon could enter into a prophet or diviner and speak through his organs of speech is attested rarely, if at all, in pre-Christian Greek writers.[125] The notion that the Pythia was possessed and could on that basis utter the oracles of Apollo is first clearly stated by Plutarch, only to be rejected by him (on rationalistic grounds) as unworthy of the god.[126]

Since the Greeks generally assumed that no one could be an intermediary for oracular responses of the gods while *ennous* ("in a normal state of mind"),[127] the terms *ennous* and *entheos* (and their synonyms) have been understood as equivalents to "rational" and "irrational." Further, to be *entheos* or in a state of *enthysiasmos* has come to be identified with frenzied, hysterical behavior. This image of the Pythia, for example, is found in one of the satires of Lucian:

> What in the world are you [i.e. Apollo] going to say, my boy? These preliminaries to your oracle are terrifying in themselves; your colour is changed, your eyes are rolling, your hair stands on end, your movements are frenzied [*korybantōdēs*], and in a word everything about you suggests demoniacal possession [*katochima*] and gooseflesh and mysteries.[128]

P. Amandry has forcefully argued that the "inspired ecstasy" of the Pythia was an invention of Plato given wider currency by Lucan (A.D. 39-65) and a number of other pagan and Christian authors.[129] He observes that authors such as Plutarch and Strabo (both of whom wrote in the second century A.D.) make no reference to any such supposed hysterical behavior on the part of the Pythia.[130] Further, in Greek vase paintings Apollo and the Pythia are always depicted as serene and tranquil.[131] Since the inspiration of a Greek oracle prophet or *promantis* can never have been spontaneous or free, Amandry argues, confined as it was to particular places and times, he denies that such persons can properly be regarded as ecstatics.[132] Ecstasy and rationality, however, should not be regarded as two mutually exclusive states of consciousness.

The kind of psychic phenomenon generally referred to as "possession" or "ecstasy" (though the terms we prefer are "vision trance" and "possession trance") can be *uncontrolled* (the only type referred to by Amandry), but it can also be *controlled*. [133] While Amandry has rightly rejected the portrait of the raving Pythia found in Lucan as spurious, all of the evidence at our disposal suggests that the Pythia, as well as other oracle intermediaries in the Greco-Roman world, experienced a controlled state of vision trance or possession trance during oracular sessions.

We have already noticed that the ancients associated the ability of the *prophētēs* or *promantis* to receive and transmit oracles from the gods with a ritual procedure which enabled them to absorb the unique oracular potencies of the site. This materialistic view of oracular inspiration is reflected in the Delphic legend of Koretas, a shepherd who accidentally fell into a crevasse on the site of the later sanctuary of Apollo and began to utter prophecies involuntarily, i.e. in an uncontrolled state of possession trance. [134] This popular materialistic view of oracular inspiration was given philosophical elaboration by Plutarch, who expressed the view that exhalations from the earth were the cause of the Pythia's inspiration. [135] One term which Plutarch and other ancient writers use for these supposed exhalations is *pneuma*; while Greco-Roman writers certainly had a concept of inspiration, they did not normally associate that conception with *pneuma*. [136] Unlike early Christianity and early Judaism, where *pneuma* is primarily a theological concept and a central means for explaining the phenomenon of divine inspiration, among Greco-Roman authors the term has no theological singificance and is marginal for their understanding of divine inspiration. The closest parallel to the use of *pneuma* in early Jewish and early Christian reflections on divine inspiration is the use of the term *enthysiasmos*. [137]

Oracular revelation, whether through a dream or vision experienced during incubation or through an inspired utterance of a cult official, could occur only in the *adyton* ("innermost sanctuary") of the oracle shrine. At inspired oracles the *adyton* was either identical with the grotto or cavern from which the oracular potency of the site was derived, or an architectural imitation of such a natural opening in the earth. Frequently the sacred waters which were central to the oracular ritual were either located in a spring in the *adyton* or were artificially piped in. The legitimation of the divine origin of the dreams or inspired speech of the oracle medium was based on the sanctity of the site and the faithful adherence to the prescribed ritual procedures rather than on the ecstatic behavior of the medium. Oracle mediums appear to have been divinely inspired in the *adyton* only after the proper ritual procedure. There is no evidence that oracle mediums were selected for their clairvoyant gifts. Rather, the occurrence of oracular inspiration was wholly dependent on the sacred site and the cultic ritual that activated its oracular potencies. Since bizarre behavior on the part of those regarded as possessed frequently occurred outside the strictures of normal social or religious institutions, such behavior functioned as a legitimation of the supernatural nature of the experience in the absence of built-in institutional guarantees. Ecstatic behavior, as we shall see, was a much more pronounced characteristic among those ancients who claimed divine inspiration but who had no permanent connection to a traditional oracle sanctuary.

III. ORACULAR PERSONS

In addition to the large number of local consultation oracles which dotted the Greco-Roman world, many professional diviners and oracle-givers had no permanent connection with local cults. Occasionally we find priests who claimed oracular gifts unconnected with oracular sites.[138] These individuals, because of their reputed skills or gifts, played an important role in mediating a knowledge of the future or the unknown to clients anxious for such information. Since they are like both early Jewish and early Christian prophets in having no connection with sacred places, these free Greco-Roman mantics deserve particularly close attention.

Four types of free diviners may be distinguished: (1) the *technical diviner,* a type which consists of two subtypes: (a) the practitioner employed by the state, and (b) the free-lance practitioner; (2) the *inspired diviner*; (3) the *collector and interpreter of oracles*; and (4) the *magical diviner.* The distinction between the technical diviner and the inspired diviner is partially based on the distinction made by many ancients between technical divination and natural divination.[139] One major problem with this distinction is that it is usually made in polemical contexts in which great value and validity is placed on natural divination at the expense of technical divination.[140] Nevertheless the distinction appears to be useful, and we have retained it for our first two types.

Plato and other ancient Greeks correctly saw that the word *mantis* ("diviner," "seer," or "prophet") and the terms *mania* and *mainesthai,* which refer to such states as "madness," "rage," and "frenzy," were cognates.[141] In spite of attempts to refute this ancient opinion,[142] modern philologists agree with Plato.[143] This etymological derivation, however, contributes little or nothing to our knowledge of the role of most diviners in the Greco-Roman period.[144]

A. THE TECHNICAL DIVINER

The technical diviner was a religious adept who professed to have the requisite knowledge and skill for the proper interpretation of the ambiguous signs and symbols that were regarded as coded indications of the will of the gods. Such signs and symbols were thought to be particularly evident in dreams, in the condition of sacrificial animals, and in the flight of birds, as well as in a variety of other strange and unusual omens and sounds. The correct interpretation of such enigmatic signs and symbols was based on an intimate knowledge of the lore of divination. The status of the technical diviner was based in part on his command of the special lore of divination that was largely inaccessible to others.

Technical diviners were customarily employed by Greek governments both to interpret the divine will in everyday affairs of state and to accompany military forces on land or sea in order to achieve victory through the careful adaptation of military tactics to the will of the gods. Whether the form of government was monarchy, tyranny, oligarchy, or democracy, the technical diviner was a ubiquitous figure whose duty was to interpret the various coded manifestations of the divine will for the advantage of the state that employed him and to minimize the risks it had to take. On military expeditions the technical diviner was a critical member of the general staff whose duty was to interpret properly omens, signs, prodigies, sacrifices, dreams, and unusual events so that victory might be achieved.[145] Before the Hellenistic period this form of divination tended to merge with magic; the diviner was not only expected to determine the most auspicious times for battle, but also to create victory. Whether employed by the state or by a general during a military campaign, one important task of the technical diviner was the interpretation of the condition and the entrails of sacrificial victims to determine whether the sacrifice was acceptable and whether the objective of the sacrifice (i.e. victory) would be achieved.[146]

Many technical mantics were free-lance practitioners who could be consulted for a price in the marketplace of any Greek city.[147] Such diviners also tended to follow military expeditions,[148] to fawn on the wealthy and the governing class,[149] and to wander to places where their arts could be profitably practiced.[150] Free-lance mantics did not always enjoy the best reputation, and they were frequently castigated for their pecuniary motivations.[151] Euripides expressed a widely held view of such diviners when he said, "What is a mantic? One who tells few truths, but many lies."[152]

Since techncal divination was as much a skill based on the possession of accumulated lore as it was a gift, it was not infrequently a hereditary vocation. Theoklymenos, the diviner who foretold the doom of the suitors shortly after arriving at the house of Odysseus, belonged to a family of mantics descended from Melampos.[153] The Telmissian mantics (one of whom was the Aristander who accompanied Alexander the Great),[154] were reportedly a large family in which women and children as well as men inherited the mantic gift.[155] The most famous family of mantics in antiquity was the Iamidae of Elis, who practiced technical divination throughout the Greek world and were sought after for their renowned skill and expertise.[156]

B. THE INSPIRED DIVINER

A generation ago it was fashionable to regard the "ecstatic" element in Greek religion as an alien intrusion of foreign "Dionysiac" elements into the rational and sober "Apolline" religion of an earlier period. Now it is widely accepted that the rational and the irrational, the sober and the ecstatic, existed side by side in Greek religion from earliest times.[157] Although some have contended that Homer knew only technical divination,[158] both the *Iliad* and the *Odyssey* appear to have a few examples of inspired divination.[159] Ancient scholars such as Plutarch found inspired as well as technical divination in Homer. The Trojan mantic Helenos is referred to as one who understood the counsel of the gods.[160] The most impressive example of inspired divination in Homer is the prediction of Theoklymenos:

> Ah, wretched men, what evil is this that you suffer? Shrouded in night are your heads and your faces and your knees beneath you; kindled is the sound of wailing, bathed in tears are your cheeks, and sprinkled with blood are the walls and the fair rafters. And full of ghosts that hasten down to Erebus beneath the darkness, and the sun has perished out of heaven and an evil mist hovers over all.[161]

While this speech has been regarded as simply a "poetic vision,"[162] it was probably modeled after a prophetic form of speech readily recognizable by the ancients.[163]

1. Sibyl and Bakis.

Several legendary prophetic figures of the past, including Orpheus, Musaeos, Sibyl, and Bakis, are mentioned frequently in Greek literature. We shall consider two of these figures, Sibyl and Bakis, in some detail. The Sibyl (a designation whose etymology is unknown)[164] was always a woman and was far more popular than Bakis, who was always regarded as male. They have several common features: (1) they belonged to the remote past, (2) their oracles were thought to have been uttered while they were in a state of divine inspiration or possession, (3) their oracles were uttered spontaneously and not in response to inquiries, and (4) collections of their oracles were extant and widely circulated in the Greco-Roman period.

The Sibyl is first mentioned in a famous statement attributed to the philosopher Heraclitus (sixth century B.C.):

> But "the Sibyl with frenzied lips," according to Heraclitus, "uttering words mirthless," unembellished, unperfumed, yet reaches to a thousand years with her voice through the god.[165]

This statement, which combines a citation with Plutarch's periphrastic comment, alludes to the divine inspiration of the Sibyl in terms of possession trance, to the spontaneity of her oracular utterances, to the gravity of their content (most were oracles of doom), and to the inelegance of their formulation (they were not retouched by a *prophētēs* or a *thespiodos*), and finally to the fact that their fulfilment was not necessarily immediate but could stretch into the indefinite future.[166] The term "Sibyl," whatever its original meaning or application, was a generic term for a wandering female prophetess who uttered spontaneous oracles in hexameter verse.[167] By the late Greco-Roman period more than forty Sibyls had been mentioned in the literature.[168]

The Sibylline traditions have a number of significant features. First, Sibyls were often located near oracles of Apollo, the god who was believed to inspire them.[169] Many Sibylline legends describe the prophetesses, not as wandering aimlessly, but as traveling from oracle to oracle. Eventually they are depicted as settling permanently at a particular oracle sanctuary. The Greek association of oracular activity with sites which possessed oracular potencies appears to have exerted a magnetic attraction on the Sibylline traditions. Second, the oracular utterances of the Sibyls are always regarded as spontaneous predictions extant in the form of written collections of oracles.[170] Third, the multiplication of Sibyls, as well as attempts to systematize the names and locations of the various Sibyls, seems to have arisen from the desire to legitimate various collections of Sibylline oracles and to anchor them to space and time in remote antiquity.[171] There was a natural tendency to associate the Sibyl with Delphi (an association which does not seem to antedate the Hellenistic period) because of the enormous prestige and reputation of that oracle. This association with Delphi served to legitimate the collections of Sibylline oracles, which enjoyed increasing circulation during the Hellenistic and Roman periods.

Sibylline oracles were immensely popular and enjoyed an excellent reputation. Even early Jewish and early Christian authors, ordinarily hostile to pagan divination and oracles, expressed respect for the Sibyl and her prophecies.[172] Many of the locations came to be associated with the Sibyls, probably because of the oracles themselves. This quotation from Pausanias reveals how such deductions were made:

> In her poem she calls herself not only Herophile but also Artemis, and the wedded wife of Apollo, saying too sometimes that she is his sister, and sometimes that she is his daughter. These statements she made in her poetry when in a frenzy and possession by the god. Elsewhere in her oracles she states that her mother was an immortal, one of the nymphs of Ida, while her father was a human. These are the verses
> "I am by birth half mortal, half divine;
> An immortal nymph was my mother, my father an eater of corn;
> On my mother's side of Idaean birth, but my fatherland was red
> Marpessus, sacred to the Mother, and the river Aïdoneus."[173]

The wide circulation and respect which the various collections of Sibylline oracles enjoyed led to the formation of a variety of legends which served to authenticate and legitimate the oracles, as well as introduce order into the discrete traditions contained in the oracles themselves. The term "Sibyl" was therefore a pseudonymous attempt to legitimate oracles which may or may not have been uttered in a state of divine possession by diviners who collected and interpreted such oracles.

The vast majority of ancient witnesses who refer to Bakis as the author of a collection of oracles refer to him in the singular.[174] Herodotus, who does not refer to the Sibyl, does mention Bakis as the author of a number of oracles.[175] Both Aristotle and Plutarch refer to a plurality of "Sibylla and Bakides,"[176] and several scholia on the plays of Aristophanes mention three Bakides, one from Attica, one from Boeotia, and a third from Arcadia.[177] On the basis of this evidence, a number of influential scholars have maintained that Bakis, like Sibyl, was a generic term for wandering male ecstatic prophets who were active ca. 700-500 B.C.[178] In Aristotle and Plutarch, however, the phrase "Sibylla and Bakides" probably means no more than "people like Sibyl and Bakis."[179] The multiplication of Bakides probably occurred through the influence of the Sibylline traditions.[180] The late accounts of wandering Bakides are legends created through the assimilation of the figure of Bakis to that of the Sibyl. In reality, all that Pausanias, Herodotus, Aristophanes, and other ancients knew of Bakis was a collection of oracles which circulated under his name.

The legendary inspired diviners called Sibyl and Bakis and the growing traditions about them functioned primarily as a means of legitimating various collections or oracles of diverse character — general predictions of judgment and destruction whose ambiguity gave ample room for the interpretative expertise of oracle interpreters. The images of Sibyl and Bakis as inspired were based on the widely accepted view that oracles in human language, providing their origin was legitimate, must be the product of persons inspired by the gods.[181]

2. Plato's *Theomanteis* and *Chrēsmodoi*.

We now turn from legendary to historical figures. Plato mentions a contemporary prophetic type (fourth century B.C.), which he calls *theomanteis* ("inspired mantics") and *chrēsmodoi* ("oracle singers").[182] Plato describes these inspired diviners as instruments through which the god speaks; the many good and true things which they say do not come from their own knowledge.[183] Although Plato mentions these inspired diviners and oracle singers only a few times, they are significant for him as models for those who speak through divine inspiration and not personal knowledge. These include poets, politicians, and philosophers as well as the Sibyl, the Pythia, and the priestesses at Dodona.[184] Since genuine divination results in a knowledge of the future,[185] such knowledge cannot come from man himself.

Plato has a fascination with *mania,* a term frequently translated "madness," but which in some contexts can more accurately be rendered "inspiration."[186] Socrates says:

> For the prophetess at Delphi and the priestesses at Dodona when they have been mad have conferred many splendid benefits upon Greece both in private and public affairs, but few or none when they have been in their right minds; and if we should speak of the Sibyl and all the others who by prophetic inspiration have foretold many things to many persons and thereby made them fortunate afterwards, anyone can see that we should speak for a long time.[187]

Here and elsewhere Plato uses a great many terms that suggest the phenomenon of divine possession or inspiration. Yet some of the more characteristic behavioral features of possession trance or vision trance can be discerned only with difficulty. In *Ion* 534d Plato seems to presuppose some visible or audible evidences of possession:

> And for this reason God takes away the mind of these men and uses them as his ministers, just as he does soothsayers [*chrēsmodoi*] and godly seers [*tois mantesi tois theiois*], in order that we who hear them may know that it is not they who utter these words of great price, when they are out of their wits, but that it is God himself who speaks and addresses us through them.

The phenomenon of divine inspiration legitimates the utterances of these inspired diviners, but Plato may be using the criterion of *content* (i.e. knowledge of the future) and not the criterion of *behavior* to reveal the inspiration of the diviner. The behavioral features which Plato associates with divine possession are the suddenness and unexpectedness of the oracular utterances of inspired persons and visionary experiences.[188] Aelius Aristides, a second-century A.D. rhetorician who was dependent on Plato, claimed that after an inspired oracle had been uttered the prophet did not know what he had said.[189]

While the picture is far from complete, we may suppose that Plato's inspired diviner (*theomantis* or *chrēsmodos*) exhibited at least some of the characteristic behavior of divine possession or divine inspiration, and that such behavior served to legitimate his oracular utterances. Although these inspired mantics may have exhibited some phenomena associated with divine possession, they spoke not ecstatic gibberish, but rational, metrical sayings which — to Plato at least — contained some profound sentiments. These inspired diviners, however, were limited in Plato's view because they did not possess knowledge.[190] Just as Plato had no serious belief in the gods of Greek myth and cult, so he did not place the highest value on inspired diviners and poets.[191]

In *Timaeus* 71e-72b Plato argues that intermediaries, whom he calls prophets, are necessary for judging and interpreting the inspired utterances of mantics:

> But it is not the task of him who has been in a state of frenzy, and still continues therein, to judge the apparitions and voices seen or uttered by himself; for it was well said of old that to do and to know one's own and oneself belongs only to him who is sound of mind. Wherefore also it is customary to set the tribe of prophets to pass judgement upon these inspired divinations; and they, indeed, themselves are named "diviners" by certain who are wholly ignorant of the truth that they are not diviners but interpreters of the mysterious voice and apparition, for whom the most fitting name would be "prophets of things divined."

Here Plato seems to refer to the practice of placing an oracle-cult official, frequently given the title *prophētēs*, between the inspired priest or priestess and the inquirer.[192] Since this quotation alludes to the famous Delphic maxim "Know yourself," Plato is probably alluding to the practice at the oracle of Apollo at Delphi.[193] The inspired diviner is described as seeing visions and mediating voices other than his own. Nowhere else is the Pythia described in ancient sources as having visionary experiences. While Plato is probably alluding to Delphi, he may be combining two or more kinds of inspired divinatory phenomena. Plato appears to use this oracular practice as a precedent for advocating the subordination of those with a less rational basis for knowledge to those with a more fully rational grasp of knowledge, i.e. philosophers and rulers.

Unfortunately, Plato does not provide an example of the kind of oracular speech which characterized the inspired diviners whom he so briefly discussed. By the second century A.D., even a writer like Pausanias no longer knew of mantics who uttered oracles.[194]

3. The Chrēsmologoi.

Another ambiguous mantic figure with a long history is known as the chrēsmologos, a term which etymologically can mean "oracle collector," "oracle interpreter," or simply "prophet."[195] When J. H. Oliver equated the chrēsmologos with the mantis, he met stiff resistance from a number of prominent European classical scholars.[196] Even though some ancient authors may have used the terms interchangeably, it was argued, originally they were quite distinct. The professional collectors and expounders of oracles were the chrēsmologoi, while the inspired individual who first uttered the oracle was called a mantis; a third figure, the exēgētēs, was the authority who interpreted questions of religious custom or ritual.[197] The problem with the distinctions made between the chrēsmologos and the mantis is that they have a more philological than historical basis.

Amphilytos the Akarnanian, a chrēsmologos according to Herodotus,[198] approached Peisistratos and uttered the following spontaneous oracle in hexameter "while inspired" (entheazon):

> Now hath the cast been thrown and the net of the fisher is outspread:
> All in the moonlight clear shall the tunny-fish come for the taking.

Herodotus understood Amphilytos, not only as one who recited selections from a collection of existing oracles, but as an inspired mantic.[199] Elsewhere in Herodotus the chrēsmologoi to which he refers act either exclusively as interpreters of oracles[200] or, in the case of Onomakritos of Athens, as a collector, reciter, and interpreter of the oracles of Musaeos.[201] That Onomakritos had been caught forging an oracle may suggest that some chrēsmologoi (such as Amphilytos and Lysistratos) were inspired diviners who produced their own oracles and yet attributed them to such ancient and legendary worthies as Orpheus, Musaeos, Sibyl, and Bakis.

In the early first century A.D. Philo of Alexandria (who had little respect for any form of pagan technical divination) remarked about the chrēsmologoi:

> just so though some oracle-mongers [chrēsmologosi] may ply their false art of divination, masked under the specious name of prophecy [prophēteias], and palm off their ecstatic utterances upon the Godhead, they will easily be detected.[202]

Again these chrēsmologoi appear to be inspired mantics, and not simply collectors and expounders of the oracles of others.

4. The Engastrimythoi.

Plutarch mentions another type of inspired mantic:

> Certainly it is foolish and childish in the extreme to imagine that the god himself after the manner of ventriloquists [engastrimythous] (who used to be called "Eurycleis," but now "Pythones") enters into the bodies of his prophets [prophētōn] and prompts their utterances, employing their mouths and voices as instruments.[203]

The term engastrimythos,[204] usually translated "ventriloquist," should rather be rendered, though less elegantly, "belly-talker." The engastrimythoi were not ventriloquists but mediums in a state of possession trance who spoke with a strange voice, perhaps one very different from the normal tone.[205] Eurycles was a famous "belly-talker" and *mantis* of the fifth century B.C.,[206] of whom the scholiast observed: "He [Eurycles] as an *engastrimythos,* say the Athenians, prophesied truthfully through a daimon resident in him."[207] Early Christian fathers regarded the *engastrimythoi* as demon possessed.[208] The third designation mentioned by Plutarch, "Pythones," is generally understood by ancient authorities as a synonym for the *engastrimythoi.* In the NT a slave girl with a "spirit of divination" (*pneuma pythōna*) is briefly described in Acts 16:16-18. As an inspired mantic the girl was a source of income for her masters. Her oracular utterances were both spontaneous and involuntary, judging by the oracle which she repeatedly cried out regarding Paul and Silas (Acts 16:17):

> These men are servants of the most high God,
> Who proclaim to you the way of salvation.

The bizarre behavior of the slave girl and her loud cry while delivering the oracle are characteristic features of possession trance.[209]

The inspired diviner who was described as an *engastrimythos,* a Eurycles, or a *python* is a type which was found as early as the fifth century B.C. in Athens and as late as the second century A.D. During this long period the central characteristic of this type of inspired mantic is the striking "possessed" behavior of speaking in a very strange voice. This behavior provided legitimation for the divine origin of the oracles uttered by such adepts.

5. Miscellaneous Types.

Syrians seem to have had a particularly notorious reputation for their prophetic arts. Arrian describes a Syrian women who, possessed by the divine spirit, followed Alexander the Great around, making a series of oracular utterances.[210] Another Syrian woman, Martha, because of the prophetic oracles which she communicated to the wife of Marius, soon became the religious advisor of Marius himself (157-86 B.C.).[211] Lucian describes the technique of a Syrian exorcist,[212] as well as that of a Syrian witch,[213] in some detail. A Syrian named Eunus is reported to have incited a slave revolt on the pretext of having received a divine revelation.[214]

One of the more significant Syrian prophetic figures or types is the one parodied by Celsus, a pagan philosopher who wrote a treatise against Christianity entitled *True Discourse* ca. A.D. 178.[215] Celsus gives a typical sample of this kind of prophetic revelation:

> I am God; I am the Son of God; or, I am the Divine Spirit;
> I have come because the world is perishing,
> and you, O men, are perishing for your iniquities.

The prophet goes on to make promises and threats, depending on the kind of response he expects to receive from his listeners. Some have thought that the prophets parodied by Celsus were pagans;[216] others more justifiably regard Celsus' portrait as an amalgam of Christian, Jewish, and pagan ingredients. The introductory "I am" has suggested similarities with the speeches of Jesus in the Fourth Gospel.[217] There are two possible interpretations of the "I am" formulations of the speech parodied by Celsus: either the speaker is claiming divine status,[218] or the prophet is a vehicle for a supernatural being who is speaking through him.[219] The phrase "I have come," which was part of the message of the prophet quoted above, indicates that the speaker is claiming divine status. In view of the structure of the entire speech, it is also probable that Celsus (who was familiar with the canonical gospels) has parodied a number of sayings of Jesus.[220] Another feature of the performance of this prophet presented by Celsus is that "strange, fanatical and quite unintelligible words" are appended to the revelatory speech.[221]

Several sources reveal a social type of inspired diviner quite different from any which we have discussed thus far. This kind of inspired mantic exercised his gifts within the context of the mystery cults. The Greek historian Polybius, reporting Cn. Manlius Vulso's foray against the Galatians (189 B.C.), mentions two Galli (eunuchs devoted to the goddess Cybele) who were sent from Attis and Battacus, priests of Cybele, and arrived in a ritual procession bearing pectorals and images to announce to Manlius that the goddess had foretold his victory. Manlius accepted this unexpected prediction graciously. The two Galli are depicted by Livy as "prophesying in frenzied chants."[222] Livy appears to have embellished the narrative by bringing one of the Galli's typical behaviors — ritual frenzy — into conjunction with their supposed prophetic activity.

Elsewhere Livy refers to the phenomenon of prophecy within the context of Dionysiac ecstasy.[223] Although the cult of Dionysos at Rome was largely composed of women, Livy describes only men as prophesying: "Men, as if insane, with fanatical tossings of their bodies, would utter prophecies."[224] Again, in view of the rarity of the evidence for prophetic activity within the framework of a mystery cult, one may suspect that Livy assumed that any speaking done in the throes of Dionysiac ecstasy deserved the label "prophesying."[225] A similar phenomenon is reported by Apuleius (born ca. A.D. 123), who describes a group of priests and followers of Cybele. One of their number was in ecstasy and noisily prophesied, accusing himself of disobedience.[226] Here "prophesy" does not concern the prediction of the future, but rather a public confession of wrongdoing.

Another witness for prophetic activity within the framework of a mystery cult is Plutarch:

> However, the thing that most filled the poetic art with disrepute was the tribe of wandering soothsayers and rogues that practised their charlatanry about the shrines of the Great Mother [Cybele] and of Serapis, making up oracles, some using their own ingenuity, others taking by lot from certain treatises oracles for the benefit of servants and womenfolk, who are most enticed by verse and a poetic vocabulary. This, then, is not the least among the reasons why poetry, by apparently lending herself to the service of tricksters, mountebanks, and false prophets [pseudomantesin], lost all standing with truth and the tripod.[227]

Although Plutarch does not mention the ecstatic behavior of these devotees of Cybele and Serapis, he does refer to two methods of producing oracles. The first method was the extemporaneous utterance of oracles in poetic form (probably hexameter), and the second was probably the use of a lot oracle consisting of prepared lists of questions and answers.[228] Plutarch is highly critical of wandering mantics who sell oracles. Unlike Livy and Apuleius, he does not link frenzied behavior with oracular speech. Another second-century writer, Arrian, reportedly observed that the Phrygians became "Corybantic" and "prophesy future events while inspired and in a state of ecstasy."[229] By the second century A.D., then, it had become widely accepted that independent inspired diviners exhibited the behavioral characteristics of possession trance while uttering oracles.

6. Eschatological Prophets.

Eschatological prophecy in the sense in which it is known in early Judaism and early Christianity was less common in Greco-Roman paganism. The Greeks and Romans, of course, had utopian visions of the future,[230] of which the most famous is perhaps the vision of an imminent golden era in Vergil's *Fourth Eclogue*.[231] Eschatological prophecy in Greco-Roman paganism, however, was much more prevalent in the eastern Mediterranean than in the west. The oracles of Hystaspes (written between the first century B.C. and the first century A.D.), with their predictions of the destruction of the world by fire and the emergence of an age of bliss, are typical of Near Eastern apocalypticism in the Roman period.[232] Such prophecies appear to have been stimulated by oriental world views combined with the experience of repressive foreign domination, first by the Greeks under Alexander and his successors and then by the Romans.

Greco-Roman Egypt gave rise to many such eschatological fantasies. The "Oracle of the Potter," which probably originated ca. 130 B.C. in Egypt, not only contains the prophecy of the potter, but also a narrative framework describing his experience. The oracle is introduced with these words: "And when the mind of the potter was displaced and he became inspired by Hermes, he said. . . ."[233] While the framework is undoubtedly a literary fiction, its intention is to legitimate the oracle in a number of ways. One such way is the description of the inspired behavior of the prophet in stereotypical conventions by saying that the potter was "out of his mind" and "inspired by Hermes."

All roads led to Rome, and at the other end of the Mediterranean world we find another example of an eschatological prophecy, delivered in the context of the plague of A.D. 166.[234] One foolish person

> continually made speeches from the wild fig tree on the Campus Martius to the effect that fire would fall down from heaven and the end of the world would come should he fall from the tree and be turned into a stork, and finally at the appointed time he did fall down and free a stork from his robe. . . .

The cosmopolitan nature of Rome makes it impossible to determine the national origin or true intentions of this pathetic figure. Such spontaneous prophetic activity seems to have broken out from time to time at Rome in response to various crises, particularly famines.[235]

C. THE COLLECTOR AND INTERPRETER OF ORACLES

The earliest reference in Greek literature to a collector and expounder of oracles is the brief account of the career of Onomakritos, an Athenian *chrēsmologos*.[236] Onomakritos reportedly both collected and arranged the oracles of Musaeos, and was banished from Athens by the tyrant Hipparchos because he was caught inserting a forged oracle into the collection. Herodotus also reports that Onomakritos would recite certain favorable oracles to Xerxes the Persian king, while ignoring other oracles which were less favorable. The role of Onomakritos, therefore, was based on a personal collection of oracles which he applied to contemporary situations by reciting and commenting upon them.

The Athenian comic poet Aristophanes (ca. 457-385 B.C.) parodied the *chrēsmologos* in one of his plays.[237] The *chrēsmologos* he depicts has a small book (*biblion*) containing a collection of the oracles of Bakis that he manipulates in order to procure clothing, sandals, and food from the unwary and credulous. Elsewhere Aristophanes portrays another *chrēsmologos* named Hierocles, who similarly quotes the oracles of Bakis in order to get a good meal from his clients.[238] Aristotle is critical of such *chrēsmologoi* because, while they are quick to make predictions, they are never very definite about the specific time when their predictions will be fulfilled.[239] Plutarch refers only once to a *chrēsmologos,* the Spartan Diopeithes who had a collection of ancient oracles in his possession:

> This man [Diopeithes] declared it contrary to the will of Heaven that a lame man should be king of Sparta, and cited at the trial of the case the following oracle: "Bethink thee now, O Sparta, though thou art very glorious, lest from thee, sound of foot, there spring a maimed royalty; for long will unexpected toils oppress thee, and onward-rolling billows of man-destroying war."[240]

The context makes it clear that other interpretations were possible, but the role of the *chrēsmologos* in reciting and interpreting oracles from his private collection is vividly depicted. Thucydides refers to this same interpretative activity of the *chrēsmologoi* several times,[241] as well as to the exegetical problems involved.[242]

In contrast to the inspired mantic, whom we have considered at length, the oracle collector and expounder based his authority not on the audible and visual behavioral phenomena associated with possession trance, but on the authority of a collection of ancient oracles attributed to Sibyl, Bakis, Musaeos, Orpheus, and others. The role of the oracle collector and interpreter complements the Greek view of the nature of oracles: because of their ambiguity, complete fulfilment was always in doubt. Nevertheless, since oracles were *always* fulfilled (unfulfilled oracles function as the exiting force in countless Greek stories), the time would come when each oracle would have its complete fulfilment. The oracle collector and expounder took advantage of this view to ply his trade in reinterpreting and reapplying "ancient" oracles, some of which he (like Onomakritos) probably composed himself.

In contrast to the kind of oracle collectors and expounders which we have been discussing, oracle interpreters (*exēgētai*) were free-lance practitioners who claimed expertise in making ambiguous oracles comprehensible for their recipients. For example, according to Lucian, near the oracle of Glykon-Asklepios managed by Alexander of Abonuteichos were numbers of interpreters who for a fee would explain ambiguous oracles to those who had received them.[243] Elsewhere Lucian satirizes the oracles of Apollo for being so obscure that they required a second Apollo to interpret them.[244] Such oracle interpreters claimed neither the authority of divine inspiration nor the status associated with owning a private oracle library. The interpreter was thought, like the technical diviner, to possess the technical lore which enabled him to clarify the meaning of obscure oracles.

D. THE MAGICAL DIVINER.

Greco-Roman revelatory magic is a subject which is rarely related to other ancient oracular and prophetic phenomena and traditions.[245] That state of affairs is unfortunate, for there are strong indications that Greco-Roman revelatory magic penetrated various phases of early Christianity. There are, for example, antimagical polemics in both the Apocalypse of John and in the Shepherd of Hermas, polemics directed against those who regarded themselves as Christians, not outsiders.[246] Our knowledge of Greco-Roman (or, more correctly, Greco-Egyptian) magic is based primarily on the fortunate survival of ancient magical handbooks written on papyrus in Egypt from the second to the fifth centuries A.D.[247] The nature of these magical texts is such that our knowledge of magical divination is of an order quite different from that of other aspects of Greco-Roman oracular traditions; we know more about the ritual procedures and their specific goals than we do about any other aspects of revelatory magic. Evidence from the magical papyri suggests that the goals of the practitioners of Greco-Egyptian magic can be placed within four broad categories: (1) protective and apotropaic magic, (2) aggressive and malevolent magic, (3) love magic and magic aimed at the acquisition of power and control, and (4) magical divination.[248] Most of the magical procedures (I prefer this term to such other possible designations as "spells," "charms," "incantations," etc.), however, focus on either erotic magic[249] or revelatory magic.[250] Our primary concern in this discussion, of course, is only with revelatory magic.

Magical texts usually consist of two structural parts, the *epiklēsis* (or invocation) and the *praxis* (or magical operation). More complicated structural analyses of these texts have been made, but they are irrelevant for present purposes. The types of revelatory magic found in the papyri can conveniently be separated into two categories, magical divination and oracular magic. Some of the more common types of magical divination include (1) lamp divination, or *lychnomanteia* (*PGM* VII.540-577), (2) bowl divination, or *lekanomanteia* (*PGM* III.276; IV.221), (3) saucer divination, or *phialomanteia* (*PGM* IV.3209-54; VII.727-739; LXII.39-46, 47-51), and (4) divination by dreams, variously called *oneiromanteia, oneiraitēton,* or *oneiropompos* (*PGM* VII.1009-16; VII.664-685, 703-726, 740-755, 795-845; VIII.64-110; XII.107-121, 121-143, 308b-318). Oracular magic, on the other hand, includes the following subtypes: (1) procedures for personal visions, variously called *autoptikos, autoptos,* or *autopsia* (*PGM* VII.319-334, 335-347; VIII.85-91a, 734-735), (2) procedures for acquiring foreknowledge, or *prognōsis* (*PGM* III.479-494, 424-465; VII.348-358), (3) procedures for acquiring an assisting divinity, or *paredros daimon* (*PGM* I.1-42, 42-132), (4) oracular questions and answers through a boy medium (*PGM* VII.348-358), a procedure very common in the Demotic magical papyri,[251] and (5) certain types of bowl divination (*PGM* IV.154-285). A frustrating feature of many of these texts is that they bring the reader to the very brink of a revelatory experience without disclosing the kind of experience involved and without providing any examples of the kinds of oracular revelation which ostensibly occurred. One very distinctive feature of magical divination and oracular magic is that there is very little evidence for the phenomenon of possession trance.[252] In an era when possession trance was regarded as a typical way of understanding oracular inspiration, the emphasis in the magical papyri is decidedly on the vision trance. However, though the magical practitioner is told in various instructions in the magical procedures that he will see and hear extraordinary things, there is no suggestion of any behavior modification. Such descriptions, however, cannot be expected given the genre of the papyri. In spite of the fact that we have proposed a number of categories of magical divination and oracular magic, it must be observed that many procedures had a multipurpose character; *PGM* IV.2145-2240, for example, is a procedure touted not only for its efficacy in securing oracles, but also for its ability to wreck chariots!

The Berlin Magical Papyrus (*PGM* I) begins with two procedures for securing an assisting divinity (I.1-42 and I.42-195), who is described as being able among other things to "reveal all things clearly to you and (as a companion) shall eat and sleep with you" (I.1-2), and to "tell you whatever you want instantly" (I.79). In *PGM* I.166b-177 the practitioner is told what to do after the *paredros daimon* has made his appearance:

> Then inquire of him using the same oaths. If he reveals his name to you, take him by the hand, go downstairs and have him recline as I said earlier and set before him the food and drink of which you (normally) partake. And when you dismiss him, after he has departed sacrifice to him whatever is spread out (on the table) and pour out wine, and thus you will be a friend of that powerful messenger [*angelos*]. When you are away, he will accompany you; when you are poor he will give you money; he will reveal future events to you, both when and specifically what time of the night or day. If anyone asks you, "What am I thinking?" or "What has happened or is about to happen to me?", ask the messenger and he will tell you silently. But you speak to the inquirer as if on your own.

Here the assisting divinity, once summoned, has become the constant companion of the magician, and even serves as an invisible silent partner who provides him instantly with oracular revelations unknown by the magician's client.

The illustrious and venerable oracle of Apollo at Delphi had a predictable influence on the tradition of oracular magic in Greco-Roman Egypt. *PGM* III.187-262 is basically a procedure for summoning Helios-Apollo. It begins with a preliminary ritual indicating the juncture at which a hymn to Helios Apollo should be sung; the hymn is then quoted *in extenso* in lines 198-229.[253] Lines 192b-196a describe the goal of the procedure:

> And the divinity will come to you, shaking before him the entire house and the tripod. And then complete acquisition of foreknowledge [*prognōstikēn*] with clear instructions as long as you wish, and then dismiss the god with thanksgiving.

The quotation describes an impressive Apolline theophany followed by an oracular interview led by the magical practitioner. In another procedure aimed at enlisting the oracular powers of Apollo (*PGM* II.1-182) fragments of what may be ancient Delphic hymns are interspersed throughout the ritual. Lines 2b-4a, in excellent hexameter, introduce the hymnic invocation:

> Phoebus, come with rejoicing to facilitate prophesying [*mantosynaisin*]
> Son of Leto, far-darting one, averter of evil, come here, come.
> Come here prophesying [*thespizōn*] and grant oracles [*manteueō*] in the night time.

Later on in the same procedure we read the following invocation in lines 53-54:

> God of gods, King of kings, compel a friendly oracle-giving daimon to come to me now.

In one of a number of examples of a procedure for a personal vision (*autoptos*), the reciter claims "I am a prophet [*prophētēs*]" (VII.323) and goes on to say in lines 329-331:

> Open my ears that you might prophesy [*chrēmatisēs*] to me concerning those matters about which I expect a response. Now, now! Quick, quick! Hurry, hurry! Tell me about those matters about which I asked you.

While the speaker might appear to be a trifle impatient, the frequency with which formulaic injunctions to haste occur in the papyri indicates that they were about as significant as RUSH stamped on a modern package. In lines reminiscent of the prophetic formula in Rev. 1:19 the magician prays for complete prophetic knowledge (III.428-29): "Enable me to know beforehand things which will happen in the future, things which are about to happen, things that have happened and all the day's happenings *en toto.*" In several procedures for personal visions the practitioner is urged to take notes: "Keep a small tablet near so that you can take down whatever he says lest you forget it after going to sleep" (*PGM* VIII.89b-91a; cf. XIII.90-91, 564-65, 646). In one procedure recommended for producing a direct, personal vision, a bronze bowl is filled with a particular type of water (depending on the results wanted), and after the performance of the requisite ritual the god will be seen in the water and can be asked questions to which he can respond in verse (IV.154-285).

Although these texts may raise many more questions than they answer, the sample procedures which we have summarized and from which we have quoted excerpts suggest that magical divination and oracular magic were a very serious business indeed. All these texts appear to presuppose that the revelatory experience occurred in a state of vision trance; one unique text is entitled a *kataptōsis,* i.e. a procedure for inducing a "falling" or "seizure," in short, a trance (IV.850-929). In one text, however, the phenomenon of possession trance appears to be contemplated (IV.1121-24): "Greetings, spirit [*pneuma*] who enters into me, seizes me and then departs from me graciously in accordance with the will of the god." Further, these magical texts all deal with the private, secret practice of oracular techniques (even if much of the ritual and liturgy is borrowed from particular religious traditions), in contrast to the public, open, and regular oracular procedures of the Greco-Roman world generally.

IV. CONCLUSIONS

The mantic arts, ranging from technical divination to inspired divination, were an integral feature of the social and religious life of the Greeks during the entire Greco-Roman period. Knowledge of the future, however obtained, was thought to be indispensable for reducing the risks inherent in a great variety of human activities. The prosecution of a war, the founding of colonies, the detection of the causes for various misfortunes, ritual prescriptions, individual decisions to marry, have children, go on a trip, train for a profession — all these and many other matters of uncertainty were the subjects of oracular inquiry. For the Greeks prophecy and divination were endemic features of socio-religious life and not activities which functioned primarily during times of social upheaval or personal calamity.

The social function of prophecy was quite different in the setting of the various mystery cults. In them, altered states of consciousness functioned as proof of the contact with supernatural powers that was a goal of participation in such cults. From the time of Plato on there was an increasing tendency to equate states of ecstatic frenzy with divine inspiration; whatever was uttered in such states was widely regarded as divinely inspired. The basic assumption was that if a god was actually speaking through an individual, that person's own mind must become inactive in order that his speech organs might become instruments of the divinity. Inevitably this notion became part of the socially recognized features of oracular speech, exhibiting itself through behavior associated with divine possession or inspiration: the use of a loud voice, abnormal tones and rhythms of speech, the physical manifestations of excitement, or a state of trance. In general the later the author the more frenzy characterizes the depiction of the inspired diviner. In all this we can discern two kinds of possession: the controlled possession which was more characteristic of inspired personnel at oracle shrines and the uncontrolled possession which was more characteristic of inspired diviners unconnected with local consultation oracles.

③ | THE FORM AND FUNCTION OF
GRECO-ROMAN ORACLES

I. INTRODUCTION

The purpose of this chapter is the presentation of an initial analysis of ancient Greek oracles in terms of their form and function. Greek oracles which have survived from antiquity have not been systematically studied by modern scholars. Of the many oracles scattered throughout ancient literature, inscriptions, and papyri, only the Delphic oracles have been collected into a comprehensive corpus.[1] The morphology of Greek oracles that we shall propose is based on a synchronic comparison of oracles from the seventh century B.C. to the third century A.D. This approach is based on the view, arising out of this study, that Greek oracles did not change greatly throughout antiquity. Further, the archaizing tendencies of the late Greco-Roman period influenced the production of oracles which were consciously patterned after ancient models. Since most oracles were given in response to inquiries, we shall also examine the form and function of oracle questions.

Since the majority of surviving oracles are found in literary contexts, serious questions have been raised about their authenticity. (Authentic or genuine oracles are those which were actually given, while spurious oracles are those invented by an author to serve a literary purpose.) These questions are valid, since ancient authors and their sources were often less concerned with the historicity of their material than with its usefulness for their own purposes. Even spurious oracles, however, were probably composed in slavish imitation of the more stereotypical features of genuine oracles. For the purpose of analyzing the form and function of oracles, therefore, the problem of authenticity is largely irrelevant.

II. GENERAL FEATURES OF ORACLES

Most Greek oracles were short, consisting of one to four lines. Longer oracles were occasionally delivered to important visitors and delegations to famous oracle sanctuaries. The original length of oracles extant only in literary settings, however, cannot always be determined. Many oracles are preserved in both shorter and longer forms, indicating that sometimes only excerpts of original oracles were quoted.[2] Most oracles were given in response to specific questions posed by individuals or representatives of states. Occasionally inspired cult officials or free-lance diviners spontaneously delivered oracles. In contrast to the responsory nature of Greek prophetic speech, most prophetic speeches in the OT and early Jewish literature were delivered spontaneously, perhaps because the social setting for oracular speech was quite different in the two cultures. The unsolicited prophecies of the OT and early Judaism were frequently delivered during periods of social crisis and upheaval, while oracular consultation in the Greco-Roman world was the regular means for reducing the risks inherent in various forms of human enterprise. In early Christianity prophetic speech was normally unsolicited, but at the same time it was ordinarily limited to those places and times designated for communal religious services.

A. POETIC FORM

From one perspective Greek oracles exhibit a striking uniformity of style.[3] They are short and written in verse, usually dactylic hexameter.[4] Other meters were used after the fifth century B.C.,[5] and prose oracles became common during the first and second centuries A.D.[6] Typical of the longer oracles is this Delphic oracle, probably the oldest genuine Delphic oracle known:

> Of all the earth, Pelasgian Argos is best,
> Thessalian horses, Lakadaimonian women,
> and men who drink the waters of fair Arethousa.
> Yet of these the best are those who dwell
> between Tirynthos and Arkadia rich in flocks,
> Argives with linen corselets, incentives for battle.
> But you of Aegium are neither third nor fourth
> nor twelfth, not in intelligence or number.[7]

The eight lines of this oracle are in dactylic hexameter, the same used in the oldest Greek literature by Homer and Hesiod (eighth to seventh centuries B.C.). The close relationship between Delphic oracles such as this one and the epic dialect of Homer and Hesiod has often been noted.[8] Seven phrases in the oracle quoted recur verbatim in either Homer or Hesiod.[9] This not only indicates a close connection between the bardic art and the mantic art, but it also suggests that trained bards were responsible for formulating the utterances of the Delphic priestess at least until the end of the fifth century B.C.[10] The epic bards did claim the inspiration of the Muses for their compositions,[11] a claim which should probably be regarded as more than mere literary convention.[12] Also, an impressive similarity in language and style is shared by the poems of Pindar and the Delphic response oracles.[13] Pindar's conscious use of oracular style indicates that he too regarded himself as divinely inspired.[14]

While most Delphic oracles were composed in dactylic hexameter, others were produced in iambic trimeter[15] and even in prose. Iambic trimeter was used in Delphic oracles which had a negative or contemptuous character.[16] One such oracle was given to the Cnidians, who had encountered great difficulties in digging a canal. When their envoys asked Delphic Apollo the cause of their difficulty, they received the following oracular response:

> The isthmus neither fence with towers nor dig through,
> For Zeus had made it an island, had he so desired.[17]

Greek meter is based on vowel quantity rather than stress (as in English), so that no translation can convey the kind of meter used in the Greek original.[18] Other oracle centers used a greater variety of meter in the composition of oracles than did Delphi. At Claros, for instance, responses were given in iambic trimeter, iambic tetrameter, trochaic tetrameter, and anapestic tetrameter as well as dactylic hexameter.[19]

The poetic form of oracles was regarded as an indication of their divine origin in the Hellenistic and Roman periods, since the Greeks widely accepted the divine inspiration of poetry. The beautiful form in which the oracles were cast revealed their divine origin.[20] While poetic oracles would have sounded both beautiful and elegant in the sixth and fifth centuries B.C., by the first century A.D. they would have sounded both elegant and archaic. The revival of oracles that began in the first century A.D. was just one expression of a widespread nostalgia for the past. Part of the archaizing tendency of the era was expressed in attempts to copy and revive ancient conventions and forms of expression. Many attempts to compose oracles in hexameter were less than successful (e.g. the Chaldaean Oracles), since few had the requisite literary skills for such a task. Since the primary function of the poetic form of oracles was to legitimate their divine origin, and also because the relationship between oracular form and poetic meter is very complex, we shall regard poetic form as an independent variable in our analysis of the form of oracles. No early Christian oracles were written in Greek meter, though the Jewish Sibylline Oracles were written in dactylic hexameter in an attempt to clothe Jewish religious ideas in Greco-Roman oracular dress.[21]

B. ENIGMATIC CONTENT

Obscurity appears to have been an essential element in the genre of ancient oracles. Heraclides is reported to have said, "The Lord whose oracle is in Delphi neither declares nor conceals, but gives a sign [*sēmainei*]."[21a] He means simply that oracles require interpretation. The ambiguity of oracular speech undoubtedly contributed to the widespread belief that an oracle would always be fulfilled, even if in a totally unexpected manner.[22] The obscurity of oracles meant that any particular interpretation was regarded with some skepticism until the fulfilment was obvious.[23] Many ancient oracles seem designed less to reveal than to conceal the will of the gods. Ambiguity and unclarity were widely regarded as characteristic and appropriate. Particularly in Greek folktales and in legends incorporated or developed in ancient literature, oracular riddles often played a central role in the development of the plot. In such literary settings oracles have two primary characteristics: they are *always* fulfilled, no matter how the characters try to circumvent their fulfilment, and they are often couched in the form of riddles which cannot easily be understood.

This literary use of oracular riddles reveals some interesting aspects of the Greek religious outlook: (1) Oracular speech, though difficult to understand, is an absolutely reliable means whereby the will of the gods is communicated to man. (2) The relationship between gods and men is a kind of game in which wit and cleverness are absolutely essential assets on the part of the latter. (3) In spite of attempts to control the gods through appropriate religious rituals, the gods and fate could at times act in unpredictable and capricious ways. One of the most famous examples of an obscure oracle is the one reportedly delivered to Croesus when he inquired of both Delphi and the oracle of Amphiaraos whether he should send an army against the Persians. The gist of the response was that if he sent an army against the Persians he would destroy a great empire (Herodotus i.53). The empire in question, of course, was that of Croesus himself. His ignorance of the true meaning of the oracle cost him his kingdom.

While the baffling and obscure nature of Greek oracles seems to be characteristic of many oracular responses, it would be inappropriate to trace that ambiguity to cult officials trying to protect the reputation of their sanctuary, or to political considerations.[24] Not all oracles were enigmatic. Questions regarding ritual protocol, for example, were usually answered clearly and unambiguously. The surviving oracles which have been preserved in literary settings are hardly representative of the normal kind of oracular response which was received in antiquity. Oracular riddles were much more interesting and appropriate for literary contexts than, for example, oracles consisting of ritual prescriptions. Nevertheless, obscurity was always thought to be characteristic of oracular responses, and this view was particularly widespread during the late Greco-Roman period. Obscurity, like poetic form, suggested the divine origin of oracular speech.

III. ORACLE QUESTIONS

Since most oracles were given in response to specific questions, it is important to review the kinds of questions which were put to cult personnel at oracle sanctuaries. Thousands of oracles and oracle fragments have been preserved, but comparatively few oracle questions. Only a small fraction of these questions are paired with responses. The oracles of Delphi and Dodona offer an interesting study in contrasts. Hundreds of Delphic oracles, both authentic and spurious, as well as scores of oracle questions, or paraphrases of such questions, have been preserved in literary contexts. Yet archeologists have recovered no actual written inquiries.[25] Quite the opposite situation exists for Dodona: few oracle questions and responses are preserved in literature, while nearly one hundred fifty oracle questions have been discovered at Dodona, as noted above.[26] Here are four examples of such questions:

> God. Good fortune.
> The Corcyraeans enquire from Zeus
> Naios and Dione to what god or
> hero by making sacrifice and prayer
> they may be of one mind for their good.

> God. Gerioton asks Zeus
> concerning a wife
> whether it is better for him to take one.

> Socrates enquires of Zeus Naios and Dione
> by engaging in what work he may do better and more well
> for himself and his family.

> Agis asks Zeus Naios and Dione
> about the blankets and the
> pillows which he has lost
> whether some one from outside may have stolen them.[27]

The structure of these and other oracle questions from Dodona consists of three basic elements: address, signature, and question. With optional elements, such as the greeting in the first question quoted, oracle questions can take on epistolary features characteristic of ancient letters of request.[28] The first and third questions cited are formulated so that a specific answer is required, while the second and fourth questions necessitate only the kind of positive or negative response characteristic of a lot oracle.

Oracle questions from other great consultation oracles are not as well or as accurately preserved as those from Dodona. The literary evidence suggests that it was a common practice at Delphi and perhaps other great oracle centers to present two related questions to cult officials. The form of the first question might be either "Shall I, or shall I not, do such and such?" or "Is it better and more beneficial that the people of X city found a colony at Y?"[29] This way of phrasing an inquiry is designed to require only a positive or negative response, the kind eminently suited to a lot oracle. If the first question received a positive answer, it was then appropriate to put a second question to the oracle, which could have the following basic forms: "What shall I do to ensure the success of such and such a venture?" or "To what god or goddess shall I sacrifice and pray to ensure the success of such and such a venture?" The object of the second question is often to ascertain the appropriate religious ritual which will ensure the success of the venture. The practice of putting double questions to oracles can be seen in this statement by the historian Xenophon (late fifth century B.C.):

> Furthermore, if you decide to go forward with the plan, I should advise you to send to Dodona and Delphi, and inquire of the gods whether such a design is better and more good for the state both now and in days to come. And should they consent to it, then I would say that we ought to ask them further, which of the gods we must propitiate in order that we may prosper in our handiwork.[30]

One form of oracle question posed commonly at Delphi is exemplified in this list of sample questions preserved by Plutarch:

> Shall I be victorious?
> Shall I marry?
> Will it be advantageous to sail?
> Should I farm?
> Shall I travel?[31]

The interrogative particle *ei* ("whether"), used in simple indirect questions, introduces each of these questions in Greek. These questions reveal the commonplace nature of most of the inquiries which were directed to Delphic Apollo. Elsewhere Plutarch provides a similar list of oracle questions in the same form as those just quoted, but in a context emphasizing the commonplace and even trivial nature of such inquiries:

> Shall I marry?
> Shall I travel?
> Shall I lend money?[32]

Such questions are parodied in Athenaeus, though the basic form is retained:

> Are there any camels stronger than those in Baktria?
> Is there anyone with a nose flatter than Socrates?[33]

From these sample lists it can be concluded that most oracle questions posed at Delphi were brief, were introduced with the interrogative particle *ei*, "whether," and posed an alternative to which the god need only respond with a positive or negative answer. The lack of an addressee in these questions may indicate that they are preserved in only a truncated form.

A similar form of oracle question is phrased in such a way that more than a positive or negative response is required. This kind of question begins with an interrogative adverb of manner such as "how" (*pōs*):

> How can I please the gods?
> What is my duty about sacrifice or about the cult of ancestors?
> How can I punish Alexander?
> How can I be relieved of madness?
> How may I get rich, son of Zeus and Leto?[34]

Several papyrus oracle questions have been discovered that are phrased almost exactly like those preserved by Plutarch.[35] These questions have been identified as part of a lot oracle consisting of previously prepared questions and answers which must be matched.[36] Here are five such questions, each of which begins with the interrogative particle (*ei*):

Am I to find what is lost?
Am I to recover from my illness?
Am I to get the dowry?
Am I to be sold?
Am I to become successful?[37]

Other papyrus oracle questions have been recovered that cannot have been part of a lot oracle with previously prepared questions and answers. These questions exhibit a basic three-part structure: address (the name of the god in the dative or, more rarely, the vocative case), question (introduced by a conditional particle and forming a protasis), and request for response (the apodosis contains a request for a response, e.g. "give this [i.e. an answer] to me," or "deliver this [i.e. the answer] to me").[38] This structure is exhibited in these two sample papyrus oracle questions:

Address:	To the Lord Soknopaios, great god, and to Ammon, greatest gods,
Question:	Sotas asks whether the monarch will not be vexed with me or will launch an investigation against me because I write vouchers for Valerius.
Request for Response:	Tell me this.
Address:	O Lord Sarapis Helios, beneficent one.
Question:	[Say] whether it is fitting that Phanias my son and his wife should not agree now with his father, but oppose him and not make a contract.
Request for Response:	Tell me this truly. Farewell.[39]

These inquiries have a marked tendency have to take on some of the structural features of letters of request, a feature evident in the concluding "farewell" in the second question.

The various kinds of oracle questions which we have considered allow us to draw several general conclusions. (1) Most oracle questions presented a predetermined alternative to the god to which he could respond only positively or negatively. This way of posing oracle questions seems to indicate that most responses to such questions were provided by lot oracles.[40] (2) Other oracle questions, however, are phrased in such a way that a more direct and specific verbal response is required. (3) The content of the oracle questions which we have considered indicates that when choices, problems, or crises confronted many ancients, they resorted to oracles in order to minimize the risks or to secure advice. Stated more positively, oracles gave the inquirer confidence and assurance in his various social and economic activities.

IV. ORACULAR RESPONSES

Many individual oracles and oracle collections of various sizes were in circulation from the archaic period through to the end of the Greco-Roman era.[41] Many of these oracles were attributed to Apollo (the Greek oracular divinity par excellence), Zeus, and the many other gods and heroes who had oracle sanctuaries. Other oracles were attributed to legendary figures such as Orpheus, Musaeos, the Sibyls, and the Bakides. Still others circulated anonymously.[42] Oracles which originated from the great oracle centers at Delphi, Dodona, Claros, Didyma, Siwah, and many lesser centers scattered throughout the Greek world were regarded as utterances of the gods who presided there. Oracles attributed to the Sibyls and Bakides, legendary or not, were formulated as the speech of the prophetesses and prophets who uttered them, and not as the speech of the inspiring divinity.[43] In our analysis of the form of Greek oracles we shall first discuss *oracular responses* and then *unsolicited oracles.*

The vast majority of oracles which have been preserved in ancient literature, papyri, and inscriptions are oracular responses. Neither these oracles nor the unsolicited oracles which we shall discuss in the next section have been subjected to a careful composition or genre analysis. This task would be superfluous had E. R. Dodds been correct in claiming that Greek oracles exhibited a conventional "oracle-style" throughout antiquity.[44] The following discussion reveals how wide of the mark Dodds' judgment was.

A. GENERAL CONSIDERATIONS

One major obstacle to the analysis of the form and function of Greco-Roman oracles is that the surviving oracular material, voluminous as it is, is not fully representative of ancient oracular speech. There are several reasons why this is so: (1) Most oracles have survived in literary settings. Ancient authors used oracles which relate to important persons, places, and events because they were more interesting and useful than oracles which concerned unimportant persons, insignificant places, and mundane affairs. (2) Oracles delivered to important persons and states, the kind most favored by ancient authors, tend to exhibit greater length, more complex structure, and more refined language and style than oracles delivered to ordinary inquirers. (3) Oracles were used in three primary ways in Greco-Roman literature, and this placed severe restrictions on the kind of oracles that could be utilized: (a) as the focal element of anecdotes and stories about famous persons, places, and events (Pausanias has numerous examples of this type, many of which he derived from the spiel of local Greek travel guides), (b) as a way of demonstrating that events have followed a divinely prescribed course (Herodotus customarily uses them in this way), and (c) as a way of demonstrating the truth of a philosophical or religious statement (Neoplatonists used the Chaldaean Oracles in this way). Oracular responses which consist of ritual prescriptions could not easily be used in any of these ways. Consequently, most oracles of this type have survived only in inscriptions. All the evidence suggests that a very large proportion of ancient oracles dealt with religious protocol. (4) Almost no oracular material which originated with inspired diviners unconnected with local consultation oracles has survived. One reason for this situation is the contempt with which ancient authors regard such manifestations of the religion of the lower class.[45] For these reasons we do not possess a fully representative sample of ancient oracles, a fact of which we must be aware.

B. THE ONE-PART RESPONSE ORACLE

The vast majority of ancient oracular responses were quite short, consisting of no more than one or two lines. This was as true for the great oracle sanctuaries as it was for the utterances of the free-lance inspired diviner. More often than not these oracular responses would be in poetic form, with dactylic hexameter the meter of preference. Ideally the genre of oracular responses should not be considered in isolation from the inquiry for which it is the answer. Unfortunately, few matching inquiries and responses have been preserved in complete form. An oracular command to sacrifice and pray to a particular god, for example, is vastly different from an unsolicited oracle if given in response to a request for ritual guidance.

The fundamental structural element of the oracular response is the short declarative sentence consisting of a single line of verse or prose. The basic purpose of the oracular response was to provide the kind of information not accessible in any other way. One-part oracular responses may be grouped into three primary categories which correspond to the three major functions of the responses: *predictive oracles,* which reveal the future course of events, *diagnostic oracles,* which provide information unknown to the inquirer about the past or present, and *prescriptive oracles,* in which the inquirer is enjoined or commanded to take a particular course of action. Predictive and diagnostic oracles are ordinarily in the indicative mood, while prescriptive oracles favor the imperative mood. Diagnostic oracles use the past and present tenses of the indicative mood, while predictive oracles use the future and the "futuristic present" tenses of the indicative.[46]

1. Predictive Oracles.

Most oracle questions were concerned with the future for very practical reasons. The inquirers sought oracular guidance in order to minimize the risks inherent in various kinds of enterprises or problematic situations. These practical concerns, which we have already glimpsed in our discussion of oracle questions, are evident in these six one-line prose oracles which were part of the prepared table of questions and answers of the *Sortes Astrampsychi*:

> You are not to escape from the slander.
> You are not to be your wife's heir.
> You are not to get the dowry.
> You are to be reconciled with your masters.
> The person who is sick will recover.
> The baby is not to be brought up.[47]

Although the verb in each response is in the present tense, it is the futuristic or oracular present.[48] Predictive oracles can be longer than a single line, but when they are they exhibit a marked tendency to take on a two-part structure (to be discussed below).

2. Diagnostic Oracles.

Diagnostic and predictive oracles can be distinguished from prescriptive oracles in that the first two types are basically responses to requests for various kinds of data, while the last type is a response to questions regarding the kind of action the inquirer should take. As examples of the diagnostic oracle we cite two oracles in dactylic hexameter produced by Glykon-Asklepios from an oracle shrine owned and operated by Alexander of Abonuteichos during the middle of the second century A.D. When asked what Epicurus was doing in Hades, Glykon-Asklepios replied:

With leaden fetters on his feet in filthy mire he sits.[49]

When Rutilianus, a high Roman official in Asia Minor, asked who should be the tutor for his son, the oracle responded:

Pythagoras and the great bard [i.e. Homer], messenger of war.[50]

In an authentic one-line hexameter incubation oracle from the diary of Aelius Aristides, the perpetually ailing rhetorician was told:

In the evening they flourished by the grassy springs.[51]

Aristides thought he knew exactly what the oracle meant, for he tells us that he immediately anointed himself in the open air (it was winter!) and bathed in the sacred well. In retrospect he later observed: "I almost got rid of all my disease." Although the oracle which Aristides received appears to be merely a brief poetic descriptive passage, its oracular origin meant that its true meaning must be symbolic.

An example of a one-part diagnostic oracle consisting of two lines is attributed to the oracle of Apollo at Claros and written in trochaics:

A man shoots stones from a whirling sling
and kills with his casts gigantic grass-fed geese.[52]

Another one-part diagnostic oracle, this one consisting of three lines, is attributed to the same oracle sanctuary:

In the land of Trachis there is a garden of Herakles,
harvested daily by all, with everything in bloom,
yet undiminished and provided continually with rain.[53]

These two oracles appear to have been stock responses which the Clarian officials delivered to more than one inquirer, a procedure which provoked the criticism of the Cynic philosopher Oenomaus of Gadara (second century A.D.) who quoted them. Again, despite the appearance of mere poetic description, the oracular origin of these statements meant that they were oracular riddles with profound significance that their recipients must interpret properly.

3. Prescriptive Oracles.

This type of one-part oracular response tells the inquirer what course of action he is to take; the verb is frequently in the imperative mood. Many inquirers at oracles were concerned with finding out the appropriate god or hero to whom sacrifices and prayers should be made to ensure the success of a venture (e.g. a military campaign) or to avert an undesirable situation (e.g. a plague). Relatively few oracles prescribing religious ritual have survived, largely because they did not lend themselves to use in literary settings. A large proportion of oracles preserved in inscriptions are concerned with matters of ritual. The double question discussed above was often used by inquirers, the first question, whether a particular course of action should be followed, and the second, the kind of ritual protocol appropriate and necessary to ensure success. A very large proportion of ancient oracles, then, were ritual prescriptions, though most have perished. The Orphic books, which consisted of oracles purportedly sung by

Orpheus and written down by Musaeos, seem to have consisted largely of charms and incantations for use in extreme need, together with directions for their use. An example of a one-part prescriptive oracle consisting of a single line is an oracle question and response from the late second century A.D. inscribed on a marble altar base at the oracle of Apollo in Didyma:

> Your prophet Damianos asks: "In your sanctuary near the altar precinct for all the gods you do not yet see an altar set up for your most holy sister, the goddess Soter Kore sprung from the father himself. But a friend of god, distressed at such a state of affairs, asks you, Lord of Didyma, Helios Apollo, to prophesy to him if you permit him to erect an altar of her child near the altar of fruit-bearing Demeter."
>
> The god declared by an oracle: "Perform this honor for Soter Kore in the altar precinct."[54]

The prophet Damianos asked an oracle question on behalf of an unnamed patron of Apollo in which a simple alternative is presented to the god. Since the question invites a specific directive, the use of the imperative is appropriate.

Prescriptive oracles, particularly those involving matters of religious ritual, could consist of one line, as the one quoted above, or they could list in parallel form a variety of ritual prescriptions. An example of a one-part prescriptive oracle consisting of a series of ritual directions is this prose oracle from Dodona quoted by the Athenian orator Demosthenes (fourth century B.C.):

> The prophet of Zeus in Dodona commands: To Dionysus pay public sacrifices and mix a bowl of wine and set up dances; to Apollo the Averter sacrifice an ox and wear garlands, both free men and slaves, and observe one day of rest; to Zeus, the giver of wealth, a white bull.[55]

Here various ritual requirements in honor of three gods are enjoined upon the Athenians.

An example of another type of prescriptive oracle is found in Lucian, who reported that Rutilianus, after asking Alexander of Abonuteichos about marriage, was told:

> Take Alexander's daughter to wife, who was born of Selene [Moon].[56]

Such oracular commands are common, though they tend to become expanded by the addition of other structural elements, as we shall see below.

C. THE TWO-PART RESPONSE ORACLE

Most ancient oracular responses were the kind of short, declarative utterances which we have just considered, but a very large number of surviving oracles exhibit a more complex structure. The tendency to expand oracles from one-part to two-part structures is observable in the manuscript tradition of the *Sortes Astrampsychi*.[57] The addition of a second structural element functions in a variety of ways, but always in a manner subordinate to the primary statement, which may be either predictive, diagnostic, or prescriptive.

There are three primary types of two-part oracular responses: *expository oracles, conditional oracles,* and *adversative oracles.*

1. Expository Oracles.

The two-part structure typical of the expository oracle can be illustrated by these six oracular responses from the *Sortes Astrampsychi*:

> You are not going to be sold just yet. It is not expedient for you.
> You have been poisoned. Help yourself.
> Your property is not to be sold at auction. Do not be afraid.
> You will not be insulted now. Do not worry.
> You are not to win. Persevere.
> You are not to inherit. Silence.[58]

In those prose responses the first element in each oracle is a predictive statement in the futuristic present or future tense (with the exception of the second response), while the second element (in all but the first instance) is in the imperative mood. The second element functions in a variety of ways, but always as an elaboration, explanation, or exposition of the basic statement. In the examples cited the second element provides: (1) comfort to a disappointed inquirer, (2) encouragement to an inquirer who has received good news, and (3) a reason or basis for the primary statement made in the response. The two-part structure evident in these examples is not unique to oracles; it is often found in epigrams, of which the following epitaph may serve as a typical example:

> Be of good courage [*eupsychei*] Cyrilla, whose beauty is like the gods,
> for now you live in the peaceful place of the immortals.[59]

The two-part structure is also found in oracular responses which consist of a single line:

> Do not trust Lepidus, for a dismal fate follows.[60]

This oracle, which occurs at the conclusion of an oracular dialogue and appears unsolicited, marks the introduction of the second element with a masculine caesura, a structural pause characteristic of a dactylic hexameter line. Two other two-part expository oracles cited by Lucian are examples of oracles in which the statement in the first part is completed by that in the second:

> Approach the shrine of the Branchidae/ and obey the oracles.
>
> Go now to Claros/ there listen to my father.[61]

Both oracles are in hexameter, and both separate the command in the first part of the line from the advice in the second part by a diaeresis (the point where a break in words coincides with the end of a metrical foot).

More commonly, the two-part expository oracle consists of two to four lines, of which the first part (often restricted to the first line) contains the primary statement (which may be either informative, predictive, or prescriptive), while the second part provides an explanation or elaboration of the primary statement. In the following example the Cnidians had difficulty in digging a canal and sent envoys to Delphi to ascertain the reason. They received the following oracle in iambic trimeter, a meter apparently used at Delphi for oracles of a generally negative or contemptuous character:

> The isthmus neither fence with towers nor dig through,
> for Zeus had made it an island, had he so desired.[62]

The first line is a prohibition in the imperative mood, while the second line provides the supporting reason.

Similar in structure is the following oracle which the rhetorician Aelius Aristides (second century A.D.) secured from the sanctuary of Apollo at Colophon:

> Asklepios will cure and heal your disease
> in honor of the famous city of Telephus,
> not far from the streams of the Caicus.[63]

In this oracle the first line consists of a predictive statement, while the supportive explanation is provided in lines two and three.

A priest of Asklepios purportedly received the following dream oracle sometime during the late first century A.D.:

> Let so-and-so depart with his possessions,
> for he is unworthy to keep his remaining eye.[64]

In this example, as in the others we have cited, the primary oracular statement is substantiated by reasons given in the second part of the response.

H. D. Betz has shown that the dream oracle received by Paul in 2 Cor. 12:9 conforms to this common oracular form:

> My grace is sufficient for you,
> for my strength is made perfect in weakness.[65]

A similar structure is evident in the dream oracles received by Joseph in the Matthean infancy narrative (Matt. 1:20-21; 2:13, 20).

2. Conditional Oracles.

One of the more common types of the two-part response oracle is the conditional oracle. When the condition(s) described in the protasis (introduced by such particles as "if" and "when") was fulfilled, then the prediction expressed in the apodosis was expected to take place. This oracular form is of particular relevance for the study of early Christian prophetic speech forms since it resembles the "pronouncement of sacral law," which we shall consider below in some detail.[66] A typical example of a conditional oracle is the following two-line oracle in hexameter preserved in an inscription from the sanctuary of Grynaion Apollo in Aetolia:

> When you honor Leto's son Phoebus [Apollo] and Zeus Patroios,
> you will receive fame; then fasten your shackles here on the tree.[67]

In this oracle the predictive statement in line two is dependent on the fulfilment of the vaguely worded ritual prescription in the first line. In another example a sick and dissolute youth from Assyria reportedly received this incubation oracle in the temple of Asklepios at Aegae:

> If you would consult Apollonius you would get better.[68]

This oracle is an uncommon example of a conditional oracle containing both protasis and apodosis in a single prose line.

Many conditional oracles were couched in such ambiguous language that the "proper" interpretation of the oracle was difficult if not impossible to determine. An example of a conditional homonymic oracle, one whose obscurity was based on a double entendre, is this Delphic oracle given to Aristomenes and Theoclus the mantic, who had come from Eira in Messene to inquire about the safety of their homeland:

> When a goat [*tragos*] drinks of the winding stream of Neda,
> No longer do I protect Messene, for destruction is at hand.[69]

Only Theoclus understood that the *tragos* did not refer to a goat, but was a distinctive Messenian term for a wild fig tree. Since such a tree was known to be bent over into the waters of the Neda River, Theoclus and Aristomenes knew that the days of Messene were numbered.

A conditional oracle in a different form is the oldest recorded oracle (third century B.C.) from the sanctuary of Apollo at Claros. It related to the refounding of Smyrna, which had been destroyed early in the third century by Lysimachus:

> Thrice, yes, four times blest [*makares*] will those men be
> who shall dwell in Pagus beyond the Sacred Meles.[70]

In this oracle the apodosis is in the first line and contains a promise, the enjoyment of which is conditional, based on the future fulfilment of the protasis, which constitutes the second line.

Many of the conditional oracles which we have discussed are conditional promises of fame, health, and general well-being. A great many conditional oracles, however, are conditional threats of disaster and destruction frequently propounded as riddles. In form such oracles resemble the conditional curse formulas found in ancient epitaphs.[71]

3. Adversative Oracles.

Adversative oracles are characterized by a sudden reversal of situation[72] or an abrupt criticism. An oracular beatitude which predicts a reversal of fortune is quoted by Athenaeus:

> Happy, thou Sybarite, all happy shalt thou ever
> be in thy abundance, whilst honouring the race of them that live for ever.
> But whensoever thou hold a mortal man in awe rather than a god,
> then shall war and civil strife come upon thee.[73]

The pronouncement of blessing dominates the first two lines, while the adversative statement in the last two has the form of a conditional oracle with a "when x, then y" pattern.

A very interesting example of an adversative oracle is perhaps the oldest genuine Delphic oracle known and which we quoted above in another connection.[74] In response to a question asking who were the best of the Greeks, this oracular response was given:

> Of all the earth, Pelasgian Argos is best,
> Thessalian horses, Lakadaimonian women,
> and men who drink the waters of fair Arethousa.
> Yet of these the best are those who dwell
> between Tirynthos and Arkadia rich in flocks,
> Argives with linen corselets, incentives for battle.
> But you of Aegium are neither third nor fourth
> nor twelfth, not in intelligence or number.[75]

The first six lines of this hexameter oracle constitute an informative statement in direct answer to the inquiry, while the last two lines consist of an unexpected attack by Apollo on the inquirers.

D. SPECIAL TYPES

The three types of one-part response oracles (diagnostic, predictive, and prescriptive) and the three types of two-part response oracles (expository, conditional, and adversative) that we have discussed above were suggested on the basis of formal features found in the structures of the oracles themselves. No particular emphasis was given to the content of the oracles examined, though a separation of form from content may appear to be an artificial analytical procedure. Many ancient oracles take on distinctive features primarily because of their content, while still others are distinctive because of an unusual combination of the formal features which we have considered above. In this section we shall examine three special types of oracles, each of which is distinguished by its particular content: the *oracular riddle,* the *didactic oracle,* and the *oracular beatitude.* We shall also discuss the *oracular dialogue,* which is a distinctive type of response oracle consisting of several of the formal features discussed above.

1. Oracular Riddles.

As already noted, ambiguity and unclarity were widely regarded in the ancient world as characteristic and appropriate features of oracular responses.[76] Most oracular riddles are preserved in literary settings, and though many of these are spurious, they were probably modeled after genuine oracles and reveal a great deal about the Greek view of oracular revelation. The simplest form of riddle oracle is the homonymic oracle in which an important term can have two meanings. Ordinarily the "correct" meaning is the more obscure and unexpected one. In the example of a homonymic oracle quoted above,[77] the term *tragos* could refer either to a goat or (less obviously) to a wild fig tree. In one of several examples of homonymic riddle oracles given by Pausanias, an oracle from Delphi had told Epaminondas to beware of *pelagos* ("ocean"). Consequently, the general feared to travel by ship. The word referred, however, to a grove of trees named *pelagos* which the general unfortunately did not avoid.[78] Pausanias mentions another homonymic riddle oracle which said that Libyan soil would cover the corpse of Hannibal. This referred not to Hannibal's home in North Africa, as the Carthaginian general mistakenly thought, but to another place named Libya outside Nicomedeia, the capital of Bithynia in Asia Minor, the site of Hannibal's tomb.[79] Pausanias was a travel guide of the second century A.D., and it is likely that such oracle stories, most of which were manufactured, were an important part of the spiel of local guides.[80]

Another type of riddle oracle was the stock oracle couched in vague and obscure terms and delivered many times to different inquirers. In practice this procedure was not much different from the lot or knucklebone oracles which used previously prepared responses.[81] The ambiguity of such oracles made it possible for the inquirer, perhaps with the aid of a professional oracle interpreter, to find almost any meaning he wished in the response. The two oracles quoted above from Oenomaus of Gadara and the one quoted by Aelius Aristides (p. 57) are typical examples of such multipurpose riddle oracles.

2. Didactic Oracles.

Oracles given in response to requests for information at times take on a character which may be regarded as didactic, particularly if the question focuses on a theological, philosophical, or moral issue.[82] Many oracles of this type emanated from the oracle sanctuaries at Claros and Didyma.[83] The surviving fragments of the Chaldaean Oracles, written toward the end of the second century A.D. by Julianus the Theurgist, the son of Julianus the Chaldaean, are prime examples of this type of oracle.[84] The oracles were apparently composed by Julianus in a flawed hexameter, though possibly dictated by various divinities (including Apollo and Hecate) to a medium in a state of trance.[85] In content the Oracles are a mixture of Platonism and popular religious and magical views which later Neoplatonists accepted as divine revelation.[86] They show a close affinity to the kind of material found in the Corpus Hermeticum. The way in which Neoplatonists used the Oracles as proof texts for their theosophical teaching can be seen in this sample quotation from Proclus Diadochus:

> Therefore the gods exhort us not to look upon them before we have been strengthened by the powers derived from the mystic rites. "For thou must not look upon them before thy body has been initiated." On this account the oracles add that "by charming souls they are ever leading them away from the mysteries."[87]

The didactic character of the Chaldaean Oracles may be seen in this eleven-line oracle quoted by Psellus; it is one of the three longest surviving fragments of the Oracles:

a	Let not the gigantic size of the earth intimidate your mind,
b	for the plant of truth is not found on earth.
a	Neither attempt to measure the size of the sun by joining rods.
b	By the eternal will of the Father it moves, not because of you.
a	Let alone the rushing motion of the moon; it moves continually by act of necessity.
b	The sidereal procession was not produced for you.
c	No truth at all is there in the far-flung paths of broad-winged birds,
c	nor in the cuttings of the entrails of sacrificial animals; such things are all diversions,
d	bases for a fraudulent trade; flee these things,
e	you who will open the sacred paradise of piety.[88]

In content this oracle is a diatribe against the divinatory sciences of astrology, oneiromancy, and haruspicy, very similar to the antidivinatory emphases of the Neopythagoreans and Philo of Alexandria. Analysis of the oracle is hampered because the extent of the original cannot be determined. In form the oracle begins with three couplets, the first and second lines of which are labeled a and b. The first line of each couplet constitutes a prohibition of a specific form of divination. In form, then, each of these three couplets is a two-part expository oracle. The final four lines have a different character. The new thought introduced in the third from last line is marked by a masculine caesura (the word division in Greek occurring after the first long syllable in a hexameter foot), while the injunction to "flee these things" is marked by a bucolic diaeresis (the word division occurring between the fourth and fifth hexameter foot). The phrase "flee these things" also indicates the hortatory or parenetic character of the entire didactic oracle.

3. Oracular Beatitudes.

The oracular beatitude, or makarism, is not a common type of Greek oracle, and the historicity of the form itself has been questioned.[89] It is of interest chiefly because of the parallels in early Jewish and early Christian prophecy and apocalyptic, where it occupies a more prominent role. In the Greco-Roman world makarisms are found in epitaphs as well as in wisdom and oracular settings.[90] Although the terminology used in Greco-Roman oracular beatitudes varies considerably,[91] there is a striking formal similarity to Judeo-Christian beatitudes: invariably the term of blessing, happiness, or joy is the first significant word in the oracle. Many Greco-Roman oracular beatitudes were spontaneous utterances by inspired mediums,[92] though many others were given in response to inquiries.

The oldest oracle from the sanctuary of Clarian Apollo relates to the refounding of Smyrna, which had been destroyed a short time earlier:

> Thrice, yes, four times blest [*makares*] will those men be
> who shall dwell in Pagus beyond the Sacred Meles.[93]

This oracle is a promise which may be realized by those who participate in the rebuilding of Smyrna; in form it is a two-part conditional oracle.

Occasionally oracular beatitudes included a prediction which made the initial promise of happiness less significant:

> Happy is this man who comes down to my temple,
> Cypselus son of Eëtes, renowned king of Corinth,
> he and his sons, but not his sons' sons.[94]

This beatitude is in the form of a two-part adversative oracle. Another adversative oracle, from Delphi, has less sting; in response to the query, "Would it be better to live at Corinth?", the Pythia replied:

> Blest [*eudaimōn*] is Corinth, but Tenea for me![95]

4. The Oracular Dialogue.

One very interesting and distinctive type of response oracle is the oracular dialogue. In the revelatory literature of the Greco-Roman period, particularly in Jewish and Christian apocalypses, Gnostic dialogues, and the Hermetic literature, divine revelation is frequently elicited through a question-and-answer format (called an *erotapokrisis*).[96] The questions are posed by a mortal and the oracular answers are provided by a supernatural being. Perhaps the simplest form of oracular dialogue, and possibly the most original, consists of two successive questions to an oracular deity.[97] Greco-Roman magical literature, particularly the Greek and Demotic magical papyri, has many recipes for gaining control of various kinds of supernatural beings for the purpose of getting oracular responses to any questions which the magical practitioner might want to pose. Once such a séance had begun, a kind of dialogue or *erotapokrisis* followed. Here are two examples from a Demotic magical papyrus that instruct the magician how to initiate a revelatory dialogue:

> You cause him (the boy [medium]) to say to Anubis "The god who will inquire for me to-day, let him tell me his name." When he stands up and tells his name, you ask him concerning everything you wish.

"The god who will ask for me, let him put forth his hand to me and let him tell me his name." When he tells you his name, you ask him as to that which you desire. When you have ceased asking him as to that which you desire, you send him away.[98]

Unfortunately, no transcriptions of such magical séances have survived; the instructions break off just at the point where the dialogue or *erotapokrisis* would begin. A very interesting feature of these two quotations is that the revelatory dialogue apparently begins with a question regarding the identity of the inspiring divinity and (presumably) an answer perhaps introduced by an "I am" formula.

Lucian has reproduced the only extensive oracular dialogue of which I am aware. He claims to have found it inscribed in golden letters on the house of Sacerdos, the inquirer:

Sacerdos:	Tell me, Lord Glykon, who are you?
Glykon:	I am the new Asklepios.
Sacerdos:	Different than the former one? What do you mean?
Glykon:	It is not lawful for you to hear that.
Sacerdos:	How many years will you remain here giving oracles?
Glykon:	One thousand and three.
Sacerdos:	Where will you go then?
Glykon:	To the region of Baktria, for it is necessary that the barbarians gain something from my presence.
Sacerdos:	Do the other oracles in Didyma and Claros and Delphi have your father Apollo delivering oracles, or are the oracles now delivered there false?
Glykon:	You must not desire to know this. It is not lawful.
Sacerdos:	Who will I be after this present life?
Glykon:	A camel, then a horse, then a wise man and prophet not less than Alexander.
Glykon:	Do not trust Lepidus, for a dismal fate follows.[99]

The questions which Sacerdos puts to the god do not conform to the usual pattern and style of oracle questions that we have considered above. All of the responses are in prose with the execption of the final spontaneous pronouncement in dactylic hexameter. Most of the responses are in the form of one-part informative oracles. However, three of the responses (lines 8-9, 13, and 17) are in the form of two-part expository oracles. The oracular dialogue begins with a request for the identity of the oracular divinity, and the response is "I am the new Asklepios." We have already suggested that oracular *erotapokriseis* or dialogues began with that kind of stereotyped interchange, similar to that in the Demotic magical papyrus quoted above. In fact, many oracular dialogues begin with what we shall designate as an "oracle of self-commendation," frequently expressed in the "I am" (*egō eimi*) formula.[100]

That this oracular dialogue is unique in Greco-Roman literature does not mean that the kind of oracular séance which formed the setting for such dialogues was rare. In our brief discussion above we have suggested several indications that the oracular dialogue was not at all uncommon in antiquity, though it was probably primarily an oral genre which did not lend itself to literary preservation. The phenomenon of the oracular dialogue and the oracular séance which formed the setting for such *erota-pokriseis* raises the question of the relationship between the oracular dialogue and the apocalyptic, Gnostic, and Hermetic dialogue. To what extent is the latter based on actual revelatory experience, and to what extent has that experience been stereotyped into literary conventions?

V. UNSOLICITED ORACLES

While most ancient oracles were given in response to specific questions posed by inquirers, some oracles were not elicited by questions but were the spontaneous utterances of mediums in a state of possession trance or trance. Perhaps the oldest type of spontaneous oracle is the unsolicited dream oracle. Our analysis of the form of response oracles indicated that they exhibit a limited number of formal features together with a relatively high degree of structural stability throughout antiquity. In content, however, response oracles display immense variety. Unsolicited oracles, on the other hand, do not easily lend themselves to formal analysis. They exhibit great diversity in both style and structure. The content of unsolicited oracles, however, is relatively limited; most of them functioned either as legitimation oracles or as predictions of doom.

A. GENERAL CONSIDERATIONS

A number of generalizations can be made about unsolicited oracles. While response oracles were a regular and reliable means for reducing the risks inherent in a variety of human enterprises or for diagnosing individual and social ills throughout the Greco-Roman period, unsolicited oracles tended to appear in extraordinary periods of social and political crisis. Unsolicited oracles also tended to be longer than response oracles. Although there are many examples of short one- or two-line unsolicited oracles, even these rarely exhibit the one-part structure which we found characteristic of many response oracles. This complexity was undoubtedly due to the fact that the unsolicited oracle had to be self-explanatory (or at least potentially so), since there was no specific inquiry which could serve as a frame of reference for the utterance or application of the oracle. Unsolicited oracles tended to occur more often after the fourth century B.C., during the Hellenistic and Greco-Roman periods, than earlier, and they also tended to occur with greater frequency in the Levant than in the western Mediterranean lands. Since the Hellenistic and Greco-Roman period was characterized by intermittent social and political upheavals, particularly in the east, and since spontaneous prophecy was a traditional feature of many Levantine nativistic traditions, all the necessary elements were present for the relatively frequent outbreak of spontaneous prophecies of doom.

B. RELATIONSHIP TO RESPONSE ORACLES

Unsolicited oracles were occasionally uttered by cult mediums at the great oracle shrines. For example, nearly five percent of the surviving Delphic oracles appear to be spontaneous pronouncements of the Pythia.[101] Although many of these oracles are probably spurious, they could have produced their desired effect and been accepted as authentic by the ancients only if they had been patterned after genuine models. If some unsolicited oracles were actually delivered at major oracle centers, it seems

inevitable that the style and form of such unsolicited oracles would closely resemble
response oracles produced at the same sanctuaries.

In one of his Pythian dialogues Plutarch observed that "the Pythian priestess is
accustomed to deliver some oracles on the instant, even before the question is put."[102]
This kind of clairvoyant oracular response cannot be regarded as an unsolicited oracle
since the oracle is given in response to a question, which, though unexpressed, is
miraculously known to the god speaking through the medium. Most of these clairvoyant oracular responses are either mythical or fraudulent attempts to enhance the
reputation of a particular oracle sanctuary.[103]

At the oracle of Glykon-Asklepios, operated by Alexander of Abonuteichos
during the mid-second century A.D., a number of unsolicited oracles were given along
with many more oracular responses. Although very few unsolicited oracles exhibit the
one-part structure characteristic of many short response oracles, the following spontaneous autophonous oracle uttered during a plague which swept the Roman empire
in A.D. 166 is an exception:

> Phoebus [Apollo] the unshorn wards off the deadly cloud of plague.[104]

This hexameter oracle, which Alexander had distributed far and wide, is an example
of an unsolicited oracle pronounced during a time of social crisis. In view of the
widespread terror evoked by the plague, the application of the oracle would have been
obvious to all. Lucian reports that the oracle was inscribed on houses as an apotropaic
magical amulet to ward off the disease.

Many unsolicited oracles emanating from oracle sanctuaries where the customary
mode of reply was the response oracle exhibit the kind of two-part structure typical
of many response oracles. Two of the three types of two-part structures characteristic
of response oracles — the expository oracle and the conditional oracle — are particularly common in spontaneous oracles. Alexander of Abonuteichos, in the act of burning
the Kyriai Doxai ("Principal Doctrines") of Epicurus, pronounced the following unsolicited expository oracle:

> I command you to burn, opinions of a blind old man![105]

In this one-line hexameter oracle the command in the first part is explained by the
accompanying statement in the second part.

In an apparently unsolicited oracle which terminated the oracular dialogue between the wealthy Sacerdos and Glykon-Asklepios (quoted above, p. 65), an expository oracle provided a warning for Sacerdos:

> Do not trust Lepidus, for a dismal fate follows.[106]

Similar in structure is this unsolicited dream oracle reportedly received by a priest of
Asklepios:

> Let so-and-so depart with his possessions,
> for he is unworthy to keep his remaining eye.[107]

Another example of a two-part unsolicited oracle with a prescriptive statement in the
first line and a supporting reason in the second line is the following fictitious oracle
said to have been delivered spontaneously by Apollo to Orpheus:

> Cease to meddle with my affairs,
> for I have already put up long enough with your vaticinations.[108]

One significant function of the unsolicited oracle is that it, like the clairvoyant response oracle, could serve to emphasize the omniscience of the oracular divinity. This kind of unsolicited oracle is exemplified by the following prose oracle attributed to Glykon-Asklepios:

> Go back; he who sent you was killed today by his neighbor Diocles, with the help of the bandits Magnus, Celer, and Bubalus, who already have been caught and imprisoned.[109]

Lucian claims that this oracle, and others like it, were not directed to specific individuals, but were fraudulent attempts to magnify the reputation of the oracular divinity by attributing clairvoyant powers to him. The specificity of this oracle supports Lucian's view that it was a fake. Although it is clear that Alexander of Abonuteichos resorted to "pious" fraud in order to enhance the reputation of his oracle,[110] such unsolicited oracles must have resembled other genuine oracles.

C. LEGITIMATION ORACLES

Unlike the unsolicited oracles which we have just considered, many unsolicited oracles preserved in Greco-Roman literature or on papyrus fragments have no demonstrable connection with ancient consultation oracles. One major category of such unsolicited oracles is the legitimation oracle, which has three types: *recognition oracles, commendation oracles,* and *oracles of self-commendation.* These three types of oracles have been designated legitimation oracles since the primary function of all three types is to provide supernatural validation for a reliable source of divine revelation or for a person of (potentially) great status.

1. Recognition Oracles.

The recognition oracle is a type of prophetic or oracular speech found in the OT, early Judaism, and early Christianity as well as in the Greco-Roman world. It provides supernatural identification for some individual of singular importance: either someone of divine parentage or one who will become a king. A recognition oracle conveniently pointed to Alexander of Abonuteichos, emphasizing his divine lineage and implying his healing and oracular abilities:

> Here in your sight is a scion of Perseus, dear unto Phoebus [Apollo];
> This is divine Alexander, who shareth the blood of the Healer![111]

Similar in content but different in form is another recognition oracle pointing to Alexander:

> I command you to honor my servant the prophet;
> the prophet, not possessions, is my great concern.[112]

A much earlier recognition oracle, spontaneously uttered, is attributed to the Pythia at Delphi:

> Thou hast come to my well-stored temple, Lycurgus,
> Dear to Zeus and to all who dwell in the courts of Olympus.
> Art thou a man or a god?
> 'Tis a god I deem thee, O Lycurgus.[113]

Homer offers one of the oldest examples of a recognition oracle in the Greek world in a short speech by Zeus:

> Hear me, all you gods and all you goddesses: here me
> while I speak forth what the heart within my breast urges.
> This day Eileithyia of women's child-pains shall bring forth
> a man to the light who, among the men sprung of the generation
> of my blood, shall be lord over all those dwelling about him.[114]

Although this oracular-style saying is a literary adaptation of a Greek folktale about the births of Herkles and Eurystheus, it is patterned after the kind of recognition oracles which we have been considering. In this case the oracle points to one who will reign as king.

According to various legendary accounts Alexander the Great was the subject of a number of recognition oracles. These recognition oracles are mentioned, though not quoted, by the Greek geographer Strabo (second century A.D.):

> The fellow [i.e. the prophet of Ammon] expressly told the king that he, Alexander, was son of Zeus. And to this statement Callisthenes [a fourth-century B.C. historian] dramatically adds that ... many oracles were carried by the Milesian ambassadors [from Didyma] to Memphis concerning Alexander's descent from Zeus, his future victory in the neighbourhood of Arbela, the death of Dareius, and the revolutionary attempts in Lacedaemon. And he says that the Erythraean Athenaïs also gave out an utterance concerning Alexander's high descent; for, he adds, this woman was like the ancient Erythraean Sibylla.[115]

Here we learn that the prophet of Ammon, the oracle of Apollo at Didyma, and the prophetess Athenaïs all delivered spontaneous recognition oracles about Alexander the Great that emphasized his divine descent. Little more is known of the oracles from Didyma or the one uttered by the prophetess Athenaïs,[116] but many references to the oracle purportedly delivered to Alexander by the prophet of Ammon at the Oasis of Siwah are found in ancient literature.[117] Regardless of what was actually said and meant at the oracle of Ammon, many versions of the story reported that the prophet of Ammon oracularly addressed Alexander with the line:

> O son of Zeus![118]

Upon becoming Pharaoh of Egypt Alexander was officially regarded as the son of Amon-Ra, whom the prophet of Ammon would have considered identical with Zeus. The greeting was probably not an unsolicited oracle proclaiming Alexander's divine parentage, but simply a recognition of his status by the cult official. The statement was quickly regarded as a recognition oracle, however, since it easily fit a well-known oracular type.

When Alexander of Abonuteichos was making preparations for the discovery of a previously concealed egg containing a snake which he wanted the populace to accept as the incarnation of Asklepios, he first addressed the people announcing that they would soon be blessed (*emakarizen*) since the city would soon receive the visible presence of the god Asklepios.[119] The context makes it clear that this prediction was intended to be taken as an unsolicited oracle apparently prefaced by a beatitude. Alexander then ran to the spot where he had concealed the egg, singing hymns to Asklepios and Apollo invoking them to come (*hēkein*) to the city, and "taking it in his hands he asserted that at that moment he held Asklepios." Although the statement is only quoted indirectly, it too is a recognition oracle.

Another example of a recognition oracle spontaneously uttered by a medium in a state of possession is reported in Acts 16:17:

> These men are servants of the Most High God,
> who proclaim to you the way of salvation.

Those who were demon possessed in Mark also identified Jesus as "the Holy One of God" (Mark 1:24; 3:11; 5:7), clearly a recognition oracle in function. The NT contains many other recognition oracles, which will be discussed in some detail below (pp. 270-74).

2. Commendation Oracles.

Commendation oracles are closely related to recognition oracles, except that they function to direct the recipients of the oracle to a trustworthy source of divine revelation other than that represented by the speaker. Three spontaneous commendation oracles, all attributed to Glykon-Asklepios, were collected by Lucian of Samosata:

> Go now to Claros, to hear the voice of my father.

> Go to the sanctuary of the Branchidae and obey the oracles.

> Depart for Mallos and the prophecies of Amphilokos.[120]

Through these oracles Glykon-Asklepios provides supernatural legitimation for these ancient oracle centers (something which they scarcely needed from him), yet in recommending other oracles (a not uncommon practice in antiquity), Glykon-Asklepios was providing legitimation for himself.

Oracles given at Colophon, Didyma, and Pergamum reportedly recommended Apollonius for his wisdom and his ability to heal.[121] Expecting a healing oracle through incubation, a dissolute Assyrian youth purportedly received a commendation oracle which referred him to Apollonius of Tyana:

> If you would consult Apollonius you would get better.[122]

Similarly, Aelius Aristides received a response oracle from Clarian Apollo sending him to the sanctuary of Asklepios for healing.[123]

If we consider Acts 16:17 again, it is evident that while the first line functions as a recognition oracle, the second line functions as a commendation oracle:

> These men are servants of the Most High God,
> who proclaim to you the way of salvation.

Another example of a combined recognition and commendation oracle is found in Mark 9:7 (Matt. 17:5; Luke 9:35):

> This is my beloved son; listen to him.

Other NT commendation oracles will be discussed below (pp. 268-69).

3. Oracles of Self-Commendation.

Self-commendation oracles are those in which the speaker claims to be an authentic vehicle of divine revelation. Functionally, self-commendation oracles serve to legitimate the medium through whom the divinity is thought to reveal his will. Pausanias quotes an example of a self-commendation oracle from a collection of Sibylline oracles with which he was familiar:

> I am by birth half mortal, half divine;
> An immortal nymph was my mother, my father an eater of corn;
> On my mother's side of Idaean birth, but my fatherland was red
> Marpessus, sacred to the Mother, and the river Aïdoneus.[124]

The divine ancestry of the Sibyl is emphasized in this four-line hexameter oracle, which may have stood at the beginning of the collection read by Pausanias. Its purpose was the legitimation of the oracle collection by underscoring the author's divine lineage. Oracles of self-commendation, like this one, are often introduced with the formula "I am," though for metrical reasons *egō eimi* cannot be used in hexameter verse.[125]

Another Sibylline oracle which begins with the "I am" formula and functions as an oracle of self-commendation is this one quoted by Proclus:

> I am a mediating spokesperson between gods and men.[126]

Again the divine status of the speaker is emphasized. In another Sibylline oracle, quoted by Clement of Alexandria, the "I am" formula is absent, but it is replaced by the "I came" (*ēlthon egō*) formula:

> O Delphians, servants of far-darting Apollo,
> I came to declare the mind of Aegis-bearing Zeus,
> though angered at my own brother Apollo.[127]

In a one-line hexameter oracle preserved by Lucian, Glykon-Asklepios announced spontaneously:

> I am Glykon, third generation from Zeus, a light for mankind.[128]

The first part of this two-part expository oracle contains a claim of divine ancestry, while the second part defines the role of Glykon-Asklepios.

Oracles of self-commendation are also found among response oracles, such as this one found at the beginning of the oracular dialogue quoted above (p. 65):

> I am the new Asklepios.[129]

When oracles of self-commendation are responsory, however, they always seem to introduce an oracular dialogue. This pattern occurs with enough frequency in oracular dialogues that it may be regarded as a convention.[130] At the beginning of Poimandres, the first tractate in the Corpus Hermeticum, the recipient of a visionary experience in which a figure appears asks, "Who are you?" The response is an oracle of self-commendation:

> I am Poimandres, the absolute *Nous*;
> I know what you desire, and I am with you everywhere.[131]

One of the most discussed oracles of self-commendation is found in Origen's treatise *Contra Celsum*. Celsus, a pagan philosopher who wrote a treatise against Christianity called *True Discourse* ca. A.D. 178, received a point-by-point rebuttal by Origen, an early third-century Christian scholar. At one point Origen quotes Celsus' parody of the kind of prophetic speech which he claims was current in Phoenicia and Palestine:

Legitimation formula:	I am God (or a son of God, or a divine Spirit). And I have come.
Possibility of deliverance:	Already the world is being destroyed. And you, O men, are to perish because of your iniquities. But I wish to save you. And you shall see me returning again with heavenly power.

Conditions of   *a*   Blessed is he who has worshipped me now!
deliverance: *b*   But I will cast everlasting fire upon all the rest, both on cities
               and on country places.
       b' And men who fail to realize the penalties in store for them
              will in vain repent and groan.
       a' But I will preserve for ever those who have been convinced
              by me.[132]

According to Celsus this kind of prophetic address was concluded with the utterance of strange, incomprehensible, and obscure words which had no rational meaning. He may be referring to a kind of glossolalia that apparently served to legitimate the divine authority of the speech by giving evidence of divine possession.[133] Although some have regarded this as a pagan prophetic speech (it is delivered "in temples"), it is more probably an amalgam of pagan, Jewish, and Christian elements.[134] Celsus had certainly read the gospels carefully, and portions of this speech are reminiscent of some of the sayings of Jesus preserved in them.[135] The phrase "I have come" indicates that the speaker claims to be a savior-god and not merely a prophetic medium with a divine message.[136] The oracle of self-commendation expressed through the "I am" formula which introduces the speech serves to provide divine legitimation for the statements which follow. The second strophe of the speech exhibits chiastic form (*a b b' a'*), and bears a suspiciously close resemblance to "pronouncements of sacral law" in the gospels (cf. Mark 8:38 and parallels). The interweaving of the themes of judgment and deliverance in this prophetic speech is characteristic of Levantine prophecy generally.

D. THE ORACULAR LETTER

While written oracle questions in the Greco-Roman world often adapted features of the ancient letter of request (see above, pp. 8, 11), oracles themselves were rarely if ever couched in epistolary form. In the Near East, on the other hand, letters were frequently used as means for communicating prophetic proclamations. A letter from the prophet Elijah is mentioned in 2 Chr. 21:12-15 (cf. Josephus *Ant.* ix.99-101). Most of the other prophetic letters in the OT and postbiblical Jewish literature are associated with the Jeremiah-Baruch tradition (Jer. 29:4-23, 24-28, 30-32 [LXX 36:4-23, 26-28]; 2 Bar. 77:17-19; 78– 87; Epistula Ieremiae [LXX]; Par. Jer. 6:15– 7:4; 7:24-35).[137] The transmission of prophecies to the reigning monarch by letter was practiced at Mari. Several letters containing prophecies sent to Zimrilim contain precise quotations of the prophecies conveyed.[138] In the NT, the Apocalypse of John has an epistolary framework, a generic feature which also characterizes several Coptic gnostic revelatory dialogues (Apoc. Jas.; Pet. Phil.; Nat. Arc.; De Res.; Eug.). Until recently, the seven letters of Rev. 2-3 were virtually the only examples of oracular letters from the Greco-Roman world. In 1968, however, several texts of oracles written on ostraca (potsherds) were published that exhibited a unique character.[139] These ostraca contain rough drafts of an oracle (apparently unsolicited) by Hermes Trismegistos to Horos a priest of Isis in 168 B.C. This oracle was then recast in the form of a letter which Horos addressed to the Egyptian sovereigns of that period. The first text below is one of the draft oracles, while the second is the oracular letter based on the draft text:

> Regarding matters disclosed to me by the thrice-great god Hermes concerning oracles for the sovereigns, I wish to announce that (the insurgent) Egyptians will quickly be defeated and that the King is to advance immediately into the Thebaid.

The epistolary revision of the oracle reads as follows:

> To King Ptolemy and to King Ptolemy the Brother and to Queen Cleopatra the Sister, greetings. Horus the priest of Isis at the sanctuary of Sebenutos in the city of Isis wishes to make an announcement about certain oracles to the sovereigns, that (the insurgent) Egyptians will be defeated quickly and that the King is to advance immediately into the Thebaid.[140]

The oracles referred to in the quotations are "(the insurgent) Egyptians will quickly be defeated," and "the King is to advance immediately into the Thebaid." In form these are simple one-part oracles, the first of which is predictive and the second prescriptive. The double oracle may not have been unsolicited, but given in response to a double question of the type discussed above (pp. 52-53, 57-58). An appropriate reconstruction of the first question would be: "Shall the insurgent Egyptians be defeated?" and the second: "What shall the King do to ensure the defeat of the insurgent Egyptians?" These two oracles may represent a short oracular dialogue between Hermes Trismegistos and Horus the priest, or perhaps the verbalizations of two successive responses to a lot oracle. The oracle is unsolicited in the sense that the king is being sent oracular advice for which he may not have asked. The letter version of the oracle is striking in that the name of the oracular divinity, Hermes Trismegistos, has been eliminated from the text.

E. ORACLES OF DOOM

Throughout the ancient Mediterranean world unsolicited oracles were frequently uttered by free-lance diviners or prophets during periods of social crisis and political oppression.[141] Those who produced such oracles, most of which focused on predictions of doom and destruction, were usually on the margins of society. Although oracles of doom could have a completely temporal reference, they were often of an eschatological character in that they anticipated a final period of bliss following an era of judgment and destruction. Oracles of doom may be divided into two categories: unconditional oracles of doom and oracles of ultimate deliverance.

1. Unconditional Oracles of Doom.

An unconditional oracle of doom is a prediction of destruction whose fulfilment was regarded as inevitable. Many of the oracles found in the ancient collections attributed to the Sibyls, Bakis, and others were of this type. Herodotus quotes an oracle of Bakis consisting of four hexameter lines that he thought was fulfilled by the Greek victory over the Persians at Plataea (479 B.C.):

> By Thermodon's stream and the grassgrown banks of Asopus
> Muster of Greeks for fight, and the ring of a foreigner's war-cry;
> Many a Median archer by death untimely o'ertaken
> There in the battle shall fall when the day of his doom is upon him.[142]

Herodotus quotes a similar unconditional oracle of doom in part, and this oracle appears to have been spontaneously uttered by the Pythia, since it was given to Argive inquirers for delivery to the Milesians, who were not present:

> In that day, Miletus, thou planner of works that are evil,
> Thou for a banquet shalt serve and a guerdon rich of the spoiler;
> Many the long-locked gallants whose feet shall be washed by thy women;
> Woe for my Didyman shrine! no more shall its ministers tend it.[143]

Although the entire oracle is a two-part conditional oracle of the type discussed above, it has the "when x, then y" pattern rather than the "if x, then y" pattern. The fulfilment of this and many other oracles similarly structured would be recognized only in retrospect, when the conditions were seen to have been completely fulfilled.

2. Oracles of Ultimate Deliverance.

Many of the unsolicited oracles of a political nature which originated in the Levant exhibit a two-part schema consisting of impending judgment and tribulation followed by a period of final deliverance, often introduced by the appearance of an ideal king. Each step in the oppressive Roman conquest of eastern Mediterranean lands was accompanied by oracular utterances which expressed the hate of the subject peoples for their Roman oppressors.[144] The same was true of native responses to the continuous conflict between the various Greek successors of Alexander the Great during the third and second centuries B.C.

One such prophecy appears to have been directed against the Jews in Egypt by a native Egyptian prophet, probably as a result of the Jewish revolt in Egypt in A.D. 115-17.[145] Although the text is fragmentary, a translation of this papyrus scrap will convey the gist of its contents:

> ... being ... unhappy Egypt ... men ... sacred things (temples?) ... placed. Therefore go against the Jews (?) ... your city become desolate ... of horses (stable?) ... shall be ... lawless ... and in place of prophets the lawbreakers ... cast out from Egypt by the anger of Isis ... they shall settle, a prophet shall have no office (?) ... serve the divine ... to the greatest....[146]

The oracle describes an unhappy period, caused in part by the Jews, followed by a time of blessing. The salvation which is expected is not from the Romans, but probably from a native king. The structure exhibited in this prophecy, unhappy present followed by a blessed future, is characteristic of many of these politically inspired prophecies. The native Egyptian origin of the prophecy is not surprising in the light of the long Egyptian tradition of unsolicited prophetic speech.[147]

The collection of Jewish Sibylline Oracles contains a number of better-preserved speeches structured in accordance with the two-part schema.[148] Pagan oracles appear to be embedded in Book 3 of the Sibylline Oracles, most of which are thoroughly Jewish in origin and content.[149] One such prophecy that is not part of the Jewish composition within which it is set is in lines 350-380, which probably originated during the war of propaganda and vituperation in 33 B.C., during Cleopatra's reign:

> 350 a For all the wealth that Rome received from tributary Asia.
> b threefold as much shall Asia receive back again
> c from Rome, and shall repay to her her hideous violence.

      a' And for all those children of Asia who served Italian homes,
        b' Italians to twenty-fold shall live in bondage and penury in Asia,
355   *c*' and shall pay back their debt ten thousand-fold.

      O Rome, pampered golden offspring of Latium!
      thou virgin oft intoxicated by thy many suitors in marriage,
      as a slave-girl shalt thou be wedded without ceremony,
      and ofttimes shall thy mistress [*despoina*] shear thy luxuriant locks,
360   and passing sentence on thee shall cast thee from heaven to earth,
      and shall lift thee up again from earth to heaven,
      because men held to a bad and lawless life.

      Samos too shall be sand [*ammos*], Delos shall vanish [*adēlos*]
      and Rome become a street [*hrymē*]: and all the oracles are being
          fulfilled.
365   Of perishing Smyrna there shall be no account.
          Outlaw shall she be,
      but with evil counsels and the villainy of her leaders.

      But tranquil peace shall make its way to the land of Asia.
      And Europe shall then be happy, the air salubrious,
      year after year bracing and free from storms, and free from hail,
370   producing everything, birds and creeping creatures of the earth.
      Thrice happy who shall live unto that time man or woman:
      happy he whose life is as among the country folk.
      For good law shall come in its fulness from the starry heaven
      upon men, and good justice, and with it
375   the best of all gifts to men, sober concord [*homonoia*],
      and affection, faithfulness, friendship from strangers and fellow-
          citizens too.
      And lawlessness, murmuring, envy, wrath, and folly
      shall flee from men: penury too, shall flee, and distress,
      and murder, and destructive strifes, and baleful feuds,
380   and thefts by night and every evil in those days.[150]

This oracle is of considerable political and social interest, since it reveals a strong current of Egyptian nationalism that regarded Cleopatra (the *despoina* of line 359) as a deliverer of eastern Mediterranean peoples and as a conqueror of Rome.[151] The basic structure of the prophecy is similar to that of the anti-Jewish oracle just discussed in that the first part (lines 350-366) deals with the times of misfortune, vengeance, and judgment, while the second part (lines 367-380)[152] focuses on the coming era of universal bliss.

The structure of lines 350-366 requires some comment. This part of the prophecy has three strophes of varying size. The first and third strophes consist of third-person predictions of judgment awaiting Rome, Samos, Delos, and Smyrna. The second strophe addresses Rome in the second-person singular. The shift from third-person to second-person address is found in the judicial speeches of OT prophets (Mic. 6:9c-15; Amos 3:10-11; Isa. 30:8-14; Hos. 12:7-9), and in OT woe oracles (Mic. 2:1-3; Isa. 10:1-4; 30:1-5). The prophecy is similar to the prophecy of the downfall of Babylon (= Rome) in Rev. 18:21-24. There Babylon is addressed in the second person in vv. 22-23, while the third person is used to frame the section in vv. 21, 24. The first strophe of Sib.

Or. iii.350-55 consists of six hexameter lines arranged in an *a b c / a' b' c'* structure and focusing on the *lex talionis,* or principle of retributive justice. This principle also figures prominently in the oracle embedded in Rev. 18:4-20; in vv. 6-7 we read:

> Render to her as she herself has rendered,
> and repay her double for her deeds;
> mix a double draught for her in the cup she mixed.
> As she glorified herself and played the wanton,
> so give her a like measure of torment and mourning.

The second section, Sib. Or. iii.367-380, which focuses on the coming era of *homonoia* ("concord"), mentioned in line 375,[153] is striking in that no note of rancor or vindictiveness is sounded. The enjoyment of blessings and the absence of woes seem to apply equally to all men.

This kind of oracle was not without its western counterparts, if Vergil's famous *Fourth Eclogue* (sometimes called the messianic eclogue) is any indication. In lines 4-10 we read:

> The last generation of the song of Cumae has now arrived;
> the great cycle of the ages is beginning afresh.
> The maiden Justice[154] is now returning, the rule of Saturn is returning,
> now a new race is being sent from the height of heaven.
> A boy is being born, with whom the race of iron will cease,
> and a race of gold be born throughout the earth.
> Be gracious to his birth, immaculate Lucina; your Apollo rules at last.[155]

Vergil's *Fourth Eclogue* is an epithalamium, i.e. a poem written for an approaching wedding.[156] The nuptial couple was probably Anthony and Octavia. The child spoken of in line 8 was the anticipated offspring of that marriage; unfortunately the child was a girl.[157] After Octavia, Anthony had twins by Cleopatra, whom he named Alexander Helios and Cleopatra Selene, to agree with other portions of the prophecy.[158] The name "Alexander" signified Anthony's intended conquest of Parthia (in emulation of the achievement of Alexander the Great), while the epithet *Helios* ("Sun") was a reference to the supreme deity of Asia. In form and content this *Eclogue* was modeled after the pattern of the Sibylline Oracles,[159] and in this putative prophecy of the Cumaean Sibyl, the rule of the Sun was to precede the arrival of the Golden Age.[160]

These two prophecies, Sib. Or. iii.350-380 and Vergil *Eclogues* iv.4-10, when taken together with many other Greco-Egyptian, Jewish, and Christian prophecies and apocalypses, indicate that in the eastern theater of the Greco-Roman world there was a general expectation of a time of peace that included the anticipation of a future ideal ruler from the east whose birth or recognition would herald the age of peace.[161]

One of the more famous Greco-Egyptian prophecies which exhibits the two-part schema is the so-called "Oracle of the Potter." The two extant recensions of this oracle date from the second to third centuries A.D., though the prophecy itself appears to reflect the historical situation which existed in Egypt ca. 130 B.C.[162] The historical framework within which the prophecy is set, and which is probably a secondary addition, places the events narrated in the reign of Amenophis (fourteenth century B.C.).

A summary of the narrative framework together with the prophecy of the potter is as follows: A potter ("potter" is one of the epithets of the god Chnum) was sent by Hermes Thoth to the Island of Helios, where he (in the opinion of bystanders) committed the sacrilege of firing pots. Outraged observers pulled the pots from the kiln and dashed them to pieces. The potter then fell into a trance and, possessed by a divine spirit, began to prophesy. The broken pots, he claimed, symbolized the destruction of Egypt. The evil god Typhon-Seth (i.e. the Greeks) will dominate the land, the Nile will provide no water, and men will suffer famine. Total chaos will prevail. Alexandria itself will be destroyed and will become a place where fishermen dry their nets. After the destruction of Alexandria (the Greek stronghold) the gods Agathos Daimon and Knephis will go to Memphis, the new capital. The era of peace and prosperity will then be introduced by a divinely appointed king:

> And then Egypt shall blossom when the king who has been in good favor for fifty-five years shall appear from the sun, a dispenser of good things, established by the great goddess [Isis], so that the living will pray that the dead will be resurrected to share the good things. And at the conclusion of this period [the plants] will put forth leaves, and the empty Nile shall be filled with water, and discordant winter shall change and run in its regular cycle. And then the summer also shall resume its regular cycle. And the storm winds shall be gently diminished into well-ordered breezes.[163]

This vivid prediction of the collapse of the political, economic, and social order of Ptolemaic Egypt, followed by its reestablishment under the leadership of a savior-king, is based on the myth and ritual of the Egyptian enthronement ideology.[164] The prophecies of the potter are patterned after the myth of Osiris: when the followers of Seth-Typhon revolt, Osiris kills Seth and a new king is installed as Horus by his mother Isis. This archaic native Egyptian tradition has been transformed into an apocalyptic scheme for the renovation of the cosmos.

A final example of oracles from the Greco-Roman world that predict doom but hold out for the ultimate deliverance of those who are worthy is the collection of oracles of Hystaspes. These oracles, of which only fragments remain, are mentioned by several church fathers.[165] They were probably a mixture of pagan, Jewish, and Christian traditions which originated some time during the first century B.C. or the first century A.D.[166] Three themes are found in the surviving fragments: (1) the fall of Rome, (2) the wickedness of the final age culminating in the gathering of the pious and the annihilation of the godless by Jupiter-Ahura Mazda, and (3) the destruction of the world by fire.[167] The oracles have a syncretistic character and are a kind of pagan counterpart to Daniel and the Jewish Sibylline Oracles, though they do not appear to be Jewish in origin.[168] The author may have been either a Hellenized Parsee or an orientalized Greek who believed in the religious and political supremacy of the east, and in the unity of Ahura Mazda, Zeus, and Jupiter.[169]

VI. ORACLE COLLECTIONS

Throughout antiquity various kinds of oracles circulated in the form of oral and written collections. These collections were composed primarily of unsolicited oracles, i.e. oracles whose interpretation was not delimited by questions. In the fifth century B.C. Herodotus knew and used collections of oracles which he ascribed to Bakis (ix.43), Musaeos (ix.43), and Laios the son of Labdacus and father of Oidipous (v.43, 89). No mention is made, however, of a collection of Delphic response oracles or indeed of a collection of oracles from any of the great oracle shrines.[170] In the second century A.D. Justin Martyr referred to collections of the oracles of Sibyl and Hystaspes,[171] while another second-century figure, Pausanias, claimed to have read the oracles of Erato, Bakis, and the Sibyl Hierophile.[172] Nowhere does Pausanias or any other ancient authority claim to have read a collection of oracles originating from such major oracle sanctuaries as Delphi, Dodona, Ammon, Didyma, or Claros. If these oracle centers had archives, and some of them certainly did, the oracles they contained were probably not circulated in the form of written collections. One of the prophets of Apollo at Claros, Nikandros, reportedly wrote three books filled with oracles, though it is not known whether he limited himself to Clarian oracles.[173] In the fifth century B.C. Euripides referred to "leather scrolls written in black ink and filled with many sayings of Loxias [Apollo],"[174] but the fragmentary nature of this statement makes any firm conclusions impossible.

Many times Greek states which had secured oracles from Delphi and other oracle sanctuaries would place them in state archives where they could be referred to if necessary. Sparta had a distinctive institution called the *Pythii,* a board consisting of two members. They went to Delphi to consult the oracle on various matters of state, and they also recorded the responses and were, together with the king, responsible for their preservation.[175] Another important source for collections of oracles was the inscriptions in which oracular responses of particular significance were permanently recorded. Pausanias speaks of the Thebans inscribing various oracles that they had received at various times from the oracles of Trophonios and the Apolline oracles at Ismene, Ptoüm, Abae, and Delphi.[176] Similarly, the Eleans had dedicated inscriptions containing their inquiries and the responses of Zeus Ammon at the temple of Ammon.[177] Many ancient collectors of oracles, such as Herodotus, Philochoros, Ister, Ephorus, Timaeus, and particularly Theopompus,[178] had only to visit various oracle sanctuaries in order to read the oracles which had been inscribed and dedicated by their recipients. At Argos, at the oracle of Apollo Deiradiotes, a collection of three oracle stories inscribed there testify to the accuracy of the oracle.[178a]

Herodotus refers to several ancient oracle collectors. One such collector was Hippias (tyrant of Athens, 527-510 B.C.), the son of Peisistratus, and Peisistratus himself had the epithet "Bakis."[179] He also reports that a certain Athenian *chrēsmologos*[180] named Onomakritos, who collected and arranged the oracles of Musaeos, was banished from Athens for forging oracles and ascribing them to Musaeos.[181] Other *chrēsmologoi* mentioned by Herodotus include Amphilytos of Acarnania (i.62), Antichares of Elis (v.43), and Lysistrates of Athens (viii.96). These figures not only collected and interpreted oracles; they also recited them on appropriate occasions.[182] The *chrēsmologoi* were probably the primary means whereby oracles ascribed to ancient figures such as Sibyl, Bakis, Orpheus, and Musaeos were collected and circulated.[183] Like Onomakritos they probably also contributed oracles to these collections.

During the later Greco-Roman period there is little evidence that the *chrēsmologoi* were still plying their ancient trade of collecting and expounding oracles. Yet it is probable that they had spiritual successors who played a similar role. By the first century A.D. another important source for the transmission of oracles was the travel guide (*periēgētēs*).[184] Pausanias himself was a travel guide, and it is clear that his repertoire of memorized oracles served him well as he interpreted his discussion of the historic sites of ancient Greece with oracle stories. Such guides were found at all the important sites in Greece, and like the guides in all places and at all times, they had an annoyingly mechanical approach to their trade. In one of Plutarch's dialogues which begins with a tour of the historic buildings of Delphi, the author observes:

The guides were going through their prearranged program, paying no heed to us who begged that they would cut short their harangues and their expounding of most of the inscriptions.[185]

Pausanias mentions one Iophon of Cnossos in Crete, a travel guide who would quote oracular responses in hexameter from memory.[186]

By the late Hellenistic and early Roman period many collections of oracles circulated freely throughout the Greco-Roman world. When fire destroyed the Roman collection of Sibylline Oracles in 83 B.C., it was not difficult to replace it with a new collection consisting of oracles gathered from various places.[187] In order to control prophecy that might not be in the interests of Rome or its emperor, in A.D. 12 Augustus had more than 2,000 prophetic writings in both Latin and Greek collected and burned.[188] Thereafter, private ownership of oracle collections became illegal.[189] Although the Romans were never as infatuated with oracles as the Greeks, the Sibylline Oracles had played an important role for the state in times of national emergency. The original collection, according to legend, was brought from the Euboean colony at Cumae by the Romans, and an administrative body was created to superintend their use.[190]

The repressive measures of Augustus and of Tiberius after him,[191] however, appear to have had little effect in impeding the circulation of oracles. Oracles with strong anti-Roman sentiment were often embedded in apocalyptic writings that expressed the repressed hopes of Levantine nativistic traditions.

4 | ANCIENT ISRAELITE PROPHECY

I. INTRODUCTION

For most Palestinian Jews of the late Second Temple period, which concluded with the capture of Jerusalem by the Romans in A.D. 70, prophecy was a phenomenon which belonged either to the distant past or to the eschatological future.[1] Since many apocalyptic groups and sects believed that the end of the age was imminent, for them prophecy could be part of present experience. Ordinarily, however, the designation "prophet" (Heb. *nabi'*; Gk. *prophētēs*) was reserved for ancient Israelite prophets or for eschatological prophets who were expected to appear just prior to the end.[2] This hiatus between canonical and eschatological prophecy has no counterpart in the history of the Greek conception of oracular divination. Political and social changes, it is true, had precipitated a decline in the popularity of oracle centers in the Greco-Roman world from the third century B.C. to the first century A.D. Yet many oracles managed to survive the lean years and continued to function in much the same way that they had in more prosperous times.[3] In Judaism, however, both the function of prophets and the more characteristic forms of prophetic speech and behavior were extensively transformed during and after the dissolution of the monarchy and the corresponding cessation of national independence in the late seventh and early sixth centuries B.C.[4] The canonization of the Hebrew scriptures, a process largely completed during the first century B.C.,[5] had the effect of elevating classical Israelite prophecy to a unique, sacrosanct, and paradigmatic status. Although verbal forms of divine revelation, particularly exemplified by apocalyptic literature, continued to flourish throughout the late Second Temple period, the special role assigned to the Jewish scriptures made it both necessary and desirable for later forms of oral and written revelation to deal seriously with canonical revelation.

Because of the discontinuities between canonical prophecy and subsequent forms of prophetic revelation that emerged during the period of the Second Temple (516 B.C.– A.D. 70), a synchronic treatment of both Israelite and early Jewish prophetic speech forms cannot be carried out successfully. The present chapter will survey Israelite prophecy and prophetic speech forms, and in the following chapter we shall turn to an analysis of the various forms of oracular speech and composition practiced in early Judaism during the late Second Temple period.

81

II. PROPHECY AND DIVINATION

Inspired prophecy was but one among many forms of divination practiced in ancient Israel.[6] Various forms of divination were widely used in the ancient world to gain information from the supernatural world in order to minimize the unpredictability and uncontrollability inherent in man's experience in the world. In ancient Israel, as in Greece, "inspired prophecy," a phrase which is interchangeable with "oracular divination," consists of comprehensible verbal messages from the supernatural world conveyed through an inspired medium who may be designated as a prophet. Divination, on the other hand, consists of the interpretation of coded messages from the supernatural world conveyed through various kinds of symbols. Both inspired prophecy and divination may be solicited or unsolicited.

The frequency of its condemnation indicates that divination was widely practiced throughout the history of Israel.[7] The folk religion of ancient Israel is rarely reflected in the Jewish scriptures and usually only in the context of condemnations of forbidden practices. However, several forms of divination met with general approval by all segments of Israelite society. One of the more common forms of approved divination was oneiromancy or divination by dreams. Many revelatory dreams in the OT had self-evident meanings, either because the recipient was directly addressed by God (Gen. 20:3, 6-7; 28:12-15; 31:10-13; 1 Kgs. 3:5-15), or because the symbolism of the dream was transparent (Gen. 37:5-11; Judg. 7:13-14). The expertise of a technical diviner or dream interpreter was required only when the meaning of the dream was elusive (Eccl. 5:3, 7). Dreams which required the skill of a technical dream interpreter are relatively rare in the OT (Gen. 40:5-8; 41:1-8; Dan. 1:17; 2:1-11). Divination by use of the sacred lot was also widely used in ancient Israel to identify a guilty individual (Josh. 7:14-15; 1 Sam. 14:41-42; Jonah 1:7), to select someone for a special task or office (1 Sam. 10:20-21;[8] 1 Chr. 24:5, 7-19; 25:8; 26:13; Neh. 10:34), to select the goat for Azazel and for Yahweh on the Day of Atonement (Lev. 16:7-10), and to give other yes or no responses to inquiries.

The provision of oracular responses to specific inquiries through divination was an important function of the priesthood in ancient Israel. The Urim and Thummim were a special form of sacred lot supervised by priests (Deut. 33:8; Num. 27:21). Although their precise form is not known (small pebbles? dice? short sticks?), they seem to have been kept in a special pocket attached to the ephod of the high priest (Exod. 28:30; Prov. 16:33). They were used to secure either a positive or negative answer to an inquiry (Num. 27:21; 1 Sam. 23:9-12), particularly the selection of goats on the Day of Atonement (Lev. 16:7-10). The priests also used the ephod for divination, though probably in conjunction with the Urim and Thummim, which it contained. The ephod, a priestly garment, is mentioned frequently in the OT, but only in 1 Sam. 23:6, 9; 30:7 is it stated that it was used for purposes of divination. The positive or negative answer received from the Urim and Thummim or ephod could be verbalized in narrative contexts, as we see in 1 Sam. 23:11-12:

> [David asks:] "Will the men of Keilah surrender me into his [Saul's] hand? Will Saul come down, as thy servant has heard? O Lord, the God of Israel, I beseech thee, tell thy servant." And the Lord said, "He will come down." Then said David, "Will the men of Keilah surrender me and my men into the hand of Saul?" And the Lord said, "They will surrender you."

The context of this dramatization makes it clear that David inquired of God through the ephod in the possession of the priest Abiathar (1 Sam. 23:9-10). After the reign of David there is no evidence that Urim and Thummim were used for purposes of divination (cf. Neh. 7:65).[9]

Another cult object used for divination was the teraphim, a collective term for images of varying size and number. Some were small and portable (Gen. 31:19, 34-35), while others were very large (1 Sam. 19:13-16) and were objects of veneration (Judg. 18:14-20). Although they were clearly used for divination (Ezek. 21:21; Zech. 10:2), precisely how they were used is not clear.

III. BASIC FEATURES OF ISRAELITE PROPHECY

Early Israelite prophecy (ca. 1000-750 B.C.) is often distinguished from classical or written prophecy, which appeared during the Assyrian crisis in the middle of the eighth century and disappeared shortly after the dissolution of the Judean monarchy in the sixth century. In many respects, however, the points of similarity and continuity between these two periods and types of prophetic activity are more significant than any differences.

A. TYPES OF PROPHETS

The oldest Hebrew terms for inspired individuals who mediate divine communications are "seer" (ḥozeh, ro'eh), i.e. one who "sees" what is hidden to others, "man of God," and "man of the Spirit."[10] The most common term for "prophet" is nabi', a word which etymologically means "one who is called,"[11] but which came to mean "speaker, spokesman (of God),"[12] or "proclaimer."[13] During the monarchical period (1000-586 B.C.) the term nabi' tended to displace the older terms ḥozeh and ro'eh (1 Sam. 9:9), though all three terms continued to be used interchangeably (2 Sam. 24:11; 2 Kgs. 17:13 [cf. 1 Chr. 21:9]; Isa. 29:10; Amos 7:12). It has become increasingly apparent that Israelite prophets had much more in common with prophets in other ancient Near Eastern cultures than was formerly thought.

1. Shamanistic Prophets.

The Israelite prophet first appears in our sources in the eleventh century B.C. This prophetic type, exemplified by such figures as Samuel, Elijah, and Elisha, combines the characteristics of the holy man, the sage, the miracle worker, and the soothsayer (1 Sam. 9; 1 Kgs. 17; 2 Kgs. 1:2-17; 6:1-7, 8-10; 13:14-21; 20:1-11). Prophets were closely associated with holy places and religious ritual (1 Sam. 7:17; 9:11-14; 10:5), and could combine the roles of priest and prophet, like Samuel (1 Sam. 2:18-20; 3:1, 19-20). They were itinerants who moved about with some freedom, apparently living off the gifts and offerings of those they served. Master prophets were given the title "father" (1 Sam. 10:12; 2 Kgs. 2:12; 6:21; 13:14) and presided over prophetic guilds called "sons of the prophets" (1 Kgs. 20:35; 2 Kgs. 2:3, 5, 7, 15; 4:1, 38; 5:22; 6:1; 9:1; Amos 7:14).[13a] Both Samuel and Elisha presided over such prophetic associations (1 Sam. 19:20, 24; 2 Kgs. 4:38; 6:22). These prophets would often prophesy in groups (1 Sam. 10:5; 19:20; 1 Kgs. 18:17-29; 22:5-10) and appear to have worn a distinctive costume consisting of a hairy sheepskin or goatskin mantle and a leather loincloth (2 Kgs. 1:8; Zech. 13:4). A system of prophetic succession may have been practiced on occasion (2 Kgs. 2:9-15; Deut. 18:15-18).[14]

2. Cult and Temple Prophets.

The oracular activities of early Israelite prophets of the shamanistic type were closely associated with, but not inseparable from, holy places and religious rituals.[15] Like Samuel the later prophets Ezekiel and Jeremiah were associated with the priesthood (Ezek. 1:1; Jer. 1:1). Priests and prophets are often mentioned together as if they shared a common sphere of activity.[16] This association, however, is attested only for the region of Judah and the city of Jerusalem.[17] Since priests were primarily attached to sanctuaries and to the temple cult in Jerusalem, the presumption is strong that prophets were also cult functionaries. Amos, though a native of Judah, traveled to the Israelite sanctuary at Bethel to prophesy (Amos 7:10-13), and Isaiah's inaugural vision took place in the Jerusalem temple (Isa. 6:1-13). Jeremiah frequented the temple in Jerusalem where he delivered prophetic messages to the priests and the people (Jer. 26:2, 7; 27:16-22; 28:1, 5). Haggai and Zechariah worked closely with Zerubbabel and the priest Jeshua ben Jozadak in the rebuilding of the temple (Ezra 5:1-2). In the preexilic period prophets whose sphere of activity was the environs of the temple in Jerusalem were apparently (like everyone else who frequented the temple) under the direct authority of the high priest (Jer. 29:26-27).[18] Many psalms, which were certainly part of temple ritual, appear to have had a "prophetic" origin, i.e. they are couched in forms of speech characteristic of prophets (Pss. 20; 21; 50; 60; 72; 75; 82; 85:8-13; 89:19-37; 108; 110; 132:11-18).[19] Furthermore, some of the classical prophets, such as Joel, Nahum, Habakkuk, and Zephaniah, seem to have used liturgical forms as a literary vehicle for their prophecies. On the basis of these various kinds of evidence it seems probable that there was, in the preexilic period, a formal relationship between some prophets and the temple cult in Jerusalem. Some prophets were undoubtedly stipended members of the temple staff and under the direct authority of the priests. On the other hand, it is clear that the priests, considering the prophets as bearers of divine relation, heeded their oracles (Jer. 5:30-31; 27:16). The temple also provided a natural center for prophets not formally associated with the cult (e.g. Jeremiah) to exercise their prophetic gifts.

The picture is complicated by the Chronicler, who regards the Levitical singers in the preexilic temple as the descendants of Asaph, Heman, and Jeduthun, all of whom were prophets or seers (1 Chr. 25:2, 3, 5; 2 Chr. 35:15; 29:30). The Chronicler appears to equate "singing" with "prophesying" (1 Chr. 25:1, 3, 6) because of the inspired nature of the former. The Chronicler also narrates the inspired prophesying of Jahaziel ben Zechariah, a Levite (2 Chr. 20:14-18), and of Zechariah ben Jehoiada, the son of a priest (2 Chr. 24:20). It is widely held that the singers in the postexilic temple were the successors of the prophetic guilds in the preexilic temple.[20] No prophetic guilds were active in the postexilic temple, however.[21]

3. Court Prophets.

There are many references to Israelite prophets who conveyed divine messages from Yahweh to the reigning monarchs.[22] Numerous examples in the Mari Letters illustrate the importance in ancient Near Eastern thought of conveying oracular messages to the king.[23] Particularly in times of war or before an impending battle prophets are reported to have delivered unsolicited oracles to Israelite kings,[24] though prophets are more frequently sought out by rulers who desire to inquire of the Lord through them.[25] Large groups of Baal prophets were employed as permanent consultants by Ahab and Jezebel (1 Kgs. 18:19; cf. 2 Kgs. 3:13). Stipended prophets kept as permanent court counsellors may be regarded as court prophets. The precise relationship of Yahweh's prophets to the king and his court is not always clear. Gad is designated as "the king's seer" (2 Sam. 24:11; 1 Chr. 21:9; 2 Chr. 29:25), a title that certainly indicates an official position. The Chronicler also names Asaph, Heman, and Jeduthun as seers of King David (1 Chr. 25:5; 2 Chr. 35:15). Nathan appears to have functioned as a court prophet for David (2 Sam. 7:4-17; 12:1-17; 1 Kgs. 1:8, 10, 22-37), though the expression "the king's prophet" is never used of him or anyone else. The Chronicler also regards various court seers as those who kept records of the reigns of various kings (1 Chr. 29:29; 2 Chr. 9:29; 33:19).

4. Free Prophets.

The threat of Assyrian expansionism in the mid-eighth century B.C. began a lengthy period in the history of Israel during which major Near Eastern powers vied with each other for political and economic control of the Near East. The central location of Palestine made Israel a pawn of the great powers until the Northern Kingdom (Israel) fell to Assyria in 721 B.C. and the Southern Kingdom (Judah) fell to the Babylonians in 586 B.C. This period of continual external danger resulted in a number of changes within Israelite life and culture. One of the institutions which dramatically mirrored those changes was Israelite prophecy.

The phenomenon of "free prophecy," in contrast to temple and court prophecy, developed dramatically during the mid-eighth century B.C. with the activity of the prophets Amos and Hosea in Israel and Micah and Isaiah in Judah. Free prophets, as the designation implies, were not stipended members of the royal court or the temple staff. The function of both royal and cultic authority was to maintain and preserve the traditional social and religious customs and values of Israel. The free prophets, on the other hand, stood on the institutional periphery of Israelite society, where they attempted to provoke both social and religious change.[26] These prophets, however, were not innovators but reformers. Acting independently of existing authority structures, they claimed divine authority to call Israel back to the ancient covenant traditions as they understood and interpreted them.[27] The free prophets claimed that they, rather than the kings or the priests, correctly understood the will of the divine "king," Yahweh.[28] The theocratic ideal of the premonarchical period was apparently a primary motivating factor in the message of the free prophets.

B. THE ROLE OF PROPHETS

Early Israelite prophets were able to control the onset of the possession trance in order to deliver oracles upon request, or, less commonly, to deliver unsolicited oracles. Oracles were requested by those who wished to learn the whereabouts of lost property (1 Sam. 9:3-10), the outcome of an illness (2 Kgs. 1:2; 8:7-15), the results of a forthcoming military engagement (1 Kgs. 22:6),[29] the proper ritual to appease an angry deity (1 Chr. 21:18-19), or appropriate ritual protocol (2 Chr. 29:25).[29a] Prophets were particularly associated with warring activities and functioned both to rouse kings to war and to predict the outcome.[30] Inquiries were regularly made of both court and temple prophets (1 Kgs. 22:5-6; 2 Kgs. 22:13; Isa. 30:2; Zeph. 1:6). Even free prophets such as Isaiah, Jeremiah, Ezekiel, and Micah were consulted by those desiring oracular responses, though the inquirers often did not receive the kind of favorable prophecy which they expected.[31] In early times priests also gave inspired oracular responses,[32] but this practice tended to decline. The phrase "inquire [darash] of the Lord" is a stereotyped formula describing the question-and-answer type of oracular consultation (Gen. 25:22; 1 Sam. 22:15; 1 Kgs. 22:5, 7; 2 Kgs. 8:8). It is identical in meaning with the phrase "inquire of a prophet" (1 Sam. 9:9; 2 Kgs. 3:11; 8:8; Ezek. 14:7).[33] Prophets were commonly remunerated by those who consulted them.[34]

Prophets are described in terms of their varied relationships with rulers and kings. Occasionally prophets are described as giving unsolicited oracles to prominent individuals, usually rulers.[35] These unsolicited prophetic speeches exhibit the same structure as many of the forms of prophetic speech preserved in the writing prophets.[36] Prophets appear to have played an occasional role in the sacral legitimation of kings.[37] Saul was anointed by Samuel (1 Sam. 10:1-8),[38] David by Samuel (1 Sam. 16:1-13), Jeroboam I by Ahijah (1 Kgs. 11:29-39; 14:7), Baasha by Jehu (1 Kgs. 16:1-2), and Jehu by an unnamed prophet (2 Kgs. 9:1-6).[39]

C. THE REVELATORY TRANCE

All inspired prophetic speech in which a religious specialist or a novice makes direct contact with the supernatural world is based on a revelatory trance experience. Several general distinctions should be made in the kinds of trance behavior characteristic of Israelite prophecy. First, it is useful to distinguish between possession trance (which can be mediumistic) and vision trance. In possession trance it is believed that an external supernatural being or power has taken control of a person, while in the vision trance it is thought that the soul leaves the body or that it is subject to visions and hallucinations of various kinds.[40] In the OT, prophetic revelations are received by persons experiencing both types of trance. Second, it is also useful to distinguish between controlled and uncontrolled possession.[41] Although initial experiences of the revelatory trance are often of an involuntary, uncontrolled, and unpredictable nature (cf. 1 Sam. 10:6; 19:23-24), with practice religious specialists can learn to control subsequent experiences of trance (1 Sam. 10:5; 19:20).[42] Third, the revelatory trance exhibits a behavioral and experiential structure which is socially communicated and "learned" by those who have such apparently "spontaneous" experiences.[43]

In ancient Israel it was widely believed that the Spirit of God caused the revelatory trance.[44] For this reason a prophet could be popularly designated a "man of the Spirit" (Hos. 9:7).[45] OT prophets also referred to their experience of revelatory trance as "Yahweh's hand" being upon them (Ezek. 3:14; 8:1; 33:21-22; Isa. 8:11; Jer. 15:17). These expressions indicate that the prophets could experience a revelatory trance in terms of divine possession or control. The revelatory trance could also be experienced in terms of a vision perceived by the prophet (Amos 1:1; 7:1, 4, 7; 8:1; Hos. 12:10; Isa. 1:1; 1 Kgs. 22:19-23). One frequent type of prophetic visionary experience involved the prophet's participation in the deliberations of the heavenly council (sod). This type is dramatized in 1 Kgs. 22:19-23 when Micaiah ben Imlah relates his prophetic experience, but it is also referred to many other times in the OT.[46]

Prophesying while in a revelatory trance was common in the ancient Near East, as indeed it is throughout the world.[47] Scholars have often emphasized the artificial nature of the "ecstasy" induced by prophets in the OT.[48] "Ecstasy," or the revelatory trance, as we prefer to call it, is said to have been induced through the rhythmical beat of music (1 Sam. 10:5; 2 Kgs. 3:15), dancing (1 Kgs. 18:21),[49] group excitement (Num. 11:24-30; 1 Sam. 10:5-13; 19:20-24), and self-flagellation (1 Kgs. 18:28-29; Zech. 13:6). It is certainly true that the revelatory trance can be induced by these and other methods, including the use of hallucinogens (4 Ezra 14:39-41).[50] It must be recognized that what many modern scholars have pejoratively designated as "artificially induced ecstasy" was never criticized or regarded as illegitimate by the ancient Israelites.[51] Further, the few references which have been interpreted as trance induction do not bear the weight assigned to them.[52] The instrumental music mentioned in 1 Sam. 10:5-13, for example, may simply have been an accompaniment to a religious ritual, while the self-laceration depicted in 1 Kgs. 18:28-29 may be more appropriately understood as a form of self-sacrifice. Further, the verbs *hitnabbe'* and *nibba'* in 1 Sam. 10:5, 6, 10; 19:20, 21, 23, usually translated "prophesy," should probably be rendered "rave."[53] The behavior of prophets was sometimes labeled as drunkenness (Isa. 28:7) or madness (Hos. 9:7; 2 Kgs. 9:11; Jer. 29:26; 1 Sam. 16:14-16, 23; 18:10-11; 19:9-10 — the irrational behavior of Saul is traced to an evil spirit).

D. PROPHETIC CONFLICT

In contrast to the free prophets, the court prophets and temple prophets often found themselves in alignment with the policies of the political and religious authorities. While there is no evidence that free prophets were in conflict with other free prophets, they were frequently in conflict with temple prophets.[54] The real conflict, however, was not between the free prophets and the temple prophets, but between the free prophets and the king.[55] The monarchy had pragmatically reinterpreted Israelite traditions in the light of changing conditions. These reinterpretations were in conflict with the theocratic ideals of the free prophets, ideals rooted in the same ancient traditions.

No distinction between "true" and "false" prophets can be made on the basis of objective, historical criteria.[56] The view that the prophets of doom (i.e. the free prophets whose message was predominantly negative) should be regarded as "true" while the prophets of salvation (the temple prophets) should be labeled "false" prophets cannot be maintained.[57] This was the view of Jeremiah (28:7-8), but he was not an objective observer. Oracles of both salvation and judgment were pronounced in cultic settings (cf. Jer. 4:10-12; Ezek. 18:9-13).[58] The oracles of judgment pronounced by temple prophets, however, appear to have been directed, not against all Israel, but against specific groups of evildoers within the nation.[59] Both the free prophet and the stipended prophet spoke with a consciousness of divine authority implied by the use of the messenger formula "thus says Yahweh" (Jer. 28:1-17; Ezek. 13:6-7; 22:28).

In a recent study of prophetic conflict and its effect upon Israelite religion, J. L. Crenshaw has synthesized the criteria used in the OT for identifying and exposing false prophets and their lying oracles.[60] He has sorted the criteria into three major categories and provided each subpoint with a short critique: (1) *Message-centered criteria*: (a) If the prophetic prediction is not fulfilled, the prophet is false (Deut. 18:22; 1 Kgs. 22:28; Isa. 30:8). The problems with this criterion are the general nature of many prophetic oracles (making the perception of their fulfilment difficult), the conditional nature of prophecy, and the limited application of this criterion only to predictive prophecy. (b) True prophets prophesy judgment, while false prophets promise salvation (Jer. 28:8; 1 Kgs. 22; Ezek. 13:10). This criterion is made problematic by the juxtaposition of promises of salvation and judgment in the same prophet. (c) False prophets receive their messages through dreams rather than visions (Jer. 23:25-28). Dreams, however, were not looked upon unfavorably in the OT (see above, p. 82). (d) Allegiance to Yahweh was the mark of a true prophet, while allegiance to Baal the mark of a false prophet (Deut. 13:1-3; cf. Jer. 2:8, 26-27; 23:13; 32:32-35). These "false" prophets, however, served Baal while believing themselves to be devotees of Yahweh in an alternate name and form. (2) *Criteria focusing on the man*: (a) The false prophet was a professional cult official. However, cult prophets were frequently faithful to the word of Yahweh. (b) False prophets were characterized by immoral conduct (Jer. 3:11; 23:14; Isa. 28:7). However, Hosea's conduct is at least open to question. (c) The true prophet was conscious of a divine commission (Amos 7:10-17; Mic. 3:8). Yet this claim was challenged (Jer. 23:21, 32; 43:2-3) and was difficult to substantiate. (3) *Chronological criterion*: Prophets not belonging to the period from Moses to Ezra were false prophets. However, this standard contributes nothing to the discernment of false prophecy within the OT itself.

In sum, Crenshaw contends that no criterion proved adequate for distinguishing true from false prophecy,[61] and that the rise of false prophecy was inevitable and resulted in the general decline of prophecy, since there was no absolutely reliable way to validate the credentials of the divine messenger.[62] Conflicting claims by prophets, he maintains, ultimately resulted in a total loss of prophetic credibility; people turned instead to wisdom and apocalyptic.[63] Although Crenshaw does provide a thorough survey of the various criteria used at various times in ancient Israel to identify "false" prophets, he does not appear to take seriously the root causes of prophetic conflict. In the words of S. DeVries,

> Prophet against prophet was only a symptom. The root cause was king against prophet, requiring prophet to oppose king. Our prophet legends record a dynamic struggle to supervise the kingship.[64]

IV. FORMS OF PROPHETIC SPEECH

A. GENERAL CONSIDERATIONS

While most oracular speech by early Israelite prophets appears to have been in response to specific inquiries, there are many other examples in the OT of unsolicited prophetic messages delivered by the nonwriting prophets.[65] Some of the writing prophets did give oracular responses to inquiries,[66] but the bulk of the material preserved in their writings is of an unsolicited nature.[67] Since the oracles of the vast majority of court and temple prophets have not survived, the oracles which have been preserved in the prophetic books of the OT cannot be regarded as fully representative from a historical point of view. The negative content and unsolicited character of many of the prophetic speeches of the classical prophets must be correlated with the fact that they were pronounced during periods of profound social and political crisis by persons who did not always enjoy official recognition.

If the form-critical analysis of Greek oracles is a task which has been almost completely neglected, the opposite is certainly true for the prophetic speech forms preserved in the OT. During the last two generations the oral and literary forms of OT prophetic speeches and narratives have been thoroughly discussed.[68] Most of the oracles of Israelite prophets were originally delivered orally. Only later were they collected and written down by others in compositions of various sizes. Form-critical analysis of this material attempts to reconstruct the preliterary forms of prophetic oracles and narratives and to establish the kinds of settings within which each oracle was spoken or each type of narrative was used.[69] Unlike the Greek oracles, which are usually identifiable in their present literary contexts, the inclusion of originally discrete oracles in longer OT literary compositions has often resulted in literary modifications of the material. Many prophetic oracles, however, are preserved within the narrative frameworks of the books of Samuel, Kings, and Chronicles, where they have presumably undergone less editorial modification.[70]

Before considering the structure of various forms of OT prophetic speech, we need to make several preliminary observations. (1) The analysis of prophetic speech forms and narratives presented below represents a simplification of the work of a number of scholars. Since the form-critical literature on OT prophecy is so vast and the opinions of specialists so diverse, the complexity of many of the forms cannot be adequately treated in this survey. (2) The form-critical analysis of OT prophetic speeches and narratives has often succumbed to the temptation of overspecifying the constituent elements of a given form.[71] The result of this overanalysis has been that optional elements are not recognized as such, nor are the individual idiosyncrasies of the speakers and writers taken sufficiently into account.[72] (3) Terminology is often confused in the study of OT prophetic speech forms.[73] Since a great deal of the research in this area has been done in Germany, the translation of terms into English has, expectedly, exhibited little consistency. We shall refer occasionally to German terms in parentheses to minimize the confusion. (4) Short forms of prophetic speech or dependent forms (those usually found in conjunction with another form) are often treated as if they were necessarily earlier stages in the historical development of more complex units.[74] This presupposition needs close supervision. (5) The span of time represented by OT literature means that prophetic speech forms have a long and complex history extending from the eleventh century B.C. to the postexilic period. In our presentation below we cannot deal with the individual history of the speech forms.

B. GENERAL FORMULAIC FEATURES

Prophetic speech in the OT is, with few exceptions, presented as a first-person address by Yahweh couched in poetic form. In spite of the variety of speech forms, a number of formulas occur with great frequency as formal introductory or concluding markers of prophetic speech.

1. The Messenger Formula.

Israelite prophets frequently used the so-called messenger formula "thus says Yahweh" to introduce oracular speeches.[75] This formula originated in the practice of transmitting oral communications through messengers (Num. 22:15-16; Judg. 11:14-15; 1 Kgs. 2:30; 2 Chr. 36:23; Ezra 1:2). Similar formulas were widely used in the oracular language of the ancient world[76] and one occurs as an introduction to a prophetic speech in the Mari Letters.[77] In the OT the prophetic use of the messenger formula indicates a consciousness of the divine origin and authority of the message, and it is always Yahweh who speaks in the first person following the formula. The earliest use of the formula in the OT is in Amos (1:1, 6, 13; 2:1, 6; 3:11, 12; 5:3, 4, 16; 7:17), yet it was in use far earlier than the eighth century B.C. A related formula, "Yahweh has said" ('amar Yahweh), is used to conclude prophetic speeches (Amos 1:5, 8, 15; 2:3; 5:17). The use of the messenger formula at the time the message is delivered has the effect of calling the recipients' attention to the earlier commissioning of the messenger by the sender of the message.

2. The Commission Formula.

This formula, which frequently introduces prophetic speech in the OT, is often a more complete form of the messenger formula.[78] The basic pattern is: "Say to X, thus says Y." Other patterns are: "Go and say to X, thus says Y," and "(Go and) say to X [messenger formula absent]." These formulas and their variants are used in narratives which report the commissioning of a messenger. In Gen. 32:3-4, for example, we read:

> And Jacob sent messengers before him to Esau his brother in the land of Seir, the country of Edom, instructing them, "Thus you shall say to my lord Esau: Thus says your servant Jacob. . . ."

The OT prophets frequently use the full commission formula to introduce oracles, and when it is present the messenger function of the prophets is being emphasized.[79] Jeremiah often uses the formula, as in Jer. 2:1-2:

> The word of the Lord came to me, saying, "Go and proclaim in the hearing of Jerusalem, Thus says the Lord. . . ."

A simpler version of the formula occurs in Jer. 8:4: "You shall say to them, Thus says the Lord. . . ." In Isa. 6:9 the commission formula is present, but the messenger formula itself is lacking: "Go, and say to this people. . . ."

3. The Proclamation Formula.

The proclamation formula, "hear the word of Yahweh," occurs frequently at the beginning of oracles in the prophets.[80] It can be used alone (1 Kgs. 22:19; 1 Chr. 18:18; Amos 7:16), with the messenger formula (Jer. 29:20; 42:15), or with the name(s) of the addressee(s) in the vocative (Jer. 2:4; 7:2; 19:3; 22:11; Ezek. 6:3; 13:2; 21:3). The formula was originally used in a number of contexts. As a summons in a court of law it was adapted for use in judicial speeches of prophets (Mic. 6:2; Jer. 2:4). The summons to hear was also used in the proclamations of divine law in the cult (Deut. 6:4; Ps. 50:7; 81:9 [Eng. 8]), in wisdom teaching (Prov. 7:24; Ps. 49:2 [Eng. 1]; Isa 28:23; Deut. 32:1), and for instruction in law (Prov. 4:1; Job 13:6; 33:1, 31; 34:2, 16; Isa. 49:1; 51:4).

4. The Divine Oracle Formula.

The divine oracle formula, *ne'um Yahweh,* is usually translated "an oracle/utterance of Yahweh," and occurs frequently at the conclusion of oracles.[81] It can take the place of the formula "Yahweh has said" (*'amar Yahweh*) at the conclusion of oracles.

5. Oath Formulas.

The oath formula, "Yahweh has sworn by," is a functional equivalent to the messenger formula used to introduce pronouncements of judgment (Amos 4:2; 8:7). The oath formula can be expressed in the third person (Isa. 14:24; 62:8; Jer. 49:13; 51:14; Amos 6:8; Ps. 110:4; 132:11), or it can be part of a first-person speech by Yahweh: "By myself I have sworn, says the Lord" (Gen. 22:16; cf. Isa. 45:23; 54:9; Jer. 44:26). Another common oath formula in ancient Israel was "as the Lord lives" (Judg. 8:19; Ruth 3:13;

Amos 8:4). This is transformed into a prophetic oath formula expressed in the first person: "As I live [ḥay 'ani], says the Lord."[82]

6. Revelation Formulas.

A number of formulaic expressions which indicate that Yahweh spoke or showed something to a prophet may be subsumed under the general rubric "revelation formulas." The more common forms of revelation formulas include "thus the Lord God showed me" (Amos 7:1, 4, 7; 8:1), "the Lord said to him/me [etc.]" (Hos. 1:4; 3:1; Isa. 7:3; 8:3; 21:16; Ezek. 44:2; Jonah 4:10; Jer. 4:27; 6:6), and "the word of the Lord/God came to" such and such (1 Kgs. 12:22; 19:9; 1 Sam. 15:10; 2 Sam. 24:11; Hag. 2:1, 20; Zech. 7:1, 8; 8:1; Hos. 1:2). Although these expressions exhibit great variety, they each stand at the beginning of an oracular saying and make an objective claim for the occurrence of revelation. Unfortunately, the formulaic nature of these expressions conceals rather than reveals the kind of revelatory trance experienced by the prophets.

C. BASIC STRUCTURAL ELEMENTS

The basic categories of literary material found in OT prophetic literature are speeches, narratives, and miscellaneous forms borrowed from other settings in Israelite life.[83] Some of the borrowed forms include the dirge (Amos 5:1-2), the national lament (Hos. 6), the taunt song (Isa. 37:22-29), the drinking song (Isa. 22:13), and the love song (Isa. 5:1-7). These borrowed forms are derived from the lyrical traditions of Israel[84] and reflect nearly every sphere of Israelite life.[85] In the following discussion only the more distinctively prophetic forms of speech and narratives will be treated.

OT prophetic speech is characterized by at least five basic elements which differ from each other mainly in content. Like parts of speech in grammar, they can be combined in only a restricted number of patterns.[86] Most prophetic oracles in the OT consist of a prediction of the future (*Weissagung*), which may be either a negative prediction, a *threat* (*Drohwort*), or a positive prediction, a *promise* (*Verheissungswort, Heilswort*). In addition three other subordinate structural elements are ordinarily attached to the threat or promise:[87] the *accusation* (*Scheltwort*), which justifies the threat, the *admonition* (*Mahnwort*), and the *statement of divine self-disclosure* (*Erweiswort*).[88]

One of the more common structural patterns is the combination of the prediction (either a threat or a promise) and a supporting reason (often an accusation).[89] If the prediction precedes the reason (*Begründung*), the latter is introduced by the causal particle "because" (*ki*). When the reason precedes the prediction, the latter is introduced with the inferential particle "therefore" (*laken*), e.g. Amos 4:11; 5:11; 6:7. In content the prediction is commonly a threat (*Drohwort*), while the reason is an accusation (*Scheltwort*). The structural pattern of statement/reason is very similar to the two-part structure of Greek expository oracles that we have examined above (pp. 55-62). It is widely held that the reason (*Begründung*) was the contribution of the prophet and not part of the prediction.[90] This view is partially supported by the fact that when the reason or accusation precedes the prediction, the "therefore" which introduces the prediction is often followed by the interjection of the messenger formula "thus says Yahweh." In Amos, for example, the accusation is *never* introduced with the messenger formula.[91] The ubiquity of the prediction/reason structure in OT prophetic speech has encouraged attempts to isolate a "basic form" of such speech.[92]

D. MAJOR FORMS OF PROPHETIC SPEECH

1. The Announcement of Judgment.

The most common type of prophetic oracle in the OT is the announcement of judgment. This form consists of a threat (a predictive statement) and an accusation (a reason for the threat). A typical example of the announcement of judgment is found in 2 Kgs. 1:6:

Messenger formula:	Thus says the Lord,
A. Accusation (*Scheltwort*):	Is it because there is no God in Israel that you are sending to inquire of Baal-zebub, the god of Ekron?
B. Threat (*Drohwort*):	Therefore [*laken*] you shall not come down from the bed to which you have gone, but shall surely die.[93]

Here the accusation precedes the threat (see also Isa. 3:12; 29:13-14; Jer. 16:11-13; Amos 3:2; 4:1-2; 8:4-8; Mic. 3:9-12), but it can also follow the threat (Jer. 29:10-11; Amos 6:11-12; Mic. 7:13). Less commonly the accusation can frame the threat or the threat can frame the accusation. Announcements of judgment can be directed to individuals (Amos 7:16-17; 1 Kgs. 21:17-19; 2 Kgs. 1:3-4), to Israel (Amos 2:6-8), or to foreign nations (Amos 1:3-5). The accusations of judgment found in collections of oracles against the nations (Isa. 13-23; Jer. 46-51; Ezek. 25-32; Amos 1-2) are prophetic speeches patterned after the war oracles used in earlier times as an element in Israelite military strategy.[94]

2 The Announcement of Salvation.

This form is not as common in the classical prophets as the announcement of judgment, a situation due to the more common use of the announcement of salvation by cult prophets. The announcement of salvation occurs only in Hosea, Jeremiah, Ezekiel, and Deutero-Isaiah.[95] This form could consist of a simple prediction lacking any supportive reason.[96] An example of a simple one-part announcement of salvation is found in Jer. 27:9, 14, a quotation of an oracle of a temple prophet:

Promise (*Heilswort*): You shall not serve the king of Babylon.

A similar oracle, also originating with a temple prophet, is quoted in Jer. 27:16:

Promise (*Heilswort*): Behold, the vessels of the Lord's house will now shortly be brought back from Babylon.

Jer. 28:2-4 is an example of the two-part structure consisting of a promise framed by a reason:

	Messenger formula:	Thus says the Lord of hosts, the God of Israel:
A.	Reason:	I have broken the yoke of the king of Babylon.
B.	Promise:	Within two years I will bring back to this place all the vessels of the Lord's house, which Nebuchadnezzar king of Babylon took away from this place and carried to Babylon. I will also bring back to this place Jeconiah the son of Jehoiakim, king of Judah,

and all the exiles from Judah who went to Babylon,
says the Lord,

A'. Reason: for I will break the yoke of the king of Babylon.

In such announcements of salvation the promise may precede the reason (1 Kgs. 11:31-32), or the reason may precede the promise (2 Kgs. 20:5-6). Or the relationship may be more complex, as in the example just quoted, in which the promise is framed by the reason. The segment containing the promise is often introduced by the phrase "Behold, I" (Jer. 32:37; 33:6; 1 Kgs. 11:31; 2 Kgs. 20:5).

3. The Salvation-Judgment Oracle.

In preexilic prophetic speech the announcement of judgment and the announcement of salvation were two distinct genres which were rarely combined, though they shared a very similar structure.[97] During the postexilic period, however, these originally distinct genres were fused into a single form of prophetic speech which may be designated the salvation-judgment oracle.[98] The development of the salvation-judgment oracle appears to have been the result of a new social situation: the Jewish community was split into competing factions on the basis of a social status informed by religious ideology.[99] This new prophetic speech form, which is largely a literary creation,[100] originated with a dissident Jewish group espousing an apocalyptic eschatology over against a more powerful hierocratic group which favored a temporally realized eschatology. The new speech form served to legitimate the ideology of the visionary group while condemning the position of the hierocratic group which enjoyed control of the Jerusalem cult. The close interweaving of salvation and judgment pronouncements characteristic of this form is exhibited in Isa. 65:13-14:

Therefore thus says the Lord God:
"Behold, my servants shall eat,
   but you shall be hungry;
behold, my servants shall drink,
   but you shall be thirsty;
behold, my servants shall rejoice,
   but you shall be put to shame;
behold, my servants shall sing for gladness of heart,
   but you shall cry out for pain of heart,
   and shall wail for anguish of spirit.

(For examples of other salvation-judgment oracles see Isa. 56:12-57:1; 57:13bc; 65:7-8, 10-11, 13-15.)[101] An example of a complete salvation-judgment oracle is found in Isa. 65:1-25, of which vv. 13-14 have just been quoted above. The general structure of the oracle is as follows: (1) accusation and threat (against a defiled cult), vv. 1-7; (2) promise (to the prophetic group), vv. 8-10; (3) second accusation and threat, vv. 11-12; (4) series of salvation and judgment announcements, vv. 13-15; (5) promise of final salvation, vv. 16-25.[102] In each accusation-threat section, the adversative phrase "but you" introduces the statement. The salvation-judgment oracle is a significant development within late Israelite prophecy, since this juxtaposition of positive and negative announcements becomes characteristic of apocalyptic literature and is found in prophetic speech in early Judaism and early Christianity.

4. The Oracle of Assurance.

A variation of the content of the announcement of salvation is found in the oracle of assurance (*Heilsorakel*), which appears to have originated within a cultic setting in which a lament (*Klagelied*) received a priestly oracular response of assurance (cf. Lam. 3:57).[103] An example of the basic form of the oracle of assurance in a cultic setting is found in 1 Sam. 1:17 (a response of Eli the priest to the complaint of Hannah):

A. Admonition: Go in peace,

B. Promise (Reason):   and the God of Israel grant your petition which you have made to him.

The classic form of the oracle of assurance consists of three elements: (1) the phrase "fear not" (or equivalent), (2) the designation of the addressee, and (3) the basic reason for the admonition expressed by a clause with the verb in the perfect tense.[104] An example of the prophetic use of the oracle of assurance is found in 2 Chr. 20:15-17, where the Levite Jahaziel, using a plural form of address, proclaimed to the people:

Proclamation formula (with *Anrede*):	Hearken, all Judah and inhabitants of Jerusalem, and King Jehoshaphat:
Messenger formula:	Thus says the Lord to you:
A. Admonition (*Heilszuspruch*):	"Fear not and be not dismayed at this great multitude,
B. Promise (Reason):	for the battle is not yours but God's. Tomorrow go down against them; behold, they will come up by the ascent of Ziz; you will find them at the end of the valley, east of the wilderness of Jeruel. You will not need to fight in this battle; take your position, stand still, and see the victory of the Lord on your behalf, O Judah and Jerusalem."
A'. Admonition:	Fear not, and be not dismayed;
B'. Promise (Reason):	tomorrow go out against them, and the Lord will be with you.

This oracle of assurance has been embellished with a brief recapitulation of the basic elements and content of the prophecy in v. 17. While the oracle of assurance began as a cultic oracular response, it was taken up particularly by Deutero-Isaiah and became a form for the literary expression of the author's message of comfort and consolation. The form stands alone in Isa. 41:8-13, 14-16; 43:1-4, 5-7; 44:1-5, though it is also used in conjunction with other prophetic speech forms.[105] Jeremiah also uses the oracle of assurance (30:10-11; 1:17-19; 42:9-12; 15:19-21).[106] The admonition "fear not" functions as a primary recognition formula for the oracle of assurance (Isa. 41:10, 13, 14; 43:1, 5; 44:2; 51:7; 54:4), though the exclamation "behold" (*hinneh*) is used also (Joel 2:19-20; Isa. 58:9; 65:1).[107]

The oracle of assurance, a prophetic speech form found throughout the Near East,[108] went through a considerable process of modification. The form reappears in Jewish apocalyptic literature (1 Enoch 95:1-3; 96:3; 104:1; 4 Ezra 12:46-47)[109] and in early Christian literature (Luke 1:30; 12:32; Acts 27:24; Rev. 1:17). The form is also very similar to the two-part Greek expository oracle which we discussed above (pp. 58ff.).

5. The Admonition.

The prophetic admonition (*Mahnwort*) has roots in various areas of Israelite life.[110] The prophetic admonition demanded that Israel do what it had neglected to do, i.e. the admonition is connected with disobedience.[111] The admonition is frequently expressed through imperatives or jussives which call for repentance and improvement. Admonitions are particularly characteristic of Jeremiah (3:12-13, 22; 4:1-2; 7:1-15; 11:1-8; 18:11), but are also found in other writing prophets (Isa. 1:10-17; Hos. 5:15; 6:1-6; 14:2-4; Amos 4:4-5; 5:4-5, 6-7, 11-15, 21-24, 27). Admonitions were an important element in the demands for repentance characteristic of the Deuteronomistic tradition (cf. 2 Kgs. 17:13).[112]

The earliest use of the prophetic admonition as an independent speech form is in Amos 5:4-5:

Messenger formula:		For thus says the Lord God
Addressee:		to the house of Israel:
A.	Admonition:	"Seek me and live; but do not seek Bethel, and do not enter into Gilgal or cross over to Beer-sheba;
B.	Reason:	for Gilgal shall surely go into exile, and Bethel shall come to naught.[13]

Admonitions can function as the central element in a prophetic saying as here (cf. Isa. 1:16-17; Amos 5:6-7, 14-15; Jer. 3:12-13, 22; 4:1-2, 3-4), or they can be used in conjunction with a promise (Jer. 3:1) or threat (Jer. 7:1-15; 13:15-17; 21:11-12). The widely held view that the classical prophets were warners and admonishers has been based on the view that individual sayings functioned as admonitions and calls for repentance. This view can be maintained only if the goals of change and improvement were real possibilities from the perspective of the prophets. The *Mahnwort* relates to a future already determined by Yahweh.[114]

6. The Oracle of Divine Self-Disclosure.

The oracle of divine self-disclosure (*Erweiswort*) is a description of the unique content of a supporting reason which is usually placed at the conclusion of a prophetic promise.[115] The core of the oracle of divine self-disclosure is the recognition formula: "You/they shall know that I am Yahweh."[116] The original setting of this kind of prophetic oracle, according to Zimmerli, was the cultic recitation of covenant law in ancient Israel.[117] Two examples of the oracle of divine self-disclosure in narrative settings are 1 Kgs. 20:13, 28:

Narrative setting:	And behold a prophet came near to Ahab king of Israel and said,
Messenger formula:	"Thus says the Lord,

A.	Reason (rhetorical question):	Have you seen all this great multitude?
B.	Promise:	Behold, I will give it into your hand this day;
C.	Recognition formula:	and you shall know that I am the Lord."

The second example is very similar:

	Narrative setting:	And a man of God came near and said to the king of Israel,
	Messenger formula:	"Thus says the Lord,
A.	Reason:	'Because [ki] the Syrians have said, "The Lord is a god of the hills but he is not a god of the valleys,"
B.	Promise:	therefore [laken] I will give all this great multitude into your hand,
C.	Recognition formula:	and you shall know that I am the Lord.'"

The recognition formula in this oracular setting is a claim that God will reveal himself in the fulfilment of the prediction announced by the prophet.[118] The statement of divine self-disclosure is particularly frequent in Ezekiel, where it occurs both in the second person, "you shall know, etc." (6:7, 13; 7:4, 9; 11:10, 12; 12:20; 13:9, 14, 21, 23, 24, 26; 29:9; etc.) and in the third person, "they shall know, etc." (6:10, 14; 7:27; 12:15, 16; 24:27; 25:11, 17; etc.). This oracular form is also found in Joel (2:25-27; 4:15-17 [Eng. 3:15-17]), Jeremiah (24:7), and Deutero-Isaiah (45:3; 49:23).

7. The Woe Oracle.

The woe oracle (*Wehe-Wort*) can be regarded as a distinctive form of prophetic speech since the woe of accusation is found only within the context of prophetic writings in the OT.[119] The form probably originated in the setting of funeral lamentation,[120] though other settings have been suggested, e.g. the recitation of cultic curses in the covenant renewal ceremony (Deut. 27:15-26)[121] and Israelite wisdom instruction.[122] The woe oracle consists of two basic elements, the woe form itself, which describes the specific misdeeds of those against whom the oracle is directed, and the threat which follows.[123] The woe oracle is never used to address Israel as a whole.[124] In many respects it is essentially a variation in form of the announcement of judgment. Mic. 2:1-3 is representative of many examples of woe oracles[125] in the prophets:

A.	Woe form (Accusation):	Woe to those who devise wickedness and work evil upon their beds!
		When the morning dawns, they perform it, because it is in the power of their hand.
		They covet fields, and seize them; and house, and take them away;
		they oppress a man and his house, a man and his inheritance.

Transition:		Therefore [laken] says the Lord:
B.	Threat:	Behold, against this family I am devising evil,
		from which you cannot remove your necks;
		and you shall not walk haughtily, for it shall be an evil time.

Characteristically, woe oracles are found in series (Isa. 5; 28:1-33:1; Hab. 2).[126] The term "woe" [hoy] itself is an indefinite announcement of judgment that prefaces an accusation.[127] The woe oracle, as well as the beatitude, is found in Jewish apocalyptic literature, the sayings of Jesus, and early Christian prophecy. The single element that most distinguishes the woe oracle from other types of oracular speech is the focus on the contrast between the heights of human audacity and pride and the depths of despair which the Day of the Lord will bring.[128]

8. The Judicial Speech.

The judicial speech, or judgment speech (Gerichtsrede), is a rhetorical form drawn by the prophets from the juridical sphere of Israelite life.[129] The judicial speech exhibits a three-part structure: (1) the summons, (2) the trial (with speeches by the prosecution and defense), and (3) the sentence.[130] Each element is not always present (the sentence is the part frequently missing), yet the juridical form of the whole speech is usually obvious. Hos. 4:1-3 exhibits the major features of a prophetic judicial speech:

A.	Summons (proclamation formula):	Hear the word of the Lord, O people of Israel; for the Lord has a controversy [rib] with the inhabitants of the land.
B.	Accusation:	There is no faithfulness or kindness, and no knowledge of God in the land; there is swearing, lying, killing, stealing, and committing adultery; they break all bounds and murder follows murder.
C.	Sentence (Threat):	Therefore [laken] the land mourns, and all who dwell in it languish, and also the beasts of the field, and the birds of the air; and even the fish of the sea are taken away.[131]

In this speech the prophet pronounces both accusation and sentence, but Yahweh can also argue his own case against the people in other judicial speeches (cf. Mic. 6:1-2).

E. PROPHETIC NARRATIVES

1. The Prophetic Call Narrative.

The term nabi', normally translated "prophet," is widely thought to have originally meant "one called," and the consciousness of having been divinely called is often thought to be integral to the prophetic role.[132] The prophetic call narrative includes both speech and narrative elements and involves a procedure similar to that involved in the commissioning of a messenger (cf. Gen. 24:34-48).[133] The focal point of the call narrative is the prophet's commissioning by God, and for this reason the narrative could well be designated "the installation of the prophet."[134] Although these narratives appear autobiographical, their similar formal features have recently led some scholars to view them not as reflections of actual experience but as proclamations serving to legitimate the prophet's vocation,[135] or (less probably) as liturgical ordination ceremonies for prophets.[136] That call narratives tend to be placed at the beginnings of oracle collections[137] indicates that they function to validate the prophet as a legitimate spokesman of Yahweh.[138] Since formal patterns are not antithetical to experiences which apparently are spontaneous and unstructured,[139] prophetic call narratives might well reflect actual experience *and* provide a vehicle for legitimating the prophetic vocation.

Jer. 1:4-10 is typical of a number of call narratives in the OT (Moses in Exod. 3:1-12; Gideon in Judg. 6:11b-17; Isaiah in Isa. 6:1-13; Ezekiel in Ezek. 1:1-3:11; Deutero-Isaiah in Isa. 40:1-11[140]):

A.	Divine confrontation (v. 4):	Now the word of the Lord came to me saying,
B.	Introductory word (v. 5a):	"Before I formed you in the womb I knew you, and before you were born I consecrated you;
C.	Commission (v. 5b):	I appointed you a prophet to the nations."
D.	Objection (v. 6):	Then I said, "Ah, Lord God: Behold, I do not know how to speak, for I am only a youth."
E.	Reassurance (vv. 7-8):	But the Lord said to me, "Do not say, 'I am only a youth'; for to all to whom I send you you shall go, and whatever I command you you shall speak. Be not afraid of them, for I am with you to deliver you, says the Lord."
F.	Sign (vv. 9-10):	Then the Lord put forth his hand and touched my mouth; and the Lord said to me, "Behold, I have put my words in your mouth. See, I have set you this day over nations and over kingdoms, to pluck up and to break down, to destroy and overthrow, to build and to plant."[141]

Although this pattern is rather elaborate, one can see that the central elements are the commission, the objection, the reassurance, and the sign.[142] In Jer. 1:4-10 the "sign" at the end is really a continuation of the commission or an actualization of the commission that occurred prior to Jeremiah's birth. Such call narratives are found occasionally in apocalyptic literature (1 Enoch 14-16, 71; 4 Ezra 14),[143] and in the NT (Acts 9, 22, 26; Rev. 1:9-20; 10:8-11).

W. Zimmerli has distinguished between two main types of prophetic call in the OT. The narrative type includes a dialogue with Yahweh, while the throne theophany type prefaces the prophetic commission with a vision of the heavenly throne of

Yahweh.[144] Jer. 1:4-10 is an example of the first type, while 1 Kgs. 22:19-22 (Micaiah ben Imlah), Isa. 6:1-13, and Ezek. 1:1-3:11 are examples of the second.

2. Prophetic Visions.

In many respects the prophetic call narrative is a distinctive type of the prophetic vision.[145] Both focus on a divine oracle and both may be categorized as *memorabilia,* i.e. first-person accounts which place oracular sayings in a narrative setting.[146] Several attempts have been made to distinguish among different types of visions, yet such refinements often contribute little to understanding or defining the genre.[147] Prophetic vision reports have at least two structural elements, the announcement of the vision and the vision sequence itself; these two elements are often joined by the term "behold" (*hinneh*).[148] The vision reported in Jer. 38:21b-23 exemplifies this form:

A.	Announcement of vision:	But if you [King Zedekiah] refuse to surrender, this is the vision which the Lord has shown to me:
	Transition:	Behold,
B.	Vision sequence:	all the women left in the house of the king of Judah were being led out to the princes of the king of Babylon and were saying, "Your trusted friends have deceived you and prevailed against you; now that your feet are sunk in the mire, they turn away from you."
C.	Meaning of vision:	All your wives and your sons shall be led out to the Chaldeans, and you yourself shall not escape from their hand, but shall be seized by the king of Babylon; and this city shall be burned with fire.

In this instance the meaning of the vision was apparently clear to Jeremiah, and the threat with which the pericope concludes is a verbalization of that which the prophet saw and which he regarded as the self-evident meaning of the vision.

A great deal of variety is evident in the vision sequence of the prophetic vision form. The vision may stand alone if its meaning is self-evident, as in the example just cited. More often the meaning of the vision requires elucidation through a dialogue between the revealer (Yahweh or an angel) and the visionary. An example of a vision with a more complex vision sequence is found in Amos 8:1-2:

A.	Announcement of vision (revelation formula):	Thus the Lord God showed me:
	Transition:	behold,
B.	Vision sequence:	
	1. Image:	a basket of summer fruit.
	2. Question by revealer:	And he said, "Amos, what do you see?"
	3. Answer by seer:	And I said, "A basket of summer fruit."

9680

4. Interpretation by revealer (revelation formula):	Then the Lord said to me, "The end has come upon my people Israel; I will never again pass by them. The songs of the temple shall become wailings in that day," says the Lord God; "the dead bodies shall be many; in every place they shall be cast out in silence."[149]

In Zechariah and Ezekiel the revealer is not always Yahweh himself, but sometimes an angel (Zech. 1:7-17, 18-21; 2:1-5; etc.; Ezek. 40-48). In apocalyptic literature the vision becomes the primary literary vehicle for communicating divine revelation.

3. Report of Symbolic Actions.

Actions which symbolize the prophetic message are more characteristic of OT prophecy than of prophecy in early Judaism, early Christianity, and Greco-Roman paganism.[150] However, in the Greco-Egyptian "Oracle of the Potter,"[151] the action of breaking pots symbolized the future destruction of Egypt.[152] The symbolic acts of the OT prophets tend to be either magical rituals[153] or dramatizations of the prophetic message that do not attempt to change the course of events. 1 Kgs. 22:11 relates how the prophet Zedekiah ben Chenaanah made iron horns and prophesied to Ahab and Jehoshaphat: "Thus says the Lord, 'With these you shall push the Syrians until they are destroyed.'" In 2 Kgs. 13:14-19 Elisha reportedly instructed Joash to shoot an arrow eastward toward Syria, thereby ensuring his victory over the Syrians. Both examples are magical rituals intended to influence particular events.

Later, among the writing prophets, symbolic actions function as dramatizations of prophetic speech. Isaiah went about unclothed and barefoot, symbolizing the manner in which the Assyrian king would lead away the Egyptians and Ethiopians as captives (Isa. 20:1-6). Jeremiah wore a yoke about his neck indicating that the people should submit to the suzerainty of Nebuchadnezzar (Jer. 27-28). Aside from this general, if nebulous, distinction between magical and dramatic symbolic actions of prophets, nearly all prophetic actions refer to the future. Magical actions attempt to influence and even determine the outcome of future events, while more purely dramatic symbolic actions simply indicate what the future holds or what course of action should be taken.

The "report of prophetic symbolic action" is a distinct and stable literary form within which the symbolic actions of the prophet are narrated.[154] This form consists of three primary elements: (1) a command of Yahweh to the prophet concerning the exact nature of the symbolic action to be performed, (2) a report of the fulfilment of the command by the prophet, and (3) a full interpretation of the prophetic action, frequently accompanied by a divine promise. These features are exhibited in Isa. 8:1-4:

A.	Command by Yahweh:	Then the Lord said to me, "Take a large tablet and write upon it in common characters, 'Belonging to Maher-shalal-hash-baz.'"
B.	Fulfilment by prophet:	And I got reliable witnesses, Uriah the priest and Zechariah the son of Jeberechiah, to attest for me. And I went to the prophetess, and she conceived and bore a son.

C. Interpretation   Then the Lord said to me, "Call his name Maher-shalal-
by Yahweh: hash-baz; for before the child knows how to cry 'My father'
or 'My mother,' the wealth of Damascus and the spoil of
Samaria will be carried away before the king of Assyria."[155]

V. THE COMPOSITION OF PROPHETIC LITERATURE

The earliest written prophecies in the form of prophetic books that have survived
from ancient Israel are only from the eighth century B.C. The earliest classical prophets,
all of whom were active during the second half of the eighth century, include Amos
and Hosea, who prophesied to the Northern Kingdom, and Micah and Isaiah, who
ministered to the Southern Kingdom. Written prophecy coincided with the expansion
of Israel's larger and more powerful neighbors, and the threat to its security provoked
internal conflict of which written prophecy is but one expression. Before the eighth
century, prophets were primarily speakers, and even after that period it was the
disciples of the prophets who collected oracles, organized, and produced the prophetic
literature.[156]

Many, if not most, of the prophetic speeches and reports were written down
soon after they were uttered, perhaps within the lifetime of the prophet, sometimes
by the prophet himself (Isa. 8:1; 30:8; Jer. 30:2; Ezek. 43:11).[157] The references within
the prophetic books themselves to the writing down of prophetic oracles indicate that
the purpose of recording oracles (and even securing witnesses for that purpose) was
to authenticate the contents of the prophecies for the time when they would be
fulfilled.[158] Shorter collections of prophetic sayings and reports can sometimes be
recognized by the way in which they are introduced (cf. Jer. 23:9; 30:1-4; 46:1; 50:1).
Shorter collections of oracles were eventually assembled into longer compositions on
the basis of such structural principles as chronology, importance, the disaster-deliv-
erance schema, etc.[159] Prophetic books compiled in the preexilic period are rarely
compositions including the oracles of a single prophet. They often exhibit a complex
traditional and literary character which can involve as many as five layers of material:[160] (1) original prophetic speeches and reports, (2) preexilic additions, (3) Deuteronomistic redaction, (4) deutero-prophetic additions, and (5) expansionist textual
traditions. The deutero-prophetic additions are collections of prophetic material by
anonymous prophets whose works were either appended to or inserted in the works
of earlier prophets. The deutero-prophetic writings include Deutero-Isaiah (Isa. 40-55),
Trito-Isaiah (Isa. 56-66); Ezek. 38-39; Joel 3-4; Zech. 9-14, and the so-called Apocalypse
of Isaiah (Isa. 24-27). These collections, all of which are postexilic, appear to reflect
a change in prophetic consciousness. With the exception of Haggai and Zechariah,
both of whom were active at the end of the sixth century B.C., no postexilic prophecy
was composed in the name of its actual author. Nevertheless, it was thought necessary
to associate collections of prophetic oracles with the name of a particular prophet.

5 | PROPHECY IN EARLY JUDAISM

I. INTRODUCTION

The opinion is widespread that prophecy ceased in Judaism during the fifth century B.C., only to break forth once again with the rise of Christianity. The evidence which we shall consider in this chapter, however, flatly contradicts that view. Israelite prophecy did not disappear. Rather, like all religious and social institutions, it underwent a number of far-reaching and even radical changes during the period of the Second Temple (516 B.C.– A.D. 70). Defined as intelligible messages from God in human language through inspired human mediums, "prophecy" can assume a wide variety of forms. In the last chapter we considered various forms of canonical prophecy in some detail. If early Jewish prophecy is compared directly with the classical prophecy of the OT, the differences are not inconsiderable. But despite the changes in form and function, prophecy continued to play an important role in the religious structures of Judaism during the Second Temple period. After discussing the early Jewish views on the role of prophecy and divine revelation in the past and present, we shall present a typology of early Jewish prophecy with representative samples of each type of prophetic speech or writing.

II. DID PROPHECY CEASE?

A number of texts from later portions of the OT, the Apocrypha and Pseudepigrapha, Josephus, and rabbinic literature are frequently cited in support of the contention that prophecy was held in low esteem during the earlier part of the Second Temple period and later vanished altogether.[1] These texts must be carefully evaluated for a number of reasons. (1) Some of these texts are relatively late (the rabbinic texts, for example, do not antedate the second century A.D.). (2) Early Judaism exhibited great variety, and the views expressed in particular texts reflect only the opinion of that segment of Judaism which produced those texts. (3) Although these texts are often lumped together, they do not all refer either to the phenomena of the low esteem in which prophecy was purportedly held or to its ultimate cessation in Judaism.

One of the rabbinic texts on the subject of the cessation of prophecy that is often quoted (not infrequently without the last sentence) is Tosephta Soṭah 13:2:

> When the last of the prophets — i.e. Haggai, Zechariah, and Malachi — died, the holy spirit ceased in Israel. Despite this they were informed by means of oracles [bat qol].[2]

Another passage quoted in the same regard is Seder Olam Rabbah 30:

> Until then, the prophets prophesied by means of the holy spirit. From then on, give ear and listen to the words of the sages.[3]

Both passages identify the "holy spirit" with the prophetic activity of the canonical prophets, for in Rabbinic Judaism the "holy spirit" was virtually synonymous with prophecy.[4] The first passage emphasizes the view that divine revelation continued in Judaism, though in a different form. The medium of revelation was no longer the inspired prophet, but rather the *bat qol* (literally, "daughter of a voice"), a heavenly voice or sound which had both oracular and divinatory functions.[5]

A related feature of these texts is that they make a qualitative distinction between canonical prophecy and that which has succeeded it. The rabbinic sages regarded themselves as the only legitimate interpreters and expounders of the Mosaic Torah, a role they had inherited from the canonical prophets who in turn were the successors of Moses. Since the sages did not consider themselves inspired spokesmen for divine revelations but rather traditionists, the view that prophecy had ceased was a means of legitimating their role as successors of Moses and the prophets.

Although these and other rabbinic texts make it clear that some rabbis did hold that prophecy had ceased during the Second Temple period, the view had a theoretical character[6] and was only one view among many.[7] According to the other rabbinic traditions, famous rabbis claimed the gift of prophecy[8] and/or the possession of the Spirit of God.[9] These mutually contradictory notions show that Rabbinic Judaism during the period following the destruction of the Second Temple in A.D. 70 was not the monolithic phenomenon that many scholars have often assumed.[10] It has been suggested, not improbably, that the rabbinic texts denying the existence of prophecy during the late Second Temple period might reflect an apologetic attempt to undermine the prophetic claims of the early Christians.[11] Indeed, it has become increasingly recognized that prophecy did not disappear in Judaism during the Hellenistic and Roman periods, but that it was alive and well, though in a form considerably different from that of classical OT prophecy.[12] According to S. Sandmel, "Outside the circle of the Rabbinic Sages the view that prophecy had ended simply did not exist."[13]

Apart from Rabbinic Judaism Jewish sects of the late Second Temple period do not appear to have regarded either prophecy or the Holy Spirit as completely absent from Jewish religious experience. The Spirit of God was widely regarded as an eschatological gift, but those apocalyptic groups which regarded the eschaton as imminent (particularly the Qumran community and early Christianity) firmly believed in the presence of the Holy Spirit. The literature produced by the Qumran community during the century prior to A.D. 66 indicates that this particular group of Essenes was persuaded that the Spirit was present and active in their community.[14] Prophecy and the presence of the Spirit may well have been regarded as normal phenomena within other Jewish apocalyptic sects also.[15] In apocalyptic literature revelatory speech is occasionally attributed to the Spirit of God (4 Ezra 14:22; 1 Enoch 91:1), and the authors frequently claim inspiration.[16] Implicit claims to divine inspiration are made when revelatory dreams together with angelic interpretations are narrated.

In addition to the rabbinic texts from the period after A.D. 70, other earlier references in Jewish literature are often used to prove that prophecy was dormant in Judaism during the Hellenistic and Roman periods. Three of these texts are clustered in 1 Maccabees (4:45b-46; 9:27; 14:41):

So they tore down the [defiled] altar, and stored the stones in a convenient place on the temple hill until there should come a prophet to tell what to do with them.

Thus there was great distress in Israel, such as had not been since the time that prophets ceased to appear among them.

And the Jews and their priests decided that Simon should be their leader and high priest for ever, until a trustworthy prophet should arise.

The first text (1 Macc. 4:45b-46) represents a conception of prophecy that involves the inspired interpretation of the relevant cultic regulations found in the Torah.[17] The type of prophet described is a kind of temple or clerical prophet who is to function in a manner similar to the priests consulted by Haggai (Hag. 2:11-13). There is little resemblance to either the classical prophets or the prophets who were the object of eschatological expectation. The second text (1 Macc. 9:27) reflects the notion that in ancient times prophets appeared in critical times and exercised a ministry to all Israel. From the author's perspective that kind of prophets no longer appeared. The third text (1 Macc. 14:41) is neither an oblique reference to John Hyrcanus (135-104 B.C.), who is described by Josephus as possessing the gift of prophecy[18] and who is the culminating figure in 1 Maccabees (16:11-24), nor to an eschatological prophet.[19] Rather, it is a way of stopping short of completely idealizing the Hasmonean program of restoration and reconstruction.[20] The general perspective of the author of 1 Maccabees is theocratic rather than eschatological, a perspective which excludes the possibility that 1 Macc. 4:46 and 14:41 refer to an eschatological prophet.[21] The type of prophecy reflected in 1 Macc. 4:45b-46 and 14:41 is "clerical" prophecy, i.e. a type of early Jewish prophecy which assumes that prophetic gifts are coextensive with the priestly-political leadership of the nation.

Several passages within the OT itself are often thought to reflect either prophecy's decline in prestige or its disappearance. Ps. 74:9 is one such text:

We do not see our signs; there is no longer any prophet, and there is none among us who knows how long.

This psalm is often thought to have originated during the Maccabean period and to reflect the Seleucid capture of the temple (Ps. 74:3-4). Yet it may reflect the situation which attended the destruction of the Solomonic temple in 586 B.C. when the temple prophets may have lost a great deal of their credibility.[22] Ezek. 13:9 and Zech. 13:2-6 are thought to reflect the decline in prestige of prophecy during the exilic and postexilic periods.[23] Yet both authors refer, not to the general deterioration in the credibility of prophets, but to the eschatological elimination of false prophets.[24] Similarly, Dan. 9:24 probably refers, not to the historical cessation of prophecy, but to the eschatological climax of the predictions of all the prophets up to and including Daniel.[25]

The early Jewish attitudes toward the past and present activity of prophecy and the Spirit of God exhibit great variety. While some of the rabbinic sages of the early talmudic period were convinced that the Holy Spirit had been taken from Israel and that the voice of prophecy had ceased, other forms of prophecy and divination were still recognized as legitimate and were practiced. These alternate forms of revelation, however, occupied a subordinate position to the Mosaic revelation codified in the Torah and expounded as oral law by the sages. Other groups within early Judaism, particularly the various apocalyptic or millenarian sects, revered the Torah while recognizing new manifestations of divine revelation through various types of written and oral prophetic activity.

The formation of the OT canon, a process which was completed by the first century B.C.,[26] appears to have had no connection with the view that prophecy had ended in Judaism. Even in the famous passage found in Josephus *Contra Ap.* i.37-41, where the Jewish historian discusses the boundaries of the Hebrew scriptures, he does not say that prophecy has ceased, only that there is no longer an "exact succession" (*akribē diadochēn*) of prophets, i.e. there is no direct relationship between the desultory appearances of various prophets.[27] The canon, it must be insisted, was not created by rabbinical fiat at the legendary "council" of Jabneh, ca. A.D. 90.[28] Rather, the Jewish canon of scriptures had been gradually defined through centuries of liturgical usage and religious study. The Torah came to occupy a position of greatest authority and sanctity, with the Prophets and Writings in positions of progressively lesser esteem. The "boundaries" between the canonical texts and other Jewish religious literature were more rigidly fixed for the Torah than for the Prophets and for the Prophets than for the Writings. Certainly there was no antithesis between a divinely inspired and centrally authoritative collection of sacred writings on the one hand and the continuing role of inspired prophecy on the other. Early Christianity itself was a sect within Judaism that revered the OT and yet was characterized by a flurry of prophetic activity.

III. TYPES OF PROPHECY

Many of the more characteristic formal features of OT prophecy are almost entirely absent from the various kinds of early Jewish revelatory speech and writing which we shall consider in the remainder of this chapter. Prose, not poetry, becomes the rule. Prophetic speeches in the first-person singular attributed to God are very rare. The various formulaic introductory and concluding phrases, such as the messenger formula, the commission formula, the proclamation formula, the divine oracle formula, and the oath formulas, are almost entirely absent. Many of the basic forms of OT prophetic speech are also strikingly absent from early Jewish sources: the announcement of judgment, the announcement of salvation, the oracle of divine self-disclosure, the judicial speech, and reports of symbolic actions. To be sure, other revelatory formulas, conventions, and genres take their place, while some OT prophetic forms are retained. Perhaps the most interesting feature of early Jewish prophecy in comparison with its OT prototypes is the general absence of the tendency to imitate OT prophetic formulas and speech forms. Even though early Jewish revelatory speech and literature must necessarily interface with canonical forms of prophecy, the integrity of the various forms of early Jewish prophecy is revealed most clearly in its independence from OT prototypes.

In one of the few attempts to characterize Jewish prophecy during the Hellenistic and Roman periods, M. Hengel has proposed three primary features:[29] (1) its method is charismatic exegesis, i.e. the inspired interpretation of OT prophecy, (2) its inspiration is through possession of the eschatological Spirit, i.e. possession trance, and (3) its content relates to the historical-political situation of the Jewish state. Unfortunately, the only consistent characteristic of early Jewish prophecy is found in the last point; the other two features are not invariably present.

J. Becker has taken the matter further by proposing a typology of prophetism in early Judaism.[30] He suggests that four basic types of prophets were active: (1) The prophet who, in continuity with the OT prophetic role, knows God's will in cases not foreseen by the law through a charismatic endowment with the Spirit (1 Macc. 4:46; 14:41). (2) The political-nationalistic prophet, without an eschatological self-understanding, of which there are two major subtypes: (a) political prophets *without* a party program (e.g. the Essenes Menahem and Simon, and Flavius Josephus),[31] and (b) political prophets *with* a party program (e.g. Zealotism).[32] (3) Eschatological prophets, of which there are five subtypes: (a) prophets who claim to perform wonders in typological imitation of Israel's wilderness period (e.g. Theudas and the Egyptian Jew),[33] (b) Elijah *redivivus,* (c) messianic prophets,[34] (d) the prophet like Moses, and (e) Moses *redivivus.* (4) The charismatic prophet who represents God and demands repentance if Israel is to escape judgment (e.g. John the Baptist, the Teacher of Righteousness).

While Becker's typology includes most of the types of prophecy which are found in early Judaism, it suffers from a number of serious weaknesses: (1) It does not adequately distinguish between *historical* prophetic types and *images* of prophets (e.g. 1 Macc. 4:46 and 14:41 do not refer to an actual prophet, nor does the Elijah *redivivus* category). (2) The social setting within which several of these prophetic types functioned is ignored (e.g. his third and fourth categories differ very little in this respect). (3) The major Jewish form of revelatory literature, the apocalypse, has been excluded from consideration. (4) Becker accepts Hengel's overly inclusive depiction of Zealot prophecy.

The remainder of this chapter will discuss the various forms of early Jewish revelatory speech and writing in terms of four major types: (1) *Apocalyptic literature* was a popular form of revelatory literature in early Judaism that both authors and readers took seriously. While the literary conventions of apocalyptic style probably mask oral speech forms and genuine revelatory experiences, our primary concern will be with the literary level of tradition. (2) *Eschatological prophecy,* primarily an oral phenomenon, has two subtypes: (a) eschatological prophecy outside the framework of a millenarian movement and (b) eschatological prophecy as a focal feature of a millenarian movement. (3) *Clerical prophecy,*[35] again primarily an oral phenomenon, is a type of historicizing, noneschatological prophecy associated with the priesthood. (4) *Sapiential prophecy,* which may be either oral or written, is associated with the sage or holy man whose purity and wisdom make him especially close to God. There are two subtypes: (a) in Palestine a kind of hasidic prophecy is found in the Pharisaic-rabbinic tradition,[36] and (b) in Alexandrian Diaspora Judaism there is a very close association between wisdom and prophecy, probably an influence of Greek tradition.[37]

IV. APOCALYPTIC LITERATURE

The term "apocalyptic" refers to three different yet related phenomena in early Judaism: a distinctive literary genre called "apocalypse," a system of religious beliefs called "apocalyptic eschatology," and a religiously motivated social movement called "apocalypticism."[38] One of the major problems in the study of Jewish apocalyptic is determining the relationship of these phenomena. Apocalyptic eschatology is a pattern of religious thought that was widespread in early Judaism and early Christianity; it was an ideology which found expression in various kinds of religious and social movements. Yet it is not clear precisely which social and religious settings provided the matrix for the composition and dissemination of apocalyptic literature. Our primary concern in this section will be to arrive at an understanding of the Jewish apocalypse as a serious form of revelatory literature.

A. MAJOR CHARACTERISTICS

The term "apocalypse" is a transliteration of the Greek *apokalypsis,* which means "disclosure" or "revelation." The first ancient composition to be labeled an "apocalypse" by its author was the book of Revelation, also called the Apocalypse of John (1:1). Since the early nineteenth century the term has been commonly used as a generic designation for literary compositions (primarily Jewish and Christian) which resemble the Apocalypse of John in both form and content.[39] Following the pattern of the Apocalypse of John, we may define an apocalypse as a form of revelatory literature in which the author narrates both the visions he has purportedly experienced and their meaning, usually elicited through a dialogue between the seer and an interpreting angel. The substance of these revelatory visions is the imminent intervention of God into human affairs to bring the present evil world system to an end and to replace it with an ideal one. This transformation is accompanied by the punishment of the wicked and the reward of the righteous.

Most of the Jewish apocalypses which contain this schema were written between 200 B.C. and A.D. 100. Daniel, usually regarded as the earliest apocalypse,[40] is the only one included in the OT canon, though portions of other canonical prophets exhibit many apocalyptic features. Other examples of Jewish apocalypses include 1 Enoch, 2 Enoch, 2 Baruch, and the Apocalypse of Abraham.[41] 1 Enoch is the longest of these apocalypses, but in actuality it is a composite work consisting of a number of shorter apocalypses: (1) 1 Enoch 1-36, (2) 37-71, the "Similitudes of Enoch," (3) 72-82, the "Book of the Heavenly Luminaries," (4) 83-90, the "Animal Apocalypse," and (5) 91-105, which contains the "Apocalypse of Weeks" (91-93).[42]

One common way to describe apocalyptic literature is through an enumeration of its salient features.[43] Some of the striking *literary* features of apocalypses are: pseudonymity, reports of visions, reviews of history presented as prophecies, number speculation, the figure of the interpreting angel (*angelus interpres*), the tendency to make frequent allusion to, but not quote, the OT, and the conscious attempt to present the compositions as revelatory literature. The more distinctive *religious* features of apocalyptic authors include: imminent eschatology, pessimism, spatial and temporal dualism, determinism, secrecy, a longing for individual, transcendent salvation, and an emphasis on the detailed knowledge of the physical and supernatural universe.

Yet a mere catalogue of the more distinctive features of apocalyptic literature reveals little about the apocalypse as a literary genre.[44] One literary characteristic of apocalypses is that they incorporate many of the genres found in biblical literature (testaments, hymns, laments, woes, visions, etc.) into patterns which show little consistency when one apocalypse is compared with another. This does not mean that the apocalypse is not a distinctive literary genre. It does mean that the structural features of the genre have not yet been satisfactorily analyzed. J. J. Collins has taken an important step in sorting out the structural features of the apocalypse, however. He has formulated this preliminary definition of the apocalypse as a literary genre:

> "Apocalypse" is a genre of revelatory literature within a narrative framework, in which a revelation is mediated by an otherworldly being to a human recipient, disclosing a transcendent reality which is both temporal, in so far as it envisages

eschatological salvation, and spatial, in so far as it involves another, supernatural world.[45]

One weakness in this definition, however, is that it neglects to address the issue of function, though it does directly address the characteristic form and content of the genre apocalypse.

B. PSEUDONYMITY

All early Jewish apocalypses are attributed, not to their actual authors, but to such ancient Israelite celebrities as Adam, Enoch, Abraham, Moses, Baruch, and Ezra.[46] Apocalyptic pseudonymity, however, was not an ancient literary convention unique to Judaism. During the Hellenistic and Roman periods literary falsification was widely practiced.[47] Since the ascription of literary works to real or fictitious persons other than the real author was perpetrated for a great variety of reasons, pseudonymity sheds no significant light on the motivations of apocalyptic writers. The real function of pseudonymity in Jewish apocalyptic literature has not yet been satisfactorily explained.[48] Scholars are divided on the question of whether the apocalyptists used pseudonymity in good faith or for purposes of deception. The following explanations for apocalyptic pseudonymity have been proposed, only the first of which emphasizes deception: (1) Pseudonymity was used to secure the acceptance of an apocalypse during a period when the canon was virtually closed and prophetic inspiration had ended.[49] (2) Pseudonymity was a means of protecting the real authors of apocalypses from reprisal.[50] (3) Apocalyptic visionaries may have had revelatory experiences mediated by those figures to whom they attributed their compositions.[51] (4) The apocalyptic seer may have identified himself with a prominent Israelite of the past and wrote as his representative and under his name.[52] None of these explanations is fully satisfactory, but the first theory appears most probable, though it requires careful qualification.

A number of important observations relate to the phenomenon of apocalyptic pseudonymity: (1) Israelite, Jewish, and early Christian prophetic literature is always attributed to specific authors and never allowed to circulate anonymously. Even the "anonymous" deutero-prophetic compositions in the OT (Isa. 24-27; 40-55; 56-66; Ezek. 38-39; Joel 3-4; Zech. 9-14) were all incorporated into the books of known Israelite prophets. Even "Malachi" (literally, "my messenger") was regarded as a proper name, though it was the title of an originally anonymous prophetic book. There was also a tendency during the late Second Temple period and the early talmudic period to attribute anonymous books in the Former Prophets to particular ancient prophets (1 and 2 Samuel, Judges, and Ruth were attributed to Samuel; 1 and 2 Kings to Jeremiah; etc.).[53]

(2) Even though the apocalypses are presented as *revelatory* literature, they are only rarely attributed to ancient Israelite *prophets.*[54] Perhaps such attribution was precluded by the practice of circulating the oracles of a particular prophet in only one collection. Even so, the tendency to avoid the pseudonymous use of the names of famous OT prophets implies that the apocalyptists did not particularly identify their function with that of the earlier prophets. In almost every instance in which revelatory genres are attributed to particular OT celebrities, the biblical account contains no comparable association of the genre with that figure. This suggests that OT figures are selected to whom "new" (or recently discovered) revelations may plausibly be attributed. Yet Ezra is called a prophet in 4 Ezra (1:1; 12:42; cf. Clement of Alex. *Strom.* iii.16), which suggests the importance of that title to the unknown author.

(3) The phenomenon of pseudonymous authorship is closely connected with historical surveys presented as predictive prophecies and the "esoteric" statements within apocalypses that they are to be "sealed" or hidden until the end of the age.[55] Each of these features is a way of asserting the antiquity and reliability of the apocalypse.

(4) Pseudonymity is not an essential feature of the apocalyptic genre, since the two Christian apocalypses, the Apocalypse of John and the Shepherd of Hermas, do not use this convention.[56]

(5) Anonymity, which characterized some postexilic prophecy (e.g. the deutero-prophetic writings), may be a stage in the development of pseudonymity, though the intervening links are not at all clear.[57]

These considerations lead to the conclusion that pseudonymity was a legitimating device intended to appropriate the prestige accorded to an illustrious ancient Israelite by affixing his name to an apocalypse. Thus the primary function of pseudonymity (and related devices) was to secure the acceptance of the apocalypse as divine revelation. This implies that the apocalypses were not primarily intended for an apocalyptic sect, for pseudonymity is functional only if readers accept the false attribution. Within the framework of a relatively small and perhaps even isolated group, such acceptance would not be possible. This conclusion leads to the consideration of the social setting within which apocalypses flourished.

C. THE SOCIAL SETTING OF APOCALYPSES

The problem of the social setting of apocalyptic literature is another issue which has not yet been satisfactorily resolved.[58] There is broad agreement that two primary religious orientations arose within postexilic Judaism, the priestly-theocratic perspective (represented by the Priestly document in the Pentateuch, the work of the Chronicler, and 1 and 2 Maccabees), and the prophetic-eschatological orientation (represented by Daniel, in addition to the deutero-prophetic writings and Malachi, mentioned above).[59] These two orientations continued to polarize Palestinian Judaism throughout the Second Temple period. The party in power during this period, whether under the succession of foreign powers that dominated Palestine during this time (Persians, Greeks, Ptolemies, Seleucids, Romans) or during the brief period of Judean independence under the Hasmoneans (142-63 B.C.), was the priestly-theocratic group. The prophetic-eschatological groups, which exhibited great diversity, were never willing or able to participate or dominate the Jewish control of the state or the cult. These two groups were polarized by a conflicting ideology; the priestly-theocratic group expected the realization of Israel's destiny within history through the restoration of an independent Jewish state in which the temple cult would play a central role. The prophetic-eschatological groups, on the other hand, expected that God would intervene in human history, bring it to an end, and establish his eternal rule within which the destiny of the chosen people would be fully realized.

Apocalyptic eschatology is the idiom of those who are oppressed and powerless and whose hopes appear impossible of realization within the existing order.[60] Apocalypses are a form of anti-Hellenistic resistance literature of a type found in other national settings in the Near East.[61] There is some agreement that apocalypticism in early Judaism was a supernaturalistic response to the social, political, and religious oppression experienced by many segments of early Judaism under foreign powers as well as under native representatives of those powers, the priestly-theocratic group.[62]

P. Hanson has demonstrated that the gradual emergence of apocalyptic eschatology from prophetic eschatology began in the sixth century B.C. and continued to develop until it reached complete form in Zech. 14 and Daniel.[63] The historical and social matrix of apocalypticism, according to Hanson, was the inner-community struggle during the Second Temple period between visionary and hierocratic elements (identical with our "prophetic-eschatological" and "priestly-theocratic" orientations respectively). The hierocratic group (composed of Zadokite priestly elements) adopted a pragmatic approach to restoration that was opposed in principle by the visionary group, who looked for the eschatological restoration of the fortunes of Israel. Hanson chronicles the conflict between the two elements through a careful analysis of select portions of the deutero-prophetic literature, stopping short of a discussion of apocalypticism in its full-blown form in Daniel. One virtue of his analysis is that he avoids identifying the visionary element in Palestinian society with a particular party.[64]

In considering the phenomenon of apocalyptic pseudonymity, we were led to the conclusion that the authors of the apocalypses did not intend that their revelations circulate within a closed group to which they might have belonged. Yet the apocalyptists were not addressing all Israel, like many of the classical prophets, but only Jewish sympathizers who shared their apocalyptic eschatological orientation and with whom they hoped for ready acceptance and response. Organized apocalyptic sects, such as the Qumran community or the movement surrounding John the Baptist, offer no evidence that pseudonymity in any form was used, since these groups completely accepted the eschatological status of their respective founders and leaders. The use of pseudonymity by an apocalyptic writer reveals his doubt that his message will be accepted on his personal authority.

Apocalyptic eschatology during the late Second Temple period was a widespread ideological matrix which gave rise to various forms of collective behavior. From the early second century B.C. on, a variety of apocalyptic sects and movements arose within Palestinian Judaism in continuity with the earlier prophetic-eschatological orientation. It has been argued that apocalyptic literature arose either within the setting of a general, unorganized, popular movement in Palestine,[65] or that it was produced by particular, organized sects. The Hasidim (literally, "pious ones"), who were the progenitors of both the Pharisees and the Essenes, are thought by many to have produced the apocalypse of Daniel as well as other such tracts.[66] The evidence for this view is slim, however, and unable to support such a hypothesis.[67] The Essenes are an example of a highly organized apocalyptic sect whose response to religious alienation was expressed in terms of self-imposed isolation from the world of Palestinian Judaism. But while the Essenes at Qumran viewed reality from the perspective of apocalyptic eschatology and collected apocalyptic literature which had arisen outside their community, there is no evidence that they used the apocalyptic genre themselves. All attempts to link apocalyptic literature to *specific* sects or movements have proven unsuccessful.[68]

Yet it is clear that Daniel and other apocalypses are a learned, scribal phenomenon produced by *maśkilim* ("the wise," Dan. 11:33, 35),[69] who are commonly (but unnecessarily) identified with the Hasidim.[70] These scribes, only loosely connected with one another if at all, wrote apocalypses as "tracts for the times" in various situations of oppression. The device of pseudonymity, however, prevented the authors from explicitly designating either the historical crisis within which they wrote (though this is hinted at in historical reviews presented as prophecy; the point at which such clear "predictions" become vague reveals the historical position of the author), or the audience for whom their work was intended. These scribes, it appears, intended their apocalypses for general distribution among those of all classes who would be sympathetic to the kind of nationalistic eschatology which they represented.

D. PROPHECY AND APOCALYPTIC

The problem of the relationship between prophecy and apocalyptic is part of the larger issue of the degree of *continuity* or *discontinuity* thought to exist between apocalyptic and Israelite religious traditions. In general it must be recognized that apocalyptic literature (together with the related phenomena of apocalyptic eschatology and apocalypticism) exhibits *both* continuity and discontinuity with Israelite tradition generally and OT prophecy in particular.

While early Jewish apocalyptic literature (Daniel, 1 and 2 Enoch, 2 Baruch, and the Apocalypse of Abraham) exhibits striking contrasts with preexilic OT prophetic literature, the trajectory from prophecy to apocalyptic becomes clearer when the exilic and deutero-prophetic literature is brought into consideration.[71] Prophecy appears to have gradually merged into apocalyptic.[72] Most of the essential features of the kind of apocalyptic literature which flourished from 200 B.C. to A.D. 100 have roots in the prophetic literature of the sixth and fifth centuries B.C. Apocalyptic is therefore an inner-Jewish development. Further, the inclusion of the more apocalyptically oriented deutero-prophetic writings (e.g. Isa. 24-27) into prophetic books indicates that they were held in equally high regard.[73]

At the same time, apocalypticism and the production of apocalyptic literature are not uniquely Jewish, but are also found in other Near Eastern countries during the Hellenistic and Roman periods.[74] Native monarchies which had fallen to the Greeks (later the Ptolemies and Seleucids) and then to the Romans often had traditions of the kingship of the national deity. In consequence of subjection to and oppression by foreign powers, "messianism" (i.e. a nostalgia for the past expressed in terms of a desire for the restoration of the native monarchy) pervaded the entire Near East.[75]

One feature common to various apocalyptic literatures of the Near East during the Hellenistic and Roman periods was the resurgence and revitalization of archaic mythical patterns of cosmic conflict in which the transition from defeat to victory, chaos to order, sterility to fertility, is brought about by a messianic figure.[76] These ancient mythical paradigms are applied to the eschaton and made the pattern for the cosmic victory of the native deity or deities over the forces of oppression. In Judaism, as in Greco-Roman Egypt and elsewhere, native traditions which were basically similar to those of neighboring cultures were subjected to the same kind of changed circumstances: subjection to foreign powers. Not surprisingly, their response was often similarly expressed by the production of apocalyptic literature.

Although Jewish apocalyptic literature used ancient Israelite and Canaanite mythical themes and patterns, it also made use of non-Israelite traditions. A. Y. Collins, for example, has shown that the particular pattern of the combat myth used in Rev. 12 is closest to the myth of Leto-Apollo-Python, even though some elements are also derived from Semitic tradition (e.g. the heavenly battle).[77] Like Israelite wisdom, which exhibits international interests and concerns, Jewish apocalyptic exhibits a receptivity to both Hellenistic and Near Eastern traditions.[78] The position of those in the apocalyptic movement, alienated from official Judaism and presumably more open to foreign influences, has been identified by O. Plöger as the principal reason for such syncretism.[79] Yet the phenomenon of syncretism itself is so widespread in the Hellenistic and Roman periods that Plöger's thesis has little explanatory value.

G. von Rad's theory that Israelite wisdom, not Israelite prophecy, was the mother of Jewish apocalyptic has found little support in the form in which he proposed it.[80] Yet the theory of the wisdom origin of apocalyptic, which tends to emphasize the discontinuity between prophecy and apocalyptic, is not completely without foundation (Wis. 7:27; Sir. 24:33). Both wisdom and apocalyptic are, after all, *scribal* phenomena.[81] Consequently, a neat distinction between wisdom and apocalyptic is not possible.[82] Yet it is important to distinguish between two related, yet different, wisdom traditions: proverbial wisdom and mantic wisdom.[83] The role of the "wise" (*maśkilim*) in interpreting dreams is well known in biblical tradition, e.g. in stories about Joseph and Daniel, both of whom were able to unravel the revelatory significance of dreams through divine wisdom (Gen. 40:8; 41:25, 39; Dan. 2:19-23, 30, 45, 47; 5:11-12). An analogous interpretive expertise is exhibited in the explanation of the meaning of the visions in Dan. 7-12, though there an angel, not Daniel, plays the role of interpreter.[84] A mode of interpretation similar to that of the wise interpreter of dreams or the *angelus interpres* of apocalyptic visionary sequences is found in the charismatic exegesis of scripture characteristic of the *pesher*-commentaries of the Qumran community. In Qumran literature the Danielic language of dream interpretation (the complementary terms *raz,* "mystery," and *peshar,* "interpretation," as found in Dan. 2:30; 4:4[Eng. 9]) has been appropriated for the interpretation of scripture (1QpHab 7:1-5).[85] Mantic wisdom, then, proves to be an important antecedent to Jewish apocalyptic literature alongside the prophetic traditions.

Apocalyptic literature is often distinguished from prophecy by emphasizing the interpretative role of the apocalyptist in contrast to the direct revelation characteristic of OT classical prophecy.[86] The increasing emphasis on "prophecy through interpretation" that characterized the sixth century B.C. and the early Second Temple period is often correlated with a growing view of the distance and transcendence of God. God does not reveal his word directly to the apocalyptists, as he did to the OT prophets, but indrectly through visions and scripture, both of which require interpretation. The primary medium of revelation in apocalyptic literature is the vision, the meaning of which is disclosed to the seer by the *angelus interpres.* In OT prophetic books it is not unusual for God to reveal the meaning of a vision to the prophet through a short dialogue (Amos 7:7-9; 8:1-3). In Zech. 1:7-6:8 and Dan. 7-12 an interpreting angel reveals the meaning of the visions. That the apocalyptists could function as biblical interpreters is indicated by the presence of midrashic-style commentaries on biblical passages in apocalyptic literature. An extensive midrash on Isa. 24:17-23 has been identified in 1 Enoch 54:1-56:4 and 64:1-68:1,[87] and one on Dan. 7:13 is found in 1 Enoch 46:1ff.[88] Yet on the whole it appears that apocalypses are not commentaries on scripture. Allusions to the OT, a characteristic feature of apocalypses, can only rarely be regarded as "midrashic" in form.[89] The role of the apocalyptists as biblical interpreters has been greatly exaggerated.[90]

Finally, the phenomena of prophecy and apocalyptic have been differentiated with regard to the basic thrust of their message. P. Hanson finds that the unique feature of OT prophecy is the tension maintained between vision and reality.[91] The OT prophets attempted to translate their visions in such a way that political, social, and religious realities were vitally affected. Prophecy became transformed into apocalyptic when the tension between vision and reality was relaxed and then broken, and the attempt to relate the cosmic vision to the realities of contemporary life was abandoned. J. J. Collins, on the other hand, finds the fundamental distinction between prophecy and apocalyptic in the type of message which is presented.[92] The prophetic oracle was addressed directly to the people and left open the possibility of repentance and change of heart in view of the imminent judgment of God. But apocalyptic had no conditional aspect to the threat of judgment, only the verdict which had already been predetermined by God.

While Hanson's view is more persuasive, the basis for the tension between vision and reality is *social,* and the transformation from prophecy to apocalyptic was inevitable. Collins' perspective is weakened by the fact that classical OT prophecy was not as conditional as many have supposed.[93] In both the OT prophets and the apocalyptists of early Judaism the judgment of God stands as a grim reality facing the people of God.

In sum, apocalyptic literature was one among many media of revelation within early Judaism. OT classical prophecy too, of course, was one among many media of revelation in Israelite religion. Apocalyptic literature is historically and genetically derived from the various revelatory media of ancient Israel, of which classical prophecy was the most important exemplar. Most scholars regard apocalyptic as the offspring of Israelite prophecy, and this view is certainly correct. Yet apocalyptic must be regarded, not simply as *the* successor of prophecy, but as one among many offspring.

E. REVELATORY FORMULAS AND GENRES

Early Jewish apocalypses are, by definition, revelatory literature. Within Judaism of the late Second Temple period the primary models of revelatory literature would have been the Mosaic Torah and the Latter Prophets. Yet the apocalyptists did not slavishly imitate OT prophetic forms and styles; rather, they developed a distinctive literary idiom of their own. Apocalypses are composed of many constituent forms or genres,[94] some of which will be analyzed in this section. In the study of OT prophetic speech the oral origin and circulation of many forms can be assumed with some confidence. During the postexilic and early Second Temple periods, however, prophecy (especially exemplified by the deutero-prophetic additions to prophetic books) became increasingly a *literary* phenomenon. During the Hellenistic and Roman periods there was a great respect for revelatory literature of all types.[95] The Septuagint, for example, enjoyed considerable prestige among pagans.[96] In spite of the obviously literary character of the apocalypses, the question of the experiential dimensions of the visionary and revelatory narratives has often been raised. Did the apocalyptists have actual visionary experiences which they then expressed in the stereotyped literary form of vision sequence reports? Although it cannot be proven, many scholars hold that apocalyptists did base at least some of their reports of visions on actual revelatory experiences.[97] Some confirmation of this view may be offered below where I hope to show that some revelatory or prophetic speech forms have been embedded in various literary settings within the apocalypses. In particular, the great concentration of "prophetic" speech forms and formulas in 1 Enoch 91-105 is significant in that it points to the prophetic consciousness of the author.[98]

1. Revelatory Formulas.

Many of the more common introductory and concluding formulas found in OT prophetic speech are either completely absent (e.g. the messenger formula) or else only marginally present (e.g. the revelation formulas).[99] The absence of the messenger formula is significant in that the apocalyptists did not conceive of themselves as messengers whose task was to convey divine messages to particular audiences. The messenger formula and the more comprehensive commission formula not only reflect the OT prophets' view of themselves as messengers, but also and more importantly they are formulaic means of affirming the divine origin and truth of the prophetic message. In apocalyptic literature the messenger formula has been functionally replaced by the *oath formula*.[100] In OT prophetic speech the oath formulas which were used (often as a substitute for the messenger formula) to introduce prophetic speech were always attributed to God himself, not the prophetic spokesman.[101] In apocalyptic literature it is the visionary who introduces his words with an oath formula in order to verify the truth of the vision or vision interpretation which follows. Since the setting in which an individual takes an oath regarding the truth of the statement he is about to make is that of a witness in a judicial process, the frequency with which these oath formulas occur in apocalyptic literature indicates that apocalyptists conceived of their role in terms of being *witnesses* to divine truth.

The apocalyptist's self-conception of being a witness survives in early Christian prophecy in the use of the verb *martyrein*, "witness, testify" (cf. Rev. 1:2; 22:18, 20).[102] A typical example of the introductory oath formula is found in 1 Enoch 103:1-2:

> Now, therefore, I swear to you, the righteous, by the glory of the Great and Honoured and Mighty One in dominion, and by His greatness I swear to you. I know a mystery and have read the heavenly tablets, and have seen the holy books, and have found written therein and inscribed regarding them. . . .

The introductory oath formulas in 1 Enoch all have a similar function: they introduce statements concerning the reward of the righteous and the punishment of the sinner.[103] The introductory use of "amen" in the sayings of Jesus functions as an oath formula, but sayings so introduced cannot always be considered prophetic in nature, though many certainly are.[104] There are also examples of an introductory oath formula functioning in prophetic speeches in Josephus (*Ant.* xviii.197ff.) and in the *Odyssey* (xvii.154ff.; xix.302-307; xx.229-231). In *Odyssey* xvii.154ff. the *mantis* Theoklymenos introduces a divination with the following words:

> But I shall prophesy [*manteusomai*] truly to you, and hold back nothing.
> Zeus be my witness, first of the gods, and the table of friendship,
> and the hearth of blameless Odysseus, to which I come as a suppliant. . . .[105]

The apocalyptic oath formula then, which might more appropriately be designated a *witness* formula, proves to be a widely distributed introductory formula in connection with oracular speech in the ancient world, though never in the OT.

Another formula found twice in apocalyptic literature is the *integrity formula*, here quoted from 1 Enoch 104:11:

> But when they write down truthfully all my words in their languages, and do not change or diminish aught from my words but write them all down truthfully — all that I first testified concerning them.

This formula is also found in Rev. 22:18-19. The prohibition from adding to, subtracting from, or in any way changing the text is used in several settings in early Judaism, all derived from the use of the integrity formula to the Mosaic covenant in Deut. 4:2; 12:32 (LXX 13:1): (1) in wisdom settings of the unalterable words and deeds of God

(Prov. 30:5-6; Eccl. 3:14; Sir. 18:6; 42:21), (2) by rabbis to comment on the inviolability of the scriptures,[106] (3) appended to the LXX to ensure its integrity (Letter of Aristeas 310-11; Josephus *Contra Ap.* i.8; *Ant.* xii.109; Philo *Vita Mosis* ii.34), and (4) in apocalyptic literature to ensure the accurate preservation of the revelatory text (1 Enoch 104:11; Rev. 20:18-19; Apoc. Paul 51; Disc. 63:15-32). In Greco-Roman paganism the formula is used by Porphyrios to show how carefully he transmitted oracular texts;[107] the formula is also used in connection with a dream revelation in an ancient Mesopotamian text.[108]

Related to the integrity formula is the *preservation formula,* which can be a reference either to the sealing or concealing of a book (Dan. 8:26; 12:4, 9; 2 Bar. 20:3; 87; 4 Ezra 12:37) or to the necessity of transmitting it (2 Enoch 54:1). A *legitimation formula* is found at the conclusion of some visions, such as the statement in Dan. 2:15: "the dream is certain, and its interpretation sure" (cf. Dan. 2:45; cf. v. 6; 8:26; 1 Enoch 90:41; 2 Bar. 40:4; 71:2).[109] This can emphasize the truth of the revelation and its inevitable fulfilment, as in 1 Enoch 90:41: "for everything shall come and be fulfilled, and all the deeds of men in their order were shown to me." Or it can be used to conclude a vision sequence: "this is the vision/dream and this the interpretation" (2 Bar. 40:4; 71:2; 4 Ezra 12:35).

2. Woe Oracles.

The woe oracle, a distinctively prophetic form in the OT, is a literary form which occurs frequently in apocalyptic literature, particularly 1 Enoch.[110] There it occurs thirty-two times and except for 1 Enoch 103:5, 8 always in a series of from two to six woes.[111] The serial arrangement of woe oracles is characteristic of the OT prophetic form. A series of three woes is found in 1 Enoch 100:7-9:

A.	Woe form (accusation):	Woe to you, Sinners, on the day of strong anguish, Ye who afflict the righteous and burn them with fire:
B.	Threat:	Ye shall be requited according to your works.
A.	Woe form (accusation):	Woe to you, ye obstinate of heart, Who watch in order to devise wickedness:
	[Transition]:	Therefore
B.	Threat:	shall fear come upon you, And there shall be none to help you.
A.	Woe form (accusation):	Woe to you, ye sinners, on account of the words of your mouth, And on account of the deeds of your hands which your godlessness has wrought,
B.	Threat:	In blazing flames burning worse than fire shall ye burn.[112]

Like its OT counterpart, the apocalyptic woe oracle consists of two basic elements, the woe form describing specific misdeeds and the threat immediately following.[113] Often a transitional term such as "therefore" or "for" joins the two parts. In Enoch the sins of the wicked are either social (95:5-6; 96:5, 8; 97:8; 98:13; 99:11-12, 15; 100:7-8) or religious (94:8; 96:4; 97:8-10; 98:1-2; 99:2, 13). The woe oracles are all found within 1 Enoch 91-105, which is a literary unit with a distinctively parenetic character. While the OT woe oracles were directed to particular groups of evildoers within Israel, the woes in 1 Enoch 91-105 see the world dichotomized into two opposing groups, the righteous and the wicked. Although the setting of the woes is a parenetic speech of Enoch to his sons, the internal character of the woes themselves suggests that they are not being used in the sense of a Two Ways tradition, but to announce the eschatological judgment of the wicked.

3. Oracles of Assurance.

The oracle of assurance is another common form of OT and Near Eastern prophetic speech that was taken up by apocalyptists.[114] A classic example of the oracle of assurance is found in 2 Enoch 1:8:

A.	Admonition (with addressee):	Have courage, Enoch, do not fear;
B.	Reason:	the eternal God sent us to thee,
C.	Promise:	and lo! you shall to-day ascend with us into heaven, and thou shalt tell thy sons and all thy household all that they shall do without thee on earth in thy house, and let no one seek thee till the Lord return thee to them.[115]

Although the classic elements are here and the oracle is addressed to an individual, it is not uttered in response to a lament or complaint, but is rather a response to Enoch's fear induced by an angelophany. The use of the basic elements of an oracle of assurance in this setting is relatively common (2 Enoch 20:3; 21:3; 22:5). In both Jewish and early Christian narrative literature the oracle of assurance is often used to structure divine revelation in a dream (Josephus *Ant.* xi.327-28; Acts 27:24; Matt. 1:20-21).

Another type of oracle of assurance occurs four times in 1 Enoch 91-105 (95:3; 96:1; 97:1; 104:2); 1 Enoch 95:3 will serve as an example:

A.	Admonition:	Fear not the sinners,
B.	Addressee:	ye righteous;
C.	Promise:	For again will the Lord deliver them into your hands, that ye may execute judgement upon them according to your desires.[116]

This oracle is in response to a lament of Enoch expressed in 95:1-2, but it is addressed to the righteous ones (plural) rather than to Enoch himself. Although most oracles of assurance in the OT are addressed to individuals, some are not, e.g. 2 Chr. 20:15-17, where the reason is omitted and only the promise is given as the basis for the admonition.

Another example of an oracle of assurance is found in 4 Ezra 12:46-47, in which Ezra responds to a lament of the people (vv. 40-45a; here he is called the last of the prophets):

A.	Admonition (with addressee):	Take courage, O Israel; be not sorrowful, O House of Jacob!
B.	Reason:	For you are remembered before the Most High, the Mighty One hath not forgotten you for ever.[117]

In this example the reason for the admonition is given but the promise is omitted.

Further, all the examples of the oracle of assurance in 1 Enoch and 4 Ezra are pronounced by the pseudonymous visionary, whereas in the OT they are uttered as the
first-person speech of God through a prophet.

4. Vision Forms.

The vision sequences in apocalyptic literature differ from those in the OT (exclusive
of Dan. 7-12) in matters of length, structure, and content. They even develop into
discourse cycles.[118] Vision reports constitute the central mode of revelation in apocalyptic literature, and they frequently are set into a stereotypical framework consisting
of four elements:[119] (1) introduction: the situation in which the vision is received,
(2) description of the visionary's state of mind (prayer and fasting are stressed), (3)
description of the vision sequence, and (4) description of the visionary's reaction (fear,
amazement, exaltation, fainting, etc.).[120] The structure of the entire vision report is
determined in part by whether the vision or dream is solicited or unsolicited. In 4 Ezra
the first four visions (3:1-5:20; 5:21-6:35; 6:36-9:25; 9:26-10:59) are given in response
to long agonizing prayers by the visionary (3:1b-36; 5:22-30; 6:36b-59; 9:27b-37). The
vision sequence itself consists of a lengthy dialogue between Ezra and Uriel, the *angelus
interpres* who guides him. These four vision sequences are not internally unified, but
consist of various images and conversations related to the problem of theodicy.

Unsolicited visions or dreams constitute a different type. They consist of the
following elements: (1) narrative setting, (2) unsolicited vision/dream sequence, (3) prayer
for enlightenment by visionary, and (4) interpretation of vision/dream segments by an
interpreting angel. This pattern is found in the fifth and sixth visions in 4 Ezra (11:1-12:39;
13:1-58) and in two lengthy vision sequences in 2 Baruch (36:1-40:4; 53:1-74:4).[121] In
the "Animal Apocalypse" (1 Enoch 83-90) the two unsolicited visions received by
Enoch concern the coming flood (1 Enoch 83:1-84:6) and the whole of world history
down to the end of the age (85:1-90:42). The first sequence is very brief and consists
of a vision of the destruction caused by the flood and an intercessory prayer to avert
total destruction. The second vision sequence consists of a transparent series of alle-
gories pretending to predict the course of world history. The clear meaning of both
visions obviates the necessity for the role of the interpreting angel. That both visions
conclude with prayer (the first with a prayer of intercession, the second with a prayer
of thanksgiving) is not unusual. In literary accounts of vision or revelatory experiences
a prayer of thanksgiving frequently concludes the account (4 Ezra 13:57-58; 2 Bar.
75:1-8; 1 Enoch 90:40; Dan. 2:20-23; 2 Chr. 20:18-19; Matt. 11:25; Josephus *Bell.* iii.351-54;
Corpus Hermeticum i.31).

5. Theophanic Salvation-Judgment Speeches.

The question of whether prophetic oracles have been embedded in apocalyptic compositions can only be answered by careful analysis. Both the Apocalypse of John and
the Shepherd of Hermas appear to contain oracular material of a less literary cast than
the apocalyptic frameworks within which they are set.[122] The problem confronting
the interpreter is determining the appropriate criteria for identifying such material.
In an analysis of the use of midrashic commentaries on prophetic texts in apocalyptic
sections of the NT, L. Hartman isolated a pattern of sequential themes that is exhibited
in many sections of Jewish apocalyptic texts.[123] The pattern of five sequential themes
includes the following elements: (1) evil times, (2) God intervenes, (3) God judges
men, (4) the wicked are punished, and (5) the righteous are delivered and rejoice.

These themes are, of course, traditional topics of central concern for Jewish eschatological expectation. More than twenty textual units that exhibit this pattern have been identified by Hartman.[124] The emphasis on the future events indicates that the basic thrust of these speeches (for they are nearly always in that form) is prophetic. However, whether they had an existence prior to insertion into their present contexts is a question which cannot be determined satisfactorily.

The first example of a theophanic salvation-judgment speech is 1 Enoch 1:3-9, where the speaker is Enoch:

[Introduction]:   Concerning the elect I said, and took up my parable concerning them:

A.   Theophany: The Holy Great One will come forth from His dwelling,
and the eternal God will tread upon the earth, (even) on Mount Sinai,
[and appear from His camp]
and appear in the strength of His might from the heaven [of heavens].

And all shall be smitten with fear,
and the Watchers shall quake,
and great fear and trembling shall seize them unto the ends of the earth.

And the high mountains shall be shaken,
and the high hills shall be made low,
and shall melt like wax before the flame.

B.   Judgment: And the earth shall be [wholly] rent in sunder,
and all that is upon the earth shall perish,
and there shall be a judgement upon all (men).

C.   Deliverance: But with the righteous He will make peace,
and will protect the elect,
and mercy shall be upon them.

And they shall all belong to God,
and they shall be prospered,
and they shall [all] be blessed.

[And He will help them all],
And light shall appear unto them,
[And He will make peace with them.]

D.   Punishment of wicked: And behold! He cometh with ten thousands of [His] holy ones
To execute judgement upon all,
and to destroy [all] the ungodly:

And to convict all flesh
Of all the works [of their ungodliness] which they have ungodly committed,
[And of all the hard things which] ungodly sinners [have spoken] against Him.[125]

In this vision of the future the theophanic language of the Sinai tradition has been revived and applied to the eschatological coming of God to judge and to save. The combination of judgment and salvation within the same prophetic form began to occur during the postexilic period with the formation of the salvation-judgment oracle.[126]

A second example of a theophanic salvation-judgment speech is 4 Ezra 6:18-28:

A. Theophany:

Behold, the days come,
and it shall be, when I am about to draw nigh to visit the dwellers upon earth,
And when I require from the doers of iniquity (the penalty of) their iniquity,
[*And when the humiliation of Sion shall be complete*,]
And when the Age which is about to pass away shall be sealed,
then [*will I show these signs*]: the books shall be opened before the face of the firmament,
and all see together.

B. Signs of the end:

(And one-year-old children shall speak with their voices,
pregnant women shall bring forth untimely births at three or four months,
and these shall live and dance.
And suddenly shall the sown places appear unsown,
and the full storehouses shall suddenly be found empty;)
and the trumpet shall sound aloud, at which all men, when they hear it, shall be struck with sudden fear.
And at that time [*friends shall war against friends like enemies*],
the earth shall be stricken with fear [*together with the dwellers therein*]
and the springs of the fountains shall stand still so that for three hours they shall not run.

C. Deliverance and Judgment in Juxtaposition:

And it shall be whosoever shall have survived all these things that I have foretold unto thee,
he shall be saved and shall see my salvation and the end of my world.
And the men who have been taken up,
who have not tasted death from their birth shall appear.
Then shall the heart of the inhabitants (of the world) be changed and be converted to a different spirit.
For evil shall be blotted out,
and deceit extinguished;
Faithfulness shall flourish,
and corruption be vanquished;
And truth, which for so long a time has been without fruit, shall be made manifest.[128]

Although the speaker is not explicitly identified, this speech is attributed to a voice "like the sound of many waters" (4 Ezra 6:17) and is certainly God himself (v. 18). This description of the eschaton, which really occupies 4 Ezra 6:11-29, has a close relationship with three other sections of 4 Ezra: 4:52-5:13a; 7:26-44; and 8:63-9:12.[129] In all these sections God himself ushers in the end (4:36; 5:4-5, 42; 6:6, 18-28; 7:43-44; 8:55-61; 9:1); elsewhere it is introduced by the Man or the Messiah. Further, all these sections are descriptions of the eschaton introduced with the formula "behold the days are coming" (5:1; 6:18; cf. 13:29) or "behold the time will come" (7:26). Such descriptions of the future are often introduced with phrases such as "in those days" or "behold the days come," both in the OT prophets (cf. Jer. 23:5, 7) and in apocalyptic literature (1 Enoch 5:6; 97:5; 99:3-5; 100:1-3, 4-6; 102:1-3; 2 Bar. 20:1; 24:1; 31:5; 39:3).

V. ESCHATOLOGICAL PROPHECY

A. INTRODUCTION

Apocalyptic eschatology, the belief that God would shortly intervene in human history to bring a catastrophic end to evil in all its forms, was a widespread ideology in Palestinian Judaism from ca. 200 B.C. to A.D. 100. This belief was a supernaturalistic response to what appeared to many Jews to be a dilemma insoluble by ordinary means: the anxiety, alienation, helplessness, and deprivation experienced in the political, economic, social, and religious spheres of Palestinian life.[130] The writing of apocalypses, i.e. religious and political protest literature, was one of the less organized responses to the oppressive conditions which existed in Palestine during this period. This literary activity can be considered a revolutionary response to oppression in view of its basic conviction that God would overthrow the present order, yet it is quiescent in that the apocalyptists take no personal, active role in the process.[131] Many more organized and active responses to the various causes of Jewish frustration occurred during the century and a half prior to the ill-fated Bar Kosiba rebellion of A.D. 132-135.[132] These movements, and those analogous to them in other times and places, have come to be designated *millenarian movements.*[133]

There can be many different types of these organized religious responses, also labeled apocalyptic movements, but they often have certain features in common. The millenarian movement usually crystallizes around a charismatic leader who is regarded as specially endowed by the supernatural to lead his followers to accomplish group goals. The leaders of millenarian movements in Palestine were often labeled "prophets" or "messiahs" because they were thought by their followers (and themselves) to have been chosen by God and endowed with supernatural powers, like the prophets and kings of old, to pave the way for the full realization of the eschatological rule of God. Palestinian millenarian movements were, in the full sense of the term, "revitalistic" movements (a term favored by contemporary anthropologists) whose purpose was the revival of ancient Israelite religious and nationalistic ideals within an eschatological framework.

As we focus on the subject of prophets and prophecy within such movements, two important factors should be kept in mind: (1) "Prophetic" or "messianic" leaders who might arise were expected to conform to various preconceived images of what such eschatological figures should say and do. Consequently, actual charismatic leaders of millenarian movements in Palestine appear to have consciously played out the eschatological roles which tradition assigned them. (2) The role of the prophet as a religious specialist who could deliver divinely inspired messages from God to the people (e.g. the classical Israelite prophets) is too narrow and confining to be an accurate description of the eschatological prophet or messiah of Jewish apocalyptic movements. The eschatological prophet/messiah has a distinctive social function in that both what he says and what he does form a unity which provides supernatural legitimation for himself and for the group which has crystallized about him. In other words, prophecy and wonder-working go hand in hand. Before discussing the types of millenarian movements which arose in Palestine during the late Second Temple period (and shortly thereafter), we shall first sketch the various images of eschatological prophets and messiahs current during that period.

B. IMAGES OF ESCHATOLOGICAL DELIVERERS

1. Messianic Deliverers.

One of the central features of apocalyptic eschatology was the programmatic belief that God would climactically intervene in human affairs to defeat and punish the wicked (pagan oppressors and reprobate Jews) and deliver the righteous (Israel or a group within Israel). He would also restore and purify Jerusalem and the temple, gather the scattered people together, and inaugurate a golden age. This eschatological program could be effected directly by God himself or indirectly through a specially chosen human agent called a "messiah" (from *mashiaḥ*), which means "anointed one." This title was derived from the ancient Israelite practice of installing kings and high priests in office with a ritual which included an anointing with oil. The phrase "Yahweh's anointed" is applied to Samuel the prophet-priest (1 Sam. 24:6, 10; 26:16; 2 Sam. 1:14, 16), to David (2 Sam. 19:21; 23:1), and to his royal successors (Lam. 4:20), but never to an eschatological deliverer. Prophets could also be anointed, though not within the framework of official institutions (1 Kgs. 19:16; Sir. 48:8), and referred to as "anointed ones" (Ps. 105:15; CD 2:12; 6:1; 1QM 11:7-8; 11QMelch 18).

When the eschatological program of divine intervention is effected by God himself, his tasks are usually conceived in terms of ancient Canaanite and Israelite combat myths in which Yahweh is depicted as a divine warrior.[134] When Yahweh's role is taken over by a human agent who is a descendant of the Davidic house, elements of the divine warrior myth are assimilated to the expectation of an eschatological restoration of the greatness of Israel under the leadership of an ideal heir of David.[135] In yet a third type of eschatology, Yahweh's role is taken over by a transcendent deliverer (e.g. "one like a son of man," Dan. 7:13-14). In such instances a greater degree of assimilation has taken place between the divine warrior pattern and the national hope for the restoration of the people of Israel through the Davidic monarchy, with an emphasis on the former. The image of the transcendent deliverer, a relatively rare image in Judaism, may have been popular in antimonarchical or anti-Hasmonean circles (e.g. Daniel), or as a response to the apparent impossibility of the prospects of a national restoration (4 Ezra 13; 1 Enoch 37-71).

The royal messianic ideology arose in response to the Davidic covenant, regarded as unconditional and eternal (2 Sam. 7; Ps. 89; 132:11-12; cf. 1 Macc. 2:57), in combination with the religious and political idealization of the Davidic reign that had already taken place by the ninth century in Judah (Isa. 7:10-16; 9:1-7; 11:1-9; Mic. 5:2-4). Davidic dynasts were expected to conform to the example set by David himself, and when they did not the desire for such model rulers was projected into the future

(Jer. 23:5-6; 33:14-22). Ezekiel even expressed the hope that David himself would appear (Ezek. 34:20-31). At the end of the sixth century, two generations after the destruction of the temple by the Babylonians in 587 B.C., the theocratic hopes of the prophets Haggai and Zechariah were quickened by the prospect of the restoration of the Davidic monarchy through Zerubbabel and the possibility of rebuilding the temple (Hag. 2:23; Zech. 3:8-10; 4:7; 6:9-14). However, the first of these expectations was disappointed. By the late Second Temple period the expectation of an eschatological Davidic messiah had permeated Palestinian Judaism.[136] The Davidic messiah of popular expectation was conceived as a military figure whose primary tasks were the defeat of Israel's enemies, the purification of Jerusalem and the temple, and the ingathering of dispersed Israelites as a prelude for a golden age. This messianic figure did not function as a prophet, a preacher of repentance, or a miracle worker.[137]

The expectation of a priestly or Levitical messiah may have had its origin in Zech. 4:14, where Joshua the high priest and Zerubbabel are called "sons of oil," i.e. "anointed ones."[138] These figures played a joint role in Haggai and Zechariah's eschatological vision of restoration. Following that model, the figures of the priestly messiah and the royal messiah are found side by side in the Testaments of the XII Patriarchs (e.g. Test. Reub. 6:5-12; Test. Levi 18:2-9)[139] and in the literature produced by the Qumran community (1QS 9:10-11; 1QSa 12-17; cf. CD 19:10-11; 20:1).[140] In these contexts the priestly messiah is consistently accorded a superior position. This combination of two quite different messianic types functions to bring more purely religious ideals into conjunction with nationalistic and political hopes. If the Qumran community originated in a secession of a group of Hasidim from the Hasmoneans, the idealized relationship between the eschatological deliverers may reflect not only an anti-Hasmonean stance, but also a projection into the future of the actual leadership structure of their community.

Two conceptions of the nature of eschatological deliverers were formerly carefully distinguished by scholars. The earthly, human, Davidic messiah, whose role was primarily military, nationalistic, and political, was contrasted with the transcendent, heavenly, messianic deliverer commonly designated as the "Son of man."[141] Yet these two messianic types are not really separable, for the Son of man traditions in Jewish apocalyptic represent a "transcendental transformation" of Davidic messianic traditions.[142] The designation "Son of man" (Heb. ben-'adam; Aram. bar-'enash) is first applied to a transcendental eschatological redeemer figure in Dan. 7:13-14:

> I saw in the night visions, and behold, with the clouds of heaven there came one like a son of man, and he came to the Ancient of Days and was presented before him. And to him was given dominion and glory and kingdom, that all peoples, nations, and languages should serve him; his dominion is an everlasting dominion, which shall not pass away, and his kingdom one that shall not be destroyed.

During the last quarter of the first century A.D. the designation "son of man" is used as a messianic title in the canonical gospels (ca. A.D. 70-100) and in the sixth vision of the apocalypse of Ezra (4 Ezra 13, after A.D. 70).[143] The designation is also used of a heavenly redeemer figure in the Similitudes of Enoch (1 Enoch 37-71, possibly after A.D. 70), but not in a titular sense.[144] In spite of the fact that each of these sources makes use of the Son of man tradition found in Dan. 7:13-14,[145] it is likely that they were also influenced by a transcendent Son of man tradition which emerged between the composition of Daniel (ca. 168-165 B.C.) and the formation of the Christian and Jewish apocalyptic Son of man traditions during the first century A.D.[146]

2. Prophetic Deliverers.

While the images of messianic deliverers focus on the task of the restoration of Israel and the inauguration of a golden age, the various conceptions of prophetic deliverers either minimize or ignore that task. Distinctions between the eschatological prophet and the Davidic messiah were often vague,[147] though at times they could be sharply contrasted (as in the Qumran community's distinction between the prophet and the messiahs of Aaron and Israel in 1QS 9:10-11). Generally, however, these eschatological deliverers are assigned distinct functions, though these functions are combined by placing various eschatological deliverers in relationship with each other. While the Davidic messiah was rarely if ever connected with prophesying (i.e. predicting the future), preaching repentance and reconciliation, and performing miracles, those tasks form the basic functions of the eschatological prophets. From the perspective of late Second Temple Judaism the functions of the eschatological prophets corresponded to those of the ancient Israelite prophets. OT prophecy was regarded as having two functions: prediction of the future and rebuke.[148] The classical OT prophets were not miracle workers, yet in legends about the prophets, such as those in the *Vitae Prophetarum* ("The Lives of the Prophets"), a collection of thumbnail biographies (first century A.D.) Jeremiah, Ezekiel, and Zechariah are depicted as miracle workers.[149] Earlier OT prophets such as Moses, Elijah, and Elisha are described as both inspired spokesmen for Yahweh and miracle workers. In Rabbinic Judaism prophecy was subordinate to the Torah,[150] a view which was common during the late Second Temple period. The OT depicts Moses as both lawgiver and prophet, and later prophets such as Elijah (1 Macc. 2:58) and Jeremiah (2 Macc. 2:1-9) are considered zealots for and guardians of the Torah. Eschatological prophets were consequently regarded as specially gifted for the interpretation of the Torah (1 Macc. 4:46). Ancient prophets were also regarded as effective intercessors between man and God (Jeremiah in 2 Macc. 15:14; Elijah in Jas. 5:17; Rom. 11:2-4), and eschatological prophets were expected to play a similar role.

Several places in the gospels refer to popular opinions on the true identity of John the Baptist and Jesus. John is asked if he is Elijah or *the* prophet (John 1:19-23), and Jesus is variously regarded as John the Baptist *redivivus*, Elijah, Jeremiah, or one of the prophets (Mark 6:14-15; 8:27-30; Matt. 16:13-16). In the Fourth Gospel Jesus is thought by some to be *the* prophet, a probable reference to the expectation of a Mosaic eschatological prophet (John 6:14-15; 7:40-41). These references, together with those in 1 Macc. 4:46; 14:41; Philo *De spec. leg.* i.65, indicate that the expectation of various types of eschatological prophets was widespread in Palestine during the late Second Temple period. In the Fourth Gospel John the Baptist's identity as an eschatological prophet is tied to his baptizing activity (John 1:24).[151] Jesus is regarded as a prophet on the basis of the miracles which were attributed to him (Mark 6:14-15; Luke 7:16; 24:19; John 6:14), as well as on the basis of the message he proclaimed (Luke 24:19; John 7:40).

The return of the "shamanistic" Israelite prophet Elijah was one very popular form of the expectation of the eschatological prophet.[152] Even in modern Jewish passover celebrations a cup of wine is poured for Elijah and the door opened for his arrival; a popular song sung during such seders is "Eliyahu ha-Nabi" ("Elijah the

Prophet"). According to tradition Elijah did not die but was taken up into heaven alive in a whirlwind (2 Kgs. 2:9-12; Sir. 48:9, 12a; 1 Enoch 89:52; 1 Macc. 2:58). This tradition made it possible to designate the messenger who will prepare the way before Yahweh (Mal. 3:1) as the returned Elijah in Mal. 4:5-6 (MT 3:23-24):

> Behold, I will send you Elijah the prophet before the great and terrible day of the Lord comes. And he will turn the hearts of the fathers to their children and the hearts of children to their fathers, lest I come and smite the land with a curse.

It is possible, but not demonstrable, that this is a conscious interpretation of Deut. 18:15-18, which refers to the coming of a prophet like Moses. Both Mal. 3:1 and 4:5-6 regard Elijah as the forerunner of Yahweh himself. According to 4 Ezra 6:26 Elijah and Enoch (who also did not experience death, Gen. 5:24; Sir. 44:6; Wis. 4:10) jointly prepare for the visitation of God. By the late Second Temple period the eschatological Elijah began to be regarded as a forerunner of the messiah. In what is probably the earliest reference to this function, 1 Enoch 90:31, he is associated in this task with Enoch. Elijah alone plays the role of the forerunner of the messiah according to Mark 9:11, while the earliest evidence apart from 1 Enoch 90:31 and the gospels is reflected in Justin's *Dialogue with Trypho* (8:3-4; 49:1; 110:1), written ca. 150.[153] The tasks of the eschatological Elijah, when synthesized, include: (1) the restoration (*apokatastasis*) of all things (LXX Mal. 3:23; Mark 9:12; Matt. 17:11), (2) intercession for the people of God to avoid the wrath of Yahweh (Mal. 4:6b; Sir. 48:10a), (3) the preaching of repentance and reconciliation in Israel (Mal. 4:5; Sir. 48:10b), (4) the gathering of dispersed Israelites (Sir. 48:10b), and probably (5) the performance of miracles (1 Kgs. 17:14-16, 17-24; 18:36-40; 2 Kgs. 2:8; Sir. 48:3-5; Jas. 5:17).

A second way of conceptualizing the eschatological prophet was in terms of the expectation of a prophet like Moses or even Moses *redivivus*.[154] The basis for this expectation is found in Deut. 18:15, 18:

> The Lord your God will raise up for you a prophet like me from among you, from your brethren — him you shall heed. . . . I will raise up for them a prophet like you from among their brethren; and I will put my words in his mouth, and he shall speak to them all that I command him.

Originally this passage probably referred to the series of prophets that would arise after Moses.[155] The first and most obvious successor to Moses in this role would be Joshua (Deut. 34:9; Josh. 1:5; Sir. 46:1), but in a codicil in Deut. 34:10-12 this is effectively denied:

> And *there has not arisen a prophet since in Israel like Moses* [italics added], whom the Lord knew face to face, none like him for all the signs and the wonders which the Lord sent him to do in the land of Egypt, to Pharaoh and to all his servants and to all his land, and for all the great and terrible deeds which Moses wrought in the sight of all Israel.

The entire succession of prophets since Moses is placed on a decidedly lower level than that of Moses himself;[156] this passage is almost certainly an allusion to Deut. 18:15-18.[157] It is not unlikely that the conception of the eschatological Elijah in Mal. 4:5-6 (MT 3:23-24) had its basis in Deut. 18:15-18, and it also appears that the prophetic features of the Suffering Servant of Isa. 40-55 (42:1-4; 49:1-6; 50:4-9; 52:13-53:12) are patterned after the expectation of a prophet like Moses.[158] Rabbinic literature has scarcely a trace of an eschatological interpretation of Deut. 18:15-18. Rather, the rabbis applied the passage to historical individuals like Jeremiah.[159] The eschatological prophet like Moses was not ordinarily regarded as the messiah in Palestinian Judaism,[160] but the combination of prophetic and royal features appears to have characterized both Samaritan Hellenistic Jewish traditions about Moses.[161] The earliest clear eschatological application of Deut. 18:15-18 is found in Qumran's Manual of Discipline compiled during the first century B.C. In 1QS 9:10-11 we read:

> And they shall be governed by the first ordinances in which the members of the Community began their instruction, until the coming of the Prophet [nby'] and the Anointed [mshyḥy] of Aaron and Israel.[162]

It is clear from this passage and from 4QTestim 1-20 (where three OT passages are quoted, Deut. 18:18-19; Num. 24:15-17; Deut. 33:8-11, which are prophetic anticipations of the prophet and the messiahs of Israel and Aaron) that the prophet must be the eschatological Mosaic prophet.[163] The Qumran sectarians regarded the Teacher of Righteousness as the eschatological Mosaic prophet,[164] just as some early Christians regarded Jesus as that prophet.[165] The Mosaic eschatological prophet combines the roles of savior and redeemer, prophet, sufferer, definitive interpreter of the Torah, and miracle worker.[166]

A number of passages in the gospels indicate that the conception of an eschatological prophet could be an inchoate figure representing a pastiche of ideas drawn from various messianic and prophetic images (Mark 6:15b; 8:28c; 7:16, 39; 24:19; John 4:19). In Matt. 16:14 (a Matthean alteration of Mark 8:28), the name "Jeremiah" is inserted into the list of possible identities of Jesus. This is one of the few references in Jewish or early Christian literature to the expectation of a Jeremiah *redivivus,* though he was more popular in Palestinian Judaism.[167]

3. Summary.

Various types of eschatological deliverers were current in Palestinian Judaism during the late Second Temple period. They all fit rather neatly into one of two categories, "messiah" or "prophet." The figure of the messiah was conceptualized as an ideal king and legitimate heir to the Davidic throne who would defeat Israel's enemies, restore Jerusalem and the temple, and gather the dispersed of Israel. Eschatological prophets, on the other hand, were expected to play a more thoroughly religious role through such activities as the preaching of repentance in preparation for the Day of Yahweh, the definitive interpretation of the Torah, intercession with Yahweh on behalf of Israel, and the performance of miracles as a display of supernatural power and authority. Prophesying, in the sense of predicting judgment or salvation in consequence of present or past behavior, is not part of the role of eschatological prophets. This may be attributed partially to the view that the eschatological prophet is himself part of the fulfilment of OT prophecy.

C. TYPES OF EARLY JEWISH MILLENARIAN MOVEMENTS

The various images of eschatological deliverers that we have just considered represent strands of early Jewish expectation, not historical realities. These images are not without importance, however, for if historical individuals wished to play the role of an eschatological deliverer (or if his followers wished to attribute such a role to him) they had to structure that role in accordance with traditional eschatological expectations. During the century and a half prior to the defeat of Bar Kosiba by the Romans in A.D. 135, a number of millenarian movements arose in Palestine. All these movements appear to have been formed around charismatic leaders of various types. Although many of these leaders regarded themselves as prophets (or were so regarded by their constituency), none except Bar Kosiba claimed to be the messiah.[168]

Millenarian movements did not always follow identical patterns, and the kinds of response exhibited by early Jewish millenarian movements fall into several types.[169] The movement associated with John the Baptist exhibited a *conversionist* response to the world, i.e. the central problem was thought to lie in human corruption. Repentance and conversion were the entrance requirements of the movement, whose members constituted an elect group which would be delivered when God came to judge the world. John, of course, was widely regarded as an eschatological prophet.[170] The Teacher of Righteousness, who was regarded by both himself and his followers as an eschatological Mosaic prophet, was responsible for the formation of the Qumran community. He and his community exhibit an *introversionist* response to the world, i.e. they regarded the world as irredeemably corrupt and sought salvation by withdrawing from it in preparation for the imminent visitation of God. Jesus of Nazareth also regarded himself as a prophet, and his followers tended to apply almost all the eschatological deliverer categories to him in the decades after his crucifixion.[171] The Jesus movement exhibits both the *conversionist* and the *thaumaturgical* modes of response to the world. The conversionist element indicates the close relationship between the Jesus movement and the John the Baptist movement, while the thaumaturgical element is found only in the former. The thaumaturgical response is characterized by an emphasis on relieving suffering individuals through miraculous healings and exorcisms. Early Christianity, that form of the Jesus movement which survived the crisis of the founder's execution by the Romans, began its existence by again combining the *thaumaturgical* with the *conversionist* response to the world, though it rapidly changed as it became increasingly institutionalized.[172]

Josephus informs us of a number of millenarian movements which conform to a type quite different from any of the movements described above — the revolutionist response. This response is based on the supposition that only the destruction of the existing order can bring salvation; God alone is able to accomplish this, but he will act very soon and his people may participate in the overthrow of the evil order. The leaders (designated "Jewish sign prophets" by P. W. Barnett) and their movements share several common features: the leader's self-conception of "prophet," the attempt to perform an eschatological "sign," close connection with the wilderness, and the involvement of a large crowd of people.[173] Both the Jewish revolt of A.D. 66-73 (in which the Zealot sect played a central role) and the revolt of Bar Kosiba (who claimed to be the messiah with the support of Rabbi Akiba and the priest Eleazar, a triumvirate reminiscent of 1QS 9:10-11) in A.D. 132-135, can be considered revolutionist responses to intolerable religious and political conditions.[174]

Both Josephus and the NT report the revolt of Theudas (ca. A.D. 44-46),[175] who tried to lead a band of about four hundred followers dryshod over the Jordan River in an apparent attempt to replicate the feat of Joshua (Josh. 3) or possibly Elijah (2 Kgs. 2:6-8). Theudas and his company were attacked and slaughtered by the Romans. Josephus reports that Theudas claimed to be a prophet, but Josephus labels him a charlatan. This revolutionist millenarian movement has a number of fascinating features: (1) Theudas claimed to be a prophet, and in view of the rarity of that label during the late Second Temple period, he must have regarded himself as an *eschatological* prophet. (2) His attempt to replicate the miracle performed by Joshua suggests that he regarded the "prophet like Moses" of Deut. 18:15-18 to be Joshua, and that he conceived of himself as a latter-day Joshua. (3) Theudas combined the claim to predict the future with the claim to be a miracle worker when he told his followers that the Jordan River would part before them. (4) Since the original miracle of the parting of the Jordan was to serve as a sign that the Israelites would be able to expel the Palestinian natives (Josh. 3:10), we may surmise that the miracle intended by Theudas was but the prelude to a holy war against the Romans and their collaborators.

Josephus and the NT also report the revolt of an unnamed Egyptian Jew ca. A.D. 55.[176] He led a band of followers (variously reported as either 4,000 or 30,000 in number) into the wilderness, where he intended to guide them back to the Mount of Olives. At his command the walls of Jerusalem were supposed to collapse, affording them an entrance to the city, which they intended to take over. This Egyptian Jew also claimed to be a prophet and was regarded as such by his followers, though Josephus predictably labels him a "false prophet" and a "charlatan." The brief reports about this short-lived millenarian revolt have a number of significant features: (1) The self-designation "prophet" must be regarded as having eschatological significance. (2) The miracle which the Egyptian Jew intended to perform, the collapse of the walls of Jerusalem, recalls the feat of Joshua at Jericho (Josh. 6:1-21), a feature which again leads us to suspect that Deut. 18:15-18 was thought to refer to Joshua, and that the Egyptian Jew regarded himself as a latter-day prophet like Joshua. (3) Again the ability to predict the future is combined with the ability to perform a wonder. (4) The miracle of the collapse of the walls of Jerusalem is regarded as a prelude to a holy war against the Romans that will be successful, just as the collapse of the walls of Jericho was a prelude to the destruction of the city's inhabitants. (5) A new element in these reports is the trek into the wilderness; the wilderness motif is found in many of these millenarian movements, and is probably a way of reenacting the ancient preconquest experiences of Israel.[177] (6) The apparent antipathy to Jerusalem inherent in his revolt[178] is not directed at the holy city itself so much as against the elements which have polluted both it and the temple. One of the regular functions of the Davidic messiah was the purification of both Jerusalem and the temple, and that objective appears to have been espoused by this movement as well.

Josephus reports a Samaritan revolt in which an unnamed Samaritan led a group of followers to Mount Gerizim in Samaria expecting to recover miraculously the ancient temple vessels which Moses had concealed there (Josephus *Ant.* xviii.85). In Judean tradition Jeremiah had concealed the vessels of the Solomonic temple, and these would be revealed at the end of the age (2 Macc. 2:4-8).[179] Within the framework of Samaritan expectations this Samaritan revolutionary probably regarded himself as the *Taheb* ("coming one"), or Mosaic eschatological prophet.[180] This revolt was also quashed by the Romans. Josephus also reports an earlier revolt, that of Judas the Galilean ca. A.D. 6-9.[181] Judas appears to have been motivated politically, and there is no evidence that he regarded himself as an eschatological figure, though he did presuppose the assistance of God in his cause.

Josephus twice characterizes the activities of millenarian movements in the first century A.D. In *Ant.* xx.167-68 he gives the following summary:

> Moreover, impostors and deceivers [*goētes kai apateōnes anthrōpoi*] called upon the mob to follow them into the desert. For they said that they would show them

unmistakable marvels and signs [*terata kai sēmeia*] that would be wrought in harmony with God's design.

A similar summary is found in *Bell.* ii.259:

Deceivers and impostors [*planoi gar anthrōpoi kai apateōnes*], under the pretence of divine inspiration [*hypo proschēmati theiasmou*] fostering revolutionary changes, they persuaded the multitude to act like madmen, and led them out into the desert under the belief that God would there give them tokens of deliverance [*sēmeia eleutherias*].

The characteristic features of such movements, not all of which are necessarily of the revolutionary type, include the charismatic leadership of an ostensible prophet who probably regards himself as an eschatological figure, the retreat into the wilderness as a kind of *Urzeit-Endzeit* pattern of recapitulating the past, and the prediction of the performance of a legitimating miracle. The function of prophecy in these movements is not simply the communication of inspired verbal messages, but rather the total activity of the prophet as a deliverer sent by God.

Since most of the movements which we have discussed were short-lived, the short prejudicial reports of Josephus and the brief notices in Acts constitute all the information we have on most of these movements. We have more information, however, about the *conversionist* movement of John the Baptist and the *introversionist* movement of the Teacher of Righteousness, and we shall focus on them in the remainder of this section. The *thaumaturgical* and *conversionist* movement represented by Jesus and his followers will be the subject of the next two chapters.

D. JOHN THE BAPTIST

One of the most widely known prophetic figures of early Judaism is John the Baptist, whose activities are reported in Josephus as well as in the NT.[182] John and his followers were part of a much larger pattern of collective behavior labeled the "baptist movement" throughout Syria and Palestine from the second century B.C. to the third century A.D.[183] John proclaimed the imminence of the eschatological judgment and administered a ritual washing (possibly a novel adaptation of proselyte baptism) for those who repented and exhibited changed behavior.[184] Yet the baptismal ritual performed by John was much more than a rite symbolizing divine forgiveness. Like the (initial) ritual bath of the Qumran community, the baptism of John appears to have functioned as a rite of passage to the eschatological community, the true Israel, who alone would be vindicated by God in the Day of Judgment.[185]

The gospels often label John a prophet or raise the question of his prophetic status.[186] The suggestion that John was Elijah is implicit in Mark, developed by Matthew, but rejected by Luke.[187] Twice in Matthew Jesus explicitly identified John with Elijah (11:13-14; 17:10-13):

For all the prophets and the law prophesied until John; and if you are willing to accept it, he is Elijah who is to come [*ho mellōn erchesthai*].

And the disciples asked him, "Then why do the scribes say that first Elijah must come?" He replied, "Elijah does come, and he is to restore all things; but I tell you that Elijah has already come, and they did not know him, but did to him whatever they pleased. So also the Son of man will suffer at their hands." Then the disciples understood that he was speaking to them of John the Baptist.

Josephus gives a very positive assessment of John as a preacher of repentance but does not designate him a prophet; this is not surprising in the light of Josephus' tendency to apply the title "prophet" only to ancient Israelite prophets.[188] Q quite clearly depicts John as both a preacher of repentance and a prophet of judgment.[189] Further, John is depicted as a prophet in a variety of ways: (1) His costume, consisting of a hairy cloak and a leather girdle (Mark 1:6; Matt. 3:4), was distinctive and consciously modeled after the garb of OT prophets (1 Kgs. 19:19; 2 Kgs. 1:8; 2:13-14; Zech. 13:4). (2) The reference in Luke 1:15 to John's being filled with the Spirit from the womb is another way of describing John as a prophet.[190] (3) In Luke 3:2 an OT prophetic revelation formula is used in connection with John: "the word of God came to John the son of Zechariah in the wilderness."[191] (4) John is depicted as boldly rebuking Herod for immorality (Mark 6:17-18) in a manner reminiscent of the classical prophets. (5) While John's message was harsh, it focused on the demand for repentance in a way which recalls the demands for repentance characteristic of the classical prophets.[192] (6) Finally, like the OT prophets John is depicted as addressing all Israel (and Gentiles as well), not just a restricted group within Israel.

Two short prophetic speeches attributed to John and preserved in the synoptic gospels have a strong claim to historicity. The first one which we shall consider was derived by Matthew and Luke from Q (Matt. 3:7-10; Luke 3:7-9). Since the Matthean and Lukan versions of the speech are virtually identical,[193] we arbitrarily quote the text of Matthew:

Address:	You brood of vipers!
Threat:	Who warned you to flee from the wrath to come?
Admonition:	Bear fruit that befits repentance,
	and do not presume to say to yourselves,
	"We have Abraham as our father";
	for I tell you, God is able from these stones to raise up children to Abraham.
Threat (conditional):	Even now the axe is laid to the root of the trees; every tree therefore that does not bear good fruit is cut down and thrown into the fire.

In form this speech bears little resemblance to prophetic speeches in the OT; neither John himself nor early Christian traditionists attempt to pattern this speech to fit OT prophetic models. Further, John speaks on his own authority and does not present his message as a first-person speech of Yahweh, as did the OT prophets. The speech does, however, have some interesting parallels with prophetic speeches in Amos. The pejorative address with which the speech begins resembles similar addresses in Amos 4:1; 8:4. Further, the admonition of John begins with a positive exhortation followed by a prohibition, a pattern also found in Amos 5:4-5. The rhetorical question "Who warned you to flee from the wrath to come?" calls to mind the OT prophetic speech form which has been designated the "summons to flee" (Jer. 4:4-5; 6:1; 48:6-8, 28; 49:8, 30; 50:8-10; 51:6, 45; Zech. 2:6-9).[194] It is as if John is asking those who flocked to him, "Who is the prophet who has advised you to flee from the imminent judgment of God?"

John stands clearly in the apocalyptic tradition in that the judgment he envisions is not a *historical* judgment conceived as a divine punishment for specific transgressions, but an *eschatological* judgment regarded by John as the final and terrifying divine judicial response to the wickedness and corruption of Israel. While the divine visitation itself is both imminent and inescapable, those who truly repent and join the eschatological community of the saved through the baptismal initiation ritual of John will escape the wrath of God.

Luke supplements this speech by appending a parenetic section (Luke 3:10-14):

> And the multitudes asked him, "What then shall we do?" And he answered them, "He who has two coats, let him share with him who has none; and he who has food, let him do likewise." Tax collectors also came to be baptized, and said to him, "Teacher, what shall we do?" And he said to them, "Collect no more than is appointed you." Soldiers also asked him, "And we, what shall we do?" And he said to them, "Rob no one by violence or by false accusation, and be content with your wages."

This parenetic appendix is introduced with the phrase "what then shall we do?", a question which has a formal parallel in Acts 2:37; at the conclusion of Peter's Pentecost sermon the crowd asks, "Brethren, what shall we do?" This Lukan pattern suggests that the evangelist has Christianized John's sermon through the addition of a sequence of exhortations in the form of a dialogue sermon.[195] Matthew appears to have attributed the message of Jesus to John in Matt. 3:2, where John reportedly proclaims: "Repent, for the kingdom of heaven is at hand" (cf. Matt. 4:17; Mark 1:15).

The second prophetic sermon of John the Baptist that we propose to discuss is found in both Mark 1:7-8 and Q (Matt. 3:11-12; Luke 3:16-17). We first quote Mark 1:7-8, followed by Luke 3:16-17:

> And he preached, saying, "After me comes [*erchetai*] he who is mightier than I, the thong of whose sandals I am not worthy to stoop down and untie. I have baptized you with water; but he will baptize you with the Holy Spirit [*pneumati hagiō*].

> I baptize you with water;
> but he who is mightier than I is coming,
> the thong of whose sandals I am not worthy to untie;
> he will baptize you with the Holy Spirit and with fire [*pneumati hagiō kai pyri*].
> His winnowing fork is in his hand, to clear his threshing floor,
> and to gather the wheat into his granary,
> but the chaff he will burn with unquenchable fire.

While the precise relationship between John the Baptist and Jesus is perhaps an insoluble problem,[196] a comparative study of the various traditions regarding John in the four gospels makes it evident that John has been "Christianized," i.e. carefully integrated into the history of salvation stretching from the OT to Christ. The gospels frequently refer to John's prediction of the "coming one" (Mark 1:7; Matt. 3:11; Luke 3:16; John 1:15, 27, 30; cf. Acts 13:25), and within the gospels and Acts the "coming one" is certainly identified with Jesus. John is assigned the role of Elijah *redivivus,* the eschatological prophet who will prepare the way for the Davidic messiah (Matt. 17:10-13; Mark 1:2-3 and parallels). Historically, however, John was probably referring to the future eschatological judge without specific reference to Jesus.[197] Originally the eschatological prophet Elijah was regarded as the forerunner of Yahweh himself (Mal. 3:1; 4:5-6); however, it is clear that the "coming one" referred to by

John could not be God but must be an eschatological judge and deliverer.[198] Complementing the ministry of John, this eschatological judge will "baptize" with the Holy Spirit and with fire, i.e. will confer salvation and judgment.[199] The reference to the Holy Spirit, if original (note that Mark 1:8 omits "fire"), referred neither to Christian baptism nor to the Spirit in a later Trinitarian sense. Some have interpreted "spirit" (regarding the adjective "holy" as a Christian gloss) to mean "wind"; the phrase "wind and fire" is then taken to include two related terms for judgment.[200] A case can be made for the originality of the phrase "holy spirit," however, since it can readily be understood in a first-century Palestinian setting as the kind of eschatological purification through the spirit of God referred to in 1QS 4:20-21:

> Then God will cleanse by His Truth all the works of every man, and will purify for Himself the (bodily) fabric of every man, to banish all Spirit of perversity from his members, and purify him of all wicked deeds by the Spirit of holiness; and He will cause the Spirit of Truth to gush forth upon him like lustral water.[201]

The second prophetic speech of John also defies categorization in terms of the major OT prophetic speech forms.[202] John speaks on his own authority and does not legitimate his message by using a messenger formula or an oath formula, nor is his proclamation couched in the first person of God. The speech may be regarded as a salvation-judgment speech, however, since it refers to the future status of those who have repented and been baptized by John (the "wheat") and those who have not (the "chaff"). The speech is addressed to followers of John, whereas the first speech we considered was addressed to outsiders (though Matthew applies it specifically to the Pharisees and Sadducees, Matt. 3:7). John was widely regarded as a prophet (Mark 11:32) primarily because he denounced immorality and wickedness and demanded repentance in the conviction that a divinely appointed eschatological judge was about to come and punish the ungodly.

E. THE TEACHER OF RIGHTEOUSNESS

The Teacher of Righteousness was the generic title for the founder of the Qumran community and his successors. The community, more or less identical with the Essenes described by Josephus, Philo, and other ancient authors, began its existence sometime during the second half of the second century B.C. and was obliterated by the Romans during the first Jewish revolt (A.D. 66-73). Although the individuality of the Teacher of Righteousness is shrouded in obscurity, many scholars agree that he regarded himself as the Mosaic eschatological prophet.[203] The rigorous study and observance of the Torah constituted the primary rationale for the existence of the community. During the latter part of the second century B.C. they had withdrawn from Palestinian society to form an introversionist center where moral and ritual impurities could be avoided and devotion to the study and interpretation of the Torah and the Prophets could be pursued without interruption. From its foundation to its dissolution two centuries later the community regarded itself as living in the last days. Their society was rigidly structured on the basis of OT models and offices,[204] for they constituted the elect people of God who alone would be delivered when God intervened to bring history to a close.

The Teacher of Righteousness is never explicitly called a "prophet" (nby') in any of the literature from Qumran, but he appears to have been regarded as such by the community. He claimed the possession of the Holy Spirit (1QH 7:6-7; 14:26; 17:26), which gave him knowledge and insight (1QH 12:11-12; 13:18-19), particularly in the understanding of mysteries (1QH 2:10, 13). The Qumran community as a whole was convinced that the Spirit of God, an eschatological gift, was present and active in their midst.[205]

Gert Jeremias summarizes the prophetic character of the Teacher of Righteousness in this manner:

> The Teacher of Righteousness is a prophet of God. All of the characteristic features of a prophet apply to him. Like the prophets he receives his instructions from the mouth of God. He has been selected by God to declare to the last generation the coming act of God. He has been sent and commissioned by God. His word necessitates a decision on the part of those who hear it. Whoever does not carry out the words of the Teacher, he is guilty and faces judgment. Whoever observes the word of the Teacher will also be saved from final judgment.[206]

One of the more significant functions of the Teacher of Righteousness was that of an interpreter of the Torah and the Prophets. In 1QpHab 2:8-9 he is described as "the Priest whom God placed in [the House of Jud]ah to explain all the words of His servants the Prophets."[207] In a frequently quoted passage in the Habakkuk Commentary we read (1QpHab 7:1-5):

> And God told Habakkuk to write down the things which will come to pass in the last generation, but the consummation of time He made not known to him. And as for that which He said, *That he may read it easily that reads it* [Hab. 2:2b], the explanation of this concerns the Teacher of Righteousness to whom God made known all the Mysteries of the words of His servants the Prophets.

Here the words of the prophets are mysteries or secrets (*rzym*) which require the inspired interpretation of the Teacher of Righteousness. He claimed that form of divine inspiration which enabled him to discern the precise time of the fulfilment of earlier prophecies.[208]

Josephus also attests the close relationship between prophecy and biblical study among the Essenes (*Bell.* ii.159):

> There are some among them who profess to foretell the future, being versed from their early years in holy books, various forms of purification and apophthegms of prophets; and seldom, if ever, do they err in their predictions.

The inspired biblical interpretation practiced by the Qumran community has been categorized as charismatic exegesis. Charismatic exegesis is a form of biblical interpretation based on two guiding principles: (1) The biblical text contains hidden or symbolic meanings which can be revealed only by an interpreter with divine insight, and (2) The true meaning of the text concerns eschatological prophecies which the interpreter believes are being fulfilled in the events and persons connected with the religious movement to which he belongs.

Members of the Qumran community produced a distinctive form of biblical commentaries which have been designated *pesher*-commentaries or *pesharim* (from Heb. *pesharim,* "interpretations"). In these *pesher*-commentaries the interpreters regarded themselves as living in the last days and approached the biblical text in terms of its secret or mystical significance. In Qumran the Danielic language for dream interpretation was appropriated for the interpretation of scripture.[209] In OT mantic wisdom (as distinguished from proverbial wisdom) the wise man's skill, which derives from God and not himself, is applied to the interpretation of dreams and visions (Joseph in Gen. 40-41, and Daniel in Dan. 2; 4-5).[210] Divine revelation in the form of enigmatic dreams constitutes an insoluble mystery (raz) until the true interpretation (pesher) is revealed (Dan. 2:30; 4:9; cf. 1QpHab 7:1-5).[211] In the pesher-commentaries the meaning of the text is always related directly to the lifetime of the interpreter and the eschatological role of the sect to which he belongs. The procedure of the interpreter is to quote a few lines of the biblical text and then to introduce his explanation with such phrases as "the interpretation of this is that...," or "the interpretation of this word concerns. ..." Most early Jewish methods of biblical interpretation do not claim any form of divine inspiration or illumination, but the pesher-commentaries are a striking exception.

As an illustration of the kind of eschatological interpretation characteristic of the pesher-commentaries, we quote the following lengthy section from the Habakkuk Commentary (1QpHab 1:16-2:15):

Habakkuk 1:5:	1:16	[Look among the nations and see, and you will be astounded, bewildered. For I will do a work in your days; you will not believe when]
	2:1	it is told.
Interpretation:		[The explanation of this concerns (pshr hdbr 'l)] those who have betrayed with the Man
	2:2	of Lies; for they [have] not [believed the words] of the Teacher of Righteousness (which he received) from the mouth
	2:3	of God. And (it concerns) those who betra[yed the] New [Covenant]; for they did not
	2:4	believe in the Covenant of God [and profaned] His [H]oly Nam[e].
Interpretation:	2:5	And likewise, the explanation of this word [concerns (pshr hdbr 'l) those who will be]tray at the end
	2:6	of days: they are the violent ... who will not believe
	2:7	when they hear all the things which will be[fall] the last generation from the mouth
	2:8	of the Priest whom God placed in [the House of Jud]ah to explain all
	2:9	the words of His servants the Prophets, by [whose hand] God has told
	2:10	all that will befall His people and [the nations].
Habakkuk 1:6a:		[F]or behold, I rouse
	2:11	the Chaldeans, that cru[el and has]ty nation.
Interpretation:	2:12	The explanation of this concerns [pshr 'l] the Kittim w[ho are] quick and valiant
	2:13	in battle, causing many to perish; [and the earth will fall] under the dominion

2:14 of the Kittim. And the wi[cked will see i]t but will not believe

2:15 in the precepts of [God. . . .][212]

While Habakkuk describes the invasion of the Babylonians (i.e. Chaldeans) in 587 B.C., the interpreter applies these prophecies to the invasion of the Kittim (i.e. Romans), to whom Palestine became subject in 63 B.C. The author sees reality polarized between the Teacher of Righteousness and those who have accepted his words (also called "the Priest whom God placed in the House of Judah"), and the Man of Lies and those who, with him, have betrayed the New Covenant and rejected the words of the Teacher of Righteousness.

Unlike John the Baptist, the Teacher of Righteousness claimed inspiration. Yet while John preached the necessity of repentance in the face of the imminent judgment of God, the Teacher of Righteousness used the gift of charismatic exegesis to unravel the eschatological mysteries which lay buried in the biblical texts. The central role of the Teacher of Righteousness for the Qumran community was that of "the seeker of the Law" (*drsh htwrh*), i.e. the definitive interpreter of the Law and the Prophets.

F. ISOLATED ESCHATOLOGICAL PROPHECY

Eschatological prophecy was not a function limited to the charismatic leaders of millenarian movements during the late Second Temple period. There are a number of examples of eschatological prophecies which were pronounced by individuals who were not part of the leadership of such religious movements, or, indeed, who were not even members of such groups. In each instance such prophecies appear to have been uttered in situations of great social or political stress.

1. Joshua ben Ananiah.

During the festival of Sukkoth held in Jerusalem during the fall of A.D. 62, a coarse (*agroikos*) peasant pilgrim at the feast named Joshua ben Ananiah was standing in the temple when he suddenly began to cry out (*exapinēs anaboan ērxato*):

> A voice [*phōnē*] from the east,
> a voice from the west,
> a voice from the four winds.
>
> A voice against [*epi*] Jerusalem and the temple,
> a voice against the bridegroom and the bride,
> a voice against all the people.[213]

This episode occurred during the procuratorship of Albinus (ca. A.D. 62-64), whose total incompetence, cruelty, and greed were significant factors leading to the Jewish revolt of A.D. 66.[214] Josephus reports that Joseph, apparently remaining in Jerusalem, repeated this oracle of doom incessantly. This led to his arrest, torture, and interrogation by Albinus; but when his only response was the cry "Woe to Jerusalem!" he was regarded as insane (*daimoniōteron to kinēma; katagnous manian*) and released. Thereafter he frequently reiterated the lament "Woe to Jerusalem!" for seven years and five months. Toward the end of the siege of Jerusalem in the spring of A.D. 70, immediately before he was killed by a Roman missile, he announced: "Woe [*aiai*] again to the city and the people and temple, and woe also to me."

The form of the first oracle of doom uttered by Joshua ben Ananiah is clearly poetic. It consists of two strophes, each composed of three stichs. The stichs in each strophe are all in synonymous parallelism. The first strophe deals with where the "voice" comes from, while the second provides the significance of the "voice." Further, the third line in each strophe summarizes the content of the unit. As an oracle of doom this speech is totally different from both OT and early Jewish forms of prophetic speech or apocalyptic writing. The utterance is not legitimated by an introductory or concluding formula but by the behavior of Joshua. He "cried out" (*anaboan; kekragōs; ekekragei; eboa*) his message, not once but repeatedly (cf. Acts. 16:16-18); such action was often regarded as a sign of possession trance. As a country peasant he appeared a rather unlikely candidate for a prophet, a fact which probably increased his credibility; his bizarre behavior was attributed to demon possession (*daimoniōteron to kinēma*). These factors combine to indicate that through the exhibition of possession behavior Joshua ben Ananiah's message received a measure of credibility.

The content of the speech suggests that a historical calamity is about to befall Jerusalem and its inhabitants and that this fate cannot be avoided. The speech resembles the woe oracles of the OT in that the pronouncement of woe itself does not specify the nature of the anticipated doom; however, it is unlike the woe oracle in that it does not specify the nature of the threat in a second part of the oracle.[215] The pronouncements of woe which Joshua uttered during his arrest and after his release do not conform to the form of the woe oracle either in the OT or in Jewish apocalyptic literature.[216] In form they are simply the kind of lamentation which is appropriate in settings of real or anticipated grief, loss, or calamity (cf. Ps. 120:5; Isa. 6:5; Mic. 7:1).

Two features of Joshua's oracle of doom bear closer examination: (1) its utterance in the temple (during the Sukkoth festival) and polemic against the temple and Jerusalem and its inhabitants, and (2) the significance of the "voice" which is referred to six times within the framework of this short speech. In the OT and in early Jewish and early Christian literature it is not unusual for references to be made to the reception of divine revelations in sanctuaries or in the temple in Jerusalem.[217] Yet only Jeremiah stood within the temple itself and there prophesied its destruction (Jer. 7:1-15; 26:4-9). Jesus also symbolically announced the overthrow of the temple through the act of "cleansing" it.[218] Many other OT prophets were critical of the temple cult, and occasionally they announced the downfall of both the city and the temple.[219] The antipathy of Joshua ben Ananiah's oracle toward Jerusalem and the temple reflects the opposition which many millenarian movements had toward the political and religious establishment of Jerusalem.[220]

The "voice" to which the oracle of doom refers is described six times as coming from all directions and as boding ill for Jerusalem, its inhabitants, and the temple. Joshua has "heard" this voice and announces publicly what he has learned. The "voice" is not that of Joshua himself, though he articulates it in his oracle of doom. What is the significance of the "voice"? In the OT and early Judaism the word "voice" (*qol*) is used in a great variety of ways;[221] in settings in which a voice signifies divine judgment (as in the speech of Joshua) it is always the "voice of the Lord" (1 Sam. 7:10; Ps. 29:3, 4, 5, 7, 8, 9; 46:6 [MT 7]; Isa. 29:6; 30:30-31; Jer. 25:30; Amos 1:2). Early Judaism tended to use the term "voice" for "voice of God," or as a surrogate in order to avoid explicitly connecting God with the act of speaking. In Jewish apocalyptic literature the mysterious voices which occasionally communicate divine revelation are often the voice of God (1 Enoch 13:8; 65:4; 2 Bar. 13:1; 22:1; 4 Ezra 6:17-18). Josephus himself exhibits a tendency to avoid explicit references to God speaking and substitutes the terms "voice" or "divine voice" (phōnē theia) in his retelling of the biblical accounts.[222] The bat qol ("daughter of a voice," or "echo of a voice") is frequently referred to in rabbinic literature, where it is sometimes but not always to be construed as the voice of God.[223] It often functions to express the judgment of God. The bat qol, of course, had prerabbinic antecedents. In Num. 7:89 Moses is said to have heard a voice from between the two cherubim; the voice turns out to be the voice of God. According to the report in Josephus (Ant. xiii.282) Hyrcanus heard a voice in the temple that delivered an oracle to him. Similarly at the baptism (Mark 1:11 par.) and transfiguration (Mark 9:7 par.) of Jesus, a voice from heaven and a voice out of the cloud reveals the divine status of Jesus; in both cases the speaker is God.

In sum, during the late Second Temple period the term "voice" was often used as a surrogate for God speaking, and in the OT the "voice of the Lord" was often used in contexts in which divine judgment was in view. When Joshua ben Ananiah repeatedly refers to the "voice" coming from all directions (cf. Ps. 29) with negative implications, he is using a well-known, recognizable idiom which refers to the voice of God pronouncing judgment. By repeating the voice he has "heard" Joshua Ben Ananiah is the voice. Remarkably, OT prophets do not refer to hearing the voice of Yahweh as a prelude to their announcement of the word of Yahweh. Yet Joshua ben Ananiah has "heard" the voice of God, and he has heard it where it was frequently heard, in the temple.

2. During the Siege of Herod.

When the Parthians invaded Palestine, they set a native Hasmonean prince, Antigonus, on the throne as a vassal (40-37 B.C.). At the same time the Roman senate declared Herod, son of Antipater, "king of the Jews." Upon returning to Palestine, Herod took three years to recapture his kingdom. In the spring of 37 B.C. Herod was besieging Jerusalem, and Josephus reports how the population responded:

> Throughout the city the agitation of the Jewish populace showed itself in various forms. The weaker gathered near the temple and became divinely possessed [edaimonia] and composed many oracles [polla theiōdesteron . . . elogopoiei] fit for the crisis.[224]

Although none of these oracles is quoted, it is clear that they were uttered in response to a crisis. In this brief notice, prophetic speech appears connected with proximity to the temple and with the phenomenon of possession trance. These features occur frequently in early Jewish prophecy.

3. During the Roman Siege.

Joshua ben Ananiah was not the only one to prophesy during the Roman siege of Jerusalem. During the last days of the siege, in August-September of A.D. 70, Josephus reports that some six thousand people who had taken refuge in one of the porticoes of the temple were incinerated when the the building was put to the torch by the Romans.[225] Josephus elaborates on the cause of this disaster:

> They owed their destruction to a false prophet [pseudoprophētēs] who had on that day proclaimed [kēryxas] to the people in the city that God commanded [ho theos . . . keleuei] them to go up to the temple court, to receive there the signs of deliverance [ta sēmeia tēs sōtērias].[226]

Again, this prophecy is uttered in a critical situation in which defeat and death appear certain. This prophecy, which is only paraphrased, appears to have been introduced by the formula "God commands," and the substance of the oracle was probably phrased as the indirect speech of God. The prediction of "signs of deliverance" appears to have been a major feature of prophetic speech within the context of a millenarian movement as well as in other settings.[227] The close relationship between prophecy and temple should also be noted. Josephus regards the man as a false prophet because he knows (with historical hindsight) that Jerusalem and the temple were doomed.

That this was not the only prophetic activity which occurred (in addition to that of Joshua ben Ananiah) is indicated by an explanatory excursus which Josephus inserts immediately after the event just discussed:

> At that time many prophets [prophētai] were planted among the people by the rulers to proclaim that deliverance from God should be expected, so that desertions might be lessened and hope might encourage even those beyond fear and precaution.[228]

This passage is significant for several reasons. First, Josephus uses the label "prophets" for those whom he obviously considers to be false prophets; he rarely uses the term for any but OT prophets.[229] Second, although Josephus claims that these prophets were bribed, it is more likely that they were simply in the employ of the leaders (cf. Neh. 6:7, 10-14, where prophets were hired by both Nehemiah and Sanballat and company), or that they spontaneously functioned as prophets of salvation. On the other hand, Joshua ben Ananiah and the unknown prophet whose oracle is referred to by Eusebius functioned as prophets of doom in the same situation.[230]

VI. CLERICAL PROPHECY

In ancient Israel priests were closely associated with oracular activity in a variety of ways.[231] Although the priestly use of the Urim and Thummim apparently ceased after the time of David, other forms of oracular activity by priests seem to have continued. The notion of clerical or Levitical prophecy has an important place in the work of the Chronicler, where we may have, not the assimilation of preexilic prophetic associations into the ranks of the Levitical temple singers, but a parallel and perhaps rival phenomenon to extracultic prophecy.[232] The close connection between the priesthood and oracular divination is indicated in Ezra 2:63 = Neh. 7:65, where we find the phrase "until a priest with Urim and Thummim should arise." While the cessation of prophecy is associated in Judaism with the absence of the Spirit since the activity of Haggai, Zechariah, and Malachi, in the first-century A.D. *Vitae Prophetarum* the cessation of the priests' ability to see visions of the angels of God, give forth visions from the inner sanctuary, or inquire of God by means of the ephod or Urim and Thummim is associated with the murder of Zechariah the son of Jehoiada. During the late Second Temple period a popular view connected the gift of prophecy with the priesthood, particularly with the high priest.[233]

A prophecy attributed to the high priest Caiaphas (ca. A.D. 18-36) is found in John 11:49-52:

> Caiaphas, who was high priest that year, said to them, "You know nothing at all; you do not understand that it is expedient for you that one man should die for the people, and that the whole nation should not perish." He did not say

this of his own accord, but being high priest that year he prophesied [*eprophē-teusen*] that Jesus should die for the nation, and not for the nation only, but to gather into one the children of God who are scattered abroad.

In form John 11:47-53 is a pronouncement story which was transmitted to the Fourth Evangelist through Christian circles, where it had been taken over from Jewish tradition.[234] The close association between the office of high priest and the gift of prophecy is assumed in this story. An interesting feature of the prophecy is that it was made unwittingly. Rabbinic literature has a number of references to prophecies made apart from the knowledge and intention of the speaker.[235] Similar notions are found in the Qumran community (4QpHab 7:1-5) and early Christianity (1 Pet. 1:10-12).

Josephus, the Jewish historian upon whom we have been so dependent for our knowledge of prophetic phenomena during the late Second Temple period, apparently regarded himself as a prophet (though he never uses the term *prophētēs* as a self-designation) and saw a close correlation between his prophetic gifts and his priestly status.[236] This is clear in *Bell.* iii.351-54:

> But as Nicanor was urgently pressing his proposals and Josephus overheard the threats of the hostile crowd, suddenly there came back into his mind those nightly dreams, in which God had foretold [*proesēmanen*] to him the impending fate of the Jews and the destinies of the Roman sovereigns. He was an interpreter of dreams [*peri kriseis oneirōn hikanos*] and skilled in divining the meaning of ambiguous [*amphibolōs*] utterances of the Deity; a priest himself and of priestly descent, he was not ignorant of the prophecies in the sacred books. At that hour he was inspired [*enthous*] to read their meaning, and, recalling the dreadful images of his recent dreams, he offered up a silent prayer to God. "Since it pleases thee," so it ran, "who didst create the Jewish nation, to break thy work, since fortune [*tychē*] has wholly passed to the Romans, and since thou hast made choice of my spirit to announce the things that are to come [*ta mellonta eipein*], I willingly surrender to the Romans and consent to live; but I take thee to witness [*martyromai*] that I go, not as a traitor, but as thy minister [*diakonos*]."

In spite of the rather obvious self-serving apologetic elements in this account, Josephus does reveal his view of himself, and the basic thrust of the report is historical.[237] Josephus regards himself as an inspired interpreter of dreams and an inspired interpreter of biblical prophecies. The particular form of inspiration claimed by Josephus (a type which he shared with the Teacher of Righteousness) was *the ability to discern the time of the fulfilment of earlier prophetic oracles*.[238] He appears to conceive of himself as a latter-day Daniel, Jeremiah, or Ezekiel. Daniel, like Josephus, was wise in the interpretation of scripture (*Ant.* x.189) and of dreams (*Ant.* x.194); he was a great prophet (*Ant.* x.266) who prophesied concerning the events which transpired under the Romans in A.D. 66-70 (*Ant.* x.276; *Bell.* iv.163ff., 318; vi.94ff., 109-10). The combination of prophetic gift and priesthood characterizes Josephus' view of Jeremiah and Ezekiel; all three — Jeremiah, Ezekiel, and Josephus — were priests and all three prophesied the destruction of Jerusalem:

> This prophet [Jeremiah] also announced the misfortunes that were to come upon the city, and left behind writings concerning the recent capture of our city, as well as the capture of Babylon. And not only this prophet predicted these things to the multitude, but also the prophet Ezekiel, who left behind two books which he was the first to write about these matters. These two men were

both priests by birth, but Jeremiah lived in Jerusalem from the thirteenth year of Josiah's reign until the city and the temple were demolished.[239]

After Josephus had surrendered to the Romans, he requested an audience with Vespasian. Standing before the general, he announced:

> You, Vespasian, think that Josephus is just another captive taken, but I come [*hēkō*][240] to you as a messenger [*angelos*] of greater things. Unless I had been sent by God to know the law of the Jews and the appropriate way for a general to die. Do you send me to Nero? For what reason? Shall those with Nero remain until your accession? *You are Caesar, Vespasian, and emperor, you and your son here* [italics added]. But bind me more securely and keep me yourself. For you Caesar are master not only of me, but also of the earth and sea and all mankind. I ask the punishment of a closer guard if I have capriciously attributed this to God.[241]

Later Josephus reports that when Vespasian became emperor he remembered this prediction and released him.[242] The essential historicity of this account is unquestionable, since it is confirmed by Suetonius and Dio Cassius.[243] Josephus regards himself here as a messenger sent by God, and indeed he calls himself (in a speech attributed to Vespasian) a "minister of the voice of God" (*diakonon tēs tou theou phōnēs*).[244] The form of the prophecy itself, indicated in italics, is that of a *recognition oracle*.[245]

If the revelatory media upon which Josephus relied were dreams and scripture, how did he know that Vespasian would become emperor? While we cannot (with some exceptions) know the content of Josephus' dreams, we can speculate about the "prophecies in sacred books" to which he refers in *Bell*. iii.352. One of the causes of the Jewish revolt of A.D. 66-73 was, according to Josephus,

> an ambiguous oracle [*chrēsmos amphibolos*], likewise found in their sacred scriptures, to the effect that at that time [*kata ton kairon ekeinon*] one from their country would become ruler of the world. This they understood to mean someone of their own race, and many of their wise men went astray in their interpretation of it. The oracle, however, in reality signified the sovereignty of Vespasian, who was proclaimed Emperor on Jewish soil.[246]

The Roman historian Tacitus (ca. A.D. 55-117), who is probably not dependent on Josephus,[247] provides us with a similar report:

> The majority firmly believed that their ancient priestly writings contained the prophecy that this was the very time [*eo ipso tempore*] when the East should grow strong and that men starting from Judea should possess the world. This mysterious prophecy had in reality pointed to Vespasian and Titus, but the common people, as is the way of human ambition, interpreted these great destinies in their own favour, and could not be turned to the truth even by adversity.[248]

A younger contemporary of Tacitus, Suetonius (ca. A.D. 69-140), preserves a similar report, again independently of Josephus, though probably dependent on Tacitus:

> There had spread over all the Orient an old and established belief, that it was fated at that time [*eo tempore*] for men coming from Judaea to rule the world. This prediction, referring to the emperor of Rome, as afterwards appeared from the event, the people of Judaea took to themselves; accordingly they revolted.[249]

A variety of OT texts have been suggested as candidates for the mysterious oracle referred to by Josephus, Tacitus, and Suetonius. These include the Judah oracle of Gen. 49:10, the seventy-weeks-of-years prophecy of Dan. 9:24-27, the oracle of Balaam in Num. 24:17, and the vision of one like a son of man in Dan. 7:13-14.[250] The Sibylline Oracles have also been suggested.[251] Whatever the biblical source of the oracle, it was basically messianic in character, and according to all three ancient historians it enjoyed popular currency. In favor of Dan. 9:24-27 as the biblical source for this oracle is the probability that the years A.D. 66-70 were reckoned to be the conclusion of the seventy weeks of years (490 years) prophesied by Daniel.[252] Josephus, however, though he believed in an Israel which could expect a glorious future if it was obedient to God, pointedly gives a *nonmessianic* and *noneschatological* interpretation to the oracle.[253] This perspective was shared with the earlier Hasmoneans[254] and very probably with the Sadducees.

Josephus was not the only Jew to predict that Vespasian would become the Roman emperor. The famous Rabbi Yoḥanan ben Zakkai, who supposedly escaped a besieged Jerusalem by pretending to be a corpse borne out in a coffin by his followers, is reported in haggadic tradition to have said to Vespasian:

Behold, you are about to be appointed king.[255]

When asked by Vespasian for justification of this prediction, Rabbi Yoḥanan quoted Isa. 10:34 with allusions to Jer. 30:21 and Deut. 3:25. Although Josephus and Rabbi Yoḥanan were probably not alluding to the same biblical oracle, both were willing to announce a noneschatological, nonmessianic fulfilment of the prediction. The similarities suggest some kind of dependence: either Josephus is dependent upon haggadic tradition (unlikely), or the redactor of the haggadic tradition is dependent on Josephus, or both represent versions of a type of story circulating at the end of the first century A.D.[256] Recognition oracles of this type are found in the OT[257] and elsewhere in the ancient Near East.[258] During the late fifth century B.C. Sanballat and Tobiah accused Nehemiah of hiring prophets to say: "There is a king in Judah" (Neh. 6:7). Regardless of the accuracy of the charge, the role of prophets in designating rulers in Israel (an ancient northern tradition) persisted into the Second Temple period. At the beginning of the revolt of Bar Kosiba (nicknamed "Bar Kochba," or "son of a star" by Rabbi Akiba with reference to the messianic prediction in Num. 24:17), Rabbi Akiba is remembered as having declared:

This is the king Messiah![259]

Here Akiba is playing a prophetic role in the oracular legitimation of the kingship of Bar Kosiba. This revolt, while undoubtedly inspired by the eschatological traditions of the restoration of the Davidic throne and the victory of the Jewish people over their oppressors, appears to have been largely noneschatological in its objectives.

The prediction of Vespasian's and Titus' future sovereignty was not the only prophetic utterance made by Josephus. In his chronicle of the Jewish revolt he persistently emphasizes the inevitability of the fall of Jerusalem. The fate of Jerusalem was made known to him, according to *Bell.* vi.312, by the inspired interpretation of dreams and of scripture. Referring to an oracle which was probably derived originally from biblical prophecy, Josephus relates:

For there was an ancient saying of inspired men [*andrōn entheōn*] that the city would be taken and the sanctuary burnt to the ground by right of war, whensoever [*ean*] it should be visited by sedition and native hands should be the first to defile God's sacred precincts.[260]

If this oracle was taken from the OT, the specific source is unclear, though Ezek. 9:1-10 is the most likely candidate.[261] The form is that of a *conditional oracle,* a type which is common in Greek oracles but almost nonexistent in Israelite and early Jewish prophetic oracles.[262] The biblical version of the oracle, then, has undergone Hellenization in form. Elsewhere Josephus claims that Jeremiah predicted the destruction of Jerusalem (*Ant.* x.79), as Daniel did also (*Ant.* x.276-77), but to what specific passage is he referring? Possibly to Lamentations, which was attributed to Jeremiah, but more probably he understood "Babylon" as a code name for Rome, and the destruction of Jerusalem by the "Babylonians" as the destruction of that city in more recent times by the Romans.[263]

Josephus also understood other OT prophecies to portend the destruction of Jerusalem:

> Thus the Jews, after the demolition of Antonia, reduced the temple to a square, although they had it recorded in their oracles that the city and the sanctuary would be taken when the temple should become four-square.[264]

Again the OT source is obscure. Ezek. 42:15-20 refers to the foursquare temple,[265] but there is no ominous connection of that with the fall of the city. More probable is the suggestion that the prophecy referred to is Dan. 9:25-26,[266] with its mention of square constructions and the destruction of the city and the sanctuary. Further, Josephus may have understood the cessation of daily sacrifices mentioned in *Bell.* vi.94 in terms of Dan. 8:11ff.; 9:27; 11:31; 12:11.[267] Although Josephus knew Daniel very well, he is strangely silent about the "stone cut out without hands" that destroyed the fourth kingdom in Dan. 3:34-35, 44-45 (he does mention it obliquely in *Ant.* x.210). He probably expected the ultimate liberation of the Jews on the basis of this prophecy, but on this subject he maintained discreet silence.[268]

Josephus is not only aware of these ancient oracles regarding the fall of Jerusalem and the temple; he professes to have been cognizant that the time of their fulfilment was near. In a long speech recorded in *Bell.* v.376-419, which bears more than a superficial resemblance to the speech of Stephen in Acts 7, Josephus draws lessons from various episodes in the history of Israel. The purpose of the speech is the condemnation of the behavior of those who are addressed. Perhaps in conscious imitation of Jeremiah, Josephus makes several attempts to persuade the Jewish leaders to surrender Jerusalem to the Romans, since the only alternative is defeat and destruction.[269] Josephus, of course, regards himself as no more a traitor to the Jewish cause than was the prophet Jeremiah.[270] In a later speech, in which Josephus urges John of Gischala and the Jews to repent and surrender (*Bell.* vi.96-110), he concludes (vi.109-110):

> Who knows not the records of the ancient prophets and that oracle which threatens this poor city and is even now coming true? For they foretold that it would then be taken whensoever [*hotan*] one should begin to slaughter his own countrymen. And is not the city, aye and the whole temple, filled with your corpses? God it is then, God Himself who with the Romans is bringing the fire to purge His temple and exterminating a city so laden with pollutions.[271]

In this paraphrase of the oracle quoted above from *Bell.* iv.388, the conditional form has been preserved, though the content has been modified. Earlier, in *Bell.* v.1ff., Josephus narrates the rebellion of Eleazar's faction against other factions in besieged Jerusalem. Eleazar seized the temple, and in the battle which followed many worshipers and priests were killed while making sacrifices and offerings. In the midst of this narrative, Josephus suddenly interjects this soliloquy:

> What misery to equal that, most wretched city, hast thou suffered at the hands of the Romans, who entered to purge with fire thy internal pollutions? For thou wert no longer God's place, nor couldest thou survive, after becoming a sepulchre for the bodies of thine own children and converting the sanctuary into a charnel-house of civil war. Yet might there be hopes for an amelioration of thy lot, if ever thou wouldst propitiate that God who devastated thee![272]

In several respects one of the closest parallels to this prophetic soliloquy of Josephus over Jerusalem is that of Jesus in Luke 13:34-35; both begin with a lament and conclude with the possibility of deliverance. Murder in the temple is a pollution which spells judgment (*Ant.* xi.299ff.).

Although Josephus nowhere claims to be a "prophet," he does claim to have the divine inspiration requisite for interpreting dreams and for understanding the true meaning and time of fulfilment of various OT prophecies, particularly those which concern the sovereignty of Vespasian and Titus and the destruction of Jerusalem and the temple. Josephus consciously identified his role with that of Daniel, Jeremiah, and possibly Ezekiel. His "prophetic" gifts were integrally related to his status as a priest, like Jeremiah and Ezekiel. In his religious party affiliation, therefore, Josephus is more closely associated with the Sadducees than with the Pharisees. Josephus claimed to be a priest by birth (*Vita* 1; *Bell.* iii.352), as well as a Hasmonean (*Vita* 1); although he claims to have sampled the various Jewish "philosophies" and settled on Pharisaism (*Vita* 2), it appears that "with his priestly charismatic exegesis Josephus is separated from the exegesis of the Pharisees."[273] In many respects Josephus shares the qualifications and outlook of the Sadducees. Certainly his interpretation of biblical prophecy, in the tradition of the clerical prophecy of the Chronicler through to 1 and 2 Maccabees, is markedly noneschatological and nonmessianic.

Josephus also refers to a dream oracle which he received that has the form of an *oracle of assurance* of the type found both in the OT and in apocalyptic literature:

Lament:	That night I beheld a marvellous vision in my dreams. I had retired to my couch, grieved and distraught by the tidings in the letter, when I thought that there stood by me [*epistanta moi*][274] one who said:
Admonition with Address:	"Cease, man, from thy sorrow of heart, let go all fear.
Promise (Reason):	That which grieves thee now will promote thee to greatness and felicity in all things. Not in these present trials only, but in many besides, will fortune attend thee.
Admonition repeated:	Fret not thyself then.
Commission:	Remember that thou must even battle with the Romans."[275]

With the exception of the final element in this dream oracle the form is that of the oracle of assurance (*Heilsorakel*). Yet the indirect nature of prophecy during the late

Second Temple period has limited the use of this form to dreams in all narrative settings outside apocalyptic literature (Luke 1:30; Acts 27:24).

In Josephus' depiction of the confrontation between the high priest Jaddua and Alexander the Great, a similar oracle of assurance is narrated:

Lament:	When the high priest Jaddūa heard this, he was in an agony of fear, not knowing how he could meet the Macedonians, whose king was angered by his former disobedience. He therefore ordered the people to make supplication, and, offering sacrifice to God together with them, besought Him to shield the nation and deliver them from the dangers that were hanging over them.
Admonition:	But, when he had gone to sleep after the sacrifice, God spoke oracularly [echrēmatisen] to him in his sleep, telling him to take courage [tharrein]
Command:	and adorn the city with wreaths and open the gates and go out to meet them, and that the people should be in white garments, and he himself with the priests in the robes prescribed by law,
Promise (Reason):	and that they should not look to suffer any harm, for God was watching over them.[276]

That such dream oracles, based on OT models, are granted to both Josephus and Jaddua, who are priests, is certainly not fortuitous from the perspective of Josephus.

VII. SAPIENTIAL PROPHECY

Like clerical prophecy, sapiential ("wisdom") prophecy is noneschatological; unlike clerical prophecy it is not connected with the gifts inherent in the priesthood, but with the faculty of wisdom, which is the peculiar specialty of the holy man, sage, or "philosopher." In Palestine sapiential prophecy is represented by a variety of figures, all of whom appear to stand in the hasidic tradition.[277] In the Diaspora there is a very close association between wisdom and prophecy, particularly in the writings of Philo of Alexandria, whom we shall consider in some detail.[278]

A. PALESTINE

Rabbi Yoḥanan ben Zakkai, whose prediction of Vespasian's accession to the Roman principate has already been mentioned, is reported to have predicted this doom for Galilee, after he was consulted only twice during his eighteen-year stay at Arav in Galilee:

Address:	Galilee, Galilee,
Accusation:	you hate the Torah.
Threat:	Your end will be that you will fall into the hands of conductores [large-scale tenant farmers].[279]

The "hatred" of the Torah with which Yoḥanan charges the Galileans is particularly evident in their rejection of the sage who is learned in the law. Jesus' prophecy of the destruction of Jerusalem in Luke 13:34-35 par. Matt. 23:37-39 has a strikingly similar structure.[280]

A similar prediction is attributed to a pupil of Yoḥanan, Rabbi Eliezer ben Hyrcanus (as well as to a number of other sages):

> With the footprints of the Messiah
> presumption shall increase and dearth reach its height;
> the vine shall yield its fruit
> but the wine shall be costly;
> and the empire shall fall into heresy
> and there shall be none to utter reproof.
> The council-chamber shall be given to fornication.
> Galilee shall be laid waste
> and Gablan shall be made desolate;
> and the people of the frontier shall go about from city to city
> with none to show pity on them.[281]

This "prophecy" consists of a list of the grave conditions in the world that will characterize the period just before the coming of the messiah. The only connection which this prediction has with the preceding is the mention of Galilee.

In addition to these examples of rabbinic prophecy Josephus reports that some of the Essenes claimed the ability to predict the future.[282] He provides several examples of Essene prophecy, and all of the examples are markedly noneschatological. In view of Josephus' great respect and admiration for the Essenes, the kind of prophetic gifts which he attributes to them appears to be based on their role as dedicated students of Torah. Josephus relates that Judas the Essene, who had a perfect track record for making correct predictions, had predicted that Antigonus would die on a particular day at Strato's Tower on the coast of Palestine.[283] When Judas saw Antigonus far from the appointed place on the fateful day, he thought that his prediction had been proven false. However, word was soon brought to Judas that Antigonus had been slain in a quarter of Jerusalem which was also called Strato's Tower. This narrative has the form and content of an *oracle story,* a particular type of Greco-Roman anecdote in which an oracular utterance which appears in danger of proving untrue is fulfilled in an unexpected way through the recognition that the oracle had a double meaning.[284] The story is typically Hellenistic and its authenticity is therefore dubious. An interesting feature of this story is that Judas himself was unsure of the real meaning of the oracle, an element emphasizing the divine origin of the prophecy. The prediction itself reflects an antipathy between the Essene pious ones (Hasidim) and the Hasmoneans. Judas is like Elijah, who predicted the death of Ahab for killing Naboth (1 Kgs. 21:19; cf. Josephus *Bell.* i.82, where the OT narrative is embellished by emphasizing that Ahab's blood will be shed on the very same spot).

Josephus tells another story of Menahem the Essene, who, while Herod was still a child, addressed him as "king of the Jews."[285] Herod remonstrated with him, whereupon Menahem (Menaēmus) explained:

> Nevertheless, you will be king and you will rule the realm happily, for you have been found worthy of this by God. And you shall remember the blows given by Menaēmus, so that they, too, may be for you a symbol of how one's fortune can change. For the best attitude for you to take would be to love justice and piety toward God and mildness toward your citizens. But I know that you will

not be such a person, since I understand the whole situation. Now you will be singled out for such good fortune as no other man has had, and you will enjoy eternal glory, but you will forget piety and justice. This, however, cannot escape the notice of God, and at the close of your life His wrath will show that He is mindful of these things.[286]

The original oracle of Menahem, recognizing the future kingship of Herod, conforms to the form of the *recognition oracle* used by Josephus and Rabbi Yoḥanan ben Zakkai of Vespasian, by Rabbi Akiba of Simon Bar Kosiba, and much earlier by Samuel of David (1 Sam. 16:1-13).

In his narratives concerning the infancy of Jesus Luke emphasizes the prophetic activity which surrounds the birth and childhood of both John the Baptist and Jesus. Particularly in Acts we find that oracles and divine revelations of various kinds regularly punctuate the narrative. This fact has both literary and theological significance. In Greek and Hellenistic literature divination and oracles frequently play critical roles in the movement of the plot.[287] While Luke has probably preserved some authentic prophetic sayings in Acts (these will be discussed below), he has also, as in Luke 1-2, composed many oracles and dream revelations himself. Yet these compositions are often modeled after the pattern of actual oracular forms. Simeon, a figure who is otherwise unknown, is presented in Luke 2:25-35 as a pious Israelite who looked forward to the consolation of Israel.[288] According to Luke the Holy Spirit revealed to Simeon that he would not die before seeing the messiah.[289] Simeon is nowhere designated a prophet, but there can be little doubt that Luke regarded him as such: it is said that "the Holy Spirit was upon him" (v. 25b), that "it was revealed to him by the Holy Spirit" (v. 26a), and that he came to the temple "in the Spirit" (v. 27a). Emerging from the temple Simeon saw Jesus, took him into his arms, and said (Luke 2:29-32):

> Lord, now lettest thou thy servant depart in peace,
>   according to thy word;
> for mine eyes have seen thy salvation
>   which thou hast prepared in the presence of all peoples,
> a light for revelation to the Gentiles,
>   and for glory to thy people Israel.

This "prophecy," however, is in reality a hymn made up of a pastiche of eschatological passages from Isaiah (in order, 52:9-10; 49:6; 46:13; 42:6; 40:5).[290] The oracular framework into which his hymn is set is secondary, and the hymn itself may have been adapted from a Palestinian Jewish Christian community.

Luke attributes a second oracle to Simeon in Luke 2:34-35:

> Behold, this child is set for the fall and rising of many in Israel,
> and for a sign that is spoken against
> (and a sword will pierce through your own soul also),
> that thoughts out of many hearts may be revealed.

This oracle was probably composed by Luke himself,[291] though it is more predictive than the other oracles of Luke 1-2. In both form and content this oracle conforms to the *recognition oracle* pattern, though oracles of this type were so widespread that they would be comparatively easy to emulate.

Anna, who is specifically identified as a prophetess,[292] is also given prominence in Luke 2:36-38. No oracle is attributed to her, and probably for that reason Luke specifically designated her a prophetess. She too recognized Jesus, apparently as the fulfilment of her hope for the redemption of Israel. Again the function of prophetic legitimation is seen to be a primary objective of Luke in chaps. 1-2. Luke presents his readers with a flurry of prophetic activity surrounding the birth and early years of John the Baptist and Jesus. Since specific oracles which Luke includes in his narrative appear to be either hymns which he has adapted to his purpose or literary compositions of his own for the same purpose, we learn nothing of real historical value 'for our investigation of the phenomenon of sapiential prophecy in Palestinian Judaism. Luke has chosen this means for communicating the theological truth that Jesus was the realization of the prophetic hope of Israel. While such prophetic activity is absent from the infancy narratives of Matthew, he more than makes up for that lack by frequently finding explicit prophetic fulfilments in the activities of Jesus and his family.

B. PHILO

Philo of Alexandria (ca. 20 B.C. to A.D. 50) is a figure of crucial importance for our knowledge of Egyptian Judaism during the Greco-Roman period. Like many of his contemporaries Philo was an eclectic Platonic philosopher; unlike most contemporary Platonists, he was a Jew. The highest kind of knowledge for Philo, as for Plato, is the knowledge of ideas; however, Philo substitutes the term "prophecy" for the Platonic term "recollection" (anamnēsis).[293] In this Platonizing sense Philo appears to have regarded himself as a prophet:

> On other occasions, I have approached my work empty and suddenly become full, the ideas falling in a shower from above and being sown invisibly, so that under the influence of the divine possession [hypo katochēs entheou] I have been filled with corybantic frenzy [korybantian] and been unconscious of anything, place, persons present, myself, words spoken, lines written. For I obtained language, ideas, an enjoyment of light, keenest vision, pellucid distinctness of objects, such as might be received through the eyes as the result of clearest shewing.[294]

If we discount the use of a hallucinogen, Philo appears to have experienced that which was highly prized and rarely achieved among the later Neoplatonists. Philo's use of the terms "divine possession" and "corybantic frenzy," not to mention the psycho-physical experiences he recounts, combine to indicate that he had himself undergone that which he elsewhere designates as "prophetic" experience.[295]

Philo regarded everything in the Pentateuch as oracular,[296] and Moses as the prophet through whom those oracles were revealed.[297] Philo distinguishes three types of oracular speech in the Pentateuch: that spoken by God himself using his prophet as an interpreter (di' hermēneōs, De vita Mosis ii.188), that in which revelation occurs through question (by the prophet) and answer (by God), and that spoken by Moses in his own person[298] when divinely inspired. This type of prophetic speech, very common in early Judaism, is rare in the OT. Oracles delivered through Moses are further divided into three categories on the basis of subject matter: the creation of the world, history, and legislation.[299] Philo is aware of the distinction between oracles and parenesis, but since he regards everything in the Pentateuch as oracular, he must nevertheless insist that parenetic material is also oracular:

Such was his [Moses'] pronouncement under divine inspiration [*katechomenos ethespisen*] on the matter of the food which came from heaven, but there are examples to follow which must be noted, though perhaps they may be thought to resemble exhortations [*parainesesin*] rather than oracular sayings [*chrēsmois*].[300]

Similarly, in *De vita Mosis* ii.258 we read:

When Moses saw it [manna], he bade them gather it, and said under inspiration [*epitheiasas*]: "We must trust God as we have experienced his kindnesses in deeds greater than we could have hoped for. Do not treasure up or store the food He sends. Let none leave any part of it over till the morrow. On hearing this, some whose piety had little ballast, thinking perhaps that the statement was no divine oracle [*chrēsmous*] but just the exhortation [*pareinesin*] of the ruler, left it to the next day; but it first rotted and filled the whole extent of the camp with its stench, and then turned into worms which are bred from corruption.

Both passages indicate that Philo did not think it natural to regard parenesis as prophecy, a view at variance with that of early Christianity in which the parenetic function of prophecy is firmly entrenched.

The faculty of inner sight was of central importance for Philo's conception of prophecy. In Philo's description of his own prophetic experience (*De migr. Abr.* 35, quoted above, p. 147) the accent lies on the heightened sense of vision. The words of God are seen as light is seen (*De migr. Abr.* 47-49); according to *De migr. Abr.* 49, "The words spoken by God are interpreted by the power of sight residing in the soul." In interpreting the phrase "all the people saw the voice" (LXX Exod. 20:18), he explains that "this shows that words spoken by God are interpreted by the power of sight residing in the soul."[301] The primary means of revelation for Moses at the burning bush was what he saw, not what he heard (*De vita Mosis* i.66). In Philo's interpretation of the speeches of Moses, he occasionally transforms them into oracular utterances even though they are not so presented in the biblical text. Within such tailored prophetic speeches the faculty of prophetic *vision* often plays a prominent role. These literary oracles exhibit a common structural pattern. In the first example Philo revises the speech that Moses made just prior to the destruction of the rebels Korah, Dathan, and Abiram (Num. 16:25-30):

Description of Inspired State:	While his [Moses'] heart was still hot within him, burning with lawful indignation, inspiration came upon him [*enthousia*] and transformed into a prophet he pronounced [*thespizei*] these words:
Accusation:	"Disbelief falls hardly on the disbelievers only. Such are schooled by facts alone and not by words. Experience will show them what teaching has failed to show that I do not lie. This matter will be judged by the manner of their latter end. If the death they meet is in the ordinary course of nature, my oracles [*logia*] are a false invention; but, if it be of a new and different kind, my truthfulness will be attested.
Visionary Threat:	I see [*horō*] the earth opened and vast chasms yawning wide. I see great bands of kinsfolk perishing, houses dragged down and swallowed up with their inmates and living men descending into Hades.[302]

After this threat the vision becomes reality and the two hundred fifty men who had led the revolt against Moses were atomized by thunderbolts. This literary oracle has two distinctive features: the description of the onset of divine inspiration as a formulaic motif introducing a prophetic utterance, and the vision of imminent judgment described in the present tense as the prophet perceives the vision. The "description of inspired state" occurs frequently in the introductions to Philo's speeches of Moses; alternately this element is placed toward the conclusion of such a speech.[303] Philo often introduces oracular speech with the introductory formula *thespizei tade*.[304]

Philo improvises a similar oracular speech for Moses, drawing at least some material from the Song of Moses in Exod. 15:

Description of Inspired State:	But, while in these helpless straits they were at death's door with consternation the prophet, seeing the whole nation entangled in the meshes of panic, like a draught of fishes, was taken out of himself [*ouket' ōn en heautō*] by divine possession [*theophoreitai*] and uttered these inspired words [*thespizei tade*]:
Lament:	"Alarm you needs must feel. Terror is near at hand: the danger is great. In front is a vast expanse of sea; no haven for a refuge, no boats at hand: behind, the menace of the enemies' troops, which march along in unresting pursuit. Whither can one turn or swim for safety? Everything has attacked us suddenly from every side — earth, sea, man, the elements of nature.
Admonition:	Yet be of good courage [*tharraite*], faint not. Stand with unshaken minds, look for the invincible help which God will send.
Promise:	Self-sent it will be with you anon, invisible it will fight before you. Ere now you have often experienced its unseen defence.
Visionary Promise:	I see [*blepō*] it preparing for the contest and casting a noose round the necks of the enemy. It drags them down through the sea. They sink like lead into the depths. You see them still alive: I have a vision [*egō phantasian lambanō*] of them dead, and today you too shall see their corpses."[305]

Like the first example cited this prophetic speech begins with a description of the onset of the inspiration of the prophet and concludes with the report of a vision which the prophet is experiencing as he relates it. In the nomenclature of OT prophetic speech, this last example has an announcement of salvation as its central element, while the first example has an announcement of judgment in the same position. In view of the distinctive nature of these Philonic oracles, we propose to label the first example a *visionary announcement of judgment,* and the second a *visionary announcement of salvation.* The second example has a very unusual feature in addition to those already noted: the *lament* has been incorporated into the oracle itself and, together with the *admonition* and *promise,* constitutes a unique literary adaptation of an oracle of assurance (*Heilsorakel*), complete with the lament (*Klagelied*) for which it is the response.[306]

Several examples of this kind of literary oracle, the two essential elements of which are the description of the prophet's inspired state and the narration of a vision while it is being experienced, are also found in Pseudo-Philo's *Liber Antiquitatum Biblicarum* (*LAB*), a haggadic midrash on Genesis– 2 Samuel composed ca. A.D. 100. *LAB* 28:6-10 presents a prophetic speech of Cenaz, one of the more prominent figures in the composition, that has no counterpart in the biblical text. After Cenaz raises a great lamentation over the possibility that Israel will be destroyed (*LAB* 28:5), we read:

Description of Inspired State:	Now while they were set, the holy spirit that dwelt in Cenez leapt upon him and took away from him his *bodily* sense, and he began to prophesy, saying [*prophetare dicens*]:
Vision Narration:	Behold now I see [*nunc video*] that which I looked not for, and perceive [*considero*] that I knew not. Hearken now, ye that dwell on the earth, even as they that sojourned therein prophesied before me, when they saw this hour, *even* before the earth was corrupted, that ye may know the prophecies appointed aforetime, all ye that dwell therein.
	Behold now I see [*nunc video*] flames that burn not, and I hear [*audio*] springs of water awaked out of sleep....
	Now out of the flame which I saw [*video*]....
	[The substance of the vision is the foundation of the earth and the prophecy by a "voice" that 7,000 years remain until the end of man's dwelling on the earth.]
Description of Cessation of Inspired State:	And it came to pass after Cenez had spoken these words that he awaked and his sense returned unto him: but he knew not that which he had spoken neither that which he had seen.[307]

This prophetic speech consists primarily of a narration of a vision experience while it is occurring. Although the vision concerns the formation of the world long before, its object is to reveal that many years of life for mankind remain in view of the 7,000-year period revealed by the "voice" (God). The new element in this speech, compared with the two we have examined in Philo, is the concluding description of the cessation of the prophet's inspiration, including that he could not remember what he had seen or spoken. Philo could never have described the conclusion of a vision trance in that way, since his view of "sober intoxication" made it possible for one in a revelatory state to be fully aware of all that had been experienced in that state. The cosmological content of Cenaz' vision resembles that of some apocalyptic visions (2 Bar. 53-74; 1 Enoch 85-90) but is completely uncharacteristic of Philo. That *LAB* was originally composed in Hebrew and does not share the distinctive views of Egyptian Judaism indicates that the oracular pattern we have discerned is not merely an idiosyncratic literary creation of Philo,[308] but a pattern of oracular speech taken over by Philo.

The expression "I saw" permeates the vision accounts of the OT and Jewish apocalyptic literature, but the present tense is never found in such literature. When the prophet or apocalyptist (or their disciples) composed accounts of revelatory visions, they were written in the form of secondary narrations of experiences which had occurred earlier. Similarly, when the OT prophets solemnly intoned "thus says Yahweh" as an introduction to their prophetic messages, they were giving a secondary account of a message which they had earlier received. In *Corpus Hermeticum* xiii (*Peri Paliggenesias*) the revelatory dialogue between Hermes Trismegistos and Tat is often couched in the present tense, especially in xiii.13: "Father, I see [*horō*] the All and myself in the Nous" (author's trans.; cf. xiii.3). These oracular speeches from Philo and Pseudo-Philo have a marked emphasis on the simultaneity of the reception of the prophetic message (in this case a vision instantly verbalized by the prophet) and its delivery to the intended audience.

This conception of prophetic revelation is characteristic of early Christianity, Greco-Roman paganism, and some Jewish apocalyptic texts, but it has one major difference: only very rarely do we find instances in which a prophet narrates a *vision* at the same time it is being revealed to him. There are, however, some widely scattered examples of this phenomenon. The earliest example is the speech of Theoklymenos in *Odyssey* xx.351-57, in which the *mantis* tells the assembled suitors what he "sees":

> Poor wretches, what evil has come on you? Your heads and faces and the knees underneath you are shrouded in night and darkness; a sound of wailing has broken out, your cheeks are covered with tears, and the walls bleed, and the fine supporting pillars. All the forecourt is huddled with ghosts, the yard is full of them as they flock down to the underworld and the darkness. The sun has perished out of the sky, and a foul mist has come over.[309]

This oracular speech has no close parallels elsewhere in the *Odyssey* or the *Iliad,* and thus has been labeled by M. Nilsson as a "poetic vision" created by the bard.[310] In Cassandra's speeches in Aeschylus *Agamemnon* 1090-1129 the prophetess "sees" what has happened in the past and what will happen in the future. This tradition is continued in Lycophron *Alex.* 86 (cf. 216, 249ff.) in which Cassandra is depicted as using the present tense in her fateful prophecies: "I see [*leussō*] the winged firebrand rushing to seize the dove" (author's trans.).

In *Vita Apollonii* viii.26 Philostratus relates how, in the midst of an oration before an audience in Ephesus, Apollonius of Tyana "saw" the assassination of the emperor Domitian in Rome. Apollonius stopped his oration and, appearing as if he were in a trance, exclaimed "Strike the tyrant! Strike him!" When he came to himself he explained what he had seen to his audience. In this example the visionary participates in the vision, but the audience is unaware of what the strange behavior means until it is explained to them. This story, unlike that regarding Theoklymenos in the *Odyssey,* includes the behavioral features associated with trance.

The closest parallel to the prophetic vision speeches of Philo and Pseudo-Philo, however, is found in the NT. At the conclusion of Stephen's long speech of condemnation, we read in Acts 7:55-56:

Description of Inspired State:	But he [Stephen], full of the Holy Spirit, gazed into heaven and saw the glory of God, and Jesus standing at the right hand of God; and he said,
Vision Narration:	"Behold, I see [*theōrō*] the heavens opened, and the Son of man standing at the right hand of God."

This short prophetic vision narrative exhibits the same two distinctive formal elements which were found in oracular speeches in Philo and Pseudo-Philo. However, Stephen does not see a vision of the past or the future in the prophetic present (as in the examples discussed above), but of the present status of the Son of man beside the heavenly throne of God. If the Son of man may be associated with the judgment motif in Luke, then perhaps the vision of Stephen is in effect a *visionary announcement of judgment,* fulfilled with the destruction of Jerusalem in A.D. 70.

Philo was a prophet only in the sense that he consciously regarded the prophetic revelatory experience as the highest source of knowledge, and he himself had experienced the heightened vision into supranormal reality. Because of Philo's close association of vision with prophetic inspiration, he appears to have transformed some of the speeches of Moses into visionary announcements of salvation or judgment.

⑥ | THE PROPHETIC ROLE OF JESUS

I. INTRODUCTION

Jesus did not clearly and explicitly claim to be a prophet, but it has been convincingly argued that precisely such a claim was implicit in his reported sayings and activities.[1] In early Judaism the designation "prophet" was ordinarily reserved for the Israelite prophets of the distant past and for a variety of prophetlike figures who were expected to appear immediately before the end of the age (which could, of course, be regarded as imminent). Josephus considered himself a prophet, though he never claimed that title for himself and only rarely used it of other figures of the postbiblical period.[2] Even the Qumran community's Teacher of Righteousness did not claim to be a prophet, though both he and his followers appear to have regarded him as such. Yet others, such as Theudas and the unnamed Jewish revolutionary from Egypt, were not so reticent about applying such an august title to themselves.[3]

The related notions of "prophet" and "prophecy" were limited to two periods, the past and the future. In early Judaism prophets of the past, whose words and deeds were recorded in scripture, were primarily regarded as predicters of the (distant) future and as miracle workers. As predicters of the future, they were considered to be divinely inspired spokesmen of the God of Israel who fulfilled their prophecies through the performance of miracles. Their predictions, recorded in scripture, were thought to consist primarily of enigmatic descriptions of the events that would unfold immediately before the end of the age. Correspondingly, a variety of eschatological prophets were expected to appear just before the eschaton and to herald the fulfilment of the ancient oracles and proclaim the imminent visitation of God. Most of the schemes of eschatological fantasy current in early Judaism called for the appearance of some kind of messenger of God whose coming could be considered a sign of the end of the age. This messenger was conceptualized primarily in terms of the two categories "prophet" and "messiah," which cannot be regarded as completely distinct from each other.[4]

II. APPLICATIONS OF THE TITLE "PROPHET" TO JESUS

A. IN POPULAR ASSESSMENTS OF JESUS

The four gospels contain a number of reflections of the popular view of the identity and significance of Jesus in which the title "prophet" is prominent. The oldest source that refers to Jesus as a prophet is the Gospel of Mark. According to Mark 6:14-15 the wonders performed by Jesus and his disciples led some of the people to suspect that he was either John the Baptist *redivivus,* Elijah, or one of the prophets.[5] A very similar popular assessment of Jesus is reflected in Mark 8:28. In response to Jesus' question, "Who do men say that I am?", the disciples respond, "John the Baptist; and others say, Elijah; and others one of the prophets."[6] The authenticity, or at the very least the antiquity, of the popular views of Jesus preserved in Mark 6:15 and 8:28 is supported both by the presence of a Semitism in both texts and by Mark's general lack of interest in depicting Jesus as a prophet.[7]

In the gospels of Matthew and Luke the crowds are also represented as acknowledging the prophetic status of Jesus. In Matt. 21:10-11 the evangelist introduces the account of Jesus' cleansing of the temple with a Semitic literary device whereby "all the city" is represented as saying, " 'Who is this?' And the crowds said, 'This is the prophet Jesus from Nazareth of Galilee.' " Similarly, in Matt. 21:46 the evangelist adds to his Markan source the detail that the authorities feared to arrest Jesus because the people held him to be a prophet. In Luke 7:16, which the evangelist draws from a special source, the crowd exclaims in response to a miracle just performed by Jesus, " 'A great prophet has arisen among us!' " and, "God has visited his people!' " Simon the Pharisee is represented as saying to himself in Luke 7:39, "If this man [Jesus] were a prophet [though he is not], he would have known who and what sort of woman this is who is touching him, for she is a sinner." Simon is used by Luke to reflect popular opinion. The Fourth Evangelist also portrays the crowd on several occasions as cherishing the belief that Jesus is "the prophet who is to come into the world" (John 6:14; 7:40, 52).

Each of the evangelists preserves traditions identifying Jesus with various eschatological prophetic figures. Elijah was the most popular of such figures, and the expectation of a Moses *redivivus* also appears to have captured the imagination of some groups, particularly the Samaritans. Still others subscribed to the vague hope that God would send a prophet, like one of the ancient prophets, who would function as his representative immediately prior to the end of the age.[8]

Several important considerations emerge from the popular assessments of Jesus as a prophet that are preserved in Mark 6:15 and 8:28: (1) The figure of the "prophet" was the object of widespread eschatological fantasy in first-century Palestine. (2) This nostalgic emphasis on prophets of the past was partially motivated by the desire to replace the dismal realities of the present with the idealized glories of Israel's past. (3) The prophetic figures of Jewish eschatological expectation were never really expected to emerge from within the existing social, political, or religious structures of first-century Palestine, but rather from the peripheral or marginal segments of Judaism.[9] (4) There was a great eagerness in first-century Palestine to assign those persons with the proper credentials to eschatological categories.[10]

B. FROM THE PERSPECTIVES OF THE EVANGELISTS

Mark preserves a number of older traditions which indicate that popular opinion regarded Jesus as a prophet, but Mark does not attempt to develop them. Matthew follows a similar pattern. While he reproduces (with some embellishment) Mark's list of those prophets with whom Jesus was popularly identified (compare Matt. 16:14 with Mark 8:28),[11] he betrays no real christological interest in the title.[12] And although Matthew utilizes a number of literary devices and theological motifs to depict Jesus as a new Moses,[13] he never attempts to identify Jesus with the eschatological Mosaic prophet.[14]

Luke shows far more interest than the other synoptic evangelists in portraying Jesus as a prophet.[15] In two places in Acts (3:22; 7:37) the OT passage which appears to predict the coming of a prophet like Moses, Deut. 18:15-18, is implicitly referred to Jesus. However, since Luke nowhere in his gospel makes any attempt to depict Jesus in terms of Moses *redivivus*, or as a prophet like Moses, it is probable that in Acts 3:22-23 and 7:37 the evangelist is reproducing older traditions. While he does not disagree with this older assessment of Jesus' identity, neither does he attempt to emphasize it.[16] In his gospel Luke presents an acclamation by the people that "a great prophet has arisen among us!" (7:16), a popular view also expressed, though in a negative way, by Simon the Pharisee (7:39). Further, the two disciples on the road to Emmaus say to their unknown companion, "Jesus of Nazareth ... was a prophet mighty in deed and word before God and all the people" (24:19). The probability that this characterization of Jesus originated as a Lukan insertion into an older Emmaus story indicates Luke's interest in the depiction of Jesus as a prophet.[17] While Luke nowhere in his gospel presents Jesus as the eschatological prophet, he does appear to confirm the general notion that Jesus was indeed a prophet.[18] Further, Luke's interest in Jesus as a prophet is intimately bound up with his conception of the violent fate of the prophets as a way of conceptualizing the meaning of Jesus' death, a subject which we shall consider in more detail below. An interesting feature of the overall structure of Luke-Acts is that the author describes a flurry of prophetic activity both *before* and *after* the appearance of Jesus, yet during Jesus' lifetime the author portrays only Jesus as a prophet.[19]

In spite of the fact that the prophetic aspects of Jesus' life and ministry are more prominently emphasized in the Fourth Gospel than in the synoptic gospels, earlier studies of the Christology of John paid little serious attention to the Johannine conception of Jesus as prophet.[20] Recent studies have more carefully analyzed the use of Mosaic themes and imagery in the Fourth Gospel and recognized the importance of "prophet" as a christological title in the Fourth Gospel.[21] It has also been cogently argued that Jesus was depicted as Elijah *redivivus* in one of the major sources used by the Fourth Evangelist.[22]

The designation "*the* prophet" occurs three times in the Fourth Gospel. In John 1:21 John the Baptist is asked if he is "*the* prophet," and he denies that he is. Again, just after a short speech of Jesus on the last day of the Feast of Tabernacles, some of those in the crowd exclaim, "This is really the prophet!" (John 7:40). Here "*the* prophet" probably refers to the Mosaic eschatological prophet, since Jesus' reference to the gift of living water is reminiscent of the incident reported in Exod. 17:1-7: in response to the people's request for water, Moses struck the rock at Horeb with his staff, and water immediately gushed forth.[23] Here John is reflecting one segment of popular belief (in 7:41 others express the belief that Jesus is the messiah), which he regards as inadequate,[24] as well as his own view that as *the* prophet Jesus is the eschatological bringer of salvation.[25]

Perhaps the most enigmatical reference to Jesus as the prophet in the Fourth Gospel is John 6:14-15:

> When the people saw the sign which he had done [i.e. the multiplication of loaves], they said, "This is indeed the prophet who is to come into the world!"

Perceiving then that they were about to come and take him by force to make him king, Jesus withdrew again to the mountain by himself.[26]

The notions of "prophet" and "king" can be regarded as casting light on each other within the framework of the prophet-like-Moses tradition,[27] in which both conceptions are closely related. Yet the fact that the early Jewish conceptions of "messiah" and "prophet" (the former emphasizing the royal element) are not always distinct makes it unnecessary (though not improbable) to appeal to the prophet-like-Moses tradition as the one tradition which unites both conceptions. Some regard the miracle of the multiplication of loaves in John 6:4-14 as a repetition of the miracle of manna that occurred in the wilderness during the time of Moses (Exod. 16), and on that basis Jesus could be regarded as a "prophet like Moses."[28] Another Johannine passage in which Jesus is identified as a prophet is John 4:19.[29] The woman at the well, after being told about her past life by Jesus, categorizes him as a prophet on the basis of his clairvoyant powers.[30] The Fourth Evangelist regards the recognition that Jesus is a prophet as an incomplete perception of his identity.[31] Those who go beyond the recognition of his clairvoyant powers as prophetic and see him as the Son of God sent from the Father have a more perfect perception of his person.

In sum, only in Acts and John is Jesus identified with the prophet like Moses. In Acts Luke apparently preserves an older Jewish Christian tradition which ultimately found fuller expression in the Clementine *Homilies* and *Recognitions* in the third century. The Fourth Evangelist consciously emphasizes the prophetic and royal aspects of the expectation of a prophet like Moses and uses them as an important, if subsidiary, christological image. In the synoptic gospels Mark and Matthew show little concern with identifying Jesus as either *a* prophet or *the* prophet. Luke shows a greater interest in the status of Jesus as a prophet, yet for him that title is primarily a vehicle for understanding Jesus as one who shared the typically violent fate of the prophets.

C. FROM THE PERSPECTIVE OF JESUS

Only two passages in the synoptic gospels have been used to demonstrate that Jesus referred to himself as a prophet. The first passage is Mark 6:4 (par. Matt. 13:57; Luke 4:24): "And Jesus said to them, 'A prophet is not without honor, except in his own country, and among his own kin, and in his own house.'" This saying is a proverbial expression which means, not that Jesus regards himself as a prophet, but that he is one who is not accepted in his homeland.[32] If the saying was actually used by Jesus, and there is no reason to doubt that it was, it could be related to the early Jewish tradition of the violent fate of the prophets, a subject which we shall discuss in some detail below. In the Lukan parallel to Mark, the Third Evangelist adds a section in which Jesus says that both Elijah and Elisha were accepted by foreigners (Luke 4:25-30). By appending such concrete illustrations to the proverb Luke shows that he at least understood the proverb to refer to the prophetic status of Jesus.

The second passage which has been understood as a reference of Jesus to himself as a prophet is Luke 13:31-33, a pronouncement story drawn from Luke's special source:

> At that very hour some Pharisees came, and said to him, "Get away from here, for Herod wants to kill you." And he said to them, "Go and tell that fox, 'Behold, I cast out demons and perform cures today and tomorrow, and on the third day I finish my course. Nevertheless I must go on my way today and

tomorrow and the day following; for it cannot be that a prophet should perish away from Jerusalem."

Originally the pronouncement story in vv. 31-32 probably circulated independently of the saying of Jesus in v. 33[33] Both traditions have a strong claim to authenticity, and both reflect the motif of the violent death of the prophets that is a significant element in Luke's Christology.[34] The saying in v. 33 has a proverbial ring, yet it cannot be regarded as a proverb, since the necessity of a prophet perishing *in Jerusalem* is found nowhere else in early Jewish or early Christian literature.[35] The conclusion that Jesus closely identified his own mission with that of the prophets of ancient Israel is very probable.[36]

III. THE MOTIF OF THE VIOLENT FATE OF THE PROPHETS

The view that suffering and martyrdom were the inescapable fate of the true prophet was widespread in early Judaism.[37] One of the oldest expressions of this tradition is found in Neh. 9:26:

> Nevertheless they [the Israelites] were disobedient and rebelled against thee and cast thy law behind their back and killed thy prophets, who had warned them in order to turn them back to thee, and they committed great blasphemies.

In early Christianity the motif of the violent fate of the prophets was used to understand the significance of the death of Jesus, who was by implication the latest and greatest of the prophets. Paul reflects this tradition in 1 Thess. 2:15, where he refers to the Jews "who killed both the Lord Jesus and the prophets."[38] One of the most forceful statements associating the motif of the violent fate of the prophets with the crucifixion of Jesus is found in the speech of Stephen (Acts 7:52):

> Which of the prophets did not your fathers persecute? And they killed those who announced beforehand the coming of the Righteous One, whom you have now betrayed and murdered.

Further, in regions where early Christianity had a strong Jewish character, it was almost expected that early Christian prophets would themselves experience suffering and martyrdom.[39]

The motif of the violent fate of the prophets occurs several times in Q, the sayings source utilized by both Matthew and Luke.[40] The first saying in which the motif is found is Matt. 5:11-12 par. Luke 6:22-23, which is here quoted in the Matthean version:

> Blessed are you when men revile you and persecute you and utter all kinds of evil against you falsely on my account. Rejoice and be glad, for your reward is great in heaven, for so men persecuted the prophets who were before you.

While this beatitude is directed to the apostles, it may also be regarded as reflecting the experience of the Q community. Those who experience persecution are said to share that fate with the OT prophets. Whether the Q community understood this saying to apply only to early Christian prophets,[41] or more generally to all Christians who experience persecution, cannot be determined. Again, in Matt. 23:29-31 par. Luke 11:47-48, part of the series of seven woes pronounced by Jesus upon the Pharisees, Jesus condemned them for decorating the tombs of the prophets, since their fathers killed them and they are implicated in their fathers' actions. Just as their fathers would not heed the prophets, but killed them, so the present generation ignores the message of representatives of the Q community and inflicts suffering upon them.

Matt. 23:34-36 par. Luke 11:49-51 records a similar saying, here quoted in the Lukan version (see also below, pp. 236-37):

> Therefore also the Wisdom of God said, "I will send them prophets and apostles, some of whom they will kill and persecute," that the blood of all the prophets, shed from the foundation of the world, may be required of this generation, from the blood of Abel to the blood of Zechariah, who perished between the altar and the sanctuary. Yes, I tell you, it shall be required of this generation.

Even though this saying of Jesus speaks of the common fate of prophets and apostles, the Q community probably understood the saying as applicable also to the death of Jesus.

In Matt. 23:37-39 par. Luke 13:34-35 a prophetic saying of Jesus preserved in Q not only reflects the motif of the violent fate of the prophets, but also indicates that Jesus regarded his own fate as linked with that of the ancient prophets.[42] The saying is here quoted in its Lukan version:

> O Jerusalem, Jerusalem, killing the prophets and stoning those who are sent to you! How often would I have gathered your children together as a hen gathers her brood under her wings, and you would not! Behold, your house is forsaken. And I tell you, you will not see me until you say, "Blessed is he who comes in the name of the Lord!"

Jesus identifies himself with a long series of messengers who have been sent in vain to Israel. The Q community recognized John the Baptist and particularly Jesus as prophets in the ancient tradition who shared the fate of their predecessors. The prophetic messengers of the Q community, though their existence and activities can only be inferred, also regarded themselves as sharing the fate of the ancient prophets and Jesus.

As we have already observed, Mark shows little concern for the christological dimensions of the title "prophet" as applied to Jesus. An apparent exception to this generalization is the parable of the vineyard in Mark 12:1-12. There the story is told of how the owner of a leased vineyard sent a series of servants to the lessees in order to collect rent in the form of produce. Some of these servants were beaten and sent away and others were killed. Finally the owner sent his beloved son, thinking that they would certainly respect him. However, the tenants killed the son, thinking that they could then claim his inheritance. The parable ends with this conclusion in Mark 12:9:[43] "What will the owner of the vineyard do? He will come and destroy the tenants, and give the vineyard to others." In Mark the parable appears to be understood allegorically. The series of messengers represents the prophets who were persecuted and killed by a rebellious Israel, while the beloved son is Jesus, the last in a long series of prophetic messengers who have experienced rejection by the people.[44] In view of Mark's lack of interest in the prophetic role of Jesus, this understanding of the parable antedated the formation of the Gospel of Mark.

Like Mark, Matthew does little to develop the motif of the violent fate of the prophets in relation to the death of Jesus, though he does contribute some embellishments to the material he used from Mark and Q that contained this motif.[45] Luke not only emphasizes the prophetic status of Jesus as a positive christological title far more than the other evangelists, but he also understands Jesus' prophetic role in terms of the motif of the violent fate of the prophets. Luke saw that the prophetic status of Jesus necessarily involved his rejection by the people in terms of suffering and death. Luke's well-known avoidance of references to the redemptive significance of the death of Jesus is probably due to his understanding of Jesus' death as the inevitable correlate of his prophetic status.[46]

Luke's view of Jesus as a prophet destined for rejection is not only a central theme of his entire gospel, but also one which is particularly emphasized in Luke 4:16-30, a scene in which Jesus delivers a homily in the synagogue at Nazareth.[47] In this passage (Luke 4:18, 21) Jesus claims that the Spirit is upon him through his comments on the scripture portion which he read from Isa. 61:1-2. In 4:24 he quotes the proverb "no prophet is acceptable in his own country," which the evangelist clearly understands as a reference to Jesus' prophetic status, since it is followed by the examples of the prophets Elijah and Elisha who were sent, not to the many Israelite widows and lepers, but to foreigners (4:25-27). Those present in the synagogue became infuriated with Jesus and led him off to a precipice from which they intended to hurl him to his death. Miraculously, he passed through their midst unharmed and went his way (4:28-30). Jesus' experience of rejection at Nazareth serves as a dramatic anticipation of the final and decisive rejection of Jesus by the Jews in Jerusalem. The prophetic status of Jesus is the key for understanding the inevitability of his rejection in Nazareth as well as in Jerusalem.[48]

Our discussion of the motif of the violent fate of the prophets has thus far been limited to the close association of suffering and death with the careers of ancient Israelite prophets, an association which suggested one way for early Christians to understand the significance of Jesus' suffering and death. In recent years it has been vigorously argued that in pre-Christian Judaism the figure of the eschatological prophet was associated with the threefold pattern of martyrdom-resurrection-ascension.[49] The earliest text cited in support of this theory is Rev. 11:3-13, where the two prophetic witnesses (probably representing Enoch and Elijah) are slain, return to life, and then ascend to heaven.[50] The notion that the martyred eschatological prophet will be resurrected is primarily attested in post-Christian sources; thus the assumption that the pattern of martyrdom-resurrection of the eschatological prophet was current in pre-Christian Judaism has not been demonstrated.[51] The theory of a pre-Christian Jewish tradition of the martyrdom of the returned Elijah, based on the assumption that the two prophetic witnesses of Rev. 11:3-13 (Enoch and Elijah) are modeled after such a pre-Christian tradition,[52] appears to have little basis.[53] Yet on the whole it would seem that the association of rejection and martyrdom with the image of an eschatological prophet is not an illogical extension of its traditional association with prophetic figures of the past.

That Jesus saw himself as a prophet is a valid inference from Luke 13:31-33, and that he regarded himself as destined to share the traditional fate of the prophets appears probable from Luke 13:31-33, 34-35. Whether or not the more complex prophetic role of martyrdom-resurrection-ascension was widely known in first-century Judaism (an assumption which appears doubtful), it seems clear that the association of suffering and martyrdom with the prophetic role was sufficiently widespread in early Judaism that such a pattern probably provided a decisive influence on Jesus' understanding of his own mission and destiny.[54]

IV. INDIRECT INDICATIONS OF JESUS' PROPHETIC SELF-UNDERSTANDING

In a characteristically brief yet comprehensive manner, C. H. Dodd suggested fifteen reasons why the category of "prophet" could appropriately be applied to Jesus, even though Dodd was convinced that he transcended that categorization.[55] While not all fifteen reasons are equally valid, they do appear to have cumulative value and they can serve the useful purpose of providing a basis for discussion and supplementation.

Dodd suggests five reasons why Jesus was popularly regarded as a prophet by his contemporaries: (1) the sovereign authority of his teaching (Mark 1:27), implied by the characteristic introductory phrase "(Amen) I say unto you," (2) the poetic character of his sayings, in contrast to rabbinic teaching, and reminiscent of the style of the OT prophets, (3) his experience of visions and auditions (Luke 10:18), (4) he, like the prophets of old, was thought to have made many predictions (Matt. 23:38 par. Luke 13:35; Mark 13:2; 14:58), and (5) Jesus, like the OT prophets, performed symbolic actions.

Turning to Jesus' teaching, Dodd finds four more reasons in features which are reminiscent of the OT prophets: (6) Jesus rejected the formalism of contemporary Judaism for a more vital form of religion, (7) Jesus rationalized the popular apocalyptic fantasies in terms of the historical possibilities of the Roman menace, (8) Jesus announced the reign of God in opposition to the power of evil, and (9) as a preacher of repentance, more than a teacher, Jesus exercised a distinctive prophetic function.

Finally, Dodd enumerated six additional personal traits of Jesus that he regarded as having an affinity with the OT prophets: (10) Jesus was conscious of a special calling which he expressed in a variety of ways (he refers to the "necessity" of his suffering, Mark 8:31; 14:36; he speaks of being "sent" by God, Mark 9:37; Matt. 15:24; Luke 4:18-26); (11) Jesus received divine revelation through intimate communion with God (Matt. 11:27 par. Luke 10:22); (12) Jesus represented God; to follow him is to obey God, to reject him is to reject God (Mark 9:37; cf. 1 Sam. 7:7; Ezek 33:30-33); (13) Jesus was conscious of a mission to all Israel (Matt. 15:24; 19:28 par. Luke 22:30); (14) like the prophets, who not only proclaimed the word of God but also consciously participated in its fulfilment, Jesus expected some momentous consequence from his death; and (15) Jesus exhibited what could be called "prophetic piety."

Dodd's points are interesting, not only for what they include, but also for what they omit. Curiously, the wonders performed by Jesus are not mentioned, though gospel tradition represents bystanders concluding on the basis of Jesus' performance of a miracle that he must be a prophet (Mark 6:15; Luke 7:16; John 6:14-15). Again, no emphasis is placed on Jesus' judgment speeches which have a formal similarity to the proclamations of doom made by OT prophets. Dodd has proceeded on the assumption that those traits which Jesus and the OT prophets have in common are sufficiently numerous that Jesus may be regarded as a prophet. This procedure, which is also used to demonstrate that Paul should be regarded as a prophet,[56] has two critical weaknesses. (1) It ignores the distinctive features which characterize the OT prophets (or types of OT prophets) as prophets for features which are marginal to their prophetic role, but important because they correspond to some trait of Jesus. (2) Dodd's perception of the OT prophet is that of a modern scholar and is not necessarily co-extensive with the image of the prophet current in early Judaism.[57] The rest of this chapter will consider further arguments that Jesus was a prophet, both in his own view and in that of his contemporaries.

A. JESUS' CONSCIOUSNESS OF A DIVINE COMMISSION

One of the distinctive features of the prophetic vocation in the OT is said to be an awareness of having been called and commissioned by God to fulfil a particular role as his spokesman.[58] Since free prophets (in contrast to cult prophets) in ancient Israel were, by definition, independent of the social, political, and religious structures of ancient Israel, the experience of a "prophetic call" provided a legitimation for their prophetic role. Cult prophets were legitimated primarily through their official association with the political and religious structures of ancient Israel or Judah.[59]

The gospels contain numerous sayings of Jesus reflecting the conviction that he had been sent by God to perform certain tasks and to announce a particular message. While some of these sayings may reflect the theology of the early church,[60] most of those preserved in the synoptic gospels have a strong claim to authenticity.[61] A sense of divine calling is presupposed by the "I came" (Mark 1:38 and parallels; 2:17 and parallels; 10:45; Matt. 5:17; 10:34-36; Luke 12:49; Matt. 11:19-20 and parallels), and the "I was sent" (Mark 9:37; Luke 10:16; Matt. 15:24) sayings. While critics have labeled some of these sayings inauthentic, they cannot all be regarded as such since they permeate all layers of gospel tradition.

The baptism of Jesus is frequently regarded as the occasion upon which Jesus became fully cognizant of his calling and mission.[62] That Jesus was baptized by John is certainly historical fact. The precise meaning which that event held for Jesus is not recoverable, however. Many critics hold that the baptism narrative has been embellished through subsequent theological reflection, but the extent to which this has occurred is difficult to determine. The narratives describing Jesus' baptism by John are not structured like a typical prophetic call narrative, and no evidence suggests that it ever had that significance.

Although it is clear that Jesus possessed a sense of divine calling and direction, the basis for that conviction is not recoverable. Further, it must be denied that a sense of divine calling is unique to the prophetic role, though it is probable that the majority of those who regarded themselves as prophets in early Judaism and who were outside the legitimating structures of existing political and religious institutions were conscious of a divine calling.

B. SYMBOLIC ACTIONS

In his capacity as a prophet in the OT tradition, Jesus is regarded as having performed a number of prophetic symbolic actions. C. H. Dodd suggested that the breaking of bread and distribution of the cup at the Last Supper, both accompanied by interpretative statements, were prophetic symbolic acts. He also regarded the cursing of the fig tree (symbolizing the rejection of Israel) and the miraculous feeding of the multitude as prophetic acts.[63] J. Lindblom has suggested a longer list of prophetic symbolic actions of Jesus, including: the messianic entrance into Jerusalem, the Last Supper, the sending of the Twelve, the miracles, the giving of symbolic names to disciples, and the purification of the temple.[64] Others would add the selection of the Twelve,[65] the miracle of walking on the water,[66] and Jesus' table fellowship with tax collectors and sinners.[67]

The major differences between these actions of Jesus and the symbolic acts of the OT prophets are that God is not represented as having commanded Jesus to perform these actions, and the OT prophets interpreted their actions by means of a word of the Lord, usually introduced with the messenger formula. When the actions referred to above by Jesus are interpreted (and few of them are), God is not represented as the authority behind that interpretation.[68] Perhaps of even greater interest is that neither Jesus nor the Christian community nor the evangelists appears to have consciously modeled any of Jesus' so-called prophetic symbolic actions after OT examples.[69] If we insist that in order to qualify as prophetic symbolic acts the actions of Jesus must incorporate a predictive element within them, i.e. as a surrogate for prophetic speech which from a first-century Jewish perspective was largely predictive, then the feeding of the multitude, the entrance into Jerusalem, the sending of the Twelve, the selection of the Twelve, the giving of symbolic names to disciples, and the miracle of walking on water cannot be regarded as prophetic symbolic actions.

One of the better examples of a prophetic symbolic action performed by Jesus is the purification of the temple in Mark 11:15-17, which consists of two primary elements, the report of a symbolic action and its interpretation:

Mark 11:15a (Transition):	And they came to Jerusalem.
Mark 11:15b-16 (Report):	And he entered the temple and began to drive out those who sold and those who bought in the temple, and he overturned the tables of the money-changers and the seats of those who sold pigeons; and he would not allow any one to carry anything through the temple.
Mark 11:17 (Interpretation):	And he taught, and said to them, "Is it not written, 'My house shall be called a house of prayer for all the nations'? But you have made it a den of robbers."[70]

Rather than interpret his actions through a word from Yahweh, Jesus bases them on a quotation from Isa. 56:7 followed by an interpretation which alludes to Jer. 7:11. Jesus' purification of the temple, a deed which has a strong claim to historicity,[71] was a symbolic gesture which at the very least indicated the necessity for the radical reformation of the Jerusalem cult. If this action is understood within the context of Jesus' predictions of the destruction of the temple,[72] then it becomes possible that the significance of Jesus' "purification" of the temple was not simply a dramatic way of emphasizing the necessity for cultic reform, but rather a symbolic overthrow of the temple that would be fulfilled in the future.[73] While Jesus' purification of the temple is commonly regarded as a prophetic symbolic act,[74] the radical nature of that action is seldom apprehended.

The story of Jesus' cursing of the fig tree (Mark 11:12-14, 20-25; Matt. 21:18-19) has been widely regarded as a prophetic symbolic act of Jesus. The magical character of the episode has been considerably diminished by the secondary addition of Jesus' sayings on faith.[75] Although Jesus' act of cursing the fruitless fig tree is not explained in either Mark or Matthew, it has frequently been interpreted as a sign of the imminent judgment of God upon Israel.[76] Yet apart from the secondary sayings on faith which have been appended to the story (Mark 11:22-25), Jesus is not remembered as having interpreted his action. If the cursing of the fig tree is understood within the framework of Jesus' predictions of the destruction of the temple and his symbolic actions in the outer court of the temple, it is perhaps correctly understood as a symbolic indication of the imminent fate of Israel.

That Jesus did perform acts which were highly symbolic is undeniable. Symbolic actions in themselves, however, are not prophetic unless they are either a surrogate for or a dramatization of oracular speech. Both Jesus' purification of the temple and his cursing of the fig tree appear to qualify as prophetic symbolic acts in that they are accompanied by verbal prophecies which provide clues for correctly interpreting the intent of his symbolic acts. Both of these symbolic acts have an eschatological orientation, and as such they may be understood as analogous to the signs which early Jewish millenarian leaders attempted to perform.[77]

C. PROPHETIC VISIONS

The only visionary experience of Jesus with prophetic features that has been preserved in gospel tradition[78] is narrated briefly in Luke 10:18:

> And he [Jesus] said to them [seventy disciples], "I saw Satan fall like lightning from heaven."

This saying, which has a strong claim to historicity,[79] exhibits a number of unique features. First, the vision is not narrated in the third person, as are the stories of the visionary and auditory experiences connected with the stories of Jesus' baptism and transfiguration. Second, the saying is tantalizingly brief and no attempt is made (or preserved) to interpret the meaning of the vision, either by Jesus himself or by Luke.[80] Third, the substance of the vision is the final conquest of Satan by God and so presupposes an earlier conflict between God and Satan in heaven.[81] Early Jewish apocalyptic used the tradition of a primordial expulsion of Satan from heaven (cf. 2 Enoch 29:4-5; Vita Adae 12-17), a motif drawn from Isa. 14:12-20, which describes the fall of the King of Babylon using the imagery and patterns of old Canaanite mythology. This vision which anticipates the eschatological defeat of Satan coheres well with other sayings of Jesus that emphasize the preliminary presence of the kingdom of God through the words and deeds of Jesus (Luke 11:20; 17:20-21).[82]

In early Judaism, as in the OT, the visions of prophets and apocalyptists were closely connected with their proclamations.[83] Such a relationship may well have existed between the anticipatory vision of Jesus' defeat of Satan in Luke 10:18 and his proclamation of the nearness and presence of the kingdom of God.[84] Jesus may have been motivated to recount this visionary experience himself by a desire to legitimate the message which he proclaimed; if so, it would function much like the commission narratives recounted by many of the OT prophets.[85] In general there are no striking similarities between this apocalyptic vision of Jesus and the visions of OT prophets, though there are striking similarities with apocalyptic visions such as those recounted in Rev. 9:1 and 12:7-8.

V. FORMAL CHARACTERISTICS OF JESUS' SPEECH

Several features of Jesus' speech that are preserved in the synoptic tradition have been regarded as characteristic of prophetic rhetoric. If these features are authentic they might corroborate the prophetic status of Jesus. If they originate with the post-Easter Christian community, then they might be considered evidence for the activity of early Christian prophets who spoke in the name of the risen Lord.[86] Few tasks confronting the modern NT scholar are as difficult as that of distinguishing authentic Jesus traditions from the embellishments of the early church. Nevertheless, it is my conviction that each of the five forms of speech which will be discussed below is authentically Jesuanic. Whether they are legitimate forms of prophetic speech is a problem which must be considered at length.

A. "(AMEN) I SAY TO YOU"

Through the use of the stereotyped messenger formula "thus says Yahweh" the OT prophets based the authority of their proclamations on the God of Israel. Nowhere in the sayings of Jesus does this messenger formula occur. In itself this fact is not surprising, since no known prophetic figure in early Judaism made use of the OT prophetic messenger formula. The formula "(Amen) I say to you," which Jesus frequently used to introduce or punctuate his sayings, has been regarded as an equivalent to the OT prophetic messenger formula.[87] The introductory formula used by Jesus, however, grounds the authority for his pronouncements not in God but in himself. First we shall discuss the expression "I say to you," and then consider the significance of the prefatory "amen" when it occurs with "I say to you."

The formulaic expression "(Amen) I say to you" occurs nineteen times in Mark, twelve times in Q, fourteen times in material unique to Luke, and twenty times in material unique to Matthew.[88] The phrase occurs some twenty-nine times in the Fourth Gospel, but always in the form "Amen, amen, I say to you." The phrase "I say to you" is rarely found in Greek literature simply because the Greeks found it to be a repugnant form of expression,[89] though it frequently occurs within the framework of quoted sayings and speeches in Judeo-Christian literature.

The expression "I say to you," whether directed to an individual or to a group, has a consistent social function wherever it occurs in early Jewish, early Christian, and (very rarely) Greco-Roman sources: the expression is used only by one whose social status is superior to the individual or group being addressed. The social situations in which this formula occurs include the following: (1) a father speaking to his son(s),[90] (2) a teacher addressing his pupil(s),[91] (3) a rabbi introducing a contrary halakhic opinion to his colleagues,[92] (4) a magician addressing the supernatural powers under his control,[93] (5) a preacher addressing a sermon of repentance or admonition to his audience,[94] (6) an apostle speaking to a Christian community whom he wishes to influence,[95] (7) two peers engaged in a dispute with each other,[96] (8) an angel addressing a man,[97] and (9) God addressing an angel.[98]

From this survey it is apparent that the expression occurs only in direct discourse in which both speaker and audience are defined. The two literary genres in which the formula appears most frequently are the dialogue,[99] found in a variety of larger literary forms (e.g. the gospel, the farewell discourse), and the letter[100] or sermon of exhortation.[101] The formula "I say (to you)" is noticeably absent in two popular literary genres which have been preserved in Greco-Roman literature, the Greco-Roman diatribe and the Hellenistic Jewish homily.[102] Both genres are impersonal since the speaker rarely refers to himself and the audience that he addresses is imaginary.[103]

The use of the formula "I say to you" in prophetic contexts is attested in both early Judaism and early Christianity. In Isa. 13:14 (LXX) God is represented as using the phrase "I say" in introducing an oracle. In a Hellenistic inscription Apollo is presented as using the expression "but I say" as an introduction to an oracular utterance.[104] In Rev. 2:4 the formula "I say to you" punctuates John's prophetic speech to the church at Thyatira. Paul uses the expression twice to introduce the oracles which he quotes in 1 Thess. 4:15 and 1 Cor. 15:51.[105] In the Shepherd of Hermas the phrase "I say to you" is occasionally used by the Shepherd, or Angel of

Repentance, when addressing Hermas.[106] More important is that four times the phrase "I say to you" introduces oracles which Hermas appears to have delivered to various Christian communities.[107] Throughout the rest of the Apostolic Fathers the phrase is virtually absent.[108]

In general the expression "I say (to you)," used in direct discourse, is an eastern Mediterranean locution indicating the relative social status of speaker and audience. It is a *legitimation formula* since it implicitly claims the authority of one of greater social status when addressing one(s) of lesser status. While the phrase can introduce or punctuate oracular speech, it can also introduce discourse in other social contexts.

Most studies of the phrase "(Amen) I say to you" have focused on the introductory use of the Aramaic and Hebrew term *'amen*.[109] Jewish and Christian sources normally use the term in a responsory manner, i.e. as a means of expressing assent to the words of others. The claim has been made that the introductory use of the term is a unique and historically authentic expression of Jesus.[110] Unimpressed by the argument that uniqueness indicates authenticity, others have argued that virtually all the sayings of Jesus introduced by the formula "Amen, I say to you" are utterances of Christian prophets speaking in the name of the risen Lord,[111] or that the introductory *amēn* originated in Hellenistic Jewish Christianity as an oath formula introducing apocalypticlike sayings.[112] The introductory *'amen* has been found on a seventh-century B.C. potsherd written in Hebrew,[113] and the fuller expression "Amen, I say to you" occurs twice in Recension A of the Testament of Abraham (8, 20), which is probably a first-century A.D. Jewish composition uninfluenced by Christianity.[114] These facts indicate that the introductory use of "Amen, I say to you" is attested in Judaism (though rarely), and that there is no compelling reason to conjecture that the phrase originated in Hellenistic Jewish Christianity, either in prophetic or apocalyptic settings. Although the introductory use of *amēn* is not unique to Jesus the rarity of its use in Judaism and early Christianity points toward its authenticity.

The foregoing discussion of the formula "(Amen) I say to you" reveals that there is no major difference between the expression "I say to you" and "Amen, I say to you" in the canonical and apocryphal sayings of Jesus. These phrases and their variants always indicate the greater status and authority of the speaker in relation to his audience. There can be no doubt that the expression is a historically authentic expression of Jesus. His use of the formula was one way of expressing his authority within the framework of a teacher-student relationship. Although "Amen, I say to you" is a legitimation formula, it is not a functional equivalent of the OT messenger formula, nor can it be said that it reflects a *unique* authority claimed by Jesus.[115]

B. "WHO AMONG YOU?"

Seven parables and similitudes in the synoptic gospels begin with the phrase "who among you" or one of its variants.[116] Many of the sayings of Jesus which are introduced with this stereotyped expression have an ending based on the "lesser to greater" principle (*a minore ad maius; a fortiori;* Heb. *qal waḥomer*).[117] The form of such sayings can be seen in this example from Matt. 12:11-12:

> He said to them, "*What man of you,* if he has one sheep and it falls into a pit on the sabbath, will not lay hold of it and lift it out? Of *how much more* value is a man than a sheep!" (italics added)

The lack of rabbinic parallels to the "who among you" formula may indicate that the expression is an authentic locution of Jesus.[118] The expression occurs occasionally in

OT prophetic literature (Isa. 42:23; 50:10; Hag. 2:3), yet it is also found in Hellenistic literature.[119] Although the introductory expression itself, therefore, may be either Palestinian or Greco-Roman, when used in combination with the "lesser to greater" argument it is a unique and distinctive pattern of speech used by Jesus. However, the meager contact which the formula alone has with OT prophetic speech patterns is insufficient to establish its prophetic character in the sayings of Jesus.[120]

C. THE TWO-PART STRUCTURE OF JESUS' SAYINGS

The sayings of Jesus often exhibit a two-part structure in which the first part is related to the present and the second to the future.[121] This present/future polarity reflects the Jewish apocalyptic conception of two ages; the present age is fundamentally evil, while the age to come, which will be inaugurated by the visitation of God and the conquest of evil, is good. Several examples illustrate this structural tendency in the sayings of Jesus:

> He who is greatest among you/ shall be your servant;
> whoever exalts himself/ will be humbled,
> and whoever humbles himself/ will be exalted. (Matt. 23:11-12)

> For whoever would save his life/ will lose it;
> and whoever loses his life for my sake and the gospels/ will save it. (Mark 8:35)

> Unless you turn and become like children/
> you will never enter the kingdom of heaven. (Matt. 18:3)

> Blessed are the merciful/
> for they shall obtain mercy. (Matt. 5:7)

These examples can be multiplied by including other sayings of Jesus that deal with such antitheses as exalt/humble (Luke 14:11; 18:14b), first/last (Luke 13:30; Mark 10:31; Matt. 19:30; 20:16); and save/lose (Matt. 10:39; Luke 17:33). The antithetical states described in the Beatitudes clearly exhibit this two-part structure.

This eschatological polarity in the sayings of Jesus has an ethical or existential dimension in addition to a temporal dimension.[122] The teachings of Jesus, therefore, show a strong tendency to use eschatological expectation as the basis for a hortatory or parenetic purpose. The presence of this two-part structure in the sayings of Jesus is no guarantee of their authenticity. On the other hand, that this structure permeates the sayings tradition points in the direction of authenticity unless there are compelling linguistic or historical arguments to the contrary. Further, this two-part structure is a basic feature of the more specific forms which we shall discuss below: the *pronouncements of sacral law* and the *eschatological correlative*. In itself the two-part structure of many of the sayings of Jesus is not a necessary feature of prophetic speech. Yet the strong future orientation of Jesus' message coheres well with his prophetic status as established on other grounds.

D. PRONOUNCEMENTS OF SACRAL LAW

In a very influential article published in 1954 E. Käsemann analyzed a form of early Christian speech which he designated "pronouncements of sacral law" (*Sätze heiligen Rechtes*).[123] The pronouncements of sacral law has five characteristics: (1) the pronouncement is structured in the form of a chiasmus, (2) the same verb is found in both parts of the pronouncement, (3) the second part of the pronouncement deals with the eschatological activity of God and has the verb in the future passive (the passive is frequently a circumlocution for divine activity), (4) the central feature of the pronouncement is the principle of retributive justice (*jus talionis*), and (5) the first part of the pronouncement is introduced by the casuistic legal form "if anyone" or "whoever," while the second part is in the style of apodictic divine law.[124] Two examples of this form are found in 1 Cor. 3:17 and 14:38:

> If anyone destroys God's temple,
> God will destroy him.

> If a man does not recognize this,
> he is not recognized.

Käsemann appeals to Rev. 22:18-19 to demonstrate the prophetic origin of such pronouncements. Sayings of Jesus which exhibit the characteristic features of pronouncements of sacral law are regarded as inauthentic, since on formal grounds they may be attributed to early Christian prophets speaking in the name of the risen Lord. Luke 12:8-9 will serve as one of many possible examples of this form of speech in the sayings of Jesus:

> And I tell you,
> every one who acknowledges me before men,
> the Son of man also will acknowledge before the angels of God;
> but he who denies me before men
> will be denied before the angels of God.

If Käsemann's analysis of the form and setting of pronouncements of sacral law in early Christianity is correct, we have a reliable formal means for distinguishing the "sayings of Jesus" which originated in the post-Easter prophetic activity of the church from those which may have originated with the historical Jesus. Unfortunately Käsemann's proposal is riddled with problems, many of which have been ignored in view of the simplicity and attractiveness of the theory: (1) The connection between the pronouncements of sacral law and early Christian prophecy has been assumed rather than demonstrated. Elsewhere in this study it will be shown that there is a close connection between prophecy and speech forms similar to pronouncements of sacral law.[125] (2) The formulation of the pronouncements is not legal, but that of conventional wisdom in which reward is matched with behavior for the purpose of ethical exhortation.[126] (3) The form analyzed by Käsemann can only be regarded as stable if one ignores the wide variations which characterize similar sayings throughout early Jewish and early Christian literature. The one fixed element is the two-part structure which describes the behavior of man in the first part and the response of God in the second part. (4) The assumption that Jesus could not and did not use a form of speech very similar to the pronouncements of sacral law cannot be demonstrated.

In sum, it appears that the pronouncement of sacral law, with its five characteristics, is only one type of pronouncement that matches present behavior with eschatological reward. The eschatological orientation of this speech form, with all its variations, lent itself to use within the framework of early Jewish and early Christian prophetic speech, though it occurs in other settings as well. The form itself does not indicate the presence of prophetic speech unless there are clearer indications of the presence of oracular speech (i.e. predictions of future events, etc.). Further, there is no compelling reason for denying that Jesus himself used that speech form, but again there is no guarantee that every occurrence of the form in the sayings of Jesus is necessarily authentic.

E. THE ESCHATOLOGICAL CORRELATIVE

The eschatological correlative was analyzed and labeled by R. A. Edwards in connection with his investigation of the sign of Jonah in the synoptic gospels (Matt. 12:39; 16:4; Luke 11:29; cf. Mark 8:11-13).[127] The eschatological correlative occurs four times in Q, once in special Matthean material, and never in Mark.[128] The basic form of the eschatological correlative is evident in Luke 11:30:

> For *as* Jonah became a sign to the men of Nineveh,
> *so* will the Son of man be to this generation. (italics added)

The first line begins with a comparative particle and has a verb in the past or present tense. The second line begins with a correlative particle and contains a verb in the future tense. The form is relatively stable and resembles the pronouncements of sacral law. Edwards supposes that the eschatological correlative, which always refers to the figure of the Son of man in the second line, arose in the Q community as an expression of their Son of man Christology.[129] He wavers on the question of whether this was a prophetic speech form used by the prophets of the Q community. The assumption that the eschatological correlative is a product of the post-Easter community is based on the close association of the speech form with the Son of man, a christological title which Edwards does not think emerged until the post-Easter period. However, if one can accept the authenticity of the eschatological Son of man sayings generally, there is no barrier to regarding the eschatological correlative as a speech form of Jesus. Certainly the two-part present/future structure of the correlative is characteristic of the sayings of Jesus.

The eschatological correlative, however, is not a unique form found only in the sayings of Jesus. The prophetic correlative, so labeled because the eschatological element is not invariably present, has been shown to occur frequently in the prophetic books of the LXX.[130] Amos 3:12 is a typical example:

> Thus says the Lord:
> "*As* the shepherd rescues from the mouth of the lion two legs, or a piece of an ear,
> *so* shall the people of Israel who dwell in Samaria be rescued, with the corner of a couch and part of a bed. (italics added)

Or again, Jer. 38:28 LXX (Eng. 31:38):

> And it shall come to pass that
> *as* I have watched over them to pluck up and break down, to overthrow, destroy, and bring evil,
> *so* I will watch over them to build and to plant,
> says the Lord. (italics added)

There is no compelling reason to regard the prophetic correlative either as a form unique to the LXX or as a distinctively prophetic form.[131] Even if we limit our selection of examples to those with the same verb in both parts of the correlative (past or present tense in the first part, and future tense in the second part), there are many occurrences of the form in the Hebrew OT. From a juridical context, reflecting the principle of retributive justice, we quote Lev. 24:19b, 20b:

as he has done/ it shall be done to him . . .
as he has disfigured a man,/ he shall be disfigured.

From a parenetic context we quote Deut. 28:63:

And as the Lord took delight in doing you good and multiplying you,
so the Lord will take delight in bringing ruin upon you and destroying you.

The so-called prophetic correlative can only be labeled prophetic because the correlative, a common rhetorical form found in the OT, is used in prophetic contexts. It could as easily be labeled the "legal correlative" or the "parenetic correlative" since it occurs in those settings as well. To muddy the waters even more, there are numerous examples of such correlatives among the Homeric similes (cf. *Odyssey* iv.335-340; xv.172-78; this last example is found within a prophetic speech uttered by Helen of Sparta). Since the rhetorical models for the eschatological correlative were as available to Jesus as they were to early Christians, there seems little reason to deny that Jesus could have used such a speech form. Further, although the correlative linking past or present and future functioned in many different kinds of contexts, in the sayings of Jesus the correlative is always eschatologically oriented. This future orientation means that the eschatological correlative functions as a prophetic speech form in the sayings of Jesus.

F. SUMMARY

In this section we have examined five forms of speech which characterize the sayings of Jesus preserved in the synoptic tradition. Each of these forms has been associated with prophetic patterns of speech. The introductory formula "(Amen) I say to you" is not a functional equivalent of the OT prophetic messenger formula, but rather an expression which defines the social relationship of the speaker and audience, particularly in Levantine rhetoric. The pronouncement of sacral law and the eschatological correlative were considered in some detail since both forms have been regarded as speech forms used by early Christian prophets. Although these speech forms are not necessarily or distinctively "prophetic," they could be used in prophetic speech. If these speech forms stem from the historical Jesus, they were used by him as a means for structuring prophetic sayings which we shall consider in some detail below. The "who among you" formula does not appear to be distinctively prophetic, though it does appear to derive from the historical Jesus. The two-part structure of many of Jesus' sayings was obviously favored by Jesus, and many of the prophetic sayings which we shall consider below, including the pronouncement of sacral law and the eschatological correlative, exhibit this structure.

7 | THE PROPHECIES OF JESUS

The prophetic status of Jesus, from his own perspective as well as from that of many of his contemporaries, was based upon his proclamation of the imminent arrival of the kingdom of God and the wonders which he performed as a way of legitimating that proclamation.[1] The various sayings of Jesus which have the form of predictions of the future, whether they concern the destruction of the temple, announcements of coming judgment, the coming of the Son of man, or his own death and ultimate victory, all relate in a fundamental way to his proclamation of the imminent arrival of the kingdom of God. Unlike the OT prophets Jesus nowhere in gospel tradition introduces any of his sayings with the characteristic OT prophetic messenger formula "thus says the Lord." While Jesus apparently regarded himself as a prophet, and some of his contemporaries regarded him as a prophet, he made no attempt to legitimate his message through the use of traditional introductory prophetic formulas. For Jesus the wonders which he performed provided a conceptual legitimation for the message he proclaimed. This close connection between prophetic speech and miracle is attested not only for the early Jewish prophetic figures that fomented millenarian movements, but also for leaders of many other millenarian movements throughout the west and the Third World.[2]

I. PREDICTIONS OF THE IMMINENT ARRIVAL OF THE KINGDOM OF GOD

Many recent treatments of the kingdom of God in the teaching of Jesus have concluded that Jesus regarded the kingdom of God as a reality which had both present and future dimensions.[3] There is a broad consensus among NT scholars on two related points: (1) In the eschatological teaching of Jesus the kingdom of God is a future reality which will appear imminently,[4] and (2) In the teaching of Jesus the kingdom of God is a present reality through the words and deeds of Jesus.[5]

One saying attributed to Jesus that clearly announces the imminent arrival of the kingdom of God is Mark 1:15:

The time is fulfilled,
and the kingdom of God is at hand;
repent, and believe in the gospel.

In this brief saying Jesus announces the imminent eschatological event of God's intervention into human history and on that basis calls for repentance, a combined emphasis which is reminiscent of the OT prophets.[6] While the basic content of this saying derives from Jesus, the formulation of the saying belongs to Mark.[7] Closely related is Matt. 10:7-8a, which contains some of Jesus' instructions to the Twelve before sending them out to proselytize:

> And preach as you go, saying,
> "The kingdom of heaven is at hand."
> Heal the sick, raise the dead,
> cleanse lepers, cast out demons.

Here the mission of the Twelve is presented as a reduplication of that of Jesus.[8] These two references to Jesus' proclamation of the imminence of the kingdom of God, while owing much to the formulation of the evangelists Mark and Matthew, must nevertheless be seen as conveying the essential intention of Jesus' message.

Two more complex sayings about the imminence of the kingdom of God are Mark 9:1 and 13:28-31. In Mark 9:1 we find this prediction:

> Truly [amēn], I say to you, there are some standing here who will not taste death before they see that the kingdom of God has come with power.

Mark 13:28-31 preserves a similar prediction:

> From the fig tree learn its lesson: as soon as its branch becomes tender and puts forth its leaves, you know that summer is near. So also, when you see these things taking place, you know that he is near, at the very gates. Truly [amēn], I say to you, this generation will not pass away before all these things take place. Heaven and earth will pass away, but my words will not pass away.

These two predictions of Jesus are related in that they do not simply announce the somewhat vague imminence of the kingdom of God, but they announce its arrival prior to the end of the generation to whom Jesus was speaking. Although many have attempted to reinterpret these sayings in order to eliminate the chronological limits which they set for the arrival of the kingdom of God, none has been successful.[9] Others have attempted to deny the authenticity of both passages,[10] or (less improbably) to claim that Mark 9:1 is a secondary construction based on Mark 13:30.[11] Arguments against the authenticity of both sayings are usually based on dubious preconceptions of what Jesus could or could not have said, or on finely tuned literary distinctions whose validity is in doubt.

Jesus did indeed predict the imminent arrival of the kingdom of God, and this proclamation provided the basis for his call to repentance and decision. The exact formulation of these predictions is no longer accessible, however, since they have all undergone extensive modification by Christian communities and evangelists. We have considered only those sayings in which Jesus predicts the imminent arrival of the kingdom of God, and not sayings or parables that mention one or another dimension of the kingdom.

II. PREDICTIONS OF THE DESTRUCTION OF JERUSALEM AND THE TEMPLE

The evangelists set all of Jesus' prophecies of the destruction of Jerusalem and the temple in or near the holy city during the last days of Jesus.[12] All four canonical gospels place a great deal of dramatic and historical importance on the final trip of Jesus to Jerusalem for the Feast of Passover. In part this emphasis is due to the significance which the events of passion week held for the Christian communities within which the gospels were formulated. More importantly, however, it appears that Jesus and his followers were irresistibly drawn to Jerusalem by the fervent expectation that God was about to act in a final and decisive way. While Jesus and those with him certainly did not intend to foment a holy war against the enemies of God,[13] neither do they appear to have been overly optimistic about the possible course of events. A considerable amount of evidence suggests that Jesus expected his visit to Jerusalem to result at least initially in tragedy, though ultimately in vindication and triumph. The tradition of the violent fate of the prophets may have played a significant role in Jesus' understanding of his own mission and destiny. It is not impossible that the twofold pattern of martyrdom-resurrection was known to Jesus and his contemporaries.[14] The sequential pattern of defeat/victory is reflected in the Markan passion predictions (8:31; 9:31; 10:33-34), which we shall consider in some detail below.

The gospels and Acts contain a number of sayings of Jesus together with rumors of his sayings to the effect that the temple in Jerusalem would be destroyed and replaced with another. At the trial of Jesus "false witnesses" reportedly made the following allegation (Mark 14:58; cf. Matt. 26:61):

> We heard him [Jesus] say, "I will destroy this temple that is made with hands, and in three days I will build another, not made with hands."[15]

The same accusation is reflected in the words of those who come to view the crucified Jesus (Mark 15:29b-30; cf. Matt. 27:40):

> Aha! You who would destroy the temple and build it in three days, save yourself, and come down from the cross!

A similar accusation is reflected in the testimony of "false witnesses" against Stephen in Acts 6:13-14:

> This man [Stephen] never ceases to speak words against this holy place and the law; for we have heard him say that this Jesus of Nazareth will destroy this place, and will change the customs which Moses delivered to us.[16]

The rumor that Jesus claimed that he would destroy the temple is properly labeled false by the evangelists, since Jesus did not claim that he himself would destroy the temple in the more direct versions of this prediction (Mark 13:2 and parallels; John 2:19-21). That claim is attributed directly to Jesus only in the Gospel of Thomas 71:

> Jesus said: "I shall destroy [this] house and no one will be able to [re]build it."

No historical authenticity can be attributed to this saying, however, in view of its lateness as well as its gnosticizing and anticultic tendencies.

While the three passages quoted above are presented by the evangelists as false rumors, a direct statement of Jesus to much the same effect is preserved in John 2:19-21.

Here Jesus, after having "purified" the temple, was asked by some of the religious authorities for a sign. He responded,

"Destroy this temple, and in three days I will raise it up." The Jews then said, "It has taken forty-six years to build this temple, and will you raise it up in three days?" But he spoke of the temple of his body.

The Fourth Evangelist has added an editorial comment (v. 21) that interprets Jesus' prophecy as a reference to his impending death and resurrection. Mark's reference to "three days" in Mark 14:58 (Matt. 26:61) and 15:29 (Matt. 27:40) makes it possible that he too understood the prophecy of Jesus in this way. The allusion to this prophecy within the testimony of false witnesses functions as dramatic irony. That both Mark and John have misunderstood the real meaning of Jesus' prophecy tends to affirm the historicity of the prediction; the original significance of the prediction will be discussed below (pp. 177-79). A more authentic version of the prediction of the destruction of the temple, and one which is directly attributed to Jesus, is found in Mark 13:2 (Matt. 24:2; Luke 21:6), where Jesus responds to a remark made by one of his disciples on the great beauty of the temple:

Do you see these great buildings? There will not be left here one stone upon another, that will not be thrown down.

In the gospels and Acts, then, are five variants of a saying of Jesus in which he predicted the destruction of the temple in Jerusalem. Since Matthew is completely dependent on Mark in 26:61 and 27:40, he provides no independent tradition of this saying. Luke appears to have shifted the rumor which he found in Mark 14:58 to Acts 6:14, where the prediction is attributed to Stephen. Both John 2:19 and Mark 13:2 preserve the only canonical attributions of this prophecy to Jesus. Did Jesus predict the destruction of the temple in Jerusalem, and if so, what is the most original form of that prediction?

The most original form of Jesus' prophecy of the destruction of the temple is preserved in Mark 14:58. Mark 13:2 is an abbreviated version of that prediction, which omits the reference to the *replacement* of the destroyed temple.[17] Both elements are preserved in John 2:19-20, independently of Mark,[18] though the Fourth Evangelist's understanding of the prediction is certainly secondary. The independence of these two versions indicates the antiquity and probably the authenticity of the tradition.[19]

Many OT prophets were critical of the temple and its worship,[20] and occasionally they went so far as to predict its destruction along with that of Jerusalem.[21] Josephus claimed to have predicted the fall of Jotopata (*Bell.* iii.406), and he refers to an ancient oracle which predicted the fall of both Jerusalem and the temple (*Bell.* vi.96-110; iv.388). Joshua ben Ananiah, active ca. A.D. 62, is said to have frequently predicted the fall of the city and the temple (Josephus *Bell.* vi.300-309). A Jewish prophet from Egypt even expected to cause the walls of Jerusalem to collapse (Josephus *Ant.* xx.169ff.; *Bell.* ii.261ff.; Acts 21:31). In view of this consistent prophetic stance against the Jerusalem cultus, it is not unlikely that Jesus would have shared that animus and made it the subject of his predictions. The numerous renewal and resistance movements which flourished during the Roman occupation of Palestine from 63 B.C. to A.D. 135 (many of which were led by prophetic figures) were united in their opposition to both Jerusalem and the cultic establishment.[22] A further argument for the historicity of Jesus' prediction (in the version represented by Mark 14:58 and John 2:19-21) is that while predictions of the destruction of the temple are known to have been made by other prophetic figures throughout the history of Israel, the prediction of destruction coupled with that of *replacement* is unique to Jesus.[23]

Jesus' prophecy of the destruction of the temple was not merely a shrewd historical prediction based on the recognition that Jerusalem and Rome were on a collision course.[24] Since the destruction of the temple and the holy city is a theme of Jewish apocalyptic, Jesus' prophecy is generally and quite correctly regarded as eschatological.[25] The reference to the replacement of the current temple with another "not made with hands" (Mark 14:58 par. Matt. 26:61) cannot refer to a physical building or the resurrection. Although most Jews expected God to build the new temple, in some strands of early Jewish eschatological expectation that task was the messiah's, a view apparently based on the oracle of Nathan (2 Sam. 7:12-14; cf. 1 Chr. 17:12-13).[26] The image of "temple" was used in both early Judaism and early Christianity to refer to a community, frequently an eschatological community.[27] Thus the "temple" which Jesus intended to build in place of the old Herodian temple was in all probability the eschatological community of the New Israel.[28] In conclusion, all the evidence suggests that Jesus could well have made a prediction of the destruction and replacement of the temple,[29] though the versions of the sayings which have been preserved make it impossible to reconstruct the original wording of the prophecy.

In addition to the prophecy of the destruction of the temple, the synoptic tradition preserves three other prophecies of the destruction of Jerusalem in the sayings of Jesus. A judgment speech of Jesus preserved in Luke 13:34-35 par. Matt. 23:37-39 begins with a lament and culminates in a pronouncement of judgment coupled with a promise of final salvation.[30] The saying originally stood in Q, and both evangelists have preserved it in almost identical wording:

Address:	O Jerusalem, Jerusalem,
Indictment:	killing the prophets and stoning those who are sent to you!
Lament:	How often would I have gathered your children together as a hen gathers her brood under her wings, and you would not!
Judgment:	Behold, your house is forsaken [*aphietai*].[31]
Promise of Salvation:	And I tell you, you will not see me until you say, "Blessed is he who comes in the name of the Lord."

While some have argued that this saying is a fragment of Jewish prophecy that Jesus quoted or the Christian community attributed to him,[32] a strong case can be made that Jesus originally uttered this oracle.[33] The basic structure of this saying is very similar to later OT prophetic speeches which include elements of both judgment and salvation (cf. Jer. 13:15-17; 8:19ff.; 23:9ff.).[34] While Jesus says nothing specifically about his own role in this prophecy, it clearly reflects the notion that just as Jerusalem has rejected the messengers of God in the past, so it is now rejecting the final messenger of God, Jesus himself. The critical nature of this rejection is revealed by the fate which awaits the holy city as the direct result of its recalcitrance. The final statement of this prophecy has frequently been rejected as inauthentic, but it appears to be integral to the structure of the entire oracle.[35] The crucial point is whether Jesus could have regarded himself as one who would, at some future time, come "in the name of the Lord," even though the tragedies of his personal destruction and that of Jerusalem would intervene. While Matthew apparently understands the oracle to refer to the parousia, it is evident that Luke historicizes it and makes it refer to the triumphal entry (cf. Lk. 19:28-40). While this juxtaposition of the themes of tragedy and triumph could be attributed to later Christian formulation, the essential elements of this conception were already associated with the tradition of the violent fate of the prophets, a tradition which appears to have played a central role in Jesus' understanding of his own mission and destiny.[36]

Another prophecy of Jesus that is structurally similar to the oracle just discussed is Luke 19:41-44; it too quickly turns into a prediction of the destruction of Jerusalem:

Address:	And when he [Jesus] •drew near and saw the city he wept over it, saying,
Lament:	"Would that even today you knew the things that make for peace! But now they are hid from your eyes.
Threat:	For the days shall come [*hēxousin hēmerai*][37] upon you, when your enemies will cast up a bank about you and surround you, and hem you in on every side, and dash you to the ground, you and your children within you, and they will not leave one stone upon another in you;
Reason for Threat:	because you did not know the time of your visitation."

This oracle has also been regarded as a prediction *ex eventu* that the Christian community later attributed to Jesus.[38] While Luke probably connected this prophecy with the historical destruction of Jerusalem in A.D. 70, there is no compelling reason for denying the original version of this oracle to Jesus.[39] The oracle is framed by references to Jerusalem's ignorance of "the things which make for peace" and the time of its divine "visitation." These phrases refer to Jesus' estimate of the significance of his mission to Israel and the negative reception which he experienced. Unlike the oracle in Luke 13:34-35, this one does not conclude with a promise of final salvation. The blindness and ignorance of Israel reflected in this oracle is a frequent theme in the OT.[40] The emphasis in the oracle, as in that just discussed, is on the grave consequences resulting from the rejection of Jesus as the legitimate and final messenger of God. The term "visitation" in Luke 19:44 represents Gk. *episkopē* and Heb. *pequddah,* which were used in early Jewish apocalyptic texts to refer to the eschatological coming of God to save and to judge, and in early Christian texts, though rarely, for the parousia of Jesus.[41] The use of the term in Luke 19:44 shows no Christian influence, since it cannot refer to the parousia of Jesus. On the other hand, neither can it refer to the eschatological visitation of God, except in the sense that Jesus himself is the visitation which Israel did not recognize. This unique use of the term points to its authenticity.

A third and final oracle of Jesus that can be related to other predictions of the destruction of Jerusalem and of the temple is located in Luke 23:28-31, where Jesus responds to the lamentation made over him as he is led to Golgotha:

Address:		But Jesus turning to them said, "Daughters of Jerusalem,
Admonition:	*a*	do not weep for me,
	b	but weep for yourselves
	c	and for your children.

Basis of Admonition (Impending Disaster):	For behold, the days are coming when they will say, 'Blessed are the barren, and the wombs that never bore, and the breasts that never gave suck!' Then they will say to the mountains, 'Fall on us'; and to the hills, 'Cover us.'
Certainty of the Disaster:	For if they do this when the wood is green, what will happen when it is dry?"

This saying is not derived from Mark; it must be regarded as a free composition by Luke, or as part of an extended passion source used by Luke,[42] or as a traditional saying of Jesus which Luke has set into its present context.[43] The close relationship of the saying to its context and the expressions uncharacteristic of Luke that form this bond make the theory of dependence on a relatively continuous source more preferable. Although the unity of the saying has been questioned,[44] the structural integrity of the saying makes the original unity of the oracle convincing.

The oracle can hardly be a Christian prophecy attributed to Jesus,[45] since its present form betrays no distinctively Christian element. On the other hand, the closest parallel to the negative beatitude at the center of the oracle is the woe of the eschatological discourse (Mark 13:17 par. Matt. 24:19; Luke 21:23): "Alas [or woe] for those who are with child and for those who give suck in those days!" In view of the composite nature of the eschatological discourse in Mark 13 and parallels, it is likely that the saying preserved in Luke 23:28-31 is the source for Mark 13:17 and parallels.[46] This argument indicates, if not the authenticity of the saying in Luke 23:28-31, at least its antiquity. Another indication of the authenticity of the oracle is that similar oracles anticipating the destruction of the temple and of Jerusalem were pronounced by Jesus; we have already considered these in some detail. The oracle can, with some confidence, be regarded as an authentic prophecy of Jesus.

The oracle has two unusual features. First, the impending disaster is not defined, but its magnitude is reflected in the cries of desperation uttered by those who would experience it. Although the specific referent of the prophecy is vague, Luke doubtless understood it to refer to the destruction of Jerusalem (Luke 21:20-24). Surprisingly, neither he nor his Christian predecessors modified the saying in order to make its meaning clearer. Second, the oracle concludes with a metaphor which some have thought inappropriate and therefore indicative of the saying's origin in a quite different setting.[47] In fact this proverb (v. 31) forms an *inclusio* with v. 28b, and thus it ties in with the thrust of the entire saying. Further, the proverb is essentially an argument from lesser to greater (*a minore ad maius,* or *qal waḥomer*), i.e. if Jesus, who is innocent, is about to be executed, how much more will those who are guilty (the Jews who rejected Jesus) pay that penalty. Elsewhere in the gospels Jesus frequently uses the argument from lesser to greater, another indication of the authenticity of this oracle.

III. PREDICTIONS OF THE DEATH AND RESURRECTION

After the major turning point in the Gospel of Mark, the confession of Peter at Caesarea Philippi (Mark 8:27-30), the evangelist inserts into the narrative a series of three predictions of the passion and resurrection of Jesus (8:31; 9:31; 10:33-34). Each of these predictions contains essentially the same elements; we shall quote the longest of them, Mark 10:33-34:

> Behold, we are going up to Jerusalem;
> and the Son of man will be delivered to the chief priests and the scribes,
> and they will condemn him to death,
> and deliver him to the Gentiles;
> and they will mock him, and spit upon him,
> and scourge him, and kill him;
> and after three days he will rise.

These three predictions have long been regarded by critical NT scholarship as prophecies *ex eventu,*[48] and it is clear that at least in their present form they have been extensively reformulated by the post-Easter Christian community. Further, even if an authentic saying in radically revised form is presented by Mark at these three junctures in his narrative, their location is determined by literary[49] rather than historical considerations. There was a widespread belief in the Greco-Roman world that those about to die were able to predict the future.[50] An important motif in the folklore relating to divine men in the Greco-Roman world was that they were expected to be able to forecast not only the death of others, but their own death as well.[51] Consequently, the Markan portrait of Jesus, a divine man according to the conceptual framework of contemporary pagan readers, is rendered more impressive by his predicting his own fate on no less than three separate occasions.

Yet such literary and theological overlays do not in themselves make it impossible that a prediction by Jesus of his own fate may underlie the three variants in Mark 8:31; 9:31; 10:33-34. That Jesus predicted his own suffering and death does not strain the imagination in view of the motif of the violent fate of the prophets, a tradition which Jesus appears to have used to structure his own perception of his mission and destiny. The reference to a resurrection after three days, though a very old Christian tradition (1 Cor. 15:4), reveals the creative hand of the Christian community. Yet once the secondary reference to three days is eliminated, the prediction of Jesus' resurrection has a greater claim to historicity. First, there is the possibility that the pattern of martyrdom-resurrection was associated with the figure of the eschatological prophet in the Judaism contemporary with Jesus.[52] Conceivably, Jesus in his role as eschatological prophet *could* have anticipated both his rejection and death, followed by his vindication and resurrection. However, since the antiquity of this tradition is still not fully known, this theory must remain in doubt. If Jesus did speak of his future resurrection, he undoubtedly used the Aramaic or Hebrew word *qum,* which basically means "to stand up" or "to raise up." If Jesus understood his own role in the light of the oracle of Nathan in 2 Sam. 7:12-14, as I think he did,[53] that passage speaks of a son of David being "raised up," i.e. "enthroned" as king. Jesus may have understood his prediction to mean that even though he might suffer death at the hands of his enemies, God would nevertheless vindicate him by enthroning him as messiah in Jerusalem.[54] Early Christians, however, understood Jesus' prediction to refer, not to his enthronement as messiah, but to his resurrection from the dead. The ambiguity in the word *qum* makes either interpretation possible.

Even though the Markan passion predictions betray the hand of the Christian community in their present form, we have argued that they may in fact conceal a prophecy of Jesus concerning his own fate. If this prediction has an authentic core, it would have consisted of a prophecy of his suffering and possibly his death, followed by an expectation of his vindication by God in terms of his enthronement as messiah. However, the three variants of the prophecy, even if they conceal an authentic prediction of Jesus, make it impossible to determine the precise form of that prophecy.

IV. JUDGMENT SPEECHES

The prophetic judgment speech, so characteristic of the preexilic prophets, almost totally disappeared in the postexilic period.[55] With John the Baptist, the Teacher of Righteousness, and Jesus of Nazareth the judgment speech reappeared, though its formal features are only loosely connected with the OT speech form.[56] Jesus' prophecies against Jerusalem and the temple, which we considered above, are essentially prophetic judgment speeches. A number of other judgment speeches of Jesus are preserved in the synoptic tradition, most of them beginning with a pronouncement of woe upon various places or persons.

The Q tradition contains a number of such judgment speeches, or oracles of doom, one of which is found in Matt. 11:21-22 (Luke 10:13-15):

Address:	Woe to you, Chorazin! woe to you, Bethsaida!
Indict- ment:	for if the mighty works done in you had been done in Tyre and Sidon, they would have repented long ago in sackcloth and ashes.
Transition:	But I tell you,
Threat:	it shall be more tolerable on the day of judgment for Tyre and Sidon than for you.

The oracle charges that the Phoenician coastal cities, largely composed of Gentiles, would have received the proclamation of Jesus, legitimated by the performance of miracles, with greater readiness than the largely Jewish enclaves of Chorazin and Bethsaida. These Gentile cities will be treated more leniently in the judgment than will the Jewish cities who have had a chance to respond to the message of Jesus but who have not. Luke places this speech in the context of the mission instructions to the Seventy, and it coheres with his earlier emphasis that Jesus would have experienced a greater reception from Gentiles, like Elijah and Elisha of old (Luke 4:23-27). The basis for this prophetic denunciation is the rejection of the mission and message of Jesus. The three structural elements in this judgment speech are address, description of offense, and pronouncement of judgment.

A similar judgment speech with an identical structure is found in Matt. 11:23-24, probably more original than the other version of this Q saying in Luke 10:15, 12:

Address:	And you, Capernaum, will you be exalted to heaven? You shall be brought down to Hades.
Indict- ment:	For if the mighty works done in you had been done in Sodom, it would have remained until this day.
Transition:	But I tell you
Threat:	that it shall be more tolerable on the day of judgment for the land of Sodom than for you.[57]

In addition to these judgment speeches directed to villages, Q contained a series of seven woes addressed to the scribes and Pharisees (Matt. 23:13-33 par. Luke 11:42-52). The form and content of these "woes" constitute a complex problem, the subtleties of which cannot be entered into here. The general form and content of these woes can be illustrated by quoting two woes from Luke 11:42, 52:

Address:	But woe to you Pharisees!
Indict-ment:	for you tithe mint and rue and every herb, and neglect justice and the love of God; these you ought to have done, without neglecting the others.
Address:	Woe to you lawyers [scribes]!
Indict-ment:	for you have taken away the key of knowledge; you did not enter yourselves, and you hindered those who were entering.

Each woe has a two-part structure, the first part of which contains the address and a very indefinite and general pronouncement of judgment expressed through the use of the term "woe." The second part contains an accusation describing the offense which has occasioned the condemnation.

A more general series of four woes is preserved in Luke 6:24-26, a section which may have existed in Q:

Address and Indictment:	But woe to you that are rich,
Threat:	for you have received your consolation. Woe to you that are full now, for you shall hunger. Woe to you that laugh now, for you shall mourn and weep. Woe to you, when all men speak well of you, for so their fathers did to the false prophets.

These woes also exhibit a two-part structure. The first line refers to those enjoying a particular state of affairs in which the offense implied is life as usual. The second line, which can have an eschatological orientation (woes two and three), indicates the reward or lack of reward which the offenders will experience. These woes were originally juxtaposed in Q with a series of beatitudes, just as we now find in Luke 6:20-26.

Several observations can be made concerning the three types of woe oracle pronounced by Jesus.[58] First, the juridical principle of *jus talionis*, frequently present in OT woe oracles, is also evident in the judgment awaiting Capernaum, which was exalted and shall be brought down to Hades (Luke 10:15 par. Matt. 21:23), and in the reversals found in the series of woe oracles in Luke 6:24-26. Second, the woe in Luke 6:25b, "Woe to you that laugh now, for you shall mourn and weep," reflects a funerary setting, one of the more ancient and persistent contexts in which pronouncements of woe are uttered. Third, woe oracles in the OT frequently refer to the Day of the Lord, or an equivalent concept, on which those independent of the sovereignty of Yahweh will experience a terrifying visitation of judgment. This biblical usage would have been familiar to Jesus' contemporaries. Fourth, the series of woes which constituted the prophecy of Joshua ben Ananiah, a near contemporary of Jesus, are laments, not pronouncements of judgment.[59] In spite of the formal similarity of the woes of Jesus and those of Joshua ben Ananiah, they function quite differently in their respective contexts.

V. PREDICTIONS OF THE COMING SON OF MAN

Few subjects have been as hotly debated in NT studies as the origin, history, and significance of the Son of man traditions preserved in the gospels.[60] The title "Son of man" is found only on the lips of Jesus, apart from two insignificant exceptions (John 12:34; Acts 7:56). The early church regarded the figure of the Son of man as identical with Jesus, though the evidence in support of this contention in the gospels appears only in the later strata of the tradition. In the Son of man oracles which we shall consider in this section, the title is consistently used by Jesus in the third person and never as a self-reference. That is, the sayings themselves do not indicate that Jesus was referring to himself, though the early Christian community and the evangelists certainly assumed that he was. Modern discussions of the Son of man traditions in the gospels have usually grouped them in three categories: (1) the "earthly," or present, Son of man sayings, (2) the "suffering" Son of man sayings, and (3) the "coming," or "eschatological," Son of man sayings. Although critical scholars have rejected the authenticity of one or another (or indeed all) of these categories, the one which is most consistently regarded as authentic is that which contains the eschatological Son of man sayings.[61] In this section we shall discuss those sayings which exhibit the form of a prediction by Jesus of the future coming of the Son of man.

One such prediction has occasioned a great deal of discussion in recent years. One version of this saying is found in Q, Matt. 10:32-33 par. Luke 12:8-9, and the other in Mark 8:38 and parallels (Matt. 16:27; Luke 9:26). The most original form of the saying appears to be the version found in Luke 12:8-9:

a   Every one who acknowledges me before men,
b   the son of man also will acknowledge before
      the angels of God;
a'   but he who denies me before men
b'   will be denied before the angels of God.[62]

The form of this saying is that of a pronouncement of sacral law in which the second couplet is antithetically parallel to the first. Although the Son of man is not identified with Jesus in the first couplet,[63] he does stand in a very close relationship to Jesus since he provides eschatological confirmation for the proclamation of Jesus. The passive "will be denied" in the last line of the second couple is a circumlocution expressing divine activity, and therefore indicative of the status of the Son of man as the plenipotentiary of God. The soteriological dimensions of this saying are striking.[64] Those who respond to the proclamation of Jesus and are admitted to the fellowship of Jesus will be confirmed in their choice by the Son of man when the kingdom of God arrives in its fulness. While Jesus does not *explicitly* identify himself with this future Son of man, the complementary function of the two figures makes such an identification implicit.[65] The saying is thoroughly apocalyptic in content and supposes that there will be a future judgment scene in which the righteous (those who acknowledge Jesus) will be separated from the sinners (those who deny Jesus). The "coming" of the Son of man, while not explicitly mentioned in this saying, is certainly presupposed; the saying was later elaborated to explicate this idea in Mark 8:38 (Matt. 16:27; Luke 9:26):

> For whoever is ashamed of me and of my words in this adulterous and sinful generation,
> of him will the Son of man also be ashamed, when he comes in the glory of his Father with the holy angels.

Along with the addition of the "coming" motif, the divine sonship of the Son of man is made explicit by the reference to "his Father." The most original form of this saying, preserved in Luke 12:8-9, is probably authentic, although many regard the structure of the saying as a speech form of early Christian prophecy.[66]

The conception of the coming Son of man is rooted in Dan. 7:13-14:

> I saw in the night visions,
> and behold, with the clouds of heaven there came one like a son of man,
> and he came to the Ancient of Days and was presented before him.
> And to him was given dominion and glory and kingdom,
> that all peoples, nations, and languages should serve him;
> his dominion is an everlasting dominion, which shall not pass away,
> and his kingdom one that shall not be destroyed.

Two other synoptic Son of man sayings are more clearly dependent on the Danielic Son of man, Mark 13:26-27 and 14:62:

> And then they will see the Son of man coming in clouds with great power and glory. And he will send out the angels, and gather his elect from the four winds, from the ends of earth to the ends of heaven.

> And Jesus said, "I am [the son of the blessed]; and you will see the Son of man seated at the right hand of Power, and coming with the clouds of heaven."

The association of clouds, the figure of the Son of man, and the verbs "see" and "come" make it quite clear that this constellation of imagery derives from Dan. 7:13-14. In addition, the reference to the seating of the Son of man at the right hand of Power is a clear reference to Ps. 110:1, which early Christians used in combination with Dan. 7:13-14 to conceptualize their faith in Jesus who had been resurrected and would some day return.[67] While the content of both sayings is clearly predictive, their authenticity is doubtful. Further, there is little in their form which would associate them with any specific forms of prophetic speech.

Another group of coming Son of man sayings is found almost exclusively in Q, and each conforms to the structure of the eschatological correlative discussed above. The first such saying is Luke 11:30 (Matt. 12:40):

> For as Jonah became a sign to the men of Nineveh, so will the Son of man be to this generation.[68]

A second correlative is found in Luke 17:24 (Matt. 24:27):

> For as the lightning flashes and lights up the sky from one side to the other, so will the Son of man be in his day.[69]

The third and fourth correlatives are preserved within a tightly structured framework in Luke 17:26-30 (Matt. 24:37-39):

I *a* As it was in the days of Noah,
  b so will it be in the days of the Son of man.
  c^1 They ate, they drank,
  c^2 they married, they were given in marriage,
  d until the day when Noah entered the ark,
  e and the flood came and destroyed them all.

II *a* Likewise as it was in the days of Lot —
  c^1 they ate, they drank,
  c^2 they bought, they sold,
  c^3 they planted, they built,
  d but on the day when Lot went out from Sodom
  e fire and sulphur rained from heaven and
   destroyed them all —
  b so will it be on the day when the Son of
   man is revealed.[70]

This saying of Jesus is characterized by a remarkably complex structure based on the principle of ring composition or chiasmus.[71] While the Semitic poetic structure alone does not guarantee that we are dealing with an authentic saying of Jesus, the presence of such an unusually complex structure is a forceful argument for authenticity.

The three sayings quoted above all exhibit the form of the eschatological correlative, and they all focus on the future judgment in which the figure of the Son of man will play a central role. As in the other coming Son of man sayings discussed above, so here the Son of man is not explicitly identified with Jesus. The correlative form is not exclusively a prophetic speech form, yet the apocalyptic content of these sayings indicates that it does function in that way here.[72]

The last prediction of the coming Son of man which we shall consider is Matt. 10:23, a saying whose form cannot easily be categorized:

When they persecute you in one town, flee to the next; for truly I say to you, you will not have gone through all the towns of Israel, before the Son of man comes.

Few sayings of Jesus have elicited as much controversy as this one, primarily because of the central role it played in A. Schweitzer's reconstruction of the life and ministry of Jesus.[73] Schweitzer regarded Matt. 10:23 as an authentic apocalyptic prediction of Jesus, who expected the present age to close and the future age to dawn before the mission of the Twelve was completed. According to Schweitzer, when this expectation failed to materialize Jesus experienced his first crisis, which led him to attempt to force the coming of the kingdom by going to Jerusalem. More recently Matt. 10:23 has been interpreted as an apocalyptic prediction which arose within early Jewish Christianity; the oracle is regarded as evidence for the lively expectation of the imminent return of the Son of man and for the urgency of the Christian mission in consequence of this belief.[74]

Several observations about this problematic text are in order. First, there is no guarantee that the saying originally was connected with the mission of the Twelve; more likely it circulated as an isolated logion.[75] Second, the time limit set for the coming of the Son of man is vague in that it is linked with the completion of a task whose scope cannot easily be defined. Third, a saying of this nature appears authentic precisely because of its difficulty; it is no less likely to have originated with the historical Jesus than with the earliest Palestinian community.

The synoptic traditions of the coming Son of man are preserved in sayings of Jesus that appear to be prophetic in that they predict a future event which will be of momentous consequences for the present ministry and message of Jesus. The coming Son of man sayings which appear to have the greatest claim to authenticity are those which exhibit a two-part structure in terms of a present-future polarity. The Son of man was the agent of God who rendered judgment and provided salvation for those who had responded to the proclamation of Jesus in a negative or positive manner. Just as the prophets of the OT were in general not concerned with the future in and of itself but rather with the future as a divine response to the present (or past) behavior of mankind, so Jesus sees the future coming of the Son of man as a eschatological confirmation of the truth of his own proclamation.

VI. THE OLIVET DISCOURSE (MARK 13 AND PARALLELS)

Jesus' eschatological discourse in Mark 13:1-32 (Matt. 24:1-36; Luke 21:5-33), sometimes referred to as the Synoptic Apocalypse, constitutes the longest and most concentrated section of the synoptic gospels devoted exclusively to the description of the events surrounding the end of the age. The content of this discourse may be summarized as follows. After emerging from the temple, one of Jesus' disciples commented on the beauty of the building, whereupon Jesus responded by predicting its total destruction (Mark 13:1-2).[76] Proceeding to the Mount of Olives, they sat down and some disciples asked Jesus, "When will this be, and what will be the sign when these things are all to be accomplished?" (vv. 3-4). Jesus then enumerated a variety of signs presaging the end: the appearance of charlatans, wars, earthquakes, and famines (vv. 5-8). Further, the disciples would experience hatred and persecution, "but he who endures to the end will be saved" (vv. 9-13). When the "desolating sacrilege" is seen, those in Judea must flee quickly; the tribulation which follows would be the worst the world has experienced (vv. 14-20). False messiahs and false prophets would appear to deceive even the elect with signs and wonders (vv. 21-23). After the tribulation there will be heavenly signs followed by the coming of the Son of man in the clouds to gather his elect from the earth (vv. 24-27). Just as one knows that summer is near when the fig tree starts to produce leaves, so when these events begin to unfold the Son of man is near (vv. 28-29). Finally, Jesus concluded by saying, "This generation will not pass away till all these things take place," yet no one — not even the Son of man — knows precisely when this will be (vv. 30-32).

The Olivet Discourse, like the Sermon on the Mount in Matt. 5-7, was not delivered by Jesus in the form in which it has come down to us in the synoptic gospels. The present unity of Mark 13 is the result of the editorial work of the evangelist, who welded together previously discrete sayings of Jesus into a relatively unified composition.[77] Since the discourse contains an apocalyptic scenario of the type frequently found in early Jewish apocalyptic literature, many have supposed that it was based on a previously existing Jewish apocalyptic tract which the evangelist adapted to its present context.[78] However, such a hypothesis is completely unnecessary.

Important progress in the modern study of Mark 13 was made by the Swedish scholar L. Hartman.[79] Through a careful analysis of the structural relationship of various apocalyptic motifs which recur in many texts together (the preliminary time of evil, divine intervention, the judgment, the fate of sinners, and the joy of the elect), Hartman demonstrated that Mark 13 is based on a midrashic interpretation of Daniel.[80] Further, those portions of Mark 13 which make up this midrashic substratum also include parenetic details, a feature which is in contrast to that which is normally found in early Jewish apocalyptic.[81] The following schematization illustrates the point which Hartman has made (the bracketed sections are those which may not have belonged to the original midrashic substratum):

Reference	Apocalyptic Prediction	Parenesis
13:5b-8	False messiahs will arise	Do not be led astray
[13:9-11]	[You will be delivered to authorities and persecuted]	[Take heed to yourselves]
13:12-16	You will be hated and killed	He who endures to the end will be saved
[13:17-18]	[Alas for those who are pregnant or who have infants]	[Pray that it will not happen in winter]
13:19-22	If anyone says "Here is the messiah"	Do not believe it
[13:23]	[I have told you all things beforehand]	[Take heed]
13:24-27	After various signs, the Son of man will come	—

While Hartman does not press the point, it is clear that he thinks that the older strata of the parenetic midrash underlying Mark 13 go back to Jesus.[82] Was Mark 13 made up of various sayings of Jesus that the evangelist wove together into a unified discourse, or does Mark 13 consist of a substratum which was a midrashic commentary on portions of Daniel that was latter supplemented with additional material before reaching Mark? The chief weakness in Hartman's position is that the literary tradition which used a particular constellation of apocalyptic motifs in the composition of the Jewish apocalyptic literature he examines could have been at work in the selection and organization of sayings of Jesus that contained similar motifs though they were not placed in association with each other. Hartman has clearly shown, however, that the pre-Markan unity of the Olivet Discourse consists in its midrashic exposition of Daniel.

The literary framework of Mark 13 is an important index to the nature and function of the eschatological discourse in its present context. This framework consists of Mark 13:1-4, 28-32.[83] In its present form, vv. 1-2 resemble a pronouncement story, i.e. a short narrative culminating in a memorable saying of Jesus:

And as he came out of the temple, one of his disciples said to him, "Look, Teacher, what wonderful stones and what wonderful buildings!" And Jesus said to him, "Do you see these great buildings? There will not be left here one stone upon another, that will not be thrown down."[84]

We have already argued that Jesus' prediction of the destruction of the temple is historical, and that Mark 13:2 is a truncated version of this prophecy that exists in more complete form in Mark 14:58. To the pronouncement story in vv. 1-2 the evangelist has added a further element in vv. 3-4 in order to complete the setting for the eschatological discourse:

> And as he sat on the Mount of Olives opposite the temple, Peter and James and John and Andrew asked him privately, "Tell us, when will this be, and what will be the sign when these things are all to be accomplished?"[85]

The widespread view that there is a literary seam between vv. 1-2 and vv. 3-4 is unfounded; the entire introduction functions well in providing a setting for the eschatological discourse.[86] The artificiality of the introduction provided by Mark is revealed by the fact that the questions posed by the disciples are answered in only the most general way. The assumption underlying the entire discourse, however, is the close relationship between the destruction of the temple and the scenario of other eschatological events. Mark 13:1-4 is unique in the NT, since it is the only place where an oracle is given in response to a question.[87] Since this form of prophetic response is entirely at home in the Greco-Roman world, but only rarely attested in early Judaism or early Christianity, the secondary nature of the framework of the eschatological discourse becomes clear.

The determination of the present genre of Mark 13 is a task which should not be confused with the problem of identifying the forms and genres of the traditions which Mark used. The genre of Mark 13 has provided a good deal of discussion. Some have identified Mark 13 as an apocalyptic tract which has been superficially Christianized by the addition of parenetic elements.[88] Others have regarded Mark 13 as an *Abschiedsrede*, or farewell discourse, a genre which is found frequently in biblical literature and which usually includes a prediction of the future within a parenetic framework.[89] A variant of these two views is the notion that Mark 13 is neither an apocalyptic tract nor a farewell discourse, but combines the literary features of both the apocalypse and the farewell discourse.[90] C. H. Dodd regarded Mark 13 as a *Mahnrede*, or speech of admonition,[91] and more recently it has been argued that Mark 13 bears several characteristic features of a genre which became increasingly popular in dissident gnostic circles: the revelatory discourse of the risen Jesus to his disciples.[92] These diverse assessments of the genre of the eschatological discourse in Mark lead one to suspect that in its present form it is a pastiche of various forms and genres which have been cemented together by the evangelist.

The introductory framework of Mark 13 contains three features of Greco-Roman literary composition: an abbreviated peripatetic dialogue (strolling conversation), a seated dialogue in full view of the temple, and two questions which are intended to elicit the prophetic speech which follows. The first two elements are formal features in the development of the Greco-Roman literary dialogue,[93] while the two questions asked by the disciples in order to elicit an oracular response from Jesus are much more appropriate in a Greco-Roman setting than a Palestinian one.[94] By adding vv. 3-4 to vv. 1-2 the evangelist has used the common Greco-Roman literary pattern of an introductory peripatetic dialogue which leads to a seated dialogue set in full view of a temple.[95] While the eschatological discourse itself can hardly be regarded as a dialogue, it is worth noting that even in the later Platonic dialogues realistic dialectic was replaced by the dogmatic lecture with some of the external features of a dialogue.[96] The lost dialogues of Aristotle, which were immensely popular in antiquity, were probably characterized by long expository speeches similar to those in the extant dialogues of Cicero. Plutarch's dialogues are also characterized by long speech; his two temple dialogues are particularly good examples of this tendency (*De defectu oraculorum* and *De Pythiae oraculis*).

Mark 13:1-4 is clearly a literary introduction using Greco-Roman literary patterns and conventions to present the eschatological discourse itself, which was formulated out of discrete sayings of Jesus. A number of prophetic sayings of Jesus are embedded in Mark 13, and we have discussed two of them in some detail above, the prediction of the destruction of the temple (13:2) and the prediction of the coming of the Son of man (13:26-27). In its present form the eschatological discourse appears to have had an important catechetical function for the community to which it was addressed,[97] yet it is hardly an important source for understanding the prophetic speech of the historical Jesus.

VII. CONCLUSIONS

Jesus was regarded as a prophet by many of his contemporaries because he conformed to their image of what an eschatological prophet should do and say. Since prophets belonged only to the distant past or to the eschatological era, those who thought of Jesus as a prophet would have regarded him in fact as an eschatological prophet. There are indications that Elijah, Moses, and Jeremiah were three figures, one of whom was expected to return at the end of the age, or to whose image the eschatological prophet was expected to conform. The evidence, though slim, does suggest that Jesus regarded himself as a prophet in the OT tradition, and in the framework of current Jewish expectation he must have thought of himself as an eschatological prophet. Jesus was also aware that the role of the prophet almost inevitably involved rejection, suffering, and death. The air of pessimism that permeates many of Jesus' predictions is due not only to the later reflection of the early church, but also to Jesus' own perceptions of his fate. The indirect indications that Jesus regarded himself as a prophet include his consciousness of being divinely commissioned, his performance of several symbolic actions in a manner reminiscent of OT prophets, and his experience of at least one prophetic vision. The deeds of Jesus, perceived by his contemporaries as miracles, function to confirm the unconventional message which he proclaimed.

The many forms of speech which Jesus used have been extensively analyzed,[98] but few of them can be regarded with any certainty as distinctively prophetic speech forms. The unique introductory formula used by Jesus, "(Amen) I say to you," is not an equivalent of the OT prophetic messenger formula; it does indicate that Jesus spoke with authority (teacher to students). Jesus' use of pronouncements of sacral law and eschatological correlatives can be regarded as an important feature of his prophetic rhetoric, but only because those forms have an essentially apocalyptic content. Many of the prophecies of Jesus have been so altered in transmission that their original form and often the full scope of their content can no longer be determined. There is no evidence that the followers of Jesus were any more impressed with his predictions than they were with other features of his message. The oracles of Jesus do not appear to have been collected or transmitted in isolation from other speech forms. Thus a focus on the more predictive elements in his sayings as more distinctively prophetic seems an artificial way to analyze the "prophetic speech" of Jesus. Certainly no general linguistic markers, like the OT messenger formula, reveal that Jesus thought that the words he spoke were in fact words of God. On the other hand, it may be that *anything* said by one who was regarded as a prophet both by himself and others in a first-century Palestinian setting would or could be regarded as "prophetic." If Jesus did not claim that his words came from God, neither did he manifest any behavioral characteristics which may be identified with divine possession,[99] at least within the context of prophetic speech. The divine legitimation from Jesus' proclamation appears to have focused in his performance of wonders, which provided a general matrix for his sayings.

One of the more interesting features of Jesus' predictions is that they are usually related to the present (or past) behavior of those to whom he has proclaimed his message. The two-part structure of present/future permeates the sayings of Jesus, so that he must be regarded as a "forth-teller" as well as a "fore-teller." This general pattern is basic to the prophetic message of the OT prophets, and certainly constitutes a distinctively prophetic thrust of Jesus' message. Another feature which permeates the prophecies which we have discussed is pessimism. Jesus anticipated his own death and the destruction of the temple and of Jerusalem. On the other hand, he also looked forward to vindication in the person of the coming Son of man and in the arrival of the kingdom of God in its fulness.

The early church, though it preserved traditions of Jesus' prophetic status both in the popular view and in terms of his own consciousness, did not regard the title "prophet" as adequate to express the developing conceptions of the significance of Jesus. For Greco-Roman audiences the status of Jesus as a divine man was important in early christological developments, yet that too was quickly abandoned for more lofty conceptions. Nevertheless, the prophetic role of Jesus remains an important index to understanding the way in which Jesus defined his own role and the ways in which many of his contemporaries responded to him.

8 | THE CHARACTER OF EARLY CHRISTIAN PROPHECY

I. INTRODUCTION

Prophets and their revelations played an integral role within early Christianity until the beginning of the second century A.D. Thereafter the inevitable forces of institutionalization banished prophets from their roles as leaders and marginalized the revelatory significance of their proclamations. The New Prophecy introduced by Montanus and his followers in the middle of the second century in Asia Minor reveals a total change in the significance of prophecy for early Christianity. Montanism was essentially a charismatic renewal movement within eastern Christianity that had more in common with the millenarian movements of Second Temple Judaism and with the Jesus movement than it had with the kind of prophetic activity which has permeated early Christianity during the second half of the first century. Montanism was labeled a heresy, and thereafter prophets and their revelations were carefully controlled and held in low esteem or even rejected as heretical. In early Christianity, as in Judaism, the gradual decline of prophetic activity is attributable to social rather than theological factors.

In contrast to the paltry evidence for prophetic activity in the popular religion of Greco-Roman paganism and early Judaism, the information regarding this phase of early Christianity is extraordinarily rich. Greco-Roman literature and inscriptions do reveal a great deal concerning the activities at the famous oracle centers, yet they turned a blind eye on the religious practices of the lower classes. The result is that very little is known about popular religion during the Hellenistic and Roman periods.[1] Most of our information about prophetic activity in early Judaism has been preserved in the form of tantalizingly brief notices by Josephus or in widely scattered references in postbiblical literature. In addition, some oracular material appears to have been embedded in Jewish apocalyptic literature. Only with great difficulty and not a little imagination can a coherent picture of the nature and function of prophecy in early Judaism be constructed from such fragmentary and disconnected evidence. Although early Christianity was not exclusively a movement of the lower classes,[2] many of its converts were necessarily drawn from the lower strata of urban populations. The NT and other early Christian literature written before the middle of the second century were intended for the internal use of Christian communities and are therefore invaluable for reconstructing the character of Christianity during this early period.[3] No other religious sect in the Greco-Roman period, with the possible exception of the Qumran community, produced a comparable body of literature which has survived.

Apart from a few insignificant exceptions, early Christian literature is the only source for our knowledge of early Christian prophecy. Two different kinds of information on this subject are found in this literature: information about prophecy and the activities of Christian prophets, and prophetic sayings and speeches of Christian prophets. These two categories of data must be treated with considerable caution, however. Information about prophecy and the activities of Christian prophets may be *idealized* (as in the Pauline letters?), *tendentious* (as in Acts?), or *idiosyncratic* (as in the Apocalypse of John?). Historical criticism is therefore a necessary tool for correcting and evaluating such evidence. Prophetic sayings and speeches, of course, may be literary creations rather than transcriptions or synopses of the utterances of prophets; or, sayings and speeches of nonprophetic origin may be incorrectly identified as prophetic (e.g. the sayings of Jesus).[4] Most previous reconstructions of the nature and functions of early Christian prophecy have been based on a synthesis of the information available on the subject from the NT and other early Christian literature. No comprehensive attempts have been made to analyze the putative oracles of early Christian prophets and to correlate the results of such an analysis with information about prophets and prophecy.[5] The present study endeavors to accomplish precisely that objective.

Information about early Christian prophecy is primarily concentrated in three sources: 1 Cor. 12-14 (addressed to the Corinthian Christians by Paul ca. A.D. 52), Did. 10-13 (addressed to rural Christian communities in Syria-Palestine by an unknown author ca. A.D. 100), and the Acts of the Apostles (written ca. A.D. 90 under the sponsorship of a wealthy Roman patron named Theophilus for the purpose of presenting Christianity in a generally favorable way).[6] Of course, many other relevant statements concerning prophets and prophecy are scattered throughout the remainder of early Christian literature, but particularly significant are the two documents which self-consciously present themselves as Christian prophecy in written form: the Apocalypse of John (written ca. A.D. 90 and addressed to a number of Christian communities in western Asia Minor) and the Shepherd of Hermas (written in various stages from A.D. 90 to 150 and addressed to the Christian congregations in and around Rome).[7] Many other oracles have been preserved in other Christian writings, and these will be isolated and analyzed in Chapter X.

The task of the present chapter is fivefold: (1) to clarify the beginnings of Christian prophecy and its role in earliest Palestinian Christianity, (2) to identify early Christian prophets and define their general relationship to other Christians, (3) to assess the relationships between prophets and other leaders within Christian communities, (4) to distinguish between various types of early Christian prophets, and (5) to consider how Christian prophets and their oracles were evaluated by other Christians.

II. THE BEGINNINGS OF CHRISTIAN PROPHECY

The earliest surviving piece of Christian literature is 1 Thessalonians, a letter written by Paul ca. A.D. 49, twenty years after the crucifixion and resurrection of Jesus of Nazareth. Within the brief span of twenty years early Christianity had spread quickly throughout the Mediterranean world until house churches were located in virtually every major urban center. Thessalonika itself was situated in Macedonia, nearly a thousand miles (as the crow flies) from Jerusalem, where Christianity began "in a corner" in A.D. 29. 1 Thessalonians reflects many of the characteristic interests and concerns of the early Christians. Perhaps in response to criticism from outsiders, the letter emphasizes strongly the necessity of living quiet, well-ordered, and morally circumspect lives. The Thessalonian Christians owed their conversion from paganism to the aggressive evangelistic efforts of Paul and his co-workers, and they in turn had sought to proselytize others. The community lived in fervent expectation of the return of Jesus, the Son of God, from heaven for their own ultimate salvation and the judgment of the ungodly (1:10; 2:19; 4:14-17; 5:2, 23). The presence and activity of the Holy Spirit in the lives of believers is taken for granted (1:5-6; 4:8; 5:19), and is connected with Christian prophecy in the first extant reference to that phenomenon (1 Thess. 5:19-22): "Do not quench the Spirit, do not despise prophesying, but test everything; hold fast what is good, abstain from every form of evil." In spite of the brevity of these statements, several tentative conclusions regarding Christian prophecy may be drawn from them: (1) the Holy Spirit and prophesying have an intimate, cause-and-effect relationship,[8] (2) prophesying was a normal congregational activity, and (3) prophesying had, for whatever reason, become a factor in intramural conflict. Although the specific problems experienced by the Thessalonian community can never be recovered, these three points are characteristic features of prophetic activity in the experience of many other Christian communities.

The first extant attempt to compose a historical narrative of the beginnings of Christianity is the Acts of the Apostles, the second part of a two-volume work, the first part of which is the Gospel of Luke. Luke-Acts was written sometime during the period A.D. 65-90, probably later rather than earlier in that period. The author, traditionally identified as "Luke" though Luke-Acts is itself anonymous, was therefore writing at least one and probably two generations after the events surrounding the beginning of Christianity. The purpose of Acts is to describe the spread of Christianity from Jerusalem to Rome through legitimate apostolic channels and to define Christianity as a legitimate religious offspring of Judaism against pagan and Jewish detractors. One of the central themes in Acts is the power and activity of the Holy Spirit (Acts 1:5, 8). In Acts 2 the initial outpouring of the Spirit upon the assembled followers of Jesus on the Day of Pentecost causes them to speak in tongues, a phenomenon which the author closely associates with prophecy (Acts 19:6). From that point on, every significant step in the spread of Christianity is attended by miracles and divine guidance. Speeches to unbelievers are made by men "filled with the Holy Spirit" (4:8; 7:55-56; 13:9-11); unbelievers are brought to faith through visionary directives (9:1-9; 10:3-6); Christian leaders are given divine guidance through both visions (10:10-16; 16:9-10; 18:9-10; 22:17-21; 27:23-24) and revelations mediated by Christian prophets (11:27-28; 13:1-3; 15:28; 20:23; 21:4, 10-11). Through the laying on of hands new groups of believers received the Holy Spirit, an experience sometimes accompanied by such manifestations as speaking in tongues, praising God, and prophesying (8:14-17; 10:44-46; 19:1-6). Further, twelve specific individuals are referred to as prophets or as regularly exercising the prophetic gift, more than are mentioned in all other early Christian literature combined: Agabus (11:27-28; 21:10-11); Judas and Silas (15:32); Barnabas,[9] Simeon Niger, Lucius of Cyrene, Manaen, and Saul (13:1); and the four virgin daughters of Philip the Evangelist (21:8-9).

In comparison with the tantalizingly brief reference to prophecy in 1 Thessalonians, Acts contains a wealth of information regarding prophecy and other revelatory phenomena in earliest Christianity. Like 1 Thessalonians, Acts reflects a close relationship between the Holy Spirit and prophecy; the Spirit is the one who speaks through prophets. The Spirit can be referred to as speaking even when an unmentioned prophet was doubtless the revelatory medium (Acts 15:28; 20:23). Prophecy, however, is but one of the many manifestations of the Spirit; others include persuasive speech, speaking in tongues, the act of praising God, the performance of miracles. Again like 1 Thessalonians, Acts depicts prophetic activity as a normal and pervasive activity often, but not always, practiced within a group. Unlike 1 Thessalonians, there is no hint that prophecy was involved in intramural conflict, though there are numerous instances of extramural conflicts in which Christian leaders who are filled with the Holy Spirit oppose and vanquish magicians and others controlling or controlled by demonic powers (Acts 8:4-8; 9:23; 13:4-12; 16:16-18; 19:11-20). Acts appears to contribute a great deal to the meager data found in 1 Thessalonians: (1) A number of early Christians are labeled "prophets" and appear to have practiced prophesying on a regular basis. (2) Prophesying is also depicted as an unexpected activity which coincides with the experience of being filled with the Holy Spirit for the first time (Acts 19:1-6; cf. 2:1-4, 15-21; 10:44-46). (3) Further, prophesying is one among many manifestations of the Holy Spirit. (4) Some of the functions of prophecy mentioned in Acts include prediction of the future (11:27-28; 20:23; 21:10-11), selection of particular individuals for special tasks (13:1-3), solving religious disputes (15:28, 32), and guidance in making various decisions (16:6-10).

1 Thessalonians, as the first extant piece of Christian writing, and Acts, as the first extant attempt to compile a history of earliest Christianity, are valuable for the study of Christian prophecy in very different ways. The mention of prophesying in 1 Thessalonians is tantalizingly brief but unquestionably historical. The wealth of material on the subject of prophets and prophecy in Acts is certainly of great value, but is not as certainly or as uniformly historical. In Luke-Acts, in contrast to 1 Thessalonians, oracles and divine revelations of various kinds have an important *literary* function. The copious references to prophecies, visions, miracles, and persons "filled with the Holy Spirit" that punctuate the narrative at critical junctures provide an exciting force which controls the movement of the plot.[10] The beginning of the Gospel of Luke also exhibits a flurry of prophetic activity surrounding the birth and early years of both John the Baptist and Jesus. Indeed, Luke takes great pains to portray Jesus as a prophet who is the last in a long series of divinely sent messengers. In Hellenistic and Roman literature divination and oracles often play critical roles in the direction and development of the plots of epics and tragedies.[11] Simply because prophetic revelation serves a literary purpose in Luke-Acts, however, does not mean that the evidence contained in Acts is unhistorical. 1 Thessalonians and Acts are two very different kinds of witnesses to the role of prophecy in early Christianity. The evidence which they present is scarcely sufficient to reconstruct a balanced picture of the nature and function of early Christian prophecy, nor have we attempted to elicit all the data which they contain.

In our brief discussion of 1 Thessalonians we noted that the Christians of the Macedonian community lived in the fervent expectation of Jesus' return to save them and judge their enemies. In contrast, Luke-Acts does not convey the notion that early Christians lived in imminent expectation of the end of the age. Luke's more relaxed attitude toward the parousia of Jesus is due in part to the fact that he wrote his two-volume treatise more than a generation after 1 Thessalonians. During the forty-year interval between the composition of those two pieces of literature the conviction that the end of all things was *imminent* appears to have lessened considerably in most phases of the early Christian movement.[12] Even Luke, however, retains remnants of the eschatological framework within which prophecy first broke out in earliest Palestinian Christianity. In Acts 2:15-21, the beginning of Peter's Pentecost sermon, the phenomenon of speaking in tongues is interpreted as the fulfilment of an ancient prophecy of Joel (Joel 2:28-32 [MT 3:1-5]):

> For these men are not drunk, as you suppose, since it is only the third hour of the day; but this is what was spoken by the prophet Joel: "And in the last days it shall be, God declares, that I will pour out my Spirit upon all flesh, and your sons and your daughters shall prophesy, and your young men shall see visions, and your old men shall dream dreams; yea, and on my menservants and my maidservants in those days I will pour out my Spirit; and they shall prophesy. And I will show wonders in the heaven above and signs on the earth beneath, blood, and fire, and vapor of smoke; the sun shall be turned into darkness and the moon into blood, before the day of the Lord comes, the great and manifest day. And it shall be that whoever calls on the name of the Lord shall be saved."

This is the only indication in Acts that the pouring out of the Spirit upon all mankind is an eschatological gift and that prophecy is a primary manifestation of this outpouring of the Spirit.

There was an apparently widespread view in early Judaism that at the end of the present age or in the age to come the Spirit of God would be poured out on all Israel and all Israelites would have the gift of prophesying.[13] In Num. 11:29 Moses is quoted as saying: "Would that all the Lord's people were prophets, that the Lord would put his spirit upon them!" In the rabbinic commentary on that passage, *Numbers Rabbah* 15:5, we read: "In this world some men have prophesied, but in the world to come, all Israelites will prophesy." The same comment is made of Joel 2:28 (MT 3:1), part of which was quoted in Peter's Pentecost address in Acts 2.[14] Earliest Palestinian Christianity lived in the imminent expectation of the end of the age and the coming of Jesus as the Son of man to save and to judge.[15] The belief that God was present in the midst of his new community was a conviction which appears to belong to the very earliest religious experience of the followers of Jesus.[16] This awareness of the divine presence was not intuitive, but was conceived in terms of a variety of epiphenomena which were all attributed to the active presence of God. This divine presence was conceptualized in a variety of ways: as the presence of the Holy Spirit (Acts 2:4; Rom. 8:9), the presence of God (1 Cor. 14:25), or the presence of Jesus (Rom. 8:10). The ability to prophesy, which was closely associated with the presence of the Spirit in Judaism, was also regarded as a natural manifestation of the presence of the Spirit in the church, a view reflected in both Acts and 1 Thessalonians.

Earliest Palestinian Christianity was a millenarian movement with basic similarities to the many other revitalistic movements within early Judaism that we have discussed above (pp. 121-38). As we saw, the movement fomented by John the Baptist was a type of millenarian movement which can be labeled a *conversionist* movement, while the movement set into motion by Jesus during his lifetime exhibited both *conversionist* and *thaumaturgical* responses to the world. The conversionist elements in the movements of John the Baptist and Jesus indicate a close relationship between the two, yet the strong thaumaturgical element in the Jesus movement constitutes a distinctive emphasis not found in other Palestinian millenarian movements. While the movement started by Jesus was characterized by a number of distinctive features, it was nevertheless only one among many such movements. Jesus himself functioned as a charismatic leader by legitimating his position in three ways: through the performance of wonders which authenticated his status as an agent of God's saving power, through a series of prophetic predictions of future events (the coming of the kingdom of God, the destruction of Jerusalem and the temple, the coming of the Son of man, etc.), and through his authoritative teaching in which he revived the religious and ethical values of the OT era.

In contrast to other millenarian movements, Christianity went through parallel stages of development as a millenarian movement during two separate periods of its growth. The first stage was that of the Jesus movement itself, prior to the execution of Jesus by the Roman authority in Palestine. The second stage began with the experience of the resurrection of Jesus, an event which breathed new life into a movement which must have appeared destined for dissolution like the many other ephemeral apocalyptic movements in Palestine. Early Christianity, however, appears to have splintered into several parallel movements quite early in its history, a fact imperfectly and indistinctly revealed in our sources (cf. Acts 6:1-6). The so-called Q community, i.e. a hypothetical group or groups of early Palestinian Christians who produced the sayings source "Q" used by both Matthew and Luke, apparently flourished in Palestine from 30 to 50 A.D. This community had millenarian aspirations coupled with a strong emphasis on prophecy.[17] Like the movement begun by Jesus, and certainly in conscious continuity with it, the Q community was a millenarian movement of the *conversionist* and *thaumaturgical* type. Although the Q community apparently placed an important emphasis on prophecy, the identities of those prophets have not survived, and we cannot reconstruct with any confidence the role of the prophet within the Q community. It is likely that, in the tradition of John the Baptist and Jesus, the prophetic activity of the Q community was directed to all Israel and not just to a sectarian elite.

Paul also appears to have functioned as the founder and leader of a group of widely separated Christian communities with a distinct millenarian focus in the tradition of Palestinian Christianity. Paul presents himself, in continuity with the image of Jesus and the early Christian leaders depicted in Acts, as a miracle worker (Gal. 3:5; Rom. 15:19; 2 Cor. 12:12; 1 Thess. 1:5; 1 Cor. 2:4) whose mighty deeds legitimated his apostolic vocation. Recent scholarship has also interpreted the community which produced the Gospel of Mark as an apocalyptic millenarian community living in the imminent expectation of the end of the age.[18] Through the early Christian mission to Diaspora Judaism (which was gradually transformed into a Gentile mission) Christian millenarianism was exported from Palestine to the entire Greco-Roman world. While most settings within which prophecy occurred in early Judaism were eschatological (either within a millenarian movement or in situations of grave social and political crisis), in the Greco-Roman world oracles and divination were generally noneschatological and prevalent everywhere. As the proportion of pagan converts to Christianity began to increase and then to outnumber Jewish Christians, some rather profound changes in the understanding of prophecy and its functions began to occur. Within the Christian communities of the Greco-Roman world prophecy had become institutionalized to the extent that it no longer had an exclusively eschatological focus or function; this is as true for the brief reference to prophesying in 1 Thessalonians as it is for the numerous references in Acts. Before the Christian movement was twenty years old, early Christian prophecy had already undergone a metamorphosis in the direction of "Christianization," i.e. a new type of prophet and prophecy had developed from early Jewish and Greco-Roman prophetic, oracular, and revelatory traditions. This "Christianization" was not a process which proceeded at the same rate throughout all phases of the Christian movement, nor did the development of the more distinctive forms of Christian prophecy (as in the Corinthian community) ever reach a state of equilibrium. Christian prophets and prophecy were in a constant state of change and development from the earliest eschatological prophecy within a millenarian setting of Palestinian Christianity to the final death rattle of prophecy with the rise and rejection of Montanism.

III. WHO PROPHESIED IN EARLY CHRISTIANITY?

There is a widespread view that in early Christianity all Christians were potential, if not actual, prophets.[18a] Further, a distinction is often made between *prophets* (i.e. those to whom the designation *prophet* is applied and who prophesy with some regularity) and *those who prophesy* (i.e. the act of prophesying by random individuals usually within a congregational setting).[19] Some scholars have held that prophesying was monopolized by a small number of Christians who were established as prophets and who formed a charismatic order which held a recognized position in the church.[20] Others have claimed that congregational prophecy was the dominant form of prophetic activity practiced in early Christianity and few occupied the role of prophet.[21] We shall first examine the application of the term *prophet* (*prophētēs*) to individuals within early Christianity, then we shall survey descriptions of the act of *prophesying* (*prophēteia*, *prophēteuein*), and finally we shall consider the validity of the view that all Christians were potential prophets.

A. EARLY CHRISTIAN PROPHETS

A number of individuals are designated as prophets or prophetesses in early Christian literature. In pagan Greek the term *prophētēs* (feminine *prophētis*) had no necessary connection with revelatory activity and meant simply "spokesman" or "announcer"; however, as a designation of the particular cultic official at Greek oracle sanctuaries who transmitted oracular responses to inquirers the term took on the technical meaning "one who speaks on behalf of the god."[22] In pagan Greek the word was never laden with such connotations as "one who predicts the future" (the prefix *pro-* meant "forth," not "fore") or "inspired spokesman," though it was given that meaning in Biblical Greek and in the literature of both early Judaism and early Christianity. Further, in pagan Greek religious contexts *prophētēs* was only one of a number of possible ways of designating "one who speaks on behalf of the god."[23] In early Christianity the exclusive use of the term *prophētēs* as a designation for a human medium of divine revelation is consciously borrowed from the widely accepted equation in Judaism of the Greek word *prophētēs* with the Hebrew term *nabi'* (reflected in the LXX).[24] The term *prophētēs* occurs 144 times in the NT, 86 of which refer to OT prophets. Similarly, in the Apostolic Fathers the word occurs 58 times, 37 of which refer to OT prophets. The early Christian application of the designation *prophētēs* to individual Christians, then, was originally determined by the prevalent conception of the prophetic role in the OT. In early Judaism the term "prophet" (*nabi'* or *prophētēs*) was rarely applied to those who were not OT prophets or eschatological prophets. In early Christianity this reluctance to apply the designation to contemporary figures was completely overcome, and the term *prophētēs* was freely applied to those who were regarded as inspired spokesmen of God. In the gospels the title is used of John the Baptist ten times and of Jesus nine times.[25] In the NT the noun *prophētēs* is used nineteen times of early Christian figures, in the Apostolic Fathers twenty-one times.[26]

In addition to the twelve prophets and prophetesses named specifically in Acts, throughout the rest of the NT (apart from the designation of John the Baptist and Jesus as prophets in the gospels) only "Jezebel" of Thyatira (Rev. 2:20) and John the Seer (implied in Rev. 22:9) are so identified. In noncanonical early Christian literature those designated as prophets include Polycarp of Smyrna (ca. A.D. 70-155), Melito of Sardis (died ca. A.D. 190), Ammia of Philadelphia (ca. A.D. 100-150), Quadratus (reign of Hadrian, A.D. 117-138), and Cerinthus (late first century, early second).[27] There were also a number of so-called gnostic prophets, including Markus, Philumene the prophetess of Apelles, Barkabbas, Martiades, and Marsianos.[28] After the middle of the second century the Montanist prophets appeared, including Montanus himself and the two prophetesses Priscilla (or Prisca) and Maximilla.[29] Tertullian tells of a woman visionary, a Montanist, who had a vision during a Sunday service and related her experience after the service.[30] In a letter to Cyprian written ca. A.D. 256, Firmilian refers to a Cappadocian prophetess who was active ca. A.D. 234, following an earthquake in the region of Cappadocia and Pontus as well as in a situation of persecution.[31] This rather meager list could be slightly expanded with the addition of the names of those early Christians who prophesied or who apparently regarded themselves as prophets though they were not labeled as prophets by others (so far as we know) or by themselves. These would include Paul, John the Seer (but cf. Rev. 22:9), Ignatius of Antioch, and Hermas of Rome.[32] These writers exhibit a reluctance to use the term "prophet" as a self-designation, a reluctance which also characterized the Teacher of Righteousness and Josephus.[33] In fact, the only use of the term "prophet" (in this instance "prophetess") as a self-designation in early Christianity is referred to in Rev. 2:20 (cf. 1 Cor. 14:37), where "Jezebel" is referred to as one "who calls herself a prophetess." Paul's primary self-conception was that of an apostle, while Ignatius presumably regarded himself as a bishop; John the Seer clearly regards himself as a prophet (e.g. he claims to have written a prophetic book, Rev. 1:3; 22:18), but the role of Hermas is more ambiguous.

In the NT the term "prophet" is used some fourteen times in contexts in which the individuals referred to are not specifically named; in the Apostolic Fathers there are twenty-one instances of the same phenomenon.[34] Further, it is noteworthy that the occurrences of the noun *prophētēs* are almost always in the plural in the NT, while in the Apostolic Fathers the situation is reversed and most occurrences of *prophētēs* are singular.[35] This suggests that prophets were primarily active in groups in the NT era, but as individual practitioners in the postapostolic period. This tentative conclusion is not related to the question of the specific settings in which prophetic activities occurred (e.g. within the setting of congregational worship). This hypothesis must be tested by examining the literary evidence.

On the basis of the evidence in 1 Cor. 12-14 it appears that prophets, or those who prophesied, were active only within the framework of Christian worship. Further, it appears that prophets were particularly active during particular segments of the service; in 1 Cor. 14:29 Paul advises: "Let two or three prophets speak, and let the others [i.e. the other *prophets*][36] weigh what is said." This passage, if we interpret it correctly, seems to imply that the prophets exercise their revelatory gifts at a particular point in the proceedings and that when they are not prophesying they are expected to participate in the evaluation of the prophetic utterances of others. Although Paul conceptualizes those who prophesy at Corinth as "prophets" (1 Cor. 14:29, 32, 37) and regards prophets as holding a particular office in the church second only to apostles (1 Cor. 12:28-29), the view held by the Corinthians themselves is not clear. Undoubtedly Paul's conception of the prophetic role was primarily informed by OT models, though the same assumption cannot be made of the Corinthian Christians themselves. Paul regards "prophets," after apostles, as a divinely appointed role in the church (1 Cor. 12:28-29); Paul specifically observes that "All are not prophets, are they?" in v. 29.

Several times in the Apocalypse of John the author uses the term *prophētēs* in the plural; he refers to "thy servants the prophets and saints" (11:18), "the blood of the saints and prophets" (16:6), "saints, apostles, and prophets" (18:20), "the blood of prophets and of saints" (18:24), "the Lord, the God of the spirits of the prophets" (22:6), and "your brethren the prophets" (22:9).[37] These references all indicate that the prophets were an identifiable group, distinguishable from saints and apostles. While there is no indication that they prophesied in groups, either within or apart from the setting of Christian worship, they appear to have constituted a "school" or "order" within the churches of western Asia Minor. The author's own revelatory experience, though it took place on Sunday (1:10), does not appear to have occurred within the setting of a prophetic group or congregational worship. If, as I suspect, the "angels" of the seven churches (1:20; 2:1, 8, 12, 18; 3:1, 7, 14) should be regarded as *prophetic messengers* rather than guardian angels or church officials, it would appear that John is functioning as a kind of master prophet in transmitting revelatory messages to the churches under his (real or assumed) jurisdiction through local prophetic messengers. But this is purely hypothetical and incapable of demonstration. The only other indication of a prophetic school in Revelation is possibly that of the prophetess Jezebel at Thyatira (Rev. 2:20-23a), whose followers are designated "my servants" (= prophets?) and "her children" (= sons of the prophetess?), though no firm conclusions can be drawn.[38] The original Jezebel had a stable of 900 prophets (1 Kgs. 18:19).

In Acts prophets ordinarily prophesy within the setting of a prophetic group (11:27-28; 13:1-3; cf. 15:32), though on one occasion Agabus is apparently the only prophet present (21:10). In the Didache (10-15) there is no indication that more than one prophet functioned at a time within the framework of Christian worship. Further, though the prophet occupies a position of great honor in the Didache (they are the Christian equivalent of OT high priests, according to Did. 13:3), their role is idiosyncratic and integral neither to Christian worship nor to the general life of the Christian community. Similarly in Hermas *Mand.* xi, the only place in that lengthy document where prophets and prophecy are mentioned, both those labeled false prophets and those regarded as true prophets give solo performances; the former in extraecclesial settings, and the latter within the framework of regular Christian services of public worship. At one point Hermas asks the Shepherd how to tell the true prophet from the false prophet (*Mand.* xi.7). The false prophet is "empty" and has the spirit of the devil, while the true prophet has the divine spirit (*to pneuma to theion*), but how can they be distinguished? The true prophet is then described in *Mand.* xi.9:

> Therefore, when the man who has the Divine Spirit comes into a meeting of righteous men who have the faith of the Divine Spirit, and intercession is made to God from the assembly of those men, then the angel of the prophetic spirit [*ho angelos tou prophētikou pneumatos*] rests on him and fills the man, and the man, being filled with the Holy Spirit, speaks to the congregation as the Lord wills.

There is no indication that Hermas is here describing the phenomenon of congregational prophecy, i.e. the act of prophesying by random individuals present at a worship service.[39] "The man who has the Divine Spirit" is a true prophet who exhibits his authenticity not only by moral irreproachability but also by delivering unsolicited prophecies only within the setting of public worship.

In sum, it appears that those designated "prophet" in early Christianity were specialists in mediating divine revelation, not simply those who occasionally prophesied. The image of the OT prophet and the term used to designate such prophets (*prophētēs*) was the primary source of this conception. In the middle of the first century A.D. in Corinth, prophets constituted a recognizable group within the Christian community that specialized in mediating a particular form of divine revelation within the setting of congregational worship. In Acts there is evidence that groups of prophets functioned in early Palestinian Christianity, though it is unclear whether they prophesied within the framework of such groups or within services of worship (probably both). At the end of the first century in western Asia Minor, John the Seer was part of a prophetic school (possibly as a kind of master prophet) whose members appear to have been scattered throughout various Christian communities but who saw themselves as a divinely instituted intramural body. No evidence suggests that these prophets functioned in a group within or apart from services of worship. At the end of the first century in Syria-Palestine (the provenance of the Didache) and in Rome (where the Shepherd of Hermas originated), prophets gave solo performances both within the setting of Christian worship (Didache, Hermas) and in private sessions (Hermas). On the basis of the evidence thus far considered we have discovered three types of prophetic activity: (1) prophets who prophesy in a prophetic group, either within or apart from Christian worship, (2) prophets who belong to a prophetic fraternity but who are scattered throughout a number of Christian communities and exercise an independent ministry in their home communities, and (3) prophets who give solo prophetic performances, either within the framework of Christian worship or in a private setting. While the differences between these types may be more apparent than real (our sources do not provide us with complete information), there is no need to reduce these types of prophetic activity to one pattern.

B. THE ACT OF PROPHESYING

In considering the title "prophet" before the activity of prophesying, we may have skewed the evidence, since it is possible that the label "prophet," with its OT associations, could have been used (particularly by Paul) to characterize those who prophesied only occasionally and who would not have regarded themselves as prophets in the specific sense of specialists in mediating divine revelation in comprehensible human language. Here we wish to consider whether the act of prophesying in early Christianity was characteristic only of specialists, or whether it was occasionally exercised by Christians who would not have regarded themselves as "prophets."

The verb "prophesy" (*prophēteuein*) occurs twenty-eight times in the NT, and in only five instances does it refer to OT prophetic activity; in all other cases it is used of prophesying in early Judaism or early Christianity.[40] In the Apostolic Fathers the verb occurs only nine times, three of which refer to Christian prophesying while the remaining six describe OT prophesying.[41] The noun which can refer to the act of prophesying (*prophēteia*), as well as to the gift of prophecy and prophetic utterance, occurs nineteen times in the NT, only three of which refer to OT activity.[42] In the Apostolic Fathers the noun occurs but four times and in only one instance describes Christian prophetic activity.[43] In pagan Greek the verb is used only rarely and very late in antiquity;[44] the verb most commonly used in Greek sources for the act of prophesying was *mainesthai*, a cognate of the most common Greek designation for a diviner (*mantis*). The verb *prophēteuein*, however, is the standard translation for the Hebrew verb *nb'* in the LXX and in early Jewish and early Christian literature. The use of the verb *prophēteuein* in early Christian literature, then (like the noun *prophētēs*), is formally derived from the Israelite-Jewish prophetic traditions.

Paul's use of the verb "prophesy" is confined exclusively to 1 Cor. 11-14, where it must be considered in the context of the use of the noun "prophet." In 1 Cor. 12-14 Paul uses his considerable rhetorical skill in attempting to persuade the Corinthian Christians that prophecy rather than glossolalia is preferable in public services of worship, since prophecy is readily comprehensible while glossolalia (unless interpreted) cannot be understood. If Paul's use of the noun "prophet" were considered in isolation (as we did above), it would appear that for him prophets were a divinely instituted static order in the leadership of the church (1 Cor. 12:28-29; cf. Eph. 2:20; 3:5; 4:11). Yet immediately following the list of gifts or services in the church in 1 Cor. 12:28-29 (where he clearly states that "all are not prophets, are they?"), he goes on to observe in v. 31: "But earnestly desire [*zēloute*] the higher gifts" (presumably the first three on the list: apostles, prophets, and teachers). Twice more Paul exhorts the Corinthians to "earnestly desire" (*zēloute*) prophecy (1 Cor. 14:1, 39). Further, he says, "I want you all to speak in tongues, but even more to prophesy" (1 Cor. 14:5a), and "if all prophesy, and an unbeliever or outsider enters, he is convicted by all, he is called to account by all."

Prophets and the act of prophesying can be understood several different ways in 1 Cor. 12-14. Perhaps the office of prophet should not be confused with the phenomenon of congregational prophecy; yet this solution seems artificial since it is doubtful whether "office" is an appropriate way of conceptualizing what Paul has in mind for the prophetic role. Further, the gift does not appear to be individual prophets sent by God to the church, but the gift of prophesying exhibited in particular individuals (cf. 1 Cor. 12:10; Rom. 12:6). Again, it is possible that by "prophet" Paul simply means those who prophesy, regardless of the frequency of that activity and the legitimacy of the gift of prophecy for all Christians. The solution which appears most satisfactory, however, is that Paul is not exhorting *all* the Corinthian Christians to desire earnestly to prophesy; rather, he is exhorting *all those who regard themselves as gifted with inspired utterance* (i.e. those who apparently designated themselves *pneumatikoi*; cf. 1 Cor. 14:37; 2:15; 3:1) to aspire to prophesy rather than to speak in tongues. It must be recognized, however, that unintelligible utterances were often part of prophetic speech in the ancient world, and that Paul was probably the first to separate glossolalia out as a distinctive category.[45] In 1 Cor. 12:14, then, "prophets" appear to be identical with "those who prophesy," yet not all Corinthian Christians prophesied, nor did Paul think that a desirable goal (1 Cor. 12:4-31). Throughout 1 Cor. 14 Paul discusses the relative merits of glossolalia and prophecy, and preference is given to the gift of prophecy in public worship because of its greater utility in providing edification for the community.

Congregational prophecy (and glossolalia) is strikingly emphasized in the book of Acts at several different points in the narrative (Acts 2:1-21; 8:14-17; 10:44-46; 19:1-6). Yet each of these incidents is depicted as the initial effect of the infilling of the Holy Spirit experienced by a group which had not previously enjoyed the divine presence in their midst. Ordinarily prophecy is exhibited only by those specifically designated as prophets, and usually within the framework of a group of prophets. Throughout the rest of the NT and early Christian literature there is little or no evidence for the existence of congregational prophecy. In the Apocalypse of John, the Didache, and Hermas *Mand.* xi the act of prophesying is inseparable from those individuals formally designated "prophets." Evidence for the phenomenon of congregational prophecy in early Christianity, then, apart from the distinctive form which it takes in Acts and its possible presence at Corinth according to 1 Cor. 12:14, is slim. This is not surprising in view of the paucity of *models* for congregational prophecy available to early Christians. Apart from a few instances of groups experiencing possession trance in the OT (Num. 11:24-25; 1 Sam. 10:5; 19:20; 1 Kgs. 18:17-29; 22:5-10) and a few instances of group prophecy in Greco-Roman mystery cults,[46] models for congregational prophecy were nonexistent. This does not mean that congregational prophecy would have been impossible in early Christian communities, but it does suggest that if it did occur it was a relatively distinctive development within early Christianity.

C. WERE ALL CHRISTIANS POTENTIAL PROPHETS?

The view that all early Christians were potential, if not actual, prophets has been mentioned above. One interpreter regards Christian baptism, not as a ritual of purification or a rite of initiation, but as a ceremony symbolizing the prophetic calling of the one baptized.[47] In general three lines of argument are advanced to support the view that all Christians were potential prophets: (1) Since all Christians possess the Spirit of God, and the Spirit was regarded as the Spirit of prophecy in early Judaism, then all Christians are prophets *ipso facto*. (2) Prophets should not be regarded as occupying an "office" in the institutional church that would separate them in a qualitative way from other Christians. (3) The functions of prophets are frequently attributed to Christians who are not specifically labeled "prophets." Against the first point it should be observed that the Spirit of God was identified as the Spirit of prophecy primarily within Rabbinic Judaism (second century A.D. and later), not within such other sects of early Judaism as the Qumran community. Against the second point we may respond that although there was no formal "office" of prophet in early Christian communities,[48] the particular role of mediating inspired utterances resulted in a tendency to label such individuals "prophets," particularly under the influence of OT conceptions. Against the third argument we may respond that while much of a prophet's activities may have been similar to other members of the Christian community, it by no means follows that all must then be regarded as prophets.[49]

The early Christian conception of the presence of the Spirit of God in the community is the primary reason why modern scholars contend that all Christians were potential prophets. Many texts in the NT and in early Christian literature indicate that the Spirit of God was regarded as the common, permanent possession of all Christians.[50] At the same time, many other texts indicate that the Spirit of God was also regarded as God's power bestowed on particular individuals for special occasions.[51] Although these two ways of conceptualizing the presence of the Spirit (the first type has been labeled "dynamistic" and the second "animistic")[52] appear contradictory, they were never so regarded by early Christians. Some scholars have suggested that the temporary manifestations of the Spirit in particular individuals on special occasions is the oldest Christian experience of the presence of the Spirit of God, while the conception of the Spirit as a general endowment shared by all Christians is a later development.[53] Similarly, it has been argued that behind 1 Cor. 12-14 lurk the clues to a general prophetism of all believers that developed into the notion that prophecy was the province of particular community leaders.[54] Such theories are interesting but in the end remain speculative and undemonstrable. There is little reason to deny that both conceptions of the presence of the Spirit — as a general endowment of all

Christians and as an exceptional manifestation of divine power in certain situations — are very old, and neither one can claim precedence over the other.[55]

If we look at the matter a bit more closely, the notion of the general and permanent endowment of the Spirit is essentially a *theological* conception which had important ramifications for the Christian understanding of religious experience, while the notion of the momentary demonstrations of divine power through a special work of the Spirit was an *empirical* phenomenon which was assigned a theological explanation in harmony with Christian presuppositions. We therefore conclude that some, but not all, early Christians acted as inspired mediums of divine revelation and that these individuals alone received the label "prophet." To regard all Christians as *potential* prophets is a theological dictum which cannot be confirmed or denied by historical or literary criticism, since it is an implication read into the early Christian belief system.

IV. CHRISTIAN PROPHETS AS COMMUNITY LEADERS

Three of the more important terms which Paul used for designating leaders in early Christian communities were apostle, prophet, and teacher, a triad which first appears in 1 Cor. 12:28:

> And God has appointed in the church first apostles, second prophets, third teachers, then workers of miracles, then healers, helpers, administrators, speakers in various kinds of tongues.[56]

The ordinals used in connection with the first three roles indicate that Paul placed particular importance on them. For him prophets occupied a special role in the leadership of the Christian community,[57] though the evidence which we shall consider below suggests that they failed to play a dominant role.[58] In the NT and early Christian literature, lists of spiritually gifted persons (1 Cor. 12:28-30; Eph. 4:11-12) and spiritual gifts (Rom. 12:6-8; 1 Cor. 12:4-11; cf. 1 Pet. 4:10-11) are found only in Pauline and deutero-Pauline letters. The limitation of such lists to one segment of early Christianity (later references to "gifts" in Justin *Dial.* 88:1; 82:1; Irenaeus *Adv. haer.* v.6.1 are also dependent on Paul and deutero-Pauline tradition) and the internal inconsistencies of the lists suggest that they originated with Paul himself and that they were *ad hoc* formulations designed to reveal the divine origin and order of various manifestations of Christian leadership.

A. TYPES OF CHRISTIAN LEADERS

According to a famous thesis formulated by A. Harnack, apostles, prophets, and teachers were held in esteem throughout the entire church, yet commissioned by no single local community; they wandered from community to community and were held in the highest respect by all.[59] Bishops, presbyters, and deacons, on the other hand, were leaders whose authority was limited to the local congregations of which they were part. Harnack later modified this schema by suggesting that teachers were normally limited to particular local congregations, while prophets could minister both within the framework of their home communities and in other Christian congregations where they could expect a hospitable reception.[60]

Harnack's reconstruction of the role of two orders of Christian leaders, one universal and the other local, has not gone without criticism, though in its modified form it is less vulnerable to attack. One critic, responding to Harnack's original formulation, correctly observed that it cannot be concluded from the Didache that most prophets were itinerants.[61] A more recent critic claims, again quite rightly, that the distinction between church offices (apostle, prophet, teacher) and local officials (bishop, deacon) has no support in Paul.[62] Paul mentions the itinerant life-style of apostles only, not prophets, and the distinctive tasks of both prophets and teachers appear to have been exercised within the framework of the local congregations where they resided.[63] While the theory of the itinerant ministry of prophets and teachers cannot be substantiated from the Pauline letters alone,[64] when we return to this subject below we shall see that objections to the view that *some* early Christian prophets were itinerants cannot be substantiated.[65]

The most important and universally recognized leadership role in early Christianity was that of the apostle (from the Gk. *apostolos,* "messenger," "one sent forth"). The term "apostle" was not originally or consistently limited to the Twelve, but was a general designation for early Christian missionaries who traveled about the Greco-Roman world for the purpose of proclaiming the gospel.[66] Apostles were apparently distinguished from other types of Christian leaders by virtue of having received a divine commission for their task,[67] and by the range of spiritual gifts at their disposal (at least according to Paul).[68] Prophets and teachers, on the other hand, exercised their ministries within the framework of the Christian community.[69] In 1 Cor. 14:22 Paul claims that "prophecy is not for unbelievers but for believers," yet the context makes it clear that it also has an effect on unbelievers (vv. 23-25). The ministry of prophets was more spontaneous and oriented toward the reception and transmission of divine revelations, while teachers were those who preserved and interpreted Christian tradition, which consisted of a christologically relevant OT, the sayings of Jesus, and the traditional belief system of earlier Christian tradition.[70] While these distinctions between apostles, prophets, and teachers are conceptually neat, they are also quite artificial. More is known about the role of the apostle in early Christianity than about those of the prophet and teacher, yet even here the primary source of information is the Pauline letters. The extent to which Paul represents views generally held in circles of early Christianity outside his own is difficult to assess. The role of the teacher in early Christianity has not yet been investigated sufficiently by modern scholars. In some respects *every* leader within early Christianity was a teacher.[71] Certainly the oral and the behavioral communication of early Christian values and norms was the implicit task of all leaders, whether they are labeled apostles, prophets, or teachers.

In many respects the NT apostle was the functional equivalent of the OT prophet. Early Christian texts often refer to "prophets" and "apostles" in contexts in which it is probable that the "prophets" are those of the OT era.[72] The divine commission of Paul as an apostle, an experience to which he frequently alludes but never describes,[73] is widely regarded by modern scholars as having formal similarities to the prophetic call narratives in the OT.[74] The three accounts of Paul's conversion that the author of Acts has intercalated into his narrative (chaps. 9, 22, 26) certainly betray a pattern and structure similar to OT prophetic call narratives.[75] In Paul's own account of his conversion in Gal. 1, the allusions to the prophetic call narratives in Jer. 1 and Isa. 6 indicate that he conceptualized his conversion-commission experience in OT categories.[76] Yet apart from Paul (who, though he does not designate himself a prophet, appears to have consciously functioned as one)[77] there is scant evidence that early Christian prophets claimed to receive inaugural visions or commissions which launched them into their prophetic careers.[78] Early Christian prophets did claim to have received commissions *for particular tasks,* however, such as the writing of a prophetic book[79] or the transmission of a divinely revealed message to particular individuals or groups.[80]

Inaugural prophetic experiences in early Christianity apparently do not occur earlier than the middle of the second century A.D. The gnostic prophet Markus played a focal role in initiating wealthy women into the prophetic role in a Eucharistic setting,[81] and the Montanist prophets not only claimed to stand in succession to earlier Christian prophets (such as Ammia and Quadratus), but also to have experienced general inaugural commissions.[82] Although the notion of a "prophetic succession" was already known in Judaism,[83] it first appears in early Christianity toward the end of the second century in Montanism and in anti-Montanist polemic.[84] With regard to the stereotypical form of the so-called prophetic commission, then, NT apostles more closely correspond to OT prophetic models than do NT prophets.[85] In the OT the prophetic commission played an important role in legitimating the mission and message of prophets who functioned largely, if not entirely, outside the boundaries of the religious establishment.[86] Presumably those prophets who functioned *within* the framework of the religious community (the cult prophets of ancient Israel and most early Christian prophets) did not need inaugural commissions to authenticate their role as prophets, since the divine authority which they claimed was not in conflict with that claimed by the religious community.

B. THE RELATION OF PROPHETS TO OTHER LEADERS

The evidence from early Christian literature strongly suggests that the prophet was never integrated into the organizational structure of local churches. The role of apostle was also never integrated into local church organizational structures, but for quite different reasons. Apostleship was, by definition, a temporary task executed in a variety of different locations; it consisted largely of evangelization and the consequent foundation of new Christian communities. Even though many (if not most) early Christian prophets were permanent residents within their communities, that factor in itself did not lead to the assimilation of the prophetic role, any more than the apostolic role, into the institutional structure of the local church.

In the lists of spiritually gifted persons found occasionally in literature emanating primarily from Paul and the deutero-Pauline tradition, emphasis is placed either on the *supralocal* nature of such leadership roles as apostle, prophet, and teacher (1 Cor. 12:28-29; Eph. 4:11), or on the *foundational* function of such gifted leaders in the past (Eph. 2:20; 3:5; Ign. Philad. 9:1). This does not mean, as Harnack originally contended, that early Christianity had a rational and coherent international organizational structure. Rather, it suggests that the ideological unity of the many scattered local congregations of Christians found concrete expression in the notion that God himself (through Jesus and/or the Spirit of God) was the central authority of the church and that his will and purposes were expedited by specially endowed persons. The emphasis placed on this supernatural unity and coherence of the church appears to have diminished in proportion to the increase in complexity and visibility of the local and regional organization of early Christianity. By the middle of the second century A.D., when the Christian communities had achieved the degree of institutionalization to which some modern scholars have affixed the unhappy label "early catholicism" (*Frühkatholizismus*), the notion of the presence of spiritually gifted persons in the church is still touted by Justin and Ireneus, though without much enthusiasm.[87]

Early Christianity had no general, comprehensive designation for those leaders who were regarded as specially endowed with gifts of the Spirit.[88] Further, recent scholarship has to deny the distinction made by Harnack and others between charismatic offices in the church and more purely administrative offices.[89] It has been correctly observed that Paul himself makes no distinction between charismatic and noncharismatic offices. Yet it must be recognized that Paul and others stressed spiritual endowments (whether conceptualized as persons or abilities) when they wished to emphasize the transcendent unity of the church. Local officials, such as bishops, presbyters, and deacons, are rarely (if ever) regarded as possessing the spiritual gift of being a bishop, presbyter, or deacon. The reason is obvious: the religious community which they represent is an empirical reality, and the authority they wield is rational. The supralocal unity of local congregations, however, was also conceptualized in early Christianity without reference to the presence and governance of the Spirit of God through the agency of specially gifted persons. At the beginning of the second century A.D., for example, Ignatius of Antioch regarded each local church as a microcosmic model of the universal church; the bishop represented Jesus Christ (or God), and the presbyters represented the apostles.[90] In this scheme there appears to be no logical necessity for supralocal leaders to function in any way other than as revered founders (Ign. Philad. 9:1).

The prophet was unique among early Christian leaders in that, unlike other functionaries, he claimed no personal part in the communication which he conveyed. Prophets acted as leaders in many early Christian communities because they were regarded by themselves and others as inspired spokesmen for the ultimate authority, God (or Jesus, or the Spirit of God, or even an angelic mediator). There is no evidence that prophets occupied a prophetic "office," nor is there any indication that they possessed personal or professional qualifications or talents other than the ability to prophesy. In early Christianity prophets flourished primarily during the period prior to the full institutionalization of the church. After the process of institutionalization was largely completed, a process which did not occur at the same rate in all parts of the Greco-Roman world,[91] the prophet became an endangered species, primarily because of the social changes which had taken place.[92] The institutionalization of early Christianity involved not only the establishment of regular leadership within a coherent organizational structure, but also the development of traditions and customs as well as specialized roles, social rules, and social values.[93] If there is any correlation between the degree of institutionalization and the presence or absence of prophets in early Christian communities, it would appear that prophecy flourished particularly in undefined or unstructured settings.[94] Since the transcendent authority claimed by the prophets was theoretically in agreement with the articulation of traditional Christian norms and values mediated by church officers and teachers, one might expect no conflict between the different types of leaders. Intramural conflict, however, flourished in early Christianity, and prophets and prophecy appear to have been enmeshed in a great deal of that conflict. When such conflicts occurred between prophets and church officials, it might appear that the advantage lay on the side of the prophets, whose messages were promulgated with divine authority. The conservative strength of Christian tradition, however, was an important mitigating factor, and prophets were increasingly expected to prophesy in harmony with accepted tradition (cf. Rom. 12:6;

1 John 4:1-3). Further, ecclesiastical authorities could always discredit a prophet by charging him with transgressing the norms of Christian behavior and thus regarding him as a charlatan, or by charging him with propagating deviant forms of teaching and associating that with demon possession.[95]

Paul names a great many individuals in his letters, but none of them are designated prophets.[96] Prophecy for Paul is a divinely bestowed gift, and the prophets who exercise that gift appear to do so only within the framework of services of worship.[97] Despite the relative gentleness of Paul's admonitions in 1 Cor. 11-14, it is apparent that at least a mild conflict between himself and the Corinthian prophets or pneumatics exists. Paul writes to the Corinthians not only with the full consciousness of his apostolic authority (1 Cor. 1:1; 9:1; 15:8-9) but also as a prophetic mediator of divine commands (1 Cor. 14:37-38). The sphere within which the Corinthian prophets were active, then, appears to have been relatively restricted, and the conflicts which they experienced were apparently limited to competition among those who claimed special endowments of the Spirit (1 Cor. 12:14-31).

The book of Acts presents a picture of the relationship between prophets and other church officials that is not essentially dissimilar. The prophets serve as resources for divinely authenticated information, but it is up to the authorities to ratify that information and to act upon it (Acts 15:28; 21:10-14). Throughout the narrative in Acts prophets and other types of Christian leaders function together in complete harmony, though Luke's purpose, of course, does not include exposing the shortcomings of Christians. Barnabas and Saul are designated prophets and teachers in Acts 13:1, and apostles in Acts 14:4, 14, while Judas and Silas are described as prophets in Acts 15:32, but as leaders (*hēgoumenoi*) in Acts 15:22. There is, however, no indication that these more formal leadership roles were exercised by virtue of the prophetic gifts of the concerned individuals. Apart from the tranquil picture presented in Acts, there are numerous indications in early Christian literature that prophets and prophecy were frequently involved in various kinds of conflict with church officials (cf. Matt. 7:15-23; 24:11; Mark 13:22; 1 John 4:1-3).[98]

The Apocalypse of John presents a more complex set of problems.[99] Although the author addresses his prophetic book to seven Christian communities in western Asia Minor, not once does he betray the existence of such local officials as bishops, presbyters, and deacons.[100] Assuming (with most scholars) that John wrote during the final decade of the first century A.D., it is impossible to believe that the churches to whom he wrote had no local organizational structure.[101] The rather tight hierarchical structure of bishop, presbyters, and deacons emphasized by Ignatius of Antioch in his letters (written ca. A.D. 117) must have existed at least in rudimentary form in the churches of Asia Minor a generation earlier.

There are at least three kinds of solutions to the problem of the relationship between the church organization of the Asia Minor communities addressed by John and the form of church leadership evident in the Johannine Apocalypse: (1) The prophets mentioned in the Apocalypse are the only office bearers in the churches addressed by John.[102] (2) The form of church leadership evident in the Apocalypse, consisting largely if not exclusively of prophets, is a literary fiction rooted in the conception of an early period of Christian history in which prophets exercised a central role in the leadership of the community.[103] (3) John the prophet intentionally ignored the officials of the local churches because his role as a mediator of divine revelation transcended petty local concerns and because his message was directed to the communities at large, not just to their leaders.[104]

This last hypothesis, though it does not look very promising at first sight, actually has the most to commend it. John in effect "democratized" the churches by emphasizing that all believers are kings and priests (1:6; 5:10) and that all (whether prophets, martyrs, or Christians generally) are obliged to remain faithful to the testimony of Jesus and the word of God (1:2, 9; 6:9; 12:17; 19:10; 20:4).[105] This egalitarian conception of the fundamental role of all Christians comes to the fore whenever John lists the various constituent elements of the church. All these lists occur within hymnic contexts; the first and most complex list occurs in Rev. 11:18:

> The nations raged, but thy wrath came,
> and the time for the dead to be judged,
> for rewarding thy servants, the prophets and saints,
> and those who fear thy name, both small and great.

The last two lines refer to Christians generally as "thy servants" and as "those who fear thy name"; "prophets and saints" constitute two groups within the church generally, as do "small and great."[106] Since the phrase "small and great" is an idiom occurring frequently in Revelation and in the OT for a group composed of those representing various stations in society,[107] it would appear that a difference of status is suggested for the parallel phrase "prophets and saints." John twice refers to the martyrdom of prophets and saints (Rev. 16:6; 18:24), and again the terms refer to two groups, both of which constitute the church as a whole. Rev. 18:20 refers to "saints and apostles and prophets," again in a context which suggests that all three groups share the same fundamental obligations and responsibilities as Christians. The apostles referred to here should probably be understood as itinerant Christian missionaries (cf. Rev. 2:2; Did. 11:3-6).[108]

However, while John does view all Christians, regardless of their role within the church, as sharing the same basic privileges and obligations, that does not mean that prophets and apostles merely exemplify the potentials of which all Christians are capable.[109] Although the data relating to the apostles is too meager to be assessed properly, the prophets in the Apocalypse constitute a group whose special task is to mediate divine revelation to the churches (Rev. 22:6, 9; cf. 1:1).[110] By emphasizing the common features of the roles of prophet and faithful Christian, John intentionally establishes a mutual relationship with the Christians he is addressing that functions to secure their acceptance of his authoritative prophetic revelation. If some scholars have been led to conclude that, according to the Apocalypse of John, all Christians are potential prophets, that is due to the author's calculated attempt to emphasize that which he and those he addresses have in common.[111] As a prophet the leadership which John exercises over the seven communities he addresses does not spring from the authority of any office which he holds (indeed, that he addresses seven communities indicates that he does not hold a formal office in any one of them), but solely from the fact that he is an inspired mediator of divine revelation. The validity of this prophetic role is underscored by the inclusion of John's commission vision at the beginning of the book (Rev. 1:9-20); the initial position of this commission (the OT prophetic call narratives are similarly positioned)[112] suggests that its chief function is to legitimate the messenger as an authentic prophet. Since we have only the Apocalypse itself, the kind of response which John received from the communities can never be known. It appears likely, however, to judge by Rev. 2:21, that earlier prophetic warnings by John were not always heeded.

Some scholars have regarded John as a completely unique type of early Christian prophet who stands in a closer relationship with Israelite-Jewish prophetic traditions than to those of early Christianity.[113] If this view is correct, the Apocalypse of John is not the best source for our knowledge of early Christian prophecy. The arguments for regarding John as a unique prophetic figure in early Christianity are the following: (1) His special role is the mediation of divine revelation to other prophets; this role sets him above or at least apart from his prophetic colleagues. (2) John claims for himself an authority comparable only to that claimed by apostles. (3) While NT prophets stand under the authority of the community (1 Cor. 12:10; 14:29),[114] John's prophetic message, like that of the OT prophets, stands over and above the community; the truth of his message cannot be questioned, for it is declared reliable and true by God himself (Rev. 21:5; 22:6). (4) In the Apocalypse, predictions of the eschatological future are central and exhortations are marginal, while in the prophetic activity reflected in the Pauline letters exhortation and admonition are central while predictions are only incidental.[115]

The uniqueness of John as an early Christian prophet has been exaggerated. Yet it is true that the Apocalypse of John is unique in many respects when compared with early Jewish apocalyptic literature (the author uses his own name, not a pseudonym, there are no historical surveys cast as prophecies of the future, etc.). Since it is our only example of a prophetic composition originating with first-century Christianity, the comparative material necessary to judge the Apocalypse is lacking. Nevertheless, a few arguments can be proposed in defense of the *representative status of John as an early Christian prophet:*

(1) Specialized social roles (such as those of the early Christian apostle, prophet, teacher, bishop, elder, and deacon) are not created by those so categorized, but are traditional and conventional and thus recognizable to the constituency for whom that role is played.[116] This means that John's presentation of himself as a prophet and his prophetic proclamation would have been accepted as such by the Christian communities he addressed *only if his modes of speech and behavior were recognizable as characteristically prophetic.*

(2) John did receive a divine revelation (or series of revelations) which he relayed to his prophetic colleagues, who in turn relayed them to the churches of western Asia Minor (Rev. 1:1; 22:16; cf. 2:1, 8, 12, etc.). Yet we have earlier noted the frequency with which we meet prophetic groups in early Christianity, and it appears that such groups were often the setting for prophetic revelations.[117] Similarly Clement and Grapte serve to transmit Hermas' revelation to various Christian constituencies (Hermas *Vis.* ii.4.3). Alexander of Abonuteichas transmitted oracles throughout the Greco-Roman world through the agency of *chrēsmologoi* (Lucian *Alex.* 36). If John's prophetic colleagues actually transmitted his revelations to others, they must have accepted the divine authority of his message (cf. 1 Cor. 14:29). While it *appears* that John acts as a master prophet (an analogous role is played by "Jezebel" in Rev. 2:20-23), it is not impossible that he in turn played a subordinate role to other members of his prophetic circle. To be sure, we are not told in the Apocalypse that any prophet other than John received divine revelations.

(3) The argument that John stands over the churches he addresses, like OT prophets, while the typical NT prophet was subject to the authority of the community, has several flaws. First, the image of the OT prophet is based only on the role of the free prophet, and even then ignores the various criteria found throughout the OT for distinguishing the true from the false prophet.[118] Second, it appears that early Christian prophets were subject to the strictures of their prophetic colleagues, not of the

community in general (1 Cor. 12:10; 14:29; Did. 11:7). Third, although John claims divine authority for his message and even appends a conditional curse for those who might tinker with his prophetic message (Rev. 22:18-19), we do not know how his message was received. Early Christians characteristically claimed divine authority for their messages, and there is no reason to regard the claims of Agabus (Acts 21:11) or Ignatius of Antioch (Philad. 7:1) as in any way inferior to those of John the prophet. John had not been unopposed in the past (Rev. 2:14-15, 20-23), and it is presumably for the purpose of overcoming any reluctance to accept and act on his message that he so carefully articulates the divine authority which stands behind that message.

(4) The differences between the types of Christian prophecy reflected in the Pauline letters (particularly 1 Cor. 11-14) and the Apocalypse of John have been overstated.[119] Exhortation and edification are for Paul the general objectives of in-tramural Christian communication, not just the task of prophets or other spiritually endowed individuals. Similarly, prediction for Paul (cf. 1 Thess. 4:13-18), no less than for John the prophet, serves to meet the present intellectual and emotional needs of Christians. In sum, one must be very careful in assessing the role of John over against early Christian prophets generally; the characteristics which he holds in common with his colleagues appear more decisive than the differences.

The Didache reflects a situation in which an undisclosed number of scattered rural Christian communities are given advice on a wide variety of practical subjects by an unknown author who uses the pseudonyms of the twelve apostles. This suggests that no Christian leader has sufficient authority to issue these directives under his own name. The author and the communities he addresses are familiar with itinerant apos-tles, prophets, and teachers, and it is apparent that a number of such figures have taken advantage of them (Did. 11-13). Bishops and deacons are mentioned only once, in a context in which it is clear that they are appointed by the community at large, and they are regarded as performing the functions of prophets and teachers (Did. 15:1-2). Apart from this one fortuitous reference all mention of local officials could easily have been omitted from the Didache. Apostles are mentioned several times (11:3, 4, 6), but their specific functions are never indicated, a fact which suggests that they belonged to an earlier period.

The author's central concern in Did. 11-13 is with the relationship between prophets and teachers and the local communities. Legitimate prophets who settle among the people are held in the highest honor, and they are supported by the firstfruits (aparchē) of crops, wine, and oil as well as the firstfruits of profits generally, "for they are your high priests" (13:1-7).[120] According to Jewish custom, the terumah (priestly dues) was separated from a person's produce and given to the priests, while the first tithe was given to Levites and the second tithe was consumed in the environs of Jerusalem or converted to money, twenty-five percent of which must be spent in Jerusalem. Originally the terumot and tithes pertained only to produce (crops, wine, and oil), but later (because of the inequities which existed between farmers and tradesmen) were extended to all profits. This extension is reflected in the Didache and presumably reflects contemporary Palestinian practice at the turn of the first century A.D. The reference in the Didache to "high priests" is probably due to the fact that during the period of the Second Temple the terumah and the first tithe were brought to the temple where they were collected and distributed by the temple authorities under the authority of the high priest. After the destruction of the temple in A.D. 70, the separation of the terumah and the first tithe was discontinued, but it was reintroduced at the end of the first century in the wake of the rabbinic reconstruction of Judaism. By the end of the second century the priestly gifts were given to those rabbis who were the spiritual leaders of the Jewish community. This development appears to have been anticipated by the Jewish Christian communities reflected in the Didache. The emphasis on giving firstfruits to prophets as surrogate high priests suggests a date for the Didache relatively late in the first century A.D., if not after the turn of the century. That the prophets of the Didache are supported by offerings formerly given to the high priest indicates that they are regarded as the highest category of spiritual leaders. Like the Jewish priests, these prophets perform their functions exclusively within the framework of cultic celebrations.

At the same time the prophets appear curiously irrelevant for the ongoing life of the community. They have an idiosyncratic way of praying during the liturgy (Did. 10:7); they are not to be tested or evaluated by the assembled church when prophesying (11:7); they are apt to make pronouncements in the spirit (e.g. "Give me money!") that are not to be taken seriously (11:12). Prophets who do not conform to the values and norms espoused by the community, expressed in the Didache in terms of a series of "tests," are regarded as charlatans. This insistence that prophets exhibit appropriate behavior is strangely divorced in the Didache from the prophetic utterances which they make. Further, not all Christian communities have a resident prophet (13:4), a fact which suggests that they were not essential to the life and worship of the church. In sum, the Didache regards the prophets with an attitude of benign neglect; they have been marginalized in a functional sense from the central concerns of the Christian communities. By insisting that true prophets conform to particular community norms, the communities exerted enormous pressure on these itinerant prophets to conform to Christian expectations. In this sense the prophets of the Didache are clearly subordinate to the communities they serve.

The Shepherd of Hermas, which came into existence in several stages between ca. A.D. 90 and 150, presents an internally inconsistent portrait of the role of the Christian prophet in the Roman churches. The most comprehensive list of Christian leaders, viewed from an eschatological perspective, is found in Hermas *Vis.* iii.5.1:

> The stones which are square and white and which fit into their joints are the Apostles and bishops and teachers and deacons who walked according to the majesty of God, and served the elect of God in holiness and reverence as bishops and teachers and deacons; some of them are fallen asleep and some are still alive.

Prophets are conspicuous by their absence, and apostles are clearly figures of the past. Elsewhere in Hermas apostles and teachers are grouped together as those who proclaimed the gospel (*Sim.* ix.15.4; ix.16.5; ix.25.2; cf. ix.17.1). Since all these lists are summaries of the earlier activities of various Christian leaders, the omission of prophets might suggest that they did not consitute a general category of church leader alongside apostles, teachers, bishops, and deacons.[121] On the other hand, the omission might well be intentional, perhaps motivated by a desire to discredit the kind of Christian prophet with which the author was familiar. Prophets and prophecy in Hermas are discussed exclusively in *Mand.* xi, and there only with regard to the ways in which the false prophet may be distinguished from the true prophet.[122] Now if the true prophecy in *Mand.* xi is primarily congregational prophecy and not the function of religious specialists, as J. Reiling has argued, then it is likely that Hermas has omitted prophets from his lists of Christian leaders because he does not consider the prophet to be an office bearer or even an unofficial Christian leader.[123] Reiling appears to be wrong, however — the true prophet in *Mand.* xi is a religious specialist, though he does not appear to be a functionary within the Christian community in which he prophesies.

One problem with Hermas' attack on false prophets and his description of the behavior of true prophets is that he himself receives and promulgates divine revelations in a manner different from the true prophet (and markedly different, of course, from the false prophet).[124] In the light of the paradigmatic behavior of the true prophet described in *Mand.* xi, one could easily conclude that the revelatory experiences described by Hermas are literary fiction and not based on actual revelatory events.[125] While it is undeniable that a great deal of the material in the Shepherd of Hermas is literary in origin, a close analysis of the document reveals the presence of prophetic speeches embedded in an apocalyptic literary framework.[126] The visions and auditions which Hermas claims to have received are always experienced while he is alone in the countryside or at home, and never within the framework of a Christian community gathered for worship, though that is precisely the setting which he claims characterizes the activity of the true prophet (*Mand.* xi.9).[127]

Revelations and explanations of previous visions are usually given to Hermas in response to prayer, sometimes accompanied by fasting and confession of sin.[128] To this extent, then, Hermas conforms to the protocol outlined in the above quotation. Further, Hermas is also frequently commissioned to transmit the revelations he receives, in both written and oral form, to various individuals, church leaders, and groups of Christians.[129] Clement and Grapte are named as messengers to relay the revelations of Hermas to various Christian groups.[130] Although Hermas does not reveal the procedure used in reading or declaring his revelations to the elect, the presbyters, and others, it is not impossible that the protocol would conform to that found in the quotation above. That is, the revelation conveyed by the "man who has the Divine Spirit" in *Mand.* xi.9 was not necessarily received following the prayer of the assembly, but an earlier revelation may have been delivered by the prophet at that point.

The false prophet whom Hermas attacks acts very differently, as we see from the description of his oracular procedure in *Mand.* xi.1-2:

> He showed me men sitting on a bench, and another man sitting on a chair [*kathedran*], and he said to me: "Do you see the men sitting on the bench?" "Yes, sir," said I; "I see them." "They," said he, "are faithful [*pistoi*], and he who is sitting on the chair is a false prophet [*pseudoprophētēs*], who is corrupting the understanding of the servants of God [*tōn doulōn tou theou*]. He corrupts the understanding of the double-minded, not of the faithful. Therefore these double-minded men come to him as to a wizard [*mantin*], and ask him concerning their future; and that false prophet, having no power of the Divine Spirit in himself, speaks with them according to their requests, and according to the desires of their wickedness, and fills their souls, as they themselves wish.

The true prophet, according to Hermas, does not give oracular responses to inquirers (xi.8), but speaks only when God wishes him to speak, and that occurs within the framework of Christian worship (xi. 9). The false prophet, on the other hand, gives oracular responses to inquiries, avoids the assembly of righteous men, and accepts payment for his services (xi.12-13). The status of the true prophet and the false prophet are markedly different. The true prophet is subordinate to the assembly of righteous men *because he comes to them* and it is the prayer of the assembly that precedes the prophesying; the false prophet has comparatively greater status *since those who wish to make oracular inquiries come to him.* That this false prophet was a Christian is indicated by the fact that he is depicted as coming to Christian assemblies but as being unable to prophesy in that setting (*Mand.* xi.14). The Christian mantic that Hermas describes is unique in early Christian literature, since he apparently stands more in the tradition of Greco-Roman magical divination than in the Jewish prophetic tradition.[131] This Christian mantic is a kind of religious entrepreneur who apparently supported himself through exercising the divinatory art. This form of activity would necessarily have eliminated him from any integral function within the framework of the Christian cult. For all his protestation, Hermas himself (here through the Shepherd) reflects some of the practices and conventions common in Greco-Roman magical divination.[132] Further, the many techniques which Hermas includes in the Shepherd for securing the acceptance of his revelations indicate that his own prophetic revelations were not immediately acceptable to the Christian communities in and about Rome.[133] That his stratagems were successful is indicated by the fact that the Shepherd was regarded as inspired by a number of church fathers from the third quarter of the second century A.D. on.[134]

This survey of the relationships which existed between early Christian prophets and other types of Christian leaders within various local congregations has confirmed the view which was proposed at the outset. Prophets were regarded as leaders only insofar as their messages were accepted as divinely inspired and authoritative articulations of the will of God. Individual prophets were not valued for their natural skills and abilities (like Christian teachers), or for their age, wisdom, and moral leadership (like bishops, presbyters, and deacons), but solely for their prophetic gifts. The primary sphere of the prophets' influence was in Christian congregations assembled for worship. In the absence of the more complex bureaucratic organization which accompanied the institutionalization of early Christianity, prophets appear to have played a more visible and active role in guiding Christian communities in decision making by reiterating the norms and values which were an integral part of Christian tradition and by providing the communities with visible evidence of the presence and activity of God and Jesus. The growth of local bureaucracies, often in the form of the triad of offices consisting of bishop, presbyters, and deacons, resulted in the increasing exclusion of prophets from active roles in the guidance of the communities. As a visible sign of the unity of the many local scattered congregations, prophets became superfluous when regional organization became a reality.[135]

V. ITINERANT AND RESIDENT PROPHETS

One important feature of A. Harnack's famous thesis which distinguished between the universal charismatic offices of the church (apostle, prophet, teacher) and the local administrative offices of the church (bishop, presbyter, deacon), in both its original and modified form, is the mobility of early Christian prophets and teachers. In the review of the evidence which follows, it will appear that early Christian prophets cannot easily be stereotyped either as itinerant or as resident leaders of Christian communities. Further, objections to the view that at least some early Christian prophets were itinerants cannot be substantiated.[136]

The most appropriate framework for understanding and appreciating the itinerant ministry of early Christian prophets, as well as other early Christian leaders, is the recognition of the astonishing degree of mobility which characterized Greco-

Roman society during the first two centuries of the Christian era.[137] The era of peace (*pax Romana*) introduced by Augustus (27 B.C.– A.D. 14) provided a stimulus for trade, commerce, and travel throughout the Roman empire. First-century Judaism particularly, with an estimated diaspora population of from four to seven million,[138] had an effective international network of communication through the active mainte- nance of contacts among the many Jewish communities which dotted the Greco- Roman world. Emissaries would gather the half-shekel temple tax from scattered Jewish communities and transport the moneys to Jerusalem. Pilgrims who traveled to Jerusalem for the three annual festivals would stay, not at the disreputable inns along the way,[139] but at Jewish homes. Jewish teachers of Torah went from community to community to deliver midrashic homilies on scripture.[140] Since Christianity began as a sect within Judaism, Jewish communities frequently became the basis for the formation of Christian communities, as the book of Acts illustrates. Paul's mission strategy was based on an initial appeal to Jews within the context of local synagogues. In Acts 13:13-43 he is welcomed as a Torah teacher and asked to deliver a homily. The high degree of mobility which characterized early Christianity is particularly emphasized in Acts and the Pauline letters. Many of Paul's opponents, against whom he argues in his letters, appear to have been outsiders who came to the Pauline churches in order to propagate their own distinctive version of Christianity.[141] Fur- thermore, many of these opponents appear to have regarded themselves and been regarded by others as charismatically endowed individuals, some of whom undoubtedly functioned as prophets and others as wonder workers.[142]

The book of Acts depicts prophets, as well as apostles and teachers, as constantly on the move. Yet this movement, at least so far as the prophets are concerned, is limited to the region of Syria-Palestine. Acts 11:27ff. reports that a group of prophets, including Agabus, traveled from Jerusalem to Antioch. It is possible, though it cannot be demonstrated, that the purpose of this trip was to announce the impending famine. Later Agabus went from Judea (presumably Jerusalem) to Caesarea for the specific purpose of delivering a prophetic warning to Paul (Acts 21:8-11). Judas and Silas, both designated prophets in Acts 15:32, were sent to Antioch from Jerusalem to interpret and expand on the letter which they carried from the apostles and elders in Jerusalem to the Antiochian Christian community (Acts 15:22-35). These three instances of pro- phetic itinerancy are the only NT examples of trips taken by prophets for the specific purpose of exercising their prophetic gifts.[143] The last two examples, and probably the first as well, are not instances of aimless wandering, but each trip is apparently undertaken for a specific purpose. All such traveling is done in the region of Syria- Palestine, and it is at least implied that such prophets returned to their home com- munities as soon as their mission had been completed.

A slightly different picture is obtained when the ministry of the author of the Apocalypse of John is considered. In Rev. 2-3 John addresses seven local churches in the western regions of Asia Minor. If John was personally known to each of the congregations he addresses, a conclusion which seems inescapable, he must have exercised an itinerant prophetic ministry.[144] It has also been proposed, with a good deal of probability, that Syria-Palestine was the original home of both John and the tradition which he represents, and that he migrated from there to Asia Minor.[145] Similarly, Philip the Evangelist, who had four daughters who prophesied, originally resided in Caesarea (Acts 21:8-9), but is reported to have later taken up residence with his daughters in Asia Minor.[146] Both John and the daughters of Philip are examples of early Christian prophets who migrated from one region to another, but for reasons which may have had little to do with their prophetic vocation. In relation to his ministry to the churches of Asia Minor, John appears to have had a circuit of congregations which he visited from time to time and over which he tried to exert an authority based on his prophetic role.

Yet a third type of itinerant prophet embodies such ascetic values as the rejection of home, family, wealth, and property. For this prophetic type wandering is a necessary correlative of the life-style which must be adopted in imitation of Jesus. Peregrinus is one such early second-century prophet who wandered from place to place and was sustained by the hospitality of his Christian admirers.[147] Later he abandoned Christianity for philosophy and became a wandering Cynic philosopher, a social type very similar to that of the itinerant Christian prophet.

The Didache is very explicit about the itinerant nature of various Christians, particularly apostles, teachers, and prophets. The communities addressed in the Didache are very familiar with visiting teachers (11:1-2) and apostles (11:3-6), but little is specifically said about the itinerant nature of Christian prophets with the exception of the directive in Did. 13:1: "But every true prophet who wishes to reside with you is worthy of his food." Unlike other Christians who visit the community, prophets are not limited to a maximum length of time for their stay.[148] If they, as well as "true teachers" (Did. 13:2), wish to settle down, they may receive the support of the community. This settlement of Christian prophets at particular locations does not necessarily indicate a gradual cessation of the itinerant style of ministry, as some scholars have suggested.[149] There were a number of patterns of itinerancy, as we have already seen, and the temptation must be resisted to make the Didache fit into a preformed theory of historical development.

Recent studies on the Jewish Christian communities responsible for the formation of the synoptic gospels and the preliterary traditions of which they are composed have found that itinerant prophets appear to have occupied an important position in such communities. A crucial presupposition in such studies is that those communities and individuals through whom the synoptic tradition was transmitted contributed to its formulation by superimposing their own perspectives onto the sayings and stories of Jesus. One important presynoptic source was the "Q" document, a sayings source used by both Matthew and Luke. This document is thought to have been transmitted and shaped by the "Q" community, a group that is thought to have been heavily involved in charismatic and prophetic activity.[150] The Q community is often portrayed as a group of Jewish Christian apocalyptic "enthusiasts,"[151] who lived in the imminent expectation of the return of the Son of man, whom they regarded as identical with the earthly Jesus. Itinerant charismatics representing these communities were sent out two by two throughout various areas of Syria-Palestine preaching a message of repentance based on the imminence of the kingdom of God and supporting that prophetic proclamation by the performance of miraculous cures and exorcisms.[152] The itinerant character of the prophetic mission of the representative of the Q community is extrapolated from the synoptic narratives of the sending of the Twelve (Mark 6:7-13; Matt. 10:5-42; Luke 9:1-6), which is widely regarded as reflecting the praxis of the Q community.[153] The specifically *prophetic* character of the Q community, however, is based largely on the supposition that many of the apparent sayings of Jesus preserved in the Q material were in reality prophetic utterances of the risen Jesus through members of the community.[154] If the case for this kind of prophetic activity has been overdrawn, as I am convinced it has, then the current conception of the emissaries of the Q community as itinerant *prophets* requires revision.

G. Theissen has made a more comprehensive analysis of the itinerant character of certain groups within early Christianity.[155] Theissen's primary concern is to describe the context and conditions within which the sayings of Jesus were transmitted in early Christianity.[156] Many of these sayings reflect radical departures from normal patterns of life in that they stress such ascetic values as homelessness (Matt. 8:20), avoidance of normal family relationships (Luke 14:26; Mark 10:29; Matt. 8:22; 19:12), and the rejection of wealth and property (Mark 10:17-31; Matt. 6:19-21, 25-28). The mission instruction of Jesus to the Twelve in the gospels and the regulations in the Didache contain most of these emphases. The radical nature of these sayings of Jesus indicates that they were probably preserved and transmitted by those who took them literally: i.e. itinerant charismatics who emulated the life-style of Jesus. Although early Christianity was largely an urban phenomenon, Theissen proposes that these itinerant charismatics were of rural origin and traveled largely among the rural Christian congregations of Syria-Palestine.[157]

A similar social type is the wandering Cynic philosopher and preacher, who shares three traits with the itinerant Christian prophet: homelessness, lack of family ties, and lack of material possessions.[158] Theissen has constructed a strong, though by no means airtight, case for the existence in rural Syria-Palestine of groups of itinerant Jewish Christian charismatics who both embodied and transmitted the radical demands found in many of the sayings of Jesus. One weakness in Theissen's reconstruction is the assumption that the radical ideals of the sayings tradition could be transmitted only by those living in accordance with these ideals. Again, evidence for the *prophetic* activity of these rural itinerants is based on the assumption that certain sayings of Jesus are in actuality sayings of the risen Jesus transmitted through early Christian prophets. These criticisms notwithstanding, Theissen has made a significant contribution to our knowledge of the contours of rural Jewish Christianity in Syria-Palestine during the middle of the first century A.D.

A great deal of recent research has been devoted to the study of the editorial contributions of Matthew to the gospel tradition which he received; Matthew is not regarded as standing in isolation, but as a representative of a Christian community (located somewhere in Syria-Palestine) during the last half of the first century A.D.[159] Matt. 10:41, a saying of Jesus found only in Matthew, has often been taken to reflect the existence of a group of itinerant prophets within the Matthean community:

He who receives a prophet because he is a prophet shall receive a prophet's reward,
and he who receives a righteous man because he is a righteous man shall receive a righteous man's reward.[160]

The setting for this saying is the Matthean version of the mission instructions to the Twelve (Matt. 10:5-42), and 10:41 therefore implies that the disciples are prophets, at least from the perspective of the First Evangelist. This identification is still clearer in Matt. 5:12:

Rejoice and be glad, for your reward is great in heaven,
for so men persecuted the prophets who were before you.[161]

The itinerant character of these disciple-prophets is made clear in Matt. 10:5-15, 23, 40-42. They travel as representatives of Jesus to the extent that their rejection implies the rejection of Jesus, as we see in Matt. 10:40:

He who receives you receives me,
and he who receives me receives him who sent me.

It is widely recognized that Matthew was involved in a dispute with a faction of prophets *within* his own community,[162] but this should not be construed to mean that Matthew rejected all charismatic and prophetic activity. The Matthean community was a settled congregation which, like the communities addressed in the Didache, was frequently visited by itinerant prophets, some of whom were illegitimate but most of whom were authentic.[163]

The evidence surveyed above permits a number of general conclusions regarding the character and activity of itinerant prophets within early Christianity. Mobility was, as we have seen, a general characteristic of Greco-Roman society shared by Judaism and early Christianity. Those Christians who regarded themselves as prophets and were so regarded by others certainly shared in this general mobility. This suggests that migrations of such prophetic figures as John and the daughters of Philip from Palestine to Asia Minor were only incidental to their prophetic roles. The itinerant prophets described in Acts were not aimless wanderers, but appear to have traveled to certain places for the specific purpose of exercising their prophetic gifts in particular ways. Similarly, Hermas received commissions directing him to deliver oracles to particular individuals and groups, though his prophetic activity was generally limited to the vicinity of Rome. The strong Jewish Christian traditions evident in Hermas confirm the connection between his practice and that of the Christian prophets in Syria-Palestine whom we meet in Acts.

The prophet John is a second distinct type of itinerant prophet. In all probability he traveled from one congregation to another (perhaps with some regularity) in western Asia Minor. If this assessment is correct, then John's activity resembles the itinerant ministry of the *apostles* in Acts and the Pauline letters more closely than it does the behavior of early Christian *prophets*.

A third type of itinerant prophet, explicitly described by Lucian and the author of the Didache, and according to many scholars implicitly described in the Q material and the Gospel of Matthew, is that which embodies the ascetic values of homelessness, lack of family ties, and the rejection of wealth and possessions, all in imitation of the life-style of Jesus. This type is not exclusively of Palestinian origin, of course, since it closely resembles the life-style of the Cynic teacher and preacher.

These three types of itinerant prophetism in early Christianity appear to have flourished primarily in Syria-Palestine and were exported from there to other parts of the Greco-Roman world. This geographical pattern of dissemination, however, reveals very little, since Christianity itself was originally a Palestinian export. More important questions relate to the reasons why certain forms of prophetism gained currency in particular regions. While the *fact* of the itinerancy of Christian prophets in early Christianity cannot be doubted, similar patterns of mobility also characterized other Christians, some of whom claimed specializations (apostle, teacher) and others who claimed none. The mobility of Christian prophets, however, as well as apostles and teachers, appears to have had an important *sociological* and *theological* function for early Christians.

From the sociological perspective, the early Christian communities which dotted the Mediterranean by the middle of the first century A.D. constituted tiny islands in a sea of paganism. The antipathy with which paganism had viewed Judaism was transferred with a vengeance to early Christianity, particularly when the latter had emerged from the former to form a distinctive and (from the Roman perspective) subversive group. The isolation and minuscule size of the early Christian congregations, complemented by the hostility and antagonism of the pagan environment, fostered and nourished the dualistic view of the world that had arisen in Palestinian Judaism centuries earlier under similar social circumstances. The world was in the grip of Satan and his demons, and the only hope for salvation from the oppression of the present evil age lay in appropriating the transcendent gift of redemption mediated by Jesus. This gift could be provisionally experienced in the present time, but only fully accomplished at the end of the age when God would remove Christians from the world, or renovate it entirely. The constant traveling of Christians, who would stop at various Christian homes along the route of their journey (many of which would have functioned as house churches) served to mitigate the feelings of isolation and alienation by fostering impressions of the international scope and cohesion of the many scattered Christian communities. In consequence of the hostility of paganism to early Christianity, the boundaries of Christian communities were firmly fixed; there was little doubt just who was and who was not a Christian. However, the internal structure of Christian congregations does not appear to have been very well defined. The identification of leaders, their succession by others, their responsibilities, the degree of authority which they could exercise, and similar issues do not appear to have been clearly defined or answered within the various Christian communities of which we have knowledge during the second half of the first century A.D.

This pattern of strong group boundaries coupled with a relatively low degree of internal social structure had advantages as well as disadvantages. The absence of normal social distinctions within Christian congregations (status, class, education, age, wealth, etc.),[164] though at variance with pagan social groups, nevertheless served to reinforce the religious beliefs of Christians that were also at variance with those of their pagan neighbors. The low level of internal structure also fostered the ideal that all men were brothers. Social distinctions which existed in the external world (e.g. the master-slave relationship) were, in view of the imminent end of the world, only temporary and hence insignificant. In the Christian congregations (at least during the first Christian generation) such distinctions were not regarded as ultimately meaningful and were left outside of meetings of the community.[165]

On the other hand, strong group boundaries coupled with imprecise and indefinite social structure inevitably leads to competition and conflict, particularly in the matter of the role of leaders. It seems clear from Acts and the Pauline letters that during the third quarter of the first century A.D. a great deal of authority was exercised over local congregations by those who were not themselves members of those groups.[166] The egalitarian ideal espoused and practiced by many Christian churches suggests that they would have been more responsive to *external* rather than internal leadership, and this of course is what the evidence indicates.[167] Leadership may be regarded as the exercise of power in social groups, and the nature of the power wielded by apostles, prophets, and teachers (among others) was also perceived as originating outside the communities themselves. Apostles based their authority on a commission by the risen Jesus that was verified by the performance of signs and wonders (1 Cor. 9:1; 2 Cor. 12:12; Rom. 15:19). Further, as *founders* of Christian communities apostles were accorded the prestige and respect associated with the founders of various Greco-Roman social and cultural institutions (1 Cor. 3:4-10; Gal. 4:12-20). Since Christian congregations were isolated from each other and alienated from the pagan environment, there was a strong inclination to identify with other Christian congregations and to conform to the "Christian" norms and values which were constantly being transmitted, inculcated, and homogenized by traveling Christians (1 Thess. 1:6-10; 2 Thess. 1:4). This is the kind of sanction used by Paul in 1 Cor. 14:33-34: "As in all the churches of the saints, the women should keep silence in the churches."

Although teaching was a function exercised by apostles and prophets as well as "teachers," those identified as teachers were apparently regarded as specialists in the transmission and inculcation of Christian norms and values. When Christian teaching was derived from the OT, both interpretative skill and charismatic exegesis were exercised. In an era when rhetorical skills were highly regarded everywhere, the most fluent and polished teachers would probably have enjoyed a greater degree of respect and admiration. Itinerant prophets differed from teachers in that as mediums of divine revelation their talents and skills had little to do with the message which they conveyed. Although Christian leaders who were not resident in the communities through which they traveled were regarded with greater respect and accorded greater authority than members of the communities accorded each other, early Christian letters indicate that there was an enormous amount of conflict among the traveling leaders and among the factions which formed their power bases in local communities. In order to understand the role which prophets played in such conflicts we must turn to a consideration of the ways in which Christian prophets were evaluated.

VI. EVALUATING PROPHETS AND THEIR ORACLES

One of the distinctions frequently made between early Christian prophets and their OT counterparts is that the former were subject to the authority of the Christian community and its leaders, while the latter exercised virtually an unlimited authority over the people of Israel and their leaders.[168] This view, which tends to regard the early Christian *apostles* as the true functional equivalents of the OT prophets, appears to oversimplify the role of the OT prophet. Both the free prophet and the cult and court prophets in ancient Israel spoke with the consciousness of divine authority evident in the use of the messenger formula "thus says Yahweh." Yet the problem of discerning the *true* prophet from the *false* prophet indicates that *no prophet was exempt from testing*, even though the criteria developed were so vague that they were virtually useless.[169] The emphasis on *testing* the prophet and his prophecy, found in both the OT and the NT, appears to arise only within the framework of intramural prophetic conflict. The testing of a prophet and his oracles was not a normal response on the part of those to whom revelations were delivered. When, however, two or more prophets communicated messages which were perceived to be at variance with each other, those who received the revelations were faced with a dilemma: which prophet spoke the truth? The problem is simpler with other divinatory techniques; it can always be claimed that the signs were not properly read or interpreted, or that the divinatory method itself was inconclusive, etc. With inspired prophecy, however, two solutions to the problem of conflicting messages can be proposed: either the spirit speaking through the prophet is a lying spirit or an evil spirit, or the prophet himself is deceitful. The procedure of testing prophets is usually invoked only when strong conflict exists between particular prophetic spokesmen and other types of political or religious leadership.[170] It will become apparent below that when the topics of testing or evaluating prophets and their messages arises in early Christian literature, a conflict between the authority of Christian leaders and the authority of prophets lurks in the background. Yet the evaluation of prophecy was not always done for the express purpose of exposing heresy (Tertullian *De anima* ix.4).

A. PROPHETIC CONFLICT IN EARLY CHRISTIANITY

Perhaps the most striking example of a conflict between prophets in the NT is reflected in the diatribe of John against "Jezebel," the false prophetess of Thyatira (Rev. 2:20-24). She is accused of inciting Christians to practice immorality and sanctioning the eating of meat previously consecrated to idols (2:20). At the social level John's tirade reflects a conflict of authority, his own versus that of "Jezebel." Some of those in Thyatira do not follow the teachings of "Jezebel" (2:24), but the entire church is charged with tolerating her (2:20). "Jezebel," of course, may equally well have opposed John as a false prophet, though her side of the story has not survived.[171] The charges of practicing sexual immorality and eating meat sacrificed to pagan deities is also made against those who follow the teaching of the Nicolaitans in Pergamum, a teaching which John claims resembles the teachings of the ancient and infamous false prophet Balaam (2:14-15). The mention of Balaam in connection with the Nicolaitan heresy at Thyatira makes it likely that the novel emphases of the movement were validated by oracular utterances. Further, it is not unlikely that the false apostles who had been repulsed by the Christian community at Ephesus also represented the views of the Nicolaitans.[172]

Outside the NT the first clear instance of a conflict between prophets is found in Hermas *Mand.* xi. Although Hermas never explicitly claims prophetic status, it is clear that he functioned as one.[173] True prophets, according to Hermas, receive divine revelations in the midst of worshiping congregations in response to communal prayer. False prophets avoid such cultic settings and give oracles in response to the questions of those who privately consult them, usually for remuneration. Hermas characterizes the whole style and technique of the Christian *mantis* whom he criticizes as pagan, and the false prophet himself as a moral degenerate. It is not the Spirit of God who speaks through the false prophet, but the spirit of the devil.

Both John and Hermas saw no point in testing their prophetic competitors to determine if they were truly inspired by God; as competitors, they were clearly false prophets. According to John the teaching and behavior of "Jezebel" and the Nicolaitans contradict Christian norms and must therefore be condemned. The condemnation takes the form of a prophetic speech in which the Lord of the church speaks through John in the first person. The charge that an evil spirit speaks through "Jezebel," however, is not made. For Hermas the content of the oracles delivered by false prophets is not as objectionable as the way in which they are delivered.

More common than conflicts among rival prophets fighting to maintain control of Christian congregations are those among various types of Christian leaders and prophets. One clear instance of such a conflict is reflected in 1 John 4:1-3:

> Beloved, do not believe every spirit, but test the spirits to see whether they are of God; for many false prophets have gone out into the world. By this you know the Spirit of God: every spirit which confesses that Jesus Christ has come in the flesh is of God, and every spirit which does not confess Jesus is not of God. This is the spirit of antichrist, of which you heard that it was coming, and now it is in the world already.

Here the term "spirits" refers to the one spirit of error (1 John 4:6), who speaks through many false prophets.[174] The test suggested by the author is based on the nature of the confession made by prophets; if they confess that Jesus Christ has come in the flesh, then they are inspired by the Spirit of God. The conflict is based on a clash in ideologies, and the ideology opposed by the author is given support by the prophetic utterances of Christian prophets. There is therefore the grave possibility that these prophets will receive a sympathetic hearing. That the physicality of the incarnation is the single doctrine which the Elder regards as most critical suggests that the social determinant for that belief is a relatively high degree of internal social structure within the Christian communities represented by the author.[175] The opposition's concern with the spirituality of Jesus reflects very probably the notion that the Christian community should reject the social structures, norms, and values prevalent in the world outside.

A second example of a Christian leader (or leaders) who expresses opposition to false prophets is the redactor of the Gospel of Matthew. Using the words of Jesus he condemns those whom he regards as false prophets in his own day (Matt. 7:15-23; 24:4-5, 23-24), both because of their behavior and because of the falseness of their eschatological prophecies.[176] A case has also been made for Mark's opposition to prophetic opponents.[177]

B. THE EVALUATION OF PROPHECY IN PAUL

In several places within his letters Paul directly addresses the subject of evaluating Christian prophecy (1 Thess. 5:19-22; 1 Cor. 12:10; 14:29).[178] These references are all-important since they constitute the earliest evidence that Christian prophecy was subject to some form of community control.

1 Thess. 5:19-22 has a string of five imperatives, all of which relate to the subject of manifestations of the Spirit within the Christian community:

> Do not quench the Spirit,
> do not despise prophesying,
> but test everything;
> hold fast what is good,
> abstain from every form of evil.[179]

The fourth and fifth lines of this quotation are an expansion of the third line, forming a basic group of three elements, a rhetorical pattern which occurs elsewhere in the same letter.[180] The injunction "Do not quench the Sprit" means that individual Christians should not repress or resist the impulses of the Spirit of God, who is trying to manifest his presence in them through prophetic speech.[181] "Do not despise prophesying" means that the Thessalonian Christians should not look down upon the prophetic utterances of others.[182] The injunction to test everything is a general principle; in all circumstances and situations, including that of congregational prophesying, the will of God must be discerned so that the good may be accepted and the evil rejected.[183] For reasons completely unknown to us some Thessalonian Christians apparently looked with disfavor upon the phenomenon of prophesying within a congregational setting. Rather than reject prophesying out of hand, Paul recommends that they allow the Spirit of God to speak through prophets and then retain that which is good and profitable and reject that which is regarded as evil and worthless.

Several observations regarding what Paul does and does not say in this short passage must be made. First, those who do the testing are not a restricted group within the congregation (unlike 1 Cor. 12:10; 14:29), but the congregation itself.[184] Second, the testing procedure is not regarded as a spiritual gift or the result of spiritual insight, but appears to be a fully rational procedure whereby prophetic utterances (among other things) are judged on the basis of their coherence with accepted customs and norms. Third, the testing of prophetic utterances (which is certainly part of the "everything" of 1 Thess. 5:21a) does not appear to have been a normal procedure which accompanied congregational prophesying. Fourth, there is no indication that any other supernatural power than that of the Spirit of God was thought to be at work in prophets whose oracles the Thessalonians had come to despise.

Let us next take a close look at 2 Thess. 2:1-2, a passage which occurs within what I take as a genuine Pauline letter and which constitutes a second example of the evaluation of prophetic speech:

> Now concerning the coming of our Lord Jesus Christ and our assembling to meet him, we beg you, brethren, not to be quickly shaken in mind or excited, either by spirit or by word, or by letter purporting to be from us, to the effect that the day of the Lord has come.

Here the phrase "by spirit" (*dia pneumatos*) very probably refers to the oracular utterance of a prophet. If so, such a prophecy is in error, according to Paul, for it contradicts what Paul himself has taught and now reiterates for the Thessalonians (2 Thess. 2:3ff.). Although Paul does not ascribe such erroneous prophetic teaching to demonic or Satanic influence, it is difficult to think that he would not have, had he chosen to comment further on the subject.

Two important references to the evaluation or testing of prophecy are found in 1 Cor. 12-14, the single most important source for our knowledge of first-century Christian prophecy. The entire section also gives a more general expression to Paul's own standard of evaluating *all* forms of religious communication within the setting of public meetings of the church. In 1 Cor. 12:8-10 Paul gives a list of nine gifts of the Spirit. The last four include prophecy, the ability to distinguish between spirits (*diakriseis pneumatōn*), various kinds of tongues, and the interpretation of tongues (*hermeneia glossōn*). The verbal cognate of *diakrisis* occurs in 1 Cor. 14:29 in what appears to be a very similar context: "Let two or three prophets speak, and let the others weigh [*diakrinetōsan*] what is said." Paul mentions the gift of "distinguishing between spirits" (the customary translation of *diakriseis pneumatōn*) only in 1 Cor. 12:10; it is absent from the other Pauline catalogues of spiritual gifts (1 Cor. 12:28-30; Rom. 12:6-8; cf. 1 Cor. 13:1-3). The close relationship between prophesying and the evaluation of prophetic utterances in 1 Cor. 14:29 indicates that there is a connection between the gift of prophecy and the gift of "distinguishing between spirits," just as there is between the gift of tongues and the gift of interpreting tongues (1 Cor. 12:10).[185]

The difficult phrase *diakrisis pneumatōn,* usually translated by such expressions as "discerning of spirits" (AV) or "the ability to distinguish between spirits" (RSV), is generally taken to mean the gift of discerning whether a particular prophetic utterance is inspired by the Spirit of God or by an evil spirit (cf. 1 Cor. 12:1-3), in a way which agrees with parallels in 1 John 4:1-3 and Did. 11:7.[186] The NEB avoids ambiguity by incorporating this interpretation into its translation of the phrase: "the ability to distinguish true spirits from false." Although this traditional interpretation of the phrase has recently come under fire,[187] it nevertheless remains thoroughly defensible. On the other hand, it does appear that the traditional understanding of the phrase is more narrow than the evidence suggests. The term "spirits" in the phrase might more appropriately be understood as "prophetic utterances," or "revelations of the Spirit," on analogy with the use of the term "spirit" (*pneuma*) in 2 Thess. 2:2; 1 John 4:1;

and particularly 1 Cor. 14:12.[188] Once *pneumata* is understood in this way, however, the term *diakrisis* presents a problem, for "distinguishing between revelations of the spirit" makes little sense. *Diakrisis* has a wide variety of meanings, including discrimination, differentiation, decision, interpretation, examination, and quarrel.[189] The most appropriate English translation for both the noun in 1 Cor. 12:10 and the verb in 1 Cor. 14:29 is "evaluation" and "evaluate" respectively, since this term combines the notions of discrimination, interpretation, and examination in a suitably ambiguous way.[190]

From Paul's perspective certain kinds of pronouncements, such as the confession "Jesus is Lord!" (1 Cor. 12:3), can appropriately be regarded as inspired by the Holy Spirit, while other kinds of statements, such as the hypothetical "Jesus is accursed!" (1 Cor. 12:3), cannot. Yet Paul does not appear to be using the introductory statements in 1 Cor. 12:1-3 to provide a rule of thumb for distinguishing between the kinds of spirits responsible for various prophetic utterances.[191] Rather, he is contrasting the former enslaved state of the Corinthian Christians in 1 Cor. 12:2 (with no reference to their "ecstatic" behavior) with their present state as those who are filled with the Spirit of God. While Paul is not formally setting out the criteria for evaluating prophetic speech, it is nevertheless clear that the *content* of such speech is the decisive criterion for determining whether or not it is an authentic utterance inspired by the Spirit of God.[192] However this may be, it is unnecessary to see the only object of "evaluating prophetic utterances" as the determination of whether the source of inspiration was the Spirit of God or an evil spirit. For a positive example of such evaluation, we may cite 1 Cor. 14:37-38:

> If any one thinks that he is a prophet, or spiritual, he should acknowledge that what I am writing to you is a command of the Lord. If any one does not recognize this, he is not recognized.

In this problematic passage[193] Paul assumes that prophets and other charismatically endowed persons have the appropriate insight to recognize that his injunctions are in fact prophetic utterances spoken with the authority of the Lord himself.[194] Prophets and other charismatically endowed individuals, then, are assumed to have the ability to "evaluate prophetic utterances" (1 Cor. 12:10). Paul may have anticipated this evaluative and interpretative procedure in Gal. 1:8-9 when he pronounces a curse on any who would preach a version of the gospel which differed from the one he originally proclaimed to the Galatians. Similarly, in John the Prophet's use of an integrity formula which contains curses leveled against those who would add or subtract anything from his prophetic book (Rev. 22:18-19), he may have anticipated the possibility that the "evaluative" and "interpretative" functions of prophets in local communities might result in the material alteration of his prophetic book.

Although Paul separates the gift of prophecy from the gift of evaluating prophetic utterances explicitly in 1 Cor. 12:10 and implicitly in 1 Cor. 14:29, this distinction may well be the product of Paul's penchant for categorizing charismatic phenomena. It may be doubted whether the Corinthians were familiar with the distinction before Paul articulated it. The function of the distinction was probably to apply controls to free-wheeling and disconnected prophesying by making the prophecies themselves the subject of discussion and evaluation. In 1 Cor. 14:29 the prophetic utterances of two or three prophets are to be evaluated by "the others" (*hoi alloi*), a phrase which probably refers to "the other prophets."[195] This evaluation of prophetic utterance, while it could certainly be concerned with distinguishing true from false prophecy, was not necessarily limited to that narrow function. Any prophetic utterance which urged a definite course of action on the part of the community or its members necessarily required some kind of response.[196] If Paul's injunctions are recognized as truly "commands of the Lord" by those who are prophetically and charismatically endowed in the Corinthian community, then they must be obeyed. This evaluative procedure may lie behind such enigmatical expressions as "it has seemed good to the Holy Spirit and to us" (Acts 15:28).[197] Similarly, when Paul was repeatedly told of the fate which awaited him in Jerusalem (Acts 20:23; 21:11), he decided to proceed to Jerusalem regardless of what might happen. Paul's decision can appropriately be labeled an evaluation of prophetic utterances. We shall see below that when Paul quotes the oracles of Christian prophets, which he does occasionally, he is both evaluating them implicitly and often providing a paraphrastic interpretation of them;[198] this procedure also reflects the "evaluation of revelations of the Spirit."

In sum, several aspects of Paul's views on the evaluation of prophetic utterances have emerged in our discussion: (1) The evaluation of prophetic speech does not appear to have been a formal procedure which usually accompanied prophetic activity within the churches addressed by Paul in his letters. (2) On the other hand, since some prophetic utterances concerned viewpoints or recommendations which had to be either accepted or rejected, the response of the community to such prophetic utterances may be considered "evaluation." (3) The most important informal criterion set forth by Paul for the judgment of prophetic speech, or indeed viewpoints expressed through a variety of oral and written forms of communication, was the content of the message. Such messages must be in agreement with what Paul himself had previously taught (2 Thess. 2:1-3; Gal. 1:8-9), or with the generally accepted beliefs and customs of the Christian community (1 Cor. 12:1-3). (4) When Paul discusses the gift of evaluating prophetic utterances (1 Cor. 12:10; 14:29), the purpose of evaluation does not appear to be negative in orientation, i.e. for the sole purpose of unmasking oracles which were inspired by demonic powers.[199]

C. UNMASKING FALSE PROPHETS

There was an increasing concern toward the end of the first century A.D. until the middle of the second century A.D. with the problems presented by false teaching and false prophecy. As in ancient Israel the difficulty of deciding which teaching is "true" and which "false," or which prophetic utterance is "true" and which "false," is a question of perspective. The historian of early Christianity cannot accept the labels which some early Christians affixed to others as objective judgments. Name-calling and the use of pejorative labels (e.g. false prophet, false apostle, false teacher) reveal the existence of crisis and conflict among those who were competing authorities in early Christian congregations. The evaluation of prophetic utterance after the time of Paul, according to our sources, became largely a negative task. In early Christian literature the most important sources dealing with the problem of testing prophets or their utterances for the purpose of exposing fraud are Matt. 7:15-23; 1 John 4:1-3; Did. 11; Hermas Mand. xi; and Acts of Thomas 79.[200]

1. Matt. 7:15-23.

Matthew, and perhaps the school he represented, was involved in an intramural dispute with prophets whom he regarded as false. This polemic is clearest in Matt. 7:15-23.

Beware of false prophets, who come to you in sheep's clothing but inwardly are ravenous wolves. You will know them by their fruits. Are grapes gathered from thorns, or figs from thistles? So, every sound tree bears good fruit, but the bad tree bears evil fruit. A sound tree cannot bear evil fruit, nor can a bad tree bear good fruit. Every tree that does not bear good fruit is cut down and thrown into the fire. Thus you will know them by their fruits.

Not every one who says to me, "Lord, Lord," shall enter the kingdom of heaven, but he who does the will of my Father who is in heaven. On that day many will say to me, "Lord, Lord, did we not prophesy in your name [tō sō onomati eprophēteusamen], and cast out demons in your name, and do many mighty works in your name?" And then will I declare to them, "I never knew you; depart from me, you evildoers [hoi ergazomenoi tēn anomian]."

If vv. 15-20 and 21-23 (here quoted as two sections) are taken together, as many interpreters do, then the false prophets mentioned in v. 15 are obviously *Christian* prophets whom the evangelist and his school oppose.[201] Matthew has used a saying of Jesus regarding the kind of fruit borne by various kinds of trees and plants (Matt. 12:33; Luke 6:43-44) and turned it into a general test to expose a false prophet. The prophets of whom he speaks appear to be itinerants,[202] and the reference to "sheep's clothing" may refer to a distinctive prophetic uniform, not unlike that affected by John the Baptist in imitation of Elijah.[203] Apparently these false prophets come under false pretenses; they say one thing but do another. This inference is supported by vv. 21-23, where the false prophets (assuming the unity of the two sections) are declared "those who commit lawless deeds" (hoi ergazomenoi tēn anomian), in spite of the fact that they prophesy, perform exorcism, and do other mighty deeds in the name of Jesus. False prophets are mentioned a second time in Matt. 24:11-12, within the framework of Jesus' Olivet Discourse:

And many false prophets will arise and lead many astray. And because wickedness [tēn anomian] is multiplied, most men's love will grow cold.

False prophets are referred to by the evangelist a third and final time in Matt. 24:23-24:

Then if any one says to you, "Lo, here is the Christ!" or "There he is!" do not believe it. For false Christs and false prophets will arise and show great signs and wonders, so as to lead astray, if possible, even the elect.

These last two texts refer to the appearance of eschatological adversaries who represent the forces of evil in their final desperate struggle against God. Even though these references have a marked eschatological character, it is by no means impossible that Matthew regarded such figures as his contemporaries. Perhaps Matthew, like the Elder, saw contemporary false prophets and false messiahs as anticipations of eschatological false prophets and false messiahs (1 John 2:18-19; 4:1-3).

Who were the false prophets Matthew and his school opposed? They do not appear to have been Gnostics, Zealots, or Pharisees,[204] but rather Christians whom Matthew regarded as a dangerous threat to the order and integrity of the Christian communities in Syria-Palestine with which he was concerned.[205] The effect of his warning against false prophets, a warning which had the authority of a prediction of Jesus himself, must have been to cast doubt on the sincerity and integrity of all itinerant prophets. The false prophets opposed by Matthew have been most frequently labeled "antinomians" (perhaps even Paulinists) because of the association of the term *anomia* ("lawlessness") and false prophets (Matt. 7:23; 24:12). Yet this conceptualization of the false prophets of Matthew as antinomians, even though widely accepted, is an exaggeration, since "lawlessness" is defined by the evangelist simply as a failure to do the will of the Father in heaven (7:21).[206] The character of this lawlessness cannot be further defined, however, for Matthew was content to deal with the subject only generally. All that can be said is that the norms of Christian behavior represented by Matthew and his circle are not completely accepted by itinerant prophets whom Matthew thinks should be exposed as charlatans. The false prophets represented a form of antistructure which posed a great threat to the existing structure of the Matthean communities. The prophetic utterances of the false prophets, however, are not attacked (unless we include the prophetic recognitions of coming messiahs in Matt. 24:23-24); it is their behavior which is objectionable.

2. I John 4:1-3.

Written during the last decade of the first century A.D., 1 John is an anonymous religious treatise in the form of a written homily. The author of 2 John and 3 John designates himself "the Elder," and in view of the common language and style of all three letters, the same author is undoubtedly responsible for all three. In 1 John 4:1-3 the author warns against the danger of false prophecy:

> Beloved, do not believe every spirit, but test [*dokimazete*] the spirits to see whether they are of God; for many false prophets have gone out into the world. By this you know the Spirit of God: every spirit which confesses that Jesus Christ has come in the flesh is of God, and every spirit which does not confess Jesus is not of God. This is the spirit of antichrist, of which you heard that it was coming, and now it is in the world already.

Here the term "spirits" refers to the one spirit of error (1 John 4:6), who speaks through many "false prophets" (1 John 4:1).[207] The warning against believing such prophetic utterances suggests that they were normally accepted as divinely inspired. The author, however, insists that the source of such prophetic utterances can be determined by applying a criterion of content: the touchstone for true prophecy is whether the prophet acknowledges that Jesus Christ has come in the flesh. The deviant teaching opposed by John, sometimes labeled Cerinthianism or docetism, but which in actuality is not historically identifiable,[208] is authenticated by prophetic utterance. The phrase "many false prophets have gone out into the world" (1 John 4:1) hints at the itinerant nature of these individuals. Yet their speaking and testing by other Christians indicates that they are still part of the local Christian communities. In 1 John 2:18-25, on the other hand, where the opponents are called "antichrists," they appear to have fully separated themselves from the community (1 John 2:19).

The doctrinal test proposed by the Elder in 1 John 4:1-3 appears completely rational in its conception, yet in 1 John 2:20, 26-27, the recognition of truth and error is said to be based on an anointing (*chrisma*) from the Holy One. The problem faced by the Elder is reiterated in 2 John 7-10, where those who deny the incarnation of Jesus are labeled deceivers (a virtual synonym for false prophets) and antichrists. The itinerant nature of these adversaries is made clear in 2 John 10: "If any one comes to you [*ei tis erchetai pros hymas*] and does not bring this doctrine, do not receive him into the house or give him any greeting." In view of the similarity between the false prophets and antichrists, the real question is whether 1 John 4:1-3 actually refers to prophetic speech within the Christian community, or whether "false prophet" is just another way of referring to a false teacher (cf. 2 Pet. 2:1; Did. 11:5, 6; Justin *Dial.* 82:1).[209] The confessions that Jesus Christ has (or has not) come in the flesh are seen as expressions of the two primary spiritual antagonists, the spirit of truth and spirit of error (1 John 4:6). In favor of the looser use of the designation "false prophet" is that when the author refers to the heresy he combats in 1 John 2:18-27 and 2 John 7-10, neither the term "false prophet" nor "spirit" is used. The position which we take, however, is that the polemic in 1 John 4:1-3, 6 is leveled against those prophets *who lend support to the deviant form of teaching opposed by the Elder through prophetic utterances.* The opposition view regarding the spirituality of Jesus may well have been based on a view of Christianity as a movement which should reject the social structures, norms, and values prevalent in the world at large. In a word, these prophets too appear to have a basic antistructural and antimaterial stance which expresses itself in the ideology of corresponding Christology. The sole test which the Elder proposes is doctrinal, and though 1 John does deal with Christian behavior to a considerable extent, no specific criterion of behavior is proposed as a test for discriminating true from false prophets.

3. Did. 11-12.

The Didache, or the Teaching of the Twelve Apostles, was apparently composed late in the first century A.D. (or early in the second) and reflects the conditions of small rural Christian congregations in Syria-Palestine. In Did. 11-12 it is recommended that all Christians who come to the communities be tested, whether they profess to be teachers, apostles, prophets, or just laymen. These instructions reflect the suspicious attitudes of rural peasants toward outsiders, even if those outsiders are Christians. The tests proposed for Christian prophets, however, when compared with those suggested for apostles, teachers, and laymen, are quite remarkable. Teachers should be received only if their teaching coheres with the kind of doctrine found in the Didache itself (Did. 11:1-2). Any apostle that stays more than three days, or accepts anything more than bed and board, or asks for money, is a "false prophet" (Did. 11:3-6).[210] Laymen can stay no more than three days unless they have a trade and are able to support themselves (Did. 12:1-3); if they have no trade, then they must still find work, for idleness is not allowed (Did. 12:4-5).

The test for determining a true prophet is given in Did. 11:7-8:

Do not test or examine [*ou peirasete oude diakrineite*] any prophet who is speaking in a spirit [*en pneumati*], for "every sin shall be forgiven, but this sin shall not be forgiven." But not everyone who speaks in a spirit is a prophet, except he have the behaviour [*tous tropous*] of the Lord. From his behaviour, then, the false prophet and the true prophet shall be known.

Several specific examples of proper behavior expected of a prophet are detailed in Did. 11:9-12. If a prophet orders a meal in the spirit,[211] well and good; but if he *eats* the meal he is a false prophet. If he teaches the truth but does not do it he is a false prophet. If he asks for money in the spirit he is not to be listened to unless he asks on behalf of others. In short, a Christian prophet must exhibit exemplary behavior.[212] On the other hand, *nothing a prophet says can be held against him,* unless his actual behavior violates community norms.

In an allusion to the Unforgivable Sin saying in Mark 3:28-29 (and parallels), Did. 11:7 forbids the testing or examination of a prophet while he speaks in the spirit.

While this is probably a secondary application of the principle enunciated in the Unforgivable Sin saying, it is not impossible that the Didache has preserved the original significance of the saying by using it to silence the real or potential critics of Christian prophets.[213] Prophets, however, are judged by the community, according to Did. 11:11, though not while they are prophesying:

> But no prophet who has been tried [*dedokimasmenos*] and is genuine [*alēthinos*], though he enact a worldly mystery of the Church, if he teach not others to do what he does himself, shall be judged by you [*ou krithēsetai eph' hymōn*]: for he has his judgment with God, for so also did the prophets of old.

This passage indicates that prophets could be certified by the communities they served. Only certified prophets could "perform a cosmic mystery of the church" (whatever that is), provided that they did not teach others to emulate them.[214] The certification process was certainly not formalized, but rather consisted of the reputation which a prophet had built up over an undetermined period of time. Prophets who settled in a community (Did. 13:1) were undoubtedly those who had been certified by the community. Nowhere else in early Christian literature do we find a reference to the process of certifying Christian prophets.

4. Hermas *Mand.* xi.

The Shepherd of Hermas is a complex document, generally regarded as sharing many of the features of the apocalyptic literary genre. This long and tedious document appears to have come into existence in various stages from the late first century A.D. to the middle of the second century A.D. Although theories of multiple authorship have been proposed,[215] the divergences in style and the contrasting patterns of thought may still be the product of one pedestrian author over a relatively long period of time.[216] One of the more complex sections of the Shepherd is *Mand.* xi, which deals almost entirely with the problem of distinguishing the true from the false prophet.[217] *Mand.* xi is the longest discussion in all of early Christian literature, prior to the middle of the second century, of the problem of true and false prophets. Yet *Mand.* xi is unique within the Shepherd, since Christian prophets are never mentioned elsewhere in the document, a fact which is significant in view of the length of the document (about 150 pages of printed Greek text, some lost sections of which are supplemented by a Latin translation).

In form *Mand.* xi is a long speech to Hermas by the Shepherd (the *angelus interpres* who reveals the meaning of the visions to Hermas), with very few questions interjected by Hermas himself; in fact, far fewer than usual. In *Mand.* xi.1-6 the primary characteristic of the false prophet, who is also labeled a *mantis* (xi.2), is that he provides oracular responses to Christians who come to him with questions. These questions are, according to the Shepherd, improperly motivated, based as they are on the lust and wickedness of those who ask them. Further, the *mantis* tells his clients what they wish to hear.[218] The Spirit of God, on the other hand, speaks spontaneously and not in response to queries, i.e. he cannot be controlled by man (xi.5).

In early Christianity only rarely do we hear of prophetic utterances being given in response to questions;[219] yet in the OT, particularly in the narratives of Samuel and Kings, but also in some of the classical prophets, a primary function of the ancient Israelite prophet was to provide divine oracles upon request.[220] The frequently occurring OT phrase "to inquire of the Lord" actually referred to the act of consulting a priest or prophet who was expected to provide an oracular response.[221] Nowhere in the OT is there any polemic against consulting prophets on particular issues in the expectation of receiving an oracular response. Philo refers to one kind of divine revelation in the Pentateuch as taking place through the process of question (by the prophet) and answer (by God) as thoroughly acceptable.[222] Solicited, rather than unsolicited, oracles were the normal means for securing divine revelation in the Greco-Roman world,[223] and it is apparently the relative absence of this phenomenon in late Second Temple Judaism that led Hermas to regard it as a thoroughly pagan religious practice. For Hermas the ability to provide oracular responses to inquirers implies control by the prophet over the supernatural power which inspires him (xi.5); since the Spirit of God is not subject to such human control, it is not he but an evil spirit who speaks through the prophet.[224] One of the distinctive emphases in *Mand.* xi is that harsh words are directed toward those who have consulted the false prophet. While those who sit before the false prophet in a private séance are designated "the faithful" (xi.1), the false prophet is said to corrupt the understanding, not of the faithful, but of the double-minded (*dipsychoi*); the double-minded ask for oracles with wicked motives (xi.2), repent frequently, and practice soothsaying and idolatry (xi.4). Hermas and the Christian *mantis* whom he attacks appear to be involved in a struggle for control over segments of the Christian communities in or near Rome. *Mand.* xi reflects a conflict between two Christian prophetic traditions within those communities. The tradition which Hermas actively opposes is that which has most in common with Greco-Roman magical divination,[225] while that which he represents has twin roots in the tradition of Christian prophecy within a congregational setting and the private revelatory experience characteristic of the apocalyptic seer.

In the next section, *Mand.* xi.7-17, the Shepherd tells Hermas that the behavior of a prophet is the appropriate basis for judging (*dokimazein*) whether he is true or false. The true prophet is meek, gentle, humble, abstains from all wickedness and evil desire, has no interest in possessions or money, and gives no answers when he is consulted (xi.8). The false prophet, on the other hand, exalts himself and wishes to have preeminence; he is impudent, impertinent, talkative, lives in luxury, and takes payment for prophesying; indeed, he will not prophesy unless he is paid (xi.12). Further, the false prophet avoids assemblies of Christians and delivers his oracular responses privately (xi.13). In an almost contradictory *volte-face,* the Shepherd tells Hermas that when the false prophet does come to a Christian assembly and those present make intercession, the prophet is struck dumb and unable to speak (xi.14). We may suspect that the prophet whom Hermas styles as "false" is one who is in association with Christian communities, and a participant in their activities, yet chooses to exercise his oracular gifts within a private context. But the word *private* needs qualification; in *Mand.* xi.1 we find the "false" prophet sitting in a room full of consultants. This assembly is not the usual gathering of Christians for public worship,[226] but a gathering of clients of the Christian *mantis* for an oracular séance. The prophet does not come to the congregation; the congregation comes to the prophet.

Hermas emphasizes the condemnation of the Christian *mantis* for prophesying only in return for remuneration. The charge that false prophets are improperly motivated, greedy, and mercenary is found only occasionally in early Christian literature.[227] The view was widespread in early Christianity that prophesying should not be a profession whereby one earned a livelihood, and the motives of those who did so were seriously questioned.[228] In the OT, however, offering a present to a seer or prophet in exchange for his services was customary, at least in the premonarchical and early monarchical periods (1 Sam. 9:6-8; Num. 22:7; 1 Kgs. 14:2-3; 2 Kgs. 4:42; 8:8-9; Mic. 3:10), though this payment was not always thought proper.[229] In early Judaism there was strong opposition to religious teachers receiving any recompense for their services.[230] Yet Paul, in 1 Cor. 9:4-18, claims that apostles are supposed to enjoy the support of Christian communities, and in 2 Cor. 11:7ff. and Phil. 4:10ff. we find that he himself did accept gifts from various Christian communities. How early Christianity came to accept the notion of financially supporting its leaders while Judaism was opposed to such practices is a problem which has no obvious solution.[231] Like Paul in 1 Cor. 9:15-18, the pagan rhetorician Aelius Aristides (second century A.D.) boasted that he never accepted fees, though many rhetoricians could and did command large fees.[232] Paul's practice of self-support (though in this matter he was less than consistent) was not necessarily part of his Jewish heritage, since Cynic and Stoic philosophers also regarded self-support and the virtues of work very highly.[233] Consultants at Greek oracles customarily gave sacrificial cakes and animals (at Delphi the sacrificial cake was later converted to a monetary equivalent) or a stated fee.[234] Free-lance mantics usually practiced their divinatory arts for a fee.[235] Philo roundly condemns those who interpret dreams for a charge (Philo *De Jos.* 125). The tradition in early Christianity appears mixed. While we do not hear of any prophet who accepted fees for his services and was not condemned for that practice, we do know that Paul thought that apostles ought to be supported by the community (1 Cor. 9:4-12). The strong Jewish Christian tradition behind both the Didache and the Shepherd of Hermas perhaps explains their repugnance at the thought of charging for a prophetic performance. The frequency of the practice of charging for oracular responses in Greco-Roman paganism together with the Jewish disdain for that practice means that the conflict in Hermas *Mand.* xi was between the Jewish Christian tradition of prophecy (represented by Hermas) and the Greco-Roman tradition of divination (represented by the Christian *mantis* attacked by Hermas).

The third section, *Mand.* xi.18-21, emphasizes that the Spirit which comes from above is infinitely more powerful than that which comes from below.

Hermas' views on the characteristic features of the false prophet may be summarized as follows. It appears that the false prophet is a moral reprobate who gives oracular responses for a fee in private settings. The charge of immorality, both because of the exaggerated character of the charge and because character assassination was one of the more common weapons used in antiquity (as in our day) against those who are rejected on other grounds, probably has little credibility. We are left with the very subjective charge that the spirit which inspires the false prophet is evil, because the prophet gives oracular responses to inquiries (thus controlling the inspiring spirit), he prophesies only for a fee, and he prophesies in private sessions. Not insignificant is that Hermas does not mention the *content* of the oracles of the false prophet. They are labeled neither heretical nor, in the event that they were of a predictive nature, untrue.

5. Acts of Thomas 79.

In Acts of Thomas 79 we find a diatribe directed against false apostles and false prophets that is attributed to a wild ass who has been given the power of speech:

> But there shall come false apostles and prophets of lawlessness, whose end shall be according to their deeds, who preach indeed and ordain that men should flee from impieties but are themselves at all times found in sins; *clothed* indeed *with*

sheep's clothing, but inwardly ravening wolves. Not satisfied with one wife, they corrupt many women; saying they despise children, they ruin many children for which they pay the penalty; who are not content with their own possession but wish that everything useful should minister to them alone, and yet profess themselves as his (Christ's) disciples. And with their mouth they utter one thing, but in their heart they think another; they exhort others to secure themselves from evil, but they themselves accomplish nothing good; who are thought to be temperate, and exhort others to abstain from fornication, theft and avarice, but secretly practise all these things themselves, although they teach others not to do them.[236]

Obviously alluding to Matt. 7:15, this speech condemns the hypocritical stance of the false apostles and false prophets; they preach one thing, but their behavior belies their words. As in Matt. 7:15-23 and Did. 11-12, behavior is the primary criterion for recognizing and unmasking the false prophet.

6. Summary.

In early Christianity, as in ancient Israel, a variety of criteria were employed at various times and places for the purpose of distinguishing the false prophet from the true. These criteria were no more successful than those used in ancient Israel, since they were both *ad hoc* formulations which in actuality were symptomatic of a deeper conflict. In all the passages in early Christian literature where tests for unmasking false prophets are discussed (with the notable exception of Did. 11-12), the primary purpose of these criteria was to denounce a particular false prophet (or group of false prophets) whom the author regarded as particularly threatening. Conflict among various prophets or between prophets and other types of Christian leaders in which prophetic *legitimacy* is questioned is a way of solving the problem of conflicting authority as perceived in what appear to be conflicting norms and values.

Unlike false teachers, false prophets were particularly difficult to deal with since they appealed to the divine authority which stood behind their pronouncements. Two basic types of charges, often combined, were used to discredit prophets regarded as a threat: they were deceivers or they were possessed by evil spirits. The charge that false prophets were mediums through which evil spirits spoke accounted for the fact that both true and false prophets claimed inspiration for their utterances. Prophets who were illegitimate were shown to be such through their *behavior,* their *teaching,* and their *prophetic protocol.* The strong emphasis on ethics that characterized early Christianity, making it appear more a philosophical than a religious sect in the Greco-Roman world, and the insistence that ethical principles be translated into behavior made the charge of immorality particularly effective. Again, the strong emphasis on doctrine found in early Christianity (also a feature which was more characteristic of philosophical schools than religious movements in the Greco-Roman world) made the charge of heterodoxy similarly effective. Violations of prophetic protocol, it seems, occur only in Hermas prior to the middle of the second century. The Christian *mantis* attacked by Hermas (aside from being a paragon of vice) infringed prophetic protocol in three ways: (1) he provided oracular responses to inquiries from clients, (2) he did this privately, and (3) he did this for money. Interestingly, all three violations of prophetic propriety appear to be status-related; that is, while prophets in early Christianity were generally without status, the prophet attacked by Hermas had a distinct and recognizable niche in the Greco-Roman social structure, and it was on that basis that he violated Christian norms.

VII. TYPES OF CHRISTIAN PROPHETS

In our discussion of Greco-Roman oracular traditions we found a rather neat and pervasive distinction between diviners or mantics who practiced the divinatory arts in close association with holy places and free-lance mantics whose divinatory gifts were personal. Further, in our consideration of Greco-Roman oracles we found a general distinction between solicited and unsolicited oracles. With regard to ancient Israel, we found several distinctive prophetic types: the earlier shamanistic prophet, the court and cult prophets, and the free prophets. The types of prophetic speech generally seemed to have no clear correlation with a specific prophetic type, except that the social position of the free prophets made them specialists in pronouncing judgment. Early Judaism had a variety of different prophetic types: apocalyptic literature (produced by visionaries), eschatological prophecy (produced by individuals connected with millennial movements), clerical prophecy (closely associated with the priesthood), and sapiential prophecy (associated with the sage, holy man, or true philosopher).

Early Christianity began as a sect within Palestinian Judaism, a Judaism which had been penetrated by pagan influences from both west and east for many centuries. During the latter half of the first century, Christianity became increasingly distinct from Judaism as more and more converts were drawn from Greco-Roman paganism. Even though early Christianity was the heir of a great variety of traditions from Judaism and Greco-Roman paganism, these traditions were not simply assimilated without change, but were "Christianized." It was perhaps inevitable that a variety of prophetic, divinatory, and oracular traditions would become combined in Christian prophetism. The most dramatic evidence for this combination is the Shepherd of Hermas, where Jewish prophetic traditions are in sharp conflict with Greco-Roman oracular traditions. Paradoxically, the champion of Jewish traditions, Hermas himself, was profoundly influenced by Greco-Roman magical divination. In this section we shall discuss the viability of formulating a typology of Christian prophetism.

Perhaps the most common way of distinguishing between types of early Christian prophecy is to differentiate the Israelite-Jewish traditional component from that of Greco-Roman paganism. In particular, the *ecstatic* element in some phases of Christian prophecy (notably the phenomenon of glossolalia at Corinth) is regarded as having a pagan origin.[237] H. Bacht, writing from a perspective which regards early Christian prophecy as far superior to its Greco-Roman counterpart, suggests five characteristic elements of Greco-Roman prophetic inspiration: (1) a state of divine possession, (2) mantic frenzy (madness), (3) dependence on artificial means for inducing the prophetic experience, (4) man takes the initiative, frequently through the use of magic, and (5) the general lack of religious or moral value in the content of inspired speech.[238] According to Bacht early Christian prophecy in its legitimate forms shared *none* of these features. In many respects, however, Bacht's depiction of Greco-Roman prophetic inspiration is a synchronic caricature of the phenomenon he attempts to describe.[239] Although Israelite-Jewish and Greco-Roman revelatory traditions have many mutually distinct features, the interpenetration of east and west during the Hellenistic and Roman period makes it very difficult if not impossible to untangle the blended elements (even if such an untangling were desirable). Christian prophecy is most adequately treated if it is regarded as a distinctively Christian institution; if so, any typology of Christian prophetism should be based primarily on internal rather than external criteria.

Scholars have proposed several types of Christian prophets and prophesy, but each proposal suffers from serious shortcomings. The first suggestion we shall consider is that which distinguishes between prophets who directed their message to all Israel and those who functioned primarily within the setting of the Christian community.[240] The first type was confined to Syria-Palestine, flourished during the generation following the crucifixion and resurrection of Jesus, and is primarily exemplified by the Q community. The second type flourished primarily in Greek-speaking Christianity and is primarily exemplified by the role of prophets within the Corinthian community (1 Cor. 12-14). The weakness in this proposal is that the prophetic activity of the Q community is known (if at all) only indirectly and very indistinctly through inferences made from the redactional study of the synoptic tradition. Since the activity of the Q community is necessarily superimposed on that of Jesus himself, the ways in which the prophetic ministry of the Q community differed from that of Jesus himself have not been preserved in the tradition.[241]

A second proposal, related to the one just considered, is that community prophecy should be distinguished from apocalyptic prophecy.[242] Community prophecy, according to this proposal, is primarily represented by the type of prophetic activity described in the Pauline letters, while apocalyptic prophecy is represented by the author of the Apocalypse of John. Against this suggestion we have already argued that the contrast between the type of prophetic activity represented in the Pauline letters and that represented by the Apocalypse of John has been exaggerated.[243] The Apocalypse of John has many distinctive features when compared with Jewish apocalypses generally, features which have a great deal in common with OT prophecy.[244] Further, we have argued that John is by no means unique when compared with Christian prophets generally.[245]

A third way of classifying early Christian prophecy is with regard to *content*. É. Cothenet has suggested that early Christian prophecy has three main aspects: apocalyptic prophecy (presumably a type which focuses on the prediction of future eschatological events), parenetic prophecy, and prophetic prayer.[246] The difficulty with this mode of classification is that the first and second categories cannot really be distinguished, while the third category involves a type of inspired speech about which very little is known.

While each of the above modes of categorizing Christian prophets or prophecy has been judged deficient in significant respects, I have no proposal to suggest in their place. The institution of Christian prophecy, it appears, does not readily lend itself to categorical conceptualization. This negative conclusion, however, is not without significance. It indicates that Christian prophecy, in all its various forms and manifestations, did not possess a dominant form or structure (or a relatively small number of dominant forms or structures); i.e. early Christian prophecy was a relatively *unstable and unstructured institution within early Christianity*. This characteristic of Christian prophecy coheres with the forms of prophetic speech, for as we shall discover in our analysis of such speech forms, *Christian prophecy produced no distinctive speech forms which would have been readily identifiable as prophetic speech*.

9 | CHRISTIAN PROPHETS AND THE SAYINGS OF JESUS

Many modern NT scholars, particularly in Germany and the United States, have theorized that early Christian prophets played a major role in the transmission, formulation, and even the creation of sayings of Jesus. This process is thought to have occurred primarily during the period when the gospel tradition had not yet been written down in the form of gospels (A.D. 30-70). According to this view the oracles of Christian prophets, proclaimed in the first person as utterances of the risen Lord, gradually became intermingled with sayings of the historical Jesus.[1] Advocates of this view are found primarily among those who confidently use the form-critical method as a reliable means for determining the authenticity or inauthenticity of the sayings and stories of Jesus preserved in the synoptic gospels. Generally, form critics adopt the standpoint of methodological skepticism on the question of the authenticity of the sayings of Jesus; such sayings are regarded as inauthentic (i.e. products of the early church rather than Jesus himself), unless they are able to pass a rigorous test of authenticity.[2] The primary concern of form criticism has not been the reconstruction or identification of the authentic teachings of Jesus, but rather the analysis of the theological concerns of the various Palestinian and Greco-Roman Christian communities which left their imprint on the Jesus traditions which they transmitted. In the judgment of these scholars, the bulk of gospel tradition was either radically reshaped and reformulated or even created in response to the post-Easter concerns of the early church. Form criticism, then, tends to emphasize the free creativity of the early church in the transmission and formulation of the sayings and stories of Jesus now preserved in the synoptic gospels.[3] Early Christian prophets have come to be regarded as primary contributors to the growing and developing tradition of the sayings of Jesus.

Since we shall attempt in the next two chapters to isolate and analyze various sayings and speeches of Christian prophets embedded in the NT and early Christian literature through the middle of the second century A.D., it is important that we determine whether some of the synoptic sayings of Jesus are in fact primary sources for our study of the form and content of early Christian prophetic speech.

I. THE "I"-SAYINGS IN THE SYNOPTIC GOSPELS

One of the central assumptions of advocates of the theory that many of the sayings of Jesus in the synoptic gospels originated in early Christian prophetic activity is that Christians made no essential or lasting distinction between sayings of the historical Jesus and post-Easter oracles from the risen Lord. Consequently, oracles in the "I"-

style supposedly uttered by the risen Lord through prophetic spokesmen gradually became assimilated to collections of sayings stemming from the historical Jesus.[4] Proponents of this view point to the oracles in the Apocalypse of John that are in the form of sayings of the risen Jesus (Rev. 1:17-20; 2-3, esp. 3:20; 16:15; 22:12ff.). Rev. 3:20 and 16:15 will serve as examples of these oracles in the "I"-style:

> Behold, I stand at the door and knock;
> if any one hears my voice and opens the door,
> I will come in to him and eat with him, and he with me.

> Lo, I am coming like a thief!
> Blessed is he who is awake, keeping his garments
> that he may not go naked and be seen exposed!

A similar oracle is found in the Odes Sol. 42:6:

> And I have arisen and am among them,
> and I speak through their mouth.

These oracles are cited for three reasons: (1) they are clear indications that early Christian prophets did in fact prophesy in the first person of the risen Lord, (2) the form of these sayings is such that they could possibly have entered the tradition of the sayings of the earthly Jesus,[5] and (3) the authority of such prophetic utterances would ensure their acceptance by Christian communities as sayings of Jesus.

Yet the inconclusive nature of these general arguments has justly drawn the fire of critics. Opponents of the theory have made the following points (some of which have weaknesses of their own, as our comments will indicate):

(1) While the examples of oracles of the risen Jesus in the Apocalypse of John and the Odes of Solomon open up the *possibility* that such utterances might have been ultimately assimilated to sayings of the historical Jesus, they nevertheless fail to demonstrate that such a process actually took place.[6]

(2) Rather than indicating that *no* distinction was made by the early church between the sayings of the historical Jesus and the oracles of the risen Lord, the examples cited indicate that oracles of the risen Jesus continued to be recognized for what they originally were: prophetic sayings of the exalted Lord.[7] F. Neugebauer, a staunch opponent of the view we are discussing, makes several subpoints under this general heading:[8] (a) If the oracles of the risen Lord were, as Bultmann claims, only *gradually* assimilated to the traditional sayings of the earthly Jesus, then a distinction was made, at least initially, between sayings of the historical Jesus and oracles of the risen Lord. (b) In both the OT and NT, oracles never circulated anonymously but were always associated with the name of a specific prophet.[9] (c) One major distinction between the literary forms *gospel* and *apocalypse* is the anonymity of the former and the clear claim to authorship (even if pseudonymous) of the latter; this basic distinction would have impeded the flow of material from the apocalyptic tradition to the gospel tradition.[10] (d) If the oracles of the risen Lord had the same authority as sayings of the historical Jesus, the early church would not have needed to place the former in a pre-Easter setting. (e) While the two types of sayings of Jesus might have been erroneously confused, they were not deliberately confused.

(3) Doubt has been cast on the claim that oracles in the "I"-style of the risen Jesus were a characteristic form of early Christian prophetic speech.[11] Yet between the extreme positions which claim that Christian prophets *always* spoke in the first

person singular of the risen Lord,[12] or that they only *exceptionally* uttered oracles in that form,[13] the evidence suggests that some, but by no means all, Christian prophetic utterances were formulated using the first person singular of the risen Jesus.[14]

(4) Paul's statements in 1 Cor. 7:10, 12, 25, 40 have been used to demonstrate that the apostle was able to distinguish between a tradition which stemmed from the earthly Jesus (1 Cor. 7:10, reflecting Matt. 5:32; Mark 10:11-12 and parallels) and his own opinions (1 Cor. 7:12, 25), even though he may well have regarded the latter as inspired (1 Cor. 7:40).[15]

(5) Prophets did not enjoy the kind of leadership positions within Christian communities that would give their oracles unquestioned authority.[16]

(6) Prophetic activity in early Christianity was generally accompanied by tests of authenticity, the most important of which was agreement with kerygmatic tradition, i.e. previous revelation (cf. Rom. 12:6).[17] Consequently it is extremely unlikely that there was a wholesale invasion of the Jesus tradition by "I"-sayings of Jesus which originated as oracles of Christian prophets. Yet this argument fails to convince on two counts: (a) The test of congruence with kerygmatic tradition was applied to other forms of Christian teaching less spectacular than that of prophecy (Gal. 1:6-9; 2 Thess. 2:2), so that radical statements in the sayings tradition (such as that which discounts the seriousness of blasphemy against the Son of man, Matt. 12:32 par. Luke 12:10) would, following this line of argument, have been rejected by the early church.[18] (b) Early Christian prophetic speech had a generally conservative tendency,[19] a characteristic which would have resulted in the close alignment between most oracles and church tradition.

In sum, it appears that at this stage in our discussion the arguments both for and against the assimilation of oracular "I"-sayings of the risen Lord into the traditional sayings of the historical Jesus are inconclusive. Such general arguments, both pro and con, are unsatisfactory because of the speculative nature of "what might have been" or "what might not have been." Thus far in our discussion no hard evidence has been presented that demonstrates conclusively that oracles of the risen Lord actually became assimilated to the sayings of the historical Jesus. Yet since Christian prophetic speech was sometimes, though not always, pronounced in the first person singular of the risen and exalted Jesus, such an assimilation is not entirely improbable. The oracles in the Apocalypse and the Odes of Solomon are inconclusive in that they only open up the *possibility* of a merging of prophetic sayings with the tradition of the sayings of the historical Jesus, but do not provide any evidence for the completion of that process.

II. SECONDARY ATTRIBUTIONS OF ORACULAR SAYINGS TO HISTORICAL INDIVIDUALS

At this point we may examine three examples of originally oracular material that has been completely assimilated to a body of sayings and teachings of a nonoracular nature associated with a particular individual. The first two examples are drawn from Greco-Roman literature nearly contemporary with first-century Christianity, and the third example is drawn from the synoptic gospels themselves.

In what is probably a local Theban legend preserved in Pausanias, Persephone is described as having appeared in a dream to Pindar (518-438 B.C.), the famous Greek lyric poet, ten days before this death.[20] The goddess complained to Pindar that he had not honored her with an ode, as he had other divinities. After his death Pindar appeared in an oracular dream to a kinswoman and sang a hymn to Persephone, which the woman wrote down upon awakening. This ode, which has survived only as a fragment,[21] was accepted as an authentic composition of Pindar even though it was composed in a postmortem oracular dream according to Theban legend.[22] This legend, which certainly antedated the second century A.D., is a striking example of a postmortem oracle attributed to Pindar that was assimilated to the premortem compositions of the poet. The *legendary* nature of this story is no objection to its relevance for our discussion, since it is popular belief, not objective history, which is at issue.

In *Vita Apollonii* Flavius Philostratus (born ca. A.D. 170) narrates an event which ostensibly occurred shortly after the death of Apollonius of Tyana, a first-century A.D. philosopher and mystic. A young disciple of Apollonius prayed to the deceased sage for enlightenment in the matter of the immortality of the soul. Eventually Apollonius appeared to the man in a dream and delivered the following six-line hexameter oracle to him; upon awakening, he delivered it to his peers:

> The soul is immortal and is no possession of your own, but of Providence.
> And after the body is wasted away, like a swift horse freed from its traces,
> it lightly leaps forward and mingles itself with the light air,
> loathing the spell of harsh and painful servitude which it has endured.
> But for you, what use is there in this? Some day when you are no more you
> shall believe it.
> So why, as long as you are among living beings, do you explore these
> mysteries?[23]

Immediately after quoting this oracle (which we would label a *didactic oracle*)[24] Philostratus makes the following observation: "Here we have a clear utterance of Apollonius, established like an oracular tripod, to convince us of the mysteries of the soul."[25] This posthumous oracular utterance is regarded by Philostratus as the authentic teaching of Apollonius. Yet this brief speech is written in hexameters, the typical Greek oracular style, while the premortem teachings of Apollonius never take this form (though he is regarded as speaking oracularly).[26] However, as in the case of the oracles in the "I"-style in the Apocalypse and the Odes of Solomon, this oracle is clearly set in a postmortem context, though it is genuinely believed to contain the authentic teaching of Apollonius.

Our third example is taken from the synoptic gospels: in dependence upon the Q sayings source, Matthew and Luke provide the following versions of a single saying of Jesus:

Matt. 23:34	Luke 11:49
Therefore	Therefore also the Wisdom of God said,
I send you prophets and wise men and scribes,	"I will send them prophets and apostles,
some of whom you will kill and crucify,	some of whom they will kill and persecute."
and some you will scourge in your synagogues and persecute from town to town.	

While the Matthean version is formulated as an "I"-saying of Jesus, the Lukan version appears to be Jesus' quotation of an utterance made by the "Wisdom of God." The future tenses in both versions of the saying indicate its basic oracular character. The Lukan introduction to the saying seems to be the more original,[27] since the attribution of such a prediction to Jesus is more probable than changing the attribution of the saying to the "Wisdom of God" rather than Jesus. The quotation attributed to Jesus in Q may be derived from a lost Jewish apocalypse,[28] but whatever its origin it is apparent that Matthew regarded Jesus as the Wisdom of God, a christological assumption which enabled him to transform an oracle of personified Wisdom into a prophetic saying of Jesus.[29] While this seems a relatively clear instance of the transformation of an oracular utterance into a saying of the historical Jesus,[30] *there is no evidence that the oracle was originally received as a prophetic utterance of the risen Jesus by a Christian prophet.*[31]

These three examples of the process whereby oracular sayings could be attributed secondarily to a historical individual do not prove that oracular utterances attributed to the risen Jesus were assimilated to collections of sayings of the historical Jesus. They do demonstrate, for both the Greco-Roman world and for early Christianity, that postmortem oracular sayings could be accorded the same status as authentic bodies of teaching or compositions. While the two Greco-Roman parallels may appear unnecessarily distant from the world of early Christianity, that distance is more apparent than real.

III. PRONOUNCEMENTS OF SACRAL LAW

Surprisingly, the theory of the creative role of Christian prophets in the composition or reformulation of the sayings of Jesus has been widely assumed as a self-evident truth rather than scientifically demonstrated. One important exception to this generalization is E. Käsemann's analysis of a particular form of early Christian prophetic speech which he labeled *pronouncements of sacral law (Sätze heiligen Rechtes)*, a speech form to which we have had occasion to refer several times during this study.[32] One example of this speech form cited by Käsemann is 1 Cor. 3:17 (see also 1 Cor. 14:38; 16:22):

If any one destroys [*phtheirei*] God's temple,
God will destroy [*phtherei*] him.

This sayings exhibits five features which Käsemann regards as characteristic of the *pronouncement of sacral law:* (1) the pronouncement is structured in the form of a chiasmus (*a b b a*), a feature more obvious in Greek than in English translation, (2) the same verb is found in both parts of the pronouncement, (3) the second part of the pronouncement deals with the eschatological activity of God, and the verb is often in the passive voice, i.e. a circumlocution for divine activity, (4) the principle of retributive justice (*jus talionis*) is a central feature of the pronouncement, expressing the intimate relationship between guilt and punishment, duty and reward, and (5) the first part (the protasis) is introduced by the casuistic legal form "if any one" or "whoever," while the second part (the apodosis) is in the style of apodictic divine law.[33] Käsemann proposes that such pronouncements of sacral law originated in prophetic proclamation and that their setting in early Christianity was within the framework of eucharistic worship. He cites Rev. 22:18-19 to demonstrate the prophetic origin of such pronouncements:

> If any one adds to them,
> God will add to him the plagues described in this book,
> and if any one takes away from the words of the book of this prophecy,
> God will take away his share in the tree of life and in the holy city, which are described in this book.[34]

On the basis of this analysis Käsemann then moves to the synoptic tradition, where he concludes that sayings such as Mark 8:38 originated, not with the historical Jesus, but as pronouncements of Christian prophets:

> For whoever is ashamed [epaischynthē] of me . . .
> of him will the Son of man also be ashamed [epaischynthēsetai].[35]

This Son of man saying is attributed to Jesus in the synoptic tradition, yet it and others which exhibit the same form are regarded by Käsemann as oracles of Christian prophets that have entered into the tradition of sayings of the historical Jesus.

Käsemann's analysis of the form and setting of pronouncements of sacral law has been widely accepted by NT scholars in both Germany and the United States.[36] His proposal, however, exhibits a number of serious flaws. First, the connection between the pronouncement of sacral law and early Christian prophecy is assumed rather than demonstrated. His claim that only apostles and prophets possessed the requisite charismatic authority with which to make such pronouncements[37] is debatable.[38] Rev. 22:18-19 constitutes a slim link connecting the pronouncement of sacral law to Christian prophecy.[39] Even more serious is the critique leveled by K. Berger against viewing pronouncements of sacral law as a form of early Christian prophetic speech.[40] Berger, who provides a much more detailed form-critical analysis of the pronouncements of sacral law than does Käsemann, isolates four types of conditional sentences that deal with reward and punishment.[41] The purpose of such sentences is hortatory or parenetic in that they match present behavior with reward or punishment; the anticipation of future eschatological judgment or reward is not essential, and the origin of such statements is wisdom literature.[42] Instead of the designation "pronouncements of sacral law," Berger suggests "pronouncements of wisdom instruction" (*Sätze weisheitlicher Belehrung*).[43] According to Berger, since the origin of such speech patterns is sapiential exhortation, there is no necessary connection between them and early Christian prophetic speech. He argues at some length that the primary setting in the life of the early church for such pronouncements was the initial instruction of converts in the Gentile mission, i.e. catechesis.[44]

Even more than Käsemann, however, Berger has erred in oversimplifying the form, setting, and function of the oral and written speech which Käsemann has labeled "pronouncements of sacral law." Both assume that the form of speech they are analyzing has stable formal features and that it was consistently used in one original identifiable setting in the life of the early church. Both these assumptions, which are often and widely used by form critics (and with some success, when applied to other speech forms), are demonstrably false when applied to the so-called pronouncements of sacral law.[45] Such features as the same verb in both parts of the pronouncement, chiastic structure, and the conditional clause in the first part of the pronouncement are optional features of this rhetorical form that are not always present, either together or separately.[46] The distinctive feature of pronouncements of sacral law is the principle of retributive justice, the very nature of which lends itself to use in a two-part pronouncement in which behavior and reward/punishment are matched. Further, the form-critical quest for the *original* situation in life in which particular speech forms were used is an interesting but often fruitless search, not unlike attempts to force etymological meanings onto words regardless of the contexts in which they are used. Pronouncements of sacral law *can* be used in early Christian prophetic speech, particularly when they have a parenetic function and an eschatological framework, but they are not always or exclusively used in that setting.[47]

Pronouncements of sacral law, focusing on the principle of retributive justice, are often used in prophetic speech both in Greco-Roman paganism and early Christianity.[48] This association, of course, is shown by the setting of Rev. 22:18-19 and 1 Cor. 14:38, where pronouncements of sacral law are clearly used in connection with prophetic speech. The eschatological orientation of the pronouncement of sacral law is also found in the prophetic speech parodied by Celsus, which also happens to exhibit chiastic structure:

a   Blessed is he who has worshipped me now,
b   but I will cast eternal fire on all the rest,
      both in cities and in country places.
b'   And men who fail to realize the penalties in store
      for them will repent in vain and groan.
a'   But I will preserve for ever those who have been
      convinced by me.[49]

In Ign. Philad. 7:1 the bishop of Antioch quotes one of his earlier prophetic utterances: "Pay attention to the bishop!" (author's trans.). In another context (Polyc. 6:1) he enjoins the same thing in a statement very similar to the pronouncement of sacral law:

Pay attention to the bishop
so that God will pay attention to you.[50]

The oracular pronouncement found in Rev. 3:5 closely resembles the pronouncements of sacral law with the confess/deny motif found in Mark 8:38 and parallels (Matt. 10:32-33; Luke 9:26; 12:8-9), even though some of the formal features of such pronouncements are lacking:

He who conquers shall be clad thus in white garments,
and I will not blot his name out of the book of life;
I will confess his name before my father and before his angels.[51]

A similar use of the "deny" motif in a pronouncement with chiastic form in the context of a prophetic speech is found in Hermas *Vis.* ii.2.7-8:

a   Blessed are you, as many as endure the great persecution
      which is coming,
b   and as many as shall not deny their life.
b'   For the Lord has sworn by his Son that those who have
      denied their Christ have been rejected from their
      life,
a'   that is, those who shall now deny him in the days to come.[52]

The common content and the formal variety of these pronouncements tends to confirm our suggestion that various features of the so-called pronouncements of sacral law could be used to structure early Christian prophetic speech, and indeed were ideally suited for such use.[53] The basic formal features of such pronouncements are that the statements consist of two parts (either of which can be elaborated in a variety of ways), the first part dealing with the activity of man in the present and the second part dealing with the eschatological response of God. Depending on the context, such pronouncements may be either conditional or absolute. However, such pronouncements are found in such a wide variety of contexts (sapiential exhortation, eschatological parenesis, prophetic proclamation) that they cannot be tied exclusively to the setting of prophetic speech. We may conclude that the presence of all or many of the features of the pronouncement of sacral law in either the sayings of Jesus or in the religious discourse of early Christian writers is not an invariable indication of the presence of prophetic speech. Nor may the presence of these features be used to deny the authenticity of a saying of Jesus that exhibits such structure.[54]

IV. THE CRITERIA OF M. E. BORING

The most comprehensive and systematic attempt to establish criteria for recognizing the presence of prophetic oracles among the sayings of Jesus in the synoptic tradition has been made by M. E. Boring.[55] Boring recognizes that the frequent claims by scholars that Christian prophets contributed to the sayings tradition have not been based on hard evidence, and sets out to rectify that situation.[56] Although the only evidence for such a process is found in the synoptic gospels, Boring believes that the inevitable circularity in argument can be broken. Features of early Christian prophetic speech must be derived, at least in part, from other primary sources for early Christian prophecy.[57] A list of the characteristics of prophetic speech, suggests Boring, should be compiled from such sources as the Apocalypse of John, the Pauline letters, the synoptic gospels and Acts, Johannine literature, and the Didache.[58] In order for any of the synoptic sayings of Jesus to be initially regarded as a possible prophetic saying, two criteria must be met: (1) the saying must be in such a form that it might easily have existed apart from its present narrative content, and (2) it must be considered an inauthentic saying of Jesus, i.e. a product of the post-Easter church.[59]

Boring selects the Unforgivable Sin saying in Mark 3:28-29 (and parallels) to serve as a test for the methodology which he proposes, since many scholars regard that saying as the product of early Christian prophetic speech, and the saying is probably inauthentic. He then presents the following arguments for the prophetic origin of the saying: (1) The saying is an independent logion resting uncomfortably in each of its present contexts in the synoptic gospels. (2) The saying exhibits three formal indications of prophetic speech: (a) the introductory formula "Amen, I say to you," (b) chiastic structure (apart from the introductory formula which gives it an "oracular quality"):

> a All sins and blasphemies shall be forgiven the sons of men
> b whatever they blaspheme.
> b′ But whoever blasphemes the Holy Spirit,
> a′ shall never be forgiven, but is guilty of an eternal sin. (author's trans.)

and (c) the principle of retributive justice (*jus talionis*). (3) The content of the saying is eschatological. (4) The authority of the statement, if it does not derive from Jesus, is such that it is more likely to have derived from a Christian prophet than a Christian scribe. (5) The saying is a *pesher* on Isa. 63:3-11, and one important function of Christian prophets was the charismatic exegesis of the OT. (6) The saying makes sense if the sin of blasphemy against the Spirit is understood as the sin of blasphemy against the Spirit of *prophecy*, i.e. opposition to the prophetic activity of early Christian prophets (the saying is clearly used that way in Did. 11:7).

Before discussing the validity of each of these points, it must be said that Boring's reconstruction of the history of tradition reflected in Mark 3:28-29 and parallels is very persuasive.[60] He proposes that the first part of the saying may derive from the historical Jesus, while the second part cannot.[61]

Although I accept the general historicity of the logion, I will accept the premise of its inauthenticity in order to test Boring's arguments. Each of the following points is a response to Boring's six points summarized above. (1) Boring is quite right in claiming that the saying had an existence independent of its present narrative contexts. (2) However, the saying does not exhibit any formal characteristics of early Christian prophetic speech: (a) The introductory phrase "Amen, I say to you," is *not* attested in Christian prophetic speech; in early Christian literature it is found only within the setting of synoptic and Johannine sayings of Jesus.[62] (b) The presence of chiasmus in the Markan version of the saying (a feature which was probably added in the post-Easter period) has no necessary connection with the formal features of early Christian prophetic speech (indeed, chiasmus is a common rhetorical form throughout the whole of the ancient Mediterranean world), though such patterning might suggest repeated use within a liturgical setting.[63] (c) The presence of the principle of retributive justice is such a widespread feature of conventional wisdom in the ancient Mediterranean world that no necessary connection can be established between it and early Christian prophetic speech. (3) The saying is eschatological, but of course not all prophetic oracles are eschatological, nor are all eschatological sayings prophetic. (4) According to Boring, since the first part of the saying may have originated with Jesus, only the second requires the authority of a prophetic spokesman. Yet the question of who in the early Christian communities had the requisite authority to speak on what subjects is a complex issue. This statement no more requires prophetic authority than the analogous one in 1 John 5:16-17. (5) Whether or not the saying is a *pesher* on Isa. 63:3-11 (which is doubtful), the intimate connection between Christian prophecy and OT interpretation has been widely assumed but never satisfactorily demonstrated.[64] (6) The final argument put forth by Boring is the strongest. Did. 11:7 does attest the use of a late version of the Unforgivable Sin saying in the context of judging Christian prophets:

> Do not test or examine any prophet who is speaking in a spirit, for every sin shall be forgiven, but this sin shall not be forgiven.

Paul seems to be giving much the same advice in the synonymous couplet in 1 Thess. 5:19-20, though he does not sanction his statement by alluding to a saying of Jesus:

> Do not quench the Spirit,
> do not despise prophesying.

The central question is whether the use of the Unforgivable Sin saying in Did. 11:7 captures or preserves the original setting in which the saying was uttered in post-Easter Christianity. When Boring limits the concept of blaspheming against the Spirit to blaspheming against the Spirit of *prophecy*, he has moved illegitimately from the general to the particular. Although the Spirit was primarily associated with prophecy in *rabbinic* literature,[65] the same association does not hold for early Judaism generally or early Christianity, where prophecy was but *one* of many manifestations of the presence and activity of the Spirit.[66] The saying in Mark 3:28-29 (and parallels) testifies to the certainty of the Christian community that it in truth possessed the Spirit of God,[67] but it is less certain that the phenomenon of prophecy is in view in the early post-Easter form of the saying. In its Markan framework the Unforgivable Sin saying is part of the larger Beelzebul pericope in Mark 3:19b-30, a pericope which is part of the antimagic polemic in the Gospel of Mark.[68] In Greco-Roman paganism magical procedures were commonly used for acquiring divine revelations and for securing the aid of an "assistant daimon" (*paredros daimōn*) who could both mediate such revelation and enable the practitioner to perform miraculous feats.[69] Both Jewish critics of early Christianity and Jewish and pagan observers naturally concluded that any manifestations of supernatural power on the part of Christians were the result of magical activities.[70] For their part Christians would have regarded such charges as blasphemy against the Spirit of God whom they believed was at work in and through them. The Unforgivable Sin saying appears to fit well in just such an apologetic context in which the Christian community's confidence that the Spirit, and not demonic powers, is at work in their midst is expressed.

In sum, Boring has not successfully argued for the prophetic origin, or even prophetic reformulation, of the Unforgivable Sin saying in Mark 3:28-29 and Q (Matt. 12:32; Luke 12:10). Many of his arguments are either invalid or of doubtful significance. The last argument, which is the strongest, is also invalid since the Unforgivable Sin saying probably originated with Jesus, who defended himself against the charge of magic. On the other hand, it is apparent that Boring has presented the strongest line of argumentation of any scholar who has held that the synoptic tradition contains sayings attributed to the earthly Jesus that in fact originated with early Christian prophets. Boring's failure, if my arguments against his position are valid, does not mean that oracles of Christian prophets did not or could not enter into the synoptic tradition. It does mean that the methodology for clearly and convincingly detecting such a process has not yet been formulated.[71]

V. THE TRANSMISSION OF SAYINGS OF JESUS

A subject which we have not yet discussed, but which is of fundamental importance for the topic of this chapter, is the problem of the channels through which the Jesus traditions were transmitted prior to the formation of the canonical gospels. The earliest bearers of such traditions must have been the disciples and followers of Jesus, and if any of the sayings of Jesus preserved in the synoptic tradition contain verbal approximations of what Jesus actually said, then *memorization* (the central method of ancient education) must have played a major role in the transmission process.[72] These bearers of tradition are labeled by the Third Evangelist as "eyewitnesses and ministers of the word" (Luke 1:2). Paul regarded himself as an apostle, yet it has often been remarked how little use he seems to have made of the Jesus tradition.[73] Apart from the early apostles, about whose role in the transmission process next to nothing is known, the early Christian teacher has been regarded by many as playing a central role in the transmission of presynoptic (and parasynoptic) tradition.[74] Many form critics have regarded the Christian preacher as the primary bearer of the Jesus tradition.[75] Whatever the merits of these views, we are primarily concerned in the present discussion with the theory that early Christian prophets were active in the process of transmitting the presynoptic tradition of the sayings of Jesus.[76] Yet this view is usually an extrapolation of the theory that prophetic sayings became assimilated to the tradition of the sayings of the historical Jesus. If the Christian prophet can be regarded as having played a major role in transmitting the sayings of Jesus, then the assimilation of oracles of the risen Lord to collections of the sayings of Jesus becomes explicable.

One of the most carefully constructed arguments for the way in which the sayings of Jesus were transmitted in early Christianity has been formulated by G. Theissen.[77] Theissen observes that many of the sayings of Jesus preserved in the synoptic tradition emphasize such radical ethical values as homelessness (Matt. 8:20), avoidance of normal family relationships (Luke 14:26; Mark 10:29; Matt. 8:22; 19:12), and rejection of possessions and wealth (Matt. 6:19-21, 25-28; Mark 10:17-31). The radical nature of these sayings, according to Theissen, indicates that they were probably preserved and transmitted by those who took them literally: itinerant charismatics who emulated the life-style of Jesus. Early Christianity was an urban phenomenon, with the exception of the rural regions of Syria-Palestine, where these itinerant charismatics were probably active. Theissen emphasizes the prophetic role of hypothetical itinerant charismatics by tying his proposal to the view (particularly espoused by E. Käsemann) that prophetic sayings entered into the stream of Jesus traditions. While Theissen's proposal has a great deal of merit, it suffers from the weakness of assuming that those who espouse radical ideals invariably practice them.[78] Again, the characterization of these itinerants as "prophets" stretches the available evidence.[79]

There are a number of reasons why it appears improbable that early Christian prophets played any extensive role in the transmission and dissemination of the sayings of Jesus in the period prior to the formation of the synoptic gospels:

(1) In the only two extant prophetic writings of early Christianity, the Apocalypse of John and the Shepherd of Hermas, and in the letters of Paul and Ignatius, both of whom can with some justification be labeled prophets, there is a surprising neglect of the direct use of the sayings of Jesus. This neglect would, at first glance, be inexplicable if early Christian prophets were important channels for the transmission of the sayings of Jesus. However, it is true that there are some oracles of the risen Lord in the Apocalypse of John that are similar to sayings of Jesus found in the synoptic gospels.[80] It is not completely clear whether John modeled some of his prophetic sayings after traditional sayings of Jesus or whether the "traditional sayings of Jesus" have been influenced by the kind of oracular speech found in the Apocalypse. Similarly, there are a few possible allusions to the sayings of Jesus in the gospels and in the Shepherd of Hermas, but there is no evidence that Hermas made any significant use of such traditions.[81] One of the clearer allusions is found in Hermas *Vis.* ii.2.6-8 (cf. Mark 8:38 and parallels; Luke 12:9), an oracle which makes use of the "deny" motif. Of the prophetic sayings embedded in the Pauline letters, only 1 Thess. 4:15ff. alludes to possible sayings of Jesus.[82] While a case has been made for the familiarity of Ignatius of Antioch with the Gospel of John,[83] allusions to sayings of Jesus have parallels in the synoptic gospels.[84] In sum, there is remarkably little use of sayings of Jesus in those authors who consciously wrote as prophets (John and Hermas), or in those who occasionally prophesied (Paul and Ignatius). This fact casts doubt on the theory that early Christian prophets specialized in the transmission of Jesus traditions.

(2) M. E. Boring has argued that there was a "fluid interplay" between prophecy and gospel tradition prior to A.D. 70, but that thereafter prophecy and the sayings

tradition parted company and followed different channels.[85] According to Boring the creation of the gospel form by Mark forced a distinction between pre- and post-Easter sayings of Jesus that had not previously been made.[86] This theory is an ingenious solution to the problem which we have just discussed. If early Christian prophets functioned as transmitters of the Jesus tradition, why are elements of that tradition so marginal in the Apocalypse of John and the Shepherd of Hermas, the only two extant prophetic writings from the early Christian period? Boring's solution is that, while Christian prophets prior to A.D. 70 functioned in that way, after that time they were no longer occupied with transmitting the sayings of Jesus. This proposal has several weaknesses: (a) The theory that Christian prophets specialized in the trans-mission of Jesus tradition is an extrapolation of the view that oracles of the risen Lord became assimilated to sayings of the historical Jesus; it appears arbitrary to eliminate the evidentiary value of the Apocalypse of John as a typical example of early Christian prophecy without strong supporting evidence.[87] (b) The selection of A.D. 70 as a turning point in the history of Christian prophecy is arbitrary and unconvincing,[88] and Boring presents no arguments substantiating his theory of a major reorientation of the role of the early Christian prophet. Further, it appears highly doubtful that the publication and dissemination of the Gospel of Mark ca. A.D. 70 could provoke such profound changes in both Christian prophecy and the transmission of the sayings of Jesus. (c) It is likely that the traditions which have been incorporated into the Apoc-alypse of John are considerably earlier than the date when the entire work was finally completed.[89]

(3) There is little evidence for the assumption that the oracles of early Christian prophets were collected and circulated by anyone other than the prophets who uttered them. This is in marked contrast to the process whereby many of the prophetic books in the OT were formed.[90] With regard to the Jesus traditions, however, recent research has emphasized that in addition to Q various collections of such traditions were in existence and circulation prior to the composition of Mark.[91] If these Jesus traditions were transmitted by Christian prophets, it appears likely that they might have collected and transmitted both their own oracles and those which originated with other prophets.[92] However, our analysis of those sayings and speeches in early Christian literature that have a formal claim to be oracular utterances does not suggest the existence of *collections* of oracles.[93] But it is true that the oracles embedded in the Apocalypse of John and the Shepherd of Hermas presuppose that the authors collected their own oracles and used them at appropriate junctures in their compositions. There is no evidence that oracles were carefully committed to memory or written down in order to be transmitted to others. Unlike the sayings of Jesus, which are well rep-resented in the NT through the synoptic gospels and in a transmuted form in the Gospel of John, the oracles of Christian prophets that have survived are few in number and often difficult to detect. The loss of these oracles may be a historical accident, or (more likely) it may indicate that they were not carefully preserved. Since teaching and learning in the ancient world were largely a matter of memorization,[94] the loss of prophetic utterances indicates that they were not spoken in settings understood as teaching-learning situations. Therefore the disappearance of the many oracles which must have been pronounced by early Christian prophets is not only due to prophetic activity being largely oral[95] (did not much of the gospel tradition also pass through an oral period?), but also and perhaps primarily to the fact that the religious settings in which prophetic speech was normally used were not those involving teaching and catechesis.

VI. CONCLUSIONS

In this chapter we have attempted to examine critically the theory that the oracles of Christian prophets, uttered in the name of the exalted Lord, became mingled with the sayings of Jesus which either originated with the historical Jesus or else were modified by the post-Easter Christian communities. While the theory is not an *a priori* impossibility, the critical methodology for detecting and demonstrating the prophetic origin of such putative sayings of Jesus has not yet been developed. On the basis of the foregoing discussion it appears unlikely that many oracles of the risen Lord became assimilated to sayings of the historical Jesus. Those that might have are now virtually undetectable. The point at issue is not whether early Christianity exercised a creative role in the formulation, reformulation, and transmission of the sayings of Jesus; they certainly did. The point at issue is the identity of those who were largely responsible for these creative additions and modifications in the traditions. German NT scholars, it appears, have seized the hypothesis of the creative role of Christian prophets because it both accounts for the additions to the sayings tradition and absolves the early Christians from any culpability in the forging of inauthentic words of Jesus. In spite of the theological attractiveness of the theory, however, the historical evidence in support of the theory lies largely in the creative imagination of scholars.

10 | THE FORM AND CONTENT OF EARLY CHRISTIAN PROPHECY: PART I

I. THE PROBLEM OF METHOD

Although prophetic activity was a significant aspect of the early developmental phases of Christianity, no collections of oracles have been preserved from the first century of Christian history. In this respect at least, early Christian prophecy stands in marked contrast to ancient Israelite prophecy and Greco-Roman oracular tradition, both of which are represented by a wealth of prophetic or oracular sayings and speeches. The two Christian documents which present themselves as written revelation, the Apocalypse of John and the Shepherd of Hermas, are exceptions to the apparent dearth of prophetic speech forms preserved from early Christianity. Yet both of these documents conform to the literary conventions constitutive of the apocalyptic genre, and it is uncertain to what extent their contents are purely literary products or actual revelatory experiences.

In this and the following chapter an attempt will be made to isolate and analyze those scattered fragments of early Christian prophetic speech forms which are preserved in early Christian literature. The major problem in achieving this objective is the formulation of objective criteria whereby such fragments of prophetic speech may be identified. In an earlier chapter we discussed at some length the theory that some of the sayings of Jesus originated as utterances of Christian prophets speaking in the name of their exalted Lord.[1] The disappointing conclusion of that discussion was that it was highly doubtful that prophets contributed a great deal of material to the Jesus tradition, and such oracles as they might have contributed would be virtually unrecognizable on the basis of formal criteria. If we are to succeed in our attempt to analyze the form and content of early Christian prophetic speech forms, we must formulate objective criteria whereby those speech forms may be recognized. While the objective criteria which we will propose below may be inadequate to reveal the presence of prophetic speech forms wherever they are embedded in the literature, they will nevertheless provide a reliable core of authentic examples of oracular material.

The criteria for identifying the presence of oracular material in early Christian literature are the following: (1) If a saying or speech is attributed to a supernatural being (i.e. to God, Jesus, the Holy Spirit, an angel, a deceased person, Satan, a demon, etc.), there is a strong possibility that we are dealing with oracular material. Such material, of course, may be literary dramatizations rather than transcriptions of revelatory experiences. Yet even in such cases there is great likelihood that such literary productions were modeled after generally recognizable oracular patterns. (2) If a saying or speech consists of a prediction of the future course of events, or reflects knowledge of the past or present that the speaker could not be expected to know by ordinary sensory means, it is possible that oracular material is present. Again, it is not unlikely that many such sayings or speeches are literary productions or that they are simply (for example) a recital of stereotyped events widely regarded as associated with the eschaton. (3) If a saying or speech is introduced by a formula which in other contexts appears to be a phrase used to introduce prophetic speech, it is possible that oracular material is present. These three criteria are not, of course, infallible means for identifying the presence of prophetic speech. However, when two or even three of these criteria are present in various early Christian texts the probability that we have discovered a fragment of prophetic speech is made even more likely. The presupposition that lies behind these criteria is that *prophetic speech tends to retain its identity* in the various literary contexts in which it is incorporated. Prophetic speech, after all, can only function as such when it is recognizable. Similarly, a prophet can be recognized as a spokesman for God only if he conforms to the social image of the prophet accepted as legitimate within the social setting in which he prophesies.

Our procedure in the next two chapters will be to analyze the prophetic sayings and speeches as they occur in various related groups of documents, beginning with the Pauline corpus. At the conclusion of this analysis we will attempt to characterize early Christian prophetic speech in terms of recurrent forms, formulas, patterns, and themes. It is our intention to discuss every fragment of prophetic speech embedded in early Christian literature to the middle of the second century A.D. The next chapter will conclude with a discussion of the Montanist oracles, the only instances of early Christian oracular speech which have been intensively analyzed by scholars.

II. THE PAULINE LETTERS

The genuine Pauline letters (not including Ephesians and the Pastorals) constitute the earliest body of Christian literature which has survived. These letters are valuable, not only for the light they shed directly on Paul himself and on the Christian communities he addresses, but also for the earlier material they contain that is derived from pre-Pauline Christianity. Paul quotes or alludes to early Christian hymns, creeds, formulas of various kinds, prayers, proverbs, fragments of liturgies, and the like. The following discussion will show that he also quoted early Christian oracles when he could use them appropriately in epistolary settings. However, since Paul himself functioned as a prophet, it is not always clear whether he quotes his own oracles or those of another.

Paul often designates himself an "apostle," but never a "prophet." Modern scholars, however, are quite willing to categorize him as a prophet.[2] From the standpoint of early Christianity the role of apostle appears to have been a functional equivalent of the OT prophet.[3] Paul's so-called conversion experience, described in different but complementary ways in Acts (9, 22, 26) and in Paul's letters (Gal. 1; 1 Cor. 9:1; 15:8), was interpreted as a *prophetic* call by both the author of Acts and Paul himself.[4] Paul is apparently called a prophet in Acts 13:1, and he was later given wider recognition as a prophet in the church (Hippolytus *Ref.* viii.20.1). Paul claims to have experienced a wide variety of revelatory phenomena.[5] In 1 Cor. 14:18 he claims to have spoken in tongues more than the Corinthians. In a sentence in which the condition is assumed as possible, he states: "If I come to you speaking in tongues, how shall I benefit you unless I bring you some revelation [*apokalypsei*] or knowledge [*gnōsei*] or prophecy [*prophēteia*] or teaching [*didachē*]" (1 Cor. 14:6); apparently he regarded himself as able to do all of these. In Gal. 2:2 Paul claims that he went up to Jerusalem "by revelation" (*kata apokalypsin*), by which he probably refers to a dream or vision experience.[6] 1 Cor. 2:13 is enigmatic, yet possibly refers to Paul's prophetic ministry:[7] "And we impart this in words not taught by human wisdom but taught by the Spirit, interpreting spiritual truths to those who possess the Spirit." In 2 Cor. 12:1-10 Paul "boasts" of two separate revelatory experiences which he had, one a heavenly journey and the other a divine oracle communicated to him in answer to prayer (this will be discussed in detail below). In 2 Cor. 13:3 he refers to the fact that Christ speaks through him, and in 1 Cor. 7:40, after giving an injunction, he observes, "I think that I have the Spirit of God." These revelatory experiences described or alluded to in Paul's letters are complemented by very similar phenomena recounted in Acts.[8] In Acts Paul is described as receiving a number of visions of the Lord apart from that which occurred on the road to Damascus (Acts 18:9-11; 20:22-23; 21:4, 10-11; 22:17-22; 23:1).[9] He also is described as experiencing night visions, which could involve the appearance of an angel (Acts 16:9-10; 27:23). All this evidence combines to suggest that Paul was a prophet who experienced many revelatory phenomena, some of which he communicated to others.[10]

A. 2 COR. 12:9

When Paul's prophetic or charismatic gifts are the subject of discussion, the passage most often referred to is 2 Cor. 12:1-10. That passage mentions two visionary or revelatory experiences of Paul, the first of which was conceptualized as an ascension to the third heaven where he learned "unutterable things" (*arrēta rhēmata*, v. 4).[11] The second revelatory experience is described in 2 Cor. 12:7-10; Paul claims that he prayed three times for deliverance from an undisclosed physical infirmity, but that a negative answer from the Lord was received through personal revelation.[12] Paul quotes this revelatory message in 2 Cor. 12:9:

> But he [i.e. the Lord; cf. v. 8] said to me,
> My grace is sufficient for you,
> for my power is made perfect in weakness.

Unfortunately, Paul supplies few concrete details that might permit us to understand more of the specific nature of this revelatory experience. Lindblom has characterized this experience of Paul as a *revelatio interna* ("interior revelation"),[13] though this educated guess does little to facilitate our understanding of this saying. The oracle could as easily have come to Paul through the medium of a dream or vision, or even through the intervention of a prophet. Paul's certainty that it was the *Lord* (i.e. the exalted Jesus) who spoke to him suggests a visionary experience,[14] but that too is merely speculation.

This revelatory saying exhibits the form of an oracular response.[15] From a Greco-Roman perspective this oracle would be regarded as a *Heilungsorakel* ("healing oracle"), i.e. the type of oracle that one might expect to receive in a dream or vision while sleeping in the inner sanctuary of a temple of Asklepios. In this instance, however, a cure is pointedly refused by the deity. From a Jewish perspective this oracle resembles a *Heilsorakel* ("oracle of assurance"), an oracular form found frequently in the OT and, indeed, throughout the entire ancient Near East.[16] The oracle of assurance was ordinarily formulated as a response to a lament or complaint, a feature that coheres well with the circumstances within which the oracle in 2 Cor. 12:9 was given. This oracle consists of two lines, the poetic nature of which is betrayed by the chiastic *a b b a* pattern: the verb "sufficient" (*arkei*) in the first line corresponds to the verb "perfected" (*teleitai*) in the second, while "grace" (*charis*) in the last part of line one corresponds to "power" (*dynamis*) in the first part of line two. The entire oracle consists of two structural units, the first part of which (coinciding with the first line) is the primary response of the deity, while the second part (coinciding with the second line) provides the theological justification for the first part and is introduced by the conjunctive particle "for" (*gar*).

In the Greco-Roman world this is one of the more common and basic oracular forms. In our formal analysis of Greek oracles we have designated this type as the *expository oracle*.[17] The expository oracle consists of two structural elements, the second of which serves to explain, support, or elaborate the meaning or significance of the primary statement. This oracular structure, however, is not unique to the Greco-Roman world. In ancient Israelite prophecy one of the most common structural patterns for oracles is the combination of a threat or promise with a supporting reason (often in the form of an accusation) introduced by the causal particle *ki*.[18] The oracle of assurance is but one type of Israelite oracle that exhibits this pattern.

2 Cor. 12:9, then, from either a Greco-Roman or Israelite-Jewish perspective, is cast in a recognizably oracular form of speech. However, whether Paul composed the oracle himself in an attempt to parody the value of Hellenistic revelatory experience,[19] or whether he is relating an actual experience, is not easily determined. But the frequency and variety of revelatory experiences claimed by Paul elsewhere in his letters and narrated in Acts make it likely that this oracle was based on an actual experience.

B. 1 COR. 15:51-52

Modern scholarship[20] widely regards 1 Cor. 15:51-52 as a prophetic revelation received by Paul:

> Lo [*idou*]! I tell you a mystery [*mystērion*].
> a   We shall not all sleep,
> b   but we shall all be changed,
>   in a moment,
> c   in the twinkling of an eye,
>   at the last trumpet.
> c'   for [*gar*] the trumpet will sound,
> a'   and the dead shall be raised imperishable,
> b'   and we shall be changed.

The oracular character of this saying is revealed, first of all, by the significance of the introductory formula. While the demonstrative particle "behold" or "lo" (Gk. *idou*; Heb. *hinneh*) functions in a variety of ways in both the OT and NT,[21] here it appears to introduce a prophetic oracle, as it often does in the Bible.[22] The oracular character of the following saying is more clearly indicated by the term "mystery" (Gk. *mystērion*; Heb. *raz*), which is virtually a technical term in prophetic and apocalyptic contexts in early Judaism and early Christianity, and to which we shall refer as the *mystery formula*.[23] The term is occasionally used this way even in Greco-Roman paganism.[24] In these settings "mystery" refers to divinely concealed information (nearly always relating to the end of the age), the true meaning of which is now disclosed to the prophet or apocalyptist through a special, divinely bestowed insight. Such divine revelation may be concealed in dreams, in texts such as the OT, and in aspects of physical reality such as the stars and planets.[25] In 1 Cor. 15:51 "mystery" refers both to the secret and its disclosure.

The oracle which follows exhibits another feature of prophetic revelation, its eschatological content. The way in which we have quoted the oracle exhibits its poetic character.[26] It consists of two strophes, each of which has three lines. Each line in the first strophe has a counterpart in the second, so that the entire oracle has a chiastic structure (*a b c c' a' b'*). The second part of the oracle, the "reason" (*Begrün-dung*), is introduced by "for," yet the reason turns out to be a reiteration of the announcement of salvation, i.e. the *form* is retained, though the content is altered. The problem of precisely where the oracle concludes is partially solved when the chiastic structure of vv. 51-52 is recognized. An interesting feature of the third line is the three prepositional phrases which begin with the same Greek preposition (*en*). The use of three synonymous phrases serially is a fairly frequent characteristic of early Jewish and early Christian prophetic speech.[27] The poetic form of the oracle, however, does not in itself suffice to prove the presence of prophetic speech; Paul continues to use poetic parallelism in vv. 53ff. One legitimate objection to viewing 1 Cor. 15:51-52 as oracular speech is the presence of the first-person plural verb forms ("we shall sleep," "we shall be changed"). The speaker, on that account, cannot be God, Jesus, or the Holy Spirit. Yet in early Jewish and early Christian prophetic speech generally, it is not uncommon that the prophet speaks in his own person.[28] The first-person plural, of course, is not inappropriate for prophetic communication within a liturgical setting in which the speaker (in homiletic fashion) might include his audience and himself in the depiction of the impending eschatological events. Nevertheless, since the first-person plural form of address is thoroughly characteristic of Paul's epistolary style, he may have reformulated an original third-person plural oracle into the first person. If so, we can suggest the following as the more original form of the oracle:

Behold! I tell you a mystery:
All shall not sleep,
but all shall be changed.
In a moment, in the twinkling of an eye, at the last trumpet.
For the trumpet shall sound,
and the dead shall be raised imperishable,
and all shall be transformed.

The content of the oracle is obviously eschatological and concerns a belief of fundamental importance for early Christianity: the final resurrection of the righteous head and the transformation of those who are yet living. This event was associated with the parousia of Jesus (cf. 1 Thess. 4:15-17, which embodies another oracle). This oracle deals specifically with the problem of the relationship of the dead to the living and their mutual destinies when the parousia occurs. The function of the oracle, then, appears to be that of providing more detail to the generally held, but somewhat vague, conviction that salvation would be fully and completely realized at the parousia of Jesus.

C. ROM. 11:25-26

This passage is another which is widely regarded as a prophetic oracle that probably originated with Paul himself.

> I want you to understand this mystery [*mystērion*], brethren:
> a hardening has come upon part of Israel,
> until the full number of the Gentiles come in,
> and so all Israel will be saved.[29]

This oracle, if that is what it is, cannot be separated from the scriptural quotation which immediately follows in vv. 26-27:

> as it is written,
> "The Deliverer will come from Zion [*ek Siōn*],
> he will banish ungodliness from Jacob";
> "and this will be my covenant with them
> when I take away their sins."

The oracle in vv. 25-26a appears to be justified by a conflated quotation from Isa. 59:20-21 and Isa. 27:9. The remarkable thing about the quotation is that the phrase "from Zion," which apparently justifies the coming of the messiah from the Jews and his proclamation among the Gentiles, is found neither in the Hebrew original nor in the LXX.[30] In other words, through the medium of an interpretative alteration in the OT text, of the sort found not infrequently in the *pesharim* from Qumran, an insight into the destiny of both Israel and the Gentiles has been extrapolated. To Paul the OT text means that a redeemer (i.e. Jesus Christ) shall come *from* Zion (for the benefit of the Gentiles) and will banish ungodliness from Jacob (i.e. "all Israel"). In all of Pauline literature this is perhaps the clearest example of the prophetic or charismatic exegesis of the OT. A characteristic feature of *midrash pesher* interpretation at Qumran is, as E. Earle Ellis has carefully pointed out, the inclusion of the interpretation into the very phraseology of the OT text itself.[31]

The use of the *mystery formula* as part of the introduction of the eschatological saying in vv. 25-26a suggests that the saying is oracular. The oracle itself consists of three lines, each of which depicts one sequence in a series of eschatological events culminating with the salvation of the entire nation of Israel.[32] If the supportive biblical quotation is regarded as part of the oracle itself, as I think it should be on form-critical grounds, we then have an oracle consisting of two strophes. The first strophe is essentially an unconditional announcement of salvation, while the second strophe provides the reason, not introduced with "for" or "because," but in this case with "as it is written."

The oracle itself is somewhat startling, since Paul has gone to the trouble of arguing in Rom. 9:6ff. that not all physical descendants of Israel are true Israelites. Certainly the notion of the eschatological salvation of "all Israel" is not found elsewhere in Paul's letters. Earlier, Paul had stated of the Jews that "the wrath of God has come upon them forever!" (1 Thess. 2:16). These two contradictory views have led B. Noack to propose a solution which at first sight seems farfetched. Noack claims that Rom. 11:25-26 was a revelation which Paul received at the very moment he was dictating Rom. 11:13-36![33] The strength of this view is that it reconciles the apparent contradiction between Rom. 9:6ff. and 11:25-26 by assuming that Paul had no idea that he would express the sentiment that all Israel would be saved until he was composing the final portions of Rom. 9-11. In support of Noack's view one might suggest that the doxology found in Rom. 11:33-36 functions as a response of praise and thanksgiving that frequently is found at the conclusion of a revelatory experience.[34] Now it is true that various strata of early Judaism assumed that Israel would experience ultimate salvation (Jub. 1:22-25; 50:5; 4 Ezra 10:38ff.), and such a view apparently characterized even the radical position of the Qumran community (1QSa 1:1-6; 1QpHab 5:3-6).[35] However, apart from Rom. 11:25-26, the notion of the eschatological salvation of all Israel never occurs in the NT or in early Christian literature. The traditional nature of the conception of the final salvation of "all Israel" (outside of Christian circles), therefore, in no way diminishes the prophetic nature of this Pauline oracle.[36]

D. 1 THESS. 4:15-17

When Paul had been forced to leave the new Christian congregation at Thessalonika after just a few weeks (Acts 17:1ff.), he sent Timothy back from Athens to continue the work he had begun (1 Thess. 3:1-2). When Timothy and Silas returned to Paul, who was now at Corinth (Acts 18:5; 1 Thess. 3:6), the apostle learned of the problems facing the Thessalonian Christians. He wrote 1 Thessalonians in an attempt to solve at least some of the major difficulties. In 1 Thess. 4:13-18 Paul particularly attempted to provide a solution to the problem of the fate of those Christians who had died prior to the expected parousia of Jesus; in so doing, he appealed to an authoritative "word of the Lord" in vv. 15-17:

> For this we declare to you by the word of the Lord, that we who are alive, who are left until the coming of the Lord, shall not precede those who have fallen asleep. For the Lord himself will descend from heaven with a cry of command, with the archangel's call, and with the sound of the trumpet of God. And the dead in Christ will rise first; then we who are alive, who are left, shall be caught up together with them in the clouds to meet the Lord in the air; and so we shall always be with the Lord.

While the meaning of this passage appears clear enough, the major problem is determining the *source* to which Paul refers with the introductory phrase "by the word of the Lord."[37] The inclusion of this passage in the present chapter indicates our conviction that it is a quotation of a prophetic saying which originated either with Paul or (more likely) with some unknown Christian prophet.

Of the six major hypotheses regarding the source of 1 Thess. 4:15ff., four appear very improbable: (1) Paul is here advising the Thessalonians in the spirit of what the Lord (i.e. Jesus) would have said on the subject.[38] (2) This pronouncement originated with Paul and proceeded from his consciousness of *Christus internus,* i.e. Paul's intimate fellowship with Christ was a means of revelation for him.[39] (3) In 1 Thess. 4:15ff. Paul reformulated one or more sayings of Jesus preserved in the canonical gospels (Matt. 24:30-31 and John 6:39-40 are most frequently cited in this regard).[40] (4) The saying was derived from the OT or from a Jewish or Jewish Christian apocalyptic writing no longer extant.[41]

The two theories of the origin of 1 Thess. 4:15ff. which appear to be the most probable are: (1) the saying is based on an *agraphon,* i.e. an independent saying of Jesus not preserved in the canonical gospels (the most famous example of which is Acts 20:35: "It is more blessed to give than to receive"),[42] and (2) the saying is based on an oracle originating either with Paul himself,[43] or with another, but unknown, early Christian prophet.[44]

Four important questions must be answered in our investigation of 1 Thess. 4:15ff.: What is the precise *extent* of the pronouncement? What is the *original form* of the pronouncement? Is there any real evidence to suggest that the pronouncement is oracular and not simply a quotation of another type of early Christian eschatological speech? Finally, assuming the oracular origin of the pronouncement, is there any evidence to suggest that the oracle originated with Paul or with another early Christian prophet? We shall discuss each of these issues seriatim in the following paragraphs.

1. The Extent of the Pronouncement.

Whether 1 Thess. 4:15ff. is regarded as an *agraphon* or an *oracle*, v. 15 is undoubtedly a Pauline summary of the content of the saying which is found in vv. 16-17a; similarly, the phrase in v. 17b ("and so shall we always be with the Lord") is generally regarded as a Pauline inference based on the pronouncement which he had just quoted.[45] Apart from any further attempts at reconstruction, the pronouncement with its introduction would look like this:

> For this we declare to you by the word of the Lord:

> "For the Lord himself will descend from heaven
>   with a cry of command
>   with the archangel's call
>   and with the sound of the trumpet of God.
> And the dead in Christ will rise first;
>   then we who are alive, who are left,
>   shall be caught up together with them in the clouds
>   to meet the Lord in the air."

2. The Original Form of the Pronouncement.

The reconstruction of the original form of 1 Thess. 4:16-17a, prior to its inclusion in 1 Thess. 4:15ff., must assume that Paul, whether quoting another source or himself, introduced alterations in order to fit the pronouncement to the epistolary setting of 1 Thessalonians.[46] In the interest of such a reconstruction of the original form of the pronouncement, a number of alterations appear required: (1) the first person plural pronoun and verb behind the expression "we ... shall be caught up" (v. 17a) appear to have been substituted for third person plurals to fit Paul's epistolary style.[47] (2) The characteristic Paulinism "in Christ" can be eliminated if the saying is non-Pauline in origin.[48] (3) The substantival participle "those who remain" (*perileipomenoi*), though found only in 1 Thess. 4:15-16 in the Pauline letters (and thus may reveal the non-Pauline origin of the saying), is redundant and should be eliminated.[49] (4) The two adverbs "first" (*prōton*) and "then" (*epeita*), while they are certainly not uncharacteristic of Paul (cf. 1 Cor. 12:28; 15:46), nevertheless do provide a temporal framework which appears to be based on Paul's interpretive inference (v. 15b) that the living shall not precede the dead at the parousia. On this basis they should be eliminated.[50] (5) The phrase "the Lord himself" (*autos ho Kyrios*) appears original, even though some would eliminate *autos ho*,[51] or substitute "Son of man" for "Lord."[52] The liturgical solemnity of the phrase "the Lord himself" points to non-Pauline formulation, perhaps in a cultic setting, within which prophetic utterances were commonly made in early Christianity. (6) The frequency with which the demonstrative particle "behold" occurs at the beginning of Christian oracles (cf. 1 Cor. 15:51-52; Rev. 1:7) suggests that this oracle originally began in that way.

On the basis of these observations and suggestions the oracle embedded in 1 Thess. 4:16-17a may have originally looked very much like this:

> This I declare to you by the word of the Lord:
> "Behold! The Lord himself
> with a cry of command,
> with the shout of the archangel,
> and with the trumpet of God,
> shall descend from heaven.
>
> And the dead shall be raised,
> and the living shall be caught up with them in the clouds
> to meet the Lord in the air."

As reconstructed above, the oracular pronouncement consists of two strophes, the first depicting the parousia, and the second the gathering of the saints, both living and dead, attendant upon that event. In this form the oracle is quasi-poetical, a fact indicated by the three parallel phrases in line two of the first strophe, each of which begins with the same Greek preposition (en).

3. The Oracular Character of the Pronouncement.

In the introductory sentence in v. 15a, where Paul says, "this we declare to you by the word of the Lord," he uses the phrase "word of the Lord" in a more specialized sense than simply the apostolic message (as "the word of the Lord" means in 1 Thess. 1:9, and the "word of God" in 1 Thess. 2:3). Paul uses the title "Lord" of the earthly Jesus in contexts in which the free citation of the transmitted words of Jesus are given (cf. 1 Cor. 7:10; 9:14).[53] Further, Paul does not use the expression "the word of the Lord" to refer to a personal revelation.[54] However, in view of the few times that Paul refers to such prophetic sayings and experiences, this argument is not compelling, nor does it touch the view that Paul is here quoting the oracle of a prophet other than himself.[55] But "the word of the Lord" is repeatedly used in the OT (LXX *logos Kyriou*) to introduce prophetic oracles (cf. 1 Kgs. 20:35; 2 Kgs.13:1ff.; 21:35; Sir. 48:3).[56] The introductory formula which Paul uses, then, while it is not exclusively used as an introduction to prophetic speech, can certainly function in that way in the present context.

The content of the saying is thoroughly eschatological, a feature which characterizes two other Pauline oracles we have investigated, 1 Cor. 15:51-52 and Rom. 11:25-26. In addition, the saying contains a new combination of traditional Christian eschatological elements: no Jewish or Christian text prior to A.D. 50 (the date of 1 Thessalonians) places the parousia of Jesus (or its Jewish equivalent, the visitation of God) in conjunction with the resurrection of the dead and the ascent of the living. Nor is the unique imagery of the meeting in the air found before this time.[57] 1 Thess. 4:16-17a thus constitutes a unique configuration of events and imagery that in itself might well require the authority of divine revelation for its successful promulgation. At the same time this new combination of elements makes it highly unlikely that the saying is derived from the tradition of the sayings of Jesus. We conclude that the arguments for regarding 1 Thess. 4:16-17a as oracular are stronger than any other hypothesis concerning the origin of the pronouncement.

4. The Non-Pauline Origin of the Oracle.

If we assume the oracular nature of 1 Thess. 4:16-17a, is there any further evidence to suggest that the oracle originated with a prophet other than Paul? Three factors suggest that this is the case: (1) If our reconstruction of the oracle is correct, the Pauline additions (apart from the use of the first person plural pronoun and verb for epistolary style) constitute Paul's interpretative comments on the oracle. He has supplied a temporal framework through the inclusion of the two adverbs of time, "first" and "then" (vv. 16b, 17a); the addition of the phrase "in Christ" is a thoroughly Pauline qualification; the redundant inclusion of the substantive participle "those who remain" appears to have been added to the oracle through the influence of Paul's statement in v. 15b. All these features indicate that Paul quoted the oracle with interpretative modifications; i.e. just as he modified the concatenated quotation of Isa. 59:20-21 and Isa. 27:9 to convey his interpretation of that passage, so he has introduced analogous modifications into the oracle quoted in 1 Thess. 4:16-17a. This analysis suggests that the oracle is not Paul's, but another's. (2) The second argument which indicates the non-Pauline origin of this oracle is the presence in vv. 15b and 17b of an inference clearly based on an interpretation of the oracle itself: "we who are alive, who are left until the coming of the Lord, shall not precede those who have fallen asleep" (v. 15b), and "and so shall we always be with the Lord" (v. 17b).[58] There is a marked incongruity between v. 17a ("to meet the Lord in the air") and v. 17b (quoted in the last sentence): the saints appear to be eternally stranded between heaven and earth, treading air! The introduction and conclusion of the oracle are Pauline inferences based on the content of the oracle itself. This indicates that Paul derived the oracle from some unknown Christian prophet. (3) It may not have escaped the reader that 1 Cor. 15:51-52 and 1 Thess. 4:15ff. are very similar in content. Although the conceptions in both passages do not exclude each other, neither do they betray any contact. If 1 Cor. 15:51-52 is a Pauline oracle, as we have assumed, then there is every likelihood that 1 Thess. 4:16-17a is not.[59]

We may hazard the suggestion that this unknown Christian prophet was that Silas/Silvanus who was at least a coauthor of 1 Thessalonians with Paul and Timothy (1 Thess. 1:1), a man of prophetic gifts (Acts 15:22, 32). Silas functioned as an amanuensis (1 Pet. 5:12) and may well have written 2 Thessalonians (2 Thess. 1:1; cf. 3:17). In reconstructing the setting of the oracle we must remember that Paul was joined by Timothy and Silas in Corinth (Acts 18:5; 1 Thess. 3:6), and that it is not unlikely that the problems experienced by the Thessalonians were not only rehearsed to Paul privately, but also before the Corinthian congregation. Within such a setting Silas or another prophet may well have brought a revelatory word which Paul then conveyed to the Thessalonian congregation.

E. 1 COR. 12:3

This verse is usually cited[60] as an example of one of the earliest Christian confessions:

> Therefore I want you to understand that no one speaking by the Spirit of God ever says "Jesus be cursed!" and no one can say "Jesus is Lord!" except by the Holy Spirit.

It is frequently assumed that both of these utterances were formulaic in nature and were familiar to the Christians at Corinth.[61] Although the possibility of a ritual cursing of Jesus in the Corinthian services of worship might appear farfetched, Origen knew of gnostics who let no one into their assembly who did not curse Jesus.[62] Projecting that phenomenon back into the NT period, some scholars have claimed that Corinthian gnostics were those who claimed to speak in the Spirit when they exclaimed "Jesus is accursed!"[63] A careful examination of the context shows that when Paul referred to the pagan background of the Corinthian Christians in 1 Cor. 12:2, he was in all probability referring to pagan religious experiences of possession trance:[64]

> You know that when you were heathen, you would be seized by some power which drove you to those dumb heathen gods.[65]

Therefore the exclamation "Jesus be cursed!" was not uttered within the Corinthian community, but is a hypothetical Pauline construct created as an antithesis to the distinctively Christian exclamation "Jesus is Lord!" It is this positive exclamation which Paul views as inspired by the Spirit, and so by definition it must be included within our survey of oracular speech embedded in the Pauline corpus.

If we regard the acclamation "Jesus is Lord!" as a prophetic utterance (as it appears we must, since Paul clearly claims that it is an utterance inspired by the Holy Spirit), the *form* of the oracle requires some comment. The form is that of a *recognition oracle*, a common type of oracular utterance in the Greco-Roman world whose object was to provide supernatural identification for some individual of singular importance; it is a type of a broader category of oracular utterances which we have designated legitimation oracles.[66] In the Greco-Roman world recognition oracles were nearly always uttered without solicitation. The recognition oracle, however, is not a type of revelatory speech confined to the Greco-Roman world, but is actually found throughout the ancient world; Israelite-Jewish prophetic tradition knows many examples of recognition oracles.[67] This type of oracle occurs with relatively great frequency in the canonical gospels and Acts, as we shall see shortly.[68] The cultic setting for the acclamation "Jesus is Lord!" suggests that Christian services of worship were at least one of the settings for those stories about Jesus in the synoptic gospels that focus on a recognition oracle.

F. THE PROBLEM OF 1 COR. 14:37-38

Near the end of Paul's lengthy discussion of spiritual gifts in 1 Cor. 12-14, he states (1 Cor. 14:37-38):

> If anyone thinks that he is a prophet, or spiritual [*pneumatikos*], he should acknowledge that what I am writing to you is a command of the Lord [*Kyriou estin entolē*]. If anyone does not recognize this [*agnoei*], he is not recognized [*agnoeitai*].

The first two lines present a host of exegetical and interpretative questions. It would appear that Paul is claiming that the foregoing injunctions have the status of prophetic speech.[69] The problem, however, is that of determining the section of instruction to which Paul refers: the whole of 1 Cor. 12-14? the larger immediate context consisting of 1 Cor. 14:26-36? the smaller immediate context consisting of 1 Cor. 14:33b-36? The problem is compounded by the apparent conflict between 1 Cor. 14:33b-36 and 1 Cor.

11:5, where Paul refers to the possibility of a woman praying and prophesying, and 1 Cor. 14:34, where women are enjoined to keep silence in the church.[70] The problem presented by 1 Cor. 14:37 cannot easily be solved. It would seem that the plural relative pronoun (*ha*), which should be translated "*the matters* about which I am writing to you are a command of the Lord," must refer to more than just the one injunction regarding the silence of women in the church in vv. 33b-36. It is our view that 1 Cor. 14:37 refers to the advice and suggestions which Paul has presented throughout 1 Cor. 14.[71]

1 Cor. 14:38, closely linked with v. 37, is frequently designated a prophetic saying.[72] The form of the saying is that of a pronouncement of sacral law (*Satz heiligen Rechts*). In our earlier discussion of this form of speech, particularly as it relates to sayings of Jesus, we concluded that while there was widespread evidence for the use of this speech form in oracular or prophetic contexts, the form was used in no *exclusively oracular forms of speech*.[73] Therefore the presence of this form does not necessarily betray the presence of oracular speech. In this context, however, Paul's reference to his own prophetic injunctions in v. 37 is a weighty argument for regarding v. 38 as a statement made in a calculatingly oracular style.

G. GAL. 5:21b

This saying has occasionally been regarded[74] as a prophetic utterance:

I predict [*prolegō*] for you now, just as I predicted [*proeipon*] formerly, that
"Those who do such things
shall not inherit the kingdom of God." (author's trans.)

In this context, the translation "predict" or "foretell" is an appropriate translation for the underlying Greek verbs.[75] On this basis, then, we consider the saying so introduced as oracular. Of particular interest is that Paul claims to have uttered the prophecy while he was with them. That is, he delivered it to them orally the first time, and now repeats it in a letter which is certainly intended to be read aloud at public worship.[76] In form the oracle is of a single line consisting of a protasis and an apodosis. The protasis contains a generic substantival participle which provides the condition (i.e. "those who do such things"), while the apodosis contains the future punishment for such present behavior. The oracle is wholly focused on the threat of eschatological judgment as a sanction for prohibiting certain types of present behavior. The oracle must be seen as having a primarily parenetic purpose; the judgment which is predicted is not absolute but is dependent on the quality of behavior presently followed. The basic structure of this oracle, then, involves the pairing of present behavior with future reward or punishment; this twofold structure characterizes a great variety of early Christian prophetic speech forms.[77]

The present form of the oracle in Gal. 5:21b does not appear to be original, since the pronoun "such things" (*ta toiauta*) in the present context refers to the items in the vice list which Paul has inserted in Gal. 5:19-21a. The reconstructed form of the oracle would look like this:

I predict that:
Those who practice vice x
shall not inherit the kingdom of God.

H. 1 THESS. 3:4

As in Gal. 5:21, here also Paul introduces a prophetic utterance into a letter, an utterance which was originally delivered orally to the Thessalonians.[78] He now has occasion to repeat the prediction in the light of its fulfilment:

> For when we were with you we predicted [*proelegomen*]:
> "We are about to suffer persecution [*mellomen thlibesthai*],"
> just as it has come to pass, and as you know. (author's trans.)

There are a number of analogous examples in Acts where such predictions of persecution are made regarding Paul, apparently by various Christian prophets (Acts 20:23; 21:4, 10-11). In 1 Thess. 3:4 the particle "that" (*hoti*) introduces direct discourse, yet we cannot on that basis be sure that we have before us the original form of the oracle. Possibly the persecution referred to was not regarded as simply an isolated, random occurrence, but as part of the great time of tribulation which would precede the end of the age. The original oracle is quoted here only in part, making reconstruction impossible.

I. 1 THESS. 4:2-6

In 1 Thess. 4:2, 6b we find statements made by Paul that suggest the presence of an oracle or oracles in vv. 3-6a. In v. 2 we read: "For you know what instructions [*parangelias*] we gave you through the Lord Jesus [*dia tou Kyriou Iēsou*]." Again, in v. 6b we read:

> (The will of God is) that no man transgress, and wrong his brother in this matter, because the Lord is an avenger in all these things, as we predicted [*proeipamen*] and testified [*diemartyrametha*] to you. (author's trans.)

Here parenesis is placed within a prophetic setting in which the primary sanction is that of the impending eschatological judgment. We have already suggested that the verb which we have translated "predict" apparently indicates the presence of oracular speech in Gal. 5:21 and 1 Thess. 3:4. The content of the oracle in 1 Thess. 4:2-6 is similar to that in Gal. 5:21 in that the present action of man is matched with a reciprocal action of God within an eschatological context. Again Paul is repeating in an epistolary context an oracle (or series of oracles) which he delivered orally to the Thessalonian Christians while he was with them. The text of 1 Thess. 4:2-6 is as follows:

> For you know what instructions we gave you through the Lord Jesus. For this is the will of God, your sanctification: that you abstain from unchastity; that each one of you know how to take a wife for himself in holiness and honor, not in the passion of lust like the heathen who do not know God; that no man transgress, and wrong his brother in this matter, because [*dioti*] the Lord is an avenger in all these things, as we solemnly forewarned you.

The solemnity with which the oracle was delivered is indicated by the two verbs "predict" (*proeipon*) and "declare" (*diamartyromai*), both of which are used of the predictions of Paul's future sufferings in Acts 20:23: "the Holy Spirit testifies [*diamartyretai*] to me in every city, [saying (*legon*)] that imprisonment and afflictions [*thlipseis*] await me." The term "testify" or "witness" (*martyromai, diamartyromai*) is used here as an introductory prophetic oath formula.[79] While oaths are not used by OT prophets to introduce prophetic sayings or speeches, they are used in that way in Jewish apocalyptic and in the Greco-Roman world.[80] We also have in this passage the very interesting reference to instructions which Paul and others (he uses the plural) gave the Thessalonians "through the Lord Jesus" (1 Thess. 4:2).[81] Paul's use of this phrase as a functional equivalent to the OT prophetic messenger formula occurs only here (where the oracular character of the instructions is confirmed by v. 6) and in 2 Thess. 3:6 (see below). In both passages Paul expressly repeats in this epistolary context prophetic parenesis which earlier he had personally delivered to the Thessalonians in oral form.

Although the original form of the oracle which Paul quotes in 1 Thess. 4:2-6 cannot be reconstructed with absolute certainty, certain modifications seem required. The introductory statement in 1 Thess. 4:2 ("For you know what instructions we gave you through the Lord Jesus") appears to be preserved in a form approximating an original oral delivery in 2 Thess. 3:6: "Now we command [parangelomen] you, brethren, in the name of our Lord Jesus Christ." Here the demands of epistolary style have required the use of the first-person plural in place of an original first-person singular. The original introductory formula, therefore, together with the oracular saying itself, probably was phrased much like this:

> I command you in the name of the Lord Jesus:
> This is the will of God,
> > that you abstain from unchastity,
> > that each one of you know how to take a wife for
> > > himself in holiness and honor, not in the
> > > passion of lust like heathen who do not know God,
> > that no man transgress, and wrong his brother in
> > > this matter,
> because [dioti] the Lord is an avenger in all these things.

Structurally the oracle consists of two parts; the first part contains a parenetic oracle consisting of three parallel elements, each dealing with proper sexual behavior on the part of men. The reason for proper behavior in this area of life is that God is the judge of all immoral behavior. The sanction is eschatological in character.

J. 2 THESS. 3:6, 10, 12

A small collection of three prophetic utterances appears to lie behind the series of exhortations found in 2 Thess. 3:6-13. Three oracular sayings are found in vv. 6, 10, and 12, which we quote seriatim:

> Now we command [parangelomen] you, brethren, in the name of our Lord Jesus Christ, that you keep away from any brother who is living in idleness and not in accord with the tradition that you received from us.

> For even when we were with you, we gave you this command [parangelomen]: If any one will not work, let him not eat.

> Now such persons we command and exhort [parangelomen kai parakaloumen] in the Lord Jesus Christ to do their work in quietness and to earn their own living.

Each of these exhortations is prefaced with a formula, the first and third of which appear to function as messenger formulas inasmuch as Paul claims that the commands or instructions were given to the Thessalonians "by" Jesus Christ. Further, each of these exhortations, though the syntactical structure is different, consists of two-part pronouncements. Here we find all the essential elements that occurred in 1 Thess. 4:2-6, with the exception that the eschatological sanction is missing. If these exhortations were originally prophetic utterances, an eschatological sanction was probably included.

K. PROPHETIC SAYINGS IN PAUL

In the preceding sections we have attempted to isolate and analyze possible examples of oracular utterances embedded within the Pauline letters. The results appear to have been moderately successful. With varying degrees of confidence, we suggest that the following passages contain oracular sayings: 2 Cor. 12:9; 1 Cor. 15:51-52; Rom. 11:25-26; 1 Thess. 4:16-17a; 1 Cor. 12:3; 1 Cor. 14:37-38; Gal. 5:21; 1 Thess. 3:4; 1 Thess. 4:2-6; 2 Thess. 3:6, 10, 12. Sayings which some might regard as oracular but which have no formal identifying features have been excluded from consideration. Many other oracles may be buried within Pauline letters, but the absence of any sure marks of identification makes their recognition dubious.

In a very interesting study of the judgment form in the letters of Paul, C. Roetzel has attempted to analyze a number of passages using the OT prophetic judgment speech as a model.[82] According to Roetzel the OT form has four parts: the summons to hear, the accusation, the introduction to the pronouncement of the sentence by the formulaic term "therefore," frequently accompanied by the messenger formula, and the pronouncement of judgment.[83] Roetzel has found this judgment form in the following passages, some fairly short and others very extensive: Rom. 1:18-32; 1 Cor. 3:16-17; 5:1-13; 10:1-14; 11:17-34; Gal. 1:6-9; 5:18-26; 6:7-10; 1 Thess. 4:3-8; 2 Thess. 1:5-12; 2:1-8; 2:9-15; 4:3-8. In contrast to the OT prophetic models, however, Roetzel rightly recognizes a strong hortatory or parenetic element in the Pauline form. Admitting that the categories in Paul's judgment structure are relatively fluid, Roetzel concludes that it cannot be determined with any certainty whether Paul was imitating the prophetic OT form consciously or unconsciously. Only in 1 Thess. 4:3-8 does Roetzel's analysis agree with our own attempt to isolate prophetic speech forms in Paul, though on other grounds. Roetzel's analysis has several weaknesses: (1) The OT prophetic judgment form which he describes is more stable in description than in reality. (2) The texts cited as Pauline examples of a judgment form do not clearly share the fourfold structure of the OT model. (3) The Pauline texts cited do not exhibit characteristics that might be identified with early Christian prophetic speech on grounds other than those suggested by Roetzel. (4) In a religious setting in which human behavior is expected to be matched by a divine response in terms of reward or punishment, such as early Christianity, it is unnecessary to suppose that Paul consciously was adopting an ancient model, especially a model which lacked the hortatory element so favored by Paul.

A more thorough attempt to isolate prophetic speech forms in the Pauline letters has been attempted in an ambitious study by U. B. Müller, *Prophetie und Predigt*. A major section of this study deals with prophetic proclamations of admonition, judgment, and salvation in the form of a speech by the prophet himself. Dealing first with Pauline formulas which may introduce prophetic speech, Müller contends that the stereotyped form of parenetic introduction in which Paul favors the verb *parakaleō* (cf. Rom. 16:17), together with a prepositional phrase such as "in the Lord Jesus"

(1 Thess. 4:1) or "through our Lord Jesus Christ" (Rom. 15:30; 1 Cor. 1:10), has the force and function of a messenger formula.[84] To account for the absence of ordinary messenger formulas in Paul the author argues that such formulas would have been subject to Hellenistic interpretation, and Paul did not want his role to be misunderstood.[85] He then argues that Pauline phrases such as "this I say" (1 Cor. 7:29; 15:50) and "I say to you" (Gal. 5:2, 16) are Pauline equivalents to the *parakaleō* formulas and that they too function as introductory legitimation formulas in Paul's prophetic speech.[86] Müller then proceeds to vitiate his own arguments by admitting that Paul's prophetic legitimation formulas do not normally introduce a prophetic pericope, since the entire letter or section in which such prophetic speeches occur has already been legitimated![87] Recognizing that this admission raises a new methodological problem, Müller contends that the interpreter must then rely on the *function* and *content* of a saying or speech in order to recognize it as prophetic.[88]

Müller then proceeds to analyze the content of various "prophetic" sections of Paul's letters, and groups them into three classifications: (1) the proclamation of the imminence of the eschaton as part of the prophetic speech of admonition (Rom. 13:11-14; 1 Thess. 5:1-11; 1 Cor. 7:29-31),[89] (2) prophetic judgment speeches (1 Cor. 5:3-5; Rom. 16:17-20; Phil. 3:17-4:1; Gal. 1:6-9),[90] and (3) prophetic proclamations of salvation for the purpose of consolation (1 Thess. 4:13; 4:15ff.; 1 Cor. 15:51-52; Rom. 11:25-26).[91] Müller does not refer to the studies of Roetzel, yet it is interesting that both have isolated only two passages as judgment speeches: Gal. 1:6-9 and 1 Cor. 5:3-5 (Müller) or 1 Cor. 5:1-13 (Roetzel).

To different degrees both Roetzel and Müller share a common methodological problem: both insist on using OT types of prophetic speech as models for determining whether oracular speech is present in the Pauline letters. Roetzel is far less insistent than Müller, however, and is unsure whether Paul followed OT prophetic speech models consciously or unconsciously. Müller's strength lies in his consideration of prophetic speech forms as a living and developing tradition through postbiblical Jewish literature, particularly the early Jewish apocalypses. However, the assumption that traditional forms of prophetic speech were alive and well in Jewish apocalyptic literature is a supposition which will require a great deal of research to substantiate.[92] The greatest difficulty with Müller's study, and one which he should have faced head-on given the title of the book, is the problem of distinguishing between prophecy and parenesis in early Christian literature.[93] An assumption which Roetzel, Müller, and many others appear to share is that prophetic speech in early Christianity had a distinctive form and content and that, even apart from the absence of formal indicators of oracular speech, it can be recognized when inserted into various kinds of literary contexts. While it is possible that prophetic speech forms have been shorn of their formal features of identity and integrated into new contexts (1 Thess. 5:16-22 is perhaps a good example), a more methodologically conservative approach to the identification of Christian oracles needs full exploration.

III. THE ACTS OF THE APOSTLES

The book of Acts is filled with references to various types of supernatural revelatory phenomena and manifestations of the activity of the Spirit of God. Each important stage in the growth and development of early Christianity is accompanied by divine guidance mediated through dreams, visions, and prophetic interventions. In fact Acts is one of the few early Christian literary sources that explicitly quotes the oracles of Christian prophets. In the following sections each occurrence of prophetic speech will be isolated and analyzed.

A. ACTS 21:11

One of the most discussed prophetic speeches in the NT is that referred to in Acts 21:10-11, a passage of extraordinary interest:

> While we were staying [at Caesarea] for some days, a prophet named Agabus came down from Judea. And coming to us he took Paul's girdle and bound his own feet and hands, and said, "Thus says the Holy Spirit [*tade legei to pneuma*], 'So shall the Jews at Jerusalem bind the man who owns this girdle and deliver him into the hands of the Gentiles.' "

This passage contains a number of unique features important for the study of early Christian prophecy: (1) In a manner reminiscent of the activities of the prophets of the OT, the prophet who suddenly appears here is specifically identified. (2) The oracle is delivered with a formality rarely preserved in early Christian literature, complete with a messenger formula which is a slight Christian variant of the OT expression "thus says Yahweh." (3) The prophet performs a symbolic action which he then interprets through a relevatory speech. Each of these features deserves further discussion.

Agabus the prophet is known only from this passage and Acts 11:28; in both instances he delivers an oracle (see below on Acts 11:28). Since he is described in Acts 21:10 as coming from Judea to Caesarea, and in Acts 11:28 as coming from Jerusalem to Antioch, we may conclude that Jerusalem was the central theater of his activity, though he also traveled on specific missions to deliver oracles on particular occasions. The models for Agabus' prophetic action and speech are derived from the OT. Possibly the author of Luke-Acts has intentionally drawn Agabus in this way, just as he has the figures of John the Baptist and Jesus.[94] Yet if Agabus is presented in a historically accurate manner, the extent to which other early Christian prophets were like him is unknown.[95] Symbolic actions performed by Christian prophets are very rare.[96] Agabus appears to have been allowed an unusual degree of freedom in his activity; that is implied by his unusual action of taking Paul's girdle, or belt, and binding himself with it.[97] After binding himself Agabus correlates his action with the impending fate of Paul by using the adverb *houtōs*, "thus," "in this manner," a linguistic feature which also characterized the symbolic prophetic actions in the OT.[98]

The oracle itself is introduced through the use of a Christianized variant of the OT messenger formula; "thus says the Holy Spirit" is certainly a very close approximation of the familiar "thus says Yahweh," and would have had an archaic ring to it.[99] While such close connections with OT prophetic style might lead to the suspicion that Luke has consciously stylized the prophecy of Agabus in accordance with OT models, it is probable that Luke derived the story of Agabus from oral tradition.[100] While the OT prophetic messenger formula "thus says Yahweh" is not completely absent from early Jewish literature (cf. Test. Job 4:3; 7:8),[101] it is never used as a formal introduction to the oracular speech of early Christian prophets. However, the introductory formula in Acts 21:11 has numerous parallels in the introductory and concluding formulas of Christian oracular speech; e.g. Rev. 2:7: "He who has an ear, let him hear what the Spirit says to the churches"; Rev. 2:18b: "Thus says [*tade legei*] the Son of God."[102] Thus the reference to the Spirit in the introductory prophetic formula of Agabus is a fairly widely distributed feature of early Christian prophetic speech.[103]

In form the oracle has two parts, of which the second is a temporal sequence of the first; Paul will be handed over to the Gentiles *after* he has been bound by the Jews. Each part contains a verb in the future tense. Structurally, then, the oracle consists of a single element: a two-stage prediction of the future fate of Paul. Thus in form this oracle has little relationship to OT prophetic speech forms, which nearly always provide a *reason* (*Begründung*) for the threat in terms of an accusation. That form is clearly irrelevant here, where the fate of Paul cannot be construed as a divine threat. Yet since OT predictions of future misfortunes are always viewed as punishments for misbehavior, the distance between OT speech forms, in both form and content, and the oracle of Agabus appears even greater. The closest formal type of prophetic speech to the oracle of Agabus is the Greco-Roman revelatory speech form which we have labeled a *predictive oracle*.[104] This form consists of a single structural element, a prediction, which is cast either in the future tense or in the futuristic present tense. The form of Agabus' oracle suggests that Luke has *not* modeled it after OT prophetic speech forms, but has in fact derived it from Christian tradition.

The content of the oracle deserves some discussion. Agabus does not tell Paul to take a particular course of action, nor does he forbid him to journey to Jerusalem. His oracle is wholly predictive; it simply warns Paul of what will transpire if he follows a certain course of action: he will be arrested and turned over to the Romans. While the oracle in its present form is not syntactically conditional, it seems understood that the predicted fate could be avoided if Paul were to stay away from Jerusalem. At least that is how Luke undoubtedly understood the oracle, since Paul's companions in Acts 21:12-14 are depicted as actively attempting to dissuade Paul from proceeding on to Jerusalem. This kind of predictive oracle in which the prediction may be avoided if a certain course of action is taken is a characteristic feature of many Greco-Roman oracles,[105] and it is occasionally exhibited in later OT prophecy and early Jewish oracles which show Hellenistic influence.[106]

From the standpoint of literary function the oracle in Acts 21:11 must be seen as a dramatic climax to a number of prophetic predictions of Paul's impending fate in Jerusalem, predictions that were delivered to Paul personally by various prophets along the route of his journey (Acts 20:23; 21:4). We have already noticed that Paul himself claims to have made similar predictions (though perhaps of a more general nature) regarding the impending persecution and suffering he would experience (1 Thess. 3:4; see above, p. 259). In contrast to the more neutral phraseology of the oracle of Agabus, the disciples at Tyre reportedly told Paul "through the Spirit" (*dia tou pneumatos*): "Do not go to Jerusalem" (Acts 21:4).[107] While this oracle is only a sample and is undoubtedly condensed, Luke understands it as a prohibition delivered by the Spirit through a prophet to Paul. Yet, in the light of Paul's "disobedience" to the oracle, which is not regarded by Luke as a violation of the will of God (Acts 21:14), this may be an instance in which prophetic speech is "evaluated."[108]

B. ACTS 11:28

The only other oracle of Agabus recorded in Acts is found in Acts 11:28, quoted here with the preceding verse:

Now in those days prophets came down from Jerusalem to Antioch. And one of them named Agabus stood up [*anastas*] and foretold [*esēmainen*] by the Spirit that there would be a great famine over all the world; and this took place in the days of Claudius.

At first sight this oracle (which is only cited indirectly) appears to be a straightforward prediction of a future historical event, a worldwide famine. In a short editorial comment Luke informs the reader that this prediction was fulfilled during the reign of the Roman emperor Claudius (A.D. 41-54).[109] A famine did occur ca. A.D. 47/48 (papyri found in Egypt indicate the sudden rise in the price of grain),[110] a year which probably coincided with the Jewish sabbatical year.[111] A difficult problem to resolve is whether Agabus was referring to a historical famine, which might be succeeded by times of plenty followed perhaps by other famines, or to the coming of the period of eschatological tribulation, of which famine was thought to be an integral part.[112] While Agabus predicts a *worldwide* famine, the famine which occurred in A.D. 47/48 seems to have been limited to Palestine.[113] On that basis, then, it appears that Agabus emphasized the universality of the famine in the expectation that it would constitute a sign of the inauguration of the end of the age.[114] Luke has, in effect, removed the eschatological features of the prediction of Agabus.

Elsewhere in Acts the expression "by the Spirit" is connected with prophetic speech only in 21:4, 11. It is not unlikely that the tradition available to Luke contained a messenger formula similar to that in Acts 21:11. The precise form of the oracle, which seems to consist merely of a prediction of a future event, is not recoverable.

C. ACTS 13:2

At the beginning of Acts 13 a list of prophets and teachers at Antioch is given that includes five names: Barnabas, Simeon Niger, Lucius of Cyrene, Manaen, and Saul (i.e. Paul). While it has been argued on the basis of syntax that the first three are prophets and the last two teachers, the terms "prophet" and "teacher" are probably interchangeable here, [115] so that all five may be considered prophets in Luke's view.[116] In Acts 13:2 we read:

While they were worshiping the Lord and fasting, the Holy Spirit said, "Set apart for me Barnabas and Saul for the work to which I have called them."

Although Luke quotes the oracle with some care, he does not mention the means whereby the Holy Spirit spoke to those assembled; it was undoubtedly through one of the five prophet-teachers mentioned,[117] though probably not Barnabas or Saul. In a number of passages in the Pentateuch and the Former Prophets God is represented as speaking directly to particular individuals without reference to the precise mode of such revelatory speech; in many of these instances Josephus, as he retells the biblical history, casually introduces prophetic figures as divine spokesmen into these scenes.[118] To leave the prophetic spokesmen unmentioned in revelatory scenes in Acts, therefore, appears to be a literary technique of the author that is reminiscent of the OT. When the council of apostles and elders depicted in Acts 15 came to a conclusion, the participants communicated to Gentile converts by means of a letter in which the phrase "it seemed good to the Holy Spirit and to us" occurs (Acts 15:28). In view of the presence of a number of prophets at that meeting (Acts 15:32), it seems probable that the will of the Holy Spirit was expressed to the gathering through one or more of the prophets.[119] Similarly, in Acts 16:6 it is said that Paul, Silas, and Timothy were forbidden by the Holy Spirit to go to Asia, and in 16:7 it is reported that the Spirit of Jesus did not permit them to go to Bithynia. Again it is not unlikely that these revelatory prohibitions were communicated through prophetic utterances,[120] though visions or dreams are equally likely. All of these references, of course, play an important literary role in emphasizing the constant guidance of God in the expansion of early Christianity.

The setting within which the oracle of Acts 13:2 is uttered deserves some consideration. Here prophecy has a close relationship to Christian worship, as in Acts 11:28, though here the group consists entirely of prophets.[121] Mention is made not only of prayer but also of fasting (Acts 13:2a); while both practices can be used as preparatory techniques for the reception of divine revelation,[122] here both practices appear to function as a general feature of Christian worship.[123]

The oracular commission was followed by a ceremony in which the four prophets laid their hands on Barnabas and Saul before sending them on their way. The close relationship between prophetic utterance and a divine commission which is ratified by the Christian community is not unique to this passage. Close parallels are found in 1 Tim. 1:18 and 4:14:

> This charge I commit to you, Timothy, my son, in accordance with the prophetic utterances ([prophēteias] which pointed to you. . . .

> Do not neglect the gift you have, which was given you [ho edothē soi] by prophetic utterance [dia prophēteias] when the council of elders laid their hands upon you.

Both passages indicate that divine commissions for various tasks were the subject of oracular utterances within the context of Christian worship.[124] The term "prophecies" in 1 Tim. 1:18 may refer to oracles uttered on more than one occasion,[125] though more probably to several oracles pronounced on one auspicious occasion.[126] The notion of a divine commission mediated through prophetic spokesmen may also be reflected in Paul's speech to the Ephesian elders in Acts 20:17ff., when he exhorts them to "Take heed to yourselves and to all the flock, in which the Holy Spirit has made [etheto] you overseers" (v. 28).[127]

In form the oracle has a single structural element consisting of a command that Barnabas and Saul be appointed to the task to which they have already been called (proskeklēmai) by the Holy Spirit. The prescriptive oracle, which we investigated in connection with Greco-Roman oracular speech,[128] is the closest formally to the oracle in Acts 13:2; yet this oracle also has an obvious affinity to the recognition oracle,[129] which has both Greco-Roman and Israelite-Jewish parallels. Recognition oracles, however, do not ordinarily consist of commands.

D. ORACLES OF ASSURANCE

The book of Acts contains three dream or vision oracles (Acts 18:9-10; 23:11; 27:23-24) which closely conform to the OT and early Jewish oracle of assurance (Heilsorakel),[130] though this particular oracular form also has close Greco-Roman and Near Eastern parallels.[131] Paul is the recipient of each of these oracles, the first two of which are narrated by the author and the third is related by Paul himself in a speech to the crew and passengers on the ship traveling to Rome. The supernatural revealer in the first two oracles is the Lord (i.e. the exalted Jesus), while in the third it is the angel of God. Each oracle is given to Paul under circumstances of great stress, though none are explicit responses to a prayer of lament or distress (unlike 1 Cor. 12:8-9).

1. Acts 18:9-10.

Narrative Setting:	And the Lord said to Paul one night in a vision [*di' horamatos*]:
Admonition:	"Do not be afraid [*mē phobou*], but speak and do not be silent,
Reason:	for [*dioti*] I am with you, and no man shall attack you to harm you; for [*dioti*] I have many people in this city."

Shortly after Paul arrived at Corinth from Athens he began to preach the gospel to the local Jewish community but was violently opposed (Acts 18:1-6). He turned his attention to Gentiles and had instant success; this oracle in Acts 18:9-10, then, serves the literary function of accounting for Paul's long stay at Corinth. The two basic elements of the OT oracle of assurance (which exhibits great formal variety) are present, the salvific exhortation or admonition ("Do not be afraid") and the reason. In this oracle the reason has two separate components. The first is the reassurance that "I will be with you," a feature in many oracles of assurance in Deutero-Isaiah (41:10; 43:1-2, 5); the second is the divine task which Paul has yet to perform in Corinth, i.e. the gathering of a large number of converts to Christianity. The admonition "Do not be afraid" does not function here as a formula of consolation intended to allay the fear inspired by a divine epiphany,[132] but is directed toward the critical situation in which Paul found himself in Corinth.

2. Acts 23:11.

While the oracle reported in Acts 18:9 was communicated to Paul through a vision trance, the following oracle was probably mediated through a dream:

Narrative Setting:	The following night the Lord stood by him [*epistas autō*] and said,
Admonition:	"Take courage [*tharsei*];
Reason:	for [*gar*] as you have testified [*diemartyrō*] about me at Jerusalem, so you must bear witness [*martyrēsai*] also at Rome."[133]

Again the basic constituent elements of the oracle of assurance are present: the admonition (here *tharsei* is virtually synonymous with the more frequent *mē phobou*) followed by the reason. The reason links the past activity of Paul to his future activity, thus providing assurance that the present perilous circumstances in which he finds himself cannot thwart the divine will. The literary function of this oracle, which takes the revelation of Agabus in Acts 21:11 one step further, is to reveal to the reader that Paul's journey to Rome is fully in line with the will of God.

3. Acts 27:23-24.

Another dream oracle which exhibits the formal features of an oracle of assurance is reported in Acts 27:23-24, where it is narrated by Paul himself:

Narrative Setting:	For this very night there stood by me [*parestē gar moi*] an angel of the God to whom I belong and whom I worship. And he said,
Admonition:	"Do not be afraid [*mē phobou*],
Address:	Paul;
Reason:	you must stand before Caesar; and lo [*idou*], God has granted you all those who sail with you."[134]

In this oracle of assurance we have, in addition to the two basic elements of admonition and reason, a third (optional) element: the address. The address is frequently found in OT oracles of assurance, but only very rarely in the Greco-Roman oracles which have a basically similar structure.[135] In this oracle the reason is introduced without the use of an inferential or causal particle. The second part of the reason contains the demonstrative particle "lo," or "behold," which is frequently found in OT oracles of assurance.

4. Summary.

All three of these oracles of assurance are placed at critical junctures in the narrative of Acts, where they facilitate the movement of the plot and underscore that the growth and development of early Christianity was a divinely superintended phenomenon. The oracles are all spoken by supernatural beings within the framework of a revelatory dream or vision. This conforms to the development of the oracle of assurance in early Judaism generally, where it is used only in dream or vision settings and pronounced only by a supernatural being. Unlike other oracular forms in Acts these oracles of assurance so closely parallel the structure of OT models that the question of formal Hellenistic influence must be answered negatively.

E. ACTS 16:17

In contrast to all the oracles we have thus far discussed from the book of Acts, this oracle is said to be inspired, not by the Holy Spirit, but by a "spirit of divination" (*pneuma pythōna*), by which the author clearly means an unclean spirit or demon. This is not the only example of speech inspired by demons in Acts, and several more instances are found in the synoptic gospels. In Acts 16:16-18 Luke describes how Paul and his companions met a slave girl with mantic powers and her owners. In v. 17 we read:

> She followed Paul and us, crying [*ekrazen*], "These men are servants of the Most High God, who proclaim to you the way of salvation."

The same oracle, or similar ones, were repeated frequently by the slave girl, until Paul exorcised the spirit (v. 18). Although the oracle has no introductory formula revealing the supernatural origin of the girl's message, her bizarre behavior and her crying out loudly while delivering the oracle were sufficient indications of possession trance.[136] This oracle exhibits two structural elements. The first constitutes a recognition oracle, in that it provides supernatural identification for an individual (or in this case, a group of individuals) of singular importance.[137] The usual form of such oracles is a demonstrative pronoun linked with an appropriate predicate ("this is ..."), or an address to the individual directly in the seccond person ("you are . . ." or "you will . . ."). The second element in the oracle indicates that those recognized in the first line are trustworthy sources of divine revelation; the form and content of this type of oracle we have earlier designated as a commendation oracle.[138] The oracle, then, combines the forms and functions of both the recognition oracle and the commendation oracle, thereby suggesting a Hellenistic provenance for the form (which one could expect). The function of this oracle in Acts is much the same as the speeches of the demoniacs in the synoptic gospels: to demonstrate that even the forces of evil recognize the emissaries of God.

Just as the "healing oracle" of 2 Cor. 12:9 functions rather to account for the fact that Paul will *not* experience divine healing, so we find in Acts a parody of the recognition oracle, which we shall designate as a persona non grata oracle. In Acts 19:13-17 the story is told of seven itinerant Jewish exorcists, all sons of a Jewish high priest named Sceva. When they attempted to exorcise victims of demonic possession with the formula "I adjure you by the Jesus whom Paul preaches," the evil spirit responded:

> Jesus I know, and Paul I know; but who are you?

The basic form of this oracle is actually that of an adversative oracle, a very common oracular type in the Greco-Roman world.[139]

F. ACTS 13:9-11

Shortly after the prophetic commission of Barnabas and Saul (Acts 13:1-3), the two emissaries arrived in Cyprus where they were summoned to appear before the proconsul, Sergius Paulus. They were opposed, however, by a Jewish magician and false prophet named Bar-Jesus or Elymas. In Acts 13:9-11 Paul pronounces judgment upon Elymas:

Description of Inspired State:	But Saul, who is also called Paul, filled with the Holy Spirit, looked intently at him and said,
Accusation:	"You son of the devil, you enemy of all righteousness, full of all deceit and villainy, will you not stop making crooked the straight paths of the Lord?
Threat:	And now, behold [*idou*], the hand of the Lord is upon you, and you shall be blind and unable to see the sun for a time."

Elymas was immediately blinded, and the proconsul believed when he saw what had happened. The brief narrative is characterized by several distinctive features. The blinding of Elymas and the deaths of Ananias and Sapphira (Acts 5:1-11) are the only two punitive miracles recorded in Acts.[140] The form of the pronouncement is that of the announcement of judgment, one of most common forms of OT prophetic speech.[141] This oracle is introduced, however, not by a messenger formula (a characteristic introductory feature of the OT announcement of judgment), but by a description of the inspired state of the speaker. In the OT the announcement of judgment is always formulated as the direct speech of Yahweh that is transmitted and amplified by the prophetic messenger. In this prophetic speech by Paul, the message is his own, yet at the same time it is uttered with the authority of the inspiration of the Holy Spirit. Finally, the use of the messenger formula as an introduction to prophetic speech in the OT implies that the message had previously been communicated to the prophet and was only later transmitted to the intended recipient. In Acts 13:9-11 the act of revelation and the transmission of the revelatory message occur at the same instant. This emphasis on the articulation of oracular speech *while in a state of inspiration,* though rare in the OT (cf. Balaam in Num. 23-24), is more frequent in early Judaism (probably through Hellenistic influence) and pervades Greco-Roman paganism and early Christianity. These considerations suggest that Luke has not modeled Paul's prophetic speech in Acts 13:9-11 *directly* from OT speech forms.

G. ACTS 7:55-56

The book of Acts contains a large number of visions, some of which we have discussed above. The vision of Stephen, which occurs at the end of a lengthy speech uttered in condemnation of unresponsive Jews in Acts 7, has a completely unique feature:

Description of Inspired State:	But he [Stephen], full of the Holy Spirit, gazed into heaven and saw the glory of God, and Jesus standing at the right hand of God; and he said,
Vision Narration:	"Behold [*idou*], I see [*theōrō*] the heavens opened, and the Son of man standing at the right hand of God."

This vision narrative is distinctive because the content of the vision is described by the recipient *while the vision is being experienced* (a feature evident from the present tense of the verb *theōrō*). The closest parallels to this form of revelatory vision are found in the writings of Philo and Pseudo-Philo's *Liber Antiquitatum Biblicarum.*[142] On the basis of these parallels and the close association of the Son of man with the judgment motif, the vision of Stephen appears to function as a visionary announcement of judgment, a literary pattern of prophetic speech which we have analyzed earlier.[143] The content of Stephen's vision contains a very unusual feature, the depiction of the Son of man *standing* at the right hand of God, rather than *seated* or *coming* or a combination of the two motifs. In view of Luke's modification of Mark 14:62 (where the Son of man is depicted as seated and coming) in Luke 22:69 (where the reference to "coming" is deleted), it seems likely that he has also modified the tradition of Stephen's vision in a similar manner.

IV. RECOGNITION ORACLES IN THE GOSPELS

The gospels contain a great deal of oracular material in addition to the prophetic speeches by John the Baptist and Jesus which we have already discussed at some length. Apart from the dream oracles of Matthew (1:20-23; 2:13-14, 19-20), all attributed to the angel of the Lord, and the visions of Luke (1:8-22, 26-38; 2:9-14), also attributed to the angel of the Lord or Gabriel, a number of pronouncements are attributed to God, angels, demons, and even divinely inspired men. The majority of these revelatory pronouncements, as we shall see below, exhibit the form of the recognition oracle. Recognition oracles are those forms of revelatory speech in which the identity and significance of an individual of exceptional importance (typically a ruler or king) are revealed. Since one of the central preoccupations of the gospels is the demonstration of the messianic, even the divine, status of Jesus, it is hardly surprising that the literary use of the recognition oracle form is prominently featured in the gospels. The wide use of the recognition oracle in both Israelite-Jewish and Greco-Roman religious traditions suggests that it was a form which had universal meaning in the ancient world.

The OT occasionally depicts prophets as playing an important role in the sacral legitimation of kings.[144] Perhaps the most famous OT recognition oracle (the heavenly voice at Jesus' baptism alludes to it) is Ps. 2:7, which reflects an oracular speech by a cult prophet upon the occasion of the coronation of an Israelite king:

> I will tell of the decree of the Lord: he said to me,
> "You are my son, today I have begotten you."

Such recognition oracles occur elsewhere in the OT as well (cf. 2 Sam. 7:14; Ps. 89:27-28 [Eng. 26-27]). In 1 Sam. 9:17 Samuel reportedly received the following revelatory message when he saw Saul for the first time:

> Here is the man of whom I spoke to you!
> He it is who shall rule over my people.

In Neh. 6:7 Sanballat writes a letter accusing Nehemiah:

> And you have also set up prophets to proclaim concerning you in Jerusalem,
> "There is a king in Judah."

In our earlier discussion of prophecy in early Judaism, we saw that both Josephus and Rabbi Yohanan ben Zakkai addressed recognition oracles to the Roman general Vespasian, who was soon after to become emperor.[145]

The following discussion will first consider recognition oracles attributed to God, then those attributed to demons, and finally those attributed to inspired men.

A. ATTRIBUTED TO GOD

The phenomenon of divine voices, uttered apart from the agency of a human messenger, was a relatively common occurrence in Israelite-Jewish tradition and in Roman tradition; in Greek literature, on the other hand, the phenomenon occurs with far less frequency.[146] In the gospels are a number of instances in which a voice is heard from heaven, obviously the voice of God, and on almost every occasion the form and content of such divine pronouncements is that of the recognition oracle.

Each of the synoptic gospels records a heavenly voice making a pronouncement regarding the status of Jesus; in the Fourth Gospel the voice is not mentioned, but a functionally analogous pronouncement is made by John the Baptist. In Mark 1:11, which Luke reproduces exactly (Luke 3:22), the heavenly voice reportedly announces:

> Thou art my beloved Son;
> with thee I am well pleased.

Grammatically this announcement is addressed to Jesus himself, while in the Matthean parallel it is apparently addressed to onlookers (Matt. 3:17):

> This is my beloved Son,
> with whom I am well pleased.

The more common forms of the recognition oracle, the "you are . . ." and the "this is . . ." forms, are both represented in the synoptic parallels. The oracle itself consists of two structural elements, the primary recognition statement followed by a brief exposition of that statement. With regard to structure this is an expository oracle,[147] while with regard to content it is a recognition oracle. The first part of the oracle alludes to Ps. 2:7, while the second part refers to Isa. 42:1. Thus, like the *bat qol* (i.e. "daughter [or echo] of a voice"), which was thought to express its utterances in phrases drawn from scripture, the heavenly voice at Jesus' baptism makes clear allusions to the OT.

The synoptic gospels also record a second heavenly voice, again obviously the voice of God, at the transfiguration of Jesus. Here, however, each of the evangelists records a slightly different version of the pronouncement. The following quotations, in order, are from Mark 9:7; Matt. 17:5; Luke 9:35:

> This is my beloved Son;
> listen to him.

> This is my beloved Son, with whom I am well pleased;
> listen to him.

> This is my Son, my Chosen;
> listen to him!

The first line is again an allusion to Ps. 2:7, while the second line does not appear to contain any allusion at all to the OT. This oracle, unlike that at Jesus' baptism, is directed according to all the gospels to the onlookers who are present; in this case, Peter, James, and John. Like the oracle at Jesus' baptism, this one also has two structural elements. The first element is the designation of the true identity of Jesus, while the second is a command to hearken to him. With respect to form alone this is an expository oracle, while the content is mixed — the first line is a recognition oracle, while the second line constitutes the whole as a commendation oracle. In form and function, then, the oracle is thoroughly Hellenistic. In the Fourth Gospel the only occurrence of a voice from heaven is in 12:28. In response to the prayer of Jesus, "Father, glorify thy name," a voice thundered from heaven: "I have glorified it, and I will glorify it again." Since this oracular response conforms to no known type of oracle, either Israelite-Jewish or Greco-Roman, it is safe to conclude that it can be attributed to the literary artifice of the evangelist.

B. ATTRIBUTED TO DEMONS

Jesus' ministry of healing and exorcism brought him into conflict with the evil spirits who controlled demoniacs. There are three places in the synoptic gospels where the demons who possess men are reported to have addressed Jesus: Mark 1:24 (Luke 4:34); 3:11 (Luke 4:41); 5:7 (Matt. 8:29; Luke 8:28). Mark 1:24 and Luke 4:34 are identical:

> What have you to do with us, Jesus of Nazareth?
> Have you come to destroy us?
> I know who you are, the Holy One of God.

Similarly, in the editorial summary in Mark 3:11 the generic statement attributed to the demons is reproduced in Luke 4:41:

And whenever the unclean spirits beheld him,
they fell down before him and cried out,
"You are [sy ei] the Son of God."

Since Mark 5:6-7 is reproduced differently in Matt. 8:29 and Luke 8:28, we quote each of those passages in succession:

And when he saw Jesus from afar, he ran and worshiped him;
and crying out with a loud voice, he said,
"What have you to do with me, Jesus, Son of the Most High God?
I adjure you [horkizō se] by God, do not torment me."

And behold, they cried out,
"What have you to do with us, O Son of God?
Have you come here to torment us before the time?"

When he saw Jesus, he cried out and fell down before him,
and said with a loud voice,
"What have you to do with me, Jesus, Son of the Most High God?
I beseech you [deomai sou], do not torment me."

Each of these five passages from the synoptic gospels contains statements attributed to demons possessing various individuals, and each statement serves the literary function of revealing the true identity of Jesus to the reader. It is not as obvious to the modern reader that the words of the demons have many parallels in ancient magical incantations, and that the demons are presented by Mark as attempting to protect themselves against Jesus by using magical formulas and techniques.[148] Since these pronouncements are all "oracular" in the general Greco-Roman sense of the term, one might expect them to take on the form, as well as the content, of the recognition oracle; however, this has really only occurred in the case of Mark 3:11 par. Luke 4:41.

C. ATTRIBUTED TO MEN

The confession of Peter is recorded in all the synoptic gospels (Mark 8:27-30; Matt. 16:13-20; Luke 9:18-21; cf. John 6:67-71). Peter's pronouncement differs from gospel to gospel, but in every instance exhibits the form and content of a recognition oracle: Mark 8:29: "You are [sy ei] the Christ"; Matt. 16:16: "You are the Christ, the Son of the living God"; and Luke 9:20: "And he said to them, 'But who do you say that I am?' And Peter answered, 'The Christ of God.' " Of course, apart from an indication that the speaker either is or claims to be divinely inspired, these are no more recognition oracles than the exclamation attributed to the Roman centurion at the foot of the cross (Mark 15:39; cf. Matt. 27:54; Luke 23:47): "Truly this man was the Son of God!" Yet in an addendum to the pericope of the confession of Peter in Matt. 16:17, a passage unique to Matthew, the oracular nature of the confession is emphasized:

And Jesus answered him, "Blessed are you, Simon Bar-Jona! For flesh and blood has not revealed [apekalypsen] this to you, but my Father who is in heaven."

Matthew, then, clearly regards the confession of Peter as a recognition oracle.

In our discussion of recognition oracles attributed to God, we noted that the Fourth Gospel has no reference to a heavenly voice which provides supernatural identification of Jesus; rather, that identification was provided by John the Baptist. In John 1 John the Baptist is presented as "a man sent from God" (1:6), i.e. a prophet. In John 1:29 we find a statement made by John the Baptist regarding Jesus that is a recognition oracle with regard to both form and content:

> Behold [ide], the Lamb of God,
> who takes away the sin of the world!

The first line of this pronouncement is repeated in John 1:36. The form of this oracle, if it may be regarded as such, is that of an expository oracle, i.e. the second part expands on the significance of the statement made in the first part. With regard to content, this two-part oracle functions as a recognition oracle. The recognition oracle was frequently used in both Israelite-Jewish and Greco-Roman tradition to designate kings and rulers. The use of this oracular form in the synoptic gospels to designate Jesus as the Son of God (reflecting the royal coronation hymn in Ps. 2) or Messiah is perfectly appropriate, since an ideal ruler was the object of Jewish messianic hopes. Although the identification of Jesus as the Lamb of God in John 1:29, 36 might at first sight seem unrelated to the normal function of a recognition oracle, the royal status of the lamb is emphasized in Rev. 5:5-14 (a document *somehow* related to the Fourth Gospel).

In a different vein, each of the synoptic gospels contains a warning against false prophets that is part of Jesus' eschatological discourse; the warning, which each evangelist varies relatively insignificantly, is derived from Mark 13:21-22 (cf. Matt. 24:23; Luke 17:23):

> And then if any one says to you, "Look [ide], here is the Christ!" or "Look [ide], there he is!" do not believe it. False Christs and false prophets will arise and show signs and wonders, to lead astray, if possible, the elect.

Although it does not say who it is that might attempt to identify the Messiah, it may well be one of the false prophets who are expected to arise; in that case their pronouncement, "Look, here is the Messiah!", might appropriately be regarded as a recognition oracle. Many interpreters have thought that the evangelist is referring to the kind of eschatological excitement which characterized Palestinian Judaism during the late Second Temple period.

V. THE APOCALYPSE OF JOHN

While modern scholars may debate whether the Apocalypse should be categorized as prophecy or apocalyptic, the author clearly intended his book to be taken as *prophecy*, a point which he makes both at the beginning and end of his composition (1:3; 22:7, 10, 18-19).[149] In form the Apocalypse is a blend of prophetic and apocalyptic elements.[150] Unlike other Jewish apocalypses and all Christian apocalypses with the exception of the Shepherd of Hermas, the author names himself, makes no mention of revelations received in dreams, and publicly reveals the substance of his revelations.[151]

One of the major questions that modern scholars have regarding the origin and composition of the Apocalypse concerns the extent to which actual experience underlies the stereotypical literary patterns and forms which characterize the book. The bulk of the Apocalypse consists of the narration of a series of visions strongly reminiscent of Jewish apocalyptic literature. While some have supposed that virtually everything designated as a vision in the Apocalypse was based on actual revelatory experience,[152] the visions appear to be a combination of prophetic experience and literary artifice; the task of untangling the two appears hopelessly difficult.[153]

G. R. Beasley-Murray has referred to the Apocalypse as a composition consisting essentially of a series of prophetlike oracles strung together.[154] It does appear that prophetic sayings and speech are sometimes found embedded in Jewish apocalypses,[155] and it is probable that the Apocalypse of John is no exception to this literary tendency. The task of the following discussion will be that of isolating and analyzing originally independent prophetic utterances which have been interwoven in the text. Earlier scholars have identified a number of passages in the Apocalypse as prophetic sayings,[156] but none to my knowledge has attempted to treat the subject systematically.

John intended the Apocalypse to be read aloud in a service of worship (1:3; 22:18), and it is very possible that this public reading would replace a prophetic address to the congregations by one or more of their local prophets.[157] The entire Apocalypse has an epistolary framework (1:4-6; 22:6-21),[158] though the seven proclamations of chaps. 2-3 probably never had a separate existence prior to their inclusion in the Apocalypse.[159] Rather, they appear to be written oracles that functioned as a surrogate for oral prophecies which the author was prevented from delivering in person.[160] The oral nature of the prophetic style exhibited by the seven proclamations is particularly evident in the central "I know" section of each letter.

A. THE PROPHETIC CHARACTER OF THE SEVEN PROCLAMATIONS

Several important studies have convincingly demonstrated that the seven proclamations of Rev. 2-3 not only contain fragments of prophetic speech (e.g. 3:20), but also represent a typical form of prophetic speech considered as a whole.[161] Interpreters are often content to point out the parallel structure which each of the seven proclamations exhibits: (1) introduction, (2) middle portion, (3) double conclusion, consisting of (a) the call for vigilance, and (b) a conquer saying. The major area of disagreement among interpreters, however, is the central section of the proclamations, which we have benignly labeled the "middle portion." We shall discuss each major structural section of the proclamations, and then turn to an investigation of particular items of interest within them. A detailed structural analysis of the proclamations is found in the following chart.[162]

1. The Commissioning Formula.

The commissioning formula, which provides an introductory narrative framework for many OT prophetic speeches,[163] provides a striking introduction to each of the seven proclamations. The messenger formula, which often represents the entire commissioning formula in the OT or is used in connection with it, is an integral feature of the commissioning formula which begins each of the seven proclamations. The basic pattern of the OT commissioning formula, together with the messenger formula, is: "Go and say to X, thus says Y." John, however, is not commanded to *go* to each of the seven churches (for that is apparently impossible; cf. 1:9), but to *write* to the churches. This command to write is certainly a functional equivalent to the sending of prophetic messengers in the OT.[164] Following the commission to write, the phrase "thus says" (*tade legei*) occurs, followed by one or more phrases or epithets which identify the speaker, who in every case is the risen and glorified Jesus.[165] The functional identity of the risen Jesus and the Spirit is made clear by the stereotypical refrain near the end of each letter (a refrain which has affinities with the OT prophetic proclamation formula): "He who has an ear, let him hear what the Spirit says to the churches."[166]

2. The Central "I Know" Section.

The central section of each letter, which we have designated the "I know" (*oida*) section, is the most varied portion of the letters with respect to both form and content. F. Hahn has suggested an analysis of this section in terms of six elements, though each does not occur in every letter. These six elements include: (1) a description of the situation of the community (found in every letter), (2) a section introduced by "I have (something) against you" (found in letters I, III, IV), (3) a demand for repentance (I, III, V, VII), (4) a "behold" clause (II, IV, VI, VII), (5) mention of the basic theme "I am coming quickly" (with variations, found in all but letter II), (6) a statement of what the church has and what it should hold to (all but II). Although this analysis has strengths, it also has a number of weaknesses. The "behold" clause, though found in four of the seven letters, is so varied in content that the formal repetition of the particle "behold" (*idou*) does not really qualify as a structural element. Two features which Hahn leaves out of consideration (he is too much occupied with formulaic expressions) are those of the threat of judgment and the promise of salvation, either of which may be tied to the "I am coming" formula found in all but one of the letters.

In contrast to Hahn, U. B. Müller disregards the stereotyped framework of each letter and focuses instead on the body, or central portion, of the letter. He finds two basic forms of prophetic speech in the seven letters, a parenetic sermon of repentance (*Bussparaklese* or *Busspredigt*) and a sermon or proclamation of salvation (*Heilspredigt*). The proclamation of salvation, according to Müller, is found in relatively pure form in Rev. 2:8-11 and 3:7-13, and mingled with the parenetic sermon of repentance in 3:1-6. Müller finds three constituent elements in the sermon of salvation, as exemplified in Rev. 2:8-11: (1) reference to the situation (v. 9), composed of (a) praise (v. 9a), and (b) depiction of need (v. 9b); (2) comfort in view of the coming tribulation (*Heilsorakel*, v. 10a); (3) admonition in the form of a conditional proclamation of salvation (v. 10b).[167]

The more characteristic prophetic form in the seven proclamations, according to Müller, is the parenetic sermon of repentance. The basic form of this type of prophetic address is found in Rev. 2:1-7, and also consists of three basic elements: (1) accusation (v. 4), (2) admonition (v. 5a), and (3) conditional threat of judgment (v. 5b).[168] With many variations, Müller finds this form in Rev. 2:12-17, 18-29; 3:1-6, 14-22.[169] He traces this form, which originated in the OT,[170] to John the Baptist (e.g. Matt. 3:7-10; Luke 3:7-9) and early Jewish apocalyptic (1 Enoch 91:3-10; Jub. 7:20-29; 36:3-11). According to Müller, therefore, these two prophetic speech forms are not merely literary imitations of OT models, but are drawn from a living, oral prophetic tradition within Judaism.[171]

There are a number of weaknesses in Müller's analysis of the central section of the proclamations, though his basic view of their prophetic character is quite correct. First, he assumes that early Christian prophetic speech forms *must be derived from antecedent Israelite-Jewish speech forms*. It is of course undeniable that there are very close links between Israelite-Jewish traditions and early Christianity, yet that does not mean that Greco-Roman traditions had no influence on the growth, development, and character of early Christianity. In our analysis of oracular speech forms in Paul, the book of Acts, and the gospels, we have already found evidence which indicates that some

Greco-Roman oracular speech forms were adapted by early Christian prophets and writers. Early Christian prophecy, it appears, borrowed from both Israelite-Jewish and Greco-Roman revelatory traditions, a process that was facilitated by the Hellenization of Judaism, both in Palestine and in the diaspora.[172] Second, when Müller posits two *basic* and *pure* types of prophetic speech in the Parenetic Sermon of Repentance and the Sermon of Salvation, which are nearly always found in *mixed* forms, he has unnecessarily placed a great gulf between the ideal and the real. An analytical approach which takes seriously the possibility of *optional elements* in a form-critical analysis seems far superior to the approach of Müller. F. Hahn has used this approach, though he has not labeled it as such, and the analysis of the basic pattern of the central section of the letters of Rev. 2-3 suggested below (and evident in the chart) also follows this method.[173] Third, Müller's attempt to trace early Christian prophetic forms back through John the Baptist and Jewish apocalyptic literature to the OT is beset with difficulties, though many of these are not ultimately insoluble. Most, if not all, examples cited by Müller are from *parenetic* sections of Jewish apocalypses. Even though these hortatory sections may have eschatological frameworks, they are not necessarily examples of prophetic speech in early Judaism.

The central section of each of the letters to the seven churches has a basically parenetic or hortatory function. Each Christian community addressed, or constituent groups within those communities, is encouraged to fully accept the norms and values of the Christian faith. Those who deserve praise for their obedience and faithfulness are assured salvation and blessing if they persevere. Those who have deviated in any way are condemned and required to change their ways. If they do not, judgment awaits; if they do, salvation and victory are the result. The prophetic speech form which the central section of the seven proclamations most resembles is the salvation-judgment oracle, a development of postexilic Israelite prophecy.[174] Yet there were apparently two groups within the postexilic Israelite community that were addressed as the "righteous" and the "wicked." The basic purpose of these early Christian salvation-judgment oracles is positive: the promise of salvation is used to encourage perseverance and commitment to the Christian faith, while the threat of judgment is used only to convince wayward Christians and Christian communities to change their behavior. Just as the announcement of salvation was a prophetic speech form in ancient Israel that was apparently more characteristic of the cult and court prophets than of the free prophets, so the salvation-judgment oracles of Rev. 2-3, which have a cultic setting in early Christianity, also have a basic salvific orientation. The constituent elements of these salvation-judgment oracles are the following: (1) praise (if appropriate), (2) censure (if appropriate; often both praise and censure are present), (3) demand for repentance, which is sanctioned by (4) the threat of judgment, and rewarded by (5) the promise of salvation. Since the seer is addressing specific communities, the elements of the salvation-judgment oracle may vary considerably from letter to letter. The basic pattern which we have suggested, however, finds expression in each letter. The *function* of these salvation-judgment oracles, however, is not distinctive to Christian prophecy but permeates the kind of religious and moral discourse exhibited in the surviving letters and homilies from early Christianity. The strongly negative tone of the kind of early Christian parenetic prophecy exhibited in the seven proclamations is occasioned by one important role of Christian prophets: to act as guardians and preservers of Christian behavior, beliefs, and customs. The necessity for prophetic intervention became acute only when deviations threatened Christian existence and no other authority structure was present or able to meet the crisis in a creative way. Thus the prophetic role is particularly important in the absence (or because of the ineffectiveness) of the leadership within local Christian communities.

3. The Call for Attention.

Each of the seven proclamations concludes with the stereotyped statement: "He who has an ear, let him hear what the Spirit says to the churches." Variations on the first phrase, such as "whoever has ears to hear, let him hear," occur seven times in the synoptic gospels as a secondary formulaic addition to parables and other sayings of Jesus (Mark 4:23; Matt. 11:15; 13:9 and par. Mark 4:9; Luke 8:8; Matt. 13:43; Luke 14:35).[175] The formula also occurs in Rev. 13:9, the only instance (out of fifteen occurrences in the NT) where it is not attributed to the earthly or risen Jesus. This short exhortation has been labeled a *Weckformel,* i.e. a formula which calls attention to the significance of what has been said.[176] Functionally this exhortation is similar to the proclamation formula (e.g. "Hear the word of Yahweh!") which often introduces prophetic oracles in the OT,[177] though there are similar examples from the Greco-Roman world. The *Weckformel* is found only in Rev. 2-3 and 13:9 within the context of Christian prophetic speech in early Christian literature.

4. The Exhortation to Conquer.

The exhortation to conquer, or to be victorious, is found in the closing portion of each letter, and begins in all but one instance with the stereotyped phrase "the one who conquers," followed by an eschatological promise (in 2:7 the phrase "to him who conquers" is the only variation). In the first three letters the exhortation to conquer is the last element in the letter and is immediately preceded by the call for attention. The reverse arrangement characterizes the last four letters; the exhortation to conquer immediately precedes the call for attention, which concludes the letters. No satisfying explanation has been given for this variation. The exhortation to conquer in many respects encapsulates the basic purpose of the salvation-judgment oracle, which is to encourage Christians to meet the challenges which face them in circumstances of religious and political oppression.

5. Elements of Interest in the Letters.

The oral character of the prophetic speeches in Rev. 2-3 is betrayed in part by the presence of an oracle within the letter to Thyatira (2:18-29). This earlier oracle to Jezebel (a code name for a prophetess active in Thyatira),[178] which is found in vv. 20b-23b, though it has been changed into a third-person narration for insertion into its present context, nevertheless contains six structural elements characteristic of John's prophetic rhetoric: (1) Censure (for encouraging God's servants to practice immorality and eat meat sacrificed to idols, v. 20b), (2) Demand for Repentance ("I gave her time to repent," but she has refused, v. 21a), (3) Threat of Judgment ("Behold, I will throw her on a sickbed, and those who commit adultery with her I will throw into great tribulation," v. 22ab), (4) Renewed Demand for Repentance ("unless they repent of her doings," v. 22c), (5) Renewed Threat of Judgment ("and I will strike her children dead," v. 23a), and (6) Conclusion ("And all the churches shall know that I am he who searches mind and heart," v. 23b). The conclusion is unavoidable that the seer has had previous contact with "Jezebel" and her followers and that he has delivered an earlier salvation-judgment oracle to them. The oracle is characterized throughout by the divine "I" style, which is apparently a characteristic of the prophetic speech of John. The final element in the oracle, "all the churches shall know that I am he," etc., is unique in the Apocalypse. It is the kind of conclusion which characterizes the self-disclosure oracles in the OT,[179] and that is apparently its source. Yet the phrase "he who searches mind and heart" appears to have particular reference to those prophets who, like John, are able through divine inspiration to search out and expose iniquity in all its various forms.

Another feature of particular interest in the seven proclamations concerns the literary form pronouncements of sacral law which many scholars, not entirely correctly, associate with early Christian prophecy.[180] Reward and punishment are matched with human behavior in accordance with the principle of *jus talionis*, or "law of retributive justice." In Rev. 3:5b, in the framework of the letter to Sardis, we read: "I will confess his name before my Father and before his angels," a statement which is strongly reminiscent of the confess/deny motifs found in the pronouncement of sacral law in Luke 12:8 (cf. Matt. 10:32-33; Mark 8:38; Luke 9:26):

And I tell you, every one who acknowledges me before men,
the Son of man also will acknowledge before the angels of God.[181]

The principle of retributive justice is also expressed in Rev. 2:23b, also within the prophetic setting of the letter to Thyatira: "I will give to each of you as your works deserve." Further, in Rev. 3:10, the basic form of the pronouncement of sacral law is retained, though apart from the structure of the conditional sentence: "Because you have kept [*etērēsas*] my word of patient endurance, I will keep [*tērēsō*] you from the hour of trial which is coming on the whole world." Actually, the conditional relative clause which focuses on reward or punishment by God in the future, based on the pursuit of a particular course of action in the present, is characteristic of all the exhortations to conquer located at the conclusion of each of the letters. All these observations confirm the notion that pronouncements of sacral law, though their form cannot be rigidly defined, could be a feature of prophetic rhetoric and indeed were ideally suited for use in such a setting. However, these pronouncements are found in such a wide variety of contexts (particularly wisdom and parenesis) that they cannot be exclusively regarded as a pattern of speech limited to prophetic utterance.

B. ADDITIONAL ORACLES IN THE APOCALYPSE

In addition to the seven proclamations a great many other prophetic oracles have been identified in the text of the Apocalypse, often on the basis of formal features thought to be characteristic of oracles. One such feature is the makarism or beatitude, of which seven examples are found in the Apocalypse (1:3; 14:13; 16:15; 19:9; 20:6; 22:7, 14). Interestingly enough, however, none of the seven beatitudes is found within the context of any of the seven proclamations.[182] The presence of a beatitude, it appears, is not an invariable indicator of the presence of oracular speech. The particle "behold" (*idou*) is often associated with prophetic speech, yet this Semitic style of speech again does not necessarily indicate the presence of prophetic speech. In the Apocalypse "behold" is always used to signal a special divine intervention; the speaker is either God (21:3, 5), Christ (1:18; 2:10, 22; 3:8, 9, 20; 16:15; 22:7, 12), an angel (5:5), or the prophet himself speaking in the Spirit (4:1, 2; 6:2, 5, 8; 7:9).[183] The single reliable feature whereby the oracles embedded in the Apocalypse may be confidently identified is the first-person singular speech of a divine revealer, whether the risen Jesus, an angel, or God.

1. Rev. 1:7-8.

In the first oracle in the Apocalypse,[184] the speaker in the last two lines is God himself:

> Behold, he is coming with the clouds, and every eye will see him, every one who pierced him; and all tribes of the earth will wail on account of him. Even so. Amen.
>
> "I am the Alpha and the Omega," says the Lord God,
> who is and who was and who is to come, the Almighty.

Here two originally separate oracles have been linked together, a phenomenon which occurs with relative frequency in the Apocalypse (cf. 13:9; 14:13; 16:15; 19:9; 21:5-8; 22:12-15; 22:18-20; see below, p. 327). The first oracle is introduced with the particle *idou*, and concluded with *amēn*, both used in Christian oracular speech (see below, pp. 327, 337).

Apart from Rev. 21:5-8 this is the only oracle in the Apocalypse in which God is the speaker, a fact which indicates the importance of these two oracles in the structure of the composition. One of the conventions of the oracular dialogue, i.e. a conversation between a mortal and a supernatural revealer, is that the identity of the revealer is often expressed at the beginning of the dialogue by an oracle of self-commendation using the "I am" formula.[185] This device legitimates the revelation which follows in the oracular dialogue, and in the Apocalypse it appears to function in much the same way. The "I am" formula is repeated in Rev. 1:17, just prior to the dictation of the seven proclamations. The oracular form in Rev. 1:8 is also reminiscent of the self-disclosure oracle (*Erweiswort*) found frequently in OT prophetic speeches, though nearly always as a concluding element.[186] The oracle has a simple chiastic construction, beginning with the divine names Alpha and Omega (probably related to the divine name "Jao" found many times in the magical papyri),[187] followed by the participial phrase "who is and who was and who is to come," and concluding with another divine name, "Almighty." The formula "who is and who was and who is to come" (*ho on kai ho ēn kai ho erchomenos*) is a syntactical anomaly[188] which has both Israelite-Jewish and Greco-Roman parallels.[189] It is also found in 1:4 and 4:8 (cf. 11:17; 16:5), and is a way of saying that the Lord is a God of prophecy, since it embodies a common Hellenistic formula used to describe prophecy (cf. 1:19: "what you see and what is and what is about to be hereafter").[190] The quotation formula, "says the Lord God," functions as a messenger formula; this particular form of the messenger formula is more characteristic of Ezekiel than of any other OT prophet (cf. Ezek. 6:3, 11; 7:2, etc.).

A very close parallel to Rev. 1:8, and one to which many commentators refer, is the oracle said to have originated with the Peleiae, or prophetic priestesses, of the oracle of Zeus at Dodona:

> Zeus was, Zeus is, Zeus shall be; O mighty Zeus.
> Earth sends up the harvest; therefore sing the praise of Earth as Mother.[191]

In this unsolicited oracular hymn each line consists of two parts. The first part makes a statement about a divinity, and the second is an expression of praise based on the preceding statement. Dione, in reality a feminine form of the name Zeus (genitive form: Dios) was closely associated with Zeus at Dodona, and the second line of the oracle is directed to her as Earth Mother. The emphasis on past, present, and future in the oracle, as in Rev. 1:8, is undoubtedly intended to characterize Zeus as a god of prophecy. In Rev. 1:8, then, a popular hymn to Zeus emphasizing his oracular capabilities has been transferred to the God of Israel and Christianity. Thus the oracle in Rev. 1:8, with regard to form, content, and literary placement, exhibits a confluence of Israelite-Jewish and Greco-Roman traditions.[192] Further, the messenger formula, usually associated almost exclusively with Israelite and ancient Near Eastern prophecy, is also used to introduce the oracles uttered in the name of Zeus at Dodona and Zeus-Ammon at the oracle of Ammon in Siwah, Libya.[193]

2. Rev. 1:17-20.

The larger commission narrative of 1:9-20 frames the oracle found in vv. 17-19:

Narrative:	When I saw him, I fell at his feet as though dead. But he laid his right hand upon me, saying,
Admonition:	"Fear not [mē phobou],
Reason:	I am the first and the last, and the living one; I died, and behold I am alive for evermore, and I have the keys of Death and Hades.
Commission:	Now write what you see, what is and what is to take place hereafter."

Fear is a common reaction to divine epiphanies in the OT as well as early Jewish and early Christian literature. The exhortation "fear not" here, while it resembles the formulaic introduction to oracles of assurance in the OT, functions very differently in this context. It is not spoken to allay the fears which motivated the recipient of the revelation to address a lament to God (as in the case of the OT oracles of assurance), but rather functions as a comfort formula meant to allay the reaction of fear at the experience of a divine epiphany. The exhortation is followed by the "I am" formula, which here (as in 1:8) functions to identify the supernatural revealer and thus to legitimate the revelations which follow. The one who utters this oracle of self-commendation is clearly the risen and exalted Jesus. John is then commissioned to write down the substance of his revelations and send them to the seven churches, a charge that has already been expressed in v. 11.

3. Rev. 13:9-10.

In Rev. 13 the seer relates two visions; the first is that of a beast rising from the sea (vv. 1-8), and the second that of a beast rising from the earth (vv. 11-18). The oracle in vv. 9-10 thus appears somewhat obtrusive in its present context:

If any one has an ear, let him hear:
"If any one is for captivity,[194]
   to captivity he goes;
if any one slays with the sword,
   with the sword must he be slain."
Here is a call for the endurance and faith of the saints!

This saying, which we take to be an originally independent oracle,[195] is framed by an introductory and concluding formula. The call for attention (*Weckruf*, or *Weckformel*) with which the oracle is introduced corresponds to similar formulas found at the conclusion of each of the seven proclamations (2:7a, 11a, 17a, 29; 3:6a, 13a, 22a; see above, p. 278). Since it is found in an introductory position before this oracle, it corresponds more closely to the proclamation formula which introduces many OT prophetic speeches, particularly judicial speeches.[196] The connection of the call for attention with Rev. 13:9-10 suggests the oracular nature of the saying. The concluding formula is found not only here but also in 14:12, with similar expressions in 13:18 and 17:9, though never in an oracular context. This conclusion is therefore to be considered an interjection of the seer.

While the text of the oracle itself has occasioned some difficulty, the translation given above probably conveys the original significance of the pronouncement. The oracle consists of two couplets, with the first and second line of each couplet in antithetical parallelism expressing the principle of retributive justice (*jus talionis*). Although the eschatological dimension of the punishment is lacking in the saying itself, it is conveyed by the context. The oracle was probably pronounced against the pagan oppressors of the church, yet it is couched not in the absolute style of OT announcements of judgment, but in the conditional style of the salvation-judgment oracles which are exhibited in Rev. 2-3 and found often in the Shepherd of Hermas (see below). It is possible that this oracle was originally uttered before pagans (cf. the situations envisaged by Matt. 10:20; Mark 13:11; Luke 12:12), but this appears highly unlikely.

4. Oracles in Rev. 14:1-12?

G. R. Beasley-Murray has identified four oracles reminiscent of OT prophetic speech in Rev. 14:1-12:[197] vv. 1-5, 6-7, 8, 9-12. The first five verses must be eliminated as oracular, however, for they consist entirely of narrative. The other three passages consist of proclamations made by three successive angels. The first proclaims an eternal gospel to all mankind (vv. 6-7); the second announces the fall of Babylon (v. 8); and the third reveals the consequences of worshiping the beast or its image (vv. 9-12). That the supernatural revealer is an angel is no real objection to the oracular nature of the pronouncements, since the relation between angels, the risen Jesus, and God himself is not always clear or even important.[198] Similarly, the loud voice with which two of the angels are said to make their announcements (vv. 7a, 9a) may indicate divine inspiration,[199] but more probably indicates the importance and solemnity of their speech.[200] The real question is whether these angelic proclamations are part of a vision or series of visions and in consequence a literary dramatization of the seer's visionary experiences, or a message which he is given to proclaim to the world (v. 6 is explicitly addressed to all mankind and this audience is presupposed for vv. 8, 9-11). The careful way in which these scenes are integrated into the plan of the Apocalypse militates against taking these three proclamations as oracular.

5. Rev. 14:13.

This passage has an entirely different character from the three pronouncements found in Rev. 14:6-11 and is probably an example of oracular speech:[201]

Revelation Formula: And I heard a voice from heaven saying,
"Write this:

Beatitude: Blessed are the dead
                who die in the Lord henceforth."

Oath Formula: "Yes," says the Spirit,

Supplement with "they shall rest from their labors,
Reason: for their works follow after them."

These two sayings, the first an oracular beatitude and the second a prophetic saying attributed to the Spirit, rest uncomfortably in their present context.[202] The interruption is signaled by a typical interjection of the author in v. 12: "Here is a call for the endurance of the saints, those who keep the commandments of God and the faith of Jesus," which is a comment on the importance of the sayings in the first part of Rev. 14. The oracular beatitude and the prophetic saying are closely related to each other, for the prophetic saying provides a brief exposition of the beatitude. The beatitude is dictated to the seer by an unidentified voice from heaven.[203] All such heavenly voices speaking in the Apocalypse have complete divine authority and approval and are ultimately to be identified with God himself.[204] The two oracles have an antiphonal relationship, for the "yes" (nai) functions here as an equivalent to "amen" (cf. Rev. 1:7b). Of the seven beatitudes in the Apocalypse only three (14:13; 19:9; 22:7) are absolute, i.e. unqualified by a phrase or sentence which expands on the meaning or implications of the pronouncement. In both Israelite-Jewish and Greco-Roman tradition beatitudes normally exhibit a two-part structure. When used in oracular contexts the form which such beatitudes exhibit can be designated that of the expository oracle.[205] In Rev. 14:13 the second saying can be construed as an interpretative expansion of the implications or significance of the oracular beatitude. As an inspired response to the oracular beatitude, the saying of the Spirit in v. 13b may constitute an example of the kind of procedure which characterized the activity of groups of prophets within cultic settings (see below, p. 327).

The content of the oracle concerns the status of those who will die "in the Lord" henceforth. They are accounted blessed because their trials have ceased though their achievements follow them. No connection is explicitly made between death and martyrdom, either in the framework of the oracle itself or in its immediate context. But since the oracle does not concern itself with those who have died in the past, it undoubtedly should be construed as a word of comfort and encouragement for those who will be faced with the possibility of martyrdom in the near future. As such the oracle touches on one of the central concerns of the seer, i.e. the comforting and encouragement of a church facing persecution.

6. Rev. 16:15.

This saying is widely regarded as either an allusion to a traditional word of Jesus[206] or a prophetic saying:[207]

> Behold [idou], I am coming like a thief!
> Blessed is he who is awake and keeps his garments
> that he might not go about naked and his shame be seen! (author's trans.)

As in the case of Rev. 1:8 and 14:3, this saying is almost completely unrelated to its context, a fact which suggests its original independence.[208] The closest parallel to the first two lines of this oracle is found in Rev. 3:3b, in the setting of a prophetic proclamation to Sardis: "If you will not awake, I will come like a thief." References to keeping one's garments are found in Rev. 3:4, 17-18. The symbol of the thief, which is foreign to the eschatological imagery of Judaism but found frequently in early Christian literature, probably entered Christian eschatological tradition through Jesus.[209] While the symbol of the thief emphasizes the unexpectedness of the Last Day (cf. 1 Thess. 5:2, 4; 2 Pet. 3:10), it is used as a metaphor for Jesus only in Rev. 3:3 and 16:15. Similar use of imagery in Rev. 16:15 and 3:3b, 4, 17-18 suggests the oracular character of 16:15. In addition to the unique metaphor of the thief, the metaphor of alertness or wakefulness also occurs in Rev. 3:2-3. The call for wakefulness, of course, is a common motif in early Christian eschatological parenesis (Matt. 24:42-43; 25:13; Mark 13:33ff.; Luke 12:37, 39; 1 Thess. 5:6, 10; 1 Pet. 5:8; Did. 16:1). The metaphor of nakedness is also found elsewhere in the Apocalypse (3:17; 17:16). That these metaphors are clustered both in Rev. 16:15 and in Rev. 3 indicates the oracular nature of both passages.

The oracle contains two formal elements, the "behold" clause and a beatitude, both of which are often (but not exclusively) used in early Christian prophetic speech. Of the seven beatitudes in the Apocalypse, four are simply indicative statements which do not further elaborate on the nature of the blessedness (1:3; 16:15; 19:9; 22:6), while three have a second structural element which performs this expository function (14:13; 20:6; 22:14). Three of the beatitudes seem clearly a part of oracles (14:13; 16:15; 19:9), while one is ambiguous (22:14) and two are not part of a prophetic speech (1:3; 22:6).

7. Rev. 18:21-24.

Rev. 18 is a prophecy of the fall of Babylon (=Rome), composed of four dirges, or songs of doom, which appear to have been consciously modeled after similar songs in the OT prophets. The first dirge (18:1-3) is sung by an angel and refers to the fall of Babylon as if it has already occurred.[210] The second dirge (18:4-8) is attributed to a voice from heaven and describes the fall of Babylon in the future. The third dirge (18:9-19) consists of sections sung by kings of the earth (vv. 9-10), merchants (vv. 11-17a), and seamen and sea captains (vv. 17b-19). These three doom songs are concluded with a cry of joy (*Jubelruf*) in v. 20: "Rejoice over her, O heaven, O saints and apostles and prophets, for God has given judgment for you against her!"

The fourth and most dramatic doom song is distinctive in that it begins with a short narrative describing a prophetic symbolic act, the throwing of a stone like a great millstone into the sea, which is then interpreted as a preview of the fall of Babylon (=Rome). However, it is an angel and not a prophet who performs the symbolic act and who then goes on to provide an interpretation:

A. Report: Then a mighty angel took up a stone like a great millstone and threw it into the sea, saying,

B. Interpretation: "So [*houtōs*] shall Babylon the great city be
   1. Threat: thrown down with violence,
   and shall be found no more;
   and the sound of harpers and minstrels, of flute
      players and trumpeters,
   shall be heard in thee no more;
   and a craftsman of any craft
   shall be found in thee no more;

and the sound of the millstone
shall be heard in thee no more;
and the light of a lamp
shall shine in thee no more;
and the voice of bridegroom and bride
shall be heard in thee no more;

2. Reason: for [*hoti*] thy merchants were the great men
of the earth,
and [*hoti*] all nations were deceived by thy
sorcery.
And in her was found the blood of prophets and
of saints,
and of all who have been slain on earth."

This oracle, as well as the first two sung by angels in Rev. 18:1-3, 4-8, is a literary oracle which appears to have been based on Jer. 25:10, an oracle of Jeremiah against Jerusalem and Judah. Further, the symbolic action of the angel seems based on a similar action of Jeremiah, accompanied by an interpretation, in Jer. 51:63-64:

> When you finish reading this book, bind a stone to it, and cast it into the midst of the Euphrates, and say, "Thus shall Babylon sink, to rise no more, because of the evil that I am bringing upon her."

Even though the prophecy of Babylon's fall is introduced as an interpretation of a symbolic action,[211] the prophecy conforms to the OT prophetic speech form called the announcement of judgment, consisting of the two basic elements of the threat and the reason, which in this case is an accusation.

Rev. 18:21-24 also contains a very interesting stylistic feature which few commentators have mentioned.[212] Vv. 21 and 24 (the first and last two lines in the quotation above) refer to Babylon in the third person, while vv. 22-23 address the city in the second person singular. This shift from third-person to second-person address is found in the judicial speeches of the OT prophets (Mic. 6:9c-15; Amos 3:10-11; Isa. 30:8-14; Hos. 12:7-9).[213] The same pattern is found in the judgment section of a prophetic speech against Rome in Sib. Or. iii.350-366.[214] This prophecy, which must be categorized as an announcement of judgment, is a literary creation in the tradition of the political prophecies of Jewish and ancient Near Eastern apocalyptic.

8. Rev. 19:9.

This oracle and the one which we discussed in Rev. 14:13 are closely related. The angel first introduced in 17:1 is apparently the speaker:

Commission Formula: And he said to me, "Write:

Beatitude: Blessed are those who are called
to the marriage supper of the Lamb."

Oath Formula: And he said to me,
"These are the true words of God." (author's trans.)

Again, this saying (along with the following verse) is not integrally related to its context and thus raises the suspicion among some scholars that it is a later interpolation.[215] Formally, these two sayings have a close relationship with Rev. 14:13, for in both passages we have an angel or heavenly voice commanding the seer to write down a beatitude. This beatitude is followed by an oracular response, which in 14:13 expands on the beatitude but in 19:9 is an affirmation of the divine origin of the saying. The beatitude should be regarded as a prophetic saying.[216] The command to write is a functional equivalent of the OT commission formula, which characterizes each of the seven proclamations (2:1, 8, 12, 18; 3:1, 7, 14), as well as the entire Apocalypse (1:11, 19). The oracular beatitude emphasizes the eschatological rewards for those believers in Christ who share the final messianic banquet.

9. Rev. 21:3-4.

The final two chapters of the Apocalypse constitute a pastiche of prophetic sayings, literary devices and patterns, and apocalyptic motifs, the complexity of which cannot be adequately dealt with in this discussion. We propose to examine several examples of what appear to be prophetic speech in Rev. 21-22, beginning with 21:3-4:

Revelation Formula:	And I heard a loud voice from the throne saying:
Promise of Salvation:	"Behold [idou] the dwelling of God is with men. He will dwell with them and they shall be his people, and God himself will be with them; he will wipe away every tear from their eyes, and death shall be no more, neither shall there be mourning nor crying nor pain any more,
Reason:	for [hoti] the former things have passed away."

Although the identity of the speaker is not mentioned, it does not appear to be God himself, for he is referred to in the third person in v. 3. In form this prophetic speech has a great deal in common with the OT prophetic speech form labeled announcements of salvation.[217] The utopian picture of the future that this speech presents also has much in common with the Greco-Roman political oracles which exhibit a two-part structure consisting of a prediction of judgment and tribulation (usually directed against the oppressive Greek monarchies or Rome), to be followed by an ideal era of peace and blessedness.[218]

10. Rev. 21:5-8.

This short section consists of three separate elements, two sayings and a speech, uttered by two different speakers.[219] The first saying is to be understood as spoken by God (the other saying attributed to God in the Apocalypse is Rev. 1:8), the second by an angel, and the third is again a speech attributed to God:

Revelation Formula:	And he who sat upon the throne said [kai eipen],
Promise of Salvation:	"Behold [idou], I make all things new."
Oath Formula:	Also he said [kai legei], "Write this, for these words are trustworthy and true."
	And he said [kai eipen] to me,

Self-disclosure Oracle:	"It is done! I am the Alpha and the Omega, the beginning and the end.
Promise of Salvation:	To the thirsty I will give from the fountain of the water of life without payment. He who conquers shall have this heritage, and I will be his God and he shall be my son.
Threat of Judgment:	But [de] as for the cowardly, the faithless, the polluted, as for murderers, fornicators, sorcerers, idolaters, and all liars, their lot shall be in the lake that burns with fire and sulphur, which is the second death.

In the midst of a rather confused combination of elements we have a prophecy which begins, in a rather unique fashion, with a self-disclosure oracle which forms an inclusio with a similar statement attributed to God and quoted in Rev. 1:8. Immediately following that oracle is a salvation-judgment oracle, i.e. a prophetic utterance in which the elements of threat and promise are combined.

11. Rev. 22:7, 12-14.

Two prophetic oracles appear to be set in this section of Rev. 22; their presence is revealed not only by an "I"-saying attributed to the risen Jesus, but also by a similar structural pattern:

Promise of Salvation:	"And behold [idou], I am coming soon." Blessed is he who keeps the words of the prophecy of this book. Behold, I am coming soon, bringing my recompense, to repay every one for what he has done.
Self-disclosure Oracle:	I am the Alpha and the Omega, the first and the last, the beginning and the end.
Promise of Salvation:	Blessed are those who wash their robes, that they may have the right to the tree of life and that they may enter the city by the gates.
Threat of Judgment:	Outside are the dogs and sorcerers and fornicators and murderers and idolaters, and every one who loves and practices falsehood.

The formal literary pattern evident in v. 7 and in vv. 12-15 consists of the "behold" [idou] clause followed by a beatitude. In vv. 12-15 this pattern is extended by the insertion of a self-disclosure oracle, which effectively identifies Jesus with God (cf. 1:8, 17; 21:6), and by the addition of a threat of judgment which may always be appended to a promise of salvation.

12. Rev. 22:18-20.

The concluding paragraph of the Apocalypse contains three distinct literary forms which are combined to form the final prophetic saying of the book:

Oath Formula:	I warn [*martyrō*] every one who hears the words of the prophecy of this book:
Threat of Judgment:	if any one adds to them, God will add to him the plagues described in this book, and if any one takes away from the words of the book of this prophecy, God will take away his share in the tree of life and in the holy city, which are described in this book.
Oath Formula:	He who testifies [*ho martyrōn*] to these things says,
Promise of Salvation:	"Surely [*nai*] I am coming soon."

The two literary forms combined here are: (1) two conditional curse formulas, combined with an integrity formula, in a prophetic oracle (vv. 18b-19), and (2) a liturgical invocation and response in reverse order, i.e. "I am coming" (spoken by the divinity) precedes the invocation "come!" (v. 20). The solemnity of this concluding oracle is indicated by the oath formula with which it is introduced (Rev. 1:2; 21:5b; 22:6, 16; cf. 1 Thess. 4:6b; Acts 20:23). In the OT, oracles are often introduced with an oath of Yahweh, but never with an oath of the prophetic spokesman.[220] In Jewish apocalyptic literature and in Greco-Roman literature, oracles are sometimes introduced with an oath taken by the speaker.[221] The basic purpose of the oath formula, of course, is the verification of the truth of the utterance which follows.

In the section labeled Threat of Judgment, we find a speech form which has been designated a pronouncement of sacral law.[222] This form is often, but not exclusively, found in early Christian prophetic speech settings. It is certainly interesting, however, that the coming of Jesus, or the Son of man, is closely connected with this particular speech form here as well as in the synoptic gospels (see above, pp. 237-240).

VI. PREDICTIONS OF LATTER-DAY HERETICS

The short letter of Jude, written to an unknown group of Christians at a date which cannot now be determined with any certainty, warns of false teachers who had entered the community he was addressing. The author, who thinks that the last days have arrived, sees the spread of heresy as the fulfilment of prophecy (Jude 17-18):

> But you must remember, beloved, the predictions [*tōn rhēmatōn tōn proeirēmenōn*] of the apostles of our Lord Jesus Christ; they said to you, "In the last time there will be scoffers, following their own ungodly passions."

A paraphrastic expansion of this "oracle" is found in 2 Pet. 3:2-4 (2 Peter is dependent on Jude),[223] with the additions italicized:

You should remember the predictions of the *holy prophets and the commandment of the* Lord and Savior through your apostles. *First of all you must understand this, that scoffers will come in the last days with scoffing, following their own passions and saying, "Where is the promise of his coming? etc."*

While Jude traces his version of the oracle to the apostles, 2 Peter obscures this clear attribution by referring the prediction to the OT prophets and awkwardly juxtaposing the apostles with the Lord as co-authors of the prediction. 2 Peter betrays no independent knowledge of the tradition derived from Jude, but whence did Jude derive this tradition? Similar predictions are attributed to scripture and the "prophetic word" in 1 Clem. 23:3 and 2 Clem. 11:2.[224]

Prophecies of an eschatological falling away are found in at least two other NT passages; these might either be the basis for Jude 17-18 or else reflect a common tradition. The first such prophecy is found in Acts 20:29-30, where Paul makes this statement toward the conclusion of his farewell speech to the Ephesian elders:

a   I know [*egō oida*] that after my departure fierce wolves
       will come in among you,
b   not sparing the flock;
a' and from among your own selves will arise men speaking
       perverse things,
b' to draw away the disciples after them.

This prediction consists of two couplets, the first couched in metaphorical terms and the second in literal terms, both in essentially parallel relationship. The wolves/flock metaphor in the first couplet continues the overseer/flock metaphor begun in v. 28. The warning focuses first on dangers from without, then on dangers from within. A close parallel is found in Matt. 7:15-20, where there is a warning against false prophets who appear like sheep but inwardly are ravening wolves. The prediction in Acts is set within the broader context of Paul's farewell address to the Ephesian elders in Acts 20:17-38, the whole of which conforms to the Israelite-Jewish literary form called the farewell address (*Abschiedsrede*); this literary form nearly always includes a section in which the speaker refers to events which will transpire after his decease or departure.[225] This prediction is introduced by the phrase "I know," which is significant in that the central section of each of the prophetic letters to the seven churches begins with the same term (2:2, 9, 13, 19; 3:1, 8, 15) and indicates the extraordinary knowledge of the speaker. In the ancient world men about to die were often thought to have prophetic powers,[226] and this popular belief appears in the farewell discourse as a literary form.

The second prophecy regarding the rise of heretics at the end of the age is found in 1 Tim. 4:1-3:

Now the Spirit expressly says [*to de pneuma rhētōs legei*],
"In later times [*hysterois kairois*] some will depart from the faith"
by giving heed to deceitful spirits and doctrines of demons
through the pretensions of liars whose consciences are seared,
who forbid marriage and enjoin abstinence from foods
which God created to be received with thanksgiving by those who believe and
       know the truth.[227]

This oracle is introduced with a formula which is very close to the messenger formula found in Acts 21:11, "thus says the Holy Spirit." Early Christian prophetic speech is, as we have seen, frequently attributed to the Spirit of God. The prophet who uttered this oracle is not mentioned, but certainly it was a prophet who mediated this prediction.[228] Determining the extent of the oracle is difficult; it may extend from vv. 1-3, as quoted above, and yet it seems (though it cannot be demonstrated) that the original oracle is limited to the single line which has been placed in quotation marks. The lines which follow, if this view is correct, function as a periphrastic interpretation of the original oracle. The phrase "in later times" (v. 1) is used here as an introductory formula for a prophetic description of the eschaton that focuses on the recrudescence of evil which will occur in that time. Analogous introductory phrases, such as "in the latter days" and "in those days," are used in OT prophets, in early Jewish apocalyptic, and in early Christian literature to begin descriptions of the renaissance of evil, the judicial activity of God, or his saving activity.[229] It is presumably implied, though rarely stated, that since the days in which the speaker lives are characterized by such phenomena, they must be in fact the last days.

In the versions of this oracle found in Jude 17-18 (followed by 2 Pet. 3:2ff.) and 1 Tim. 4:1ff., the rise of heretics or a falling away of the faithful is viewed as an integral part of an eschatological scenario. Since these oracles cannot be reduced to one early exemplar, they must be regarded as detachable motifs from a more complete sequence of eschatological events that prophets could repeat, with endless variations, within the setting of Christian worship.

11 | THE FORM AND CONTENT OF EARLY CHRISTIAN PROPHECY: PART II

The important role which prophecy played in early Christianity permeates the literature of the NT, but prophetic activity did not disappear at the end of the apostolic era. In this chapter we shall discuss some of the remnants of early Christian prophetic speech which have been preserved primarily within that body of postapostolic Christian literature commonly designated the "Apostolic Fathers." This literature, some of which was regarded as canonical by various segments of the church prior to the end of the fourth century A.D., when the extent of the NT canon was decisively fixed, all came into existence between the last decade of the first century and ca. A.D. 150. In addition, we have used the Odes of Solomon, which probably belong to the same period. Our discussion of the command to flee Jerusalem and the Montanist oracles, however, is based primarily on the information preserved by fourth- and fifth-century Christian historians and heresiologists.

I. IGNATIUS OF ANTIOCH

Ignatius was an early bishop of Antioch who died as a martyr in Rome near the end of the reign of Trajan (A.D. 98-117). On the way to Rome under arrest he traveled overland through western Asia Minor. During this journey he wrote seven letters, five to local churches which he passed (Ephesus, Magnesia, Tralles, Philadelphia, and Smyrna), one to the church at Rome, and one to Polycarp the bishop of Smyrna. Ignatius is perhaps most remembered for his heavy emphasis on the monarchical episcopate, i.e. that form of church which ascribes unlimited authority to the local bishops who, with their circle of presbyters and deacons, are earthly representatives of God or Jesus and the apostles. Ignatius refers to Christian prophets only once in his letters (Philad. 5:2),[1] and in view of his emphasis on church order and discipline he appears an unlikely figure to be considered as a prophet or a pneumatic.[2] However, Ignatius preserves several oracles in his letters that he, and possibly others also, uttered in liturgical settings.

A. PHILAD. 7:1-2

When writing to the church at Philadelphia shortly after having paid that congregation a visit, Ignatius recalls:

> Revelation Formula: I cried out [ekraugasa] while I was with you,
> I spoke with a great voice [megalē phōnē],

with the voice of God [theou phōnē]:

Admonition: "To the bishop give heed,
and to the presbytery,
and to the deacons."[3]

This short oracular utterance is immediately followed by another prophetic saying, or rather a string of sayings:

Narrative: But some suspected that I said these things because I already knew of the division caused by certain people.

Oath and But he is my witness [martys] in whom I am bound
Revelation Formulas: that I learned nothing from any human being,
but the Spirit was proclaiming [ekēryssen] by speaking in this manner [tade]:

Admonitions: "Apart from the bishop do nothing";
"Guard your flesh as the temple of God";
"Love unity";
"Flee divisions";
"Be imitators of Jesus Christ as he was of the Father!"

Ignatius clearly regards these exhortations as prophetic utterances directly inspired by God and/or the Spirit. The setting in which these oracles were uttered was that of a service of worship. The first oracle caused the Philadelphians to suspect Ignatius of having gained some previous knowledge of the situation in Philadelphia, a charge which he vehemently denied through the use of an oath formula. It is precisely the Spirit from God, claims Ignatius, who "exposes secrets" (ta krypta elenchei, Philad. 7:1). Here prophecy functions in a way very similar to 1 Cor. 14:25, where Paul focuses on the fact that prophecy discloses the secrets of men's hearts.

The first oracle is short and in poetic form, features which some regard as essential characteristics of prophetic speech.[4] Before quoting the oracle itself, Ignatius provides an introductory triplet which is itself in poetic form in that it exhibits climactic (or stairlike) parallelism. In using a poetic triplet as an introductory formula for an oracular triplet, Ignatius is undoubtedly introducing a literary embellishment. In spite of the elaborate introduction to the oracle, Ignatius does not reveal the specific introductory formula which was used when the oracle was originally delivered, apart from his reference to the fact that it was uttered "with a loud voice, the voice of God." The loud voice indicates a state of excitation or possession trance and is a frequent accompaniment of oracular speech.[5] The second oracle, or series of oracles, however, was probably introduced by the early Christian prophetic messenger formula "thus says the Spirit" (tade legei to pneuma) or words to that effect (cf. Acts 21:11; 1 Tim. 4:1; Rev. 2:7. 11, 17, 29; 3:6, 13, 22; 14:14; etc.). In all probability, therefore, the exhortations in Philad. 7:2, as well as those in 7:1, were introduced individually or as a group with the formula "thus says the (Holy) Spirit." In spite of the fact that the divine "I" does not occur in these oracles, their divine origin was indicated at least in part by both the loud voice with which they were uttered and the use of the early Christian messenger formula.

In form the first oracle is a triplet in which each short line stands in synonymous parallelism with the other lines. We have already mentioned that the poetic triplet seems to be used with relative frequency in early Christian (as well as early Jewish) prophetic speech.[6] The oracle contains one main verb in the imperative mood, a feature which also characterizes each of the five lines of the second oracle (or series of oracles). If Ignatius had not labeled these exhortations as prophetic, they would be formally indistinguishable from ordinary parenetic statements, which are also succinct, make use of the imperative mood (or the hortatory subjunctive), and can stand in series with little or no overall unity.[7] Formally, the oracles in Philad. 7:1-2 are very similar to the Pauline injunctions found in 1 Thess. 5:15-22. In fact, in view of the context and content of that passage, Paul himself may have joined together several injunctions which the Thessalonians would recognize as having a prophetic origin.

The second oracle in Philad. 7:2 contains five short statements of oracular parenesis which may reflect the utterances of more than one prophet.[8] Although these pronouncements are juxtaposed in their present epistolary context, it does not seem likely that they would have been uttered in that form orally before the Philadelphia congregation. Further, Ignatius' insistence that he was unaware of the situation in Philadelphia when he made the oracular utterance quoted in Philad. 7:1 would have been strengthened if he were not the only one to have uttered such prophetic parenesis.

The content of these oracles is wholly parenetic, with no eschatological emphasis whatsoever. The first oracle on giving heed to the church officials is a motif which permeates the Ignatian letters and is hardly surprising on the lips of Ignatius, inspired or not. The second group of oracles, with the exception of the last, also has numerous parallels in the letters of Ignatius: "apart from the bishop do nothing" (cf. Smyrn. 8:1-2; Trall. 2:2; 7:2; Magn. 4:1; 7:1); "guard your flesh as the temple of God" (cf. 1 Cor. 3:16-17; 6:19; 2 Cor. 6:19; 2 Clem. 9:3); "love unity" (Magn. 13:2; Trall. 11:2); "flee divisions" (Philad. 2:1; Smyrn. 7:2); "be imitators of Jesus Christ as he was of the Father" (1 Cor. 11:1; John 5:19). The content of these oracles, therefore, is hardly innovative. Ignatius views these inspired utterances as a divine confirmation of the very values which he himself seeks to inculcate in the congregations he visited and addressed by letter.

B. OTHER INDICATIONS OF PROPHETIC SPEECH

These clear instances of oracular utterances preserved in the letters of Ignatius encourage us to look for other indications of prophetic speech. In writing to the Romans Ignatius observed (7:2):

Narrative: My lust has been crucified, and there is in me no fire of love for material things;

Revelation Formula: but only water living and speaking in me, and saying to me from within [esōthen moi legon],

Admonition: "Come to the Father."

O. Michel has emphasized the close connection between prophecy and martyrdom in early Christianity (as in early Judaism) and has suggested that Ignatius saw his prophetic role in intimate relationship to his impending martyrdom.[9] Certainly in this passage Ignatius has combined his desire to die the death of a martyr with an inner voice (perhaps in the Socratic tradition) in an oracular style that encourages him to pursue this path. The reference to living and speaking water has been interpreted as referring both to baptism (i.e. one who is baptized may be required to follow Christ even to the point of death) and to the Spirit of God.[10] Both baptism and the Spirit are so intertwined in the thought of Ignatius, however, that the two conceptions should probably not be separated. The exhortation directed to Ignatius by the living water is probably a metaphorical use of an oracular form to indicate the implications for him of his baptism and subsequent possession of the Spirit of Christ.

In his letter to the Ephesian congregation Ignatius proposes to write a second little book about the dispensation of the new man Jesus Christ "if the Lord reveals" (*ean ho kyrios moi apokalypsē*) to him the unity displayed by their faith and worship (20:1-2). Since the lack of unity which characterized the Philadelphia congregation was the substance of the revelation to Ignatius implied by the oracles in Philad. 7:1-2, here Ignatius is probably expecting a divine revelation concerning the state of the faith of the Ephesian congregation. Here too, then, divine revelation is the disclosure of the secrets of men's hearts.

In Trall. 4 and 5 Ignatius seems to model his discussion after that of Paul in 2 Cor. 12. In Trall. 4:1 he begins, "I have many thoughts in God," but he is careful not to boast about them and on that account to perish. He goes on in Trall. 5:1 to pose the rhetorical question, "Am I not able to write to you concerning heavenly things [*ta epourania*]?" Immediately he responds, "Yes, but I am afraid that I should do you harm since you are babes." He goes on to make the following claim in Trall. 5:2:

> For I myself, though I am in bonds and can understand heavenly things, and the places of the angels and the gatherings of principalities, and "things seen and unseen," not for this am I a disciple even now, for much is lacking to us, that we may not lack God.

Ignatius does not, it should be observed, claim to have had visionary experiences whereby such cosmological secrets were conveyed to him. It appears that Ignatius regarded himself as the recipient of divine revelations whereby such knowledge was communicated to him. Again, the function of prophetic revelation, if we may designate this as such, is primarily the disclosure of secrets normally hidden from human beings.

C. PRONOUNCEMENTS OF SACRAL LAW

One further indicator of the possibility of the presence of oracular speech patterns in the letters of Ignatius is the frequent occurrence of a rhetorical form which is very similar to E. Käsemann's pronouncements of sacral law (*Sätze heiligen Rechtes*). However, since the occurrences of such speech forms in Ignatius are, with one exception, unconnected with any of the formal indicators of the presence of oracular speech, we shall not press the case. R. M. Grant, in following and expanding on suggestions made by Bishop Lightfoot, has identified a characteristic feature of Ignatian rhetoric which he labels the *Statement of Reciprocity*.[11] These statements or pronouncements function as parenetic arguments for Ignatius. They consist of a couplet in which the action of man in the first line is paralleled by a corresponding action or reward by God in the second line. Most often the reference in the second line is to the future. These statements embody the principle of *jus talionis*, i.e. the law of retributive justice. Often, but not invariably, the same verb is found in both parts of the pronouncement.

There are some nineteen examples of these pronouncements in the letters of Ignatius:

Eph. 2:1   Crocus . . . has relieved me in every way,
            may the Father of Jesus Christ refresh him in like manner.

Eph. 2:2   It is appropriate in every way to glorify [*doxazein*]
            Jesus Christ,
            who has glorified [*doxasanta*] you.

Eph. 21:16 Remember me,
            as Jesus Christ does you.

Trall. 5:2 Much is lacking [*leipei*] to us,
            that we might not lack [*leipōmetha*] God.

Rom. 8:1   Desire it [*thelēsate*]
            that you might be desired [*thelēthēte*].

Philad. 10:1-2 Appoint a deacon to glorify [*doxasai*] the Name,
                . . . and you yourselves shall be glorified [*doxasthēsesthe*].

Philad. 11:1 You received them,
              as the Lord did you.

Philad. 11:2 Byrrhus was sent . . . as a mark of honor [*timēs*],
              the Lord will honor [*timēsei*] them.

Smyrn. 9:1   He who honors [*ho timōn*] the bishop,
             has been honored [*tetimētai*] by God.

Smyrn. 9:2   In all respects you have refreshed me,
             and may Jesus Christ do the same for you.

Smyrn. 6:1   The one who receives [*ho chōrōn*],
             let him receive [*chōreitō*].

Smyrn. 5:1   There are some who ignorantly deny [*arnountai*] him,
             but rather were denied [*ērnēthēsan*] by him.

Smyrn. 2:1   Some unbelievers say that his Passion was merely in
             semblance [*to dokein*],
             but it is they who are merely in semblance [*to dokein*].

Smyrn. 10:2 You treated (my bonds) with neither haughtiness nor
             shame [*epēschynthēte*],
             and he who is perfect hope, Jesus Christ, shall not
             be ashamed [*epaischynthēsetai*] of you.

Smyrn. 12:1 Byrrhus . . . has in every way refreshed me,
             . . . In all things grace shall reward him.

Polyc. 1:2   Help all men,
             as the Lord does you.

Polyc. 3:1   But especially must we endure [*hypomenein*] all things for
             the sake of God
             that he also may endure [*hypomeinē*] us.

Polyc. 6:1   Give heed to the bishop,
             that God may do the same to you.

Polyc. 6:2   Be therefore longsuffering with one another in gentleness,
             as God is with you. (author's trans.)

One of these statements of reciprocity, that found in Polyc. 6:1, is very similar to the parenetic exhortation of Ignatius found in Philad. 7:1.[12] Further, some of the themes found in the pronouncements of sacral law in the synoptic gospels, such as "to deny" (Matt. 10:33; Luke 12:9) and "to be ashamed" (Mark 8:38; Luke 9:26), are found in some of these Ignatian statements of reciprocity (Smyrn. 5:1; 10:2). None of Ignatius' statements of reciprocity is couched in the form of a conditional sentence with a protasis and an apodosis, like the pronouncements of sacral law. Nevertheless it is clear that the basic principle of retributive justice wherein human behavior is matched with punishment or reward permeates Ignatius' parenetic rhetoric. One must beware of relating too closely particular rhetorical forms such as the pronouncement of sacral law/statement of reciprocity and prophetic speech in early Christianity.

II. THE ODES OF SOLOMON

The Odes of Solomon are a collection of forty-two early Christian hymns written in Syriac by a single author and dating from the first quarter of the second century A.D.[13] The Odes, probably originating in Syria (the area of Edessa is more likely than that of Antioch), preserve a very distinctive type of early Christian prophetic utterance: the prophetic hymn.[14] Although prophetic hymns are occasionally referred to in early Christian literature (1 Cor. 14:15; Col. 3:16; Eph. 5:19), there do not appear to be any examples of this prophetic genre preserved in the NT itself.[15] The hymns of the Apocalypse of John share some features with the Odes of Solomon (e.g. an emphasis on realized eschatology, an antiphonal structure), but there appears to be no firm basis upon which to posit a *prophetic* origin and character of the hymns of the Apocalypse.[16]

In spite of their potential importance for understanding a type of eastern Christianity not otherwise well attested, the Odes have sometimes been overhastily categorized as "gnostic"[17] and on that basis ignored.[18] In view of the uniform style of the Odes it is not feasible at this point in the history of research to propose that earlier prophetic speech forms have been embedded in the Odes and can confidently be identified. Nor can we analyze all forty-two Odes as clear examples of early Christian prophetic hymns. Rather, we shall discuss a number of aspects of the Odes that appear to contribute to our knowledge of an important, but neglected, aspect of early Christian prophecy.

The Odes are not primarily oral compositions written down only later, for the author refers to the process of writing them down (Ode 26:8). They have been designated "odes" (a term synonymous with "song") because they are so designated by the author himself (Syriac *zmyrt'*): he refers to the "odes of Thy truth" (14:7), "I will recite His holy ode" (26:2), "the odes of His rest" (26:3), "the odes of the Lord" (26:8), "the composition of His odes" (36:2), "my members are anointed by His odes" (40:3). The close association between the Lord and the Odist's songs, reflected in each of these six references, suggests their inspired character. This impression is confirmed by the frequent claims which the author makes to divine inspiration in the composition of his odes (6:1-2; 10:1-3; 11:4-6; 12:1-2; 15:3-4; 16:5; 42:6). The author can also conclude a prophetic speech with a claim to inspiration that functions as a prophetic signature (3:10; 18:5). In two instances Odes begin with a proclamation formula exhorting the hearers to pay close attention (8:1; 9:1; cf. 8:9-10).

The Odes contain a number of problematic passages where it appears that the speaker is Christ (8:8-19; 10:4-6; 17:6-16; 22:1-12; 28:9-20; 31:6-13; 36:3-8; 41:8-10; 42:3-20).[19] These passages occur abruptly, with only a grammatical change from first-person plural verb forms and pronominal suffixes (where the Odist speaks on behalf of the community) to first-person singular forms. Nowhere in the Odes is the speaker in the passages mentioned above ever explicitly designated as Christ, yet the content strongly suggests that the speeches are *ex ore Christi* (see particularly 8:15-20; 10:6; 22:5; 28:17; 31:13; 36:3). One example is Ode 10:6:

> And they walked according to my life and were saved,
> And they became my people for ever and ever.

In some instances speeches of Christ are preceded by the Odist's claim to be uttering inspired song (10:1-3; 17:5; 36:1). One of the most quoted passages of the Odes expresses a programmatic claim for the *ex ore Christi* speeches in the Odes (42:6):

> Then I arose and am with them,
> And will speak by their mouths.[20]

Here "arose" (Syriac *qmt*) refers to the resurrection of Jesus, and the second line apparently refers to prophetic utterances made in the name and person of the risen Lord (such as the *ex ore Christi* speeches in the Odes). An example of one such speech of Christ is found in Ode 10:4-8, here quoted with the introductory statements in vv. 1-3:

> The Lord hath directed my mouth by His word.
> And He hath opened my heart by His light.
> And He hath caused to dwell in me His deathless life.
> And gave me that I might speak the fruit of His peace.
> To convert the souls of them who are willing to come to Him.
> And to lead captive a good captivity for freedom.
>
> I was strengthened and made mighty and took the world captive.
> And it became to me for the praise of the Most High, and of God my Father.
> And the Gentiles were gathered together who were scattered abroad.
> And I was unpolluted by my love for them,
> Because they confessed me in high places.
> And the traces of the light were set upon their heart.
> And they walked in my life and were saved and became my people for ever
> and ever.[21]

The speeches of Christ in the Odes, such as this one, emphasize soteriology, including such constituent topics as the mysterious appearance of the messiah, the persecution he endured (frustrated by his resurrection), his task of calling forth predestined believers, and his proclamation to the dead and their response to him. The repeated emphasis on the experience of persecution within these speeches (29:8-19; 31:8-13; 42:5) apparently provided a paradigm for the experience of the Odist's community so that the liturgical recitation of these songs may have functioned to provide the community with a vivid reminder of the nearness of their Lord.

The Odist refers with some frequency to visionary trips to paradise (11:1-21;

21:1-7; 36:1-8; 38:1-21). In Ode 36:1-2, for example, the Odist describes a trip to the heavenly world, where he continues to offer praise to God:

> I rested on the Spirit of the Lord,
> And She lifted me up to heaven;
> And caused me to stand on my feet in the Lord's high place,
> Before His perfection and His glory,
> Where I continued glorifying (Him) by the composition of His Odes.

This forms the introduction to a speech *ex ore Christi* in vv. 3-8. The Odist's prophetic experience of a heavenly ascent is but one feature of the perspective of realized eschatology that permeates the Odes.[22] By "realized eschatology" I simply mean that paradigmatic events and conditions normally regarded as belonging to the temporal future are spoken of *as if* they were already wholly or partially present realities.[23] There are many passages in the Odes in which the future is somehow conceived as merging with the present, as in Ode 11, where the Odist experiences a *Himmelsreise* and sees all the trees in paradise, watered by the river of gladness.[24] The trees symbolize Christians who have already been "planted" in paradise, as vv. 18-21 reveal:

> And I said, Blessed, O Lord, are they
> Who are planted in Thy land,
> And who have a place in Thy Paradise;
> And who grow in the growth of Thy trees,
> And have passed from darkness into light.
> Behold, all Thy labourers (are) fair,
> They who work good works,
> And turn from wickedness to Thy pleasantness.
> For they turned away from themselves the bitterness of the trees,
> When they were planted in Thy land.

Like the hymns in the Odes of Solomon, those in the Apocalypse of John sometimes speak of future realities as if they were already present.[25] The eschatological perspective of the hymns of the Apocalypse varies from total anticipation (Rev. 7:10b), to partial realization (11:15b; 12:10), to total realization (19:1-2).[26] The view of L. L. Thompson thus appears to be as applicable to the Odes of Solomon as to the Apocalypse of John:

> The writer of the Apocalypse used hymnic liturgical materials as they were used by prophets in the worship of the Christian community: to realize in the present realities otherwise apprehended only as future eschatological events.[27]

The Odes also contain a scene in which an eschatological theophany is envisioned with its salvific effects (Odes 7:16b-20):

> And the Most High will be known by His holy ones
> To announce to those who have songs of the coming of the Lord,
> That they may go forth to meet Him and may sing to Him
> With joy and with the harp of many tones.
> The Seers [ḥzy'] shall go before Him,
> And they shall be seen [wmtḥzwn] before Him.
> And they shall praise the Lord in His love,
> Because He is near and does see [wḥzy'].

And hatred shall be removed from the earth,
And with jealousy it shall be drowned,
For ignorance was destroyed upon it,
Because the knowledge of the Lord arrived upon it.

This scene is somewhat unusual in that it is predicted (the verbs are in the imperfect), while most depictions of eschatological conditions or events in the Odes are described as already present (with verbs in the perfect, i.e. the *perfectum propheticum*). This excerpt from Ode 7 exhibits the features of the "eschatological theophany oracle" in that lines 1-8 anticipate the eschatological arrival of the Lord, while the concluding four lines deal with the salvific effects of the divine presence.[28] The Odist favors paronomasia as a stylistic device,[29] and here he uses cognates with the basic meaning of "see" in several ways. Though the common word for prophet in Syriac (*nby'*, as in Hebrew) does not occur in the Odes, the passage quoted above refers to the "Seers" (Syriac *ḥzy'*), who are themselves "seen" by God. These seers may be identical with the "holy ones" referred to in line 1, or they may constitute separate, identifiable groups within the Odist's community.

Although the Odes do not easily surrender their secrets, it appears that they are best regarded as a distinctive type of prophetic hymnbook which, while it has connections with other types of early Christian prophetic speech, nevertheless remains unique.

III. THE SHEPHERD OF HERMAS

The Shepherd of Hermas is a long, loosely structured Christian apocalypse which gradually came into existence between the last decade of the first century and A.D. 150 in Rome. In its final form the Shepherd comprises three sections containing five visions, twelve mandates, and ten parables. The central emphasis of the book is the problem of a second repentance. The document purports to consist of a series of divine revelations granted to Hermas first by an old woman, then by an angel in the form of a shepherd, and it is from this last figure that the name of the entire work is derived. For the purpose of the present discussion one of the central issues in the interpretation of the Shepherd of Hermas is whether the visions and auditions which Hermas claims to have experienced were entirely literary creations based on the conventions of Jewish and Christian apocalyptic literature, or (in addition to the undoubted presence of literary artifice) did they have some basis in the religious experience of Hermas? In posing this problem we must admit that the method does not exist which can clinically separate accounts of authentic experience from the later overlays of literary conceptualization or even complete literary fabrication.

One way of dealing with the question of the legitimacy of the revelatory experiences claimed by Hermas is to see whether there are any prophetic sayings or speeches embedded in the Shepherd. A preliminary assessment of a number of such oracles has been proposed by J. Reiling, and our discussion is a development and modification of some of his proposals.[30] The Shepherd of Hermas contains two basic forms of prophetic oracles. The first form is found only in *Vis.* i-iv, the oldest section of the document, and occurs just four times. The second form is found eight times, twice in the *Mandates* and six times in the *Similitudes*. Both forms of oracular speech are similar in that they exhibit a balanced emphasis between the promise of salvation and the threat of judgment which we have found frequently combined in the Apocalypse of John and to which we have assigned the general term salvation-judgment oracle.

A. SALVATION-JUDGMENT ORACLES IN *VIS.* I-IV

1. Criteria for Identification.

The primary criteria for isolating and identifying the prophetic oracles in the *Visions* are: (1) the occurrence of an introductory commissioning formula spoken by the ancient lady to Hermas, followed by (2) a shift from the second-person singular pronouns and verbs to the second-person plural.[31] Using these two criteria, we find four prophetic speeches in the *Visions*: ii.2.6-8; ii.3.4; iii.8.11— 9.10; and iv.2.5-6. The texts of each of these oracles will be given first, with marginal indications of their internal structure, followed by a more detailed discussion of their form, content, and function.

2. Text and Structure of Oracles.

a. *Vis. ii.2.6-8.*[32]

Commission Formula:	You shall say, therefore, to the leaders of the church that they reform their ways in righteousness, that they receive in full the promises with great glory:
Admonition:	"You, therefore, who work righteousness must remain steadfast and be not double-minded
Reasons:	
1. Conditional Promise:	that your way might be with the holy angels. Blessed are you, as many as endure the great persecution which is coming, and as many as shall not deny their life.
2. Conditional Threat:	For the Lord has sworn [*ōmosen*] by his Son that those who have denied [*arnēsamenous*] their Christ have been rejected from their life, that is, those who shall now deny him in the days to come.
3. Conditional Promise:	But those who denied him formerly have obtained forgiveness through his great mercy."

b. *Vis. ii.3.4.*

Commission Formula:	But you shall say to Maximus:
Conditional Threat:	"Behold [*idou*], persecution is coming [*erchetai*], if it seems good to you to deny the faith again.
Conditional Promise:	'The Lord is near those that turn to him,' as it is written in the Book of Eldad and Modat, who prophesied to the people in the wilderness."

c. Vis. iii.8.11 — 9.10.

Commission Formula:	But I command you first, Hermas, with these words, which I am going to relate to you, to speak them all into the ears of the saints, that they may hear them and do them and be cleansed from their wickedness, and you with them:
Proclamation Formula:	"Listen to me, children:
Accusation:	I brought you up in great simplicity and innocence and reverence by the mercy of God, who instilled righteousness into you that you should be justified and sanctified from all wickedness and crookedness. But you do not wish to cease from your wickedness.
Admonition:	Now, therefore, listen to me and be at peace among yourselves and regard one another and help one another and do not take a superabundant share of the creatures of God for yourselves, but give also a part to those who lack.
Reason:	For [*gar*] some are contracting illness in the flesh by too much eating and the flesh of the others who have nothing to eat is being injured by their not having sufficient food and their body is being destroyed. So this lack of sharing is harmful to you who are rich, and do not share with the poor. Consider the judgment which is coming.
Admonition:	Let therefore they who have over-abundance seek out those who are hungry, so long as the tower is not yet finished
Reason (Conditional Threat):	for when the tower is finished you will wish to do good, and will have no opportunity. See to it, then, you who rejoice in your wealth, that the destitute may not groan, and their groans go up to the Lord, and you with your goods be shut outside the door of the tower.
Address:	Therefore I speak now to the leaders of the church and to those who take the chief seats:

Accusation: Be not like the sorcerers, for sorcerers carry
           their charms in boxes,
but you carry your charms and poison in your
           hearts.
You are hardened, and will not cleanse your hearts,
and mix your wisdom together in a pure heart that
           you may find mercy by the great king.

Admonition: See to it, therefore, children,
that these disagreements do not rob you of your
           life.
How will you correct the chosen of the Lord
if you yourselves suffer no correction?
Correct therefore one another
and be at peace among yourselves,

Reason (Condition-   that I also may stand joyfully before the Father,
al Promise):   and give an account of you all to the Lord."

d.   *Vis. iv.2.5-6.*

Commission   Go then and tell the Lord's elect ones of his
Formula: great deeds,
and tell them that this beast is a type of the
           great persecution which is to come:

Conditional   If then you are prepared beforehand,
Promise: and repent with all your heart toward the Lord,
you will be able to escape it,
if your heart be made pure and blameless,
and you serve the Lord blamelessly for the
           rest of the days of your life.
Cast your cares upon the Lord
and he will put them straight.
Believe on the Lord, you who are double-minded,
that he can do all things,
and turns his wrath away from you,
and sends scourges on you who are double-minded.

Conditional   Woe [*ouai*] to those who hear these words and
Threat: disobey;
it were better for them not to have been born."

3. Analysis.

In each instance the speaker who commissions Hermas and who addresses the recipients of the prophetic speeches he mediates is the ancient lady, i.e. a personification of the church (*Vis.* ii.4.1), elsewhere identified as the Holy Spirit who is the Son of God (*Sim.* ix.1.1), whom Hermas confuses with the Sibyl of Cumae. The Lord is spoken of in the third person in all these oracles except the third, where the speaker uses the first-person singular in the final sentence of the oracle and thereby indicates that he is none other than the Son of God. Although the entire book which Hermas is writing is intended for general circulation among Christian congregations, both at Rome and elsewhere (Vis. ii.4.3), each of the prophetic speeches which we have isolated is loosely inserted in its present literary context and probably existed alone originally. In each case the ancient lady delivers an oracle to Hermas that he is to deliver at a later date to its intended recipients in a manner reminiscent of many OT prophets. Each of these four oracles begins with a commission formula, an introductory narrative element of a type found frequently in the OT,[33] but only occasionally in early Christian prophecy.[34] Further, in these oracles of Hermas (unlike the OT and Rev. 2-3) the speaker is never identified through the inclusion of a messenger formula such as "thus says X." On the other hand, the commission formulas in Hermas, apart from the one which introduces the message to Maximus, all contain a synopsis of the message which follows or the reason for which the message is being transmitted. Although Hermas is again and again commanded to write down the messages which he receives, it is clear that he (or his emissaries) is to proclaim the message in person, i.e. to read or recite it to the appropriate audience (Vis. iv.3.6; Mand. xii.3.3; Sim. viii.11.1). The second element in the third oracle quoted above (Vis. iii.8.11 — 9.10) is labeled a proclamation formula in the marginal analysis, since it introduces the prophetic speech with a call to attention in a manner often found in the OT.[35] The formula was used in wisdom, judicial, and forensic settings as well as in prophetic settings, however, and here it is appropriate both as a prophetic call for attention and as a common rhetorical feature of the Hellenistic Jewish homiletical style.[36]

The prophetic speeches themselves exhibit numerous features of the style of the Hellenistic Jewish homily, an eclectic speech form which itself is in many respects indistinguishable from the Cynic-Stoic diatribe.[37] If Hermas had not labeled these prophetic speeches with a commission formula, it would be virtually impossible to distinguish them from a homiletic or epistolary parenesis. The structure of these speeches exhibits a certain degree of variety and flexibility, yet within defined limits. The basic purpose of these speeches is parenetic; the recipients are enjoined to exhibit certain kinds of behavior. These hortatory or parenetic statements are sanctioned in two ways: appropriate behavior is encouraged through conditional promises, while inappropriate behavior is discouraged through conditional threats. These two elements are present in each oracular speech, though they occupy no particular position or order in relationship to other elements. Two additional elements are optional — at least they are not found in all the oracular speeches in the Visions — the admonition and the accusation. The admonition consists of one or more commands in the imperative that either demand or prohibit certain forms of behavior. The accusation describes the iniquitous behavior of the recipients of the oracle, and in its two occurrences in the oracles quoted above it is followed by an admonition. The function of the accusation, therefore, is not to justify an unconditional threat of judgment, as in the OT, but rather to prepare the recipient for the parenetic admonition which follows. Although this sample of prophetic speech is rather limited, it will be expanded by a consideration of the other forms found in the Mandates and the Similitudes below.

All of the oracles discussed above either explicitly or implicitly support a new theologoumenon which Hermas claimed to receive through divine revelation: the possibility of a second repentance. This notion of a second and final repentance is reinforced through the eschatological framework within which it is located. *Each oracle makes explicit reference to the coming persecution (thlipsis) or judgment (krisis), which must be understood as eschatological events.*[38] In view of the general absence of eschatological thought in the Shepherd, the preservation of this element in each of the oracles is the more remarkable and lends further confirmation to the view that each of these prophetic speeches was originally independent of its present literary context.

Several specific observations can now be made about particular elements within the four oracles quoted above. In the first oracle, in the sections labeled conditional threat and conditional promise, we have a relatively clear allusion to the kind of tradition found in Mark 8:38 (and parallels) and Luke 12:9 (and parallel): "But he who denies me before men will be denied before the angels of God."[39] Even though this oracle of Hermas does not refer to the parousia as the synoptic passages just mentioned do, and the death of the individual is referred to instead (cf. the scene before the Father in the last sentence of the third oracle quoted), reference is still made to the angels. Taken together, the conditional threat and conditional promise contain the essential elements of the pronouncements of sacral law described by E. Käsemann. In *Vis.* ii.2.8 these two elements are introduced by an oath formula: "For the Lord has sworn by his Son that . . ."; this formula resembles OT oath formulas in that they are pronounced by God and never by the prophet,[40] whereas in Jewish apocalyptic literature it is often the seer himself who swears the truth of the revelation he is about to relate.[41] Variations on the oath formula occur within oracular settings of the Apocalypse of John, as we have seen above.[42] The first oracle also contains a beatitude, a form which is often but not exclusively found in oracular sayings and speeches in early Judaism, early Christianity, and even Greco-Roman paganism. Other beatitudes are found in the Shepherd of Hermas in *Sim.* ii.10; v.3.9; ix.29.3; ix.30.3). A pronouncement of woe is found at the conclusion of the fourth oracle (*Vis.* iv.2.6): "Woe to those who hear these words and disobey; it were better for them not to have been born." The second line following the woe may refer or allude to Mark 13:7, which refers to the time of tribulation that each oracle mentions. In the Apocalypse of John a blessing is pronounced on those who read, hear, and keep the word (Rev. 1:3; 22:7), rather than a woe upon those who do not. The woe pronouncement which comes at the end of this oracle, like the two pronouncements of blessedness which frame the Apocalypse, functions as a legitimation formula in that it associates an eschatological sanction with the value, truth, and necessity of obeying the prophetic words with which it is associated.

As in the case of the oracles of Ignatius the prophetic speeches of Hermas exhibit the features of the Hellenistic Jewish homily. The implication of this similarity, as in the case of Ignatius, is that one of the major sources of prophetic rhetoric and diction for Hermas was the early Christian sermon. To be sure, the necessity that the prophetic nature of his messages be recognized as such made it imperative that such speeches be framed by certain formal and recognizable features of oracular utterance. The appeal to divine authority for Hermas' condemnation of the lax morality of his Christian brothers and his introduction of the notion of a second and final repentance were necessary in view of the lack of status of the messenger.

B. ORACLES OF ASSURANCE IN THE *MANDATES*

1. Criteria for Identification.

The second form of oracular speech found in the Shepherd of Hermas occurs only twice in the *Mandates* (xii.4.5-7; xii.6.1-3). In contrast to the four parenetic salvation-judgment oracles discussed above, the commission formula does not introduce these oracles or the six additional oracles found in the *Similitudes,* which will be discussed in a separate section below. Rather, the speaker is always identified (in all oracles in the *Mandates* and the *Similitudes*) as the angel of repentance, who speaks in the first-person singular and addresses his audience through Hermas in the second-person plural. Unlike the oracles just discussed, these contain no eschatological element whatsoever. After quoting the two oracles with a marginal indication of their structure, a short analysis will follow.

2. Text and Structure of Oracles.

a.   *Man.* xii.4.5-7.

Admonition:	Do you, therefore, who are empty and light in the faith, put the Lord into your heart, and you shall know that nothing is easier or sweeter or more gentle than these commandments.
	Be converted, you who walk in the commandments of the devil, which are difficult and bitter and cruel and foul.
Oracle of Assurance:	
1. Admonition:	And do not fear [*mē phobēthēte*] the devil
2. Reason (Promise):	because [*hoti*] there is no power in him against you. For [*gar*] I, the angel of repentance, who master him, will be with you. The devil can only cause fear, but fear of him has no force.
3. Admonition:	Therefore do not fear [*mē phobēthēte*] him
4. Reason (Promise):	and he will fly from you.

b.   *Man.* xii.6.1-3.

Introductory Formula:	But I, the angel of repentance, say to you,
Oracle of Assurance:	
1. Admonition:	Do not fear [*mē phobēthēte*] the devil.
2. Reason (Promise):	For [*gar*] I was sent, said he, to be with you who repent with all your heart, and to strengthen you in the faith.
Conditional Promise:	Believe, therefore, in God, though you have renounced your life through your sins, and have added to your sins, and have made your life heavy, that if you turn to the Lord with all your heart and do righteousness for the rest of the days of your life,

and serve him in uprightness according to his will,
he will heal your former sins,
and you shall have the power to master the works
of the devil.

Oracle of
Assurance:

  1. Admonition: But do not fear [$m\bar{e}$ $phob\bar{e}th\bar{e}te$] the threat of the
devil at all,

  2. Reason: for [gar] he is powerless as the sinews of a
dead man.

Conditional
Promise: Listen, therefore, to me,
and fear him who has all power to save and to
destroy
and keep these commandments,
and you shall live to God.

3. Analysis.

In many respects these oracles bear a close relationship, in both form and content, to the six oracles from the *Similitudes* which are quoted and analyzed below; some of our remarks will be postponed until that discussion. The distinctive feature of these oracles, however, is that their center is an oracle (or oracles) of assurance. This oracular form is found often in the OT and early Judaism, yet it also has close phenomenological similarities with Greco-Roman oracles.[43] In early Judaism and early Christianity this oracular form survives in two very different contexts. In non-apocalyptic Jewish and Christian literature the oracle of assurance is found exclusively in revelatory dreams,[44] while in Jewish and Christian apocalyptic literature oracles of assurance are pronounced exclusively by supernatural beings or prophetic personages in revelatory messages conveyed through media other than dreams.[45] These two oracles are also remarkable because of their very positive orientation: they contain no conditional threats, but only oracles of assurance, admonitions, and conditional promises. Generalizations can hardly be made on the basis of two oracles, but it appears again as if the sequence of these elements is optional. The final conditional promise of the second oracle quoted is introduced by the phrase "listen, therefore, to me," a phrase which we have earlier identified as a proclamation formula.

C. PARENETIC SALVATION-JUDGMENT ORACLES IN THE SIMILITUDES

1. Criteria for Identification.

The criteria for identifying the following six oracles are the same used to identify the two oracles in the *Mandates*: the speaker in every case identifies himself as the angel of repentance, and the speech which he makes exhibits a change from second-person singular pronouns and verbs to the second-person plural. The six oracles which we have isolated on this basis are: *Sim.* vi.1.4; ix.23.5; ix.24.4; ix.28.5-8; ix.31.3— 32.5; ix.33.1. Again we shall quote the oracles, indicate their structure in the margins, and conclude with an analysis of their form and content.

2. Text and Structure of Oracles.

a. Sim. vi.1.4.

Addressee:	You, therefore, who repent
Admonition:	put away the wickednesses of this world which lead you astray, but if you put on all the virtue of righteousness, you shall be able to keep these commandments, and no longer add to your sins.
Conditional Promise:	Therefore, walk in these commandments of mine, and you shall live to God.
Legitimation Formula:	All these things have been spoken to you by me (the angel of repentance).

b. Sim. ix.23.5.

Legitimation Formula:	And I, the angel of repentance, say to you:
Conditional Promise:	"As many of you as have this heresy, put it aside and repent, and the Lord will heal your former sins, if you cleanse yourselves from this demon.
Conditional Threat:	But if not you shall be delivered to him to death."

c. Sim. ix.24.4.

Legitimation Formula:	And I, the angel of repentance, say to you who are such:
Conditional Promise:	"Remain as you are, and your seed shall not be blotted out for ever, for the Lord has proved you and written you in among our number, and all your seed shall dwell with the Son of God, for of his Spirit have you received."

d. Sim. ix.28.5-8.

Conditional Threat:	Watch, therefore, you who have these thoughts, lest this thought remain in your hearts, and you die to God.
Admonition:	But you who are suffering for the Name ought to glorify God, that God deemed you worthy to bear this name, and that all your sins should be healed. So then count yourselves blessed; but think that you have done a great deed, if any of you suffer for God's sake.

Reason:	The Lord is giving you life, and you do not consider it; for your sins have weighed you down, and except you had suffered for the name of the Lord, you would have died to God because of your sins.
Legitimation Formula:	I (the angel of repentance) say this
Addressee:	to you who are hesitating as to denial or confession:
Conditional Threat:	"Confess that you have a Lord, lest you deny him and be delivered into prison. If the heathen punish their servants if one deny his lord, what think you will the Lord, who has power over all, do to you?
Conditional Promise:	Put away these thoughts from your heart that you may live for ever to God."

e. Sim. ix.31.3 — 32.5.

Legitimation Formula:	I, the angel of repentance, judge you all happy who are innocent as babes, for your part is good and honorable with God. But I say to you all:
Admonition:	"Keep simplicity and bear no malice, and do not remain in your guilt, or in remembrance of the bitterness of offences. Be of one spirit and put away these evil schisms, and take them away from yourselves that the lord of the sheep may rejoice over them.
Conditional Promise:	But he will rejoice if all be found whole;
Conditional Threat:	but if he will find some of them fallen away, it will be woe to the shepherds. But if the shepherds themselves be found fallen away, what shall they answer to the Master of the flock? They will not be believed, for it is incredible that a shepherd should be harmed by the sheep, and they will rather be punished for their lie.
Legitimation Formula:	And I am the Shepherd, and am very exceedingly bound to give account for you.

f. Sim. ix.33.1.

Legitimation	All these things which have been written above,

Formula:	I, the Shepherd, the angel of repentance, have declared and spoken to the servants of God.
Conditional Promise:	If then you shall believe and shall listen to my words, and shall walk in them, and shall correct your ways, you shall be able to live.
Conditional Threat:	But if you shall remain in malice and in the memory of offences, none of such kind shall live to God.
Legitimation Formula:	All these things that I must tell have been told to you.

3. Analysis.

Since the angel of repentance, or the shepherd, is the speaker to whom each of the oracles in the *Mandates* and *Similitudes* is attributed, a closer determination of his identity is important. In *Mand.* xi.9 Hermas refers to the "angel of the prophetic spirit" as the divine agent which produces prophetic utterances in men who have the divine Spirit. In *Vis.* v.2 the shepherd, who is identical with the angel of repentance (*Vis.* v.7), claims to have been sent to Hermas by "the most reverend angel" (*semnotatos angelos*). In *Sim.* ix.1.1-2, the ancient lady (= church) is identified with the Holy Spirit, and the Spirit is identified with the Son of God, and the same Spirit is said to be equivalent of the angel (of repentance). The complexity of Hermas' Christology is well known,[46] yet despite the conceptual unclarity of Hermas' Christology, pneumatology, and angelology, it is virtually certain that the angel of repentance is to be identified with Christ, the Son of God.[47] One might argue that it is precisely the theological ambiguity of Hermas' theological thought that points toward the authenticity of his revelatory experiences.[48] Although we have labeled those sections in which the speaker identifies himself as the angel of repentance legitimation formulas, their basic function is analogous to the messenger formula in that the original words of the speaker are preserved and related to the intended audience in the form of a quotation.

Unlike the first four oracles which we identified in the *Visions,* the element which we have labeled accusation occurs in none of the oracles in the *Mandates* and *Similitudes.* Rather, the charges of misbehavior of various kinds are made explicit in the conditional threat. Again the structure of each of these speeches appears rather loose. In general, however, the conditional promise tends to be placed immediately before the conditional threat.

D. CONCLUSIONS

Although one might suspect that a number of other oracles could be successfully identified in Hermas (e.g. *Sim.* x.4.4), we have insisted that the mere change from second-person singular to second-person plural is not in itself a decisive criterion for identifying oracular speech. It must be accompanied by a formal indication of the presence of such speech forms as the commission formula (as in the case of the oracles in the *Visions*), or by a legitimation formula, i.e. the direct attribution of the speech to a supernatural being (as in the case of the oracles in the *Mandates* and the *Similitudes*). The results of our inquiry make it probable that at least twelve prophetic oracles have been integrated by Hermas into the final composition of the Shepherd. Thus, in spite of the charge (which is probably not without some basis in fact) that the element of deliberate fiction looms large in the Shepherd,[49] there is a strong probability that a core of prophetic speech has been preserved and elaborated through literary artifice and stylization to produce the finished document known as the Shepherd of Hermas.

The oracles of Hermas share a number of common elements with the prophetic sayings and speeches, suggesting that both authors stand in a particular stream of early Christian prophetic tradition. The seven proclamations of Rev. 2-3 and the oracles which we have identified in Hermas can all be characterized as parenetic salvation-judgment oracles. Although this form is loosely structured, its basic purpose is to encourage proper behavior and to discourage misbehavior by supporting the former with admonitions and conditional promises, and the latter with accusations and conditional threats. The rhetoric of the speeches themselves appears to be drawn from early Christian homiletic style, which in turn owes a great deal to the Hellenistic Jewish homily on the one hand and the Cynic-Stoic diatribe on the other.

IV. DIDACHE 11:12

Although Did. 11-13 contains a great deal of important information concerning early Christian prophets and their relationships to congregations in Syria-Palestine at the turn of the first century, it contains but two possible oracles (11:12):

> Whoever shall say in the Spirit,
> "Give me money (or something else)."
> You shall not listen to him.
> But if he tells you:
> "Give to others who lack."
> Let no one judge him. (author's trans.)

The way the Didache refers to a prophet as one who speaks "in the Spirit" (Did. 11:7, 8, 9, 12) makes it apparent that such inspired speech was recognizably oracular. However, the Didache nowhere indicates how such inspired speech was either behaviorally or linguistically recognizable. While physical agitation and loud speech is one possibility, the references to "speaking in the Spirit" appear to refer rather to the use of some kind of legitimation formula analogous to "thus says the Holy Spirit."

The first oracle, "Give me money (or something else),"[50] while it is in direct discourse, is probably a sample of the kind of oracular utterance that could be expected from a prophet: a short, imperative utterance. The second sample oracle, given this time in indirect discourse, would be similar in form to the first, yet because of the unselfish nature of the request would be honored as a command of the Spirit (i.e. "Give (to me) on behalf of others who are lacking"). Neither of these sample oracles is in any way concerned with eschatology. In form the oracles are very similar to those in Ign. Philad. 7:1-2: short, concise statements with the main verb in the imperative mood, i.e. prescriptive oracles.

V. THE ORACULAR COMMAND TO FLEE JERUSALEM

In narrating the events which occurred just prior to the first Jewish revolt of A.D. 66-73, Eusebius of Caesarea (writing in the early fourth century) refers to the effect which a certain oracle had on the Christian community in Jerusalem at that time:[51]

> Now the people of the church in Jerusalem were commanded in an oracle [chrēsmon] given by revelation [di' apokalypseōs] before the war to those in the city who were worthy of it, to depart and dwell in one of the cities of Perea which they called Pella.

This account is so brief that any attempt to reconstruct the original form of the oracle would be very difficult if not impossible. Nevertheless, the oracle apparently consisted of two elements, first a command to flee (in the imperative), and then a directive indicating the destination of the flight. This is the famous Pella tradition reflected in a number of early Christian writings.[51a] Many scholars have noted the correspondence between this oracle and that portion of the Olivet Discourse found in Mark 13:14-20 (and parallels):

> But when you see the desolating sacrilege set up where it ought not to be (let the reader understand), then let those who are in Judea flee to the mountains; let him who is on the housetop not go down, nor enter his house, to take anything away; and let him who is in the field not turn back to take his mantle.
>
> And alas for those who are with child and for those who give suck in those days! Pray that it may not happen in winter. For in those days there will be such tribulation as has not been from the beginning of the creation which God created until now, and never will be. And if the Lord had not shortened the days, no human being would be saved; but for the sake of the elect, whom he chose, he shortened the days.[52]

This pericope consists of two sections: the first is the command to flee (vv. 14-16), and the second a description of judgment (vv. 17-20). Since neither Eusebius nor any other Christian author who has occasion to refer to the Pella tradition expresses any awareness of a relationship between that tradition and Mark 13:14-20, if there is a relationship it must be based on dependence upon a common source or tradition.[53]

If we assume a hypothetical correspondence between the Pella tradition of Eusebius and Mark 13:14-20, there are three primary motifs which must be taken into account: (1) the oracular command to flee, (2) Pella as the specific destination of flight, and (3) the description of judgment. Motifs (1) and (3) are found in Mark 13:14-20, while (1) and (2) are found in Eusebius. The Pella tradition is also found in Epiphanius (Haer. xxix.7; xxx.2), but both references contain motifs (1) and (2) and are probably dependent upon Eusebius.[54] However, Epiphanius preserves a third mention of the Pella tradition, which appears to be independent of Eusebius (De mens. et pond. xv; Migne, PG, xliii, p. 261B):

> When the city was on the point of being captured by the Romans and laid waste, all the disciples were forewarned by an angel to depart from the city which was about to be completely destroyed. They departed and took up residence in Pella.

While this version of the Pella tradition might appear to be a conflation of that found in Eusebius and Mark 13:14-20, since it contains all three motifs, this is not the case. First, Pella as the destination of the flight is not part of the oracle. Second, the oracle is given, not before the war, but at a critical point during the war. Third, the threat of judgment is quite different from that found in Mark.

In scholarly discussions of the Pella tradition the primary concern is usually the problem of the historicity of that tradition; the weight of opinion favors the historicity of the flight to Pella.[55] Gerd Lüdemann, however, has recently argued persuasively that the Pella tradition arose in a Jewish Christian community, associated with Pella, in the post-A.D. 70 period in order to present itself as the true successors of the pre-A.D. 70 Jewish Christian community in Jerusalem.[56] Lüdemann, however, has not recognized that the Pella destination has been added to an oracle which must originally have consisted of two elements, the command to flee enforced by a prediction of judgment. In terms of OT oracular patterns it is clear that we are dealing with a familiar type of prophetic speech, the summons to flight (*Aufforderung zur Flucht*), a type found in historical narratives (1 Sam. 15:6; 22:5) that became a pattern for the writing prophets, particularly Jeremiah (Jer. 4:4-5; 6:1; 48:6-8, 28; 49:8, 30; 50:8-10; 51:6, 45).[56a] In the OT examples of this oracle form, the initial summons to flee is usually followed by a threat of judgment. These two features are found both in Mark 13:14-20 and Epiphanius De mens. et pond. xv. A similar oracle is exhibited in two dream revelations to Joseph in Matt. 2:13 and 2:19-20, which share three elements: (1) command to arise and flee, (2) destination, and (3) reason.

There is every probability that a prophetic summons to flight was mediated to the Christian community in Jerusalem by a prophetic or angelic messenger just before or during the first Jewish revolt. That such a flight in fact occurred is assured by the survival of the oracle in several variant forms, even though its specific association with Pella must be regarded as a secondary development. The flight to Pella itself was thought by early Christians to be related to the martyrdom of James, which occurred in A.D. 62/63 according to Josephus (*Ant.* xx.9.1), or A.D. 66 according to Hegesippus (Eusebius *Hist. eccl.* ii.23.18); the latter date is probably more accurate.[57] The account in Eusebius dates the oracle "before the war," while the version preserved in Epiphanius De mens. et pond. xv suggests that the revelation occurred when the city of Jerusalem was on the point of capture. The latter possibility has the most to be said for it, since there are really no circumstantial historical reasons why the oracle enjoining flight and the flight itself could not have occurred in (or near) A.D. 68.[58]

The summons to flight, then, may well have been an oracular pronouncement mediated by a prophet or angelic messenger to the Jerusalem Christians, and it would certainly have implied if not badly stated the imminent destruction of Jerusalem. Pronouncements regarding the destruction of Jerusalem were made by OT prophets, early Jewish prophets, and Jesus himself. In spite of all the prophetic activity in and around Jerusalem both before and during the first Jewish revolt, there is very little evidence in Josephus (our chief source of knowledge for this period) that prophetic oracles in the form of a summons to flight were uttered. It is perhaps significant, however, that Josephus (who appears to have regarded himself as a prophet and as a kind of latter-day successor to Jeremiah) depicts himself as urging his compatriots to surrender in view of the imminent victory of the Romans and the inevitable destruction of the city and temple (*Bell.* v.362-419). That the flight motif occurs in some OT oracles in connection with impending judgment suggests the eschatological orientation of the motif.[59] Thus the summons to flight reported by Mark, Eusebius, and Epiphanius was probably not enjoined for the purpose of rescuing a group of Christians from an imminent historical calamity, but as a motif which was integral to an eschatological scenario of the events of the end time.

VI. THE MONTANIST ORACLES

Montanism was a prophetic movement within Christianity that began during the third quarter of the second century and spread to all corners of the Greco-Roman world.[60] Eusebius, who quotes an unknown opponent of Montanism who has come to be called the Anonymous, provides an account of the origins of this movement (*Hist. eccl.* v.16.6-9):

> In Phrygian Mysia there is said to be a village called Ardabau. There they say that a recent convert called Montanus, when Gratus was proconsul of Asia, in the unbounded lust of his soul for leadership gave access to himself to the adversary, became obsessed [*pneumatophorēthēnai*] and suddenly fell into frenzy and convulsions [*en katochē tini kai parekstasei genomenon*]. He began to be ecstatic [*enthousian*] and to speak and to talk strangely [*xenophōnein*], prophesying contrary to the custom which belongs to the tradition and succession of the church from the beginning. . . . But by some art, or rather by such an evil scheme of artifice, the devil wrought destruction for the disobedient, and receiving unworthy honours from them stimulated and inflamed their understanding which was already dead to the true faith; so that he raised up two more women and filled them with the bastard spirit so that they spoke madly and improperly and strangely [*ekphronōs kai akairōs kai allotriotropōs*], like Montanus. The spirit gave blessings [*makarizontos*] to those who rejoiced and were proud in him, and puffed them up by the greatness of its promises [*epangelmatōn*].

Eusebius and his source are obviously very critical of Montanus and the movement which he began. They impugn his motives and describe his and his followers' possession trance experiences with terminology drawn from pagan divination. Further, it appears that Eusebius' source has intentionally modeled his depiction of Montanus' inaugural prophetic experience, as well as that of the two women, Maximilla and Prisca, after Lucian's satire on the prophet Alexander of Abonuteichos.[61] This deliberate attempt by Christian heresiologists to paganize Montanus has led many modern scholars to agree that Montanist prophecy was an intrusion of pagan revelatory ecstasy into Christianity.[62] This view is completely false. All of the major features of early Montanism, including the behavior associated with possession trance, are derived from early Christianity.[63] Montanism is particularly closely associated with the Gospel of John and the Apocalypse of John; their emphasis on the Paraclete was drawn from the former, and their preoccupation with the New Jerusalem (which was expected to appear in Pepuza) was gleaned from the latter.

The Montanists called their movement the "New Prophecy,"[64] while their Christian critics more often referred to them as the Phrygian Heresy. In addition to their full acceptance and use of the Apocalypse of John and the late first-century prophetic movement which John apparently represented, the Montanists also saw themselves as standing in the same tradition as Ammia, the prophetess of Philadelphia, who was active during the first half of the second century.[65] In general, Montanism should be viewed as a renewal movement within the second-century church; more specifically it was a millenarian movement similar to the many millenarian movements in early Judaism including that of Jesus himself.[66] The rise of Montanism was probably encouraged by an oppressive political environment which characterized the principate of Marcus Aurelius.[67] Their acceptance of the value of martyrdom and emphasis on a rigorous ethical position tended to place distance between them and non-Montanist Christians.

Neither Montanus nor his immediate followers appears to have written any treatises, or if they did, none have survived.[68] A number of Montanist oracles, however, have survived in quotations made by various early Christian writers.[69] In one of the most recent collections and assessments of these oracles K. Aland has listed sixteen oracles which he regards as authentic.[70] We shall quote each of these and follow them with a brief analysis.

1. (Montanus says:) "I am [*egō eimi*] the Father and I am [*egō eimi*] the Son and I am [*egō*] the Paraclete."

   Or, "I am [*egō eimi*] the Father and the Son and the Spirit."

   Or, "I am [*egō eimi*] the Father and the Son and the Holy Spirit."

2. (Montanus said:) "I am [*egō eimi*] the Father, and the Son, and the Paraclete."

3. (Montanus says:) "I the Lord, the Almighty God, remain among men."

4. (Montanus says:) "Neither angel, nor ambassador, but I, the Lord God the Father, have come [*ēlthon*]."

5. (Montanus said:) "Behold [*idou*], man is like a lyre,
       and I rush thereon like a plectrum.
       Man sleeps and I awake.
       Behold [*idou*], the Lord is he who arouses the
          hearts of men,
       and gives a heart to men."

6. (Montanus says in his so-called prophecy:)

       Why do you call the more excellent man saved?
       For the righteous man shall shine a hundred times more
          than the sun,
       but the little ones who are saved among you will shine
          a hundred times more than the moon.

7. (The Paraclete in the new prophets says:)

       The Church can forgive sins, but I will not do it,
       lest they sin again.

8. (The Spirit says:)

       You will be publicly displayed; that is good for you,
       for whoever is not publicly displayed before men
          will be publicly displayed before God.
       Let it not perplex you!
       Righteousness brings you into the midst.
       What perplexes you about winning glory?
       Opportunity is given, when you are seen by men.

9. (The Spirit speaks:)

       Desire not to die in bed,
       nor in the delivery of children,
       nor by enervating fevers,
       but in martyrdom,
       that He may be glorified who has suffered for you.

10. (The Paraclete says through the prophetess Prisca:)

They are flesh and they hate flesh.

11. (The holy prophetess Prisca proclaims:)

A holy minister must understand how to minister holiness.
For if the heart gives purification, they will also see visions.
and if they lower their faces, then they will perceive
    saving voices,
as clear as they were obscure (occultas).

12. (Quintilla or Priscilla says:)

In the form of a woman arrayed in shining garments,
came [elthe] Christ to me and set wisdom upon me
and revealed [apekalypse] to me that this place is holy
and that Jerusalem will come down hither from heaven.

13. (Maximilla says:)

After me there will be no longer a prophet,
but the consummation [synteleia].

14. (Maximilla says:)

Listen not to me, but listen to Christ.

15. (Maximilla says:)

The Lord has sent me [apesteile me]
as adherent, preacher and interpreter
of this covenant and this promise;
he has compelled me, willingly or unwillingly,
to learn the knowledge of God.

16. (The Spirit says through Maximilla:)

I am chased like a wolf from the sheep;
I am not a wolf;
I am word and spirit and power.

The first four oracles (and possibly the fifth) are remarkable in that either God the Father or the Trinity appears to be speaking through Montanus. Here Montanus is neither claiming that he is the Father and the Son and the Paraclete nor that all three divine persons constitute an undifferentiated unity.[71] Through the first four oracles Montanus is claiming that God is speaking through him. In form and content these oracles conform to the type which we have designated oracles of self-commendation, i.e. oracles whose function it is to legitimate the prophetic spokesman as a reliable source of divine revelation.[72] While it is likely that these oracles of self-commendation prefaced and legitimated a longer prophetic speech, the ecclesiastical authors have preserved only these fragments. These oracles are unusual in that inspired speech is rarely attributed to God in early Christianity; there are at least two instances of this phenomenon in the Apocalypse (1:8; 21:5-8) and one possible instance in Ignatius (Philad. 7:1). Most often the divine spokesman whose words are mediated by Maximilla and Prisca is the Spirit or Paraclete (nos. 7-10, 16). Yet some oracles are clearly uttered in the person of the prophet (nos. 11-15). Oracles 8 and 9 are parenetic and exhort believers to desire to suffer and even die for their faith voluntarily. Tertullian refers to these oracles as "oracles of the Spirit" (*sermones Spiritus*) and "divine exhortations" (*divinae exhortationes*) in *De Fug.* 9.4; 10.1. In oracle 12 Priscilla relates a vision experience in which Christ revealed to her that Pepuza was to be the site of the New Jerusalem, an important and highly original feature of Montanist eschatology. Oracle 13 is perhaps the only genuine oracle which reflects an imminent eschatological perspective; Maximilla in effect claims for herself the status of an eschatological prophet. Oracle 14 constitutes what we have earlier designated as the proclamation formula, and one suspects that it originally prefaced a prophetic speech of unknown length. Oracle 15 is, as we have noted earlier,[73] a prophetic commission which Maximilla apparently referred to as a means of legitimating her status as a prophetess. The final genuine oracle, no. 16, apparently reflects the rejection which Maximilla had experienced by other Christians who regarded her, in the words of Matt. 7:15, as a wolf in sheep's clothing.

The fragmentary nature of these oracles provides only the most tentative glimpse into the prophetic activity of the Montanist prophets, the true nature of which can probably never be understood. One early Montanist, Theodotus, was apparently accustomed to experiencing ascents to heaven while in a state of trance (Eusebius *Hist. eccl.* v.16.14-15); the Anonymous further claimed in the same passage that a spirit of deceit hurled Theodotus down to earth, where he died from the fall.

12 | THE BASIC FEATURES OF EARLY CHRISTIAN PROPHETIC SPEECH

I. INTRODUCTION

In our discussion of the fragments of early Christian prophetic speech in the NT (Chapter 10) we analyzed some fifty-nine texts (counting the seven prophetic proclamations in Rev. 2-3 separately) which have some claim on formal grounds to be considered oracular. Similarly, in Chapter 11, we identified and analyzed forty-eight texts (counting the sixteen Montanist oracles separately) from early Christian post-canonical literature.[1] In our discussions of each of these 107 texts we endeavored to pay close attention to matters of form, structure, style, setting, and function, and to understand these various features in relationship to prophetic traditions of ancient Israel and early Judaism on the one hand, and Greco-Roman paganism on the other. The purpose of this final chapter is to synthesize these many discrete analyses and to attempt to present as coherent a description of early Christian prophetic speech as possible, given the fragmentary state of the evidence.

One of the more surprising results of our investigation was the relatively large number of texts, or fragments of texts, which appeared to qualify on formal grounds for consideration as possible examples of early Christian prophetic speech. While not all these fragments are legitimate, they were identified on formal rather than critical grounds. The criteria which we used to identify potential oracles of Christian prophets included the following: (1) If a saying or speech is attributed to a supernatural being (i.e. God, Jesus, the Spirit, an angel, Satan, a demon, etc.), it may be an example of prophetic speech. (2) If a saying or speech consists of a prediction of the future course of events, or involves special knowledge, it is again possible that we are dealing with a fragment of prophetic speech. (3) If a saying or speech is introduced or concluded (or otherwise punctuated) by a formula or formulas which in other contexts appear to be used to introduce prophetic speech, it is possible that oracular material is present. (4) If reference is made in the context of a particular saying or speech to the inspiration of the speaker, the pronouncement may have a prophetic origin. (5) If a saying or speech which has some claims to being regarded as oracular (on the basis of the first four criteria) does not rest comfortably in its present literary setting, the saying or speech may be prophetic. If individual texts can be identified as possibly oracular on the basis of several of the above criteria, there is increasing probability that we have before us a fragment of early Christian prophetic speech.

II. LITERARY ORACLES

One of the major problems in identifying and analyzing early Christian prophetic speech is determining the extent to which they are wholly or partially literary productions. If an ancient author chose to include authentic oracular material in a literary text, there appear to be four major ways in which he could do so. First, he could remove all formal features which indicate an oracular origin in adapting an oracular text for use in literary settings so that its oracular character is no longer obvious and can no longer be detected with any certainty. Second, an author could insert an oracle (in whole or in part) directly into an appropriate literary setting without making any substantial modifications. If he does this, it is apparent that he wants to capitalize on the divine and authoritative character of the oracle. Third, an author can insert an oracle (in whole or in part) directly into a literary setting by making certain editorial modifications so that the prophetic material will fit in more smoothly and appropriately with the genre and style of the literary work into which it is set. These modifications can be placed anywhere on a continuum from minor to major surgery, depending on the purpose of the author. Fourth, an oracle or prophetic speech can be created out of whole cloth by an author for inclusion in a literary setting. Here there are two further possibilities: he can model his oracular material after popular conceptions of oracular speech, or he can follow stereotyped literary traditions describing the behavior of prophets and the style and content of their utterances. In short, it is possible that despite the spurious character of strictly "literary" oracles, they may exhibit stereotypical features of authentic oracles and oracular traditions.

Within the NT twenty-two oracles are found in the narrative settings of the gospels and Acts. Of these twenty-two, we have judged eight to be authentic. In ancient narrative, both in Israelite-early Jewish and Greco-Roman literary traditions, oracles and prophetic speeches frequently punctuate the plot and are used as exciting forces to move the action along. It is thus to be expected that oracles and prophetic sayings or speeches will be used in the gospels and Acts as important devices for moving the plot toward the desired goal. Each of the ten oracles in the gospels, for example (with one exception, Mark 5:7 and par.),[2] exhibits the form and content of the legitimation oracle. The reason, of course, lies in the fact that the focal concern of the gospels is the identification and legitimation of Jesus of Nazareth. Legitimation oracles, therefore, are appropriately attributed to the heavenly voice (i.e. God) at the baptism of Jesus (Mark 1:11 and par.) and on the occasion of his transfiguration (Mark 9:7 and par.). The way in which Matthew and Luke have introduced variations into the Markan exemplar suggests that all worked consciously within the framework of a well-known and easily recognizable pattern of prophetic speech. Similarly, the originally nonoracular form of the confession of Peter (Mark 8:29) has been adapted by Matthew (16:16-17) into an oracular form through the suggestion that Peter speaks by divine revelation, not from his own human knowledge. In the Fourth Gospel John the Baptist plays the role of a prophet sent by God (John 1:6-8) who points to Jesus as the Lamb of God in language whose royal and messianic overtones would have been unmistakable to the Johannine community (John 1:29, 36). Further, Mark uses the witness of a demon-possessed man to express the fact that Jesus is "the Son of God" (Mark 3:11; cf. Luke 4:41).

All of this oracular material appears to have entered into the Jesus tradition and received embellishment at various stages in the preliterary, and especially in the literary, history of that tradition. These literary oracles, however, are functionally and formally similar to the prophetic utterance "Jesus is Lord" (1 Cor. 12:3), apparently pronounced in the setting of cultic worship by those believed to be inspired by the Spirit. The central significance of the literary oracles of the gospels, of course, is to legitimate the royal status of Jesus by using a style which resonated with the ancient belief in the divine selection of kings by the gods.[3] Oracular legitimation of a ruler is particularly important when the succession is contested or when a usurper has taken over the reins of power and intends to found a new dynasty. All of the oracles of the gospels that we have briefly discussed above, then, appear to be literary creations modeled after a form of oracle widespread throughout the ancient Mediterranean world.

There are, however, a few legitimation oracles which we have not yet discussed. In the eschatological discourse of Mark, taken over by both Matthew and Luke, those who are identified as "false prophets" and "false Christs" are presented as proclaiming "Look, here is the Christ," or, "Look, there he is!" (Mark 13:21-22 and par.). In the same context another form of the legitimation oracle is used by those who come, under false pretenses, in the name of Jesus and say "I am he," or, "I am the Christ" (Mark 13:6 and par.). Rather than being purely literary creations, these brief oracular pronouncements appear to be caricatures of the kind of prophetic activity which the early Christian church experienced in its contacts with the Jewish liberation movement in Palestine before A.D. 70.

Twelve fragments of oracular speech from the Acts of the Apostles have also been discussed in some detail. Just as demons were given cameo roles in the Gospel of Mark, so they also make brief, but literarily significant, appearances in Acts. In two passages in particular, Acts 16:17 and 19:15, the author has parodied common oracular forms. In Acts 16:17 we are told that a slave girl pestered Paul and his friends by frequently proclaiming: "These men are servants of the Most High God, who proclaim to you the way of salvation." The form of this oracle is thoroughly Hellenistic and one form of the legitimation oracle. Similarly, in a parody of oracular speech in Acts 19:15, which we have labeled a "persona non grata" oracle, the evil spirit in a demoniac addressed the seven Jewish exorcists with the two-part pronouncement: "Jesus I know and Paul I know, but who are you?" Both these oracles are obviously literary creations, but they accurately reflect particular types of oracular forms which circulated in the ancient world, and they testify as well to the care and technical artistry of the author.

Within both Israelite-Jewish and Greco-Roman literary traditions it appears that rather distinct images of inspired speakers and prophetic speech became concretized into specific literary *topoi*.[4] The author of Luke-Acts demonstrates his literary virtuosity by drawing on both eastern and western literary traditions in which such *topoi* are used. The clearest example is found in Acts 7:55-56, where the author, at the conclusion of Stephen's speech, inserts a visionary announcement of judgment. This form consists of three elements: (1) a description of the inspired state of the speaker (Stephen), (2) the use of the present tense of a verb meaning "see," followed by (3) a narration of the vision, presented as a preliminary experience of a future event. There are many examples of this literary form in Philo, Pseudo-Philo's *Liber Antiquitatum Biblicarum,* Greek epic and dramatic literature, and the Acts of the Christian martyrs.[5] Although this form is found only once in Luke-Acts (and nowhere else in the NT), it is related to the author's concern to show that the life of Jesus and the experience of the earliest Christians were constantly guided and legitimated by God, who spoke through inspired persons, visions, and dreams. The author frequently designates one who is about to speak as "filled with the Holy Spirit" (Luke 1:15, 41, 67; 4:1; Acts 2:4;

4:8, 31; 6:3, 5, 8; 7:55; 9:17; 11:24; 13:9), thereby demonstrating his strong literary interest in this motif. Similar to the concluding section of the speech of Stephen discussed above is the announcement of judgment described in Acts 13:9-11. Beginning with a description of the inspired state of the speaker (Paul), it continues with a two-part oracle consisting of an accusation and threat. Although this literary prophecy is modeled after similar prophetic speeches in the OT, it nevertheless draws upon a literary tradition in which it is appropriate and important to focus attention on the inspired state of the speaker (cf. Acts 4:8, 31).

Another very literary type of prophetic speech in Acts is embedded in the lengthy farewell speech of Paul to the Ephesian elders (Acts 20:18-38), in which a prediction is made, introduced by the phrase "I know" in vv. 29-30. Since the entire literary form is that of the farewell speech, in which a predictive element is nearly always present, the literary character of vv. 29-30, is assured. Nevertheless, the use of the phrase "I know," with its parallels in each of the seven proclamations in Rev. 2-3, suggests that the author has been influenced by actual prophetic style. Similarly, Luke's characterization of the prophetic activities of Agabus in Acts 11:28 and 21:11 appears to exhibit a primarily literary character. But in the case of Acts 11:28, where Luke has both removed the eschatological features from what appears to be an originally eschatological oracle and provided it with a historical interpretation, we are almost certainly in possession of an authentic oracle. Acts 21:11 is more complicated. First, the almost total absence of prophetic actions on the part of NT prophets suggests that the scene has been modeled consciously on OT exemplars. Second, the introductory prophetic formula used by Agabus ("thus says the Holy Spirit") is so close to the familiar OT messenger formula found in the LXX ("thus says the Lord") that it may have been consciously composed with that formula in mind. Third, there is the structural correspondence between the predictions of Paul's imprisonment in Acts with those of Jesus' fate in Luke. In spite of these arguments for the literary origin of the oracle of Agabus in Acts 21:11, there appears to be a historical basis for it.[6]

In the gospels and Acts, therefore, most of the instances of oracular or prophetic speech have a literary origin and were modeled after stereotypical popular conceptions of oracular speech or were based on traditional literary *topoi*. While the formulas, forms, and structures of prophetic speech in the narrative portions of the NT may exhibit some of the stereotypical features of prophetic speech, they themselves do not constitute legitimate examples of such speech. With a few exceptions (e.g. Mark 13:6, 21 and par.; Acts 11:28; 18:9; 21:11; 23:11; 27:23-24), the twenty-two "fragments" of early Christian prophetic speech are not fragments at all, but literary compositions. However, once we shift our attention to the thirty-seven prophetic fragments in the rest of the NT and the forty-eight fragments from early postcanonical literature, the situation changes dramatically. With some exceptions (i.e. Rev. 18:21-24; 22:6-7; 22:16; 22:18-20; Hermas *Sim.* ix.33.1) these texts appear to be predominantly genuine, even though they have often been drastically modified to fit their present literary contexts. In the remainder of this chapter, then, we shall discuss the basic forms of early Christian prophetic speech, then the more complex forms, followed by the stylistics of early Christian prophecy.

III. BASIC FORMS OF CHRISTIAN PROPHETIC SPEECH

The relatively few extant examples of authentic fragments of early Christian prophetic speech make it virtually impossible to synthesize the material either diachronically or regionally. The present discussion, therefore, is essentially a synchronic description of Christian prophecies. Despite the methodological difficulties involved, the absence of a viable alternative makes a synchronic phenomenological description of the morphology of Christian prophetic speech necessary. We shall first describe six types of prophetic speech, each of which can occur alone or in combination with others into larger and more complex units. These six basic forms include: (1) oracles of assurance, (2) prescriptive oracles, (3) announcements of salvation, (4) announcements of judgment, (5) legitimation oracles, and (6) eschatological theophany oracles.

A. ORACLES OF ASSURANCE

Oracles of assurance are a relatively stable form of revelatory speech that occurs frequently in Israelite-Jewish tradition and also in Near Eastern and Greco-Roman revelatory traditions.[7] Oracles of assurance usually exhibit a three-part structure consisting of (1) an introductory formula, followed by (2) an admonition introduced by such stereotypical phrases as "fear not" or "have courage," and then (3) a promise which constitutes the reason for the admonition, usually introduced by such inferential or causal particles as "for" or "because." There are four oracles of assurance among the 107 texts we have analyzed: three in Acts (18:9; 23:11; 27:23-24) and one in Paul (2 Cor. 12:9). In addition to sharing the three-part structure typical of oracles of assurance, they also share two additional features: they are presented in the form of dream or vision reports, and they are presented as the first-person speech of a supernatural being. The form of this type of oracular speech is so stable that it is virtually impossible to distinguish purely literary productions from authentic oracles experienced and narrated in terms of fixed, socially determined perceptions and structures. The distinctive form of the oracle of assurance in 2 Cor. 12:9, however, argues in favor of its authenticity. Later we shall consider how such oracles of assurance can be used in more complex types of prophetic speech, i.e. the parenetic oracle of assurance (Hermas *Mand.* xii.4.5-7; xii.6.1-3).

B. PRESCRIPTIVE ORACLES

Prescriptive oracles are a type of prophetic speech in which the supernatural speaker enjoins a particular type of action or behavior. Among the 107 fragments of prophetic speech which we have isolated, fifteen examples of this type of oracle are found (Gal. 5:21; Acts 13:2; 21:4; 2 Thess. 3:6, 10, 12; 1 Thess. 4:2-6). In early Christianity most of the examples of the prescriptive oracle concern ethical issues and on that basis might be more appropriately designated parenetic oracles. In form they use either the imperative or hortatory subjunctive on the one hand, or conditional and participial constructions on the other. Particularly in their parenetic form, prescriptive oracles are often part of more complex types of prophetic speech (see below). Six prescriptive oracles are quoted in serial form by Ignatius (Philad. 7:1-2):

> Give heed to the bishop, and to the presbytery and deacons. . . .
> Do nothing without the bishop,
> Keep your flesh as the temple of God,
> Love unity,
> Flee from divisions,
> Be imitators of Jesus Christ, as was he also of his Father.

While these oracles all exhibit a parenetic character, an oracle which enjoins action rather than moral behavior is found in Acts 13:2: "The Holy Spirit said, 'Set apart for me Barnabas and Saul for the work to which I have called them.'" Similarly, Acts 21:4 reports that the disciples at Tyre told Paul, through the Spirit, not to go to Jerusalem.

Early Christian literature exhibits a strong emphasis on ethical exhortation, often expressed in the form of ethical catalogues (virtue and vice lists), station codes (*Haustafeln*), the "Two Ways" teaching, and other eclectic and apparently loosely arranged structures.[8] Parenesis is found in both Greek and Jewish literature, and current opinion favors the Hellenistic synagogue as the mediating institution. Parenesis, or ethical exhortation, appears to have been a focal concern in early Christian preaching, though no authentic examples of such sermons have been preserved.[9] A great many patterns and features of Christian homilies are nevertheless evident in various sections of the gospels, Acts, and the letters of the NT, as well as in many of the documents that make up the Apostolic Fathers.[10] The content of the ethical exhortations often has a self-authenticating character insofar as it is accepted by all as common knowledge, even though there are occasional deviations.

In considering *oracular* parenesis, however, a new element is introduced. First, while the general or universal character of oracular parenesis is still evident, it appears that their application to the specific circumstances in which the addressees find themselves is virtually assured. That is the case, not only with oracular parenesis which exists independently of larger and more complex forms of prophetic speech, but also in the case of those more complex forms themselves. Second, the appeal to divine authority for prescriptive injunctions of an ethical nature suggests a situation of conflict in which the inspired speaker (or the author who makes use of such oracular material) cannot assume that his audience fully shares his convictions. The claims of divine inspiration and the optional inclusion of divinely sanctioned threats serve as means of convincing the audience of the wisdom of obedience. Third, the oracular parenesis exhibited in some types of early Christian prophetic speech presupposes a relationship between man and God that mirrors the oriental and Hellenistic-Roman authority structure of king-subject and emperor-citizen in which master-slave imagery is appropriate. Most of the Greek oracles which prescribe certain actions or behaviors are oracular *responses*. The master-slave relationship, therefore, is not presupposed in Greek oracles prior to the Hellenistic-Roman period,[11] though it does become more common in the postclassical period with the arrival of oriental religions within the framework of autocratic rule.[12] Finally, the sources suggest that the literary tendency to serialize oracular parenesis (e.g. Ignatius Philad. 7:2; 2 Thess. 3:6-10) may reflect an original *Sitz im Leben* in which several oracles of a similar type are uttered one after the other.[13]

C. ANNOUNCEMENTS OF SALVATION

The announcement of salvation is a prophetic speech form found occasionally in the OT,[14] though it occurs more frequently in Israelite-Jewish tradition as part of a more complex speech form which we have designated the "salvation-judgment oracle."[15] Further, although the announcement of salvation itself does not occur in Greco-Roman sources very often, oracles which juxtapose a period of judgment with an epoch of ultimate salvation do occur with some frequency in the Hellenistic and Roman periods.[16] The oracle of assurance, discussed above, is essentially an announcement of salvation which exhibits such a distinctive and stable structure that it deserves description in its own right. Further, there is another distinctive form of the announcement of salvation which we shall discuss below under the rubric "eschatological theophany oracles." In early Christian prophetic utterance, as in late Israelite, early Jewish, and Hellenistic-Roman traditions, the promise of salvation is found much more frequently within the framework of a larger and more complex form of prophetic speech that we describe below under the designation "parenetic salvation-judgment oracles." Among the 107 fragments of early Christian prophetic speech which we have identified, only three can be designated as announcements of salvation: Rev. 14:13 (a text which really consists of two oracles joined together); 19:9; 22:7. All are found in the Apocalypse of John, and all are in the form of a beatitude.

D. ANNOUNCEMENTS OF JUDGMENT

The announcement of judgment, the most common form of prophetic speech in the OT, is exceedingly rare in early Christianity. In early Christian prophetic traditions the threat of judgment is usually conditional, and usually occurs in conjunction with conditional promises of salvation. Acts 13:9-11 and Rev. 18:21-24, which conform most closely to OT models of the announcement of judgment, are clearly literary creations fashioned by their respective authors expressly for their present literary settings. One example of the announcement of judgment in the NT, however, is 1 Cor. 14:37-38, which culminates in a threat expressed within the framework of a conditional clause: "If any one does not recognize this, he is not recognized." The curse which Paul prefixed to his letter to the Galatians (1:8-9) and the speeches of Peter to Ananias and Sapphira (Acts 5:1-11) appear very similar to OT pronouncements of judgment; yet on formal grounds we have not designated them as possible examples of prophetic speech.

One very particular form of the announcement of judgment is the summons to flight, found in the difficult oracle preserved in Eusebius (and par.), to the effect that Christians should flee Jerusalem in view of its imminent destruction. Yet the very fact that a select group is allowed to escape a local form of judgment means that the summons to flight functions as both an oracle of salvation and an oracle of judgment. This type of oracle is parodied in the speech of John the Baptist (Matt. 3:7-10; Luke 3:7-9) that begins, "You brood of vipers! Who warned you to flee from the wrath to come?" The summons to flight also occurs in the eschatological discourse of Jesus (Mark 13:14-18) and in an angelic warning to Joseph by dream in the birth narrative of the Gospel of Matthew (2:13).

E. LEGITIMATION ORACLES

There are two types of legitimation oracle in early Christian literature, the recognition oracle (which is used to identify and hence to give divine "legitimation" to a special person, usually introduced with the stereotyped phrase "this is") and the oracle of self-commendation (used by the speaker to identify himself and hence to "legitimate" himself as a divine spokesperson, usually introduced with the phrase "I am"). We have already had occasion to mention the frequency with which the first type of oracle occurs in the narrative portions of the NT. Although many of these oracles owe their formulation to the demands of narrative, some evidence suggests that even the purely literary products were modeled after ancient conceptions of legitimation oracles, and that oracles exhibiting such patterns were an authentic part of early Christian prophetic speech. One authentic example of such a legitimation oracle is found in 1 Cor. 12:3, and another example is found in Mark 13:21-22 (and par.), where "false Christs" and "false prophets" say such things as "Look, here is the Christ!" or "Look, there he is!" Here, however, the reference is doubtless to the typical pronouncements of Jewish prophets connected with the Palestinian Jewish liberation movement during the first century A.D.[17]

More common in early Christian sources is the oracle of self-commendation, which usually begins with the "I am" formula followed by various predications. Its shortest form is epitomized by Mark 13:6 (and par.): "Many will come in my name, saying, 'I am he!' " In the NT the literary adaptation of the "I am" revelatory speech is most fully developed in the Fourth Gospel.[18] In extracanonical early Christian literature this type of revelatory speech emanates from varieties of Christianity that deviate from the norms and practices of the Great Church. The "I am" oracles in early Christian sources usually occur in relation to larger and more complex oracular forms, for which they form either the introduction or conclusion. Nevertheless, there are at least six instances in which a brief oracle of self-commendation appears to have originally stood alone: Rev. 1:8; 1:17; Montanist oracles 1, 2, 3, 4. Let us briefly review the major features of Rev. 1:8, where we read:

"I am the Alpha and the Omega," says the Lord God,
Who is and who was and who is to come, the Almighty.

The function of this brief oracle can be understood better in conjunction with Rev. 1:17-20:

Fear not, I am the first and the last, and the living one;
I died, and behold I am alive for evermore,
and I have the keys of Death and Hades.
Now write what you see, what is and what is to take place hereafter.
As for the mystery of the seven stars. . . .

It is obvious that the function of a legitimation oracle which commends the speaker is to mobilize the acceptance of the authority and prestige of the speaker by appealing to his role as spokesperson for a divinity. Of course, such an oracle of self-commendation may be used as only one part of a more complex prophetic speech, as indeed it is in several parenetic salvation-judgment oracles in the Shepherd of Hermas (Sim. vi.1.4; ix.23.5; ix.24.4; ix.31.3; ix.33.1; Mand. xii.6.1). A similar feature found in the OT is the self-disclosure oracle (Erweiswort), which is appended to oracles and is characteristically phrased: "You/they shall know that I am Yahweh." In a fragmentary Christian oracle embedded in Rev. 2:21-23 we find a similar conclusion: "And all the churches shall know that I am he."

In considering Greco-Roman oracular forms we observed that oracular dialogues often began with an "I am" self-presentation formula in response to an explicit or implicit "Who are you?"[19] This convention is widespread enough in Greco-Roman sources to suggest a function for Rev. 1:8 and 1:17ff. in the Apocalypse as a whole. In Rev. 1:8 the "I am" formula is intimately connected with the phrase "the Lord God, who is and who was and who is to come," i.e. God is the Lord of prophetic knowledge.[20] A similar reference to "what is and what is to take place hereafter" (i.e. prophecy) is connected with the "I am" formula in Rev. 1:17ff. Placed at the beginning of the Apocalypse, these legitimation formulas serve to identify and emphasize the divine source behind John's inspired message. Further, the first speaker (Rev. 1:8) is God himself (in the Apocalypse, God speaks only here and in Rev. 21:5-8), whose modes of existence and relationship to the world of man (is, was, is to come) define the basic character, origin, and possibility of prophecy. The second speaker is Jesus, who is the central mediator and agent of the prophetic message (1:17ff.). Significantly, the legitimation formula in 1:17 is followed by a commission formula in 1:18, thus providing divine validation for John's prophetic book.

F. ESCHATOLOGICAL THEOPHANY ORACLES

This type stands out as one of the more distinctive forms of early Christian prophetic speech. These oracles all emphasize specific aspects of eschatological salvation regarded as the immediate consequence of the "coming" of Jesus, i.e. the "presence" of God in its final and most complete form. Eight oracles in early Christian sources exhibit this "eschatological theophany" pattern: Rom. 11:25-26; 1 Cor. 15:51-52; 1 Thess. 4:16-17; Rev. 16:15; 21:3-4; 21:6-8; 22:12-15; Odes Sol. 7:16b-20. These oracles all consist of two main parts, the first of which usually centers on the experience of an eschatological theophany (only in Rom. 11:25-26 and 1 Cor. 15:51-52 is this order reversed), while the second focuses on the effects of that salvific theophany upon human experience, particularly upon the experience of the elect.

Further, all these oracles (with the exception of Rom. 11:25-26) are preserved in a distinctive poetic form. Three of the oracles consist of two strophes of three lines each (1 Cor. 15:51-52; 1 Thess. 4:16-17; Rev. 21:6-8), though the last oracle contains a third section, a prose description of the fate of the unrighteous. Rev. 21:3-4 has two strophes of four lines each, while Rev. 22:12-15 has three strophes of three lines each followed by a more prosaic section describing the fate of the wicked (similar to 21:6-8). Rev. 16:15 consists of four lines, the first of which describes the anticipated theophany, while the next three focus on the results. In Odes Sol. 7:16b-20, though it is not justifiable to divide this passage into strophes, it is clear that the first eight lines exhibit an internal unity in that they describe the praise which shall meet the Lord upon his arrival, while the last four lines describe the consequences of that arrival in terms of the elimination of hatred and jealousy from the earth. Throughout the Odes various modes of experiencing the final presence of God are paired with the elimination of the negative aspects of mortality: sickness, ignorance, weakness, persecution.[21] Unlike the other forms which we have discussed above, eschatological theophany oracles are never found as substructures within larger and more complex types of prophetic speech.

IV. COMPLEX FORMS OF PROPHETIC SPEECH

The several types of early Christian prophetic speech which we have just discussed not only occur alone, but are combined in various ways to form more complex prophetic utterances. While there are some phenomenological similarities between these complex forms of prophetic speech and prophetic traditions in the OT and early Judaism, there are more differences than similarities. The manner in which various types of basic prophetic speech are combined to form larger units appears neither stereotypical nor predictable. I suspect that even if we were in possession of more samples of early Christian prophetic speech than we now possess, no firm patterns would emerge. It appears that early Christian prophetic speech, particularly in its more complex forms, used optional elements and optional arrangements. The major types of complex prophetic speech in early Christianity are three: (1) parenetic salvation-judgment announcements, (2) parenetic oracles of assurance, and (3) amplified oracles.

A. PARENETIC SALVATION-JUDGMENT ORACLES

Among the 107 fragments of early Christian prophetic speech which we have analyzed, there are nineteen examples of parenetic salvation-judgment oracles: the seven proclamations in Rev. 2-3; Rev. 13:9-10; 22:18-20; Hermas *Vis.* ii.2.6-8; ii.3.4; iii.8.11 — 9.10; iv.2.5-6; *Sim.* vi.1.4; ix.23.5; ix.24.4; ix.28.5-8; ix.31.3-5; ix.33.1. The number of examples suggests that this type of prophetic speech is the most common complex genre of prophetic utterance in early Christianity. Yet we must beware of generalizing from fragmentary data, and of assuming that all these texts exhibit a rigidly stereotypical and comparable structure. In spite of the many examples, only two sources are involved, and both are apocalypses.

We have designated these prophetic speeches as "parenetic salvation-judgment announcements" because all of them exhibit a strong emphasis on moral and behavioral exhortation. Proper behavior is encouraged by admonitions and conditional promises, and misbehavior is discouraged by accusations and conditional threats. The formulators of these prophetic speeches regarded themselves as members of the groups or communities to whom they directed their messages. That a recommended course of action or behavior is sanctioned by promises of salvation and threats of judgment within the framework of a divinely inspired speech suggests that the behavior in view is not one which everyone addressed either agrees to or practices, and that no suitable authority structure exists upon which to base a more rational appeal. Both the author of the Apocalypse and the author of the Shepherd of Hermas regarded themselves as confronted with a crisis: for John it was the problem of Christian conformity and compromise in a pagan environment, and for Hermas it was moral laxity which must now cease upon a second and final opportunity to repent. The homiletic and hortatory character of these prophetic speeches makes them essentially indistinguishable from more rational forms of early Christian discourse.

B. PARENETIC ORACLES OF ASSURANCE

The oracle of assurance is, as we have noted earlier, one of the more stable forms of prophetic speech in the ancient world. In early Christian sources it is always presented as the direct speech of a supernatural being, usually through the medium of a dream or vision and in a situation in which the recipient lacks comfort, encouragement, or assurance. In two instances in early Christian sources the characteristic form of the oracle of assurance is used along with more conventional kinds of ethical exhortation or parenesis (Hermas *Mand.* xii.4.5-7 and xii.6.1-3). While two examples cannot constitute a separate "type," or even be regarded as a significant development within early Christian prophecy, they are of interest in that they exhibit the tendency to combine various simpler elements into new and more complex units. In *Mand.* xii.4.5-7 two exhortations in the imperative are followed by two connected oracles of assurance. In *Mand.* xii.6.1-3 two oracles of assurance bracket a section which consists of an exhortation to believe God, followed by a promise conditional upon that belief. In both oracle complexes that which is not to be feared is the devil, and the speaker is explicitly the angel of repentance. The path of belief and behavior demanded of the angel is opposed by the devil, so that the basic pattern exhibited in both oracles is that of the "Two Ways."

C. AMPLIFIED ORACLES

All the oracles and fragments of oracles which we have identified and isolated from early Christian literature have been preserved only because they were thought useful for various literary purposes by some early Christian authors. If genuine oracles were left relatively intact, they exhibit those formal features which marked them out and identified them to ancient readers as oracular. These oracles have been put into three kinds of literary settings: narratives (the gospels, Acts), essays (letters and homilies), and vision reports (the Apocalypse of John and the Shepherd of Hermas). In conventional narrative discourse, oracles were created for the situation and are relatively clear, comprehensible elements in the plot. In the other two forms of discourse, however, where genuine oracles are most often to be found, they are often amplified in a number of ways. Occasionally the tendency to amplify an oracle takes the form of an interpretation of the real meaning of the oracle (Acts 11:28; 1 Thess. 3:4; cf. John 11:49-52). In Greco-Roman literature a widely used form of anecdote is the oracle story, in which an oracle is fulfilled in a totally unexpected manner.

One distinctive form of amplifying oracles in early Christianity appears to have been the prophetic interpretation of earlier oracles; the interpretation is then quoted along with the original oracle. Several examples of this type of complex oracle occur in the Apocalypse of John (1:7-8; 13:9; 14:13; 16:15; 19:9; 21:5-8; 22:12-15; 22:18-20). Let us examine Rev. 14:13 more closely in this connection:

> And I heard a voice from heaven saying, "Write this: 'Blessed are the dead who die in the Lord henceforth.' " "Yes," says the Spirit, "They shall rest from their labors, for their works follow after them." (author's trans.)

This short oracle actually consists of two oracles, one uttered by a heavenly voice, the other by the Spirit. The second oracle, furthermore, is both a responsory affirmation of the first oracle and an amplification or interpretative expansion of it. Although this combination of elements may be preliterary, there is no way of demonstrating that possibility with any confidence. An explanation for this phenomenon has been suggested by H. Kraft. In commenting on Rev. 1:7-8 Kraft suggested that some of the dialogues and responses in the Apocalypse should be understood as sequences of inspired speech that, as in Christian worship, were followed by inspired speeches of individuals.[22] Although Kraft uses this explanation far too broadly, it does appear that each of the oracles from the Apocalypse mentioned above exhibits a composite character that may best be explained by appealing to this hypothesis. Paul mentions the fact that a prophetic utterance could receive a responsory "amen" (1 Cor. 14:16), and 1 Cor. 14:29 suggests that the process of prophetic evaluation of previous prophetic utterance in serial fashion occurred within the framework of Christian worship.[23]

V. THE STYLE OF PROPHETIC SPEECH

In view of the great diversity exhibited by the fragments of early Christian prophecy analyzed in Chapters 10 and 11, it is difficult to generalize on the stylistics of Christian prophetic speech. Yet in spite of the wide-ranging diversity a number of features recur again and again. These stylistic features are particularly evident when analogies exist with Israelite-Jewish and Greco-Roman oracular and prophetic traditions.

A. FRAMING DEVICES

The method which we have followed in identifying early Christian prophetic speech insists on the presence of distinctive framing devices which mark off prophetic discourse from other forms of Christian discourse. With no access to the behavior of the speaker (i.e. to the distinctive behaviors associated with possession trance), linguistic markers are all that remain. There are six types of formulas which require discussion, though the term "formula" should not be taken to mean unvarying expressions: (1) messenger formulas, (2) commission formulas, (3) proclamation formulas, (4) legitimation formulas, (5) oath formulas, and (6) the "mystery" formula.

1. Messenger Formulas.

These formulas, widely used in the OT but rare in early Judaism and in the Greco-Roman world, function to alert the hearer to the fact that the message borne by the prophet is not his own, but originates with a supernatural being. Messenger formulas are closely related in function to commission formulas and legitimation formulas. In early Christianity the messenger formula which most closely resembles OT usage (mediated by the LXX) is the phrase "thus says" (*tade legei*), usually followed by an identification of the supernatural speaker. This formula is rare in Greco-Roman sources, though "thus says Zeus" (*tade legei Zeus*) is found in connection with the oracle of Dodona,[24] and "thus says Ammon" (*tade legei Ammōn*) is used at the oracle of Ammon in Libya.[25] In early Christianity this formula is characteristic of the praescriptio of each of the proclamations in Rev. 2-3 (2:1, 8, 12, 18; 3:1, 7, 14), and is found in a form which even more closely parallels OT usage in Acts 21:11 ("thus says the Holy Spirit"). It is important to note that by the first century A.D. *tade* (a demonstrative pronoun declined from *hode*) was largely limited to official formulas, and would therefore convey a very special, ancient, and authoritative significance.[26] This technical use of *tade* is also found in Ignatius Philad. 7:2, where an early Christian messenger formula is clearly preserved: "But the Spirit was proclaiming by speaking thusly [*tade*]. . . ." Yet the total number of fragments of early Christian prophetic speech which use this formula is only nine.

More frequently the divine source of the message is identified and coupled with a verb of saying/speaking, most commonly *legei*. In the introductions to the seven proclamations in Rev. 2-3 the speaker is identified as Jesus, but he is identified only by a series of descriptive phrases (drawn from the inaugural vision of chap. 1) and titles, the most familiar of which is "Son of God" (2:18). These literary introductions are balanced by concluding formulas in which the Spirit is identified as the speaker: "He who has an ear, let him hear what the Spirit says to the churches" (2:7, 11, 17, 29; 3:6, 13, 22). In most instances, however, we are dealing not with formulas but with a variety of expressions all of which function to identify the divine speaker and to emphasize his role as the true author of the prophetic message. The speaker, however, can be Jesus, the Spirit, God, an angel, or even the Trinity.

We have already noted that Jesus is presented as the speaker in formulas which introduce each of the proclamations in Rev. 2-3. Elsewhere the "Lord" (presumably Jesus) is identified as the speaker in oracles of assurance (2 Cor. 12:9; Acts 18:9; 23:11; yet cf. Acts 27:23, where an "angel of God" is the messenger in an oracle of assurance). In 1 Thess. 4:15ff. Paul quotes an oracle using the phrase "by the word of the Lord," presumably referring to Jesus. In 1 Cor. 14:37-38 he claims that what he has written is "a command of the Lord," again presumably referring to Jesus. Further, Paul appears to be preserving oracular material in several instances in which he appeals to the authority of Jesus for his own instructions, using such expressions as "through the Lord Jesus" (1 Thess. 4:2), "in the name of our Lord Jesus Christ" (2 Thess. 3:6), and "in the Lord Jesus Christ" (2 Thess. 3:12). Jesus is implicitly identified as the speaker in the oracles preserved in Rev. 16:15; 22:12-15, 16, 20. We have a total of fifteen oracles where Jesus is identified as the speaker, and four in which he is identified as the source or authority of prophetic speech. If we add to this the nine speeches of Jesus found in the Odes of Solomon, the number of oracles attributed to Jesus totals twenty-eight.

The Spirit is also frequently identified as the source of prophetic speech, as we have seen above in connection with the messenger formulas of Acts 21:11 and Ignatius Philad. 7:2. Yet there is a degree of fluidity in early Christian conceptions of divinity that blurs modern attempts to introduce clarity and logic into ancient Christian texts.[27] For example, even though the exalted Jesus is presented as the speaker in the introductory messenger formulas to each of the seven proclamations in Rev. 2-3, the Spirit is also identified as the speaker in the formulaic conclusion to each speech (2:7, 11, 17, 29; 3:6, 13, 22). In addition to these oracles the Spirit is clearly identified as the speaker in Acts 13:2; 21:11; 1 Tim. 4:1-3; Rev. 14:13; Ignatius Philad. 7:2; Montanist oracles 7, 8, 9, 10, 16; and one version of the oracular command to flee Jersusalem in Epiphanius De mens. et pond. xv. The Spirit is also referred to as the means by which prophetic speech is uttered, using such expressions as "through the Spirit" (Acts 11:28; 21:4), "by the Holy Spirit" (1 Cor. 12:3), "in the Spirit" (Did. 11:12), or speech uttered while the speaker is "full of the Holy Spirit" (Acts 13:9; 7:55-56). Thus the Spirit, like Jesus, can be either the source or means of oracular speech. Here we have a subtle distinction which is nevertheless important for understanding the early Christian view of prophetic speech. If the speaker is a divine being, then the message transmitted by the messenger possesses the divine authority of its originator. But if the speaker is a mortal, then the authority and inspiration of the message can only be guaranteed if the Spirit or another divine entity mediates the message in some effective way. This is an important distinction for, as we shall see below in greater detail, there are two styles of early Christian prophetic speech: that in which a supernatural being speaks in the first person, and that in which the Christian prophet speaks in his own person, though in an inspired state.

God is designated as the speaker only very rarely in early Christian prophetic speech (Rev. 1:8; 21:5-8; Ignatius Philad. 7:1; Montanist oracles 3 and 4; cf. 1 Cor. 14:25). To these we must add Rev. 14:13 as a possibility, which refers only to a "voice from heaven," and Rev. 21:3-4, which refers to the "loud voice from the throne." There is oscillation here as well, for Rev. 19:9 identifies an angel as the one who commands John to write, yet the words are then described as "true words of God." Similarly, Philad. 7:1 refers to God as the authority for Ignatius' prophetic utterance, yet 7:2 attributes prophetic speech to the Spirit.

Angels can also be identified as the supernatural source for oracular utterances, yet in most cases it appears tacitly understood that the angelic messenger is actually a spokesperson for God (clearly the case in Acts 27:3 and Rev. 19:9). A special case is presented by the Shepherd of Hermas, where the angel of repentance is identified as the speaker in several oracles received and transmitted by Hermas (Mand. xii.6.1; Sim. ix.23.5; ix.24.4; ix.31.3; ix.33.1). In the four oracles embedded in the Visions (ii.2.6-8; ii.3.4; iii.8.11 — 9.10; iv.2.5-6), the speaker is identified in the context as the ancient lady (= the church, Vis. ii.4.1), elsewhere identified as the Holy Spirit who is the Son of God (Sim. ix.1.1). On the basis of the evidence presented in Hermas it appears that the angel of repentance should be identified with Christ, the Son of God.[28] If so, then these oracles should be placed with those which attribute prophetic speech to

Jesus. It must be pointed out in addition that outside of *Mand.* xi, inspiration is not mentioned anywhere in Hermas in connection with prophetic speech.

2. Commission Formulas.

In the OT the commission formula, for which the messenger formula is a kind of abbreviation, occurs frequently.[29] In the OT there are several basic patterns for commission formulas: "Say to X, thus says Y," "Go and say to X, thus says Y," and "(Go and) say to X [messenger formula absent]." The commission formula is nearly always used in connection with the delivery of an oral message. One of the rare instances in which a prophet is commissioned to *write* rather than to go and tell is found in Jer. 29:30-31: "Then the word of the Lord came to Jeremiah: 'Send [this message] to all the exiles, saying, "Thus says the Lord. . . ." ' " In contrast to Israelite-Jewish tradition there is a longer and more venerable tradition in the Greco-Roman world in which individuals are, for various reasons, commanded by the gods to write.[30]

Early Christian prophets are only very rarely commissioned to go and tell, while commissions to write are much more frequent. The commission to go and tell, while often implied (Acts 11:27-28; 21:10-11; Rev. 2:21; Hermas *Mand.* xi.9), is made explicitly only in the Shepherd of Hermas (*Vis.* ii.2.6; ii.3.4; iii.8.11; iv.2.5). These references exhibit homogeneity, for in each instance (with the exception of *Vis.* ii.3.4) Hermas is commanded to go and proclaim a message to a particular individual or group, and that commission is accompanied by a brief summary of the message, e.g. *Vis.* ii.2.6:

> You shall say, then, to the leaders of the Church that they reform their ways in righteousness, to receive in full the promises with great glory.

The message itself, addressing the recipients in the second-person plural, follows. These commission clauses, while they resemble OT exemplars in function, nevertheless do not appear to have been modeled after them on the literary level.

In a kind of compromise between the "go and tell" and the "write this" types of commission, we find a commission given to Hermas to write two copies of the revelatory book he had received, one for Clement and one for Grapte (Hermas *Vis.* ii.4.3):

> Therefore you shall make two copies and send one to Clement and one to Grapte. Clement is to send it to the cities abroad, for it is his duty. And Grapte is to exhort the widows and orphans. But in this city you shall read it yourself with the elders who preside over the church. (author's trans.)

Here the book in question is the central medium of revelation, and Hermas, Clement, and Grapte are messengers commissioned to go and read it aloud to the groups mentioned. Since the ancient lady has herself read the heavenly book aloud to Hermas (*Vis.* i.3.3-4), Hermas, Clement, and Grapte are commissioned to recapitulate her procedure.

The most common type of commission formula in early Christian prophecy is the command to write. This commission formula is found in a fixed form repeated in the praescriptio of each of the seven proclamations found in Rev. 2-3: "To the angel of the church in — — — write: 'Thus says. . . .' " A similar commission introduces the double oracle found in Rev. 14:13: "And I heard a voice from heaven saying, 'Write this: . . .' " (cf. Rev. 19:9; 21:5). In addition to these ten instances of a commission formula standing before individual oracles, two uses of the commission formula suggest that the entire composition is written under divine command and for that reason constitutes a prophetic book (Rev. 1:11, 19). This literary commission is not regarded by the author as any less significant than a commission to go and tell, as Rev. 10:11 indicates by implication: "And I was told, 'You must again prophesy about many peoples and nations and tongues and kings.' "

The commission to write also occurs several times in the Shepherd of Hermas, but never in the immediate context of the twelve oracles which we have identified therein. Commands for Hermas to write down the substance of the revelations given to him are found in *Vis.* ii.4.3 and v.5-7. The latter passage is of particular interest, for it concludes the *Visions,* and it is a legitimation of all that precedes:

> First of all write my commandments and the parables; but the rest you shall write as I shall show you. This is the reason," said he, "that I command you to write first the commandments and parables, that you may read them out at once, and be able to keep them." So I wrote the commandments and parables as he commanded me.

> If then you hear and keep them, and walk in them, and do them with a pure heart, you shall receive from the Lord all that he promised you, but if you hear them and do not repent, but continue to add to your sins, you shall receive the contrary from the Lord.

> All these things the shepherd commanded me to write thus, for he was the angel of repentance.

This concluding paragraph consists of three elements: (1) the command to write, so that the revelation may be read aloud before the appropriate groups, (2) two conditional clauses elaborating on the consequences of obeying or disobeying the revelatory message, and (3) a legitimating clause in which the completeness of the written revelation and its supernatural source are indicated.

3. Proclamation Formulas.

Proclamation formulas are essentially injunctions to audiences to pay attention to the message which is about to be, or has been, delivered. Such formulas usually consist of a verb meaning "listen" or "pay attention" in the imperative. The original settings of such formulas are both public speeches, in which the importance of the announcement requires emphasis, and the introductory clauses of prayers. Proclamation formulas are often used in connection with OT prophetic speech,[31] but more rarely in Greco-Roman oracular tradition. Since the latter consists of responses to queries, however, the attention of the recipients can be assumed. The proclamation formulas are often used in the context of early Christian prophetic speech, though in a variety of ways. At the conclusion of each of the seven proclamations in Rev. 2-3 the following stereotyped phrase occurs: "He who has an ear, let him hear what the Spirit says to the churches" (2:7, 11, 17, 29; 3:6, 13, 22). In Rev. 13:9 the same formula is used to introduce an oracle. A different formulation is used in Hermas *Vis.* iii.9.1 (immediately following a commission formula): "Listen to me, children" (repeated in *Vis.* iii.9.2). In *Mand.* xii.6.3 essentially the same proclamation formula is found ("Listen, therefore, to me"), but this time at the conclusion of the prophetic speech. In Odes Sol. 8:8 we find a proclamation formula which introduces a speech of Christ that extends to v. 19: "Hear the word of truth, and receive the knowledge of the Most High." Finally, in Montanist oracle 14 Maximilla is reported to have said, "Listen not to me, but listen to Christ." Christ, of course, has chosen to speak through her, so one had better listen after all.

4. Legitimation Formulas.

Legitimation formulas and clauses function to underscore the truth and authority of the prophetic oracle (as well as the prophet) by identifying the divine speaker, by appealing to the inspired state in which the oracle was uttered, or by utilizing conditional threats and curses. Messenger formulas and commission formulas have a similar function. More often than not, the legitimation formula occurs at the conclusion of the oracle, as a kind of prophetic signature. In the OT the so-called "divine oracle formula," which usually takes the form "an oracle/utterance of Yahweh," constitutes a common way of concluding a prophetic oracle.[32] The stereotyped conclusions of the seven proclamations of Rev. 2-3 clearly function as legitimation formulas: "He who has an ear, let him hear what the Spirit says to the churches." Similarly, we find in Hermas *Sim.* vi.1.4 the following conclusion to an oracle: "All of these things have been spoken to you by me [the angel of repentance]." Similarly, the oracle in *Sim.* ix.31.3-6 concludes with this statement: "And I am the shepherd, and am very exceedingly bound to give account for you."

Another type of prophetic signature, or legitimation clause, is found at the conclusion of two prophetic speeches in the Odes of Solomon (3:10-11 and 18:15).[33] In 3:10-11, for example, we read:

This is the Spirit of the Lord, which is not false,
Which teaches the sons of men to know His ways.
Be wise and understanding and vigilant.[34]

A more complex concluding legitimation formula is found at the conclusion of the entire collection of six oracles which have been embedded in Hermas *Sim.* vi and ix. In *Sim.* ix.33.1 we read:

All these things which have been written above I, the shepherd, the angel of repentance, have declared and spoken to the servants of God.

If then you shall believe and shall listen to my words and shall walk in them, and shall correct your ways, you shall be able to live.

But if you shall remain in malice and in the memory of offences, none of such kind shall live to God.

All these things that I must tell have been told to you.

Although this concluding statement is long and complex, it consists of only three basic elements: (1) a legitimation formula identifying the speaker, (2) two conditional clauses revealing the consequences of obedience and disobedience, and (3) a statement attesting the completeness of the revelation. With regard to both content and structure, then, this passage bears a striking resemblance to *Vis.* v.5-7 (quoted above, p. 331). Both these passages, in turn, bear a close resemblance to Rev. 22:18-20, which contains a legitimation formula in the form of an oath, and also two conditional curses guarding the integrity of the entire prophetic book and clearly implying its completeness. Rev. 22:6-7 and 1 Cor. 14:37 function in a similar way and with a similar structure in relationship to their respective literary contexts. These examples suggest that the legitimation formula, which often functioned as a conclusion to a prophetic speech, could be expanded in a restricted manner to bring a series of oracles to a conclusion.

The most complete examples are found in Hermas *Sim.* ix.33.1; Rev. 22:18-20; 22:6-7, yet each of the conclusions of the seven proclamations in Rev. 2-3 contains two of the three basic elements. It is perhaps worth noting in passing that two of the three possible elements are also found at the beginning of Paul's letter to the Galatians. In Gal. 1:8-9 Paul repeats a conditional curse and then in vv. 11-12 identifies the real source of "his" gospel as a revelation of Jesus Christ.

5. Oath Formulas.

Oaths are often associated with prophecy in the Greco-Roman world, for the normal function of an oath is to ensure the truthfulness of a given statement or deposition. Oath formulas are also used with some frequency in connection with OT prophetic speech,[35] but the oath is always presented as an utterance of Yahweh himself, never the prophet. The oath formula also occurs often in portions of Jewish apocalyptic literature in connection with eschatological material, but in these contexts it is always used by the prophet or seer, never by the deity.[36] Oath formulas are also found in prophetic speeches in the *Odyssey* (xvii.154ff.; xix.302ff.; xx.229ff.). Josephus preserves at least one prophetic oath formula of a pagan (*Ant.* xviii.198), at the beginning of a long prophetic speech made by a German prisoner to Agrippa (*Ant.* xviii.195-202). The Greek terms *diamart-* and *mart-* and cognates are very important for understanding the prophetic task (Rev. 1:2; 19:10; 22:16, 18, 20). Oath formulas are used to introduce oracles in Acts 20:23; Rev. 21:5; 22:6-7; 22:18ff.; Ignatius Philad. 7:2, and to conclude them in 1 Thess. 4:6; Rev. 19:9. In what appears to be an older oracle reworked in Hermas *Vis.* ii.2.8, the author includes an oath formula using the style of OT prophetic speech:

> For the Lord has sworn by his Son that those who have denied their Christ have been rejected from their life, that is, those who shall now deny him in the days to come.

6. The "Mystery" Formula.

Two early Christian oracles use the term "mystery" (Greek *mystērion*) in introductory clauses. 1 Cor. 15:51 begins, "Behold! I tell you a mystery," whereupon an oracle is quoted, and Rom. 11:25 begins, "I want you to understand this mystery, brothers," and again an oracle follows. The term "mystery" is virtually a technical term in early Jewish and early Christian apocalyptic and prophetic texts.[37] The close connection between "mystery" and prophecy in early Christianity is suggested not only by Rev. 10:7 ("the mystery of God, as he announced to his servants the prophets, should be fulfilled"), but also by a number of other important passages (Rev. 1:20; 17:7; 1 Cor. 2:7; 13:2; 14:2).[38] The stereotyped phrase "the mystery of God hidden for ages but now revealed" (occurring in a number of variant forms) has been labeled the "revelation schema."[39] Further, in Jewish apocalyptic the phrase "I know a mystery" is used three times as a preface for the unfolding of a schema of future events (1 Enoch 103:1; 104:10, 12).[40]

B. COMPOSITIONAL FEATURES

1. The Prophet Speaks in His Own Person.

In connection with the use of messenger formulas in early Christian prophetic speech we focused on those supernatural beings (primarily Jesus, the Spirit, God, and angels) who are frequently claimed as sources for oracular utterance. Yet there is another style of prophetic speech in early Christianity in which the prophet speaks in his or her own person, not using or conveying the words of the inspiring deity.[41] Occasionally, however, a supernatural figure is mentioned, "through," "in," or "by" whom the prophet speaks. In early Christianity prophetic speeches are made that claim the instrumentality of the Spirit (1 Cor. 12:3; Acts 7:55-56; 11:28; 13:9; 21:4) or Jesus (1 Thess. 4:2, 15; 2 Thess. 3:6, 12). There are yet other oracular fragments in which the prophet speaks in his own person without any appeal to an inspiring supernatural authority (Rom. 11:25-26; 1 Cor. 15:51-52; Gal. 5:21; 1 Thess. 3:4; 2 Thess. 3:10; Rev. 1:7; 13:9-10; 22:18-19; Did. 11:12; Montanist oracles 5, 6, 11, 12, 13, 14, and 15). This group contains sixteen oracles, though several scholars would include a great many more, particularly from the Pauline letters.[42] It is of course possible that material of oracular origin has been shorn of its framing devices and embedded in early Christian literature, thereby taking on the appearance of ordinary forms of discourse. We have consciously chosen to include only those possible fragments of prophetic speech which still retain in their present literary setting some of the framing devices typical of oracular discourse.

In this context it is important to consider whether other oracular traditions in the Hellenistic and Roman periods use this same style. A great deal of evidence suggests that this is so. First, there are sixteen "Delphic" oracles, out of a corpus of more than six hundred, which are styled as the direct speech of the Pythia rather than that of the inspiring divinity (Apollo).[43] One of the more famous oracles of Zeus from Dodona refers to both Zeus and Dione in the third person (Pausanias x.12.10). Further, all the oracles of Sibyl and Bakis are formulated as the direct speech of their authors (see above, p. 55).

Although the vast majority of oracles in the OT are presented as messages from God to be transmitted by prophetic messengers, the oracles of Balaam (a pagan prophet) are expressed in the person of the prophet himself (Num. 23:7-10, 18-24; 24:3-9, 15-24). Similarly, some of the prophetic speeches of the later prophets are couched in the form of speeches in the person of the prophets themselves (Nah. 1:2-11; 1:14-2:12; Hab. 1:2-4, 12-17; the latter two passages form a dialogue between the prophet and God, with God's response in 1:5-11).[44] From early Judaism the oracle found in 1 Enoch 1:3-9 is expressed in the person of the prophet, as are the speeches of John the Baptist in the NT (Matt. 3:7-10; Luke 3:7-14; Mark 1:7-8 and par. Matt. 3:11-12; Luke 3:16-17), the prophecy of Joshua ben Ananiah (Josephus *Bell.* vi.301), and that of the high priest Caiaphas (John 11:49-52). From early Christianity it is instructive that the Montanist oracles (referred to above) share this style side by side with an oracular style which attributes prophetic utterance directly to an inspiring divinity. There is then no methodological or formal objection to regarding prophetic discourse in the person of the prophet as a legitimate oracular style in early Christianity.

2. The Length of Oracles.

H. Weinel once proposed that authentic early Christian oracles were characterized by both brevity and poetic form.[45] More recently it has been suggested that the reforms proposed by Paul for the protocol of Christian worship at Corinth in 1 Cor. 12-14 probably resulted in the development of longer, more homiletic forms of prophetic speech.[46] Of the 107 prophetic texts which we have analyzed, some are written in a poetic style (i.e. using Semitic parallelism as a basic poetic structure) and are for that reason easier to divide into constituent stichoi or sense lines. The more prosaic oracles I have resolved into stichoi on the basis of clauses (I recognize the relative arbitrariness of this procedure). The following statistics emerge: oracles of one line: twenty-three; oracles of two lines: sixteen; oracles of three lines: nine; oracles of four lines: nine; oracles of five lines: seven; oracles of six lines: five; oracles of seven lines: one; oracles of eight lines: four; oracles of ten to fifteen lines: nine; oracles of eighteen to twenty-four lines: six; oracles of twenty-six to thirty lines: five; oracles of thirty-one lines: one; oracles of forty-four lines: one.[47]

While these figures do not reveal very much about the nature of early Christian prophetic speech, they do exhibit some interesting correlations. Oracles of one to three lines in length, for instance, occur frequently in the gospels and Acts (twenty instances of a total of forty-eight), and many of these, as we have seen, have a purely literary origin. All the oracles longer than seven lines are found either in the Apocalypse of John, the Shepherd of Hermas, or the Odes of Solomon (as one might expect). A survey of the evidence indicates that it is not possible to maintain that shorter oracles have a greater claim to authenticity than do longer ones.

3. The Poetic Form of Oracles.

Although evidence from early Christian literature suggests that the prophetic hymn was an important genre of prophecy (Col. 3:16; Eph. 5:19; 1 Cor. 14:15), the only surviving hymns which claim a prophetic origin are the Odes of Solomon.[48] Yet aside from the Odes there are many fragments of Christian prophecy that have a lyrical quality which is difficult to pin down to any precise definition of "poetry." In Hebrew, Aramaic, and Syriac the chief formal features of poetry include parallelisms of various types (the couplet thereby constitutes the basic poetic unit), and in some instances a pattern of stressed and unstressed syllables is evident. Greek and Latin poetry, of course, is not based on rhyming schemes any more than Semitic poetry, but rather on prescribed sequences of vowel quantity. Early Christian poetic compositions are identifiable chiefly by virtue of their utilization of Semitic types of parallelism (with couplets or triplets as the basic units) and a few associated structures. Several purely literary oracles in the NT are written in poetic form, including Luke 1:14-17 within the larger text in vv. 11-20, and Luke 1:32-35, which is similarly encased in vv. 28-37. There is also the Benedictus of Zechariah in Luke 1:67-79, and the angelic hymn in Luke 2:9-14.

Yet the real issue is whether there are any genuine fragments of early Christian prophecy that exhibit poetic form and structure. One type of early Christian prophetic speech particularly exhibits poetic features: eschatological theophany oracles (see above, p. 325). Since the basic structure of this type of oracle is determined by the juxtaposition of the motif of an eschatological theophany and the motif of the salvific effect of that theophany on the world of man, all these oracles exhibit a two-part structure which in most cases takes the form of two strophes of very nearly equal size. Strophes of three lines occur several times in this type of oracle (1 Cor. 15:51-52; 1 Thess. 4:16-17; Rev. 21:6-8; 22:12-15).

The two-part structure in oracles is not limited to eschatological theophany oracles; it is a comparatively widespread phenomenon throughout the ancient world.[49] This structure is often exhibited in oracles of two lines or more and lends itself rather neatly to expression in the characteristic types of Semitic parallelism. In synthetic parallelism, where the second line completes the thought of the first, we have the pattern exhibited in Mark 1:11 and par.; 9:7 and par.; John 1:29; Acts 13:2, 9-11; 16:17; Gal. 5:21; 2 Thess. 3:6, 12. Perhaps the most common type of relationship between the two structural elements in ancient oracles is causal: the pronouncement made in the first part is substantiated in the second part, often introduced with such causal particles as "for," "because," or "therefore." Just as antithetic parallelism is a common form of Semitic parallelism, so we find that it is also a common device in Greco-Roman oracles.[50] Although this type of oracle is very rare in early Christianity, it is found in six instances among the genuine Montanist oracles (nos. 4, 7, 9, 10, 13, 14). A partial explanation for this phenomenon suggests itself when the content of these oracles is considered in the light of the social circumstances of the Montanist groups. Let us consider oracle no. 7 in this connection:

> The Church can forgive sins,
> but I will not do it,
> lest they sin again.

This oracle provides divine legitimation for the rigorist position espoused by the Montanists, and also validates the separatist existence of the Montanist movement by placing a wide chasm between the normal ecclesiastical practice and the desire of the Paraclete (whose views, not surprisingly, coincide with those of the Montanist community). A further example of antithetic parallelism is found in Rev. 13:9-10, in which the first line of each of the two couplets which constitute this oracle are in antithetic relationship.

Chiasmus is a device frequently used in Semitic poetry, though it is also found in classical literature, where it often designated "ring composition." The oracle of assurance in 2 Cor. 12:9 has a two-part saying (the second line is introduced with the inferential particle "for") in which an *a b b a* pattern is evident. A chiastic structure is also evident in 1 Cor. 15:51-52 where the slightly more complex arrangement *a b c c' a' b'* is found. Chiasmus is closely associated with the pronouncements of sacral law, to which we now turn.

4. Pronouncements of Sacral Law.

During this study we have had more than one occasion to refer to this form, first identified by E. Käsemann and then subjected to rigorous criticism by K. Berger.[51] Käsemann described five stylistic features which he regarded as characteristic of pronouncements of sacral law: (1) the pronouncement has a chiastic structure, (2) the same verb is used in both parts of the pronouncement, (3) the second part of the pronouncement deals with the eschatological activity of God with the verb often occurring in the passive voice (i.e. as a circumlocution for divine activity), (4) the principle of *lex talionis* ("retributive justice") is a central feature of the pronouncement, expressing the intimate relationship between guilt and punishment, duty and reward, and (5) the first part is introduced by the casuistic legal forms "if any one" or "whoever." Although all five features do occur in some early Christian oracles (e.g. Rev. 22:18-19; 1 Cor. 14:37-38), the same style also occurs in pronouncements which cannot automatically be presumed to have an oracular origin, and in many instances an oracular origin must necessarily be excluded as a possibility.[52]

Both Käsemann and Berger assume that pronouncements of sacral law (or, as Berger prefers to designate them, pronouncements of wisdom instruction) exhibit a rigid stability, and both propose different (and mutually exclusive) original settings. However, many of the features of these pronouncements that Käsemann has regarded as essential are in actuality optional features (e.g. the same verb in both parts, chiastic structure, the conditional clause in the protasis), while the really distinctive element is the principle of *lex talionis*. This principle lends itself to formulation in two-part pronouncements in which present behavior is matched with (eschatological) reward or punishment. Further, since this basic form together with some or all of the optional elements is used in various settings, the mere identification of the form itself cannot prove the presence of prophetic speech. Nevertheless, it must also be observed that the eschatological application of this speech form did lend itself to the basic concerns of early Christian prophetic speech.

5. The Use of Conditional Clauses.

Since the purpose of many of the oracles which we have analyzed is to encourage certain types of behavior and to discourage other types, conditional clauses are frequently part of the grammatical structure of such oracles. Conditional particles are used in fourteen of the 107 oracles which we have discussed (1 Cor. 14:37-38; 2 Thess. 3:10; Rev. 2:1-7, 12-17; 3:1-6, 7-13; 13:9; Hermas *Vis.* ii.3.4; iv.2.5-6; *Sim.* vi.1.4; ix.23.5; ix.28.5-8; ix.31.3-6; ix.33.1). Yet the conditional element can be implicit as well as explicit. For example, in the oracles which warn Paul against going to Jerusalem (Acts 21:4, 11; cf. 20:23), it appears that he might avoid arrest *if* he did not go. Further, participial constructions are often used in clauses where a particular type of behavior is paired with a certain kind of reward; the implication is certainly that *if* such behavior is not maintained or forthcoming, the reward will certainly not be granted (Gal. 5:21; Rev. 2:8-11, 18-29; 21:6-8; Hermas *Vis.* ii.2.6-8; *Sim.* ix.24.2). The stereotyped endings of the seven proclamations of Rev. 2-3 should also be included here ("To the one who conquers . . .").

6. Miscellaneous Features.

The particle "behold!" is a Semitism used in early Christian literature in a variety of ways: to enliven a narrative, to introduce new elements, to emphasize the size or importance of something, or to introduce a prophetic oracle.[53] Yet the use of "behold!" in oracles is not really rhetorically different from the first three types of usage mentioned. "Behold!" is used some twelve times in early Christian oracles (1 Cor. 15:51-52; Acts 7:55-56; 13:9-10; 27:23-24; Rev. 1:7, 18; 2:22; 16:15; 21:3, 5; 22:7, 12). In several instances it introduces an oracle (1 Cor. 15:51-52; Acts 7:55-56; Rev. 1:7; 16:15; 21:3, 5; 22:12), and in three very interesting passages (Acts 13:9-11; 27:23-24; Rev. 2:22) it serves to introduce the second part of a two-part oracle. Prophecy is connected with punitive miracles in both Acts 13:9-11 and Rev. 2:22, though the former passage is of a more literary character, and in both cases the threats are introduced with "behold!" Here we find a suggestion of the close relationship between prophecy and magic.[54]

Beatitudes occur in six early Christian oracles (Rev. 14:13; 16:15b; 19:9; 22:7, 14; Hermas *Vis.* ii.2.7). Five of the seven beatitudes of the Apocalypse (1:3 and 20:6 are the exceptions) are found within prophetic pronouncements. Yet beatitudes are predominantly used in eschatological and wisdom settings in early Christianity where no oracular origin can be presumed.

VI. CONCLUSIONS

Prophetic sayings and speeches preserved in early Christian sources exhibit a wide variety of forms and styles. Even though we have somewhat overconfidently proposed a typology of six types of basic forms of prophetic speech and three kinds of complex forms, it is apparent that only the presence of formal framing devices betrays the possible presence of Christian prophetic speech. This is the case because nearly all of the types and styles of prophetic speech which we have considered are either drawn from or so closely similar to other forms of Christian discourse that they are virtually indistinguishable from one another. There is therefore no such thing as a distinctively characteristic form of Christian prophetic discourse that is recognizable apart from the presence of formal framing devices. The only real exception to this generalization is the apocalyptic vision report, a literary form which we have not considered in any detail and which requires careful study in its own right. It will also be readily apparent that the stylistic features of early Christian prophetic speech, discussed above, are no more characteristic of oracles than of other forms of Christian discourse. Attempts to delineate the characteristics of prophetic diction, therefore, can only be successful in a limited way.[55] Further, if there are no stylistic or generic features which can confidently be identified as characteristic of prophetic speech, the accumulation of such hypothetical elements cannot increase the probability that a given text is oracular in origin.[56]

At the same time the present study has shown that early Christian prophets favored particular types and styles of discourse more than others, and the present chapter consists of a synthesis and typology of those favored modes of discourse. The essential indistinguishability of early Christian prophetic speech from other forms of discourse in the early church, however, has several important implications. First, it suggests that the distinctive feature of prophetic speech was not so much its *content* or *form*, but its *supernatural origin*. Christian prophetic speech, then, is Christian discourse presented with divine legitimation, either in the absence of more rational structures of institutional authority, or in conflict with them. Second, the much-discussed problem of the decline of prophecy in early Christianity must be viewed as a social rather than a theological issue. With the institutionalization of Christianity and the rationalization of its authority structures, prophecy became redundant as well as dysfunctional. Throughout the entire second century the phenomenon of prophecy was primarily tied to dissenting voices and movements within various phases of Christianity. This does not mean that prophets became an endangered species primarily because of their increasing association with heretical movements, but it does suggest that the earlier role of the prophets as articulators of the norms, values, and decisions of the invisible head of the church was taken over by the visible figures of the teacher, preacher, theologian, and church leader.[57]

Appendix

CHRISTIAN PROPHECY AND CHARISMATIC EXEGESIS

"Charismatic exegesis," as now understood by biblical scholars, is a very particular form of biblical interpretation based on two presuppositions: (1) The sacred text contains hidden or symbolic meanings which can only be revealed by an interpreter gifted with divine insight, and (2) The true meaning of the text concerns eschatological prophecies which the interpreter believes are being fulfilled in his own day. Charismatic exegesis, then, appears to have three essential features: it is *commentary,* it is *eschatological,* and it is *inspired.* The designation "charismatic exegesis" was apparently first proposed by H. L. Ginsberg as a description of the mode of biblical interpretation practiced by the Teacher of Righteousness of the Qumran community as exhibited in the Habakkuk Commentary.[1] Charismatic exegesis has come to be regarded as a characteristic feature of Jewish prophetism in the Hellenistic and Roman periods.[2] By analogy, early Christian biblical interpretation has also been labeled charismatic exegesis, a form of divine revelation closely associated by many NT scholars with the role of the early Christian prophet. The purpose of this Appendix is to examine the validity of this theory.

I

Prophecy is a specific form of divination that consists of intelligible verbal messages believed to originate with God and communicated through inspired human intermediaries. Divination proper, on the other hand, is the art or science of interpreting symbolic or coded messages from God. Prophecy is direct revelation while divination is indirect revelation. Greco-Roman thinkers originated this distinction when they differentiated between "technical divination" (*artificiosa divinatio*), dependent on the knowledge, training, and skill of the diviner, and "natural divination" (*naturalis divinatio*), which involved the direct inspiration of a medium through a possession trance or vision trance.[3]

Charismatic exegesis, as defined above, cannot be accurately characterized as either prophecy or divination. It resembles divination in that it deals with the interpretation of coded messages, yet it is like prophecy in that the inspiration of the intermediary is involved.[4] On the whole, however, charismatic exegesis is closer to divination than to prophecy for the following reasons: (1) Like divination, charismatic

339

exegesis is indirect revelation, while prophecy is direct revelation. (2) Prophetic speech usually involves a trance experience (possession trance or vision trance), while charismatic exegesis does not. (3) The product of charismatic exegesis (whether oral or written) stands in a secondary, dependent relationship to the inspired text from which it arises, whereas prophetic speech (whether oral or written) possesses an intrinsic authority. The inspired text, in spite of the activity of the charismatic exegete, remains the primary locus of divine revelation; it is never replaced or rivaled by the "inspired" commentary. (4) There is no material difference between the interpretation of dreams, one of the more popular forms of divination in the ancient world, and the inspired interpretation of scripture.[5]

II

The OT was the single most important source of religious knowledge in early Judaism. The divine origin of scripture was a central presupposition held in common by all the diverse sectarian movements within synagogue Judaism, including the Qumran community and early Christianity.[6] Yet the primary concern of the sages, the apocalyptists, and the early Christians was not the original, literal meaning of the Bible, but rather what it had come to mean, i.e. its actualized or contemporized meaning.[7] For the sages this meant that derash (creative exegesis, free rabbinic interpretation) took precedence over peshaṭ (the plain, literal sense of scripture) in the composition of the midrashim ("commentaries" on scripture).[8] In the midrashim, scripture was actualized or contemporized by the sages, but not within an eschatological framework. From the perspective of content there are two types of midrashim: halakhic midrashim (expositions of legal material), and haggadic midrashim (expositions of nonlegal material). From the standpoint of literary structure, however, there are three types of midrashim:[9] exegetical midrashim (the verse-by-verse exegesis of a biblical text practiced in rabbinical academies), homiletical midrashim (explanations in sermonic form of the sederim, or lections from the Torah, and haphtaroth, or lections from the Prophets read in the synagogue on Sabbaths, festivals, and special occasions), and narrative midrashim (literary compositions, like Jubilees, the Genesis Apocryphon, and Pseudo-Philo's Liber Antiquitatum Biblicarum, which are paraphrastic expansions of the biblical narrative using legends and other nonbiblical materials). The midrashim of the sages are not eschatologically oriented nor do they claim to be the product of inspired insight into the true meaning of the biblical text.

The apocalyptic literature of early Judaism presents a very different picture. One of the striking features of this literature is that while frequent allusions are made to various OT texts, they are rarely quoted. This means that, whatever an apocalypse is, it is not a commentary on the biblical text. Nor, for that matter, can apocalyptic be viewed as the interpretation of revelation previously given.[10] A second striking feature of apocalyptic literature is the claims their authors make (masked, of course, by pseudonyms) to divine inspiration that appear to place their compositions on a par with Mosaic revelation.[11] Thus far it has not been possible to determine the social setting or sectarian framework within which apocalyptic literature arose.[12] This may indicate that the apocalypses were written within the setting of a more general form of collective behavior which had not yet crystallized into coherent social movements or sects. If charismatic exegesis is an activity characteristic of religious sectarianism, the general absence of it from apocalyptic literature is readily comprehensible.

Judeo-Christian charismatic exegesis originated in the phenomenon of mantic wisdom (as distinguished from proverbial wisdom), in which the skill of the wise man (which derives from God and not himself) is applied to the interpretation of dreams and visions (Joseph in Gen. 40-41, and Daniel in Dan. 2, 4-5).[13] Divine revelation in the form of enigmatical dreams constitutes an insoluble mystery (*raz*) until the proper interpretation (*peshar*) is revealed (Dan. 2:30; 4:6 [Eng. 9]; cf. 1QpHab 7:1-5).[14] This kind of indirect revelation is a two-stage process which is only completed when the coded message has been deciphered. The same phenomenon is characteristic of the revelatory visions of apocalyptic literature (e.g. Dan. 7-12). The meaning of the visions must always be explained to the seer by an interpreting angel (*angelus interpres*), so that the revelatory process, consisting of both vision and interpretation, may be completed.[15] It is not surprising, then, that in Qumran the Danielic language for dream interpretation has been appropriated for the interpretation of scripture.[16]

The practice of charismatic exegesis by the Essenes became evident upon the discovery of a distinctive form of biblical commentary, the examples of which have been labeled *pesharim* ("interpretations"). In these *pesharim* the interpreters regarded themselves as living in the last days and approached the biblical text in terms of its secret or mystical significance. The meaning of the text always related very directly to the lifetime of the interpreter and the eschatological role of the sect to which he belonged. The procedure of the interpreter is to quote a few lines of the biblical text and then to introduce his explanation with the phrases "the explanation [*pesher*] of this is that . . ." or "the explanation [*pesher*] of this word concerns. . . ." While most early Jewish methods of biblical interpretation do not claim any form of divine inspiration or illumination, this is not true for the Qumran *pesharim*. In the Habakkuk Commentary (1QpHab 7:1-5) we read:

> And God told Habakkuk to write down the things which will come to pass in the last generation, but the consummation of time He made not known to him. And as for that which He said, *That he may read it easily that reads it* [Hab. 2:2], the explanation of this concerns the Teacher of Righteousness to whom God made known all the Mysteries of the words of His servants the Prophets.[17]

Here the words of the prophets are mysteries or secrets (*razim*) which require the interpretation of the Teacher of Righteousness. The Teacher of Righteousness claimed that form of divine inspiration which enabled him to discern the precise time of the fulfilment of earlier prophecies.[18] Elsewhere he is described as "the Priest whom God placed in [the House of Jud]ah to explain all the words of His servants the Prophets" (1QpHab 2:8-9).[19] The close relationship between prophecy and biblical study among the Essenes is also attested by Josephus (*Bell.* ii.159):

> There are some among them who profess to foretell the future, being versed from their early years in holy books, various forms of purification and apophthegms of prophets; and seldom, if ever, do they err in their predictions.

The Teacher of Righteousness, probably the founder of the sect, regarded himself and was regarded by his followers as an eschatological figure, possibly the "prophet like Moses" of Jewish expectation.[20] He claimed (if he was the author of the Hodayoth, or "Hymns") that the Holy Spirit had been poured out upon him (1QH 7:6-7; 14:26; 17:26) and given him knowledge and insight (1QH 12:11-12; 13:18-19), particularly concerning the mysteries (1QH 2:10, 13). The Qumran community as a whole was convinced that the Spirit of God, an eschatological gift, was present and active in their midst.[21] Although the Holy Spirit is primarily regarded as the Spirit of prophecy in Rabbinic Judaism,[22] in Qumran the Holy Spirit has a function which is more broadly conceived in terms of cleansing, truth, holiness, and divinely mediated knowledge and insight.[23] Apart from the phenomenon of charismatic exegesis, prophecy (as direct revelation mediated through inspired speech or writing) does not appear to have been practiced by the Teacher of Righteousness or other members of the Qumran community.[24] For the Qumran community charismatic exegesis played a functionally equivalent role to prophecy, yet it is readily apparent that the differences between the two phenomena are not small.[25]

III

The earliest Christian communities, as many recent studies have made clear, expended an enormous amount of effort in establishing a relationship between prophecies and antitypes in the OT and their eschatological fulfilments in the history of Jesus and the formation of the earliest Christian community.[26] Like the Qumran community, the earliest Christians were convinced that they possessed the eschatological gift of the Spirit of God. The Spirit was thought to provide supernatural insight into spiritual matters generally (1 Cor. 2:6-16; 1 John 2:21, 27) as well as into the true meaning of the words of Jesus (John 2:22; 12:16; 14:26; 16:12-15) and the OT (Luke 24:45; 2 Cor. 3:14-18). In 1 Cor. 2:6-16 Paul advanced the claim that Christians through the Spirit are enabled to understand the secret and hidden wisdom of God that was concealed for ages but now revealed to those who possess the Spirit of God. The notion of the "mystery of God hidden for ages but now revealed" has been labeled the "revelation schema" and occurs elsewhere in Pauline and deutero-Pauline literature (Col. 1:26-27; Eph. 3:5, 9-10; Rom. 16:25-26; cf. 2 Tim. 1:9-10; Tit. 1:2-3; 1 Pet. 1:20).[27] In one of these passages, Rom. 16:25-26, the revelation schema is placed in conjunction with OT interpretation:

> Now to him who is able to strengthen you according to my gospel and the preaching of Jesus Christ, according to the revelation of the mystery which was kept secret for long ages but is now disclosed and through the prophetic writings is made known to all nations, according to the command of the eternal God.

There appears to be more than a superficial resemblance between the *mystery*/*revelation* and *kept secret*/*disclosed* dialectic expressed here and the *raz*/*pesher* pattern found in both Daniel and the Habakkuk Commentary from Qumran. From this preliminary survey it appears very likely that some early Christians practiced charismatic exegesis. Divine illumination into the true meaning of the OT, however, cannot be separated from other forms of spiritual discernment; all are based on the presence and activity of the Spirit of God.

IV

Not surprisingly, a number of NT scholars have attempted to demonstrate that one major task of early Christian prophets was the charismatic exegesis of the OT.[28] Two approaches are used to substantiate this thesis. One is to examine the descriptive or theoretical statements made by various early Christian authors about the prophetic or charismatic interpretation of the OT. The second approach analyzes actual texts thought to be the products of charismatic exegesis.

In spite of the confident claims which have been made that Christian prophets could function as charismatic exegetes, a survey of the underlying arguments proves disappointing. While there is an enormous amount of eschatological exegesis of the OT in the NT, such exegesis is rarely labeled "inspired" or "charismatic." Two related problems present themselves: (1) Can eschatological exegesis be regarded as "inspired" or "charismatic" even though explicit claims are lacking? (2) Is there any demonstrable connection between charismatic exegesis, whenever and wherever it occurs in early Christian texts, and Christian prophecy? We shall attempt to answer these questions at the close of our discussion.

Since the parenetic role of prophecy is well established in Paul and Acts,[29] one argument runs, and the parenetic function of the OT is emphasized (among other places) in Rom. 15:4 ("For whatever was written in former days was written for our instruction [*paraklēsis*]"), the intimate association of prophecy, *paraklēsis*/*parenesis*, and OT interpretation is demonstrated.[30] Unfortunately, parenesis is a common function of virtually all varieties of the ministry of the word in early Christianity. When parenesis is not tied explicitly to prophecy in early Christian texts, that connection cannot be demonstrated.

A more formal indicator of the presence of both charismatic exegesis and prophetic activity has been proposed by E. E. Ellis. Nine quotations of the OT in the NT exhibit modification of the text and contain the formula "says the Lord" (*legei kyrios*); Ellis suggests that these quotations are the products of early Christian prophecy.[31] He has summarized his argument in four points:[32] (1) "Says the Lord" (*legei kyrios*) is a characteristic formula used by OT prophets. (2) Early Christian prophets sometimes used the same phrase, or its equivalent, in citing their own revelations.[33] (3) The phrase is inserted within some NT quotations of the OT in such a way as to preclude its function as an introductory formula or as part of the cited OT text. (4) These quotations consistently diverge from extant OT texts and their source is often within a "testimony" pattern evident elsewhere.

One example of such an OT quotation is found in Rom. 12:19: "For it is written, 'Vengeance is mine, I will repay, says the Lord.'" The most likely source for this quotation is Deut. 32:35: "Vengeance is mine, and recompense, for the time when their foot shall slip; for the day of their calamity is at hand, and their doom comes swiftly." Here the insertion of "says the Lord" in Rom. 12:19 appears to be a way of identifying the original speaker (Deut. 32 consists of a long speech which commences in v. 19 with the identification of the Lord as speaker). An examination of each of the *legei kyrios* quotations reveals that, although each may be labeled "implicit midrash," i.e. interpretive renderings cited as part of an OT text, there is no persuasive evidence to suggest any connection with early Christian prophetic activity.

Unaccountably Ellis does not consider the *legei kyrios* formula used in connection with OT quotations in the Apostolic Fathers, where it occurs sixteen times in fifteen quotations.[34] Most occurrences of the *legei kyrios* formula are found in Barnabas; of the eleven uses of the formula in ten OT quotations, six of the quotations in Barnabas have the phrase though it is not used in the OT texts cited.[35] The author of Barnabas was a Christian teacher (1:8; 4:9) who claimed (with his audience) to have divinely bestowed insight into the true meaning of the OT (1:7):

For the Lord made known to us through the prophets things past and things present and has given us the firstfruits of the taste of things to come; and when we see these things coming to pass one by one, as he said, we ought to make a richer and deeper offering for fear of him.

Again, in Barn. 5:3,

Therefore we ought to give great thanks to the Lord that he has given us knowledge of the past, and wisdom for the present, and that we are not without understanding for the future.

The same theme recurs in Barn. 6:10b: "Blessed be our Lord, brethren, who has placed in us wisdom and understanding of his secrets." In these and other passages (Barn. 2:4; 8:7; 10:12) the author does not claim an exclusive insight into the true meaning of the OT, but claims to share that knowledge with those whom he addresses. Barnabas never mentions the role of the Spirit in his understanding of the OT, nor does he refer to his interpretations of the OT as in any way "prophetic." Barnabas is thoroughly parenetic in content, not unlike other compositions written in the style of the Hellenistic Jewish homily.[36] Further, the OT texts which Barnabas cites in abundance are not simply drawn without alteration from known OT texts and versions, but give evidence of interpretative textual alteration within the framework of a general, if somewhat muted, eschatological setting.

We are now in a better position to determine whether the *legei kyrios* formula is in fact a sign of the activity of early Christian prophets. The case for such an hypothesis is weak for the following reasons:

(1) The *legei kyrios* formula, used in the citation of OT prophetic texts, is never used as an introductory formula in early Christian prophetic speech.[37] The early Christian prophetic speech formula "thus says the Spirit" is not equivalent to "says the Lord," since the latter is used in contexts very different from those in which the former is used.[38]

(2) The *legei kyrios* formula is simply a useful way of identifying God as speaker when that is not obvious. Since the phrase occurs a great many times in the OT, this application cannot be regarded as unusual for early Christian authors.

(3) While the *legei kyrios* formula is used in the NT and Apostolic Fathers with OT texts in which there is evidence of "implicit *midrash*," i.e. interpretative alterations in the text, no clear evidence suggests any connection between "implicit *midrash*" and early Christian prophecy.

(4) The *legei kyrios* formula is used more frequently by the author of Barnabas than by any other early Christian writer; Barnabas is clearly a teacher, not a prophet, though he does claim (with his audience) charismatic insight into the meaning of the OT.

(5) Among all the authors who may be considered Christian prophets (John the author of the Apocalypse, Ignatius, Hermas; Paul is an exception), there is a notable absence of the use of the *legei kyrios* formula. The formula is entirely absent from the letters of Ignatius, the Shepherd of Hermas, and the Apocalypse of John, though it is found in Paul (Rom. 12:19; 14:11; 1 Cor. 14:21; 2 Cor. 6:16ff.); yet there is no reason to associate Paul's use of the *legei kyrios* formula with prophetic activity, since the formula simply functions to identify God as the speaker.

In sum, there is no evidence suggesting that the *legei kyrios* quotations were formulated by Christian prophets.[39] There is undoubtedly a connection between such altered quotations and early Christian "scribal" or "school" activity, yet to label that kind of activity "prophetic" goes beyond the available evidence.[40]

Apart from formal indications of the presence of charismatic exegesis and its connections with prophetic activity, a number of scholars have sought to identify exegetical patterns in NT texts and to connect that interpretative activity with charismatic exegesis and Christian prophecy. A number of studies have focused on the existence of midrashic homiletic patterns in various sections of the NT.[41] The identification of the presence of such exegetical structures, however, does not in itself demonstrate either that such exegesis was thought inspired or that it was the product of prophetic activity.

The mission speeches of Acts, of which Peter's Pentecost sermon in Acts 2 is a particularly good example, have been pointed to as idealized presentations of the form of Christian prophetic preaching.[42] Acts 2 of course, as B. Lindars has shown,[43] exhibits a very complex exegetical substructure based on a number of eschatologically interpreted OT texts. A corollary of this view is that prophetic speech had an important kerygmatic function in early Christianity, a perspective that has little to commend it.[44] In Acts 2, even though Peter's sermon is set within the framework of the pouring out of the Spirit on the day of Pentecost, there is no explicit connection between the sermon and either charismatic exegesis or prophetic speech. The most ambitious attempt to analyze the genre of the "prophetic sermon," that of U. B. Müller, makes no attempt to use the speeches of Acts as examples of prophetic sermons.[45]

Paul's sermon at Pisidian Antioch, found in Acts 13:16-41, has been proposed as a prime example of a prophetic homily.[46] Paul, it states, accepted the invitation of the synagogue rulers to present a word of exhortation (*logos paraklēseōs*, Acts 13:15). The resultant sermon in Acts 13:16-41 is very probably a midrashic homily based on 2 Sam 7.[47] Yet despite the midrashic structure of Acts 13:16-41, there is no evidence that the sermon itself should be regarded as in any way "prophetic."[48] That the author of Acts once identifies Paul as a prophet (13:1), and that the activity of *parakl ēsis* is associated with the work of the Holy Spirit (Acts 9:31; 15:28, 31; cf. 1 Cor. 14:23),[49] are discrete phenomena which do not compel the conclusion that Paul preached a prophetic sermon at Pisidian Antioch.

V

While there is not an abundance of evidence that charismatic exegesis was widely practiced in early Christianity, the evidence is sufficiently distributed throughout the NT to indicate that it was indeed widely practiced. There is virtually no evidence, however, that this activity was carried out by those who were labeled "prophets" in early Christianity. Of the many studies of the use of the OT in the NT, only one — that of E. E Ellis — suggests that OT exegesis was a task carried out by early Christian prophets.[50] The probable reason why the connection is not made between eschatological exegesis and the role of the Christian prophet is simply that the evidence for making such a connection is not readily apparent in the source material. In fact, while little is known about the role of the prophet in early Christianity, even less is known about the role of the teacher. The negative result of the present inquiry suggests that exegesis of the OT, whether simply eschatological or both charismatic and eschatological, was the primary province of the teacher.

One of the major differences between the Qumran community and early Christianity, aside from the roles of their respective founders, was that the phenomenon of prophecy (direct revelation) was an integral part of early Christian religious experience. While the designation "prophet" (*nabi'* or *prophētēs*) was only used by the Qumran community to label those of the distant past or eschatological future, in early Christianity the term was often employed as a designation for inspired mediums of divine revelation. Because of the early Christian perception that divine revelation was directly available through inspired persons, charismatic exegesis did not and probably could not occupy the central place that it did in the Qumran community. That is not to say, however, that prophetic speech in early Christianity was unquestionably authoritative. The OT continued to occupy a central place in the early Christian quest for divine knowledge.

Notes

Chapter 1

1. In addition to the books and articles which will be discussed in this chapter, note the following studies: G. Dautzenberg, *Urchristliche Prophetie*; E. E. Ellis, *Prophecy and Hermeneutic in Early Christianity*; J. Panagopoulos (ed.), *Prophetic Vocation in the New Testament and Today*, containing a number of excellent articles by scholars who participated in a consultation at the Ecumenical Institute in Bossey, Switzerland held on September 12-17, 1975; U. B. Müller, *Prophetie und Predigt im Neuen Testament*. In addition, from 1972-77 a Seminar on Early Christian Prophecy was sponsored by the Society of Biblical Literature, chaired first by M. E. Boring, and later by D. E. Aune.

2. Guy, *NT Prophecy*, p. 27.

3. Ibid., p. 153.

4. Ibid., pp. 9-10.

5. Ibid., p. 50.

6. Ibid., p. 63.

7. Ibid., p. 94.

8. Ibid., p. 104.

9. Ibid., pp. 142-43.

10. Ibid., p. 143.

11. *TDNT,* VI, 787.

12. See below, pp. 32-34.

13. See below, p. 66.

14. *TDNT,* VI, 791.

15. Ibid.

16. Ibid., p. 795.

17. Ibid., pp. 796-812.

18. Ibid., pp. 812-828.

19. Ibid., pp. 828-861.

20. Ibid., p. 829.

21. Ibid., p. 848.

22. Ibid., p. 849.

23. Ibid.

24. Ibid.

25. Ibid., p. 851.

26. Ibid.

27. Ibid., p. 853.

28. Ibid., p. 851.

29. This forms the major thesis for the 1978 Cambridge dissertation of Wayne A. Grudem, now published with a few additions as *The Gift of Prophecy in 1 Corinthians*, and is also the view of D. Hill (see below, p. 13).

30. Cothenet, "Prophétisme," col. 1233.

31. Ibid., cols. 1233-64.
32. Ibid., col. 1262.
33. Ibid., cols. 1267-75.
34. Ibid., cols. 1275-85.
35. Ibid., col. 1276.
36. Ibid., col. 1285.
37. Ibid., col. 1286.
38. Ibid., cols. 1301-1303.
39. Ibid., cols. 1297-99.
40. Ibid., cols. 1299-1301.
41. Ibid., cols. 1316-31.
42. Ibid., col. 1318.
43. Ibid., col. 1331.
44. Crone, *Early Christian Prophecy*, pp. 1-186.
45. Ibid., pp. 11-52.
46. Ibid., pp. 53-151.
47. Ibid., pp. 152-186.
48. Ibid., p. 170.
49. Ibid., p. 204.
50. Ibid., p. 226.
51. Ibid., p. 247.
52. Ibid., p. 263.
53. Ibid., pp. 284-85.
54. Hill, *NT Prophecy*, pp. 4-5.
55. Ibid., p. 5.
56. Ibid., p. 129.
57. Ibid., p. 167.
58. Ibid., p. 117.
59. Ibid., p. 113.
60. Ibid., pp. 9-47.
61. Ibid., p. 15.
62. Ibid., p. 21.
63. Ibid., p. 43.
64. Ibid., p. 68.
65. Ibid., p. 75.
66. Ibid., p. 97.
67. Ibid., p. 103.
68. Ibid., pp. 111-18.
69. Ibid., p. 111.
70. Ibid., p. 116.
71. Ibid., p. 121.
72. Ibid., p. 123.
73. Ibid., p. 126.
74. Ibid., p. 128.
75. Ibid., p. 129.
76. Ibid., p. 132.
77. Ibid., p. 135.
78. Ibid., p. 191.
79. See J. Charlot, *New Testament Disunity*, and more recently, J. D. G. Dunn, *Unity and Diversity in the New Testament*.
80. Hill, *NT Prophecy*, p. 121.
81. E. Bourguignon, *Possession*; idem, *Religion, Altered States of Consciousness, and Social Change*. I have used the phrase "vision trance" in place of her term "trance."

82. E. Bourguignon, *Possession*, p. 7.
83. Wilson, *Prophecy*, p. 84.
84. H. Bacht, "Wahres und falsches Prophetentum," pp. 249-251.
85. See below, pp. 32-34.
86. D. E. Aune, "Magic in Early Christianity," p. 1515.

Chapter 2

1. This point is emphasized by R. Martin and H. Metzger, *La religion Grecque*, pp. 13-14.
2. See the remarks of U. von Wilamowitz-Moellendorff, *Der Glaube der Hellenen*, II, 27, and O. Kern, *Die Religion der Griechen*, II, 147ff. In contrast, the Romans had a college of scholarly diviners, the *quindecemviri sacris faciundis*, who had custody of the Sibylline books and consulted them in times of national emergency.
3. In Pausanias x.12 the author lists women and men who prophesied spontaneously (i.e. without solicitation), all legendary figures from the remote past. He concludes by observing that since time is long, perhaps similar things may occur again.
4. O. Weinreich, *Ausgewählten Schriften*, I, 535-36.
5. D. E. Aune, "Divination," pp. 971-74.
6. H. W. Parke, *Greek Oracles*, p. 9.
7. Based on the categories of Greek divination suggested by K. Latte, "The Coming of the Pythia," p. 10.
8. Important general studies on Greek divination include A. Bouché-Leclercq, *Histoire de la divination dans l'antiquité* (4 vols.; 1879-82), still indispensable; W. R. Halliday, *Greek Divination*; M. P. Nilsson, *Geschichte der griechischen Religion*, I, 164-174; R. Bloch, *Les prodiges dans l'antiquité classique*.
9. Cicero *De divin.* i.6.12, apparently following Posidonios of Apamea (ca. 135-50 B.C.), who in turn was dependent on Plato (e.g. *Ion* 534c), distinguished between *artificiosa divinatio* (variously translated as "artificial," "technical," or "inductive divination"), and *naturalis divinatio* ("natural," "nontechnical," or "intuitive divination"). Similarly, Plutarch (A.D. 40-120), using the character of Simmias in *De gen. Socr.* 593c-d, reads into Homer a twofold distinction in the mantic art. The first kind involves divination through various kinds of signs and sacrifices, while the second consists of an actual understanding of the conversation of the gods. This latter kind of divination is reminiscent of the convention of the throne vision of ancient Israelite prophets (e.g. the vision of Micaiah ben Imlah in 1 Kgs. 22:19-23; on which see S. J. De Vries, *Prophet against Prophet*.
10. This kind of divination is described by Plato in *Ion* 534d: "And for this reason God takes away the mind of these men and uses them as his ministers . . . in order that we who hear them may know that it is not they who utter these words of great price, when they are out of their wits, but that it is God himself who speaks and addresses us through them."
11. Some dissatisfaction with this traditional distinction is expressed by W. R. Halliday, *Greek Divination*, pp. 54ff., and P. Amandry, "La divination en Grèce," pp. 171ff.
12. Of the recent general treatments of Greek religion, that of R. Martin and H. Metzger, *La religion Grecque*, pp. 15-16, 24-61, shows sensitivity to the importance of the sacred site of local consultation oracles and the distinctive natural feature which embodies the oracular potencies of the site. For the significance of sacred places in various religious systems see M. Eliade, *Patterns in Comparative Religion*, pp. 367-387; idem, *The Sacred and the Profane*, pp. 20-65.
13. The theme that all men are potential prophets is occasionally mentioned by Plutarch (*De sera numinis* 566c; *De def. orac.* 431e-432b, 432c, 435b; *De gen. Socr.* 588d-e, 589b-c), and found also in Philostratus *Vita Apoll.* iii.42.
14. See below, note 18.
15. Greek religion in the Hellenistic and Roman period, according to G. Murray, *Five Stages of Greek Religion*, pp. 114-165, experienced a "failure of nerve." For a more positive assessment of late antiquity, see P. Brown, "Sorcery, Demons, and the Rise of Christianity," pp. 34-35.

16. Plutarch *De def. orac.* 410b ff., 411e ff., 434c ff. Strabo (xvii.1.43) comments on the decline of the once great oracle centers (writing ca. A.D. 160), a subject which formed the basis for Plutarch's Pythian dialogue *De defectu oraculorum.*

17. Lucian *Alex.* 29. In *Deor. conc.* 12 Lucian refers, with Epicurean sarcasm, to what H. D. Betz has aptly termed "oracle inflation" (*Lukian von Samosata*, p. 58). In this latter passage Lucian refers only to the healing oracles of various heroes which are springing up all over (Polydamas at Olympia, Theagenes in Thasos, Hector in Troy, and Protesilaus in the Chersonese).

18. Pausanias i.40.6; ii.24.1.

19. Lucian *Alex.*

20. P. Amandry, *La mantique Apollinienne*, pp. 81ff., and H. W. Parke, *Greek Oracles*, pp. 80-81.

21. Cicero *De divin.* i.34.

22. H. W. Parke, *The Oracles of Zeus*, pp. 108-109. Callisthenes (F. Jacoby, *Die Fragmente der griechischen Historiker*, 124 F 22) mentions lots in a vessel in connection with the oracle of Zeus at Dodona.

23. For a description of this oracle see Pausanias vii.25.10.

24. "Astragalomanteia," Pauly-Wissowa, *Realencyclopädie der klassischen Altertumswissenschaft* (Stuttgart, 1896), II, 1793. I am indebted to Roy D. Kotansky for very enlightening discussions regarding the functioning of this type of oracle.

25. The most complete collection of these inscriptions is found in the now outdated dissertation by F. Heinevetter, "Würfel- und Buchstabenorakel in Griechenland und Kleinasien" (1912).

26. G. Kaibel, *Epigrammata Graeca*, p. 455 (no. 1038), author's trans.

27. G. Björck, "Heidnische und christliche Orakel mit fertigen Antworten," pp. 86-98; more recently see G. M. Browne, "The Composition of the Sortes Astrampsychi," pp. 95-100; idem, *The Papyri of the Sortes Astrampsychi.*

28. G. M. Browne, "The Composition of the Sortes Astrampsychi," pp. 95-96, contains a detailed description of how this lot oracle was consulted.

29. B. Kötting, *Peregrinatio Religiosa*, p. 13.

30. See C. A. Behr, *Aelius Aristides and the Sacred Tales*, which has an extended discussion of the life of Aristides, as well as the only English translation of his Sacred Tales (*Orat.* 47-52). Behr is currently translating the works of Aristides for the Loeb Classical Library.

31. Pausanias i.34.5; see also Plutarch *De def. orac.* 412a-b; *Arist.* xix.1-2.

32. Plutarch *Consol. ad Apoll.* 109b-c.

33. W. M. Calder, "Two Phrygian Epitaphs," pp. 214-15; L. Robert, *Études anatoliennes*, pp. 129-133.

34. Some striking exceptions are found in the oracles of Alexander of Abonuteichos quoted in Lucian *Alex.*

35. E. Rohde, *Psyche*, II, 290-91. Rohde regarded the oracle of Dionysos at Emphikleia in Phokis (reported in Pausanias x.33.11) where a priest gave oracles in a state of inspiration as typical of early Dionysiac religion. Rohde has needlessly confused Dionysiac ecstasy with oracular mediumship (E. R. Dodds, *Greeks and the Irrational*, p. 69).

36. E. R. Dodds, *Greeks and the Irrational*, pp. 68-69; H. W. Parke, *Greek Oracles*, p. 41; O, Kern, *Die Religion der Griechen*, II, 116-17.

37. O. Kern, *Die Religion der Griechen*, II, 136.

38. Pausanias vii.3.1 (Claros); Strabo vii.7.10 (Dodona). A fragment of Strabo suggests that the oak at Dodona was the first plant (frag. 7. 1c, in H. L. Jones, *Geography of Strabo*, III, 322-23).

39. H. W. Parke, *The Oracles of Zeus*, pp. 35-43.

40. Philostratus *Imag.* ii.33; here "Hellos" is the eponymous ancestor of the *Selloi* or *Helloi* mentioned in *Iliad* xvi.233ff. as the interpreters of Zeus at Dodona. See the scholion on *Iliad* xvi.234 (H. Erbse, *Scholia Graeca in Homeri Iliadem*, 4, 222).

41. Herodotus ii.55; a rationalizing interpretation of this legend, typical of Herodotus, follows in ii.56ff.

42. Aeschylus *Eumenides* 1-19; Pausanias x.5.5-6; Apollodoros i.4.1; Euripides *Iph. in Taur.* 1259ff.

43. Plutarch *De def. orac.* 433c-d, 435d-e; Pausanias x.5.7; Diodorus Siculus xvi.26.

44. Pindar *Nem.* ix.23ff. Athenaeus *Deip.* vi.232e-f.

45. For the oracle of Apollo at Claros, see Pliny *Hist. nat.* ii.96.232; Tacitus *Annals* ii.54; Macrobius *Saturn.* i.18.1; Eusebius *Praep. evang.* ii.3.2. For the oracle of Mopsos and Amphilokos see Pausanias i.34.4. For the oracle of Apollo at Branchidae see Strabo xvii.1.43; Ammianus Marcelinus xxix; Iamblichus *De myst.* iii.11; most of the references are collected in W. Günther, *Das Orakel von Didyma,* p. 114 n. 30 and p. 120. On Delphi see Pausanias x.24.7; Lucian *Hermot.* 60; *Bis accus.* i.792; *Jup. trag.* 30, 675. See P. Amandry, *La mantique Apollinienne,* pp. 135-39. For the oracle of Demeter at Patrae see Pausanias vii.21.11. For the oracle of Apollo Thyrxeus see Strabo ix.3.5: Diodorus Siculus xvi.26; Iamblichus *De myst.* iii.11. For the oracle of Glykon-Asklepios see Lucian *Alex.* 14.

46. On Delphi see Strabo ix.3.5. On Trophonios see Pausanias ix.39.5-14; Strabo ix.2.37 (Strabo here refers to "Trophonian Zeus"); Trophonios appears to have been a local fertility divinity who had "faded" to heroic status (L. R. Farnell, *Greek Hero Cults,* p. 21; W. K. C. Guthrie, *The Greeks and Their Gods,* pp. 223-231). On Clarian Apollo see Tacitus *Annals* ii.54; Valerius Flaccus 299. On Herakles Buraikos see Pausanias vii.25.10.

47. The earliest reference to the oak at Dodona (*Odyssey* xiv.327ff., repeated in xix.296ff.) refers to hearing "the will of Zeus from the oak." This probably gave rise to the legend of the talking tree. Sacred trees were more loquacious in Italy than Greece, since only the Oak at Dodona had this particular distinction in Greek tradition, while there are numerous instances of talking trees in Roman tradition. Pausanias (viii.23.5) speaks of the oak at Dodona as still in existence, though H. W. Parke, *Oracles of Zeus,* p. 31, plausibly argues that the oak could not have survived later than ca. 500 B.C.

48. Strabo ix.3.5.

49. The Pythia is designated a *promantis* in Herodotus vi.66; vii.111, 141; Thucydides v. 16; Lucian *Hermot.* 60; Pausanias iii.4.4, and a *prophētis* in Plato *Phaedrus* 244a; Euripides *Ion* 42, 321. For further data and references see M. van der Kolf, "Prophetes," col. 815.

50. Plutarch *Quaest. Graec.* 292d. Nikander is called a *prophētēs* in Plutarch *De def. orac.* 438b, and a *hiereus* ("priest") in Plutarch *De E apud Delphos* 386b. According to Herodotus viii.37 Akeratos was also a Delphic prophet. On Plutarch as one of the priests of Delphi see Plutarch *An seni resp.* 792f; *De def. orac.* 437a (R. Flaceliere, *Plutarque sur la disparition des oracles,* p. 14); *De Pyth. orac.* 409b-c; *De E apud Delphos* 391d-e (R. Flaceliere, *Plutarque sur l'E de Delphes,* pp. 5-6, 10-11, 61). W. Dittenberger, *SIG³,* 829A, reproduces an inscription from a statue of Hadrian, dedicated ca. A.D. 117-120, in which Plutarch is called a priest. In Plutarch *Quaest. conv.* 717d the plural nouns "prophets and priests" are connected by *kai* and have a single article, indicating that both terms describe the same group. On the identity of Delphic priests and prophets see W. R. Halliday, *Greek Questions,* pp. 59-60; R. Flaceliere, *Plutarque sur la disparition des oracles,* pp. 259-260 n. 305; idem, *Plutarque sur l'E de Delphes,* pp. 10-11; P. Amandry, *La mantique Apollinienne,* pp. 118-123.

51. These officials are all carefully discussed by P. Amandry, *La mantique Apollinienne,* pp. 115-125.

52. The tripod probably represented the throne of Apollo; cf. H. W. Parke, *Greek Oracles,* p. 74. Greek vase paintings represent both the Pythia and Apollo as seated on the tripod.

53. Plutarch *De def. orac.* 414b; Strabo ix.2.4.

54. Plutarch *De Pyth. orac.* 405c-d; A. Bouché-Leclercq, *Histoire de la divination dans l'antiquité,* III, 93ff. Diodorus Siculus xvi.26.6 claims that originally a virgin was chosen, but that later a matron of fifty or more years was chosen and clad in the garb of a virgin. Lucian *Astr.* 23 says that a virgin held the office of *prophētis* at Delphi.

55. This last point is argued by P. Amandry, *La mantique Apollinienne*, p. 175.

56. *Iliad* xvi.233ff.

57. Cf. H. W. Parke, *Oracles of Zeus*, pp. 1-19. Strabo (vii.7.10) regarded the *Selloi* as barbarians. One of the latest attempts to find foreign (in this case Semitic) influence in the practices of the *Selloi* is the article by M. Delcor, "The Selloi of the Oracle of Dodona," pp. 116-123. Another unusual feature of the oracle of Zeus at Dodona is the lack of a sanctuary until very late in the history of the oracle (fourth century B.C.). Strabo (ix.2.4) mentions the Dodonaean custom of male cultic officials delivering oracles to the Boeotians.

58. Herodotus ii.55ff. The names of the three prophetesses which he recorded are Promeneia, Timarete, and Nikandra. Sophocles, frag. 456 (ed. A. C. Pearson), mentions "the prophetic priestesses of Dodona." Strabo (vii.7.12) mentions the change from male to female prophets. The three priestesses are designated *prophētides* ("prophetesses") in Herodotus ix.93; Strabo vii.7.12; ix.2.4.

59. K. Buresch, *Klaros*, p. 36 (contra Iamblichus *De myst.* iii.11).

60. O. Schneider, *Nicandrea*, p. 18; K. Buresch, *Klaros*, p. 35.

61. Nikander *Alex.* 11.

62. A. S. F. Gow and A. F. Scholfield, *Nicander*, p. 5; O. Schneider, *Nicandrea*, pp. 17-18.

63. W. Dittenberger, *SIG*³, 633, 20.

64. W. Günther, *Das Orakel von Didyma*, p. 118; cf. *CIG*, 2884.

65. Origen *Contra Celsum* i.70; Iamblichus *De myst.* iii.11. Like the Delphic Pythia, she is not mentioned in inscriptions (W. Günther, *Das Orakel von Didyma*, p. 119).

66. W. Günther, *Das Orakel von Didyma*, p. 119.

67. W. Dittenberger, *SIG*³, 1157.

68. Pausanias x.33.11.

69. Herodotus i.182.

70. Herodotus viii.135; Strabo ix.2.34; W. Dittenberger, *SIG*³, 635; W. R. Halliday, *Greek Questions*, p. 59.

71. J. Wackernagel, *Vorlesungen über Syntax*, II, 239-240; E. Fascher, *PROPHĒTĒS*, p. 51; M. van der Kolf, "Prophetes," col. 798; H. Krämer, *TDNT*, VI, 783.

72. P. Amandry, "La divination en Grèce," p. 175; M. van der Kolf, "Prophetes," col. 798. O. Kern, *Die Religion der Griechen*, II, 112.

73. E. Fascher, *PROPHĒTĒS*, p. 6; H. Krämer, *TDNT*, VI, 795.

74. Scholium on *Iliad* xvi.235 (H. Erbse, *Scholia Graeca in Homeri Iliadem*, IV, 222-23). See the instructive discussion in M. van der Kolf, "Prophetes," cols. 799-800; E. Fascher, *PRO-PHĒTĒS*, pp. 27-32; Eustatius *Commentarii ad Homeri Iliadem*, II, 318-19 (on *Iliad* xvi.235); Lucian *Alex.* 24, 26. Attempts on the part of scholiasts to distinguish the role of the *prophētēs*, as one who predicts the future, from the *hypophētēs*, as one who interprets the words of the *prophētēs*, is a refined usage not reflected in the literature (cf. the scholium on Theocritus xxii.116).

75. Plutarch *De Iside* 378c.

76. Philostratus *Vita Apoll.* iii.42.

77. Pausanias ix.39.5-14 is the basis for the summary which follows. The assumption that this was an incubation oracle is refuted by R. J. Clark, "Trophonios," pp. 63-75.

78. Plutarch *De def. orac.* 398a.

79. P. Amandry, *La mantique Apollinienne*, pp. 81-85; H. W. Parke, *Greek Oracles*, pp. 80-81.

80. Diodorus Siculus xvi.26; Plutarch *De def. orac.* 435b, 437b, 438a-b.

81. In Plutarch *De def. orac.* 438b it is said that after taking the proper auspices the Pythia *descended* (*katebē*) to the oracle shrine (*manteion*). *De def. orac.* 437c mentions the room (*oikos*) in which the consultants are seated where perfumed odors are sometimes wafted in from the *adyton*.

82. Pausanias x.24.7; Lucian *Hermot.* 60; *Bis accus.* i.792; *Jup. trag.* 30, 675.

83. On the sacred spring Kassotis see P. Amandry, *La mantique Apollinienne*, pp. 135-39. On water as a means of inspiration see Pausanias vii.21.13; ix.2.1; x.24.7; Plutarch *De def. orac.* 432d. Aristides *Or.* i.46.

84. H. W. Parke, *Greek Oracles*, p. 75; P. Amandry, *La mantique Apollinienne*, pp. 126-134; H. W. Parke and D. E. W. Wormell, *The Delphic Oracle*, I, 24.

85. Pausanias ii.24.1.

86. R. Flaceliere, *Greek Oracles*, pp. 44-45.

87. Tacitus *Annals* ii.54; Pliny *Hist. nat.* ii.103 (106).232; K. Buresch, *Klaros*, p. 35.

88. W. Günther, *Das Orakel von Didyma*, p. 114, esp. n. 30.

89. H. W. Parke, *Greek Oracles*, pp. 83-84.

90. Lucian *Dial. deor.* 12; *Alex.* 19.

91. *Inscriptiones Graecae*, VII, 235.

92. Lucian *Alex.* 23; *Ep. Sat.* 21; *Tim.* 6.

93. Plutarch *De gar.* 512e; Herodotus vi.19 (both of the Pythia); Plutarch *De def. orac.* 434c-f (oracle of Mopsos); Lucian *Alex.* 19, 49, 50, 52. For the same phenomenon in magical divination see K. Preisendanz, *Papyri Graecae Magicae*, I.174-77; III.263-275.

94. On the unusual form of the lot oracle there see above, p. 25.

95. On Corope see W. Dittenberger, *SIG*[3], 1157 (discussed in some detail in H. W. Parke, *The Oracles of Zeus*, pp. 104ff.); on Mallos see Plutarch *De def. orac.* 434d-e (an attempt to test the oracle); on Alexander of Abonuteichos, see Lucian *Alex.* 19, 49.

96. Strabo (ix.3.5) observed that the Pythia delivered oracles in both poetry and prose, and that the prose oracles were versified by poets.

97. This is the suggestion of P. Amandry, *La mantique Apollinienne*, p. 120; similar proposals are made by M. P. Nilsson, "Das delphische Orakel," p. 244.

98. Plutarch *De Pyth. orac.* 397a ff.

99. W. R. Halliday, *Greek Questions*, pp. 59-60, referring to Plutarch *De Pyth. orac.* 407b and Strabo ix.3.5.

100. H. W. Parke, *Greek Oracles*, p. 139.

101. W. Günther, *Das Orakel von Didyma*, p. 119.

102. Herodotus viii.135; A. Bouché-Leclercq, III, 214-17; P. Guillon, *Les trépieds du Ptoion*, II, 137ff.

103. S. Eitrem, *Orakel und Mysterien*, p. 42, finds the closest parallel in Paul's insistence in 1 Cor. 14:13-19, 27-28, that incomprehensible glossolalia be interpreted in what he regards as the Delphic procedure whereby the *prophētēs* interprets the Pythia's incomprehensible speech for inquirers. This view is based largely on conjecture, not on hard evidence.

104. *Odyssey* xiv.327ff.; xix.296ff.; Apollodorus *Bibl.* i.16.6 refers to the talking plank in the ship *Argo* which was gotten from the oak at Dodona.

105. Dionysius Halicarnassensis i.14.

106. H. W. Parke, *The Oracles of Zeus*, pp. 129-163.

107. The Suida, s.v. *Dōdōnē* (A. Adler, *Suidae Lexicon*, II, 135).

108. Lucian *Alex.* 26-27.

109. Lucian *De dea Syria* 36.

110. Lucian *Alex.* 49.

111. Lucian *Alex.* 19.

112. H. W. Parke, *The Oracles of Zeus*, pp. 194-241.

113. Pausanias iii.18.3.

114. The function of this oracle is described by two relatively late authors, Diodorus Siculus and Quintus Curtius, both of whom appear to be dependent on a lost work of Callisthenes (H. Meltzer, "Der Fetisch im Heiligtum des Zeus Ammon," pp. 186-223). The reports on the oracle of Ammon are found in Diodorus Siculus xvii.50-51 and Quintus Curtius iv.7. See also Strabo xvii.1.43.

115. Diodorus Siculus xvii.51.2.

116. H. W. Parke, *Oracles of Zeus*, p. 200.

117. Quintus Curtius iv.7 reports the existence of silver bells on the litter, while Diodorus Siculus xvii.51.2 makes an enigmatic reference to "certain symbols of sound."

118. H. Klees, *Orakel und Seher,* pp. 46-47. Cf. Herodotus i.46-49; Plutarch *De def. orac.* 412a (in both examples, the tests are applied by non-Greeks).

119. Hermias *In Platonis Phaedrum Scholia* 94.5ff.

120. The oracle of Dodona quoted in Pausanias x.12.10 refers to Zeus and Dione in the third person. Sixteen Delphic oracles are expressed in the third person; cf. J. Fontenrose, *The Delphic Oracle,* p. 207.

121. Plutarch *De def. orac.* 414e. The assumption has frequently been made that this is the dominant view which Plutarch expresses (through Lamprias), only to reject it (E. Rohde, *Psyche,* II, 312-13). W. D. Smith, "So-called Possession in Pre-Christian Greece," p. 415, regards this view as a relatively recent innovation due to oriental influence. In Plutarch *De def. orac.* 414e the term *Pythōnes,* the contemporary designation for those earlier called *Eurykleis* (mantics who claimed that a god entered their bodies and spoke through them) is obviously derived from *Pythō,* the ancient name for the site of the Delphic oracle. The prominence of Delphi together with the use of the term *Pythōn* as a designation for those who believed themselves divinely possessed makes it virtually certain that the popular view of the Pythia was that she was divinely possessed when she uttered the oracles of Apollo. The antiquity of this view, however, cannot be determined. A related view of inspiration attributed oracular activity to the influence of *daimones,* i.e. supernatural beings located midway between gods and men on the scale of being (Plutarch *De def. orac.* 418c-e; 421b; 431a-c). Here the precise means whereby *daimones* inspire the mantis is not discussed by Plutarch. This theory can be traced to Plato (*Timaeus* 71a-72a; 86e-87a; *Phaedrus* 244a ff.; 265a; *Rep.* 503a; cf. Plutarch *Amat.* 758d-e, where he summarizes Plato *Timaeus* 86e-87a). Plutarch's own view, which he shared with Plato, was that the human mind is the daimon of each man. This daimon is capable of receiving impressions from other daimones, a process which is essentially divine inspiration (Plutarch *De def. orac.* 431c). However, the daimon theory of inspiration is not really important for Plutarch, since it is not found at all in *De Pythiae oraculis.*

122. H. Frisk, *Griechisches etymologisches Wörterbuch,* I, 517, s.v. *enthousiazō.* *Entheos* is made up of the preposition *en* ("in") prefixed to the noun *theos* ("god"); etymologically, however, the term does not mean "in (a) god," but rather "wherein a god is."

123. W. D. Smith, "So-called Possession in Pre-Christian Greece," pp. 403-426, has attempted to refute the widespread notion that the Greeks believed in divine possession prior to the first century A.D. The idea of divine possession, which occurs frequently in both pagan and Christian literature from the second century A.D. on, according to Smith, is the result of oriental influence. A careful review of the evidence which Smith discusses, and some that he does not (for example, he does not come to grips with some of the texts cited by A. Delatte, *Les conceptions de l'enthousiasme,* indicates that while the dominant view in ancient Greece was that spiritual beings used external means to influence man to prophesy and to write poetry, the notion of divine possession was not unknown (cf. Eurycles, discussed below, pp. 40-41).

124. Smith observes, quite correctly, that there is no description of exorcism in pagan literature prior to Lucian ("So-called Possession in Pre-Christian Greece," p. 409). On p. 413 Smith summarizes the conclusions of one part of his study: ". . . madness conceived as divine visitation and punishment, whether by *daimones* or gods, is not conceived or described as entry and possession by the hostile spirit, but is imaged as a physical and psychic disturbance caused by any of a number of means of attack — from chemical means like poison to simple physical shock." Smith discusses various Greek terms for divine "breath," which was believed to exert an influence on man and was regarded as a source for prophetic inspiration; yet he denies that possession is a necessary correlate of such divine inbreathing (pp. 419ff.).

125. W. D. Smith, "So-called Possession in Pre-Christian Greece," pp. 404, 414 n. 36 (Ps.-Longinus *Peri Hypsous* 13 cannot be as easily explained away as Smith would like).

126. Plutarch *De def. orac.* 414e.

127. A. E. Taylor, *A Commentary on Plato's Timaeus,* p. 513.

128. Lucian *Jup. trag.* 30.

129. P. Amandry, *La mantique Apollinienne,* pp. 20ff., 234-35. Lucan *De bello civili* v.102-197 is, as Amandry points out (pp. 20-21), dependent on the description of the ecstatic Sibyl in Vergil *Aeneid* vi.42ff. Vergil's depiction of the Cumaean Sibyl is itself historically suspect because it contains an element not found elsewhere in connection with Sibylline prophecy: the granting of oracular responses to questions posed by inquirers. Elsewhere the traditions of the Sibyl's prophetic behavior is always depicted as spontaneous and unsolicited.

130. The only hysterical behavior of the Pythia described by Plutarch is the result of her attempt to give oracular responses under unfavorable circumstances (*De def. orac.* 438b). On the other hand, Plutarch does refer to the Pythia as "regaining her composure" after descending from the tripod (*Amatorius* 759b), a reference which seems to presuppose a prior state of excitation, and in *De Pyth. orac.* 404e he describes the Pythia as unable to keep silent.

131. P. Amandry, *La mantique Apollinienne,* pp. 66-77.

132. P. Amandry, "La divination en Grèce," p. 175. On p. 176 he observes: "The only form of revelation which fully merits the designation 'intuitive' is that which is received directly, without intermediary, at any moment and in any place by a human being capable of immediately understanding and communicating the divine message." E. Fascher, whose main concern was a comparison of the basic features of Greek and Israelite prophecy, expressed doubt whether "real prophecy was possible within the framework of an institution" (*PROPHĒTES,* p. 59). Fascher ignores the very different social settings of prophecy in ancient Israel and Greece. In Israel the free prophet (the figure Fascher uses for the purposes of comparison, ignoring the court and cult prophet) stood outside all political and religious structures, while in Greece the oracle *prophētēs* and *promantis* were regular and integral features of Greek religious institutions.

133. In his study of the sociology of possession, I. M. Lewis distinguishes between two types of possession, uncontrolled, involuntary, and unsolicited possession as opposed to controlled, voluntary, and solicited possession (*Ecstatic Religion,* pp. 55, 64). Earlier, N. K. Chadwick, *Poetry and Prophecy,* pp. 58-72, with frequent discussions of Siberian shamanism, discussed mantic technique and the regulation of ecstasy.

134. Plutarch *De def. orac.* 433c-d, 435d-e; Pausanias x.5.7; Diodorus Siculus xvi.26.

135. This view is presented by Lamprias in Plutarch *De def. orac.* 431d-438e. Plutarch used Lamprias in this dialogue (his brother in real life) as a vehicle for expressing his own views (F. E. Brenk, *In Mist Apparelled,* pp. 116ff.). While Plutarch's theory of exhalations (the terms which he uses include *pneuma* ["breath," "vapor"], *rheuma* ["breath"], *anathymiasis* ["vapor," "exhalation," "breath"], *aponoia* ["effluence," "radiation"]) has been widely regarded as Stoic, Plutarch regards it as compatible with Aristotelianism (*De def. orac.* 434b), and it is articulated by Lamprias who, like Plutarch, is a Platonist (*De def. orac.* 431a). F. E. Brenk, *In Mist Apparelled,* pp. 117-18, 126-27, argues for a Platonic origin of Plutarch's theory of exhalations. The exhalation theory, though more systematically elaborated by Plutarch than any one before him, was not original with him (H. W. Parke and D. E. W. Wormell, *The Delphic Oracle,* I, 19ff.). Cicero was familiar with the theory (*De divin.* i.38, 79, 114; ii.117), which he regarded as Stoic. Aelius Aristides (*Or.* i.46) also speaks of "mantic waters and exhalations."

136. M. E. Isaacs, *The Concept of the Spirit,* p. 15.

137. W. C. van Unnik, "Den Geist löschet nicht aus," pp. 265ff.

138. In his epitaph Athanatos Epityncharos (ca. A.D. 313-14), who was a pagan high priest, emphatically claims that he had the gift of dispensing oracles: *alēthōs dōron elabon chrēsmodotin* (W. M. Ramsay, *Cities and Bishoprics of Phrygia,* II, 566-67).

139. See above, n. 9.

140. This motive is readily apparent in Plato, who did not value technical divination as highly as inspired divination (*Phaedrus* 244c-d; *Timaeus* 72b), and in Posidonios, who shared the Stoic preference for natural over technical divination. Cicero himself, an adherent of the New Academy, was skeptical of all forms of divination and sought to discredit them thoroughly in his treatise on the subject (*De divinatione*). The distinction which Plutarch makes between

the two forms of divination (*De genio Socr.* 593c-d), however, appears devoid of value judgments.

141. Plato *Phaedrus* 244b-245c; cf. Herodotus iv.79.

142. E. Rohde, *Psyche,* II, 314 n. 1, where he erroneously contends that *mantis* is derived from *manyō.*

143. H. Frisk, *Griechisches etymologisches Wörterbuch,* II, 172-73; E. Boisacq, *Dictionnaire etymologique de la langue grecque, ad loc.*; E. R. Dodds, *The Greeks and the Irrational,* p. 70; E. Fascher, *PROPHĒTĒS,* p. 7.

144. U. von Wilamovitz Moellendorff, *Der Glaube der Hellenen,* I, 40 n. 2.

145. W. K. Pritchett, *The Greek State at War,* III, 47-90 ("The Military Mantike").

146. Plutarch *Arist.* xiv.1; *Aratus* xliii.4; *Crassus* xix.6; *Quaest. conv.* 631a.

147. Plutarch *Mul. vert.* 252e-f; Artemidorus *Oneirocriticus* i. praef.

148. Plutarch *Reg. et imp.* 201b-c.

149. Plutarch *Caius Marius* xvii.1-3 (here Martha, a Syrian prophetess, worms her way into the confidence of Marius); xlii.2 (Octavius is presented as the victim of his own superstitions and as the prey of charlatans and mantics).

150. Plutarch *Lyc.* ix.3; *De Pyth. orac.* 407c.

151. Lucian *Demonax* 37; Aristophanes *Pax* 1050; *Aves* 959-991.

152. Euripides *Iph. at Aulis* 956ff.

153. *Odyssey* xv.222-256.

154. Arrian *Alex.* i.11.2; i.25.6-8; iii.2.2.

155. Arrian *Alex.* ii.3.3-4.

156. The eponymous ancestor of the Iamidae, Iamos, reportedly received the gift of divination from Apollo (Pausanias vi.2.5). Among his descendants was Tisamenos a Klytid, who was the state diviner at Sparta (Herodotus ix.35; Pausanias iii.11.6-8). Thrasybulos son of Aeneas practiced at Mantinea (Pausanias vi.2.4); Theoklos son of Eumantis practiced for the Messenians (Pausanias iv.16.1); Hegistratus son of Tellias divined for the Persians (Herodotus ix.37); Tellias of Elis divined for the Phocians (Pausanias x.1.8).

157. This thesis was brilliantly demonstrated by E. R. Dodds, *The Greeks and the Irrational.*

158. M. P. Nilsson, *Geschichte der griechische Religion,* I, 166; E. Fascher, *PROPHĒTĒS,* p. 60.

159. R. Flaceliere, *Greek Oracles,* pp. 20-21.

160. Plutarch *De gen. Socr.* 593c-d; cf. *Iliad* vii.44-45. The first kind of divination, according to Plutarch, is divination through various kinds of signs and sacrifices, while the second involves an actual understanding of the conversation of the gods. The first kind is common, the second is rare. In Plutarch's notion of divination there is an apparent conflict between divination as an art or skill and divination as a universal human faculty, particularly in those who are cultivated and educated. Plutarch's notion of the nature of man is that he is characterized by a tripartite division of body (*sōma*), soul (*psychē*), and mind (*nous*) (*De facie* 943a). As the soul is superior to the body, so the mind is superior and more divine than the soul. Elsewhere, Plutarch emphasizes the bipartite division in man consisting of body and soul (*Consol. ad Apoll.* 108b-c). Dreams and visions are actually generalized oracles not limited by time and space (*De sera numinis* 566c). In *De def. orac.* 432c-d the intelligent man is the best of diviners if he follows the guidance of his soul. All souls are possessed of this mantic power, although it is dimmed by the body (*De def. orac.* 431e-432c). When the body is asleep, the soul is less hindered by the body and is able to receive divine communications with greater ease (*De gen. Socr.* 588d-e). Those who are the most sensitive to divine communications in various forms are those who restrain the desires of the body in order to give full rein to the soul.

161. *Odyssey* xx.351-58.

162. M. P. Nilsson, *Geschichte der griechische Religion,* I, 166.

163. H. W. Parke, *Greek Oracles,* pp. 14ff.; R. Flaceliere, *Greek Oracles,* pp. 20-21; W. B. Stanford, *Commentary on the Odyssey, ad loc.*

164. H. Frisk, *Griechisches etymologisches Wörterbuch,* II, 700.

165. Plutarch *De Pyth. orac.* 397a (H. Diels, *Die Fragmente der Vorsokratiker*, I, 96; frag. 92), LCL trans. with modifications. See C. H. Kahn, *Art and Thought of Heraclitus*, pp. 44-45 (frag. 34), with commentary on pp. 124-26. The parts of the quotation in quotation marks are probably the words of Heraclitus quoted by Plutarch (Kahn, pp. 125, 310-11 n. 105).

166. The last line of this quotation ("yet reaches to a thousand years with her voice through the god") has been attributed by many to Plutarch, not Heraclitus (see the instructive note in A. Delatte, *Les conceptions de l'enthousiasme*, pp. 6-7 n. 1; cf. C. H. Kahn, *Heraclitus*, p. 125, with references). The difficulty with the line is whether Heraclitus could have placed the activity of the Sibyl a millennium before his own time. That difficulty is obviated if we regard his statement as referring, not to the time when the Sibyl was active, but to the extent of time during which her oracles could be fulfilled. This view makes it probable that Heraclitus was familiar with a collection of Sibylline oracles and that, in spite of their antiquity, they were thought to find fulfillment in various contemporary events.

167. The earliest evidence for multiple Sibyls comes from the fourth-century writer Heraclides of Pontus, quoted in Clement of Alex. *Strom.* i.108.3 (K. Müller, *Fragmenta Historicorum Graecorum*, II, 197).

168. Pausanias x.12.1-9 names three Sibyls: Herophile of Marpessus (where she lived near the temple of Apollo Smintheos, from which she traveled to Samos, Claros, Delos, Delphi, and back again to Marpessus), Demo of Cumae, and Sabbe (a Hebrew, Babylonian, or Egyptian Sibyl). Varro, in Lactantius *Div. inst.* i.6, names ten Sibyls: (1) Persian, (2) Libyan, (3) Delphic, (4) Cimmerian, (5) Erythraean, (6) Samian, (7) Cumaean, (8) Hellespontine, (9) Phrygian, and (10) Tiburtine. Another list of ten Sibyls, nearly identical to that of Varro, is found in the scholium on Plato *Phaedrus* 244b (G. C. Greene, *Scholia Platonica, ad loc.*). References to the Sibyls in ancient literature are collected and discussed extensively in C. Alexandre, *Excursus ad Sibyllina*. For a short summary of the various Sibyls and references to them, see V. Nikiprowetzky, *La troisième Sibylle*, pp. 4-5.

169. V. Nikiprowetzky, *La troisième Sibyelle*, p. 4.

170. Apart from Vergil's imaginative description of the Cumean Sibyl in *Aeneid* vi.42ff., there is no evidence that the Sibyls were thought to have given oracular responses to inquiries. See J. J.Collins, *The Sibylline Oracles*, p. 2, where he takes the possibility of consultation too seriously, as if the Sibyls were historical figures.

171. Plutarch's reference to the first Sibyl who uttered prophecies while seated on a rock at Delphi near the Bouleuterion (*De Pyth. orac.* 398c; cf. Clement of Alex. *Strom.* i.15.70.3) was probably based on information gleaned from the Delphic guides. The rock (to which modern guides still point) provided a concrete way of relating the Sibyl to Delphi. While Plutarch states that the first Sibyl had come from Helikon where she had been reared by the Muses, he also cites another opinion that she had come from the Malians and was the daughter of Lamia, whose father was Poseidon. By the time Pausanias wrote (ca. A.D. 160), the variant traditions of the Delphic Sibyl found in Plutarch (ca. A.D. 100) had been integrated into a consistent account. In Pausanias x.12.1ff. the first Sibyl is the daughter of Zeus and Lamia, who was the daughter of Poseidon. The second Sibyl was Herophile.

172. Josephus *Ant.* i.118 (a prose paraphrase of *Orac. Sib.* iii.97ff. quoted from Alexander Polyhistor), Hermas *Vis.* ii.4; Justin *1 Apol.* 20, 44; Ps.-Justin *Coh. ad Graecos* 37.

173. Pausanias x.12.1ff.; cf. C. Alexandre, *Excursus ad Sibyllina*, pp. 10-11.

174. Herodotus viii.20, 77, 96; ix.43; Plato *Theag.* 124d; Pausanias iv.27.4; ix.17.5; x.12.11; x.32.8ff.; Aelius Aristides *Or.* ii.46; Aristophanes *Equites* 1002ff.; *Pax* 1071ff.

175. Herodotus viii.20, 77, 96; ix.43.

176. Aristotle *Prob.* 954a; Plutarch *De Pyth. orac.* 399a; M. P. Nilsson, *Geschichte der griechische Religion*, I, 620, mistakenly claims that Plato refers to Bakis in the plural.

177. Scholium on Aristophanes *Equites* 123 (F. Dübner, *Scholia Graeca in Aristophanem*, p. 38). Cf. Clement of Alex. *Strom.* i.21.1 (where only the Boeotian and Arkadian Bakides are mentioned.

178. E. Rohde, *Psyche*, II, 394 n. 58; E. Fascher, *PROPHĒTĒS*, p. 55.

179. E. R. Dodds, *The Greeks and the Irrational,* p. 88 n. 45.

180. This process of assimilating the Bakis traditions to those of the Sibyl is apparent in the scholium on Aristophanes *Aves* 962 (F. Dübner, *Scholia Graeca in Aristophanem,* p. 232), in which Philetas of Ephesus is quoted as saying that there were three Sibyls (one the sister of Apollo, one the Sibyl of Erythrae, and the third of Sardis) and three Bakides (one from Eleon in Boeotia, one an Athenian, and the third an Arkadian).

181. A. E. Taylor, *A Commentary on Plato's Timaeus,* p. 513.

182. Plato *Apol.* 22c; *Meno* 99c; *Ion* 534c; cf. E. R. Dodds, *The Greeks and the Irrational,* p. 88 n. 46; E. Fascher, *PROPHETES,* pp. 66ff.

183. According to R. S. Bluck, *Plato's Meno,* p. 427, the term *theomantis* in *Apol.* 22c and *Meno* 99c means an inspired *mantis* as opposed to a *mantis* who interprets omens, prodigies, and dreams. However, it is clear from *Meno* 99d that *theomantis* and *mantis* can be used interchangeably by Plato. It is true that Plato did not value augury and hepatoscopy as highly as inspired divination (*Phaedrus* 244c-d; *Timaeus* 72b).

184. In Plato *Theag.* 124d, Sibyl, Bakis, and Amphilytos (originally from Akarnania; cf. Herodotus i.62) are described as *chrēsmodoi.*

185. Plato *Charmides* 173c.

186. In *Phaedrus* 244b-249e Plato discusses four kinds of inspiration (*mania*): (1) inspired divination (244b), (2) the inspiration of the priest who finds a way to free men from diseases and other ills (244d-e), (3) the inspiration of poets (245a), and (4) the inspiration of the philosopher who recollects ideas not perceived by the senses (249d).

187. Plato *Phaedrus* 244a-b.

188. Plato *Cratylus* 396d.

189. Aelius Aristides *Or.* ii.43. The same claim is made by Ps.-Justin *Coh. ad Graecos* 37 (also dependent on Plato). Yet Plato does not say that after the occurrence of inspired speech the prophet or prophetess does not *remember* what was said; rather, he asserts that what they said did not originate with their own knowledge (Plato *Apol.* 22c; *Meno* 99c). W. Burkert, *Griechische Religion,* p. 185, accepts as historical the view of Aristides, not recognizing that Aristides has considerably amplified Plato.

190. R. S. Bluck, *Plato's Meno,* pp. 424ff.

191. E. R. Dodds, "Plato and the Irrational," pp. 117ff.; *The Greeks and the Irrational,* pp. 217-18. In *Rep.* 415c Plato approves of the practice of forging oracles to achieve good ends.

192. U. von Wilamovitz Moellendorff, *Der Glaube der Hellenen,* I, 40.

193. H. Krämer, *TDNT,* VI, 787-88.

194. Pausanias i.34.4; cf. W. R. Halliday, *Greek Divination,* p. 92.

195. The first two meanings are insisted upon by M. P. Nilsson, *AJP,* 71 (1950), 422, in a review of J. H. Oliver, *The Athenian Expounders* (see next note). H. Frisk, *Griechisches etymologisches Wörterbuch,* II, 1118, translates *chrēsmologos* as *weissagend* ("prophetic") or *Wahrsager* ("prophet, seer"). Clement of Alex. *Strom.* i.21.132 produces a list of Greek prophets, all of whom he designates as *chrēsmologoi.*

196. J. H. Oliver, *The Athenian Expounders.* Oliver's equation of the *chrēsmologos* with the *mantis* was strongly opposed by M. P. Nilsson, *AJP,* 71 (1950), 422; D. Hanell, *Gnomon,* 25 (1953), 525.

197. These distinctions are those formulated by H. W. Parke and D. E. W. Wormell, *The Delphic Oracle,* II, xv.

198. Amphilytos is referred to, along with Sibyl and Bakis, by Plato *Theag.* 124d, as *chrēsmodoi* ("oracle singers"). The quotation is from Herodotus i.62. In Herodotus viii.96 an oracle by the Athenian *chrēsmologos* Lysistratos is quoted.

199. Both meanings are suggested by W. W. How and J. Wells, *Commentary on Herodotus,* I, 85. J. H. Oliver has collected a number of texts which show that the same individual could be called both a *chrēsmologos* and a *mantis* (*The Athenian Expounders,* p. 11, where references are made to the texts collected in the appendix).

200. Herodotus vii.142-43.

201. Herodotus vii.6.

202. Philo De spec. leg. iv.52.

203. Plutarch De def. orac. 414e; cf. Lucian Lex. 20; Josephus Ant. vi.329. Engastrimythos is found fifteen times in the LXX, and is several times applied to the witch of Endor (1 Kgs. 28:3-9). For the use of the term in early Christian literature see Lampe, Patristic Greek Lexicon, p. 397.

204. Three synonyms are: (1) sternomantis (found only in Sophocles, frag. 59 [A. C. Pearson, The Fragments of Sophocles, I, 37] and Hesychius, s.v. engastrimythos [K. Latte, Hesychii Alexandrini Lexicon, II, 5], (2) engastromantis (only in Hesychius, s.v. engastrimythos [K. Latte, Hesychii Alexandrini Lexicon, II, 5]), and (3) thymomantis (Aeschylus Persae 224).

205. This has been convincingly argued by E. R. Dodds, The Greeks and the Irrational, pp. 71-72 and notes; P. Amandry, "La divination en Grèce," p. 175, agrees with Dodds.

206. Plato Soph. 252c; Aristophanes Vespae 1019-20.

207. Scholium on Aristophanes Vespae 1019 (F. Dübner, Scholia Graecam in Aristophanem, p. 158).

208. Origen De princ. iii.4.5; Jerome Ep. ad Avitum 8.

209. On the significance of the loud voice see F. J. Dölger, "Theou Phōnē," pp. 218-223. Several examples of possession coupled with involuntary speech are found in Mark 1:24-26; 3:11; 5:7-12 (cf. F. Bauernfeind, Die Dämonenworte im Markusevangelium) and Lucian Philops. 15-16.

210. Arrian Alex. iv.13.5-6.

211. Plutarch Caius Marius xvii.1-3; E. Peterson, "Beiträge," p. 267 n. 74, suggests a connection between Martha's prophetic technique (sitting upon a litter; cf. 2 Macc. 9:8) and magical divination.

212. Lucian Philops. 15-16.

213. Lucian Dial. Meretricii 288.

214. Florus ii.7.4-8. Enus is described as "counterfeiting an inspired frenzy" (fanatico furore simulato), and he hid a nut filled with fire and sulphur in his mouth which sent forth flames as he spoke. His activity is dated ca. 135 B.C.

215. Origen Contra Celsum vii.9.

216. G. Hölscher, Die Propheten, p. 134; W. Schneemelcher, NTA, II, 685. The pagan setting for the activity of Celsus' prophet is "in temples" (Origen Contra Celsum vii.9; cf. P. de Labriolle, La Crise Montaniste, pp. 95-101 (cannot be Montanist).

217. R. Reitzenstein, Poimandres, pp. 222-23, draws attention to the similarity of the speech of Celsus' Syrian prophet and the style of the Johannine Jesus in John 8:42ff. E. Norden, Agnostos Theos, pp. 18ff., agrees with Reitzenstein and supposes that the Fourth Evangelist, familiar with such revelatory speeches as that reproduced by Celsus, transformed that basic pattern into the dialogue form found in John 8:42ff. For a bibliography on the "I"-style of aretalogies and the egō eimi formula in early Christian and gnostic sources, see J. Z. Smith, "Native Cults in the Hellenistic Period," p. 243 n. 12.

218. There were those who made such claims in antiquity. Menekrates, a fourth-century B.C. Syracusan physician, thought that he was Zeus (Athenaeus Deip. vii.289a-290a). On the borderline between a mystic and a psychotic, Menekrates wanted to be taken seriously as a divine man. The most comprehensive study on Menekrates is O. Weinreich, Menekrates Zeus und Salmoneus, pp. 305-331.

219. E. R. Dodds, Pagan and Christian, p. 59.

220. See the discussion of this oracle below, pp. 71-72.

221. The phenomenon described by Celsus could either be glossolalia (ecstatic speech) or the use of voces magicae. If this prophet concluded his oracle with incomprehensible ecstatic speech, that could be considered a form of legitimation underscoring the supernatural origin of the revelatory message (cf. T. W. Gillespie, "A Pattern of Prophetic Speech in First Corinthians," pp. 74-95).

222. Polybius xxi.37.5-7; cf. Livy *Annals* xxxviii.18.9 (dependent upon Polybius), where we read *vaticinantes fanatico carmine.*

223. Livy *Annals* xxxix.8ff.; cf. A. D. Nock, *Conversion*, pp. 72-73.

224. Livy *Annals* xxxix.13.12: *Viros, velut mente capta, cum iactatione fanatica corporis vaticinari.*

225. The phenomenon reported by Livy is taken seriously by R. Reitzenstein, *Hellenistische Mysterienreligionen*, pp. 97, 99 (cf. p. 12).

226. Apuleius *Metamorphoses* viii.28: *Infit vaticinatione clamosa conficto mandacio semet ipsum incessere atque criminari.* E. Fascher, *PROPHETES*, p. 205, observes that "He is more an ecstatic and a flagellant than a proclaimer of a divine message." Fascher's "comparative" method seems designed to depreciate anything not fashioned after the Judeo-Christian pattern.

227. Plutarch *De Pyth. orac.* 407c.

228. This lot oracle was probably similar to the *Sortes Astrampsychi* discussed above, p. 25.

229. Dionysius Periegetes, active during the second century A.D., attributed this statement to Arrian according to Eustatius *On Dionysius Periegetes* 809 (ed. Bernhardy, I, 256); cf. I. M. Linforth, "The Corybantic Rites in Plato," p. 123.

230. J. Ferguson, *Utopias of the Classical World.*

231. See the discussion of the *Fourth Eclogue* below, p. 76.

232. J. Z. Smith, "Wisdom and Apocalyptic," pp. 131-156.

233. L. Koenen, "Die Prophezeiungen des 'Töpfers'," p. 196, lines 16-18 (frag. P_1).

234. *Scriptores historiae Augustae*, Marcus Antoninus 13.6. During the same plague, which swept the entire empire, Alexander of Abonuteichos reportedly sent an oracle consisting of a single line of hexameter verse to all nations: "Phoebus the unshorn wards off the deadly cloud plague" (Lucian *Alex.* 36; author's trans.).

235. Dio Cassius lv.31.2-3 describes such prophetic activity during a famine in A.D. 7; cf. the announcement of a universal famine by Agabus the Christian prophet according to Acts 11:27-30.

236. Herodotus vii.6. We have already underlined the ambiguous nature of the term *chrēsmologos* (see above, p. 40), which can refer either to an inspired diviner, a collector and expounder of oracles, or an interpreter of oracles.

237. Aristophanes *Aves* 959-991.

238. Aristophanes *Pax* 1043-1126.

239. Aristotle *Rhet.* 1407b (iii.5.4).

240. Plutarch *Agesilaus* iii.3-5.

241. Thucydides ii.8.2; ii.21.3; viii.1.1.

242. Ibid., ii.54.2-3.

243. Lucian *Alex.* 49.

244. Lucian *Jup. trag.* 28.

245. The most important treatment of the subject is still the magisterial work of T. Hopfner, *Griechisch-ägyptischer Offenbarungszauber.* The best survey of Greco-Roman magic in English is that of J. M. Hull, *Hellenistic Magic and the Synoptic Tradition.* For a survey of Greco-Roman magic and its relationship to early Christianity with extensive bibliographical references, see D. E. Aune, "Magic in Early Christianity," pp. 1507-57. Two other indispensable studies are by M. Smith, *Clement of Alexandria and a Secret Gospel of Mark*, pp. 195-278; idem, *Jesus the Magician.*

246. On the Apocalypse see D. E. Aune, "The Social Matrix of the Apocalypse of John," pp. 26-29 (the mixture of magical and anti-magical traditions in the Apocalypse will be treated extensively in my forthcoming commentary on that book). On the Shepherd of Hermas see E. Peterson, "Beiträge zur Interpretation der Visionem im Pastor Hermae," pp. 254-270, and particularly J. Reiling, *Hermas and Christian Prophecy.*

247. K. Preisendanz, *PGM* (2 vols.; 1973-74); other published Greek and Coptic magical papyri and inscriptions on amulets are listed in D. E. Aune, "Magic in Early Christianity," p. 1516 n. 32.

248. T. Hopfner, *Griechisch-ägyptischer Offenbarungszauber*, II, 41ff.; cf. D. E. Aune, "Magic in Early Christianity," pp. 1517-18.

249. D. F. Moke, "Eroticism in the Greek Magical Papyri."

250. T. Hopfner, *Griechisch-ägyptischer Offenbarungszauber*.

251. F. L. Griffith and H. Thompson, *The Leyden Papyrus*.

252. Possession trance is presupposed in *PGM* IV.1121-24 (quoted on p. 47).

253. Presented in a fully restored form in *PGM* vol. 2, 241-42.

Chapter 3

1. An exhaustive collection of Delphic oracles is available in H. W. Parke and D. E. W. Wormell, *The Delphic Oracle*, II; see also H. W. Parke and D. E. W. Wormell, "A Neglected Delphic Oracle," pp. 18-20. Ten oracles of Clarian Apollo are collected and discussed in K. Buresch, *Klaros*. R. R. Hendess, *Oracula Graeca*, has collected 212 oracles, primarily from literary sources. Another collection is found in G. Wolff, *Porphyrii de Philosophia ex Oraculis Haurienda*, in which the many oracles of Claros, Didyma, and Hecate quoted by Porphyrius, excerpts of which were in turn quoted by Eusebius in *Praeparatio evangelica*, are assembled and discussed. The fragments of the Chaldaean Oracles are available in the collection of E. des Places, *Oracles Chaldaïques*. Fragments of the original Sibylline oracles are collected by C. Alexandre, *Excursus ad Sibyllina*. Some oracles preserved in inscriptions from the sanctuary of Apollo at Didyma are found in T. Wiegand, *Didyma*, 2. Teil: *Die Inschriften*, pp. 299ff. Other oracles in inscriptions are collected by G. Kaibel, *Epigrammata Graeca*, pp. 447-460, and W. Dittenberger, *Sylloge Inscriptionum Graecarum*, nos. 1915-24.

2. H. W. Parke and D. E. W. Wormell, *The Delphic Oracle*, II, xxii.

3. E. R. Dodds, "New Light," p. 265; H. W. Parke and D. E. W. Wormell, *The Delphic Oracle*, II, xxiii.

4. Apollonios of Molon (first century B.C.) thought that only hexameter oracles were genuine; scholium on Aristophanes *Nubes* 144 (F. Dübner, *Scholia Graeca in Aristophanem*, p. 88).

5. G. Wolff, *Porphyrii*, gives examples of oracles in iambic trimeter (pp. 69-80), trochaics (pp. 80-83), and elegiacs (pp. 84-87). Parke-Wormell, *The Delphic Oracle*, II, xxi, regard all Delphic elegiac responses as fictitious. Some elegiac oracles attributed to Delphi are preserved in the *Greek Anthology* xiv.71, 74. Oenomaus of Gadara, quoted in Eusebius *Praep. evang.* v.23, cites an oracle of Claros in trochaics.

6. Prose oracles are briefly discussed in Parke-Wormell, *The Delphic Oracle*, II, xxii. A prose oracle of Glykon-Asklepios is quoted by Lucian *Alex.* 52; Lucian does not call attention to this feature, though he would certainly have done so if the practice were unusual. Plutarch devoted his dialogue *De Pythia oraculis* to a discussion of why oracles were no longer given in verse at Delphi.

7. Author's translation based on the text printed in Parke-Wormell, *The Delphic Oracle*, II, 1.

8. U. von Wilamowitz-Moellendorff, *Der Glaube der Hellenen*, II, 39; Parke-Wormell, *The Delphic Oracle*, II, xxx ff.; R. Crahay, *La littérature oraculaire chez Hérodote*, pp. 34, 98, 150, 172, 186, 193, 237, 296-97.

9. W. E. McLeon, "Oral Bards at Delphi," pp. 317-18.

10. This has been demonstrated by W. E. McLeod, "Oral Bards at Delphi," pp. 317-325.

11. *Iliad* i.1: "Sing, goddess, the wrath of Achilles son of Peleus"; Hesiod *Theog.* 22: "These [Muses] once taught Hesiod beautiful song." See also *Odyssey* i.1, 10; viii.481, 488; Hesiod *Opera* 1.

12. E. R. Dodds, *Irrational*, p. 117.

13. Parke-Wormell, *The Delphic Oracle*, II, xxxiv-xxxv.

14. C. M. Bowra, *Pindar*, pp. 210-11, 225-26; O. Kern, *Die Religion der Griechen*, II, 112.

15. E.g. Herodotus v.67; vii.169.

16. H. W. Parke, "Delphic Oracles," pp. 58-66.

17. Herodotus i.174.

18. For an excellent introduction to ancient Greek poetry see P. Maas, *Greek Metre*. Occasionally scholars have attempted to translate Greek dactylic hexameter using English iambic pentameter.

19. H. W. Parke, *Greek Oracles*, p. 139.

20. Longinus *Peri Hypsous* 8.4. The beautiful language of dream oracles serves Aristides as a rhetorical model (Aelius Aristides *Or.* 1.25 [B. Keil, II, 432]). That the beauty of oracles in verse indicates their divine origin is a presupposition held by the participants in Plutarch's dialogue *De Pyth. orac.* 396c-d.

21. Josephus *Ant.* iv.303 refers to the Song of Moses (Deut. 32:1-43) and the predictions it contains as a composition in hexameter. The poem was actually written using the Semitic poetic device *parallelismus membrorum*; even the LXX version makes no attempt to translate the poem into hexameter. Josephus used the term "hexameter" to convey to a Greek audience the poetic and oracular character of Deut. 32. J. T. Milik has conjectured that 1 Enoch 37-71 was originally composed in Greek hexameters using a pseudo-Homeric dialect in "Problèmes de la littérature Hénochique," pp. 373ff., and more recently in *The Books of Enoch*, (p. 92).

21a. Plutarch *De Pyth. orac.* 404d (Diels, frag. 93), translation of C. H. Kahn, *Heraclitus*, p. 43 (frag. xxxiii).

22. H. Klees, *Orakel und Seher*, pp. 68-91.

23. Ibid., p. 91.

24. Parke-Wormell, *The Delphic Oracle*, II, xxiii, xxvi.

25. P. Amandry, *La mantique Apollinienne*, p. 149.

26. See above, p. 25; see also H. W. Parke, *The Oracles of Zeus*, pp. 100-114; the author has translated a selection of thirty-eight inquiries on pp. 259-273.

27. The four questions quoted are taken from H. W. Parke, *The Oracles of Zeus*, pp. 260, 265, 268, 272.

28. J. L. White and K. A. Kensinger, "Categories of Greek Papyrus Letters," pp. 79-81, 85.

29. The customary formulaic introduction to many oracle questions was *ei lōion kai ameinon* ("Is it better and more beneficial. . . ?"); cf. Xenophon *Vect.* vi.2; Demosthenes *Or.* xliii.86. For a short discussion of the normal form of inquiries see H. W. Parke, *Greek Oracles*, p. 45.

30. Xenophon *Vect.* vi.2-3 (LCL trans. slightly revised by author). Similar double questions are evident in Xenophon *Anab.* iii.1.5-7; Thucydides i.134.4; Dionysius Halicarnassensis *Antiq. Rom.* i.23.4; T. Wiegand, *Didyma*, 2. Teil: *Die Inschriften*, p. 301. The convention of the double question is discussed briefly in M. P. Nilsson, *Geschichte der griechische Religion*, I, 628.

31. Plutarch *De E apud Delphos* 386c; each of the questions is in the third person in Plutarch, but I have placed them in the first person.

32. Plutarch *De Pyth. orac.* 408c (author's trans.).

33. Athenaeus *Deip.* v.219a (author's trans.).

34. Xenophon *Mem.* iv.3.16; i.3.1.; Athenaeus *Deip.* vi.232f; vi.232e; v.219a (author's trans.).

35. Several oracle questions from P. Oxy. 1477 are printed and translated in A. S. Hunt and C. C. Edgar, *Select Papyri*, I, 436ff. (nos. 193-95).

36. G. Björck, "Heidnische und christliche Orakel mit fertigen Antworten," pp. 86-98.

37. These five oracle questions are quoted from G. M. Browne, *Sortes Astrampsychi*, pp. 22-23.

38. The basic collection and analysis of papyrus oracle questions is W. Schubart, "Orakelfragen," pp. 110-15. Schubart's three-part structural analysis of oracle questions has been corrected at points by A. Henrichs, "Zwei Orakelfragen," p. 116. Greek and Demotic oracle questions are very similar in form; cf. W. Erichsen, *Demotische Orakelfragen*, p. 17. For a basic bibliography on the subject of Greek and Demotic oracle questions, see A. Henrichs, "Zwei Orakelfragen," p. 115 nn. 1 and 2, p. 116 n. 4.

39. The first oracle question is the author's translation of K. Preisendanz, *PGM*, XXXe (two collections of oracle questions are found in *PGM*, XXXa-f and XXXIa-c). The second oracle question quoted is from the short collection of such questions in A. S. Hunt and C. C.

Edgar, *Select Papyri*, I, 436-37.

40. P. Amandry, *La mantique Apollinienne*, pp. 155-56, 179ff. Amandry attributes the vagueness and ambiguity of ancient oracles to the difficulty which Apollo may have had in choosing between the two alternatives offered him (p. 167). While most of the oracle questions which have survived support Amandry's contention that such inquiries were always phrases in terms of two alternatives, others presuppose a more open-ended inquiry.

41. On the subject of ancient oracle collections see below, pp. 77-79.

42. M. P. Nilsson, *Cults, Myths, Oracles*, pp. 130ff.

43. H. W. Parke, *Greek Oracles*, pp. 49-55; Parke supposes that the personality of the Sibyl was not submerged in her ecstatic utterance, unlike that of the Pythia. He offers a psychological solution for a sociological phenomenon.

44. E. R. Dodds, "New Light," p. 265. The style and meter of the Delphic responses, which alone exhibit great variety, are discussed by Parke-Wormell, *The Delphic Oracle*, II, xxi-xxxvi.

45. R. MacMullen, *Roman Social Relations*, p. 41.

46. G. M. Browne, *Sortes Astrampsychi*, p. 5.

47. Ibid., pp. 54-55.

48. H. W. Smyth, *Greek Grammar*, par. 1882 (he uses the designation "oracular present"); F. Blass, A. Debrunner, and R. W. Funk, *Greek Grammar*, par. 323; N. Turner, *Syntax*, p. 63.

49. Lucian *Alex.* 25 (LCL trans. with slight changes).

50. Lucian *Alex.* 33 (author's trans.).

51. Aelius Aristides *Or.* xlviii.71 (ed. B. Keil, II, 410); trans. C. A. Behr, *Aelius Aristides*, p. 238 (*Sacred Tales* ii.71).

52. Eusebius *Praep. evang.* v.23.3 (author's trans.).

53. Eusebius *Praep. evang.* v.22.1 (author's trans.).

54. I. M. Linforth, *Orpheus*, pp. 125, 137.

55. Author's translation of an inscription reproduced in T. Wiegand, *Didyma*, 2. Teil: *Die Inschriften*, p. 301.

56. Demosthenes *Orat.* xxi.53.

57. Lucian *Alex.* 35.

58. A comparison of the two editions of the *Sortes Astrampsychi* reveals a tendency to expand single-line (one-part) responses into two-part responses (cf. G. M. Browne, *Sortes Astrampsychi*, pp. 3-4).

59. G. M. Browne, *Sortes Astrampsychi*, pp. 36-37, 55-56.

60. *Sammelbuch Griechischer Urkunden aus Ägypten*, I (1915), 301 (no. 4230).

61. Lucian *Alex.* 43 (author's trans.).

62. Herodotus i.174.

63. Aelius Aristides *Or.* xlviii.12 (ed. B. Keil, II, 397); trans. C. A. Behr, *Aelius Aristides*, p. 243 (*Sacred Tales* ii.12).

64. Philostratus *Vita Apoll.* i.10 (author's trans.).

65. H. D. Betz, "Eine Christus-Aretalogie," pp. 293-303. This is the only analysis of the two-part oracle with which I am familiar. Some of the comparative material to which Betz appeals, however (such as sayings of Apollonius), is not clearly and convincingly oracular, even though uttered by a "divine man."

66. See below, pp. 237-240.

67. Translated by the author from the text published by H. Hommel, "Das Versorakel des gryneischen Apollon," pp. 84-92. For a slightly different reconstruction of the text, see R. Merkelbach, "Ein Orakel des gryneischen Apollo," p. 48.

68. Philostratus *Vita Apoll.* i.9 (author's trans.).

69. Pausanias iv.20.1.

70. Pausanias vii.5.2, also found in R. Hendess, *Oracula Graeca*, no. 142, and discussed by K. Buresch, *Klaros*, p. 32. See below, p. 64.

71. Several examples of conditional curse formulas in epitaphs are discussed in R. Lattimore, *Epitaphs*, pp. 110ff.

72. Often presented in a totally unexpected manner.

73. Athenaeus Deip. xii.520a.

74. See above, p. 50.

75. Author's translation of text reproduced in Parke-Wormell, The Delphic Oracle, II, 1. In the Greek Anthology xiv.73 the same oracle is applied to the Megarians.

76. See above, pp. 51-52. See also Heraclitus in Plutarch De Pyth. orac. 404e (H. Diels, Die Fragmente der Vorsokratiker, I, 172 [frag. 92]). See also Plutarch De Pyth. orac. 407c-d; Lucian Alex. 10, 22; J. J. Collins, Sibylline Oracles, p. 5; K. Ohlert, Rätsel und Rätselspiele der alten Griechen, pp. 134-145; W. Schultz, Rätsel aus dem hellenischen Kulturkreise, I, 65-81.

77. See above, p. 61 (Pausanias iv.20.1).

78. Pausanias viii.11.10.

79. Pausanias viii.11.10-11. The same oracle story is found in Diodorus xxv.19.

80. Other homonymic riddle oracles are collected in Strabo vi.1.5.

81. See above, p. 25.

82. An excellent discussion of this type of oracle, designated "theological oracle," is the article by A. D. Nock, "Oracles Théologiques," pp. 280-290.

83. See the fragments collected by G. Wolff, Porphyrii.

84. The Suida, s.v. Ioulianos; cf. H. Lewy, Chaldaean Oracles, p. 5; E. des Places, Oracles Chaldaïques, p. 7.

85. E. R. Dodds, Irrational, p. 284; R. MacMullen, Enemies of the Roman Order, pp. 106-107.

86. The best exposition of the religious and philosophical thought of the Chaldaean Oracles is H. Lewy, Chaldaean Oracles; see the review by E. R. Dodds, "New Light," pp. 263-273. For a more recent summary of the major ideas expressed in the Oracles see E. des Places, Oracles Chaldaïques, pp. 11-18.

87. Proclus In Alc. 50 (trans. J. O'Neill, Proclus Diadochus, p. 25). These fragments are found in W. Kroll, De Oraculus Chaldaicus, p. 55, and in a slightly longer form in E. des Places, Oracles Chaldaïques, p. 99 (frag. 135).

88. Psellus Comm. 1128b, quoted in W. Kroll, De Oraculis Chaldaicus, p. 64 (author's trans.). The same fragment is also quoted in E. des Places, Oracles Chaldaïques, pp. 92-93 (frag. 107).

89. J. Fontenrose, The Delphic Oracle, pp. 151, 171-72.

90. R. Lattimore, Epitaphs, p. 49.

91. The more common terms for blessing in the oracles are eudaimon (Parke-Wormell, The Delphic Oracle, II, 7-8 [no. 16], 53-54 [no. 121]); eudaimōn (Athenaeus Deip. xii.520a; xiii.602c); olbios (Parke-Wormell, II, 5 [no. 8], 85 [no. 206], 128 [no. 319], 201 [no. 497], 202 [no. 498, an alternate version to no. 497]; dysdaimōn (Parke-Wormell, II, 128 [no. 319]; makar (Pausanias vii.5.2).

92. Of the oracular beatitudes (largely Delphic) listed below in n. 108, those in Parke-Wormell, II, 5 (no. 8), 85 (no. 206), 128 (no. 319), and that in Pausanias vii.5.2 appear to be spontaneous.

93. Pausanias vii.5 2; also found in R. Hendess, Oracula Graeca, no. 142, and K. Buresch, Klaros, p. 32. See above, p. 61.

94. Herodotus v. 92 (author's trans.).

95. Strabo viii.6.22; also in Parke-Wormell, The Delphic Oracle, II, 172 (no. 424).

96. H. Dörrie and H. Dörries, "Erotapokriseis," cols. 342-370.

97. See above, pp. 52-53 and n. 30.

98. These two quotations are taken from L. Griffith and H. Thompson, Demotic Magical Papyrus, p. 33 (iii.3-5), and p. 123 (xix.32-33).

99. Lucian Alex. 43 (author's trans.).

100. Cf. Acts 9:4-6; 22:7-8; 26:14-18; Rev. 1:8, 17 (here the oracles of self-commendation serve to introduce the entire composition); Corpus Hermeticum i.2; Apocryphon of John 2:11-15; Apocryphon of Paul 18:21; Apocalypse of Adam 66:19ff.; Letter of Peter to Philip 134:15ff.

101. The twenty-eight Delphic oracles which Parke-Wormell suggest might be unsolicited are nos. 4 (p. 3), 6 (p. 5), 8 (p. 5), 29 (p. 14), 82 (p. 36), 101 (p. 44), 114 (p. 51), 162 (p. 71), 206 (p. 85), 216 (p. 89), 233 (p. 95), 240 (p. 98), 258 (p. 104), 287 (p. 117), 294 (p. 120), 319 (p. 128), 321 (p. 129), 377 (p. 153), 431 (p. 175), 446 (p. 182), 469 (p. 190), 503 (p. 204), 514 (p. 207), 515 (p. 208), 516 (p. 208), 599 (p. 232), 601 (p. 233), 607 (p. 235).

102. Plutarch *De gar.* 512e.

103. For examples of oracular clairvoyance see Herodotus vi.19; Plutarch *De def. orac.* 434c-f; Lucian *Alex.* 19, 49, 50, 52.

104. Lucian *Alex.* 36 (author's trans.).

105. Lucian *Alex.* 47 (author's trans.).

106. Lucian *Alex.* 43 (author's trans.).

107. Philostratus *Vita Apoll.* i.10 (author's trans.).

108. Philostratus *Vita Apoll.* iv.14.

109. Lucian *Alex.* 52.

110. Anthropological studies have shown that sincerity and fraud can be found in the same individual who claims to possess some form of supernatural power. See A. L. Kroeber, *The Nature of Culture*, p. 311; C. Lévi-Strauss, *Structural Anthropology*, pp. 161-180. Alexander cannot simply be dismissed as a fraud on the basis of the biased reports of Lucian.

111. Lucian *Alex.* 11.

112. Lucian *Alex.* 24 (author's trans.).

113. Herodotus i.65.

114. *Iliad* xix.101-105. Translation of R. Lattimore, *The Iliad of Homer*, pp. 394-95.

115. Strabo xvii.1.43.

116. Athenaïs is elsewhere mentioned only in Strabo xiv.1.34, where she is again compared with the Erythraean Sibyl. Athenaïs, like the Sibyl, uttered spontaneous oracles. In actuality, figures like Athenaïs were probably the models for the creation of Sibylline legends.

117. A fine discussion of the events which may have taken place at Siwah and the various extant sources are found in an appendix to P. A. Brunt (trans.), *Arrian*, I, 467-480.

118. Plutarch *Alex.* xxvii.5-11 reflects a number of opinions regarding what the prophet of Ammon said and the significance of the statement. The statement quoted is one version recorded by Plutarch.

119. Lucian *Alex.* 13-14.

120. Lucian *Alex.* 29 (author's trans.). These three recognition oracles placed so closely together suggest that Lucian had a written collection of the oracles of Alexander.

121. Philostratus *Vita Apoll.* iv.1.

122. Philostratus *Vita Apoll.* i.9.

123. Aelius Aristides *Or.* xlviii.12 (ed. B. Keil, II, 397).

124. Pausanias x.12.3.

125. The "I am" formula, according to R. Bultmann, *John*, pp. 225-26 n. 3, can be used in several ways: (1) as a "presentation formula" (in answer to the question "Who are you?"), (2) as a "qualificatory formula" (in answer to the question "What are you?"), and (3) as an "identification formula" (speaker identifies himself with another person or object). The oracle of self-commendation combines the first two classifications suggested by Bultmann.

126. Proclus Diadochus *In Plat. Tim.* 325e (ed. H. Diel, III, 282) (author's trans.).

127. Clement of Alex. *Strom.* i.21.108 (author's trans.). The *ēltho egō* formula is equivalent to the *egō eimi* formula; cf. O. Weinreich, *Ausgewählte Schriften*, I, 285-89.

128. Lucian *Alex.* 18 (author's trans.).

129. Lucian *Alex.* 43 (author's trans.).

130. See above, pp. 64-66, and esp. n. 100.

131. Corpus Hermeticum i.2 (author's trans.).

132. Origen *Contra Celsum* vii.9 (trans. H. C. Chadwick, p. 402).

133. T. W. Gillespie, "A Pattern of Prophetic Speech," pp. 74-95, has sought to dem-

onstrate that comprehensible prophetic speech followed by glossolalia is a pattern found in the Corinthian community as well as Greco-Roman paganism. D. Georgi, *Die Gegner des Paulus*, pp. 120-21, thinks that this prophet is clearly an ecstatic. The category "ecstatic," however, is one that has little meaning.

134. See above, pp. 41-42.

135. John 8:42ff.; Luke 12:8-9; Mark 8:38 and parallels.

136. M. Smith, "Aretalogies," p. 180. The formula *hēkō* ("I have come") and its equivalents is a formula placed in the mouths of savior gods (cf. the references in H. Chadwick, *Origen: Contra Celsum*, p. 402 n. 5). D. Georgi, *Die Gegner des Paulus*, p. 125, sees a relation between the "I have come" formula of Celsus' parody and the phrase "I have come to you" (*hēkō soi*) used by Josephus in *Bell.* iii.400 in his prophetic speech to Vespasian (first noted by O. Michel, "Ich Komme," pp. 123-24, who described the idiom as "Hellenistic presentation style"; cf. R. Bultmann, *Geschichte*, p. 168 n. 2, where he too refers to Origen *Contra Celsum* vii.9). *Hēkō* (= *ēlthon*) is technical epiphanic language attributed to divinities and supernatural revealers in first-person speeches. *Hēkō* is used by Dionysos (Euripides *Bacchae* 1), a ghost (Euripides *Hecuba* 1), Poseidon (Euripides *Troades* 1), Hermes (Euripides *Ion* 5); cf. O. Weinreich, *Ausgewählte Schriften*, I, 285ff. (with other examples). The verb *ēlthon* is also used in epiphanic settings by Athena (*Iliad* i.207) and Apollo (Euripides *Orestes* 1628). The ancient lady who appeared to Hermas (*Vis.* iii.1.4) said *hēxō ekei, hopou theleis*. The *hēkō* speeches are the counterpart of invocations to divinities to "come" (*elthe*) found frequently in the Orphic Hymns (Praef. 43; 1.9 (*pareinai*); 9.11; 11.4; 12.14; 14.12; 27.11; 33.8; 34.1; 35.7 (*baine*); 36.13; 40.18; etc. (A. N. Athanassakis, ed., *The Orphic Hymns*). A similar invocation to Apollo is found in a fragment of what may be an old Delphic hymn in *PGM* I.297ff. Invocations to supernatural beings to "come" permeate the magical papyri (e.g., *PGM* I.29, 90).

137. K. Berger, "Apostelbrief," p. 213. D. Pardee, "Ancient Hebrew Epistolography," p. 331, shows that a prophetic formula, not an epistolary formula, introduces Jeremiah's prophetic letters.

138. See W. von Soden, "Verkündigung des Gotteswillens," pp. 397-403, who translates four such texts. See also W. Beyerlin, *Near Eastern Texts*, pp. 122-28. An oracular letter containing a response to an oracle question posed by Zimrilim is published and translated in A. Lods, "Une tablette inédite de Mari," pp. 103-110.

139. T. C. Skeat and E. G. Turner, "An Oracle of Hermes Trismegistos," pp. 199-208; all data regarding the text are derived from this article, including the dating. The five texts were later published in *Sammelbuch Griechischer Urkunden aus Ägypten*, 10 (1969), 159-160 (no. 10574).

140. The first text is a translation by the author of text "B" and the second of text "E"; cf. n. 139.

141. See the discussion above on eschatological prophets in the Greco-Roman world, p. 43.

142. Herodotus ix.43.

143. Herodotus vi.19.

144. E. Norden, *Kleine Schriften*, p. 264.

145. This is the view of L. Koenen, *Gnomon*, 40 (1968), 258.

146. This translation is found in V. Tcherikover, A. Fuks, and M. Stern, *Corpus Papyrorum Judaicarum*, III, 119-121 (no. 520). A full discussion of the fragment and its points of contact with the Oracle of the Potter is included.

147. On this subject see G. Lanczkowski, *Altägyptischer Prophetismus*, and idem, "Eschatology in Ancient Egyptian Religion," pp. 129-134. See also C. C. McCown, "Hebrew and Egyptian Apocalyptic Literature," pp. 357-411.

148. The best general discussion of the Jewish Sibylline Oracles and their relationship to contemporary and antecedent prophetic activity in the Levant is J. J. Collins, *Sibylline Oracles.*.

149. M. Nilsson, *Geschichte der griechische Religion*, II, 112. Nilsson sees lines 381-400 as directed to Alexander the Great by the Persian Sibyl, lines 314-18 to Antiochus IV Epiphanes (ca. 215-163 B.C.), and lines 350-362 as a piece of anti-Roman propaganda from the period

of the Third Mithridatic War (188-184 B.C.).

150. W. W. Tarn, "Alexander Helios," pp. 137-38; the oracle is discussed extensively in J. J. Collins, *Sibylline Oracles*, pp. 57-64. The translation is that of H. C. O. Lanchester in R. H. Charles (ed.), *APOT*, II, 385.

151. W. W. Tarn, "Alexander Helios," pp. 142-43.

152. This section has been judged by M. P. Nilsson, *Geschichte der griechischer Religion*, II, 112, and others as a *chiliastischer Schluss* which has been secondarily appended. That many such Greco-Egyptian prophecies are characterized by a similar two-part schema makes the hypothesis of interpolation or expansion both unnecessary and undetectable.

153. The importance and significance of this conception, which is the central point of the prophecy, has been underlined by W. W. Tarn, "Alexander Helios," p. 141: "This [*homonoia*] is a noble conception. It shows that there were Greeks in the East to whom Cleopatra's struggle with Rome appeared in a very different light from that in which Roman history represents it; for it was to be a rising of the oppressed against the oppressors, not for revenge alone, but for a better world, in which both sides, victors and vanquished, should alike share."

154. The phrase "maiden Justice" represents the Latin *virgo*, which some have taken to be an allusion to Isa. 7:14 (H. W. Garrod, "Fourth Eclogue," pp. 37-38).

155. The translation is that of J. Ferguson, *Utopias*, p. 164.

156. D. A. Slater, "Fourth Eclogue," pp. 114-19.

157. W. W. Tarn, "Alexander Helios," pp. 153ff.; idem, *Cambridge Ancient History*, X, 66ff.

158. W. W. Tarn, "Alexander Helios," p. 158.

159. R. E. A. Palmer, *Roman Religion*, p. 151.

160. W. W. Tarn, *Cambridge Ancient History*, X, 68-69; J. Ferguson, *Utopias*, pp. 163ff.

161. W. Weber, *Der Prophet und sein Gott*, pp. 87-101, 134-36; J. J. Collins, *Sibylline Oracles*, pp. 1-19; E. Norden, "Josephus und Tacitus," pp. 637-666, reprinted in E. Norden, *Kleine Schriften*, pp. 241-275. Other oracles reflecting this schema include those spontaneous hexameter oracles quoted by Phlegon of Tralles (F. Jacoby, *Die Fragmente der Griechischen Historiker*, II/B, 1174-77 (257. Phlegon v. Tralles, F. 36), and the apocalypse in Asklepios 24-26 (A. D. Nock and A. J. Festugière, *Hermès Trismégiste*, II, 326-331; now in a Coptic version translated in J. M. Robinson, *Nag Hammadi*, pp. 300-307.

162. The most recent text, based on two recensions existing in three papyrus fragments, is that of L. Koenen, "Die Prophezeiungen des 'Töpfers'," pp. 178-209; see also L. Koenen, "The Prophecies of a Potter," pp. 249-254. Koenen cites all of the important previous literature; the following discussion closely follows his views.

163. Translation by the author of the text of P$_2$ published in L. Koenen, "Prophezeiungen des 'Töpfers'," pp. 180ff.

164. L. Koenen, "Prophecies of a Potter," pp. 249-250; idem, "Die Prophezeiungen des Töpfers'," pp. 180ff. See also the important discussion by J. Z. Smith, "Wisdom and Apocalyptic," pp. 140-154.

165. A bibliography of previous studies on the oracles of Hystaspes is found in J. R. Hinnels, "Salvation," pp. 126-27 n. 2. Ancient references include Justin *1 Apol.* 20, 44; Clement of Alex. *Strom.* vi.43.1; Lactantius *Inst.* vii.15.19; vii.18.2-3. The oracles of Hystaspes are also referred to by Aristokritos (the relevant texts are collected and translated in J. R. Hinnels, "Salvation," pp. 127-133). See also J. J. Collins, "Persian Apocalypses," p. 210. S. Eddy, *The King is Dead*, pp. 16-20, 32-36, points out numerous parallels between the oracles of Hystaspes and one section of the Bahman Yasht.

166. H. Windisch, *Hystaspes*, p. 96.

167. Ibid.

168. Ibid., p. 98.

169. Ibid., p. 97.

170. On the oracle collections in Herodotus see R. Crahay, *La littérature oraculaire chez Hérodote*, pp. 11-14. Since Herodotus does not refer to a collection of Delphic oracles, one probably never existed (M. P. Nilsson, "Das delphische Orakel," p. 246).

171. Justin *1 Apol.* 20, 44.

172. Pausanias viii.37.11-12; x.32.8-9; x.12.2-3.

173. O. Schneider, *Nikandrea*, p. 18; K. Buresch, *Klaros*, p. 35.

174. Euripides, Frag. 627 (A. Nauck, *Tragicorum Graecorum Fragmenta*, 2nd ed., p. 556; in the 1856 edition it is numbered as Frag. 629, p. 438).

175. Herodotus vi.57; Parke-Wormell, *The Delphic Oracle*, II, xiv; H. W. Parke, *Greek Oracles*, p. 58.

176. Pausanias iv.32.5.

177. Pausanias v.15.11.

178. Plutarch *De Pyth. orac.* 403e; Clement of Alex. *Strom.* i.21.134-35.

178a. W. Vollgraff, *Bulletin de Correspondence Hellénique*, 33 (1909), 450-55 (no. 22).

179. Herodotus v.90; v.93. In v.91-92 there is an excellent example of how such oracles could be utilized to manipulate political situations. On Peisistratus see Aristophanes *Aves* 1071 (F. Dübner, *Scholia Graeca in Aristophanem*, p. 203).

180. See our discussion of the role of *chrēsmologoi* above, pp. 40, 43-44.

181. Herodotus vii.6. Pausanias had also read the oracles of Musaeos and he thought that some of them had been forged by Onomakritos (i.22.7).

182. Herodotus vii.142-43.

183. In Aristophanes *Pax* 1095 a *chrēsmologos* with a collection of Sibylline oracles is mentioned, and Aristophanes *Aves* 959-991 refers to a *chrēsmologos* who has a collection of the oracles of Bakis that he can recite from memory.

184. Plutarch *De Pyth. orac.* 396c.

185. Plutarch *De Pyth. orac.* 395a.

186. Pausanias i.34.4.

187. Dionysius Halicarnassensis iv.62.6.

188. Suetonius *Oct.* 31.1.

189. Tacitus *Annals* vi.12; cf. R. MacMullen, *Enemies of the Roman Order*, p. 130.

190. This administrative group was called Decemviri Sacris Faciundus; cf. K. Latte, *Römische Religion*, pp. 160-61.

191. Tiberius made an investigation of oracle collections, accepting some but rejecting others, according to Dio Cassius lvii.18.4.

Chapter 4

1. Two kinds of oracular speech in early Judaism are an exception to this generalization: the phenomenon of clerical prophecy and the prophetic gifts of the sage or holy man (discussed below, pp. 138-152).

2. That *nabi'* and *prophētēs* were terms usually reserved for canonical prophets and/or eschatological prophets among early Jewish writers does not mean that the phenomenon of prophecy was unknown to those authors. It does mean that canonical and eschatological prophecy had a special status that distinguished them from prophetic activity in the intervening period. Some leaders of early Jewish millenarian movements appear to have designated themselves as prophets, notably Theudas (Josephus *Ant.* xx.97-98) and the unnamed Egyptian Jew (Josephus *Ant.* xx.169-172; *Bell.* ii.261ff.). J. Reiling, *"Pseudoprophētēs,"* p. 156, incorrectly claims that Josephus never designated contemporary seers with the term *prophētēs*; cf. Josephus *Bell.* vi.285, and D. E. Aune, "The Use of *PROPHĒTĒS* in Josephus," 419-421.

3. The problem of the cessation of many oracles is discussed directly in Plutarch *De defectu oraculorum*. The reasons discussed are all rationalizations based on various religious and philosophical presuppositions. Popular views on the subject are not reflected in the dialogue.

4. Changes in Israelite social structure, including the dissolution of the monarchy, resulted in the transformation of Israelite prophecy into (among other things) Jewish apocalyptic; cf. F. M. Cross, "Apocalyptic," p. 161; O. Plöger, *Theocracy*, p. 29; E. Hammershaimb, *Prophecy*, pp. 91-112; J. Blenkinsopp, *Prophecy and Canon*, p. 2; D. Petersen, *Late Israelite Prophecy*, pp. 2-5.

5. For a thorough recent discussion of the texts bearing on the canonization of the Jewish scriptures, see S. Z. Leiman, *Canonization*. For an excellent treatment of the dynamics which led to canonization, see J. Blenkinsopp, *Prophecy and Canon*.

6. For what follows, see D. E. Aune, "Divination," pp. 971-74.

7. Lev. 19:26; Deut. 18:10; 1 Sam. 15:23; 28:2; 2 Kgs. 17:17; 21:6; Isa. 3:2; Jer. 27:7; 29:8; Ezek. 13:6, 9; 22:28; Mic. 3:11; Zech. 10:2.

8. Lot oracle used to select Saul; see A. Lods, "Le rôle des oracles," p. 92.

9. R. de Vaux, Ancient Israel, II, 352-53.

10. For "seer" see 1 Sam. 9:11, 18-19; 2 Sam. 15:27; 24:11; Amos 7:12. For "man of God" see Judg. 13:6; 1 Sam. 9:6; 1 Kgs. 12:22; 17:18, 24; 2 Kgs. 5:8. The title "man of the Spirit" is found only in Hos. 9:7, but was probably a popular term for a prophet in the eighth century (J. Lindblom, Prophecy, p. 175; H. W. Wolff, Hosea, p. 157). It refers to one overcome by the Spirit of God (1 Sam. 10:6; 1 Kgs. 18:12; 22:21-22; 2 Kgs. 2:9, 16; Isa. 61:1; 2 Chr. 20:13; etc.).

11. W. F. Albright, Stone Age, pp. 303ff. For a broader discussion of possibilities see A. Jepsen, Nabi, pp. 5ff.; H. W. Robinson, Inspiration, p. 173 n. 1; R. Rendtorff, TDNT, VI, 796-97.

12. T. J. Meek, Origins, pp. 150-51, emphasizing the meaning of nabi' in Exod. 7:1.

13. H. Junker, Prophet, pp. 27-28, 36-37; W. Eichrodt, Old Testament, I, 312; H. W. Robinson, Inspiration, p. 173 n. 1.

13a. A. Phillips, "The Ecstatics' Father," 183-194, contends that 'ab is a technical term for a person able to disclose information hidden to others; J. G. Williams, "The Prophetic 'Father,'" pp. 344-48.

14. J. Blenkinsopp, Prophecy and Canon, p. 44 n. 68, where Deut. 18:15-18 is convincingly regarded as referring to prophetic succession generally.

15. On this subject generally, see S. Mowinckel, Psalms, II, 53-73; A. Johnson, The Cultic Prophet; H.-J. Kraus, Worship, pp. 101-112; R. de Vaux, Ancient Israel, II, 384-86.

16. 2 Kgs. 23:2; Isa. 28:7; Jer. 2:26; 23:11; 26:7, 8, 11, 16; 29:1; Lam. 2:20; Hos. 4:4-5; Ezra 5:1-2; etc.

17. A. Jepsen, Nabi, p. 161.

18. G. Hölscher, Die Profeten, p. 143.

19. S. Mowinckel, Psalms, II, 58-68.

20. Ibid., 56-57; A. Johnson, The Cultic Prophet, pp. 68-74.

21. R. de Vaux, Ancient Israel, II, 385; H. Ringgren, Israelite Religion, p. 212; D. L. Petersen, Late Israelite Prophecy, p. 87.

22. On the court prophet see A. Jepsen, Nabi, pp. 94-99, 152-59.

23. F. Ellermeier, Prophetie in Mari, pp. 150-56.

24. 1 Kgs. 20:13-15, 22, 28, 35-42; 2 Kgs. 6:8-10, 15-23; 2 Chr. 12:5-8; 15:1-7; 16:7-10; 19:2-3; 20:13-17; 20:37; 21:12-15; 24:20; 25:7-8, 14-16.

25. 1 Sam. 28:5-6; 1 Kgs. 22:5-6, 15-17; 2 Kgs. 3:11-20; 13:14-19.

26. R. R. Wilson, "Early Israelite Prophecy," pp. 9-10. Although the problems of the social setting and function of Israelite prophecy have been largely neglected by biblical scholarship, this issue is now being addressed. See R. R. Wilson, "Prophecy and Society," pp. 341-358; idem, "Early Israelite Prophecy," pp. 8-11; idem, Prophecy and Society.

27. R. E. Clements, Prophecy and Covenant, pp. 119-129.

28. K. Baltzer, "Prophet," pp. 575-581, observes that the title "king" is not applied to the Israelite ruler by a number of prophets including Isaiah, Jeremiah, and Ezekiel. The title is applied to God, however, and the office of prophet is placed above that of the Israelite king.

29. See above, n. 25.

29a. B. O. Long, "Divination," pp. 493-97; idem, "Question and Answer," pp. 129-139.

30. See D. L. Christensen, War Oracle.

31. Isa. 30:3; Jer. 21:2; 23:33, 35, 37; 37:17; 38:14-23; 42:4; Ezek. 20:1, 3; Mic. 3:4, 7.

32. Judg. 18:5-6; 1 Sam. 14:36-37; 23:9-12; 30:7-8; Ps. 60:6 and 50:1-7 appear to be priestly oracles. See R. de Vaux, Ancient Israel, II, 349-353; A. Bentzen, Old Testament, pp. 185-191.

33. C. Westermann, "Die Begriffe für Fragen," pp. 16-22.

34. 1 Sam. 9:6-8; Num. 22:7; 1 Kgs. 14:2-3; 2 Kgs. 4:42; 8:8-9; Mic. 3:10. In retelling the story found in 1 Sam. 9, Josephus noted that Saul was ignorant that prophets accepted

no reward for their services (*Ant.* vi.48). This may reflect a view prevalent in early Judaism that religious teachers should not receive recompense for their services (cf. G. F. Moore, *Judaism,* II, 96-97).

35. 1 Kgs. 11:29-39; 12:22-24; 13:1-2; 20:35-43; 2 Kgs. 1:3-4, 6, 15-16.

36. C. Westermann, *Basic Forms,* pp. 90-93; K. Koch, *Biblical Tradition,* pp. 210-11.

37. T. N. D. Mettinger, *King and Messiah,* pp. 74ff., 167ff. S. Mowinckel, *He That Cometh,* pp. 5-6, emphasizes the occasional nature of this prophetic function, largely exercised in the case of usurpers.

38. According to 1 Sam. 10:17-24, Saul was selected the first ruler of Israel by a lot oracle. See the discussion of this passage in the light of Egyptian and Greek parallels in A. Lods, "Les rôle des oracles," pp. 91-100.

39. R. de Vaux, *Ancient Israel,* I, 103ff.

40. E. Bourguignon, *Religion,* pp. 12, 42-43, 336; idem, *Possession,* pp. 3-4.

41. I. M. Lewis, *Ecstatic Religion,* pp. 64, 93.

42. Ibid., p. 55.

43. H. G. Barnett, *Indian Shakers,* p. 226; P. Worsley, *Trumpet Shall Sound,* p. xxxiv; J. Mooney, *Ghost-Dance Religion,* pp. 178-200.

44. Hos. 9:7; Isa. 30:1-2; 48:16; 59:21; 61:1; Ezek. 3:12-15; 8:3; 11:5-24; 37:1; 43:5.

45. See above, n. 10.

46. Isa. 6:1-5; Jer. 23:18, 22; cf. F. M. Cross, "Council of Yahweh," pp. 274-77.

47. T. J. Meek, *Origins,* p. 155; J. Leipoldt and S. Morenz, *Heilige Schriften,* p. 33.

48. J. Pedersen, *Israel,* I-II, 158; J. Lindblom, *Prophecy,* pp. 58-59; W. Kornfeld, *Religion,* p. 185; see esp. W. Jacobi, *Ekstase,* pp. 7-15.

49. On the cultic dance see W. Eichrodt, *Old Testament,* I, 310ff.

50. M. J. Harner (ed.), *Hallucinogens and Shamanism.*

51. Contrary to H.-J. Kraus, *Worship,* p. 102, Hos. 9:7 is not a criticism of ecstatic prophecy, but instead is a quotation of a popular criticism of the prophet based on his predictions of doom (J. Lindblom, *Prophecy,* p. 175 n. 108; H. W. Wolff, *Hosea,* pp. 156-57).

52. For an excellent recent discussion see S. B. Parker, "Possession Trance," pp. 271-285.

53. A. Jepsen, *Nabi,* pp. 7ff., sees the hithpael of the verb *hb'* as taking on the following meanings in chronological order: (1) to rave, (2) to proclaim while raving, and (3) to proclaim (p. 9). More recently see S. B. Parker, "Possession Trance," pp. 271ff.

54. The theme of prophetic conflict in ancient Israel has been recently treated in three very different ways: J. L. Crenshaw, *Prophetic Conflict*; J. Blenkinsopp, *Prophecy and Canon*; and S. DeVries, *Prophet Against Prophet.* A very important earlier study on the subject is G. Quell, *Wahre und falsche Propheten.*

55. S. DeVries, *Prophet Against Prophet,* p. 150.

56. G. Quell, *Wahre und falsche Propheten,* pp. 160-61; J. L. Crenshaw, *Prophetic Conflict,* pp. 49-61.

57. G. von Rad, "Die falschen Propheten," p. 112.

58. H. G. Reventlow, *Liturgie und prophetisches Ich,* pp. 132-38.

59. Jörg Jeremias, *Kultprophetie und Gerichtsverkündigung,* pp. 196-97.

60. J. L. Crenshaw, *Prophetic Conflict,* pp. 39-61.

61. Ibid., p. 61.

62. Ibid., p. 103.

63. Ibid., pp. 110-11.

64. S. DeVries, *Prophet Against Prophet,* p. 150.

65. See above, nn. 24, 35.

66. See above, n. 31.

67. G. M. Tucker, "Prophetic Speech," p. 34.

68. Important reviews of the literature include J. H. Hayes, "Form-Critical Study of Prophecy," pp. 60-99; R. R. Wilson, "Form-Critical Investigation," pp. 100-127; G. M. Tucker, *Form Criticism,* pp. 54-77; idem, "Prophetic Speech," pp. 31-45; W. E. March, "Prophecy," pp. 141-177.

69. H. Gunkel, "Israelite Prophecy," pp. 61-62.

70. C. Westermann, *Basic Forms*, pp. 90-93; K. Koch, *Biblical Tradition*, pp. 210-11.

71. See the critique by R. R. Wilson, "Form-Critical Investigation," p. 113.

72. The notion of optional elements is derived from the structural study of folklore, while the idiosyncratic modifications of traditional forms and genres reflect the "rhetorical criticism" of J. Muilenburg, "Form Criticism and Beyond," pp. 1-18.

73. A short discussion of terminology is found in C. Westermann, *Basic Forms*, pp. 64-70.

74. H. Gunkel, "Israelite Prophecy," pp. 63-66; O. Eissfeldt, *Old Testament*, p. 79; E. Sellin and G. Fohrer, *Old Testament*, pp. 252-53.

75. On the messenger formula see J. Lindblom, *Die literarische Gattung*, pp. 97-110; idem, *Prophecy*, pp. 103-104; C. Westermann, *Basic Forms*, pp. 98-128; H. W. Wolff, *Joel and Amos*, pp. 135-37.

76. J. Lindblom, *Die literarische Gattung*, pp. 102-108.

77. F. Ellermeier, *Prophetie*, pp. 27 (A 15, lines 32ff.), 114-16.

78. This formula is discussed by J. Lindblom, *Die literarische Gattung*, pp. 110-15; H. W. Wolff, *Joel and Amos*, pp. 135-37; C. Westermann, *Basic Forms*, pp. 98-128.

79. Jer. 2:2; 8:4; 11:3; 13:12, 13; 15:2; 18:11; 19:11; 21:8; 25:27, 28; 26:4; 28:13; 29:24-25; 34:2; 36:29; 39:16; 43:10; 45:4; Ezek. 2:4; 3:11, 27.

80. On the proclamation formula see H. W. Wolff, *Joel and Amos*, pp. 92-93; idem, *Hosea*, pp. 66, 97.

81. On this formula see F. Baumgärtel, "Formel," pp. 277-290; H. W. Wolff, *Joel and Amos*, pp. 143-44.

82. Num. 14:21, 28; Deut. 32:40; Isa. 49:18; Jer. 22:24; 46:18; Ezek. 5:11; 14:16, 18, 20; 16:48; 17:16, 19; 18:3; 20:3, 31, 33; 33:11, 27; 34:8; 35:6, 11; Zeph. 2:9.

83. E. Sellin and G. Fohrer, *Old Testament*, p. 351. This threefold classification is more useful than C. Westermann's distinction between accounts, speeches, and prayers (*Basic Forms*, pp. 90-93). Westermann is followed by G. M. Tucker, "Prophetic Speech," pp. 33-34; idem, *Form Criticism*, p. 57.

84. J. H. Hayes, "Form-Critical Study of Prophecy," p. 68.

85. G. M. Tucker, "Prophetic Speech," p. 35.

86. Among the more helpful recent introductions to OT prophetic speech forms are A. Bentzen, *Old Testament*, pp. 185-202; E. Sellin and G. Fohrer, *Old Testament*, pp. 77-78, 347-358; G. M. Tucker, *Form Criticism*, pp. 54-77; A. Weiser, *Einleitung*, pp. 48-53; O. Eissfeldt, *Old Testament*, pp. 76-81.

87. C. Westermann, *Basic Forms*, pp. 96-98. Westermann's attempt to isolate a "basic form" of prophetic speech has been criticized by, among others, R. R. Wilson, "Form-Critical Investigation," pp. 100-112. Wilson concludes (p. 120) by observing that little progress has been made in uncovering a basic form of prophetic speech.

88. W. Zimmerli, "Das Wort des göttlichen Selbsterweises," pp. 120-132. Zimmerli's analysis of the *Erweiswort* indicates that it is sufficiently distinctive to deserve mention here.

89. H. W. Wolff, "Begründungen," pp. 1-22. Wolff's basic position is discussed in some detail by C. Westermann, *Basic Forms*, pp. 56-61.

90. H. W. Wolff, "Begründungen," pp. 11-17; idem, *Joel and Amos*, p. 92.

91. H. W. Wolff, *Joel and Amos*, p. 92.

92. C. Westermann, *Basic Forms*, pp. 86-87, 129-179, sees the judgment speech (*Gerichtsankündigung*), which we have designated as the announcement of judgment, as basic, while K. Koch, *Biblical Tradition*, pp. 207-208, finds a common pattern in prophecies of disaster and prophecies of salvation, but does not designate either type as the root of the other.

93. The same oracle, with minor variations, is repeated three times in 2 Kgs. 1:3-4, 6, 15-16. We have simplified the analysis of this oracle presented by K. Koch, *Biblical Tradition*, pp. 191-94.

94. D. L. Christensen, *War Oracle*, p. 283; J. H. Hayes, "Oracles Against the Nations," p. 93.

95. E. Sellin and G. Fohrer, *Old Testament*, p. 354, limit the use of the announcement of salvation to Hosea, Jeremiah, and Ezekiel. C. Westermann, *Isaiah 40-66*, p. 13, has shown that the form also occurs in Deutero-Isaiah (Isa. 41:17-20; 42:14-17; 43:16-21; 49:7-12).

96. C. Westermann, *Basic Forms,* pp. 97-98.

97. K. Koch, *Biblical Tradition,* p. 215.

98. This has been convincingly demonstrated by P. D. Hanson, *Dawn of Apocalyptic,* pp. 106-108, 142, 163, 166-173.

99. Ibid., pp. 209-279.

100. Ibid., p. 145.

101. Ibid., p. 162.

102. Ibid., pp. 144-45; here I have replaced Hanson's terms "indictment" and "sentence" with "accusation" and "threat."

103. J. Begrich, "Das priesterliche Heilsorakel," pp. 87-91.

104. Ibid., p. 83; C. Westermann, *Isaiah 40-66,* pp. 11-13. C. Westermann, "Heilswort," pp. 355-373 (esp. p. 359), gives the following analysis of the *Heilswort* (oracle of assurance): (1) *Anrede* (address); (2) *Heilzuspruch* (salvific exhortation), e.g. "fear not!"; (3) *Begründung* (reason), (a) nominal clause ("I am with you," etc.), or (b) verbal clause using past tense; (4) *Folge* (sequel), using the future tense.

105. C. Westermann, *Isaiah 40-66,* pp. 11-13; idem, "Heilswort," p. 359.

106. J. M. Berridge, *Prophet,* pp. 184-209.

107. H. W. Wolff, *Joel and Amos,* p. 58 (the use of *hinneh* in this context appears to be a postexilic development).

108. H. Ringgren, "Israelite Tradition," pp. 38-39; A. Guillaume, *Prophecy and Divination,* pp. 42-45.

109. These examples are discussed by U. Müller, *Prophetie und Predigt,* pp. 215-220.

110. See E. March, "Prophecy," pp. 168-69; most recently see G. Warmuth, *Das Mahnwort.* Warmuth summarizes the variety of roots proposed for the prophetic admonition on pp. 17-20. These include: (1) priestly Torah (Amos 4:4-5; 5:4-5, 21-22; Hos. 6:6; Isa. 1:10-17; 66:2b-3; Mal. 1:10, all prophetic derivations from this source); (2) judicial settlement proposals (Hos. 2:4ff.); (3) proclamation in response to communal lamentation (Jer. 36:9; 1 Kgs. 21:12; Amos 5:16; Isa. 22:12); (4) wisdom instruction; (5) war speeches (Jer. 7:4), i.e. from all cultic, juridical, and ethical spheres of Israelite life.

111. G. Warmuth, *Das Mahnwort,* p. 170.

112. O. H. Steck, *Israel,* pp. 142-43, 152-53, 180ff. See also the discussion in U. Müller, *Prophetie und Predigt,* pp. 76-92.

113. H. W. Wolff, *Joel and Amos,* p. 232.

114. G. Warmuth, *Das Mahnwort,* p. 170. He particularly advances his argument of the unconditional nature of the admonition on pp. 35-36, 55ff., 82-83, 166ff., 170-71.

115. This section is based on W. Zimmerli, "Selbsterweises," pp. 120-132.

116. The "I"-style in revelatory speech is a common form used in the ancient Near East in a variety of ways. See E. Norden, *Agnostos Theos,* pp. 186ff., 201, 207-220.

117. W. Zimmerli, "Selbsterweises," pp. 125-26.

118. Ibid., p. 125.

119. This discussion is based primarily on E. Gerstenberger, "Woe-Oracles," pp. 249-263, and H. W. Wolff, *Joel and Amos,* pp. 242-45 (an excellent, succinct survey of the form-critical discussion of the woe oracle). See also C. Westermann, *Basic Forms,* pp. 190-94; W. Janzen, *Mourning Cry and Woe Oracle*; and J. Vermeylen, *Du Prophète Isaïe,* II, 603-652, for a very complete review of the literature on the subject.

120. W. Janzen, *Woe Oracle,* p. 83, also the view of J. Vermeylen, *Du Prophète Isaïe,* II, 618-621.

121. C. Westermann, *Basic Forms,* pp. 190-94.

122. E. Gerstenberger, "Woe-Oracle," pp. 254-262.

123. E. Gerstenberger, "Woe-Oracle," p. 253, finds three basic elements in the woe oracle. The second is a juncture (i.e. "therefore" [*laken*] between the first and third parts). In the interests of simplification, I have omitted this as a *basic* element characteristic of the form.

124. C. Westermann, *Basic Forms,* p. 191.

125. Amos 5:18-20; 6:1-7; Isa. 1:4; 5:8-10, 11-14, 18-19, 20, 21, 22-24; 10:1-3; 28:1-4; 29:15; 30:1-3; 31:1-4; Mic. 2:1-4; Jer. 22:13-14; 23:1; Zeph. 3:1; Ezek. 34:2; Isa. 45:9-10; Nah. 3:1; Hab. 2:6, 9, 12, 15, 19. For a complete survey, see R. J. Clifford, "The Use of HÔY," pp. 458-464.

126. C. Westermann, *Basic Forms,* p. 191, where he describes the series of woes as the original form of the woe oracle.

127. A. Bentzen, *Old Testament,* p. 199.

128. W. Janzen, *Woe Oracle,* pp. 81-82.

129. G. M. Ramsey, "Speech-Forms in Hebrew Law," pp. 45-58; H. J. Boecker, *Rede-formen des Rechtsleben,* pp. 91-94, and *passim.* For a review of recent literature on prophecy and law see M. Clark, "Law," pp. 135-36.

130. C. Westermann, "Sprache und Struktur," pp. 135-144.

131. See the discussion in G. M. Tucker, *Form Criticism,* pp. 66-67.

132. G. W. Ahlström, "Prophet," p. 62; W. F. Albright, *Stone Age,* p. 305.

133. For a review of the literature on the call narrative see E. March, "Prophecy," pp. 170ff. On prophetic call narratives generally, see J. Lindblom, *Prophecy,* pp. 182-197; G. von Rad, *Old Testament Theology,* II, 50-69.

134. K. Baltzer, "Prophet," p. 569. Baltzer compares the "installation" of the prophet by God to the installation of a royal vizier by the Egyptian pharaoh (pp. 570ff.). The parallels are formally similar, but the legitimating function of the OT prophetic call narrative is not found in the Egyptian materials.

135. N. Habel, "Call Narrative," p. 317.

136. H. G. Reventlow, *Liturgie und prophetisches Ich,* pp. 24-77, esp. p. 68. Reventlow sees the prophetic call narratives as stereotyped liturgical ordination ceremonies for prophets, very similar in structure to the oracle of assurance (*Heilsorakel*), which also had a liturgical setting. However, it appears that Jeremiah has consciously adapted the oracle of assurance for inclusion in the call narrative in Jer. 1:4-10 (J. M. Berridge, *Prophet,* pp. 28, 52-53).

137. E. Sellin and G. Fohrer, *Old Testament,* p. 361.

138. J. Blenkinsopp, *Prophecy and Canon,* pp. 144-45.

139. See above, n. 43.

140. On this last passage see the reservations of D. L. Petersen, *Late Israelite Prophecy,* pp. 20-21.

141. This analysis is based on N. Habel, "Call Narrative," pp. 297-323. A compelling analysis of Jer. 1:4-10, and one which is mildly critical of Habel's analysis, is that of J. M. Berridge, *Prophet,* pp. 26-62.

142. E. Kutsch, "Gideons Berufung," pp. 79-82.

143. H. L. Jansen, *Die Henochgestalt,* pp. 114-18; M. Black, "Similitudes of Enoch," pp. 1-10; idem, "The Throne-Theophany," pp. 57-73. G. Scholem, *Major Trends,* p. 44, observes that 1 Enoch 14-16 is the earliest Jewish account of a heavenly ascent extant.

144. W. Zimmerli, *Ezekiel,* I, 97-100.

145. For a review of the recent literature, see E. March, "Prophecy," p. 170, and B. O. Long, "Reports of Visions," pp. 353ff.

146. H. W. Wolff, *Hosea,* pp. 10-11, 57-58.

147. F. Horst, "Visionsschilderungen," pp. 193-205, distinguishes between *Anwesenheits-visionen* ("presence" visions), *Geschehnisvisionen* (event visions), and *Wortassonanzvisionen* (word-association visions). B. O. Long, "Reports of Visions," pp. 353-365, distinguishes between oracle visions, dramatic word-visions, and revelatory-mysteries-visions. In the last two categories Long confounds content with structure. For example, the revealer in his second category is Yahweh, while in the third it is an *angelus interpres,* and the identity of the revealer is a partial reason for distinguishing between types, according to Long.

148. The following analysis is a modification of B. O. Long, "Reports of Visions," pp. 353-365.

149. This is a modification of B. O. Long, "Reports of Visions," p. 357.

150. E. Fascher, *PROPHĒTĒS,* p. 184, correctly observes that symbolic actions belong to the Jewish, not the Hellenistic, prophetic type. Yet isolated symbolic prophetic actions

are found in early Judaism, early Christianity, and Greco-Roman paganism.

151. See above, pp. 76-77.

152. This symbolic action is remarkably similar to Jer. 19:1-15, where the breaking of pottery presages the destruction of Israel.

153. G. Hölscher, *Die Profeten,* pp. 30-31; G. Fohrer, *Die symbolischen Handlungen,* pp. 10-15, 21-24. Fohrer sees the origin of the symbolic action in magical ritual ("Prophetie und Magie," pp. 25-47; *Die symbolischen Handlungen,* p. 19), and in this he is probably correct. J. Lindblom, *Prophecy,* p. 164, makes an artificial distinction between primitive magical action and symbolic acts of the OT prophet.

154. G. Fohrer, *Die symbolischen Handlungen,* p. 17, has enumerated 32 examples of symbolic prophetic actions in the OT. The analysis which follows is dependent on G. Fohrer, "Die Gattung," pp. 101-120; idem, *Die symbolischen Handlungen,* pp. 17-19, 20-71.

155. Other prophetic symbolic acts include Isa. 7:10-17; 20:2-6; Jer. 19:1-15; 28:10-11; 32:6-44; Ezek. 4:1-3, 4-8, 9-17; 5:1-17.

156. On this subject, see E. Sellin and G. Fohrer, *Old Testament,* p. 358. For a specific treatment of the transmission of Hosea's prophecies, see H. W. Wolff, *Hosea,* pp. xxix-xxxii, and for a complicated theory on the formation of the book of Amos, see H. W. Wolff, *Joel and Amos,* pp. 106-113.

157. G. Fohrer, *Die Propheten,* I, 13. According to H. W. Wolff, *Hosea,* p. xxix, the prophet himself was responsible for part of the written tradition. See also the references below in n. 158.

158. Isa. 8:16-22; 29:11-12; 30:8-14; Hab. 2:2-3; Jer. 30:2-3; 45:1; 51:60-64. The writing of prophecies in Jer. 29:1-23, 26-28, 31-32 (three letters); and 36:2-8 was done as a substitute for the prophet's presence. The view that prophecies were written so that their authenticity would be vindicated upon fulfilment is advanced by J. Blenkinsopp, *Prophecy and Canon,* pp. 26-27. E. Sellin and G. Fohrer, *Old Testament,* p. 360, espouse the view that prophecies were rapidly written down to preserve and increase their magical efficacy.

159. E. Sellin and G. Fohrer, *Old Testament,* pp. 361-62.

160. D. L. Petersen, *Late Israelite Prophecy,* p. 14.

Chapter 5

1. These include: Ps. 74:9; Ezek. 13:9; Zech. 13:2-6; Dan. 3:38 (LXX); 9:24; 1 Macc. 4:46; 9:27; 14:41; Josephus *Contra Ap.* i.37-41; 2 Bar. 85:3; Seder Olam Rabbah 30; Tosephta Soṭah 13:2; T. B. Sanhedrin 11a-b; T. B. Yoma 9b; T. B. Soṭah 48b. For a general discussion of many of these texts see R. Meyer, *TDNT,* VI, 812-19.

2. S. Z. Leiman, *Canonization,* p. 66.

3. Ibid.

4. J. Levy, *Wörterbuch,* III, 323-25; P. Schäfer, *Die Vorstellung vom heiligen Geist,* pp. 21-26; Strack-Billerbeck, III, 27ff.; E. Sjöberg, *TDNT,* VI, 381-82.

5. J. Lindblom, *Gesichte,* p. 17 n. 2; J. Blenkinsopp, *Prophecy and Canon,* p. 119; R. Meyer, *TDNT,* VI, 818. On the *bat qol* generally see G. F. Moore, *Judaism,* I, 422; III, 127. J. Lindblom, *Gesichte,* p. 17, points out that in the OT the voice of Yahweh was sometimes compared to the sound of thunder (Job 37:4-5; Ps. 18:14; 29:3ff.; 68:38; Isa. 30:30; cf. John 12:28-29. On the divinatory function of the *bat qol* see S. Lieberman, *Hellenism,* pp. 194-99. For an extensive discussion on the *bat qol* see L. Blau, "Bat Ḳol," pp. 588-592.

6. J. Lindblom, *Gesichte,* pp. 168-69.

7. P. Schäfer, *Die Vorstellung vom heiligen Geist,* p. 147.

8. Strack-Billerbeck, II, 128; P. Schäfer, *Die Vorstellung vom heiligen Geist,* p. 145; O. Michel, "Prophetentum," pp. 63-65.

9. E. Sjöberg, *TDNT,* VI, 386.

10. A recent caveat against this approach has been given by E. P. Sanders, *Paul and Palestinian Judaism.* The author emphasizes the diversity of rabbinic views on almost every subject.

11. E. E. Urbach, *"Mty psqh hnbw'h?" Tarbiz,* 17 (1945-46), 1-11. The article is discussed briefly by R. J. Zwi Werblowsky, "Le prophétisme," p. 42, and more extensively by P. Schäfer,

Die Vorstellung vom heiligen Geist, pp. 144-46.

12. A. Harnack, *Ausbreitung,* I, 344-45; H. Lewy, *Sobria Ebrietas,* pp. 105-106 n. 1; O. Plöger, "Prophetisches Erbe," pp. 291-96; D. Georgi, *Die Gegner des Paulus,* p. 121; W. Foerster, "Der heilige Geist," pp. 119-121; O. Michel, "Spätjüdisches Prophetentum," pp. 60-66; F. Hahn, *Titles of Jesus,* pp. 352-54; R. Meyer, *TDNT,* VI, 812-828; M. Hengel, *Die Zeloten,* pp. 235-251.

13. S. Sandmel, *Judaism and Christian Beginnings,* p. 174.

14. H. Braun, *Qumran und das Neue Testament,* II, 252-53; M. Hengel, *Die Zeloten,* p. 241; H.-W. Kuhn, *Enderwartung und gegenwärtiges Heil,* pp. 117-139. For a summary and critique of Kuhn's views see D. E. Aune, *Realized Eschatology,* pp. 31-37.

15. W. Bousset and H. Gressmann, *Religion des Judentums,* pp. 394-99.

16. J. Alizon, *Étude sur le prophétisme chrétien,* p. 12; D. S. Russell, *Apocalyptic,* pp. 82, 158-177; M. E. Stone, "Apocalyptic — Vision or Hallucination," pp. 47-56. See 1 Enoch 91:1; 93:1; Vita Adae 29; 2 Enoch 22:4-13; Jub. 1; 4 Ezra 14; 2 Bar. 6:3; 10:1-3; 59; Sib. Or. iii.162, 489-491, 306, 395-96, 809-811; Mart. Isa. 1:7; 5:14.

17. J. Giblet, "Prophétisme," p. 105.

18. Josephus *Bell.* i.68-69.

19. That 1 Macc. 14:41 refers to John Hyrcanus is supported by R. Meyer, *TDNT,* VI, 815-16; M. Hengel, *Die Zeloten,* p. 240; E. Bammel, *"ARCHIEREUS,"* pp. 351-56. The view that 1 Macc. 14:41 refers to an eschatological (Mosaic) prophet is supported by Strack-Billerbeck, II, 479-480; J. Jeremias, *TDNT,* IV, 857-58; G. Jeremias, *Die Lehrer der Gerechtigkeit,* pp. 286-87; A. S. van der Woude, *Die messianischen Vorstellungen,* p. 80. P. Volz, *Eschatologie,* p. 193, leaves the question open. J. Becker, *Johannes der Täufer,* p. 45, does not think that the expected prophet refers to John Hyrcanus (no hint of that identity is found in 1 Maccabees) or to an eschatological prophet (no eschatological characteristics are referred to in 1 Maccabees). He thinks that the passage reflects the expectation of a prophet like the OT prophets whose charisma will make decisions possible that cannot now be made.

20. D. Arenhoevel, *Die Theokratie,* p. 68; E. Janssen, *Das Gottesvolk,* pp. 45-46.

21. D. Arenhoevel, *Die Theokratie,* pp. 58, 169.

22. R. Meyer, *TDNT,* VI, 813-14; F. Hahn, *Titles of Jesus,* p. 388 n. 1.

23. Zech. 13:2-6 is interpreted in this way by J. J. Collins, *Daniel,* p. 68; and D. L. Petersen, *Late Israelite Prophecy,* pp. 33-38.

24. R. Meyer, *TDNT,* VI, 812-13. Against an aspect of Meyer's argument, however, there is no evidence that Zech. 13 is against the *ecstatic* prophetic type *per se.*

25. In the view of A. Lacocque, *Le livre de Daniel,* p. 143, "Daniel has consciously put a final end to prophecy in Israel and that gives his book a unique, impressive character." However, this "end to prophecy" is eschatological and not historical.

26. The most satisfactory discussion of the canonization of the Jewish scriptures is S. Z. Leiman, *Canonization* (1976).

27. W. C. van Unnik, "Die Prophetie bei Josephus," pp. 47-48.

28. J. Blenkinsopp, *Prophecy and Canon,* p. 3, rightly regarded this as a scholarly myth unsupported by historical evidence, yet Blenkinsopp is wrong in calling it a "Christian" myth (according to Blenkinsopp going back to H. E. Ryle, *The Canon of the Old Testament* [1892]). The view is in fact expressed earlier by the Jewish historian H. Graetz, *Kohelet* (1871), p. 149, and before him by the seventeenth-century Jewish philosopher B. Spinoza, *Tractatus Theologico-Politicus,* cap. X (Gebhard, *Spinoza Opera,* III, 150), where Spinoza sees the collection of sacred books as achieved by a "concilium Pharisaeorum."

29. M. Hengel, *Die Zeloten,* pp. 240-42.

30. J. Becker, *Johannes der Täufer,* pp. 44-60 (followed in this paragraph).

31. Josephus *Ant.* xv.373ff.; *Bell.* ii.113; *Ant.* xiii.299, 282-83, 311-12.

32. M. Hengel, *Die Zeloten,* pp. 235-251. Hengel, I think, overemphasizes the role of prophecy in Zealotism by including in his discussion examples of prophetic activity which have no demonstrable connection with Zealotism.

33. On Theudas see Josephus *Ant.* xx.97-98; Acts 5:36; on the Egyptian Jew see Josephus *Bell.* ii.261ff.; *Ant.* xx.169-170.

34. Josephus *Ant.* xviii.85ff.

35. J. Blenkinsopp, *Prophecy and Canon*, pp. 132-38; D. L. Petersen, *Late Israelite Prophecy*, pp. 55-96; R. Meyer, *TDNT*, VI, 825-26; E. Bammel, *"ARCHIEREUS,"* pp. 351-56; J. D. Newsome, "Chronicler," pp. 201-217.

36. R. Meyer, *TDNT*, VI, 823-25; cf. G. Vermes, *Jesus the Jew*, pp. 58-82 (on charismatic Judaism).

37. R. Meyer, *TDNT*, VI, 821-23.

38. These distinctions are carefully made by P. D. Hanson, "Apocalypticism," pp. 29-31.

39. The use of the term "apocalypse" as a designation for a distinctive literary genre was coined by K. I. Nitzsch in 1822 on the basis of Rev. 1:1, where John the Seer styles his composition "the revelation [*apokalypsis*] of Jesus Christ" (J. M. Schmidt, *Die jüdische Apokalyptik*, pp. 98-99).

40. W. Bousset and H. Gressmann, *Die Religion des Judentums*, p. 12; P. Volz, *Eschatologie*, p. 11.

41. Most scholars agree that these documents at least deserve the designation "apocalypse"; cf. J. J. Collins, "Pseudonymity," p. 329; K. Koch, *Apocalyptic*, p. 23 (see pp. 18-22, where Koch eliminates other compositions from consideration).

42. For a very full review of the literature on apocalypses generally see J. H. Charlesworth, *Pseudepigrapha* (1976).

43. Cf. H. Ringgren, "Apokalyptik," p. 464; a number of lists by scholars of the characteristics of apocalyptic literature are tabulated by F. Dexinger, *Apokalyptikforschung*, p. 59.

44. H. D. Betz, "Apocalypticism," pp. 135-36.

45. J. J. Collins, "Apocalypse," p. 364. This definition is only part of an elaborate paradigm of the essential and optional elements of apocalyptic literature developed by Collins.

46. On apocalyptic pseudonymity see D. S. Russell, *Apocalyptic*, pp. 127-139; B. M. Metzger, "Literary Forgeries," pp. 3-24; J. J. Collins, *Daniel*, pp. 67-74; idem, "Pseudonymity," pp. 329-343; K. Koch, "Pseudonymous Writing," pp. 712-14; F. Dexinger, *Apokalyptikforschung*, pp. 60-64.

47. For a comprehensive discussion of this subject see W. Speyer, *Die literarische Fälschung* (1971); J. A. Sint, *Pseudonymität im Altertum* (1960); N. Brox (ed.), *Pseudepigraphie in der heidnischen und jüdisch-christlichen Antike* (1977); B. Metzger, "Literary Forgeries," pp. 3-24.

48. K. Koch, "Pseudonymous Writing," pp. 712-14; idem, *Apocalyptic*, p. 26, and the instructive n. 21 on p. 134.

49. R. H. Charles, *APOT*, II, viii-ix; R. Bauckham, "Rise of Apocalyptic," p. 18; J. J. Collins, *Daniel*, p. 68; idem, "Pseudonymity," p. 331 (Collins sees this as one factor among many).

50. P. D. Hanson, *Dawn of Apocalyptic*, p. 252.

51. M. Stone, "Apocalyptic," pp. 47-56. A similar theory for early Christian pseudepigraphy has been proposed by K. Aland, "Anonymity and Pseudonymity," pp. 39-49.

52. D. S. Russell, *Apocalyptic*, pp. 132-39.

53. T.B. Baba Bathra 14b, 15a.

54. Among the exceptions are: the Book of Eldad and Modad (Num. 11:24-30 inspired this composition which is referred to in Hermas *Vis.* ii.3-4), the Apocryphon of Ezekiel (portions as early as the first century A.D.), the Ascension and Martyrdom of Isaiah (the Martyrdom is as early as the second century B.C.; the Ascension is Christian and from the first century A.D.), and the Apocalypse of Zephaniah (Jewish, earlier than the second century A.D.). On these writings see the relevant sections of J. H. Charlesworth, *Pseudepigrapha*.

55. J. J. Collins, "Pseudonymity," pp. 329-343.

56. Ibid.

57. P. D. Hanson, *Dawn of Apocalyptic*, pp. 70-71.

58. K. Koch, *Apocalyptic*, pp. 21-22, 28-35; F. Dexinger, *Apokalyptikforschung*, pp. 45-57.

59. W. Kornfeld, *Religion und Offenbarung*, pp. 243-264; however, Kornfeld incorrectly associates Haggai and Zech. 1-8 with the prophetic-eschatological perspective. They are correctly linked to the theocratic group by P. D. Hanson, *Dawn of Apocalyptic*, pp. 174-76 (in opposition to Trito-Isaiah), and J. D. Newsome, "Chronicler," p. 216.

60. P. Volz, *Eschatologie*, pp. 121-23; J. Bloch, *Apocalyptic*, pp. 18-19; M. Eliade, *Quest*, pp. 110-11; J. J. Collins, "Apocalypse," p. 365; G. Theissen, *Sociology*, p. 29.

61. J. J. Collins, "Environment," pp. 27-36; idem, *Daniel*, pp. 191-93.

62. H. Ringgren, "Apokalyptik," p. 464; M. Hengel, *Judaism and Hellenism*, I, 194-96; O. Plöger, *Theocracy and Eschatology*; P. D. Hanson, *Dawn of Apocalyptic*, p. 232, and *passim*; D. L. Petersen, *Late Israelite Prophecy*, pp. 6-8 (a brief review of the literature).

63. P. D. Hanson, *Dawn of Apocalyptic*; for a critique of Hanson, see R. J. Bauckham, "Rise of Apocalyptic," pp. 10-23; J. Blenkinsopp, *Prophecy and Canon*, pp. 113-14.

64. Hanson, *Apocalyptic*, p. 20.

65. J. Bloch, *Apocalyptic*, pp. 130-143; F. Dexinger, *Apokalyptikforschung*, p. 51; D. S. Russell, *Apocalyptic*, pp. 23-28.

66. M. Hengel, *Judaism and Hellenism*, I, 175-210, esp. pp. 176, 194.

67. V. Tcherikover, *Hellenistic Civilization*, pp. 175-203; J. J. Collins, *Daniel*, pp. 201-205; F. Dexinger, *Apokalyptikforschung*, pp. 45-48.

68. E. Janssen, *Das Gottesvolk*, pp. 98-99. But the recent theory of J. J. Collins ("Court Tales," p. 232; *Daniel*, pp. 54-59), that Dan. 7-12 was the product of a group which had produced Dan. 1-6 in Mesopotamia and then migrated to Palestine, is very attractive, though necessarily tentative.

69. D. S. Russell, *Apocalyptic*, p. 28; J. J. Collins, "Environment," p. 31; idem, *Daniel*, pp. 210-18; S. Mowinckel, *He That Cometh*, p. 282; E. Janssen, *Das Gottesvolk*, pp. 96-100 ("Die Apokalyptiker als Schriftgelehrte").

70. M. Hengel, *Judaism and Hellenism*, I, 194.

71. F. M. Cross, "Apocalyptic," p. 10; P. D. Hanson, *Dawn of Apocalyptic*, pp. 5-8, 395-401.

72. J. Bloch, *Apocalyptic*, pp. 25, 28-39; P. D. Hanson, *Dawn of Apocalyptic*, pp. 27-29.

73. F. Dexinger, *Apokalyptikforschung*, pp. 26-32.

74. J. Z. Smith, "Wisdom and Apocalyptic," pp. 131-156; idem, "Native Cults," pp. 236-249; C. C. McCown, "Hebrew and Egyptian Apocalyptic Literature," pp. 357-411; cf. above, pp. 76-77, on the Oracle of the Potter.

75. J. J. Collins, "Environment," pp. 27-30.

76. The renewed use of ancient paradigmatic myths in late prophetic and early Jewish apocalyptic literature has been emphasized by A. Bentzen, *King and Messiah*, pp. 73-80 (cf. pp. 12-15, 24), and demonstrated by P. D. Hanson, "An Ancient Ritual Pattern," pp. 37-59 (for Zech. 9); cf. idem, *Dawn of Apocalyptic*, pp. 299-316. A. Y. Collins, *Combat Myth*, has done this for portions of the Apocalypse of John. The central elements of the so-called Divine Warrior Hymn (identified by F. M. Cross and P. D. Hanson) are: (1) the cosmic battle of the divine warrior (Yahweh); (2) his temple-building activity, (3) the banquet, and (4) his glorious reign (P. D. Hanson, *Dawn of Apocalyptic*, p. 300).

77. A. Y. Collins, *Combat Myth*, pp. 57-100.

78. Two important and complementary studies: H. D. Betz, "Apocalypticism," pp. 134-156, and A. Y. Collins, "History-of-Religions Approach," pp. 367-381.

79. O. Plöger, *Theocracy and Eschatology*, pp. 47ff.

80. G. von Rad, *Old Testament Theology*, II, 301-308; idem, *Wisdom in Israel*, pp. 268-283. P. von der Osten-Sacken, *Die Apokalyptik*, and F. Dexinger, *Apokalyptikforschung*, pp. 39-43, argue against von Rad's thesis. E. Janssen, *Das Gottesvolk*, pp. 69-81, shows the apocalyptists' concern with *Heilsgeschichte*, a feature von Rad denies to apocalyptic.

81. J. Z. Smith, "Wisdom and Apocalyptic," p. 140; J. Blenkinsopp, *Prophecy and Canon*, pp. 112, 128-132. S. Schulz, *Spruchquelle*, p. 58, places prophets and scribes in opposition and the composition of Daniel, 1 Enoch, and Testaments XII are all attributed to the latter. This polarity is inappropriate.

82. G. Nickelsburg, "Apocalyptic Message," pp. 327-28; J. J. Collins, *Daniel*, pp. 210ff.

83. H. P. Müller, "Mantische Weisheit und Apokalyptik," pp. 268-293; cf. J. J. Collins, "Court Tales," p. 232; R. Bauckham, "Rise of Apocalyptic," p. 13.

84. J. J. Collins, *Daniel*, p. 75.

85. A. Finkel, "The Pesher of Dreams and Scripture," pp. 357-370; L. H. Silberman,

"Unriddling the Riddle," pp. 323-364; K. Elliger, *Studien zur Habakuk-Kommentar,* pp. 154-57.

86. J. J. Collins, "Environment," pp. 31-33; idem, *Daniel,* pp. 74-87; R. North, "Prophecy to Apocalyptic," p. 54; J. Schreiner, "Bewegung," pp. 237-39.

87. D. Suter, "Tradition and Composition," pp. 57-113; idem, "Apocalyptic Patterns," pp. 2-7.

88. M. Black, "The Eschatology of the Similitudes of Enoch," p. 3. For more examples cf. E. Janssen, *Das Gottesvolk,* p. 98 n. 40. See also the exhortations of G. W. Buchanan, "Apocalyptic Vision," pp. 183-192, which I think are basically misguided.

89. The current emphasis on the identification of midrashic patterns of exegesis in apocalyptic and early Christian literature runs the risk of regarding all biblical allusions as "midrashic." This tendency is particularly evident in E. E. Ellis, *Prophecy and Hermeneutic.* A broad approach to the subject of midrashic exegesis is A. Wright, *Midrash,* which should be read in the light of R. Le Déaut, "Definition of Midrash," 259-282.

90. M. Stone, "Apocalyptic," p. 52.

91. P. D. Hanson, "Apocalyptic Reexamined," pp. 458-469.

92. J. J. Collins, *Daniel,* pp. 75-76.

93. G. Warmuth, *Das Mahnwort,* pp. 35-36, 55ff., 82-83, 166ff., 170-71, where the author stresses the unconditional nature of the prophetic admonition and challenges the widespread view of the prophets as preachers of repentance.

94. K. Koch, *Apocalyptic,* p. 28.

95. O. Weinreich, *Ausgewählte Schriften,* I, 535-36.

96. C. H. Dodd, *The Bible and the Greeks,* pp. 243-48.

97. M. Stone, "Apocalyptic," pp. 47-56; H. Kraft, "Die altkirchliche Prophetie," p. 253; J. Lindblom, *Gesichte und Offenbarungen,* pp. 206-239, attempts to separate the authentic visionary experiences of John in the Apocalypse from the strictly literary visions.

98. G. Nickelsburg, "Apocalyptic Message," pp. 325-28.

99. Note the occurrence of the following formulas, which have points of contact with the OT: "and the Lord said to me" (2 Enoch 37:2 [A]), "the word of the Lord came to" (2 Bar. 1:1; 10:1), "and the Lord [answered and] said to me" (2 Bar. 4:1; 15:1; 17:1; 19:1); "and thus spoke the Lord to me" (2 Enoch 37:2 [B]).

100. K. Berger, *Die Amen-Worte Jesu,* pp. 20-27, has a very comprehensive discussion of the oath formula in eschatological sayings in apocalyptic literature. He lists the following passages where the oath formula occurs: 1 Enoch 98:1, 4, 6; 99:6; 103:1; 104:1; 2 Enoch 49:1; Asc. Isa. 1:8; 3:18; Apoc. Mosis 18; 3 Bar. 1:7; Test. Sol. 1:13; Rev. 10:6; 1 Clem. 58:2. See also G. W. E. Nickelsburg, "Apocalyptic Message," p. 316.

101. See above, pp. 90-91.

102. E. E. Ellis, *Prophecy and Hermeneutic,* p. 131 n. 8.

103. K. Berger, *Die Amen-Worte Jesu,* p. 24.

104. See below, pp. 164-65.

105. Translation of R. Lattimore, *The Odyssey of Homer,* p. 257.

106. T. B. Megillah 14a; T. B. Erubin 13a, 100a; T. B. Sanhedrin 101a; T. B. Shabbat 116b; Midrash Ruth 2.4 (103b); Numbers Rabbah 10 (159b); cf. E. Stauffer, "Der Methurgeman des Petrus," pp. 283-293.

107. G. Wolff, *Porphyrii,* p. 109 (Eusebius *Praep. evang.* iv.7).

108. W. G. Lambert, "The Fifth Tablet of the Era Epic," p. 122 lines 43-44: "It was revealed to him in the night and he did not leave out a single line, nor did he add one to it."

109. E. Janssen, *Das Gottesvolk,* p. 95.

110. G. W. E. Nickelsburg, "Apocalyptic Message," pp. 310-12; R. A. Coughenour, "Woe Oracles in Ethiopic Enoch," pp. 192-97.

111. 1 Enoch 94:6-8; 95:4-7; 96:4-8; 97:7-8; 98:9, 11-16; 99:1-2, 11-16; 100:7-9; 103:5, 8.

112. Translation of R. H. Charles, *APOT,* II, 272.

113. See above, pp. 96-97.

114. On the OT form of the oracle of assurance see above, pp. 94-95. On the oracle

of assurance in 1 Enoch 91-105 see G. W. E. Nickelsburg, "Apocalyptic Message," pp. 312, 320; in apocalyptic generally see U. Müller, *Prophetie und Predigt*, pp. 215-220.

115. Translation of R. H. Charles, *APOT*, II, 431-32.

116. Translation of R. H. Charles, *APOT*, II, 266.

117. Translation of G. H. Box, *APOT*, II, 615.

118. K. Koch, *Apocalyptic*, pp. 24-25.

119. M. Stone, "Apocalyptic," p. 55.

120. This four-part structure characterizes the first four visions of 4 Ezra: (1) 3:1-5:20: (a) 3:1a, (b) 3:1b-36, (c) 4:1-5:19, (d) 5:20; (2) 5:21-6:35: (a) 5:21, (b) 5:22-30, (c) 5:31-6:34, (d) 6:35; (3) 6:36-9:25: (a) 6:36a, (b) 6:36b-59, (c) 7:1-9:25, (d) [missing]; (4) 9:26-10:59: (a) 9:26-27a, (b) 9:27b-37, (c) 9:38-10:59a, (d) 10:59b.

121. This four-part structure is found in the fifth vision of 4 Ezra: (1) 11:1a, (2) 11:1b-12:3a, (3) 12:3b-9, (4) 12:10-39, and again in the sixth vision of 4 Ezra: (1) 13:1a, (2) 13:1b-13a, (3) 13:13b-20ab, (4) 13:20c-56. It is also found in the vision in 2 Bar. 36:1-40:4: (1) 13:1, (2) 13:2-37:1, (3) 38:1-4, (4) 39:1-40:4, and again in the vision sequence in 2 Bar. 53:1-74:4: (1) 53:1a, (2) 53:1b-12, (3) 54:1-22, (4) 55:1-74:4.

122. See below, pp. 274-288, 299-310.

123. L. Hartman, *Prophecy Interpreted*, pp. 23-49, 50-70.

124. Among them are Jub. 23:11-31; 1 Enoch 10:16-11:2; 80:2-8; 91:6-11; 99:1-16; 100:1-9; 102:1-11; 103:1-15; 104:1-105:2; Test. Lev. 4:1-4; Test. Judah 21:6-22:3; Test. Zeb. 9:5-9; Ass. Moses 10:1-10.

125. Translation of R. H. Charles, *APOT*, II, 188-89. Cf. L. Hartman, *Prophecy Interpreted*, pp. 112-18.

126. See above, p. 93.

127. L. Hartman, *Prophecy Interpreted*, pp. 132-37.

128. Translation of G. H. Box, *APOT*, II, 576-77.

129. W. O. E. Oesterley, *II Esdras*, pp. xv-xvi. For a brief overview of the source theories of 4 Ezra see J. M. Myers, *I and II Esdras*, pp. 119-120 (the unity of 4 Ezra is maintained by Myers).

130. S. R. Isenberg, "Millenarianism in Greco-Roman Palestine," pp. 20-37; idem, "Power through Temple and Torah in Greco-Roman Palestine," pp. 24-52; S. Applebaum, "Economic Life in Palestine," pp. 631-700.

131. E. Fascher, *PROPHETES*, p. 163.

132. D. M. Rhoads, *Israel in Revolution*.

133. See B. R. Wilson, *Magic and the Millennium*; N. Cohn, *The Pursuit of the Millennium*; S. Thrupp (ed.), *Millennial Dreams in Action*; K. Burridge, *New Heaven, New Earth*. For further bibliography and discussion see J. G. Gager, *Kingdom and Community*, pp. 20-37 (and notes).

134. For example, see the analysis of Zech. 9 by P. D. Hanson, "Zechariah 9," pp. 37-59. On the divine warrior myth see F. M. Cross, *Canaanite Myth and Hebrew Epic*, and P. D. Miller, *The Divine Warrior in Early Israel*. On ritual combat as a feature of the Israelite royal ideology, see A. Bentzen, *King and Messiah*, pp. 12-15, 24.

135. The main elements of the divine warrior hymn, according to P. D. Hanson (*Dawn of Apocalyptic*, p. 300) are: (1) the cosmic battle of the divine warrior (Yahweh), (2) his temple-building activity, (3) the banquet, and (4) his glorious reign.

136. The literature on the subject of Jewish messianism is voluminous. Among the more significant studies and surveys of the subject are: S. Mowinckel, *He That Cometh*; A. Bentzen, *King and Messiah*; J. Klausner, *The Messianic Idea in Israel*; W. Bousset and H. Gressmann, *Die Religion des Judentums*, pp. 213-242, 259-268; P. Volz, *Eschatologie*, pp. 173-186; R. H. Fuller, *Foundations*, pp. 23-34; D. S. Russell, *Apocalyptic*, pp. 304-323; F. Hahn, *The Titles of Jesus*.

137. That the Davidic messiah was not expected to be a miracle worker is generally recognized; cf. J. Klausner, *The Messianic Idea in Israel*, p. 506; J. L. Martyn, *History and Theology in the Fourth Gospel*, pp. 181-88. Mark 13:22 (and par. Matt. 24:24) which refers to signs and wonders (*sēmeia kai terata*) performed by false messiahs and false prophets (*pseudochristoi kai*

pseudoprophētai) represents a conflation of traditions. John 7:31, which refers to the miracles performed by a messiah, is a distinctively Christian element (R. Schnackenburg, *Das Johannesevangelium*, II, 205-206; M. de Jonge, *Jesus*, pp. 91-92).

138. On the priestly or Levitical messiah see P. Volz, *Eschatologie*, pp. 190-93; F. Hahn, *The Titles of Jesus*, pp. 229-239; D. S. Russell, *Apocalyptic*, pp. 310-16.

139. G. R. Beasley-Murray, "The Two Messiahs," pp. 1-12; K. G. Kuhn, "The Two Messiahs," pp. 57-58; A. S. van der Woude, *Die messianischen Vorstellungen*, pp. 190-216.

140. A. S. van der Woude, *Die messianischen Vorstellungen*, pp. 54ff., 75ff. (see index under "Hohepriester, endzeitlicher"); H. Ringgren, *Faith of Qumran*, pp. 167-173, 176-180.

141. S. Mowinckel, *He That Cometh*, pp. 280-84.

142. On the Son of man in Jewish tradition see particularly C. Colpe, *TDNT*, VIII, 400-430; E. Sjöberg, *Der verborgene Menschensohn*; U. B. Müller, *Messias und Menschensohn*.

143. On the use of the title Son of man in early Christian literature see A. J. B. Higgins, *Jesus and the Son of Man*; H. E. Tödt, *The Son of Man*; F. Hahn, *The Titles of Jesus*, pp. 15-67; R. H. Fuller, *Foundations*, pp. 119-125; N. Perrin, *Rediscovering*, pp. 173-206; particularly excellent is the article on *ho huios tou anthrōpou* by C. Colpe, *TDNT*, VIII, 430-477.

144. This is demonstrated by C. Colpe, *TDNT*, VIII, 423-26.

145. N. Perrin, *Rediscovering*, pp. 164-173.

146. R. H. Fuller, *Foundations*, pp. 34-43; C. Colpe, *TDNT*, VIII, 427-29; E. Sjöberg, *Der verborgene Menschensohn*, pp. 154-59, 165-67.

147. A. S. van der Woude, *Die messianischen Vorstellungen*, pp. 83, 248; E. Fascher, *PROPHĒTĒS*, p. 181.

148. J. Bowman, "Prophets and Prophecy," pp. 107, 205-206, 210-11; cf. Ass. Moses 1:10-10:15 in the light of 3:11. The hermeneutical assumption behind the Qumran *pesharim* is that all that the prophets wrote was predictive, and those predictions are now being fulfilled (F. M. Cross, Jr., "Qumran Community," p. 83; F. F. Bruce, *Biblical Exegesis*, p. 9; idem, *Second Thoughts*, p. 77).

149. C. C. Torrey, *The Lives of the Prophets* (Jeremiah: 3, 5; Ezekiel: 8-10, 11, 12; Zechariah: 1).

150. J. Giblet, "Prophétisme," pp. 96-97.

151. This may reflect the notion that the eschatological prophet is a forerunner whose task is the designation of the messiah, or it may indicate that John's preaching of repentance coupled with a rite of ritual washing was perceived as prophetic, a perception visually aided by John's prophetic costume (Mark 1:6; cf. 1 Kgs. 19:19; 2 Kgs. 1:8; 2:13-14; Zech. 13:4).

152. On Elijah see J. Jeremias, *TDNT*, II, 928-941; P. Volz, *Eschatologie*, pp. 195-97, 200-201; Strack-Billerbeck, IV/2, 764-798.

153. John 1:26 appears to reflect a similar tradition (M. de Jonge, *Jesus*, p. 87), and CD 7:18-19, with its allusion to 1 Kgs. 19:15, may refer to the returning Elijah as a way of conceptualizing the role of the Teacher of Righteousness (A. S. van der Woude, *Die messianischen Vorstellungen*, p. 55).

154. The conception of a Moses *redivivus* is based on legends that Moses, like Enoch, Elijah, and Ezra (on Ezra see 4 Ezra 14:9; cf. W. O. E. Oesterley, *II Esdras*, p. 167), did not actually die but was translated to heaven. Evidence for this notion is found in Josephus *Ant.* iv.326; cf. iii.96; Philo *Quaest. in Ex.* ii.29; this in spite of the record of Moses' death and burial in Deut. 34:5-8. On the ascension of Moses see J. Jeremias, *TDNT*, IV, 854; Jeremias thinks that the conception of Moses' ascension is primarily a Hellenistic Jewish development. On the whole question see H. M. Teeple, *The Mosaic Eschatological Prophet*, pp. 41-43.

155. This interpretation may be reflected in Josephus, who refers to a "failure of the exact succession of the prophets" (*tēn tōn prophētōn akribē diadochēn*) in *Contra Ap.* i.8. See above, p. 106.

156. J. Blenkinsopp, *Prophecy and Canon*, p. 86.

157. Ibid., pp. 86, 176 n. 16.

158. A. Bentzen, *King and Messiah*, pp. 65-67.

159. Strack-Billerbeck, II, 626.

160. J. Jeremias, *TDNT,* IX, 857-58.

161. W. Meeks, *The Prophet-King.*

162. Translation of A. Dupont-Sommer, *Essene Writings,* p. 94.

163. A. S. van der Woude, *Die messianischen Vorstellungen,* pp. 78-80; R. Brown, "The Messianism of Qumran," pp. 59-61.

164. N. Wieder, "The 'Law Interpreter'," pp. 158-175; O. Betz, *Offenbarung und Schrift-forschung,* pp. 61-68, 88-99; A. Dupont-Sommer, *Essene Writings,* pp. 360-64; A. S. van der Woude, *Die messianischen Vorstellungen,* pp. 75-89; G. Jeremias, *Der Lehrer der Gerechtigkeit,* pp. 268-307.

165. See below, pp. 154-56.

166. R. H. Fuller, *Foundations,* pp. 46-49; J. Jeremias, *TDNT,* IV, 848-864. The most comprehensive treatment of the Mosaic eschatological prophet is that of H. Teeple, *The Mosaic Eschatological Prophet.*

167. All the references to Jeremiah *redivivus* are collected in K. Berger, *Die Auferstehung des Propheten,* pp. 256ff. n. 72. See also L. Ginzberg, *The Legends of the Jews,* VI, 341. On the impact of Jeremiah on early Judaism and early Christianity see C. Wolff, *Jeremia im Frühjudentum und Urchristentum* (1976).

168. Bar Kosiba (also known as Bar Kochba, meaning "son of a star," a title coined by Rabbi Akiba with reference to Num. 24:17 and Simon bar Kosiba's messianic status, and Bar Koziba, meaning "son of a lie," a pejorative title coined by his opponents) called himself "prince" (*naśi'* or *nasi'*) of Israel (Y. Meshorer, *Jewish Coins,* nos. 167, 169-172, 181-82, 186-87, 192-93, 199, 201, 204, 206, 209B, 210-12, 215). See G. Vermes and F. Millar, *History of the Jewish People,* I, 543ff.
192-93, 199, 201, 204, 206, 209B, 210-12, 215). See G. Vermes and F. Millar, *History of the Jewish People,* I, 543ff.

169. The typology which follows is based on that developed by B. R. Wilson, *Magic and the Millennium,* which the author summarizes on pp. 16-30, and develops in some detail in the remainder of the book.

170. See below, pp. 129-132.

171. See below, pp. 156-57.

172. J. G. Gager, *Kingdom and Community,* pp. 20-65, discusses early Christianity in terms of a millenarian movement. G. Theissen, *Sociology of Early Palestinian Christianity,* discusses early Christianity (particularly in its earliest Palestinian phase) as a pacifistic Jewish renewal movement.

173. P. W. Barnett, "The Jewish Sign Prophets," pp. 679-697. Barnett regards Jesus as sharing the same pattern, but since he preceded all the Jewish sign prophets, he may have served as a paradigm for them. Barnett is probably wrong, for social movements with similar features in the same culture do not necessarily have a direct relationship.

174. On the Zealots see M. Hengel, *Die Zeloten,* a book which should be read in the light of the correctives supplied by M. Smith, "Zealots," pp. 1-19.

175. Josephus *Ant.* xx.97-98; Acts 5:36.

176. Josephus *Ant.* xx.169-172; *Bell.* ii.261-63; Acts 21:38.

177. The motif of the retreat into the wilderness as a widespread nostalgic phenomenon in early Judaism is discussed by M. Hengel, *Die Zeloten,* pp. 255-261.

178. G. Theissen, "Die Tempelweissagung Jesu," pp. 144-158; idem, *Sociology of Early Palestinian Christianity,* pp. 47-58, places many of the religious movements which focus on Jerusalem within the interpretative framework of the antipathy which existed between country and city. The revolutionary and renewal groups accepted the essential holiness of Jerusalem and the temple, according to Theissen, but not in their present condition. Theissen's interpretation is quite compelling.

179. This episode and the various traditions which are related to it are fully discussed by M. F. Collins, "Hidden Vessels," pp. 97-116.

180. Ibid. See also J. A. Montgomery, *The Samaritans,* pp. 234-251; M. Gaster, *The Samaritans,* pp. 90-91; W. A. Meeks, *The Prophet-King,* pp. 246-254.

181. Josephus *Ant.* xviii.4-10; xx.102; *Bell.* ii.117-18; Acts 5:37.

182. One of the more recent critical studies of John the Baptist is that of C. H. H. Scobie, *John the Baptist* (1964), generally excellent though deficient in his conception of Jewish eschatological expectations of the late Second Temple period. A fine redaction-critical study is available in W. Wink, *John the Baptist in the Gospel Tradition* (1968). Both books contain extensive bibliographies. A short but significant study is the more recent book by J. Becker, *Johannes der Täufer* (1972). Still indispensable is C. H. Kraeling, *John the Baptist* (1951).

183. W. Brandt, *Die jüdischen Baptismen* (1910); J. Thomas, *Le mouvement baptiste en Palestine et Syrie* (1935); J. Schmitt, "Le milieu baptiste de Jean le Précurseur," pp. 391-407.

184. W. Brownlee, "John the Baptist," pp. 36-37.

185. C. H. H. Scobie, *John the Baptist*, pp. 110-16.

186. Mark 11:32 (and par. Matt. 21:26; Luke 20:6); Matt. 14:5; Luke 1:76; 7:26 (and par. Matt. 11:9); John 1:21, 25. For discussions of the prophetic status of John see C. H. H. Scobie, *John the Baptist*, pp. 117-130; E. Fascher, *PROPHĒTĒS*, pp. 174-76; F. Schnider, *Jesus der Prophet*, pp. 39-54; J. Lindblom, *Gesichte und Offenbarungen*, pp. 172ff.; J. Becker, *Johannes*, pp. 41-62.

187. W. Wink, *John the Baptist in the Gospel Tradition*, pp. 42-43.

188. Josephus *Ant*. xviii.116-19. In *Ant*. xviii.116-17 Josephus describes the ministry of John as follows:

> But to some of the Jews the destruction of Herod's army seemed to be divine vengeance, and certainly a just vengeance, for his treatment of John, surnamed the Baptist. For Herod had put him to death, though he was a good man [*agathon andra*] and had exhorted the Jews to lead righteous lives, to practise justice towards their fellows and piety towards God, and so doing to join in baptism. In his view this was a necessary preliminary if baptism was to be acceptable to God. They must not employ it to gain pardon for whatever sins they committed, but as a consecration of the body implying that the soul was already thoroughly cleansed by right behavior.

For the reticence of Josephus in using the term *prophētēs* of postbiblical figures, see J. Reiling, "The Use of *PSEUDOPROPHĒTĒS*," p. 156; for a qualification of Reiling's judgment see D. E. Aune, "The Use of *PROPHĒTĒS* in Josephus," 419-421.

189. P. Hoffmann, *Studien zur Logienquelle*, pp. 1-33; S. Schulz, *Spruchquelle*, pp. 366-378; F. Schnider, *Jesus der Prophet*, p. 39.

190. R. E. Brown, *Birth of the Messiah*, pp. 274-75.

191. See above, p. 91.

192. A. Sand, *Das Gesetz und die Propheten*, p. 127; F. Schnider, *Jesus der Prophet*, p. 39; cf. the analyses of P. Hoffmann and S. Schulz referred to above in n. 189.

193. In the Greek text Matthew has 63 words, while Luke has 64; the additional word in Luke is *kai*.

194. R. Bach, *Aufforderung zur Flucht*, pp. 15-50. The summons to flee is found in Mark 13:14-19, in an anonymous oracle preserved in Eusebius *Hist. eccl.* iii.5.3, and in Epiphanius *De mens. et pond.* xv (Migne, *Patrologia Graeca*, XLIII, 261B); see below, pp. 311-12.

195. H. Conzelmann, *Theology of St. Luke*, p. 26. On parenesis in the message of John see C. H. Kraeling, *John the Baptist*, pp. 65-94.

196. See the excellent discussion in J. Jeremias, *New Testament Theology*, pp. 43-49.

197. C. H. H. Scobie, *John the Baptist*, p. 63; P. Hoffmann, *Studien zur Theologie der Logienquelle*, pp. 28-29.

198. This is demonstrated by C. H. Kraeling, *John the Baptist*, pp. 53-55; cf. O. Cullmann, *Christology*, pp. 25-26. Scobie's discussion of whether the messianic figure of John's expectation of an earthly (Davidic) messiah or a heavenly (Son of man) redeemer figure is flawed by an oversimplified typology of first-century Jewish eschatology (C. H. H. Scobie, *John the Baptist*, pp. 62ff.). Recently J. H. Hughes, "John the Baptist: the Forerunner of God Himself," pp. 191-218, has attempted to refute Kraeling's arguments that the "coming one" in John's speech cannot be God. Kraeling argues that (1) John would not have compared himself with

God, (2) God would not be described as "mightier," and (3) God would not be described as wearing sandals. Hughes' counter arguments are trivial, and his interpretation of Matt. 11:2-6; Luke 7:18-23 (the embassy sent to Jesus by John to ask if he were the "coming one") strains credulity. A further argument that John regarded himself as the forerunner of an eschatological prophetic-messianic figure is that wonder-working is never associated with him in the tradition, though such activity was widely thought to be integral to the work of an eschatological prophet.

199. See the discussion in J. D. G. Dunn, *Baptism in the Holy Spirit*, pp. 8ff.; idem, "Spirit-and-Fire Baptism," pp. 81-92.

200. E. Best, "Spirit-Baptism," pp. 236-243.

201. Translation by A. Dupont-Sommer, *Essene Writings*, p. 81.

202. J. I. H. McDonald, *Kerygma and Didache*, p. 17, thinks John uses neither the typical announcement of judgment nor the salvation oracle, but combines elements of both into a new form which he labels "the announcement of imminent messianic salvation."

203. O. Betz, *Offenbarung und Schriftforschung*, pp. 61-68, 88-99; N. Wieder, "The 'Law-Interpreter'," pp. 158-175, esp. p. 171; A. Dupont-Sommer, *Essene Writings*, pp. 360-64; G. Jeremias, *Der Lehrer der Gerechtigkeit*, pp. 268-307; A. S. van der Woude, *Die messianischen Vorstellungen*, pp. 75-89; W. Brownlee, "Messianic Motives," pp. 17-20.

204. This is very clearly demonstrated by B. J. Roberts, "Biblical Exegesis and Fulfilment in Qumran," pp. 195-207.

205. H. Braun, *Qumran und das Neue Testament*, II, 252: "The new element in the pneumatology of Qumran in comparison with ordinary Judaism is the *complete presence of the Spirit.*" See also M. Hengel, *Die Zeloten*, p. 241. This has been carefully demonstrated through a detailed exegesis of the relevant Qumran texts by H.-W. Kuhn, *Enderwartung und gegenwärtiges Heil*, pp. 117-139.

206. G. Jeremias, *Lehrer*, p. 141.

207. This translation and the next are from A. Dupont-Sommer, *Essene Writings*, pp. 259, 262.

208. F. F. Bruce, "Josephus and Daniel," p. 159; idem, *Second Thoughts*, p. 93.

209. A. Finkel, "The Pesher of Dreams and Scripture," pp. 357-370; L. H. Silberman, "Unriddling the Riddle," pp. 323-364; K. Elliger, *Studien zum Habakuk-Kommentar*, pp. 154-57.

210. H.-P. Müller, "Mantische Weisheit," pp. 283-85. According to Müller mantic wisdom was one of the primary antecedents of Jewish apocalyptic.

211. F. F. Bruce, *Biblical Exegesis*, pp. 7-17.

212. Translated by A. Dupont-Sommer, *Essene Writings*, p. 259; the structure of this particular selection is discussed by P. Weimar, "Formen frühjüdischer Literatur," pp. 155-160.

213. Josephus *Bell.* vi.301 (author's trans.); the report by Josephus on Joshua ben Ananiah is found in *Bell.* vi.300-309. Part of the discussion which follows is based on O. Michel, "Spätjüdisches Prophetentum," pp. 61-62.

214. Josephus sketches the major features of Albinus' tenure as procurator in *Bell.* ii.272-77.

215. See above, pp. 96-97.

216. See above, pp. 116-17.

217. Num. 7:89; 1 Sam. 3:2-14; Isa. 6:1-13; Josephus *Ant.* xiii.282; Luke 1:8-23; Acts 22:17-21.

218. See below, pp. 161-62.

219. On prophetic critiques of the temple cult see Hos. 6:6; Amos 5:4-7, 21-23; Isa. 1:10-12; Jer. 7:21-26; Ps. 50:9; 51:18-21 (Eng. 16-19). For predictions of the destruction of the temple (and Jerusalem) see Jer. 7:14; 26:4-9; Dan. 9:26; 11:31; Ezek. 9:1-10. At Jeremiah's trial for treason Micah's prediction of the destruction of Jerusalem is quoted in Jeremiah's defense (Jer. 26:18; cf. Mic. 3:12). Uriah ben Shemaiah, who also prophesied against the city and was killed on that account is also mentioned (Jer. 26:20-23). In the *Vitae Prophetarum* Jonah and Zechariah ben Iddo are said to have predicted the fall of Jerusalem, while Habakkuk is said to have prophesied the destruction of the temple.

220. See above, n. 65.

221. O. Betz, *TDNT,* IX, 278-292.

222. Josephus *Ant.* i.85 (cf. Gen. 15:13); ii.267-69 (cf. Exod. 3:2-4:23); iii.88-90 (cf. Exod. 19:16-20:1); viii.352 (cf. 1 Kgs. 19:9).

223. O. Betz, *TDNT,* IX, 288-290; E. Bevan, *Sibyls and Seers,* pp. 106-111; Strack-Billerbeck, I, 125-134; L. Blau, "Bat Ḳol," pp. 588-592.

224. Josephus *Bell.* i.347 (author's trans.).

225. Josephus *Bell.* vi.281-87.

226. Josephus *Bell.* vi.285.

227. Josephus *Ant.* xx.97-98 (Theudas); *Ant.* xx.169-172; *Bell.* ii.261-63 (unnamed Egyptian Jew); the "signs of deliverance" motif is also found in two summaries of millenarian activity by Josephus in *Ant.* xx.167-68; *Bell.* ii.259.

228. Josephus *Bell.* vi.286 (author's trans.).

229. J. Reiling, *"PSEUDOPROPHĒTĒS,"* p. 156, claims that contemporary seers are never designated *prophētēs* in Josephus. This statement by Josephus shows Reiling's judgment to be incorrect; cf. D. E. Aune, "The Use of *PROPHĒTĒS* in Josephus," pp. 419-421.

230. The oracle referred to by Eusebius is found in *Hist. eccl.* iii.5.3, and also in Epiphanius *Haer.* xxix.7; xxx.2; *De mens. et pond.* xv (Migne, *Patrologia Graeca,* xliii, 261b); see the discussion on this oracle below, pp. 311-12.

231. See above, pp. 82-83, 94.

232. On clerical or Levitical prophecy see J. Blenkinsopp, *Prophecy and Canon,* pp. 132-38; R. Meyer, *TDNT,* VI, 825-26; E. Bammel, *"ARCHIEREUS,"* pp. 351-56. On the clerical prophecy espoused by the Chronicler see D. L. Petersen, *Late Israelite Prophecy,* pp. 55-96; J. D. Newsome, "Chronicler," pp. 202-217. The theory that bands of cult prophets were absorbed into the ranks of Levitical singers has been carefully argued by A. Johnson, *Cultic Prophet.*

233. C. H. Dodd, "The Prophecy of Caiaphas," pp. 139-140; E. Bammel, *"ARCHIEREUS,"* pp. 351-56; S. Mowinckel, *Psalms,* II, 57. There is a close relationship between prophecy and priesthood in Philo *De praem.* 55-56; *De spec. leg.* 192; *De vita Mosis* ii.2, 187, 275. At the end of the fourth century B.C. the high priest Jaddua reportedly had an oracular dream (Josephus *Ant.* xi.327-28). The Hasmonean John Hyrcanus was not only a ruler and a priest but also had prophetic powers (*archēs tou ethnous kai tēs archieraitikēs timēs kai prophēteias*), according to Josephus *Ant.* xiii.299; *Bell.* i.68-69. In *Ant.* xiii.282-83 Hyrcanus is said to have received an oracle in the temple while burning incense in his capacity as high priest; other prophecies are attributed to him in *Ant.* xiii.300; *Bell.* i.169. The prophetic powers of Hyrcanus are not regarded as eschatological by Josephus.

234. C. H. Dodd, "The Prophecy of Caiaphas," pp. 134-143.

235. According to Strack-Billerbeck, II, 546: "Prophecies apart from the knowledge and intention of the speaker are frequently mentioned in rabbinic literature." Among the several examples given is this quotation from Midrash Ps. 90 (194a): "R. Eleazar [ca. A.D. 270] said in the name of R. Jose ben Zimra [ca. A.D. 220]: 'All prophets who have prophesied have not been aware of what they prophesied, only Moses and Isaiah were fully aware.'" This is reminiscent of Greco-Roman theories of divine inspiration; cf. above, pp. 32-34, 38-40, esp. n. 189.

236. J. Blenkinsopp, "Prophecy and Priesthood in Josephus," pp. 239-262, is an excellent study on the subject; cf. O. Betz, *Offenbarung,* pp. 105-108; D. M. Rhoads, *Israel in Revolution,* pp. 8-11.

237. H. Lindner, *Geschichtsauffassung,* p. 144.

238. F. F. Bruce, "Josephus and Daniel," p. 159. Bruce cites 1QpHab 7:1-4 as an instance of such insight on the part of the Teacher of Righteousness. In *Ant.* x.267, 277ff., Josephus emphasizes that Daniel's vision shows not only *what* will happen, but also *when* it will happen. Bruce justifiably suspects that Josephus has his own prophetic gift in mind here.

239. Josephus *Ant.* x.79-80.

240. O. Michel, "Ich Komme," pp. 123-24, has called attention to the occurrence here, within the context of a prophetic speech, of the term *hēkō,* which he describes as "Hellenistic presentation style." He cites a parallel with the speech of the Syrian prophet parodied by

Celsus in Origen *Contra Celsum* viii.9. He is followed by D. Georgi, *Die Gegner des Paulus*, p. 125. In fact, there is formal but not material similarity. The formula *hēkō* is an expression attributed to savior gods (=*ēlthon*). See above, p. 72, n. 136.

241. Josephus *Bell.* iii.400-402 (author's trans.).

242. Josephus *Bell.* iv.622-29.

243. Suetonius *Vesp.* 5.6; Dio Cassius lxv.1.4. In the latter author we read: (Josephus speaking) "You may imprison me now, but a year from now, when you have become emperor, you will release me." R. Lattimore, "Portents and Prophecies," pp. 441-49, lists twelve portents or prophecies connected with Vespasian's assumption of the principate. The most extensive recent discussion of this oracle is that of A. Schalit, "Die Erhebung Vespasians," pp. 208-327, who thinks that there are basic historical kernels behind the prophecies of both Josephus and R. Yohanan ben Zakkai (pp. 262-64). Recently, J. W. Doeve has revived H. Grätz's view that Josephus appropriated R. Yohanan's prophecy for himself ("The Flight of Rabban Yohanan," pp. 61-62.)

244. Josephus *Bell.* iv.626.

245. For the recognition oracle in Greco-Roman paganism see above, pp. 68-70; for the recognition oracle in early Christianity see below, pp. 270-74, 323-25.

246. Josephus *Bell.* vi.312.

247. According to H. St. J. Thackeray, *Josephus,* pp. 37-38, Tacitus and Josephus are probably dependent on a common source. H. Lindner, *Geschichtsauffassung,* p. 72, opines that Suetonius and Tacitus are both independent of Josephus.

248. Tacitus *Hist.* v.13.

249. Suetonius *Vesp.* 4.5; on the independence of Suetonius from Josephus see above, n. 247.

250. In support of Gen. 49:10 see J. Blenkinsopp, "The Oracle of Judah," pp. 55-64 (the author thinks that this passage is also presupposed by the gospel accounts of Jesus' triumphal entry); in support of Dan. 9:24-27 see F. F. Bruce, "Josephus and Daniel," p. 158; L. Gaston, *No Stone on Another,* pp. 461ff.; in support of Num. 24:17, P. Corssen, "Die Zeugnisse des Tacitus und pseudo-Josephus," p. 122; I. Hahn, "Josephus und die Eschatologie von Qumran," p. 169; it is suggested as a possibility by F. F. Bruce, "Josephus and Daniel," p. 158.

251. E. Norden, "Josephus und Tacitus," pp. 656ff.

252. I. Hahn, "Josephus und die Eschatologie von Qumran," pp. 167-191; L. Gaston, *No Stone on Another,* p. 463.

253. M. de Jonge, "Josephus und die Zukunftserwartungen seines Volkes," pp. 210ff.

254. O. Michel and O. Bauernfeind, *Josephus,* I, 406 n. 35. The noneschatological perspective of 1 Maccabees is sympathetic with the aims of the Hasmoneans, even though some slight reservations are apparent (see D. Arenhoevel, *Theokratie,* pp. 58-66).

255. Aboth de Rabbi Nathan (Rec. A) 4.5 (J. Goldin, p. 36); T. B. Gittin 56a-b. In spite of the fact that this story is frequently regarded as historical by Jewish scholarship (cf. M. D. Herr, "Historical Significance," p. 128), it is most probably legendary (A. Schalit, "Die Erhebung Vespasians," pp. 264, 316ff.; P. Schäfer, "Johanan ben Zakkai," pp. 84-88.

256. The last possibility, which appears most likely, is supported by A. J. Saldarini, "Johanan ben Zakkai's Escape," pp. 198-99.

257. See above, p. 86; cf. S. Mowinckel, *Psalms,* II, 61-62.

258. K. Sethe, "Die Berufung eines Hohenpriester," pp. 30-35; A. Lods, "Le rôle des oracles," pp. 91-100. Lods (p. 95) gives an example from an inscription executed under Ramses II: "You are henceforth the first prophet of Amon."

259. Midrash Rabbah Lamentations ii.2 (H. Freeman, *Midrash Rabbah,* VII, 157); T. J. Taanith 4.7 (68d); see L. Finkelstein, *Akiba,* p. 269.

260. Josephus *Bell.* iv.388.

261. F. F. Bruce, "Josephus and Daniel," pp. 155-56, suggests Jer. 7:14; 26:6; and Dan. 11 (all highly unlikely) in addition to Ezek. 9.

262. See above pp. 60-61.

263. These are the reasonable suggestions of C. Wolff, *Jeremia im Frühjüdentum und Urchristentum,* p. 11.

264. Josephus *Bell.* vi.311.
265. Suggested by O. Michel and O. Bauernfeind, *Josephus,* II/2, 190 n. 149.
266. F. F. Bruce, "Josephus and Daniel," p. 155.
267. Ibid., p. 156.
268. Ibid., p. 160.
269. Josephus *Bell.* v.591-93 (a passage indicating Josephus' conscious emulation of Jeremiah); cf. C. Wolff, *Jeremias im Frühjüdentum und Urchristentum,* pp. 11-12; M. de Jonge, "Josephus und die Zukunftserwartungen seines Volkes," p. 207.
270. H. Lindner, *Geschichtsauffassung,* p. 73.
271. In Sib. Or. iv.115-127, which (with all of Book iv) is of Jewish origin and generally dated after A.D. 70 because it refers to the Roman conquest of Jerusalem, we find an oracle very similar in form and content to that mentioned by Josephus (trans. R. H. Charles, *APOT,* II, 395):

> To Solyma [Jerusalem] too the evil blast of war shall come from Italy, and shall lay in ruins God's great temple, whenever, confident in their folly, they shall cast godliness to the winds and commit hateful murders before the temple. . . . And a Roman leader shall come to Syria, who shall burn down Solyma's temple with fire, and therewith slay many men, and shall waste the great land of the Jews with its broad way.

272. Josephus *Bell.* v. 19.
273. H. Lindner, *Geschichtsauffassung,* p. 146.
274. This phrase and its synonyms are technical terms in the narration of revelatory dream experiences (E. R. Dodds, *Irrational,* pp. 105-106); cf. the phrase *parestē gar moi* in Acts 27:24.
275. Josephus *Vita* 42.
276. Josephus *Ant.* xi.326-27.
277. See R. Meyer, *TDNT,* VI, 823-25; G. Vermes, *Jesus the Jew,* pp. 58-82.
278. R. Meyer, *TDNT,* VI, 821-23.
279. T. J. Shabbat xvi, 15d (trans. A. Oppenheimer, *The 'Am Ha-Aretz,* p. 202); cf. L. Finkelstein, *Akiba,* p. 62. Here "conductores" is a translation of *msykyn,* possibly a transliteration of the Latin *mesicius,* a retired Roman soldier who settled in a colony, the kind of thing that occurred in second-century Galilee (see Loftus, "The Anti-Roman Revolts," p. 81 n. 16).
280. See below, pp. 175-76.
281. M. Soṭah 9.15 (trans. H. Danby, *Mishnah,* p. 306); the same prophecy is attributed to various other sages of different periods (A. Oppenheimer, *The 'Am Ha-Aretz,* p. 203 n. 13): to R. Judah in T. B. Sanhedrin 97a; to Resh Laḳish in Canticles Rabbah ii.13; to R. Abbun in *Pesiḳta de-Rav Kahana* v, *and Pesiḳta Rabbati* xv.
282. Josephus *Bell.* ii.159, quoted above, p. 133.
283. Josephus *Ant.* xiii.311-12; *Bell.* i.78-80; discussion here follows O. Betz, *Offenbarung,* pp. 99-102.
284. See above, pp. 51-52.
285. Josephus *Ant.* xv.373; cf. O. Betz, *Offenbarung,* pp. 102-103.
286. Josephus *Ant.* xv.374-79.
287. Prophecy plays a critical role in the plots of the *Iliad,* the *Odyssey,* the *Argonautica* of Apollonius Rhodius, the *Aeneid* of Vergil, Lucan's *Bellum Civile,* Silius Italicus' *Punica,* Valerius Flaccus' *Argonautica,* and Statius' *Thebais*; cf. C. H. Moore, "Prophecy in the Ancient Epic," pp. 99-175. Oracles and oracular fulfilment play an important role in Herodotus as well as the Athenian tragedians. Among later writers Plutarch makes extensive use of oracles, especially dream oracles, to punctuate the lives of great men, as does Arrian in his life of Alexander. No comparable study (to that of C. H. Moore) for the role of prophecy as a literary device in Luke-Acts has been done.
288. *Paraklēsis* (= Heb. *nḥm*) is an important term in the LXX version of Deutero-Isaiah (40:1; 49:13; 51:3) and Trito-Isaiah (61:3; 66:13); cf. É. Cothenet, "Les prophètes chrétiens comme exégètes," pp. 81ff.
289. The term "revealed" (*kechrēmatismenon*) by the Holy Spirit does not betray the means whereby this revelation came to Simeon.

290. R. E. Brown, *Birth of the Messiah,* p. 458.

291. Ibid., pp. 455-56.

292. OT women who are identified as prophetesses include Miriam (Exod. 15:10), Deborah (Judg. 4:4), Huldah (2 Kgs. 22:14; 2 Chr. 34:22), the wife of Isaiah (Isa. 8:3), and Noadiah (Neh. 6:14). NT women prophets include only the daughters of Philip (Acts 21:9) and the prophetess "Jezebel" (Rev. 2:20).

293. H. A. Wolfson, *Philo,* II, 10.

294. Philo *De migr. Abr.* 35; *De cher.* 27.

295. The use of the verb *korybantian* in Philo as a metaphor for one who has the vision of ideas in all their beauty is discussed by I. M. Linforth, "The Corybantic Rites in Plato," p. 154. D. Lührmann, *Offenbarung,* p. 32, states that "Philo of Alexandria knows ecstasy as the highest form of revelation." Lührmann is not strictly correct; he is focusing on ecstasy in general, while Philo enumerates various kinds of ecstasy, one form of which concerns the prophets (Philo *Quis rer. div.* 249). The behavioral characteristics of divine possession in the view of Philo must be considered, since Philo designates the experience paradoxically as "sober intoxication" (*De op. mundi* 70-71).

296. Philo *De vita Mosis* ii.188. Philo, who apparently did not know Hebrew, is referring to the LXX version (cf. *De vita Mosis* ii.37-40; cf. J. Leipoldt and S. Morenz, *Heilige Schriften,* p. 35). While Philo rarely refers to the Prophets or other OT writings, when he does he regards them as fully inspired and prophetic (*De conf. ling.* 44, 62; *Quis rer. div.* 290; *De somn.* 172; *De mut. nom.* 139, 169; *De cher.* 49).

297. On the prophetic role of Moses in Philo see E. R. Goodenough, *By Light, Light,* pp. 192-96; H. A. Wolfson, *Philo,* II, 3-72; E. Fascher, *PROPHETES,* pp. 152-53.

298. Philo *De vita Mosis* ii.188-191; Philo then proceeds to give several examples of the second and third kind of oracular utterance.

299. Philo *De praem.* 1.

300. Philo *De vita Mosis* ii.270.

301. Philo *De migr. Abr.* 47-49; cf. 190-91.

302. Philo *De vita Mosis* ii.280-81.

303. Philo *De vita Mosis* i.57, 175.

304. Cf. *De vita Mosis* i.201.

305. Philo *De vita Mosis* ii.250-52.

306. Another example of the three-part visionary announcement of salvation is attributed to Balaam in *De vita Mosis* i.283-84.

307. *LAB* 28:6-10 (trans. of M. R. James, *The Biblical Antiquities of Philo,* pp. 165-67); the Latin text is that of G. Kisch, *Pseudo-Philo's Liber Antiquitatum Biblicarum.* For a bibliography on the study of this document see J. H. Charlesworth, *Pseudepigrapha,* pp. 170-73. The text and translation of the Hebrew document called the Chronicles of Jerahmeel, in those sections which preserve extracts or paraphrases of *LAB,* is now available in D. J. Harrington, *Hebrew Fragments.* Since the fragments of the *LAB* in the Chronicles of Jerahmeel were translated into Hebrew from a Latin version, they are of little value for our discussion.

308. In the account of Balaam in *LAB* xviii.10-12 we have a prophetic speech by Balaam based on Num. 23-24. Here, however, in contrast to the biblical account, it is explicitly stated that "the spirit of God abode not in him" (*non permansit in eo spiritus Domini*); cf. Num. 23:5, 16; 24:2. The explicit mention of (the lack of) divine inspiration is, on the basis of form-critical considerations, in the appropriate position. Next comes a brief soliloquy on the impossibility of doing what Balak wishes. Finally, there is a vision sequence in which the present tense "I see" (*video*) is used three times to describe the glorious destiny of Israel, which, though far in the future, is described as if it were present.

309. Translation of R. Lattimore, *The Odyssey of Homer,* p. 307.

310. M. P. Nilsson, *Geschichte der griechische Religion,* I, 166; see the brief discussion on this oracle above, p. 36.

Chapter 6

1. See the succinct discussion in R. H. Fuller, *The Foundations of New Testament Christology,* pp. 125-131. Fuller contends that Jesus understood himself as an eschatological prophet and

that this self-understanding unifies what is known of his proclamation and activities.

2. Following the precedent of the OT, where both "true" and "false" prophets are simply designated "prophets," Josephus labels as "prophets" those who vainly proclaimed victory through God's imminent intervention on behalf of the besieged Jews near the end of the rebellion of A.D. 66-70 (*Bell.* vi.286). Josephus also refers to "Cleodemus the prophet, also called Malchus" in a quotation from Alexander Polyhistor (*Ant.* i.240-41); cf. D. E. Aune, "The Use of *PROPHĒTĒS* in Josephus," pp. 419-421.

3. Josephus *Ant.* xx.97-98, 169ff.

4. Strack-Billerbeck, II, 480; E. Fascher, *PROPHĒTĒS*, p. 178. The idea of an anointing of prophets was not uncommon in NT times; cf. F. Hahn, *The Titles of Jesus,* pp. 360-61; H. Kraft, "Anfänge," p. 83. The conceptual ambiguity of these terms finds expression in the statement of H. Windisch, *Paulus und Christus,* pp. 175ff., that Jesus (like Paul) was a messianic-prophetic pneumatic!

5. This passage is discussed extensively by O. Cullmann, *Christology,* pp. 31-35. The expression "one of the prophets," found in Mark 6:15b and also in 8:28, is a Semitism. The word *heis* ("one") represents the indefinite relative pronoun *tis* ("any"), so that a more appropriate translation of the entire phrase would be "a prophet like any (true) prophet" (M. Black, *An Aramaic Approach,* p. 105).

6. Secondary assessments, i.e. those with a lesser claim to reflect authentically the popular views which his contemporaries held of Jesus, are found in Luke 9:8, 19 (expanded parallels to Mark 6:15; 8:28), "one of the ancient prophets," and Matt. 16:14 (an altered parallel to Mark 8:28), where the name "Jeremiah" is inserted into the list of possible identities of Jesus.

7. F. Schnider, *Jesus der Prophet,* pp. 147-158, discusses the Markan perspective on Jesus as prophet; the results are quite meager.

8. H. Teeple, *The Mosaic Eschatological Prophet,* pp. 9-10.

9. All of the would-be eschatological prophets mentioned by Josephus were social deviants. The Hasmoneans and Josephus, on the other hand, tried to fit the eschatological expectations surrounding the figure of the prophet or messiah into existing social and religious structures. Josephus speaks approvingly of John Hyrcanus (135-104 B.C.) assuming the roles of ruler, high priest, and prophet (*Bell.* i.68; *Ant.* xiii.299), while Josephus himself placed his own prophetic gifts in close relationship to his priestly office (*Bell.* iii.351-54).

10. This tendency is emphasized by O. Betz, *What Do We Know About Jesus?* pp. 80-81.

11. It is perhaps significant that Mark 6:15 is not used by Matthew.

12. J. D. Kingsbury, *Matthew,* pp. 88-92.

13. Many of these literary devices and theological motifs are discussed by H. M. Teeple, *The Mosaic Eschatological Prophet,* pp. 74-83, and F. Hahn, *The Titles of Jesus,* pp. 385-86. One of the more extensive treatments of the subject is that of W. D. Davies, *The Setting of the Sermon on the Mount,* pp. 14-108. For an extensive bibliography on the subject see J. D. Kingsbury, *Matthew,* pp. 88ff.

14. H. M. Teeple, *The Mosaic Eschatological Prophet,* pp. 74-83, erroneously claims that Matthew did make this identification.

15. On this subject see the brief discussions in F. Hahn, *The Titles of Jesus,* pp. 386-87; E. Franklin, *Christ the Lord,* pp. 67ff.; C. F. D. Moule, "The Christology of Acts," pp. 161-63.

16. G. Lampe, "The Holy Spirit," pp. 175-76; H. M. Teeple, *The Mosaic Eschatological Prophet,* pp. 87-88; C. F. D. Moule, "The Christology of Acts," pp. 162-63, supposes that Luke is making a subtle distinction between the recognition of Jesus as a prophet (largely by unbelievers) prior to the resurrection, and the recognition of the post-resurrection church. Such a distinction appears too finely drawn.

17. Luke 24:13-27 is a dialogue which appears to have been inserted by Luke into the framework of an older Emmaus legend (P. Schubert, "Structure," p. 170; F. Schnider, *Jesus der Prophet,* pp. 124-27).

18. See the brief but convincing discussion in E. Franklin, *Christ the Lord,* p. 67.

19. On this see the very interesting article by W. B. Tatum that starts with H. Conzelmann's threefold periodicization of Luke's view of salvation history and applies it to Luke 1-2; "The Epoch of Israel," pp. 184-195.

20. For a short review of the literature see W. A. Meeks, *The Prophet-King,* pp. 21-25.

21. Two important studies are T. F. Glasson, *Moses in the Fourth Gospel* (1963), and W. A. Meeks, *The Prophet-King* (1967).

22. J. L. Martyn, "We Have Found Elijah," pp. 181-219; Martyn argues that Jesus was depicted as Elijah in the Signs Gospel, the major source for the Fourth Gospel.

23. T. F. Glasson, *Moses in the Fourth Gospel,* p. 28; R. Schnackenburg, *Das Johannesevangelium,* II, 218.

24. C. H. Dodd, *Interpretation of the Fourth Gospel,* pp. 239-240; idem, *Historical Tradition,* p. 215.

25. F. Schnider, *Jesus der Prophet,* pp. 214-221; unlike Dodd, Schnider views John 7:40 in a positive sense.

26. T. F. Glasson, *Moses in the Fourth Gospel,* pp. 28-29, struggles unsuccessfully with the interpretation of this passage. C. H. Dodd, *Historical Tradition,* p. 213, suggests that John 6:14 may have stood in the primitive tradition upon which the Fourth Evangelist drew.

27. Wayne A. Meeks has carefully and meticulously argued that the "prophet-king" of John 6:14-15 must be understood in relation to the tradition of a prophet like Moses which ultimately stems from Deut. 18:15-18 (*The Prophet-King,* pp. 32-99).

28. C. H. Dodd, *Historical Tradition,* p. 213; F. Schnider, *Jesus der Prophet,* p. 210.

29. See the excellent discussion of this passage in its context in F. Schnider, *Jesus der Prophet,* pp. 191-99.

30. The clairvoyance of Jesus is referred to in John 1:42, 45-48; 5:6; 11:11, 14, in addition to 4:16-18.

31. F. Schnider, *Jesus der Prophet,* p. 199; see above, n. 24.

32. This passage is discussed by F. Schnider, *Jesus der Prophet,* pp. 147-152.

33. The various possibilities are discussed by R. Bultmann, *Geschichte,* p. 35. In the more recent discussion of this pericope by F. Schnider, *Jesus der Prophet,* pp. 167-172, the author concludes that two originally independent sayings have been joined together by Luke.

34. The reference to the "third day" might appear secondary, in view of the events of passion week, yet the three days referred to are not those spent in the grave, but relate to the active ministry of Jesus (J. Jeremias, *New Testament Theology,* p. 285). The puzzling metaphor of the "fox" may provide evidence substantiating the authenticity of the saying. If Jesus saw himself pursued with deadly intent by Herod, much as his ancestor David had been by Saul, then "fox" (Heb. *shu'al*) might be understood as a pun referring to Herod in his role as a latter-day Saul (Heb. *sha'ul*).

35. O. H. Steck, *Israel,* p. 46. R. H. Fuller, *Foundations,* p. 127, incorrectly regards Luke 13:33 as proverbial.

36. F. Gils, *Jésus Prophète,* p. 28.

37. For discussions of various aspects of this tradition see O. Michel, *Prophet und Märtyrer*; O. H. Steck, *Israel und das gewaltsame Geschick der Propheten* (an exceptionally valuable study); H. J. Schoeps, "Die jüdischen Prophetenmorde," pp. 126-143; H. A. Fischel, "Martyr and Prophet," pp. 265-280, 363-386.

38. The prophets referred to here are undoubtedly OT prophets, though it has been argued that Christian prophets are being referred to. That Christian prophets did experience suffering and martyrdom and that their experience was seen in the light of the fate of OT prophets is clear from Matt. 5:11-12 par. Luke 6:22-23; Matt. 23:34-35.

39. According to O. Michel, "Struggle and conflict, suffering and martyrdom are necessary features of true prophetism" (*Prophet und Märtyrer,* p. 10). He argues that suffering and martyrdom were as characteristic of early Christian prophets as they were of their OT counterparts (pp. 73-74). Yet he appears to have overstated the case, since it is not clear that early Christian prophets were regarded as any more liable to experience suffering and martyrdom than other Christians (see H. Kraft, "Anfänge," p. 92).

40. What follows is generally dependent on the discussion of F. Schnider, *Jesus der Prophet,* pp. 133-172, in which this motif is discussed in great detail.

41. O. H. Steck, *Israel,* p. 283.

42. This prophetic saying is discussed in greater detail below, pp. 175-76.

43. Mark 12:10-12 appears to be a secondary expansion of the original parable which uses a quotation from Ps. 118:22-23 to apply the parable to the rejection of Jesus.

44. J. Jeremias, *Parables*, pp. 70-77.

45. For specific details see the discussion in F. Schnider, *Jesus der Prophet*, pp. 158-163.

46. W. Schmeichel, "Christian Prophecy in Lukan Thought," pp. 293-304.

47. This point is emphasized in two fine analyses of Luke 4:16-30: J. A. Sanders, "From Isaiah 61 to Luke 4," pp. 75-106; W. Schmeichel, "Christian Prophecy in Lukan Thought," pp. 293-304.

48. These two points are convincingly argued by W. Schmeichel (see above, n. 47).

49. This position is argued by R. Pesch, "Auferstehung Jesu," pp. 201-228, and more recently (and comprehensively) by K. Berger, *Die Auferstehung des Propheten* (1976).

50. J. M. Nützel, "Zum Schicksal der eschatologischen Propheten," pp. 59-94, contends that the ascension motif was not present in the source of Rev. 11:3-13 (p. 76) or in the Apocalypse of Elijah 37:7-21 (pp. 60-67).

51. The post-Christian dates for most of the texts adduced by R. Pesch are emphasized by M. Hengel, "Ist der Osterglaube noch zu retten?" pp. 252-269. J. M. Nützel, "Zum Schicksal der eschatologischen Propheten," pp. 59-94, after a careful examination of the texts used by Pesch, concludes on p. 94: "We have seen that the expectation of a murder and resurrection of an eschatological prophet existed at the time of Jesus. Nevertheless, the evidence is so quantitatively slight that the assumption of a wide dissemination of this expectation in Palestine ca. A.D. 30 is without foundation."

52. The pre-Christian date for the tradition of the martyrdom of the returning Elijah is maintained by J. Jeremias, *TDNT*, II, 939ff.

53. R. Bauckham, "The Martyrdom of Enoch and Elijah," pp. 447-458, has concluded that the martyrdom of the two witnesses in Rev. 11:3-13 (Enoch and Elijah) is a Christian innovation which is the basis for the use of the same motif in later Christian literature. Therefore the Christian tradition of the return and martyrdom of Enoch and Elijah provides no evidence for a pre-Christian Jewish tradition of their martyrdom.

54. O. Michel, *Prophet und Märtyrer*, p. 22; F. Schnider, *Jesus der Prophet*, p. 258; R. H. Fuller, *Foundations*, p. 127.

55. C. H. Dodd, "Jesus as Teacher and Prophet," pp. 53-66.

56. J. M. Myers and E. D. Freed, "Is Paul Also among the Prophets?" pp. 40-53.

57. On the basis of these criticisms the points made by Dodd that are of little value in assessing the role of the OT prophets or that of Jesus include 1, 2, 6, 7, 11, 12, 14, and 15.

58. J. Lindblom, *Prophecy in Ancient Israel*, pp. 182-197; G. W. Ahlström, "Prophecy," p. 62; R. E. Clements, *Prophecy*, pp. 33, 38.

59. Prophets attempted to invalidate the messages of their prophetic opponents by claiming that they had not been sent by God (Jer. 28:15; 43:2-3).

60. This tendency is particularly evident in the Fourth Gospel, in which "sending" terminology occupies a central place in Johannine Christology. For a recent comprehensive treatment of this motif see J. P. Miranda, *Der Vater, Der Mich Gesandt Hat* (1972), and a review by D. E. Aune, *Interpretation*, 29 (1975), pp. 100-102.

61. See the brief but important arguments of R. H. Fuller, *Foundations*, pp. 127-28.

62. V. Taylor, *The Person of Christ*, p. 157; O. Cullmann, *Christology*, pp. 66ff.

63. C. H. Dodd, "Jesus as Teacher and Prophet," p. 60.

64. J. Lindblom, *Gesichte und Offenbarungen*, p. 174 n. 24.

65. H. Schürmann, "Die Symbolhandlungen Jesu," pp. 37ff.

66. E. Lövestam, "Wunder und Symbolhandlung," pp. 124-135.

67. H. Schürmann, "Die Symbolhandlungen Jesu," p. 38.

68. F. Schnider, *Jesus der Prophet*, pp. 84-85.

69. Ibid., p. 85.

70. The structure of Mark 11:15-17 that accompanies the quotation of that passage is based on the analysis of F. Schnider, *Jesus der Prophet*, pp. 83ff.

71. This is forcefully argued by J. Roloff, *Das Kerygma*, pp. 89-110, who also contends that the purification of the temple by Jesus was a prophetic sign dramatizing the necessity of Israel's repentance and conversion in the last days.

72. These predictions are discussed in detail below, pp. 173-77. The necessity of understanding the purification of the temple in connection with Jesus' predictions of the destruction of the temple is correctly advocated by F. Hahn, *The Worship of the Early Church*, pp. 26-30.

73. In Josephus *Bell.* vi.96ff. and Syb. Orac. iv.115ff., the act of committing murders within the temple precincts is regarded as a sacrilege which spells the doom of both temple and city. While the form of the sacrilege is different in Mark 11:15-17, the significance is much the same; the cleansing of the temple as a prophetic anticipation of its destruction is also the view of D. Juel, *Messiah and Temple*, p. 198.

74. Ps. Sol. 17:33: "And he [the Davidic Messiah] shall purge Jerusalem, making it holy as of old." See C. Roth, "The Cleansing of the Temple," pp. 174-181; R. J. McKelvey, *The New Temple*, pp. 62-67.

75. L. Brun, *Segen und Fluch*, pp. 75-76; M. Smith, *Jesus the Magician*, p. 119.

76. J. Roloff, *Das Kerygma*, p. 168; H. Giessen, "Der verdorrte Feigenbaum," pp. 103ff., 110. H. W. Bartsch, "Die 'Verfluchung' des Feigenbaums," pp. 256-260, suggests that, on the basis of the ambiguity of the original (reconstructed) Aramaic, Jesus' statement, "No one will ever eat fruit from you again [because the end will come before it has ripened]" was misunderstood as a cursing miracle: "May no one ever eat fruit from you again." This interpretation is supported by J. Jeremias, *New Testament Theology*, p. 87.

77. See above, pp. 126-29. These and other examples, however, function more as legitimating miracles than as prophetic-symbolic actions on analogy with OT examples.

78. J. Lindblom, *Gesichte und Offenbarungen*, pp. 65-66. H. Windisch, "Jesus und der Geist," p. 235, suggests (without any possible means of substantiation) that Jesus had many other such visionary experiences which were not preserved in gospel tradition.

79. R. Bultmann, *Geschichte*, pp. 113, 174, 176, expresses no real doubts about the authenticity of the saying, but hesitates to say much about it due to its fragmentary nature. More recently U. Müller, "Vision und Botschaft," pp. 416-448, defends the authenticity of this saying and finds many common features between this report of Jesus' vision and the visions of OT prophets. Müller virtually turns Luke 10:18 into the central prophetic experience upon which Jesus based his proclamation of the presence of the kingdom of God. Müller attempts to go too far and base too much on a saying of such a fragmentary nature.

80. U. Müller, "Vision und Botschaft," p. 423, calls attention to these features, yet wishes to demonstrate the distance between this vision of Jesus and typical apocalyptic visions. This tendency is also evident in R. Bultmann, *Geschichte*, p. 113, when he states that in late Judaism visions and auditions were the concerns of apocalyptists, but Jesus was not an apocalyptist in the proper sense of that term.

81. J. Jeremias, *New Testament Theology*, p. 95, observes that the participle *pesonta* is a Semitic-type quasi-passive which should probably be translated "be cast out."

82. Numerous parallels are cited by U. Müller, "Vision und Botschaft," pp. 421-22. Müller emphasizes Rev. 12:7-9 as a close parallel to Luke 10:18 (as does J. Jeremias, *New Testament Theology*, p. 95). There a battle in heaven is depicted between Michael and his angels on the one hand and Satan on the other; Satan is defeated and thrown down to the earth. M. E. Boismard, "Rapprochements," pp. 56-57, calls attention to the close verbal parallel between Luke 10:18 and Rev. 9:1: "I saw a star fallen from heaven to earth." The "star" is apparently Satan (Rev. 9:11).

83. G. Dautzenberg, *Urchristliche Prophetie*, pp. 202-207; see Sir. 46:15; 48:22, 24; 1 Enoch 1:2; 40:2, 8; 2 Enoch 13:8; 11QPs^a 22:13-15; 1QM 10:10-11.

84. U. Müller, "Vision und Botschaft," pp. 422-29.

85. Ibid., p. 428. Call narratives in OT prophetic books were primarily means of legitimating prophetic status; cf. N. Habel, "Call Narrative," p. 317; H. G. Reventlow, *Liturgie*, p. 68.

86. Chapter 9 is devoted to a thorough discussion of this subject.

87. H. A. Guy, *New Testament Prophecy,* pp. 52-53; T. W. Manson, *The Teaching of Jesus,* pp. 105ff., 207; H. Schürmann, *Traditionsgeschichtliche Untersuchungen,* p. 96; J. Jeremias, *New Testament Theology,* p. 36; R. A. Edwards, "An Approach to the Theology of Q," p. 255.

88. Statistics by H. Schürmann, *Traditionsgeschichtliche Untersuchungen,* p. 97.

89. The expression presupposes a situation in which a real or imagined audience is spoken to in the form of direct address; Greek rhetoricians studiously avoided this kind of locution. Aelius Aristides once lapses into using the related expression "for I say" in *Or.* 28.114, but this is rare. The expression is also rare in Greco-Roman oracular speech, though in a putative oracle Apollo begins his oracular response with "But I say" (W. Dittenberger, *SIG,* 735).

90. Test. Reuben 1:7; 4:5; 6:5; Test. Gad 5:2; Test. Naphtali 4:1; Test. Levi 16:4 (var. lec.); Test. Benjamin 9:1 (var. lec.); 1 Enoch 92:18; 94:1, 3, 10; 2 Enoch 2:2; Prov. 31:2 (LXX); Jub. 36:11.

91. Prov. 24:38 (LXX 23); Teachings of Silvanus (VII,4) 93.24; 94.5; Treatise on Resurrection (I,3) 48.20; 50.13 (here the use of the phrase by Jesus and Paul fits very well).

92. M. Smith, *Tannaitic Parallels,* pp. 27-31. Jesus' use of the phrase "But I say to you" in the antitheses of the Sermon on the Mount (Matt. 5:22, 28, 32, 34, 39, 44) does not imply a claim of authority far exceeding that of the rabbis, even rivaling that attributed to Moses himself, as some would assert (E. Käsemann, "The Problem of the Historical Jesus," p. 37). On the contrary, most of the features of Matt. 5:21-48 are paralleled in tannaitic literature, as Smith has demonstrated. See also E. Lohse, "Ich aber sage euch," pp. 75-80. See the brief speech of R. Gamaliel in Acts 5:35-39 to his colleagues in the Sanhedrin; he reportedly uses the phrase "I say to you" in v. 38.

93. K. Preisendanz, *PGM* IV.2088; XII.131; XII.1074; XXXVI.286; LVIII.8.

94. 1 Enoch 99:13; 102:9; John the Baptist in Matt. 3:9 par. Luke 3:8.

95. Paul in Rom. 11:13; 1 Cor. 6:5; 15:51; Gal. 5:2; 1 Thess. 4:15. More often Paul uses such expressions as "But I say" or "again I say" (Rom. 10:18, 19; 11:1, 11; 12:3; 1 Cor. 7:6, 8, 12, 35; 2 Cor. 11:16, 18; Gal. 1:9; 3:17; 5:16).

96. Baldas to Job in Test. Job 37:1; Abraham to Death in Test. Abraham (Rec. A) 18; more frequently Death to Abraham in Test. Abraham (Rec. A) 16, 18, 20 (twice); Test. Abraham (Rec. B) 13.

97. Michael to Abraham in Test. Abraham (Rec. A) 8.

98. God to Michael in Test. Abraham (Rec. A) 16. "I say" is used in Isa. 13:14 (LXX) in which God is represented as the speaker.

99. In the canonical gospels the sayings of Jesus which are prefaced or punctuated by the phrase "(Amen) I say to you" are not infrequently set in a dialogue framework. Similarly, among the Nag Hammadi documents the formula "(Amen) I say to you" is set in a dialogue with Jesus as the speaker and the disciples as the audience in the Apocalypse of James (I,2) 2.29; 6.2, 14-15; 10.1, 15; 12.9; 13.9; "I tell you this," 12.20; "therefore I say to you," 3.34-35; 8.27-28; "this is what I say to you," 10.28; The Book of Thomas the Contender (II,7) 142.27; 142.29f. ("truly I tell you"); Dialogue of the Savior (III,5) 120.8-14 (3 times); 128.2; 140.4-5 ("I say to you"); First Apocalypse of James (V,3) 32.9 ("truly I say to you"); Second Apocalypse of James (V,4) 57.21 ("therefore I tell you"); Second Apocalypse of James (V,4) 51.14; 52.14-15 ("[This is] what I say to you").

100. The phrase occurs in the context of a letter to the Church at Thyatira in Rev. 2:24, and many examples of its occurrence have already been cited in the Pauline corpus (above, n. 95). The Treatise on the Resurrection (above, n. 91) is also a letter.

101. The letter form frequently reflects the characteristics of oral communication, so that rigid distinctions between written letters and oral sermons are not always appropriate. See U. Müller, *Prophetie und Predigt,* pp. 109-117. The structure of the Pauline letters is not based exclusively on the Greco-Roman letter genre but has been influenced by rhetorical

forms and conventions; cf. H. D. Betz, *Galatians*, pp. 14-25 (cf. the review by D. E. Aune, *Religious Studies Review*, 7 [1981], 323-28); B. H. Brinsmead, *Galatians*, pp. 37-55; R. Scroggs, "Paul as Rhetorician," pp. 272-73, and J. A. Fischer, "Pauline Literary Forms," p. 209.

102. The Greco-Roman diatribe has been carefully discussed recently by S. K. Stowers, *Diatribe*; see also R. Bultmann, *Der Stil* (the literary sources used in this book are much too limited). For the so-called Hellenistic Jewish homily see H. Thyen, *Der Stil der jüdisch-hellenistischen Homilie*. The Hellenistic Jewish homily has many common elements with the Greco-Roman diatribe.

103. Paul frequently makes use of a style very similar to the Greco-Roman diatribe. While he does use the device of an imaginary interlocutor, he is nevertheless speaking to a concrete situation and the audience he addresses is very real.

104. W. Dittenberger, *SIG*, 735.

105. For a discussion of these oracles, see below, pp. 250-51, 253-56.

106. Hermas *Mand.* iv.3.6; xii.3.6; *Sim.* v.1.3; cf. above, n. 97.

107. Hermas *Vis.* iii.9.7; *Mand.* xii.6.1; *Sim.* ix.23.5; ix.28.7. Each of these oracles is discussed in some detail below, pp. 298-310.

108. In 2 Clem. 8:5 "I say to you" occurs within the context of a quotation from Luke 16:10-12. In Ign. Rom. 8:2 the expression "I speak truly" functions as an oath formula.

109. Two of the most recent and comprehensive studies are those by V. Hasler, *Amen*, and K. Berger, *Die Amen-Worte Jesu*.

110. Strack-Billerbeck, I, 243-44; J. Jeremias, *The Prayers of Jesus*, pp. 112-15; idem, *New Testament Theology*, pp. 35-36.

111. V. Hasler, *Amen*, pp. 173-74.

112. K. Berger, *Die Amen-Worte Jesu*, pp. 4-28; Berger theorizes that the prepositive *amēn* originated in Hellenistic Judaism as an oath formula introducing apocalyptic statements as a substitute for the homophonic asseveration *ē mēn*.

113. J. Strugnell, " 'Amen I say to you'," pp. 177-181.

114. These references are discussed in detail by K. Berger, *Die Amen-Worte Jesu*, pp. 4-6, and the implications of this discussion are summarized on p. 28.

115. Cf. above, n. 92.

116. Matt. 7:9-10 par. Luke 11:11-12; Matt. 12:11 par. Luke 14:5; Luke 11:5-8; 14:28-30, 31-32; 15:4-7, 8-10; 17:7-10; Matt. 6:27 par. Luke 12:25.

117. H. Greeven, " 'Wer unter euch ... ?' " pp. 86-101. The Semitic origin of such questions, which function as conditional clauses, is discussed by K. Beyer, *Semitische Syntax*, I, 287-293.

118. H. Greeven, " 'Wer unter euch ... ?' " pp. 99-101.

119. K. Berger, "Gleichnisse," pp. 58-61. Berger has attempted to demonstrate that the phrase "who among you" at the beginning of parables is a widespread Hellenistic tradition, though the only valid example which he cites is Epictetus i.27.15-21.

120. S. Schulz, *Spruchquelle*, p. 63, has accepted the form-critical analysis of Greeven, but has adroitly attributed the form to the prophets of the Q community, without providing any rationale for such an ascription.

121. J. M. Robinson, "The Formal Structure of Jesus' Message," pp. 91-110. Our discussion is dependent on this article.

122. J. M. Robinson, "The Formal Structure of Jesus' Message," p. 99, wants to deny the significance of the temporal element in the sayings of Jesus and focus almost exclusively on the existential dimensions of his message. This tendency to reduce NT teaching to its existential dimensions was more popular in post-World War II Germany than in America or England, through the influence of R. Bultmann. This tendency appears to be on the wane.

123. E. Käsemann, "Sentences of Holy Law in the New Testament," pp. 66-81. This subject is discussed in greater detail below, pp. 237-240.

124. E. Käsemann, "Sentences of Holy Law," pp. 66ff.; idem, "Beginnings," p. 86.

125. See the discussion below, pp. 237-240.

126. K. Berger, "Zu den sogenannten Sätzen heiligen Rechts," pp. 10-40. Berger's objections are stated in greater detail below, pp. 237-240.

127. R. A. Edwards, *The Sign of Jonah*, pp. 47-58; idem, "The Eschatological Correlative," pp. 9-20.

128. Luke 11:30 par. Matt. 12:40; Luke 17:24 par. Matt. 24:27; Luke 17:26 par. Matt. 24:37; Luke 17:28, 30 par. Matt. 24:38-39; Matt. 13:40-41.

129. R. A. Edwards, *The Sign of Jonah*, p. 58.

130. This has been demonstrated by D. Schmidt, "The LXX *Gattung* 'Prophetic Correlative'," pp. 517-522.

131. Unfortunately, D. Schmidt in the article cited in n. 130 omitted consideration of the correlative form in the Hebrew OT, or in contexts other than that of the prophetic writers. In Hebrew the correlative particles *ke/ka'asher . . . ken* ("as . . . so") are found many times in the OT, often with the first line of a correlative statement containing a past- or present-tense verb, and the second line containing the same verb in the future tense.

Chapter 7

1. N. A. Dahl, *Das Volk Gottes*, pp. 269-270. Dahl does not connect Jesus' performance of miracles with his prophetic status, yet it is clear that both aspects of Jesus' ministry were intimately related and mutually interpretative (cf. Luke 11:20).

2. See the broad comparative study of modern millenarian movements by B. Wilson, *Magic and the Millennium*.

3. The fundamental study in this area remains that of W. G. Kümmel, *Promise and Fulfilment*. More recently, see the following three surveys, done independently, which arrive at much the same conclusions as Kümmel: G. Lundström, *The Kingdom of God in the Teaching of Jesus* (1963); N. Perrin, *The Kingdom of God in the Teaching of Jesus* (1963); and G. E. Ladd, *Jesus and the Kingdom* (1964).

4. A number of scholars have disputed Kümmel's emphasis on the imminence of the kingdom in the teaching of Jesus. He has forcefully defended his views in "Die Naherwartung in der Verkündigung Jesu," pp. 457-470.

5. This thesis has recently been disputed by (the long overdue translation of) J. Weiss, *Jesus' Proclamation of the Kingdom of God*, and R. Hiers, *The Kingdom of God in the Synoptic Tradition* (1970).

6. The prophetic demand that Israel return to God is similar to Jesus' demand for repentance; cf. Isa. 6:13; 10:21-22; 19:22; 21:12; 35:10; 40:22; 51:1; 55:7; 63:17; Jer. 3:11, 22; 4:1; 12:15; Hos. 6:1; 7:10; 14:1; Mal. 3:7. See. E. Würthwein, *TDNT*, VI, 982-86.

7. K. L. Schmidt, *Die Rahmen der Geschichte Jesu*, p. 33; R. Bultmann, *Geschichte*, p. 366; W. Marxsen, *Mark the Evangelist*, pp. 132ff.

8. G. Theissen, "Wanderradikalismus," p. 253. Matthew places the proclamation of Jesus (4:17) on the lips of John the Baptist (3:2). That John used the term kingdom of God/heaven is doubtful (C. Kraeling, *John the Baptist*, p. 67). The subject of the kingdom of heaven in Matthew is discussed at length by J. D. Kingsbury, *Matthew*, pp. 128-160. He discusses Matt. 3:2; 4:17; and 10:7 and the theme of imminence on pp. 138ff.

9. W. G. Kümmel, *Promise and Fulfilment*, p. 87; D. E. Aune, "Delay of the Parousia," p. 97; G. R. Beasley-Murray, *Mark Thirteen*, pp. 9, 99.

10. N. Perrin, *Rediscovering the Teaching of Jesus*, pp. 199-202. Those who regard both passages as "words of comfort" formulated by the post-Easter community (E. Grässer, *Parusieverzögerung*, p. 130) have pushed the problem of nonfulfilment one step forward, but not solved it.

11. A. Vögtle, "Exegetische Erwägungen," pp. 642-47; L. Gaston, *No Stone on Another*, p. 451, holds that Mark 9:1; 13:30; Matt. 10:23; 23:39 are not four separate sayings, but rather four versions of a single saying. His inclusion of Matt. 10:23 and 23:39 appears unwarranted.

12. The single exception is Luke 13:34-35, yet the parallel in Matt. 23:37-39 is set in Jerusalem within the temple precincts. Matthew's setting is historically more probable.

13. G. Theissen, *Sociology of Early Palestinian Christianity,* pp. 59-76, rightly regards the Jesus movement as "the peace party among the renewal movements within Judaism" (p. 64). On the recent debate about whether Jesus was a political revolutionary (a view promoted by S. G. F. Brandon, among others), see the refutations by O. Cullmann, *Jesus and the Revolutionaries* (1970); M. Hengel, *Was Jesus a Revolutionist?* (1971); idem, *Victory over Violence* (1975).

14. See the discussion above, pp. 157-59.

15. F. Flückiger, "Zukunftsrede," pp. 404-405, thinks that Jesus' prediction of the destruction and replacement of the temple, found in its most original form in Mark 14:58, was abbreviated by the evangelist in Mark 13:2.

16. Here one must reckon with the real possibility that Luke has displaced this saying from Mark 14:58 (for which he has no parallel) and placed it in this new context. This position is convincingly argued by R. Pesch, *Die Vision des Stephanus,* pp. 44-45.

17. F. Flückiger, "Zukunftsrede," pp. 404-405, thinks that Mark 13:2 is a variant of 14:58, as does R. Pesch, *Naherwartungen,* p. 91 (on pp. 83-96 Pesch has discussed Mark 13:2 and parallels in great detail).

18. C. H. Dodd, *Historical Tradition,* pp. 89ff.

19. R. Bultmann, *Geschichte,* pp. 126-27, 132, 135 (together with the supplementary remarks in the *"Ergänzungsheft"*). For a fuller discussion supportive of the basic historicity of the saying, see W. G. Kümmel, *Promise and Fulfilment,* pp. 99ff.

20. Hos. 6:6; Amos 5:4-7, 21-23; Isa. 1:10-12; Jer. 7:21-26; Ps. 50:9, 13-14; 51:18-21 (Eng. 16-19).

21. Jer. 7:14; 26:4-9, 12; Dan. 9:26; 11:31; Ezek. 9:1-10. At Jeremiah's trial for sedition Micah of Moresheth's prediction of the destruction of Jerusalem is quoted in Jeremiah's defense (Jer. 26:18=Mic. 3:12). Uriah ben Shemaiah, who prophesied against the city and was killed on that account, is also mentioned (Jer. 26:20-23). In the *Vitae Prophetarum,* Jonah (8) and Zechariah son of Iddo (6) are remembered as having predicted the destruction of Jerusalem, while Habakkuk (2, 11) is said to have prophesied the destruction of the temple.

22. G. Theissen, "Die Tempelweissagung Jesu," pp. 144-158, discussed the basic antipathy which characterized the renewal and resistance movements of the countryside toward Jerusalem and the religious-political establishment. See also his *Sociology of Early Palestinian Christianity,* pp. 47-58. It is to Theissen's credit that his analysis of the social structure of first-century Palestine leaves the problem of the social and economic status of the 'am ha-'areṣ ("people of the land") completely aside. In his recent study *The 'Am Ha-Aretz* (1977), A. Oppenheimer is so eager to dispel the myth that the 'am ha-'areṣ constituted the rural proletariat whose cause Jesus took up against the urban artisans, merchants, and religious establishment that he ignores or minimizes the tensions between Jerusalem and rural Palestine. See the review by D. E. Aune, *CBQ,* 40 (1978), 441-43.

23. This point is made by G. Theissen, "Die Tempelweissagung Jesu," pp. 144-158.

24. This is the view of C. H. Dodd, *The Parables of the Kingdom,* pp. 43-48; idem, "Jesus as Teacher and Prophet," pp. 61-62.

25. R. Bultmann, *Geschichte, "Ergänzungsheft,"* pp. 46-47 (supplementing pp. 126-27).

26. The connection between the expectation of an eschatological Davidic king and the building of the temple is already evident in Zech. 6:12-13 and Isa. 53:5. On this expectation see M. Goguel, *The Life of Jesus,* p. 510; O. Betz, "Die Frage nach dem messianischen Bewusstsein Jesu," pp. 34-37; idem, *What Do We Know about Jesus?* pp. 87-97. One of the motifs of the so-called Divine Warrior Hymn is the building of a temple; cf. P. Hanson, *Apocalyptic,* p. 300.

27. B. Gärtner, *The Temple and the Community* (1965), and R. J. McKelvey, *The New Temple* (1969), have provided thorough discussions of this subject.

28. B. Gärtner, *The Temple and the Community,* pp. 105-122; R. J. McKelvey, *The New Temple,* pp. 67-74. McKelvey concludes, on p. 72, that "the new age would have its temple, and he as Messiah would erect it," yet he does not equate this new temple with the eschatological community, as does Gärtner.

29. R. Pesch, *Naherwartungen,* pp. 88, 91-92.

30. According to F. Christ, *Jesus Sophia,* pp. 136-152, Jesus speaks here as wisdom personified.

31. The verb *aphietai* is an oracular present, and the line as a whole refers to the conviction that God must leave his dwelling before its destruction can occur.

32. R. Bultmann, *Geschichte,* pp. 120-21. A more recent and extensive discussion of Luke 13:34-35 par. Matt. 23:37ff. is found in O. H. Steck, *Israel,* pp. 40-58, where the saying is thought to be an early Jewish prophetic proclamation of judgment that the early Christian church attributed to Jesus. Steck thinks that Luke 13:34-35 par. Matt. 23:37ff. and Luke 11:49ff. par Matt. 23:34ff. (both sayings deal with the tradition of the violent fate of the prophets) are sayings of Wisdom formulated like prophetic pronouncements of judgment and that both are drawn from the same Jewish source (pp. 50-51). This is also the opinion of M. J. Suggs, *Wisdom,* pp. 63-71.

33. The authenticity of the saying is supported by, among others, F. Schnider, *Jesus der Prophet,* pp. 142-47; P. Hoffmann, *Studien zur Theologie der Logienquelle,* pp. 171-180. One crucial issue is the interpretation of the phrase "how many times I have desired" (*posakis ēthelēsa*), which some have understood as personified Wisdom's suprahistorical perspective on the entire history of Jerusalem's negative response to prophetic messengers (R. Bultmann, *Geschichte,* pp. 120-21; O. H. Steck, *Israel,* pp. 53-56). Yet the phrase may refer equally well to the experience of Jesus, since the present participles in the first lines of the prophecy, *apokteinousa* and *lithobolousa* ("killing" and "stoning"), need not refer to the suprahistorical perspective of the speaker, but to examples drawn from past history (F. Schnider, *Jesus der Prophet,* p. 145). This interpretation is confirmed by the change in tense from present to aorist, expressing the change from general historical experience to the specific vantage point of the speaker (P. Hoffmann, *Studien zur Theologie der Logienquelle,* p. 173). M. J. Suggs, *Wisdom,* p. 66, contends that the speaker *cannot* be Jesus, since the metaphor of a hen gathering her brood under her wings "requires a heavenly, indeed, a divine being." Although such imagery is normally used in this way, an interesting exception is found in Ruth 2:12, where the *kanap,* "wings," under which Ruth took refuge are Yahweh's, while *kanap* is also used in 3:9 for the "skirt" of Boaz' garment with which Ruth covers herself. This play on words is certainly intentional.

34. M. Plath, "Der neutestamentliche Weheruf über Jerusalem," pp. 455-460; Plath sees a threefold structure in Luke 13:34-35 par. Matt. 23:37-39, consisting of *Anklage* ("Complaint"), *Drohung* ("Threat"), and *Hoffnungsstrahl* ("Ray of Hope").

35. P. Hoffmann, *Studien zur Theologie der Logienquelle,* p. 177.

36. See R. Pesch, "Auferstehung Jesu," p. 223; and see the discussion above, pp. 157-59.

37. Phrases like "then" or "in those days" introduce descriptions of future judgment in 1 Enoch 97:3-6; 99:3-5; 100:1-3, 4-6, 10-13; 102:1-3. Cf. G. Nickelsburg, "Apocalyptic," pp. 312-13.

38. R. Bultmann, *Geschichte,* pp. 37, 130. Bultmann suspects the saying of being quite old, possibly originating in the Aramaic-speaking Palestinian church.

39. See B. Reicke, "Synoptic Prophecies," pp. 121-23, where the author convincingly argues that the details of Luke 19:41-44 coincide with what usually happened when an ancient city was besieged and conquered. The various motifs found in the prediction are also found in prophetic portions of the OT (Isa. 29:3; Ezek. 4:2; Isa. 37:33; Ezek. 4:2-3; 26:8; Isa. 3:26; 26:6; 63:18; etc.). For an earlier discussion (unmentioned by Reicke) which emphasized that the motifs in both Luke 19:41-44 and 21:20-24 (a passage which will be discussed shortly) are commonplace conceptions of the circumstances attending ancient siege warfare, see C. H. Dodd, "The Fall of Jerusalem," pp. 47-54. These and similar studies are referred to by J. A. T. Robinson, *Redating the New Testament,* pp. 13-30, in an attempt to demonstrate that gospel predictions of the destruction of Jerusalem do not conform to the historical events of A.D. 70 and consequently could not be predictions *ex eventu.* While I do not think that Luke can be dated before A.D. 70, neither does it appear that Jesus' prophecies

of the destruction of Jerusalem and the temple have been radically tranformed to bring them into conformity with actual historical events.

40. In Isa. 6:9-13 the ignorance and blindness of Israel is combined with the motifs of destruction and desolation; cf. Ezek. 3:4-11; Jer. 5:21; CD 1:11-13. The theme of Israel's blindness occurs frequently in early Christian literature, and on that basis Luke 19:41-44 might conceivably be regarded as a Christian formulation. Yet the fact that a similar sentiment was expressed in the Damascus Document (CD) 1:11-13 may indicate that such an attitude was entirely at home within the framework of a dissident religious renewal movement in first-century Palestine.

41. The Greek term *episkopē* ("visitation"), found here in Luke 19:44, is occasionally used in early Christian literature as a designation of the parousia (1 Pet. 2:12; 1 Clem. 50:3), and it was undoubtedly understood by Luke in that way. The term occurs far more frequently in Jewish literature, where it refers to the eschatological day of judgment or salvation; cf. Wis. 3:7 and H. W. Beyer, *TDNT*, II, 606-608. The Hebrew equivalent, *pequdah,* occurs frequently in the Dead Sea Scrolls as a reference to the eschatological coming of God: CD 7:9, 21; 8:3; 4QD^b 1:6, 10; 1QS 3:14, 18; 4:6. See H. Ringgren, *The Faith of Qumran,* pp. 152ff.

42. V. Taylor, *The Passion Narrative,* p. 90, argues that Luke 23:27-31, peculiar to Luke, is part of an extended pre-Lukan passion narrative. He argues against free composition by Luke on the basis of the occurrence of expressions not characteristic of Luke.

43. M. Dibelius, *Formgeschichte,* p. 203; R. Bultmann, *Geschichte,* p. 341.

44. W. Käser, "Erwägungen," pp. 240-254, argues that the beatitude in vv. 29-30 has been inserted by Luke into vv. 27-28 and 31.

45. The contention of R. Bultmann, *Geschichte,* p. 37.

46. T. W. Manson, *The Teaching of Jesus,* p. 262.

47. M. Dibelius, *Formgeschichte,* p. 203 n. 1.

48. R. Bultmann, *Geschichte,* p. 163; M. Dibelius, *Formgeschichte,* pp. 227-28.

49. K. L. Schmidt, *Die Rahmen der Geschichte Jesu,* pp. 217ff.

50. *Iliad* xvi.851ff. (cf. scholium ad *Iliad* xvi.854); xxii.358; Sophocles *Oed. Col.* 1370ff.; Xenophon *Cyrop.* viii.7.21; Plato *Apol.* 39c; Diodorus Siculus xviii.1; Cicero *De divin.* i.63; Plutarch *De def. orac.* 40; Vergil *Aeneid* iv.614; x.739; Plotinus iv.3.27; Cyprian *De mortal.* 19; Lactantius *Div. inst.* vii.12.27ff.

51. L. Bieler, *Theios Anēr,* I, 91-93. Apollonius is said to have predicted the death of Titus (Philostratus *Vita Apoll.* vi.22), and he predicted the death of the governor of Cilicia in three days (i.12). He is said to have "seen" the assassination of Domitian (viii.26). According to Philo *De vita Mosis* ii.291, Moses predicted his own death. Jesus is represented as predicting the death of Peter in John 21:18-19, and in Mark 10:39 we have an oblique prediction of the deaths of James and John.

52. See above, pp. 157-59.

53. D. E. Aune, "Messianic Secret," pp. 21ff.

54. J. H. Hayes, "The Resurrection as Enthronement," pp. 333-345; D. E. Aune, "Messianic Secret," pp. 23-24.

55. C. Westermann, *Basic Forms of Prophetic Speech,* p. 206, observes that the judgment speech was abandoned in the postexilic period and did not recur again until the proclamation of Jesus in his pronouncement of woes over various cities (Matt. 11:20-24 par. Luke 10:13-15) and his announcement of the fall of Jerusalem (Luke 11:49-51). See also E. Hammershaimb, *Aspects of Old Testament Prophecy,* pp. 109-112, where the disappearance of the oracle of doom is attributed (somewhat nebulously) to changes in the structure of Israelite society during the postexilic period.

56. N. A. Dahl, *Das Volk Gottes,* p. 269.

57. R. Bultmann, *Geschichte,* pp. 117-18.

58. The following remarks are based on the conclusions of the excellent study by W. Janzen, *Mourning Cry and Woe Oracle,* pp. 91ff.

59. Josephus *Bell.* vi.300-309 (for a discussion of these oracles see above, pp. 135-37).

60. Scholarly output on this subject has been enormous. Among the more important and comprehensive studies are those of A. J. B. Higgins, *Jesus and the Son of Man*; H. E. Tödt, *The Son of Man in the Synoptic Tradition*; R. H. Fuller, *The Foundations of New Testament Christology*, pp. 34-43, 119-125; N. Perrin, *Rediscovering the Teaching of Jesus*, pp. 164-199; an excellent survey is found in R. H. Fuller, *The New Testament in Current Study*, pp. 44-49.

61. This is the general conclusion of two important studies, A. J. B. Higgins, *Jesus and the Son of Man*, pp. 185-209, and H. E. Tödt, *The Son of Man*, pp. 224-26. Those who regard *all* Son of man sayings as secondary productions of the church include P. Vielhauer, "Gottesreich und Menschensohn," pp. 51-79 (he bases this view on the fact that the Son of man is never used in combination with the kingdom of God in the sayings of Jesus), and N. Perrin, *Rediscovering the Teaching of Jesus*, pp. 197-99. H. E. Tödt attempts to refute Vielhauer in *The Son of Man*, pp. 298-316.

62. H. E. Tödt, *The Son of Man*, pp. 55-60; R. H. Fuller, *Foundations of New Testament Christology*, pp. 122-23; N. Perrin, *Rediscovering the Teaching of Jesus*, pp. 187-191.

63. In the Matthean version of this Q saying the pronoun "I" twice replaces the title "Son of man." Luke's version is clearly the more original, though the Matthean version is an early interpretation of the saying.

64. These are discussed by H. E. Tödt, *The Son of Man*, pp. 55-60, and carried further by R. H. Fuller, *Foundations of New Testament Christology*, pp. 122-23.

65. Cf. A. J. B. Higgins, *Jesus and the Son of Man*, pp. 200-203, where the theory is advanced that Jesus adopted the Son of man concept to refer to himself as the Son of God he already believed himself to be, though not yet installed in his heavenly seat. This viewpoint implicitly rejects the authenticity of the earthly and suffering Son of man sayings.

66. See above, pp. 166-68.

67. See D. Hay, *Glory at the Right Hand*, an examination of the use of Ps. 110:1 in early Christianity, and N. Perrin, *Rediscovering the Teaching of Jesus*, in which he examines the combination of Dan. 7:13-14 and Ps. 110:1 in terms of their function as an early Christian passion apologetic.

68. The Matthean form of the saying, expanded by reference to the death of Jesus, is secondary.

69. The Matthean version substitutes the term "the coming" (*hē parousia*) for the phrase "in his day," which Luke has probably derived from Q.

70. Matthew again substitutes the phrase "the coming" for the more original Q phrase which Luke reproduces as "and in the days." This saying is regarded as authentic by R. Bultmann, *Geschichte*, p. 128; H. E. Tödt, *The Son of Man*, p. 224; F. Hahn, *Titles of Jesus*, pp. 31-32. Its authenticity is disputed by N. Perrin, *Rediscovering the Teaching of Jesus*, pp. 195-96; R. A. Edwards, "Eschatological Correlative," pp. 9-20; and P. Vielhauer, "Gottesreich und Menschensohn," pp. 67-68.

71. The structural analysis of the text is that of T. W. Manson, *The Teaching of Jesus*, p. 54.

72. See above, pp. 168-69.

73. A. Schweitzer, *The Quest of the Historical Jesus*, pp. 358-360.

74. H. E. Tödt, *The Son of Man*, pp. 60ff. This saying is frequently thought to be the oracle of an early Christian prophet that was eventually accepted as one of the sayings of the historical Jesus.

75. H. E. Tödt, *The Son of Man*, p. 60; W. G. Kümmel, *Promise and Fulfilment*, pp. 61-62.

76. For a discussion of this oracle, see above, pp. 173-77.

77. W. Marxsen, *Mark the Evangelist*, pp. 158, 161, 167; W. G. Kümmel, *Promise and Fulfilment*, p. 98. Kümmel emphasizes that the discourse was constructed out of detached sayings and small groups of sayings of various origin. The unity of Mark 13 is emphasized by L. Hartman, *Prophecy Interpreted*, *passim*; F. Busch, *Zum Verständnis der synoptischen Eschatologie*; J. Lambrecht, *Die Redaktion der Markus-Apokalypse*, pp. 299-300.

78. E. Meyer, *Ursprung und Anfänge des Christentums,* I, 129-130; M. Albertz, *Die Botschaft des Neuen Testaments,* I/1, 180-81. A more recent exponent of the *Flugblatt* theory is R. Pesch, *Naherwartungen,* pp. 207-223. According to Pesch this apocalyptic tract consisted of vv. 6, 22, 7b, 8, 12, 13b, 14-17, 18(?), 19-20a, 24-27.

79. L. Hartman, *Prophecy Interpreted.*

80. Ibid., p. 235, finds traces of a *midrash* on Dan. 2:31-45; 7:7-27; 8:9-26; 9:24-27; 11:21-12:4(13) in Mark 13:5b-8, 12-16, 19-22, 24-27.

81. L. Hartman, *Prophecy Interpreted,* p. 208.

82. Ibid., pp. 245-48.

83. Ibid., pp. 219-226; R. Pesch, *Naherwartungen,* p. 27 (in agreement with Hartman); Pesch provides an excellent analysis of Mark 13:1-2, 3-4, on pp. 83-106.

84. According to J. Wellhausen, *Das Evangelium Marci,* p. 107, Mark 13:1-2 is an authentic saying of Jesus to which an inauthentic saying (vv. 3-4) has been added. R. Bultmann, *Geschichte,* pp. 36, 64, conjectures that the prophetic saying of Jesus may be very old, while the framework itself could be of Hellenistic origin.

85. K. L. Schmidt, *Der Rahmen der Geschichte Jesu,* p. 290, regards Mark 13:3-4 as a composition of the evangelist that was formulated to join the saying against the temple with the eschatological discourse which follows.

86. W. Kelber, *Kingdom in Mark,* pp. 111ff., has rejected the widespread assumption of a literary seam between Mark 13:1-2 and 3-4 in favor of a serious appreciation of the redactional function of the entire introduction. The following discussion will provide further evidence in support of Kelber's view.

87. Oracular responses to queries was the normal way in which oracles were delivered in Greco-Roman religions, while unsolicited prophetic utterances were the norm in early Judaism and early Christianity. In Hermas *Mand.* xi.2-6 the author attacks the question-answer method of eliciting prophetic utterances as pagan. The practice is also disapproved in Ap. Jas. 6:21-31 (J. M. Robinson, *Nag Hammadi Library,* p. 32). In the Gospel of Thomas, oracles are requested of Jesus in logia 18, 51, 113, but without any negative implications. In apocalyptic literature questions are regularly put to the *angelus interpres* for the purpose of eliciting information about the future, but this is primarily a literary device.

88. See above, n. 78.

89. E. Lohmeyer, *Das Evangelium des Markus,* p. 267; F. Busch, *Zum Verständnis der synoptischen Eschatologie,* p. 44; E. Schweizer, *Mark,* p. 262; L. Gaston, *No Stone on Another,* p. 42. However, in studies of the genre of the farewell discourse in the NT, Mark 13 is rarely classified as such. E. Stauffer mentions Mark 13 only under the section entitled "Revelations about the Future" in his morphological breakdown of the genre into components (*New Testament Theology,* pp. 344ff.). Mark 13 is not classified as a farewell discourse either by J. Munck, "Discours d'adieu," pp. 155-170, or H.-J. Michel, *Die Abschiedsrede des Paulus,* pp. 57-72 (where he reviews the sections of the NT which are connected with this genre).

90. D. E. Nineham, *The Gospel of St. Mark,* p. 340.

91. Quoted in G. R. Beasley-Murray, *Jesus and the Future,* p. 100; cf. F. Busch, *Zum Verständnis der synoptischen Eschatologie,* p. 48.

92. L. Gaston, *No Stone on Another,* pp. 13, 43-45; N. Perrin, "Towards an Interpretation of the Gospel of Mark," p. 36.

93. The peripatetic dialogue, or *peripatos,* is a literary account of a philosophical or religious discussion which takes place during a stroll; it is essentially an introductory setting for a literary dialogue. The *peripatos* and the dialogue were first combined by Epicurus (R. Hirzel, *Der Dialog,* I, 364 n. 2). Diogenes Laertius frequently refers to a certain Athenodoros as the author of a literary work entitled *Peripatoi* (iii.3; v.36; vi.81; ix.42). In the Greco-Roman period the term peripatetic was applied to Epicurean philosophers (Cicero *Letters to Atticus* vii.1.1: *ut philosophi ambulant*; cf. Hirzel, *Der Dialog,* I, 364 n. 1). By the second century A.D., when Plutarch and Lucian had revived the dialogue as a literary form suitable for ethical, religious, and philosophical discussion, the *peripatos* had become, to judge by Plutarch's fourteen surviving dialogues, an essential feature (Plutarch *Amatorius* 771d; *De facie*

937c; *Non posse suav.* 1086d; etc.). In Plutarch's dialogues one frequently finds a seated conversation following a *peripatos* (R. Hirzel, *Der Dialog,* II, 187); thus a *peripatos* can provide the setting for part or all of a Plutarchian dialogue, or it may be regarded as having already occurred prior to the beginning of the seated dialogue. Thus *De defectu oraculorum, De E apud Delphis, De Pythiae oraculis,* and *Septum sapientium convivium* all begin with a *peripatos* and conclude with a seated dialogue. *De sera numinis* contains a dialogue that occurs during a *peripatos* which lasts throughout the entire composition.

Another form of the Greco-Roman dialogue which influenced the formulation of Mark 13:1-4 is what Hirzel designated the *Kirchen-* or *Tempeldialog* (church or temple dialogue), so named because a religious sanctuary is either the locale where the dialogue occurs or the place from which a *peripatos* commences during which a dialogue occurs. Ordinarily the dialogue is occasioned by religious questions concerning something observed or said in or near the sanctuary. The *De re rustica* of Varro is the earliest surviving example of such a temple dialogue. It begins with Varro entering the temple of Tellus on the occasion of the festival of the Sementivae, where he meets those who will participate in the ensuing conversation (ii.1). An imperfectly preserved temple dialogue is the *Vergilius orator an poeta* of Florus, which was set in a temple in Tarraco (Spain), and written ca. A.D. 122 (R. Hirzel, *Der Dialog,* II, 66). Other temple dialogues include one by Cebes of Thebes (first century A.D.) and one by Numenius (late second century A.D.) (R. Hirzel, *Der Dialog,* II, 258, 359). Plutarch wrote two dialogues which can be designated temple dialogues, *De defectu oraculorum* and *De E apud Delphos.*

94. See above, n. 87, and the discussion below, pp. 217-19.

95. See above, n. 93.

96. For this observation and what follows see W. Jaeger, *Aristotle,* p. 28.

97. C. H. Dodd, "The 'Primitive Catechism'," pp. 18-24.

98. Perhaps the most succinct survey of the distinctive features of Jesus' speech is that of J. Jeremias, *New Testament Theology,* pp. 8-37; see also idem, *The Prayers of Jesus,* pp. 108-115. Another very fine and more detailed treatment is found in H. Schürmann, *Traditionsgeschichtliche Untersuchungen,* pp. 83-108 (reprint of "Die Sprache des Christus: Sprachliche Beobachtungen an den synoptischen Herrenworten," *BZ,* 2 [1958], 54-84). For the poetic features of Jesus' speech see C. F. Burney, *The Poetry of Our Lord,* and for a thorough investigation of possible Aramaisms in the gospels see M. Black, *An Aramaic Approach.*

99. C. Bonner, "Traces of Thaumaturgic Technique," pp. 171-181.

Chapter 8

1. On this subject see A. J. Festugière, *Personal Religion among the Greeks;* A. D. Nock, *Conversion;* M. P. Nilsson, *Greek Popular Religion;* E. R. Dodds, "The Religion of the Ordinary Man in Greece," pp. 140-155. A. Momigliano, "Popular Religious Beliefs," pp. 1-18, has observed on p. 18: "Thus my inquest into popular religious beliefs in the late Roman historians ends in reporting that there were no such beliefs."

2. Recent studies on social aspects of early Christianity have tended to show that people from all strata of ancient society were drawn to Christianity: E. A. Judge, *The Social Pattern of Christian Groups,* p. 60; W. Wuellner, "Sociological Implications," pp. 666-672; E. A. Judge, "The Early Christians," pp. 2-15, 125-137; A. J. Malherbe, *Social Aspects of Early Christianity,* pp. 29-59 (essentially a review of recent research on the subject); R. M. Grant, *Early Christianity and Society.*

3. This has been appropriately emphasized by A. J. Malherbe, *Social Aspects of Early Christianity,* pp. 11-28.

4. See below, Chapter 9: "Christian Prophets and the Sayings of Jesus."

5. Mention should be made of the recent work of U. B. Müller, *Prophetie und Predigt im Neuen Testament: Formgeschichtliche Untersuchungen zur urchristlichen Prophetie.* In the third major section of his book Müller attempts to identify and provide a form-critical analysis of prophetic sermons in Paul.

6. On prophecy in 1 Cor. 12-14 see H. Greeven, "Propheten, Lehrer, Vorsteher bei Paulus," pp. 1-43; idem, "Die Geistesgaben bei Paulus," pp. 111-120; K. Maly, *Mündige Gemeinde,* pp. 186-228; G. Dautzenberg, *Urchristliche Prophetie,* pp. 122-304, and the literature there cited; idem, "Botschaft und Bedeutung der urchristliche Prophetie," pp. 131-161. On Did. 10-13: G. Schille, "Das Recht der Propheten," pp. 84-103; A. Harnack, *Die Lehre der zwölf Apostel,* pp. 93-158; idem, *Mission und Ausbreitung,* I, 340-379. On Acts: E. E. Ellis, "The Role of the Christian Prophet in Acts," pp. 55-67 (= *Prophecy and Hermeneutic,* pp. 129-144).

7. On the Apocalypse of John: D. Hill, "Prophecy and Prophets in the Revelation of St. John," pp. 401-418; on the Shepherd of Hermas: J. Reiling, *Hermas and Christian Prophecy;* idem, "Prophecy, the Spirit and the Church," pp. 58-76.

8. On this passage see W. C. van Unnik, " 'Den Geist löschet nicht aus,' " pp. 255-269.

9. The patronym "Barnabas" is interpreted to mean "son of consolation" (*huios paraklēseōs*) in Acts 4:36. E. E. Ellis takes this to mean "son of prophecy" through a far-fetched equation of *paraklēsis* with *prophēteia* (using a kind of logic of the excluded middle); "The Role of the Christian Prophet in Acts," p. 57 (=*Prophecy and Hermeneutic,* p. 132). "Son of consolation" should rather be regarded as a popular and incorrect etymology of "Barnabas." The true etymology is "son of Nabu" (S. P. Brock, "Barnabas," pp. 93-98; cf. E. Haenchen, *Acts,* p. 232, where he suggests "son of Nebo").

10. E. Benz, *Paulus als Visionar,* p. 84.

11. Prophecy plays a critical role in the plots of the *Iliad,* the *Odyssey,* the *Argonautica* of Apollonius Rhodius, the *Aeneid* of Vergil, Lucan's *Bellum Civile,* Silius Italicus' *Punica,* Valerius Flaccus' *Argonautica,* and Statius' *Thebais;* cf. C. H. Moore, "Prophecy in the Ancient Epic," pp. 99-175. Oracles and their inevitable fulfilment also play a critical role in Greek tragedy: R. Stählin, *Das Motiv der Mantik im antiken Drama* (1912); E. H. Klotsche, *The Supernatural in the Tragedies of Euripides* (1918); R. P. Winnington-Ingram, "The Role of Apollo in the Oresteia," pp. 97-104; E. Bächli, *Die künstlerische Funktion von Orakelsprüchen, Weissagungen, Träumen usw in der griechischen Tragödie* (1954); H. H. Cordes, Jr., "The Religious Use of Oracles in Attic Tragedy." For the use of oracles in the comedies of Aristophanes see N. Lichtenberg, "The Literary Use of Oracles in Aristophanes."

12. See D. E. Aune, "The Significance of the Delay of the Parousia," pp. 87-109, and the literature there cited.

13. E. Sjöberg, *TDNT,* VI, 384ff.

14. T. B. Baba Meṣia 59b.

15. See below, n. 17.

16. For this statement and those which follow see D. E. Aune, "The Presence of God," pp. 454-55.

17. See R. A. Edwards, "An Approach to a Theology of Q," pp. 247-269; idem, *A Theology of Q* (1976); S. Schulz, *Q: Die Spruchquelle der Evangelisten* (1972). The reconstruction of the Q Community and its activities that I find the most convincing is that of P. Hoffmann, *Studien zur Theologie der Logienquelle* (1972).

18. H. C. Kee, *Community of the New Age.*

18a. For the Apocalypse this claim is made by H. Kraft, *Offenbarung,* pp. 21, 38; D. Hill, "Prophecy and Prophets," p. 414; E. Schweizer, *Church Order,* pp. 134-35. For the Johannine community see J. R. Michaels, "The Johannine Words of Jesus," pp. 240, 248ff., 256. For the Roman churches addressed by Hermas see J. Reiling, *Hermas and Christian Prophecy,* pp. 124-25, 135-36, 146.

19. E. Cothenet, "Les prophètes chrétiens comme exégètes," pp. 78, 101; C. Perrot, "Prophètes et prophétisme," p. 27 (Perrot distinguishes between three types: the individual prophet, the group of prophets, and those who prophesy).

20. H. B. Swete, *Holy Spirit,* p. 377.

21. J. Reiling, "Prophecy, the Spirit and the Church," pp. 58-76.

22. J. Wackernagel, *Vorlesungen über Syntax,* II, 239-240; E. Fascher, *PROPHĒTĒS,* p. 51; M. van der Kolf, "Prophetes," col. 798; H. Krämer, *TDNT,* VI, 783. On the technical meaning

of *prophētēs* as "one who speaks on behalf of the god," see P. Amandry, "La divination en Grèce," p. 175; M. van der Kolf, "Prophetes," col. 798; O. Kern, *Die Religion der Griechen*, II, 112.

23. Other terms used in similar contexts include *hypophētēs*, *mantis*, *promantis*, *theomantis*, *theopropos*, *chrēsmologos*, *chrēstēs*, etc.

24. E. Fascher, *PROPHĒTĒS*, pp. 166ff.

25. For the application of the term "prophet" to John the Baptist see above, pp. 129-132; for the application of the title to Jesus see above, pp. 153-57.

26. The nineteen NT references are: Acts 11:27; 13:1; 15:32; 21:10; 1 Cor. 12:28, 29; 14:29, 32 (2x), 37; Eph. 3:5; 4:11; Rev. 11:10, 18; 16:6; 18:20, 24; 22:6, 9. The twenty-one references in the Apostolic Fathers are: Did. 10:7; 11:3, 7, 8(2x), 9, 10, 11; 13:1, 3, 4, 6; 15:1, 2; Hermas *Mand.* xi.7 (3x), 12 (2x), 15, 16.

27. For Polycarp see Mart. Polyc. 16:2 where he is called a *didaskalos*; cf. 5:2; 12:3 where he speaks *prophētikōs*; Melito of Sardis: Eusebius *Hist. eccl.* iv.26.2; Polycrates of Ephesus in Eusebius *Hist. eccl.* v.24.5; Jerome *De vir. illustr.* 24; on Ammia of Philadelphia see Eusebius *Hist. eccl.* v.17.3-4; W. M. Calder, "Philadelphia and Montanism," pp. 329-330; on Quadratus see Eusebius *Hist. eccl.* iii.37.1; A. Harnack, *Chronologie*, I, 320ff., placed both Ammia and Quadratus under the reign of Hadrian; on Cerinthus see Dionysius of Alexandria, quoted in Eusebius *Hist. eccl.* iii.28 (Dionysius regards Cerinthus as a prophet partially because he thinks he is the author of the Apocalypse); on Peregrinus see Lucian *Peregr.* 11, 16.

28. For Markus see Ireneus *Adv. haer.* i.13-21; Hippolytus *Ref. omn. haer.* vi.39-55; Epiphanius *Haer.* xxxiv; Markus flourished just after the middle of the second century, according to A. Harnack, *Chronologie*, I, 294ff. Hippolytus and Epiphanius are both dependent on Ireneus, who is in effect our sole source of information regarding Markus; cf. F. M. Sagnard, *La Gnose Valentinienne*, pp. 358-386. Most recently on Markus see J. Reiling, "Marcus Gnosticus," pp. 161-179. On Philumene, the prophetess of Apelles, see Hippolytus *Ref. omn. haer.* vii.38.2; Tertullian *De praescr.* 6.6; 30.6. On Barkabbas: Epiphanius *Haer.* xxvi.2.2; on Martiades and Marsianos: Epiphanius *Haer.* xl.7.9.

29. On Montanus and Montanism: Eusebius *Hist. eccl.* vi.20.3; Hippolytus *Ref. omn. haer.* vii.19.1.

30. Tertullian *De anima* ix.4; cf. the comments of J. H. Waszink, *Tertullian: De Anima*, pp. 167-173.

31. Cyprian *Ep.* 75.10.

32. See below, pp. 209-211, 248-49.

33. See above, pp. 132-35, 139-144.

34. In the NT these include all the references in n. 26 above except for those in Acts; the references in the Apostolic Fathers are identical to those in n. 26 above.

35. The only NT reference to *prophētēs* in the singular (apart from places where the prophet is specifically named) is 1 Cor. 14:37; the references to *prophētai* in the plural in the Apostolic Fathers include Did. 10:7; 11:3; 13:6; 15:1, 2; Hermas *Mand.* xi.7, 12, 15, 16. All these plurals, however, are generic plurals, as in Did. 10:7: "But permit the prophets to offer prayers of thanksgiving as they wish."

36. G. Friedrich, *TDNT*, VI, 855; J. Moffatt, *1 Corinthians*, p. 228; K. Maly, *Mündige Gemeinde*, p. 218; E. C. Selwyn, *Oracles*, p. 401; H. von Campenhausen, *Ecclesiastical Authority*, p. 62. The interpretative problem centers in the phrase *hoi alloi*, "the others," which may refer to "the other prophets" or the other Christians present. In 1 Cor. 14:31, where Paul says *dynasthe gar kath' hena pantes prophēteuein* ("for you can all prophesy one by one"), he is specifically addressing the prophets, not everyone (cf. H. Conzelmann, *1 Corinthians*, p. 245). That would make it more probable that *hoi alloi* in v. 29 means the other *prophets*.

37. E. E. Ellis, *Prophecy and Hermeneutic*, p. 23 n. 1, incorrectly claims that "in Revelation (1,9; 4,11; 12,10; 19,10; 22,9) *adelphos* always means prophet." There is no evidence in Revelation to support this view. John may refer to himself as "your brother" (1:9), but it is faulty logic to conclude that because John is a prophet and John is a brother that prophet=brother.

38. At first sight it might appear that the term *doulos* is a synonym of *prophētēs*, particularly in the light of Rev. 10:7, where the OT prophets are referred to as *tous heautou doulous tous prophētas*. Yet in 11:18 we find the term considerably expanded: *tois doulois sou tois prophētais kai tois hagiois kai tois phoboumenois to onoma sou*. John calls himself a servant (1:1), but there is no necessity for regarding the term here as a synonym for prophet, any more than the term "brother" in 1:9.

39. J. Reiling, *Hermas and Christian Prophecy*, pp. 97, 125, 146; idem, "Prophecy, the Spirit and the Church," pp. 73-74, claims that Hermas' reference to "the man having the Divine Spirit" is "not a man bearing the title prophet, but just a man and a member of the church." Also critical of Reiling's view is H. Paulsen, *"DIADOCHĒ TĒN PROPHĒTŌN,"* pp. 445-46 n. 23.

40. The verb *prophēteuein* is used of OT activity in Matt. 11:13; 15:7; Mark 7:6; 1 Pet. 1:10; Jude 14; of early Judaism in Luke 1:67; John 11:51; of early Christianity in Matt. 7:22; 26:68; Mark 14:65; Luke 22:64; Acts 2:17-18 (a quotation from Joel 3:1); 19:6; 21:9; 1 Cor. 11:4, 5; 13:9; 14:1, 3, 4, 5 (2x), 24, 31, 39; Rev. 10:11; 11:3.

41. The verb is used of early Christian prophesying in Barn. 16:9; Hermas *Mand.* xi.12, 13; of OT prophesying in Barn. 5:6, 13; 9:2; 12:10; Hermas *Vis.* ii.3.4.

42. The noun *prophēteia* refers to OT prophecy in Matt. 13:14; 2 Pet. 1:20, 21; to NT prophecy in Rom. 12:6; 1 Cor. 12:10; 13:2, 8; 14:6, 22; 1 Thess. 5:20; 1 Tim. 1:18; 4:14; Rev. 1:3; 11:6; 19:10; 22:7, 10, 18, 19.

43. The noun refers to early Christian prophecy only in Hermas *Mand.* xi.12; to OT prophecy in Barn. 13:4; 1 Clem. 12:8; Ign. Smyrn. 5:1.

44. E. Fascher, *PROPHĒTĒS*, p. 53.

45. N. J. Engelsen, "Glossolalia," pp. 20-21, 60.

46. See above, pp. 41-43.

47. H. Kraft, "Anfänge," p. 92.

48. See below, pp. 201-211.

49. One of the theses of the present study is that when the function of early Christian prophets was gradually taken over by other representatives of the Christian community the need for prophets considerably diminished.

50. Acts 2:38; 5:32; 10:45; Rom. 8:9-12, 23; 5:5; 1 Cor. 3:16; 2 Cor. 1:22; 5:5; Gal. 3:2-5; 1 Thess. 4:8; Tit. 3:5-6; 1 Clem. 2:2; 46:6; Barn. 1:3; Hermas *Sim.* ix.13.7. Cf. E. Schweizer, *TDNT*, VI, 398-400, 406.

51. Acts 4:8; 6:3, 5, 8; 7:55; 16:6-7; 20:23; 1 Cor. 14:12; 12:4-11; Ign. Philad. 7:2; Hermas *Mand.* xi.9.

52. The conception of the Spirit of God as the general possession of all Christians has been labeled "dynamistic," i.e. the Spirit is conceived as an impersonal force which fills a person like a liquid, while the conception of the Spirit as an independent personal force which can possess a man and inspire him to work deeds of power or to speak inspired words has been termed "animistic" (cf. R. Bultmann, *NT Theology*, I, 153-164; E. Schweizer, *TDNT*, VI, 406).

53. H. Gunkel, *Die Wirkungen des heiligen Geistes*, pp. 2-43; on p. 28 Gunkel observes that "originally the conception of the Spirit had nothing to do with that of the community." In the second part of his study Gunkel argues that Paul was the first to view the Spirit in close connection with the everyday moral and religious life of Christians. Against Gunkel, however, it appears that that view is pre-Pauline.

54. H. Greeven, "Propheten," p. 8.

55. This is the conclusion of J. Reiling, *Hermas and Christian Prophecy*, p. 139; idem, "Prophecy, the Spirit and the Church," pp. 63, 65.

56. The three roles of apostle, prophet, and teacher are found together only in 1 Cor. 12:28 in the NT and early Christian literature. Apostles and prophets are linked in Eph. 2:20; 3:5; 4:11; Did. 11:3. In Rev. 18:20, saints, apostles, and prophets are mentioned, and in Ign. Philad. 9:1 prophets and apostles are mentioned as members of the same group (*hoi prophētai kai apostoloi*), making it difficult to decide whether the reference is to OT or NT prophets

(F. Schnider, *Jesus der Prophet,* p. 62, referring to Eph. 2:20; É. Cothenet, "Les prophètes chrétiens comme exégètes," p. 78 n. 3). Apostles and teachers are listed together in 2 Tim. 1:11; Hermas *Sim.* ix.15.4; ix.16.5; ix.25.2; *Vis.* iii.5.1. Prophets and teachers are linked in Did. 15:1, 2. On the other hand, the triadic local structure consisting of bishop(s), presbyters, and deacons is frequently referred to in Ignatius (Magn. 6:1; 13:1; Trall. 7:2; Philad. inscr. 4:1; 7:1; 10:2; Smyrn. 8:1; 12:2; Polyc. 6:1), and bishops and presbyters are linked by Ignatius almost as often (Eph. 4:1; 20:2; Magn. 2:1; 7:1; Trall. 2:2; 3:1; 12:2; 13:2). Paul mentions bishops and deacons together in Phil. 1:1.

57. N. Bonwetsch, "Prophetie," p. 411.

58. A. Schlatter, *Church,* p. 22.

59. Both this statement and the following are made in A. Harnack, *Die Lehre der zwölf Apostel,* pp. 104-105. Harnack's entire reconstruction of the role of universal and local offices in early Christianity is found in *Die Lehre der zwölf Apostel,* pp. 93-158, which was later incorporated into his *Mission und Ausbreitung,* I, 340-379.

60. A. Harnack, *Constitution and Law,* p. 24.

61. B. H. Streeter, *The Primitive Church,* p. 77.

62. H. Greeven, "Propheten, Lehrer, Vorsteher," p. 42.

63. H. Greeven, "Propheten," p. 9; H. von Campenhausen, *Ecclesiastical Authority,* pp. 61, 65ff.

64. H. Greeven, "Propheten," p. 9.

65. M. E. Boring, "Christian Prophets," pp. 75ff., not only objects to the view that early Christian prophets were wanderers, but also challenges Harnack's interpretation of the role of prophets in the Didache. Harnack may have been guilty of overgeneralizing the major features of the prophetic role on the basis of data preserved in the Didache, but his exegesis of the Didache itself is, on the whole, unassailable.

66. In Rom. 16:7 Andronicus and Junias are designated apostles; Epaphroditus is designated an apostle in Phil. 2:25; Titus and others not named are called apostles in 2 Cor. 8:23; Barnabas is called an apostle (with Saul=Paul) in Acts 14:4, 14; Titus and Silvanus are so designated if 1 Thess. 1:1 is compared with 2:6; and Apollos may be designated a prophet in the light of 1 Cor. 4:6, 9. This unrestricted use of the title "apostle" is preserved in the Didache, a feature which either reveals the antiquity of the tradition or is a self-conscious archaization (the latter view is espoused by G. Schille, "Das Recht der Propheten," pp. 84-103), though the former view appears much more probable. On this subject see D. Lührmann, *Offenbarungsverständnis,* p. 95.

67. H. Kraft, "Anfänge," p. 91; O. Betz, "Die Vision," p. 121.

68. E. Fascher, *PROPHETES,* p. 185.

69. Ibid., p. 186; A. Harnack, *Die Lehre der zwölf Apostel,* p. 119; J. Reiling, "Prophecy, the Spirit and the Church," p. 69.

70. E. Cothenet, "Les prophètes chrétiens comme exégètes," p. 102; G. Friedrich, *TDNT,* VI, 854.

71. F. V. Filson, "The Christian Teacher," p. 322; D. Hill, "Christian Prophets as Teachers," p. 109.

72. The motif of the violent fate of the prophets is mentioned in connection with the killing of Jesus and the (OT) prophets and the persecution of "us" (= apostles?); on this motif see above, pp. 157-59. Other passages which place OT prophets and NT apostles in functionally equivalent roles include: Matt. 5:12; Eph. 2:20 (but NT prophets could be referred to here, since the phrase *tōn apostolōn kai prophētōn* [one article governing two nouns connected by *kai*] indicates that the same group is described by both nouns; cf. F. Schnider, *Jesus der Prophet,* p. 62; E. Cothenet, "Les prophètes chrétiens comme exégètes," p. 78 n. 3); 2 Pet. 3:2; Ign. Philad. 9:1; Hermas *Sim.* ix.15.4.

73. The introductory signature of Rom. 1:1 has a counterpart in many other places in Paul's letters: "Paul, a servant of Jesus Christ, called [*klētos*] to be an apostle, set apart

[aphorismenos] for the gospel of God" (cf. Rom. 11:13; 1 Cor. 1:1; 9:1-2; 15:9; 2 Cor. 1:1; Col. 1:1). Paul is similarly referred to in the deutero-Pauline letters: Eph. 1:1; 1 Tim. 1:1; 2:7; 2 Tim. 1:1; Tit. 1:1.

74. G. Sass, *Apostelamt und Kirche*, pp. 40ff.; T. Holtz, "Zum Selbstverständnis des Apostels Paulus," pp. 321-330; E. Lohmeyer, *Grundlagen paulinischer Theologie*, p. 202; N. A. Dahl, *Das Volk Gottes*, p. 270; O. Betz, "Die Vision des Paulus," pp. 113-123. The precise relationship between the three narratives of Paul's conversion in Acts 9, 22, 26 and references to that experience in his letters (Gal. 1; 1 Cor. 9:1; 15:8) remains problematical.

75. W. Zimmerli, *Ezekiel*, I, 97-100, distinguishes between two kinds of prophetic call in the OT, the narrative type of call that includes a dialogue with Yahweh, and the divine call and commission preceded by a "throne vision." According to Zimmerli the narratives of Paul's conversion in Acts 9, 22, and 26 conform to the second pattern (ibid., p. 100). More recently, C. Burchard, *Der dreizehnte Zeuge* (who did not refer to Zimmerli's earlier analysis), has categorized Acts 9 on form-critical grounds as a conversion (*Bekehrung*) narrative (pp. 87-88), while Acts 22 (p. 96) and Acts 26 (pp. 119ff.) narrate the conversion of Paul in terms of prophetic call (*Berufung*). O. H. Steck, "Formgeschichtliche Bemerkungen," pp. 20-28, has denied the form-critical connection between the OT prophetic call narratives and the narratives of Paul's conversion in Acts. The distinctions which Burchard and Steck make are too finely drawn.

76. O. Betz, *Was Wissen Wir von Jesus?* p. 67; idem, "Die Vision des Paulus," pp. 118-19.

77. See below, pp. 248-49.

78. H. Kraft, "Die altkirchliche Prophetie," p. 250.

79. Rev. 1:9-20 (cf. H. Kraft, *Die Offenbarung des Johannes*, pp. 38-49). Each of the seven proclamations to the churches of Asia Minor also begins with a command to write (Rev. 2:1, 8, 12, 18; 3:1, 7, 14; cf. 21:5). Hermas is similarly commanded to write in *Vis.* ii.4.3; v.5, 6, 7; *Sim.* ix.33.1. Aelius Aristides also claimed to have received a divine command to write down the substance of his dreams (*Or.* xlviii.2; ed. B. Keil, p. 395). These early Christian references indicate that prophecy cannot be considered primarily an oral phenomenon, since they represent a development of OT commission formulas (see above, p. 90).

80. This is presupposed in Acts 21:10-11, and clearly stated in Hermas *Vis.* ii.2.6; ii.3.4; iii.8.11; iv.2.5.

81. See the important recent discussion of J. Reiling, "Marcus Gnosticus," pp. 170-79. See also the earlier discussion in R. Reitzenstein, *Poimandres*, pp. 220-22; idem, *Hellenistic Mystery-Religions*, pp. 315-16. Reitzenstein makes an important form-critical observation regarding the prophetic initiation supervised by Marcus when he emphasizes the concluding offering of thanks by the initiant to the priest (*Poimandres*, p. 222). This has an exact parallel in Corpus Hermeticum i.27-29 (noted by Reitzenstein).

82. On the possibility of a prophetic line of succession at Hierapolis and Philadelphia see the quotation from an anonymous author of an anti-Montanist treatise preserved in Eusebius *Hist. eccl.* v.17.4: "For if the Montanist women succeeded [*diedexanto*] to Quadratus and Ammia in Philadelphia in the prophetic gift [*to prophētikon charisma*]. . . ." The Anonymous is apparently reproducing a claim of the Montanists. On this point see F. C. Klawiter, "The New Prophecy," pp. 170-71. Maximilla, a Montanist prophetess, reflects the conviction that she had been divinely commissioned in this quotation from Epiphanius *Haer.* xlviii.13.1: "The Lord of this work and covenant and promise sent me as its elector and revealer and interpreter as one who had been compelled willingly or unwillingly to learn the knowledge of God."

83. Cf. Josephus *Contra Ap.* i.8.

84. Cf. the connection between the *prophētikē taxis* and *diadochē* in P. Oxy. I.5. See A. Harnack, "Über zwei . . . altchristliche Fragmente," pp. 516-520; H. Paulsen, *"DIADOCHĒ-TŌN PROPHĒTŌN,"* pp. 443-453.

85. J. Panagopoulos, "Die urchristliche Prophetie," pp. 7-8, observes (with, I think, some exaggeration) that there are very few common links between OT and NT prophets,

and that the former contribute very little to our knowledge of the latter.

86. See above, pp. 97-99.

87. Justin *Dial.* lxxxii.1; lxxxviii.1; Ireneus *Adv. haer.* v.6.1. In *De Antichristo* 2 Hippolytus argues that the age of prophecy is past.

88. O. Linton, *Das Problem der Urkirche,* p. 104.

89. Ibid., p. 104; E. Schweizer, *Church Order,* pp. 181-87; H. Conzelmann, *TDNT,* VI, 406; idem, *I Corinthians,* p. 211; J. G. Gager, *Kingdom and Community,* pp. 68-74. Harnack, it appears, was less theologically motivated than many of his critics.

90. D. E. Aune, *Cultic Setting,* pp. 143-44. The notion that each church represents *the* Church is also implied in several places in Paul (1 Cor. 1:2; 2 Cor. 1:1; cf. K. L. Schmidt, *TDNT,* III, 506). This view of the significance of the local church is still preserved in Eastern Orthodoxy.

91. H. Kraft, "Anfänge," p. 81.

92. Among many German NT scholars the institutionalization of early Christianity, which in its early stages is frequently referred to as *Frühkatholizismus,* is regarded as symptomatic of the deterioration of true Christianity. Against this theological evaluation of the negative significance of institutionalization it must be observed that *all* social movements either become institutionalized or disappear. Recently, J. G. Gager, *Kingdom and Community,* pp. 66-76, has argued that the routinization of early Christianity was an inevitable (and irreversible) social process.

93. The general framework for these remarks is adapted from H. Blumer, "Collective Behavior," p. 199. An important theoretical study based on a great deal of empirical research is that of N. Smelser, *Theory of Collective Behavior.*

94. According to B. Wilson, *Magic and the Millennium,* p. 188 (and here he could have been addressing the analogous, or even homologous, situation faced by Paul in Corinth): "Inspirationalism always creates problems of institutionalization. Where prophets abound, order is difficult to attain." Here Wilson seems to attribute disorder to prophets. It would be more prudent to see prophets as one of the consequences of lack of structure, even the conscious rejection of structure, characteristic of new social and religious movements in their early stages of development. Such movements often tend to reject the "equilibrium" characteristic of existing society, and particularly the values and norms espoused by that society (cf. N. Smelser, *Theory of Collective Behavior,* B. R. Wilson, *Magic and the Millennium,* and K. Burridge, *New Heaven, New Earth*).

95. See below, pp. 217-229.

96. For a very interesting discussion of the kinds of people that Paul tends to mention in his letters see E. A. Judge, "The Early Christians as a Scholastic Community," pp. 125-137. Also important is E. E. Ellis, "Paul and His Co-Workers," in *Prophecy and Hermeneutic,* pp. 3-22.

97. On the various settings of early Christian prophecy see below, pp. 189ff.

98. On prophetic conflict see below, pp. 218-19.

99. On this subject the three most significant studies are A. Satake, *Die Gemeindeordnung in der Johannesapokalypse*; D. Hill, "Prophecy and Prophets," pp. 401-418; U. B. Müller, *Zur frühchristlichen Theologiegeschichte,* pp. 27-38 (surprisingly, Müller makes no reference to the article by D. Hill).

100. Some commentators have regarded the *angeloi* to whom the seven proclamations are addressed as prominent leaders or bishops of their respective communities (Strack-Billerbeck, III, 790-92; T. Zahn, *Introduction,* III, 413-17; see the brief surveys of scholarly opinion in W. Bousset, *Die Offenbarung Johannis,* pp. 200-201; R. H. Charles, *Revelation,* I, 34-35). The most widely accepted view is that they are angelic beings who are heavenly counterparts and representatives of each of the seven churches (G. Kittel, *TDNT,* I, 86-87; R. Mounce, *Revelation,* p. 82; G. R. Beasley-Murray, *Revelation,* pp. 68-70; U. B. Müller, *Zur frühchristlichen Theologiegeschichte,* pp. 33-34; R. H. Charles, *Revelation,* I, 34; J. M. Ford, *Revelation,* pp. 386-87). The best recent discussion of this problem is found in H. Kraft, *Die Offenbarung des Johannes,* pp. 50-52; Kraft concludes correctly that the seven proclamations

are each addressed to messengers who will relay them to their respective communities. The twenty-four elders (*presbyteroi*) referred to frequently in Revelation (4:4, 10; 5:6, 8, 11, 14; 7:11; 11:16; 14:3; 19:4) are probably OT saints; cf. Heb. 11:2 and the convincing discussion by A. Feuillet, "Les Vingt-quatre Viellards," pp. 5-32.

101. G. Bornkamm, *TDNT*, VI, 669.

102. A. Satake, *Die Gemeindeordnung in der Johannesapokalypse*, pp. 155-161.

103. G. Bornkamm, *TDNT*, VI, 669-670.

104. U. B. Müller, *Zur frühchristlichen Theologiegeschichte*, p. 31.

105. D. Hill, "Prophecy and Prophets," pp. 406-411, argues that prophets, though distinguished from other Christians, are not accorded positions of precedence. On pp. 411-14 he argues that the role of all Christians, prophets included, is basically similar. However, he moves beyond the evidence when he suggests that all Christians are potential prophets.

106. A. Satake, *Die Gemeindeordnung in der Johannesapokalypse*, pp. 39, 52-53.

107. Gen. 19:11; Deut. 1:17; 25:13-14; 1 Sam. 5:9; 20:2; 30:2, 19; 1 Kgs. 22:31 (=2 Chr. 18:30); 2 Kgs. 23:2 (=2 Chr. 34:30); Est. 1:5, 20; Job 3:19; Ps. 115:13. The idiom occurs several times in the Apocalypse: 11:18; 13:16; 19:5, 18; 20:12.

108. A. Satake, *Die Gemeindeordnung in der Johannesapokalypse*, pp. 56, 135.

109. Against the conclusions of D. Hill, "Prophecy and Prophets," pp. 411-14 (see above, n. 105).

110. In Rev. 22:16 the *hymin* probably refers to the Christian prophets who are John's colleagues; similarly, it is possible that the *douloi* of Rev. 1:1 are John's prophetic brothers.

111. See above, n. 105.

112. See above, p. 98.

113. G. Friedrich, *TDNT*, VI, 849-850; D. Hill, "Prophecy and Prophets," pp. 406-411, 415-16; idem, "Christian Prophets as Teachers," pp. 119-122. The following statements are drawn from these sources.

114. H. Kraft, *Offenbarung*, p. 38. This view of the role of the early Christian prophet has been disputed by G. Dautzenberg, *Urchristliche Prophetie*, pp. 126-148, esp. pp. 129, 147. However, Dautzenberg's argument has been demolished by W. Grudem, "A Response to Gerhard Dautzenberg," pp. 253-270.

115. G. Friedrich, *TDNT*, VI, 853.

116. I. Goffman, *The Presentation of the Self in Everyday Life* (New York, 1955).

117. See above, pp. 195-98.

118. See above, pp. 87-88.

119. G. Dautzenberg, *Urchristliche Prophetie*, pp. 40-42, 301-302.

120. The following discussion is based on the chapter section on "Tithes and Ritual Purity" in A. Oppenheimer, *The 'Am Ha-Aretz*, pp. 23-51.

121. D. van den Eynde, *Les Normes de l'Enseignment*, p. 91; N. Bonwetsch, "Die Prophetie," p. 462. M. Dibelius thought that the prophet stood in a position of inferiority within the Christian community in Rome (*Der Hirt des Hermas*, p. 541).

122. The most important recent study of *Mand.* xi is that of J. Reiling, *Hermas and Christian Prophecy*, which focuses specifically on *Mand.* xi and refers to the significant earlier literature on the subject.

123. J. Reiling, *Hermas and Christian Prophecy*, pp. 124-25, 135-36.

124. Ibid., pp. 157-170, where Reiling discusses at length the contrasts between Hermas' description of the true prophet in *Mand.* xi and the way in which he himself apparently received and communicated divine revelations. Reiling is of the opinion that *Mand.* xi describes not a religious specialist designated as a "prophet," but rather the phenomenon of congregational prophecy.

125. D. van den Eynde, *Les Normes de l'Enseignment*, p. 88; E. Bevan, *Sibyls and Seers*, p. 175 n. 1.

126. See below, pp. 299-310.

127. Quoted above, p. 197.

128. Hermas *Vis.* i.1.3; i.2.1-2; ii.2.1; iii.1.2; iii.1.5; iii.10.7; iv.1.3-4; v.1.

129. Hermas *Vis.* ii.1.3; ii.2.3-4, 6; ii.3.4; ii.4.2-3; iii.3.1; iii.8.10-11.

130. Hermas *Vis.* ii.4.3; compare this with Alexander of Abonuteichos who transmitted oracles throughout the empire through *chrēsmologoi,* i.e. collectors and expounders of oracles (who could themselves prophesy; cf. Philo *De spec. leg.* iv.52; see above, pp. 38-40), in Lucian *Alex.* 36. A similar pattern is evident in the relationship between John the prophet and his prophetic colleagues (see above, pp. 206-208).

131. This has been demonstrated by J. Reiling, *Hermas and Christian Prophecy,* pp. 79-96; cf. pp. 41-47. The classic treatment of Greco-Roman revelatory magic remains that of T. Hopfner, *Griechisch-ägyptischer Offenbarungszauber* (2 vols.; Leipzig, 1921-24), presented in condensed form in his article "Mageia" in Pauly-Wissowa, *Real-Encyclopädie der klassischen Altertumswissenschaft,* XIV (1928), 301-393.

132. See the articles by E. Peterson, "Beiträge zur Interpretation der Visionen im Pastor Hermae" and "Kritische Analyse der fünften Vision des Hermas" in a collection of his essays published under the title *Frühkirche, Judentum und Gnosis* (Rome, Freiburg, and Vienna, 1959).

133. L. W. Barnard, "Hermas, the Church and Judaism," pp. 153-54.

134. Ireneus *Adv. haer.* iv.20; Origen *In Rom.* xvi.4; Eusebius *Hist. eccl.* v.8.

135. Perhaps the best account of the development of ecclesiastical organization and ideology during the second and third centuries A.D. is found in C. Andresen, *Die Kirchen der alten Christenheit,* pp. 3-115.

136. M. E. Boring, "Christian Prophets," pp. 75ff., not only objects to the view that early Christian prophets were itinerants; he also vainly challenges Harnack's interpretation of the Didache.

137. A. J. Malherbe, *Social Aspects of Early Christianity,* pp. 62-70; idem, "The Inhospitality of Diotrephes," pp. 222-232; W. M. Ramsay, "Roads and Travel (in the New Testament)," pp. 375-402; idem, *Letters to the Seven Churches,* pp. 15-20; L. Casson, *Travel in the Ancient World,* pp. 122, 127, 147-48.

138. The lower estimate is that of A. Harnack, *Mission und Ausbreitung,* I, 13, while J. Juster, *Les Juifs dans l'Empire Romain,* I, 209-210, estimated the Jewish population at between six and seven million. The evidence is reviewed by S. Baron, *Social and Religious History of the Jews,* I, 165ff., who thinks a total of eight million is possible.

139. The vulgar nature of such inns is described by L. Casson, *Travel in the Ancient World,* pp. 197-218.

140. *Compendia Rerum Judaicarum ad Novum Testamentum,* I/2, 762; J. Juster, *Les Juifs,* I, 455-56; D. Georgi, *Die Gegner des Paulus,* pp. 98-99 (on pp. 105-114, Georgi summarizes the attitudes of various Greco-Roman authors on Jewish beggars).

141. See E. E. Ellis, "Paul and His Opponents," in *Prophecy and Hermeneutic,* pp. 80-115, which is an extensive review of the literature on the subject.

142. D. Georgi, *Die Gegner des Paulus,* pp. 219-246 (see also the critique of some of Georgi's views in C. H. Holladay, *Theios Aner,* pp. 34-40); E. E. Ellis, "Paul and His Opponents," in *Prophecy and Hermeneutic,* p. 115, provides an excellent summary of his findings: "The Pauline mission was an enterprise of pneumatics, persons who claimed special understanding of the Scripture and who experienced manifestations of inspired, ecstatic speech and of visions and revelations. The primary opposition to that mission arose from within a segment of the ritually strict *Hebraioi* in the Jerusalem church and with variations in nuance continued to pose, sometimes as a counter mission and sometimes as an infiltrating influence, a settled and persistent 'other' gospel. It also laid claim to pneumatic powers and experiences. Each group claimed to be the true voice of Jesus, each claimed to give the true *gnōsis* of God and, on occasion, each made its higher appeal to apostolic status. It was, in a word, a battle of prophets, and the congregations were called upon to choose—Paul or his opposition."

143. Although Paul, Barnabas, and Silas are designated as prophets in Acts (13:1; 15:32), and all three are depicted as traveling extensively, their itinerant ministry is nowhere explicitly connected with their prophetic roles.

144. Rev. 2:21, where Jesus through the prophet John says of the prophetess "Jezebel," "I gave her time to repent," may be an oblique reference to an earlier oracle directed to "Jezebel" herself by the prophet John (W. Bousset, *Die Offenbarung Johannis*, p. 219; R. H. Charles, *Revelation*, I, 71; E. Lohmeyer, *Die Offenbarung des Johannes*, p. 28; G. R. Beasley-Murray, *Revelation*, p. 21; U. B. Müller, *Prophetie und Predigt*, p. 68). Whether John personally delivered this oracle, however, cannot be decided with any confidence. H. B. Swete, *Revelation*, p. 43, assumes without evidence that "Jezebel" was an itinerant prophetess. John the prophet is, I think, correctly regarded by U. B. Müller, *Zur frühchristlichen Theologiegeschichte*, pp. 46-50, as an itinerant.

145. U. B. Müller, *Zur frühchristlichen Theologiegeschichte*, pp. 46ff.; G. Bornkamm, *TDNT*, VI, 669-670; A. Satake, *Die Gemeindeordnung der Johannesapokalypse*, pp. 194-95.

146. Papias in Eusebius *Hist. eccl.* iii.39.9, and Polycrates of Ephesus in Eusebius *Hist. eccl.* iii.31.3; v.24.2.

147. Lucian *Peregrinus* 11-12. On Peregrinus see F. C. Klawiter, *The New Prophecy*, pp. 130-142.

148. Apostles, who appear to be regarded with some suspicion, are allowed to stay one day, or at the most two (Did. 11:4-5). If an apostle stays longer, or asks for money, he is a *pseudoprophētēs* (Did. 11:5-6). This does not mean that legitimate apostles are prophets (contra H. A. Guy, *New Testament Prophecy*, p. 174). Rather, the label "false prophet" is affixed to those who illegitimately claim to be sent by God and to speak and act under his authority (Mark 13:22; Matt. 24:11, 24; 2 Pet. 2:1; 1 John 4:1). Apart from apostles, other Christian travelers may stay two or at most three days (Did. 12:2). Christians who wish to reside with the community must work for their keep (Did. 12:3ff.).

149. Against G. Schille, "Das Recht der Propheten und Apostel," p. 86.

150. R. A. Edwards, *A Theology of Q*, pp. 44-57; idem, "Christian Prophecy and the Q Tradition," pp. 119-126; idem, "An Approach to a Theology of Q," pp. 247-269. The characteristics of the prophetic speech of members of this community are summarized by S. Schulz, *Spruchquelle*, pp. 57-65. See also G. Schille, *Das vorsynoptische Judenchristentum* (1970).

151. S. Schulz, *Spruchquelle*, pp. 34, 65.

152. P. Hoffmann, *Studien zur Theologie der Logienquelle*, pp. 236ff., 312ff., 329ff.; cf. the review by D. E. Aune, *CBQ* 35 (1973), 93-95.

153. R. A. Edwards, *A Theology of Q*, pp. 99-100; F. W. Beare, "The Mission of the Disciples," pp. 1-13.

154. S. Schulz, *Spruchquelle*, pp. 57-65.

155. G. Theissen, "Wanderradikalismus," pp. 245-271.

156. See below, pp. 242-44.

157. G. Theissen, "Wanderradikalismus," pp. 264ff.

158. Ibid., p. 256.

159. The more important recent studies are referred to by J. D. Kingsbury, *Matthew: Structure, Christology, Kingdom*.

160. E. Meyer, *Ursprung und Anfänge des Urchristentums*, I, 143; É. Cothenet, "Les prophètes chrétiens dans l'Evangile selon saint Matthieu," pp. 293-99.

161. A. Sand, *Das Gesetz und die Propheten*, pp. 171-72; P. Minear, "False Prophecy," pp. 76ff.

162. E. Schweizer, *Matthäus und seine Gemeinde*, pp. 140-41; É. Cothenet, "Les prophètes chrétiens dans l'Évangile selon Matthieu," pp. 299ff.; G. Barth, "Matthew's Understanding of the Law," pp. 73-75; R. Hummel, *Die Auseinandersetzung zwischen Kirche und Judentum*, p. 27.

163. P. Minear, "False Prophecy," p. 80; E. Schweizer, *Matthäus und seine Gemeinde*, pp. 140-48. J. D. Kingsbury has recently claimed that E. Schweizer has depicted Matthew's entire community as a group of Christians living a life parallel to that of Jesus, i.e. wandering

charismatic prophets ("The Verb *Akolouthein*," pp. 62-63). Kingsbury effectively argues that the Matthean community is a well-to-do urban church which is not heavily involved in healing activity. Yet it appears, contra Kingsbury, that Schweizer does not argue that the *entire* Matthean community was not domiciled, i.e. "largely itinerant in character" (as Kingsbury claims in "The Verb *Akolouthein*," p. 64 n. 44), since Schweizer distinguishes leaders (prophets, scribes, "the righteous") from the community at large (E. Schweizer, *Matthäus und seine Gemeinde*, p. 160). It is clear from his discussion of the prophets (pp. 140-48) that Schweizer thinks that there were prophets in the Matthean community (Matt. 23:34; 10:41), and that they, in addition to other groups, served the community. It was the prophets, more than others, who literally embodied the ascetic community ideals of homelessness, lack of family ties, and the forsaking of wealth and property (p. 143). In conversation with Prof. Kingsbury he and I concluded that Schweizer himself presented his views in an inconsistent and confusing manner in *Matthäus und seine Gemeinde*.

164. F. Cumont, *Oriental Religions*, pp. 27-28; V. Turner, *Ritual Process*, p. 98.

165. The interrelationship of structure and communitas (i.e. the absence of structure) in human society is the subject of a provocative study by V. Turner, *Ritual Process*.

166. The problem of apostolic authority is dealt with in a recent study of J. H. Schütz, *Paul and the Anatomy of Apostolic Authority*, though not very successfully. Schütz is primarily concerned with the theological basis of Paul's authority, yet it appears that he mixes that issue with sociological issues.

167. The model used for the following analysis is that proposed by M. Douglas, *Natural Symbols*.

168. G. Friedrich, *TDNT*, VI, 849; D. Hill, "Prophecy and Prophets," p. 410. This view is disputed by G. Dautzenberg, *Urchristliche Prophetie*, pp. 126-148.

169. Two of the more recent studies on this problem are J. L. Crenshaw, *Prophetic Conflict*, and S. J. DeVries, *Prophet against Prophet*. On this subject see above, pp. 87-88.

170. According to S. J. DeVries, *Prophet against Prophet*, p. 150: "Prophet against prophet was only a symptom. The root cause was king against prophet, requiring prophet to oppose king. Our prophet legends record a dynamic struggle to supervise the kingship." The root cause for the phenomenon of prophetic conflict in ancient Israel was *social* (i.e. competing claims to authority) based on an ideological stance (the prophet's understanding of God's will for his people). This subject is discussed within a broader context by J. Blenkinsopp, *Prophecy and Canon*, pp. 1-9, 96-123, 139-152.

171. See W. Bauer, *Orthodoxy and Heresy*, pp. 77ff.

172. W. Bousset, *Die Offenbarung Johannis*, pp. 204, 219; R. H. Charles, *Revelation*, I, 50.

173. A. Harnack, *Die Lehre der zwölf Apostel*, p. 102; L. Pernveden, *Shepherd of Hermas*, p. 150; R. J. Bauckham, "The Great Tribulation," p. 27; W. J. Wilson, "The Prophet Hermas," pp. 21-62. Hermas' prophetic status is emphatically denied by G. Snyder, *Shepherd of Hermas*, p. 10; H. Opitz, *Ursprünge frühkatholischer Pneumatologie*, pp. 111-15.

174. R. Bultmann, *Johannine Epistles*, pp. 61-62; G. Therrien, *Le discernement*, pp. 56ff.

175. This correlation is based on M. Douglas, *Purity and Danger*, who argues that the body furnishes a set of natural symbols for the social system. The body, with its head, can symbolize the centrally authoritative social system, and it is used for that purpose in Paul (1 Cor. 12:12-31).

176. The dominant view among scholars is that the false prophets condemned in Matt. 7:15-23 were promulgators of an antinomian heresy. Yet on closer examination it appears that Matt. 7:15-20 and 7:21-23 may not be referring to the same group. Matthew's polemic in 7:15-20 does not appear to be an intramural Christian conflict according to K. Stendahl, *School of St. Matthew*, p. xii. D. Hill, "False Prophets and Charismatics," pp. 327-348, argues that the false prophets of Matt. 7:15 are the Pharisaic opponents of the Matthean community. In spite of Hill's careful marshalling of the arguments, the false prophets described in Matthew still appear to me to be Christian opponents of the evangelist and his school.

177. M. E. Boring, "The Paucity of Sayings in Mark," pp. 371-77.

178. Paul also alludes to the process of prophetic evaluation in 2 Thess. 2:1-2; 1 Cor. 2:6-16; 12:1-3; 14:37-38; Rom. 12:6.

179. One of the better recent discussions of this passage is that by G. Therrien, *Le discernement*, pp. 72-79; see also G. Dautzenberg, *Urchristliche Prophetie*, pp. 129-132.

180. G. Therrien, *La discernement*, p. 73, and the references there cited. Cf. faith, hope, love (1 Thess. 1:3); power, Spirit, assurance (1:5); error, uncleanness, guile (2:4).

181. The interpretation of 1 Thess. 5:19-20 here presented follows that of W. C. van Unnik, " 'Den Geist löschet nicht aus,' " pp. 255-269.

182. In Paul the noun *prophēteia* can refer both to the gift of prophecy (Rom. 12:6; 1 Cor. 12:10; 13:2; 14:22) and to the utterance of a prophet (1 Cor. 14:6; cf. 1 Tim. 1:18; 4:14). In 1 Thess. 5:20 the latter meaning is probable, though the former is also possible (G. Friedrich, *TDNT*, VI, 830; G. Therrien, *Le discernement*, p. 74).

183. G. Therrien, *Le discernement*, pp. 75-79; the author places the notion of "testing" or "discernment" within the broad significance which it has in the Pauline letters.

184. G. Dautzenberg, *Urchristliche Prophetie*, p. 132.

185. W. Grudem, "A Response to Gerhard Dautzenberg," pp. 256-58, is unnecessarily skeptical about the connection between 1 Cor. 12:10 and 14:29.

186. C. K. Barrett, *The First Epistle to the Corinthians*, p. 286; J. Moffatt, *The First Epistle of Paul to the Corinthians*, p. 182; W. F. Orr and A. Walther, *I Corinthians*, p. 282; A. Robertson and A. Plummer, *I Corinthians*, p. 267.

187. G. Dautzenberg, *Urchristliche Prophetie*, pp. 122-148. Dautzenberg understands the phrase *diakrisis pneumatōn* in 1 Cor. 12:10 to mean "*interpretation* of revelations of the Spirit" (*Deuttung von Geistesoffenbarungen*), a form of charismatic speech which specialized in the interpretation of prophetic revelations. The background for this view is early Judaism, which the author shows exhibits a consistent emphasis on the interpretation of earlier revelations (pp. 43-121). Recently Dautzenberg's interpretation of *diakrisis pneumatōn* has been subject to a point-by-point critique which has shown it to be unfounded (W. Grudem, "A Response to Gerhard Dautzenberg," pp. 253-270). The major weakness with Dautzenberg's proposal is that early Christian prophetic utterances do not appear to have required the specialized intervention of a charismatic interpreter.

188. G. Dautzenberg, *Urchristliche Prophetie*, pp. 135-142, argues for this interpretation at great length and, I think, successfully.

189. Liddell-Scott-Jones, *Greek-English Lexicon*, p. 399.

190. J. D. G. Dunn, *Jesus and the Spirit*, pp. 233-36, esp. p. 236: "To sum up, 'discerning of spirits' is to be understood as *evaluation of prophetic utterances, an investigating and interpreting which throws light on their source and their significance.* "

191. Here I follow K. Maly, "1 Kor 12,1-3, eine Regel zur Unterscheidung der Geister?" pp. 82-85, whose interpretation of this passage is also followed closely by G. Dautzenberg, *Urchristliche Prophetie*, pp. 143-46.

192. K. Maly, *Mündige Gemeinde*, p. 244.

193. G. Dautzenberg, *Urchristliche Prophetie*, pp. 257-273, argues that 1 Cor. 14:33b-36 is a post-Pauline interpolation, and that the statement which we have just quoted from 1 Cor. 14:37-38 belongs with that interpolation (p. 297). Whether or not 1 Cor. 14:33b-36 belongs in its present position (the basic problem is the apparent contradiction between this section and 1 Cor. 11:5), the problem is determining the extent of the section which Paul refers to as a command of the Lord in 1 Cor. 14:37. Does it refer only to 1 Cor. 14:33b-36 (here we assume, with J. Lindblom, *Gesichte und Offenbarungen*, p. 140, that the contradiction with 1 Cor. 11:5 is only apparent), or to the larger section composed of 1 Cor. 14:26ff., or to the entire section on spiritual gifts in 1 Cor. 12-14 (J. Lindblom, *Gesichte und Offenbarungen*, p. 137, opts for this last possibility).

194. H. Greeven, "Propheten, Lehrer, Vorsteher," pp. 11-12, sees 1 Cor. 14:37 as an

example of testing the utterance of a Christian prophet, as does G. P. Wetter, "Damascus-vision," p. 87.

195. See above, n. 36.

196. One example is the anonymous prophetic oracle delivered to the Jerusalem church warning them to flee to Pella (Eusebius *Hist. eccl.* iii.5.3; Epiphanius *Haer.* xxix.7; xxx.2; *De mens. et pond.* xv.2-5); see the discussion of this oracle below, pp. 311-12.

197. This view has been expressed by M. E. Boring, "Christian Prophets," p. 59; E. Käsemann, "Sentences of Holy Law," p. 74. E. E. Ellis, "The Role of the Christian Prophet in Acts," pp. 57, 61 (=*Prophecy and Hermeneutic,* pp. 132, 137), thinks that the apostolic decree of Acts 15 was essentially a prophetic utterance. Although that view cannot be substantiated, there is no doubt that the formulation and promulgation of the apostolic decree is closely associated with prophetic activity.

198. See below, pp. 248-262.

199. This view is opposed to that of J. D. G. Dunn, "Prophetic Utterances," p. 185: "Of the first-generation Christians no one appears to have more clearly grasped the danger of an inspiration whose source was demonic and whose utterance could not be trusted than Paul." In a more general vein Dunn observes (p. 183): "Since other spiritual forces were recognized to be at work and could be the inspiration behind a prophetic word, consequently *no* prophecy could command acceptance in and of itself, and *all* prophecy has to be subjected to scrutiny and tested." These statements are not at all supported by the evidence.

200. See also Ps.-Cor. ad Paul 3; Clementine Recognitions iv.21; *Hom.* ii.6-11; Eusebius *Hist. eccl.* v.16.16 (a special commission examined Maximilla); Tertullian *Adv. Marc.* i.21.6; *De anima* ix.4.

201. The more important recent studies on this passage include: W. D. Davies, *Sermon on the Mount,* pp. 199ff.; É. Cothenet, "Les prophètes chrétiens dans l'Evangile selon saint Matthieu," pp. 281-308; H.-T. Wrege, *Die Überlieferungsgeschichte der Bergpredigt,* pp. 136-152; D. Hill, "False Prophets and Charismatics," pp. 327-348 (includes an excellent review of the literature); M. Krämer, "Hütet euch vor den falschen Propheten," pp. 349-377.

202. J. Reiling, *Hermas and Christian Prophecy,* p. 8; this is clear from the phrase *hoitines erchontai pros hymas.*

203. This is the view of O Böcher, "Wölfe in Schafspelzen," pp. 405-426.

204. The view that the false prophets of Matthew are Gnostic heretics is discussed and refuted by W. D. Davies, *Sermon on the Mount,* pp. 199ff. The Zealot theory has been criticized by D. Hill, "False Prophets and Charismatics," pp. 329-333. Hill himself proposes that Matthew has two groups in view, the false prophets of Matt. 7:15 (whom he identifies with Pharisees, though I think incorrectly) and the charismatics of Matt. 7:22-23 (pp. 340-48).

205. See above, nn. 162, 163.

206. Matthew's use of *anomia* is discussed by W. D. Davies, *Sermon on the Mount,* pp. 202-206; he concludes that its legal connotation cannot be pressed, and that it merely signifies sin in a general sense. D. Hill, "False Prophets and Charismatics," pp. 333-340, critiques and rejects the antinomian hypothesis.

207. R. Bultmann, *The Johannine Epistles,* pp. 61-62; G. Therrien, *Le discernement,* pp. 56ff.

208. See the excellent discussion in I. H. Marshall, *The Epistles of John,* pp. 14-22.

209. H. C. C. Cavallin, "The False Teachers," pp. 263-270, has made a vain attempt to equate the false teachers of 2 Pet. 2:1 with false prophets.

210. The term "false prophet" as used here does not imply that the apostles depicted in the Didache functioned as prophets; rather, the term "false prophet" is used here as a general term for a charlatan; cf. J.-P. Audet, *La Didache,* p. 205 n. 2.

211. *PGM,* I.103-112, describes how revelatory magic can be used to provide the practitioner with food and even fancy banquets.

212. The one exception to this is if a tried and true, i.e. a certified, prophet performs a "cosmic mystery of the church" (*mystērion kosmikon ekklēsias*), as long as he does not teach others to emulate him (Did. 11:11).

213. M. E. Boring, "The Unforgivable Sin Logion," pp. 258-279.

214. The meaning of this obscure statement is debated (cf. J.-P. Audet, *La Didache,* pp. 451ff.), but the most accepted interpretation is that proposed by A. von Harnack, who suggested that a "spiritual marriage" was effected by the prophet as an enactment of the relationship between Christ and his church (cf. Eph. 5:32).

215. Most recently by S. Giet, *Hermas et les Pasteurs,* and W. Coleborne, "The Shepherd of Hermas," *Studia Patristica,* X/1, 65-70.

216. L. W. Barnard, "The Shepherd of Hermas," p. 32.

217. The most important study of *Mand.* xi is J. Reiling, *Hermas and Christian Prophecy.*

218. D. E. Aune, "Herm. Man. 11.2," pp. 103-104.

219. Apart from questions asked of the *angelus interpres* by apocalyptic seers, there are few instances of question-and-answer revelation schemas in early Christian literature. In its present form, Mark 13 is a prophetic speech of Jesus in response to a question put to Jesus by several disciples (Mark 13:4); see above, pp. 186-87. A less pertinent parallel is the response of Paul in 1 Cor. 12-14 to questions put to him by the Corinthians; at least part of the answer he regards as a "command of the Lord" (1 Cor. 14:37).

220. See above, pp. 85-86, 88.

221. See above, pp. 85-86.

222. Philo *De vita Mosis* ii.188-192; this form of oracular procedure is closely related to the question-and-answer revelatory dialogues between an *angelus interpres* and a seer in apocalyptic literature, both Jewish and Christian. See the discussion of the oracular dialogue (*erotapokrisis*) above, pp. 64-66.

223. See above, Chapters 2 and 3.

224. This distinctively Christian view, no doubt formulated in opposition to pagan modes of divination, is clearly articulated by Ireneus *Adv. haer.* i.13.3-4. (cf. J. Reiling, *Hermas and Christian Prophecy,* pp. 13, 64). According to H. Bacht, "Wahres und falsches Propheten-tum," pp. 249-251, one of the characteristics of Greco-Roman prophetic inspiration is that the initiative for prophetic inspiration is taken by man, and frequently through the use of magic. In Rabbinic Judaism, to prophesy or not to prophesy is the prerogative for God to decide, a view possibly formulated vis-à-vis magical revelation (J. Bowman, "Prophecy," pp. 307-308).

225. This has been discussed in detail by J. Reiling, *Hermas and Christian Prophecy,* pp. 41-48, 73-96.

226. J. Reiling, *Hermas and Christian Prophecy,* p. 31, thinks that the school scene in *Mand.* xi.1 serves only the literary function of introducing the *dramatis personae,* whereas it appears to me (contrary to an earlier view expressed in D. E. Aune, *Cultic Setting,* p. 180) that an oracular séance is being depicted. It is true, as Reiling has noted (p. 31 n. 1), that the opening scene of *Mand.* xi does not reflect what we know of Greco-Roman divinatory procedure.

227. Did. 11:12; Herm. *Mand.* xi.12; Asc. Isa. 3:28; Ireneus *Adv. haer.* ii.32.4; cf. Aristides *Apol.* 11.1. This subject, with numerous references to ancient literature, is discussed in J. Reiling, *Hermas and Christian Prophecy,* pp. 52ff.

228. E. R. Dodds, *Pagan and Christian,* p. 58 n. 2.

229. See above, p. 86 n. 34.

230. G. F. Moore, *Judaism,* II, 96-97.

231. See the informative note on this problem in D. Dungan, *The Sayings of Jesus,* pp. 12-13 n. 1.

232. For references see C. A. Behr, *Aelius Aristides,* p. 8 n. 12.

233. See A. Malherbe, *Social Aspects,* pp. 24-25; R. F. Hock, "The Working Apostle" (1974), a Yale Ph.D. thesis referred to by Malherbe on p. 4 n. 7.

234. The oracle of Amphilocus in Cicilia charged two obols (Lucian *Deor. conc.* 12), while Alexander of Abonuteichos collected one drachma and two obols for each oracular consultation (Lucian *Alex.* 23). More references are collected in J. Reiling, *Hermas and Christian Prophecy,* p. 54 n. 2. For a discussion of the wandering Greek mystagogues who taught and

prophesied for remuneration see D. Georgi, *Die Gegner des Paulus,* pp. 234-241.

235. Mantics were often suspected of pecuniary motives (Lucian *Demonax* 37; Aristophanes *Pax* 1050; *Aves* 959-9); free-lance mantics could usually be consulted for a price in the marketplace of Greek cities (Plutarch *Mul. vert.* 252e-f), and they were generally despised by members of the upper class (Artemidorus *Oneirocriticus* i. praef.).

236. Quoted from Hennecke-Schneemelcher, *NTA*, II, 485.

237. U. B. Müller, *Prophetie und Predigt,* pp. 31-37. By consigning the Testament of Job 48-50 (where the daughters of Job speak with angelic language, *tē angelikē dialektō*) to the limbo of *Hellenistic* Judaism, Müller thinks that the Greco-Roman origin of glossolalia in early Christianity is assured.

238. H. Bacht, "Wahres und falsches Prophetentum," pp. 249-251. Most of the points made by Bacht are reiterations of arguments advanced by early church fathers against the validity of Greco-Roman or heretical prophecy. The ecstasy of Montanus was attacked by the Anonymous (Eusebius *Hist. eccl.* v.16.7, 9); dependence on artificial means of inducing prophetic experience was condemned by Clement of Alex. *Strom.* i.21.135; the argument that God must take the initiative in inspiring prophets was advanced by Hermas *Mand.* xi.5, 8; Ireneus *Adv. haer.* i.13.3-4.

239. Of the five points which Bacht makes, the first is certainly valid, though there were no clear-cut behavioral features associated with the phenomenon of divine possession in Greco-Roman paganism. The significance of Bacht's point, however, is undermined by the consideration that *the presupposition of divine possession underlies all ancient theories of oracular speech,* whether Greco-Roman, Israelite-Jewish, or early Christian. Mantic frenzy is sometimes associated with inspired divination in the Greek world, but only commonly at a relatively late date (see above, pp. 32-34). The presence of bizarre possession behavior cannot simply be inferred from the use of such terms as *mania, enthousiasmos, entheos,* and *katochē,* where no description of possession behavior is found. Ritual frenzy characteristic of some mystery cults was not the same phenomenon as divine possession enabling individuals to give utterance to divine oracles, through the two were frequently associated. There is some evidence that means were used to induce prophetic experience, yet in local consultation oracles the media used were not intended to induce ecstasy but to put the medium into direct contact with the oracular potencies of the holy place. Magical means for securing oracles was certainly a dominant interest of the late Greco-Roman period, though it was certainly not the only means. Finally, that pagan oracles are only occasionally concerned with religious or moral values means only that divine revelation functioned in a very different way for the Greco-Roman pagan than it did for the Jew or the Christian.

240. For a very brief survey of scholarship in support of this view (which is also represented by the author) see U. B. Müller, *Prophetie und Predigt,* pp. 19-23.

241. See above, pp. 213-15.

242. J. Panagopoulos, "Die urchristliche Prophetie," pp. 3-4.

243. See above, n. 119.

244. This is well argued by D. Hill, "Prophecy and Prophets," pp. 401-418.

245. See above, pp. 205-208.

246. É. Cothenet, "Les prophètes chrétiens comme exégètes," p. 79; idem, "Prophétisme et Ministère d'apres le Nouveau Testament," *La Maison-Dieu,* 107 (1971), 29-50.

Chapter 9

1. Although this theory did not originate with him, R. Bultmann was the first scholar to assign a major creative role to early Christian prophets in the formation of the synoptic tradition of the sayings of Jesus. In his influential book *Die Geschichte der synoptischen Tradition,* with the *Ergänzungsheft,* ed. G. Theissen and P. Vielhauer, first published in 1921, Bultmann proposed that many of the prophetic and apocalyptic sayings of Jesus (pp. 113-138), as well as many of the "I"-sayings of Jesus (pp. 161-179), actually originated with early Christian

prophets (pp. 134-35, 176). The extent to which this seminal proposal has come to be regarded as one of the assured results of modern gospel criticism may be seen by consulting D. E. Aune, "An Index to Synoptic Pericopae Ostensibly Influenced by Early Christian Prophets." Bultmann was not the first to suggest the creative role of Christian prophets, however, as the references collected by M. E. Boring, "Oracles of Christian Prophets," p. 501 n. 2, demonstrate.

2. This methodological skepticism of form criticism is clearly articulated by N. Perrin, *Rediscovering the Teaching of Jesus,* pp. 15-53. Perrin discusses three criteria for authenticity (pp. 39-47): the criterion of dissimilarity (the earliest form of a reconstructed saying of Jesus may be regarded as authentic if it is dissimilar to the characteristic emphases of both early Judaism and early Christianity); the criterion of coherence (sayings of Jesus may be regarded as authentic if they cohere with sayings shown to be authentic by the criterion of dissimilarity); and the criterion of multiple attestation (sayings of Jesus may possibly be authentic if they are found in all or most of the sources lying behind the synoptic gospels). The criterion of dissimilarity, central to the historical methodology of most form critics, does facilitate the isolation of the irreducible minimum of authentic Jesus traditions. Yet the method has been justifiably criticized insofar as it is used to reconstruct the *characteristic* emphases of Jesus' message (M. D. Hooker, "Christology and Methodology," pp. 480-88; I. H. Marshall, *Historical Jesus,* pp. 201-203). For a careful review of the criteria used to determine the authenticity of sayings of Jesus see D. G. A. Calvert, "Authentic Words of Jesus," pp. 209-218.

3. N. Perrin, for example, certainly one of the foremost exponents of form criticism in America until his premature death in 1976, claimed that *all* of the Son of man sayings in the synoptic gospels originated in the post-Easter Christian communities (*Rediscovering the Teaching of Jesus,* pp. 164-199; *A Modern Pilgrimage,* pp. 10-22, 23-40, 57-83). In contrast, most German exponents of form criticism assume that at least a basic core of Son of man sayings are authentic (C. Colpe, *TDNT,* VIII, 438). This basic core is generally thought to consist of the apocalyptic Son of man sayings (H. E. Tödt, *The Son of Man,* pp. 222-283; A. J. B. Higgins, *Jesus and the Son of Man,* pp. 185-209; F. Hahn, *The Titles of Jesus,* pp. 15-42). Using the theory of the creative contributions of Christian prophets to the Jesus tradition, M. E. Boring has observed, "When these two phenomena are placed side by side, (1) that practically all extant Son of Man sayings are secondary, but (2) they occur only as words of Jesus, an apparent solution presents itself: they are the sayings of Christian prophets" ("Christian Prophets," p. 200).

4. R. Bultmann, *Geschichte,* pp. 134-35, 176. This view has been cogently expressed by N. Perrin, *Rediscovering the Teaching of Jesus,* p. 15: "The early Church made no attempt to distinguish between the words the earthly Jesus had spoken and those spoken by the risen Lord through a prophet in the community, nor between the original teaching of Jesus and the new understanding and reformulation of that teaching reached in the catechesis or parenesis of the Church under the guidance of the Lord of the Church."

5. R. Bultmann, *Geschichte,* pp. 134-35, 176; P. Vielhauer in Hennecke-Schneemelcher, *New Testament Apocrypha,* II, 606; J. Jeremias, *New Testament Theology,* I, 2; G. F. Hawthorne, "Christian Prophecy," p. 112.

6. D. Hill, "The Creative Role of Christian Prophets," pp. 268-69. This is a recent and comprehensive attempt to rebut the thesis that early Christian prophets made major contributions to the tradition of the sayings of Jesus.

7. V. Taylor, *Gospel Tradition,* p. 108.

8. F. Neugebauer, "Geistessprüche und Jesuslogien," pp. 218-228.

9. See above, p. 102. In early Christianity, however, we can point to the following *anonymous* oracles: Rom. 11:25-26; 1 Cor. 15:51-52; 1 Thess. 4:15ff.; Acts 13:2; 1 Tim. 4:1ff.; Jude 17-18 (cf. 2 Pet. 3:2-4); Eusebius *Hist. eccl.* iii.5.3.

10. The fallacy of this argument is the assumption that the *tradition* which lies behind gospels and apocalypses flows in separate channels.

11. D. Hill, "The Creative Role of Christian Prophets," pp. 269-270.

12. M. E. Boring, "Christian Prophets," pp. 107ff.; idem, "Oracles of Christian Prophets," p. 502. Boring is so convinced of that that he regards Agabus' attribution of his prophetic message to the Holy Spirit in Acts 21:11 as primarily due to the influence of Lukan theology ("Oracles of Christian Prophets," p. 508). K. Berger, *Die Amen-Worte Jesu,* pp. 117-124, presents evidence suggesting that the attribution of prophetic speech to the Holy Spirit was characteristic of early Christian prophecy.

13. D. Hill regards the prophet John as an atypical example of an early Christian prophet ("Prophecy and Prophets in the Revelation of St. John," pp. 401-418; idem, "The Creative Role of Christian Prophets," pp. 269-270), a view which I regard as fundamentally erroneous (see above, pp. 206-208). John's prophetic proclamation would have been accepted as such by the Christian communities which he addressed only *if his modes of speech were such that they would be recognized as characteristically prophetic.* Hill discounts the significance of the quotation from Odes Sol. 42:6 by making an artificial distinction between Christian prophets and inspired men (Ode 42:6, he claims, refers only to the latter). Hill's view of the Gnostic character of the Odes is not correct (cf. the review of the literature in D. E. Aune, *Cultic Setting,* pp. 171-72), nor is his acceptance of J. H. Bernard's view that the "I" of Ode 42:6 stands for believers generally (cf. R. Abramowski, "Der Christus der Salomooden," pp. 44-69). Abramowski underlines the *prophetic* character of the Odes in her discussion; cf. D. E. Aune, *Cultic Setting,* pp. 174-77, and idem, "Odes of Solomon," 435-460.

14. H. Weinel, *Die Wirkungen des Heiligen Geistes,* p. 83, correctly pointed out that the Spirit, God, Christ, an angel, or even a demon could be represented in the "I"-style of early Christian prophecy. In many early Christian oracles there is no indication of the identity of the speaker. In others, like the proclamations of John the Baptist and Jesus, the pronouncements are made under the authority of the speakers themselves. U. B. Müller, *Prophetie und Predigt,* p. 17, rightly objects that too exclusive a focus has been placed on the "I"-style of early Christian prophetic speech to the exclusion of other styles.

15. F. Neugebauer, "Geistesprüche und Jesuslogien," p. 224; V. Taylor, *Gospel Tradition,* pp. 107-108; J. D. G. Dunn, "Prophetic Utterances," p. 180. Some difficulties with this argument are discussed by G. F. Hawthorne, "Christian Prophecy," pp. 112-14. See D. Dungan's convincing discussion of the conservative manner in which Paul used Jesus traditions (*Sayings of Jesus,* pp. 100-101, 141-45). Paul, however, can hardly be regarded as *typical* of early Christianity in spite of the fact that he is so well represented in the NT canon.

16. See above, pp. 217-229; F. Neugebauer, "Geistesprüche und Jesuslogien," p. 226; D. Hill, "The Creative Role of Christian Prophets," pp. 273-74. Hill is in error, however, when he states on p. 274 that "honour and authority surely belonged to apostles in the primitive church, and they were witnesses to the ministry of Jesus: *another group, however important, can hardly have possessed the authority to speak in the name of the risen Lord and have such declarations accepted*" (italics added). On the other hand, G. F. Hawthorne also goes too far when he claims that what the prophet said was accepted by the community *"to be obeyed without question"* ("Christian Prophecy," p. 109, italics added). The view of J. D. G. Dunn, "Prophetic Utterances," pp. 183-88, is more balanced; he recognizes the authority of Christian prophets within their communities, yet insists that their utterances were usually tested by various criteria. For a discussion of the leadership roles of Christian prophets and the kinds of authority which they exercised, see above, pp. 203-211.

17. J. D. G. Dunn, "Prophetic 'I'-Sayings and the Jesus Traditions," pp. 175-198; idem, *Unity and Diversity,* pp. 192ff. In "Prophetic 'I'-Sayings" Dunn errs when he writes: "The implication is that the early churches were as suspicious of anonymous prophetic oracles as their Jewish forebears, and prompts the question, was there ever a stage when a mass of 'sayings of Jesus' were circulated without any concern as to who first gave them utterance?" (p. 179).

18. J. D. G. Dunn, "Prophetic 'I'-Sayings and the Jesus Traditions," pp. 193-96. Dunn's choice of the Q version of the Unforgivable Sin saying in Mark 3:28-29 and Matt. 12:32 par. Luke 12:10 (widely regarded as the product of Christian prophetic activity; see the bibliographical references in D. E. Aune, "An Index to Synoptic Pericopae Ostensibly Influenced by Christian Prophets") to test his argument reveals its lack of utility in discussing particular sayings of Jesus suspected of having a prophetic origin. M. E. Boring, who argues for the prophet origin of Mark 3:28-29 and parallels, does *not* argue that the earliest form of the saying produced by a Christian prophet contained the clause discounting blasphemy against the Son of man ("The Unforgivable Sin Logion," pp. 274-76).

19. See above, pp. 203-204. There are also numerous instances of early Christian prophetic sayings which are at variance with received tradition, hence the appeal to the legitimating force of divine revelation for support. One example of a radical prophetic utterance appears to be that of the prophetess "Jezebel," who is condemned by the risen Jesus, speaking through the prophet John, for teaching immorality and the permissibility of eating meat previously sacrificed to idols (Rev. 2:20), a practice which (under certain circumstances) is permissible for mature Christians according to Paul (1 Cor. 8:1-13; Rom. 14:1-4). Another instance of a prophetic proclamation at variance with ecclesiastical tradition is Hermas' announcement of a second, and final, opportunity for repentance (Hermas *Vis.* ii.2.6-8; ii.3.4; iii.8.11-9.10; iv.2.5-6; *Mand.* xii.4.5-7; xii.6.1-3; *Sim.* vi.1.4; ix.23.5; ix.24.4; ix.28.5-8; ix.31.3-32.5; ix.33.1), a singular emphasis which required the composition of the entire Shepherd of Hermas with its elaborate appeals to divine revelation to convince Hermas' audience.

20. Pausanias ix.23.4.

21. B. Snell, *Pindarus* (3rd ed.; Leipzig, 1959-64), II, frag. 37; A. Boeckh, *Pindari Opera* (Leipzig, 1811-19), II, frag. 18.

22. In an alternate version of the story, filtered through the rationalism of Alexandrian critics but appearing more authentic to many scholars (U. von Wilamowitz-Moellendorff, *Pindaros* [Berlin, 1922], pp. 279ff.; F. Schwenn, "Pindaros," *RE*, xx [1950], col. 1612; C. M. Bowra, *Pindar* [Oxford, 1964], p. 51), Demeter (or, more probably, Persephone) appeared in a dream to Pindar and he subsequently composed an ode in her honor. For references to ancient sources see C. M. Bowra, *Pindar*, p. 51.

23. Philostratus *Vita Apoll.* viii.31. (LCL translation with modifications by the author).

24. See above, p. 63.

25. Philostratus *Vita Apoll.* viii.31.

26. E. Fascher, *PROPHĒTĒS*, pp. 199-203; Philostratus *Vita Apoll.* iii.42; iv.1, 6, 44; vii.18; viii.26.

27. G. Strecker, *Der Weg der Gerechtigkeit*, p. 124 n. 11; O. H. Steck, *Israel*, p. 29 n. 3; P. Hoffmann, *Studien zur Theologie der Logienquelle*, pp. 164-171; D. R. A. Hare, *Jewish Persecution of Christians*, p. 92; F. Christ, *Jesus Sophia*, p. 120.

28. R. Bultmann, *Geschichte*, pp. 119-120, 163; O. H. Steck, *Israel*, pp. 50-51; J. Jeremias, *New Testament Theology*, p. 128; M. J. Suggs, *Wisdom*, pp. 13-29, 58-61.

29. M. J. Suggs, *Wisdom*, pp. 58-61.

30. M. Dibelius, *Formgeschichte*, p. 286.

31. Against E. E. Ellis, "Luke 11:49-51," pp. 157-58.

32. E. Käsemann, "Sentences of Holy Law in the New Testament," pp. 66-81. Throughout our discussion we shall translate Käsemann's phrase *Sätze heiligen Rechtes* with the English phrase "pronouncements of sacral law," which is more felicitous than "sentences of holy law" or N. Perrin's periphrastic translation "eschatological judgment pronouncements" (*Rediscovering the Teaching of Jesus*, p. 186).

33. E. Käsemann, "Sentences of Holy Law," pp. 66-68; idem, "Beginnings of Christian Theology," p. 86.

34. E. Käsemann, "Sentences of Holy Law," p. 76.

35. Ibid., pp. 77-78. In addition to Mark 8:38 Käsemann also discusses Mark 4:24; Matt.

5:19; 6:14-15; 10:32-33; 16:27.

36. For an indication of the widespread acceptance of Käsemann's proposal see D. E. Aune, "An Index to Synoptic Pericopae Ostensibly Influenced by Early Christian Prophets," under Matt. 10:32-33; Mark 8:38; Luke 12:8-9. N. Perrin, *Rediscovering the Teaching of Jesus,* p. 22, characterizes Käsemann's argument as "careful and convincing."

37. E. Käsemann, "Sentences of Holy Law," p. 68.

38. This point has been forcefully made by D. Hill, "The Creative Role of Christian Prophets," pp. 271-74. The inadequacy of Käsemann's argumentation is also admitted by M. E. Boring, "Oracles of Christian Prophets," p. 502.

39. Rev. 22:18-19 is an "integrity formula" which some commentators think reflects the prophetic confidence of the author (W. Bousset, *Die Offenbarung Johannis,* p. 460; E. Lohmeyer, *Die Offenbarung des Johannes,* p. 182). Some interpreters see this saying as a pronouncement of the risen Jesus (H. B. Swete, *Apocalypse,* p. 311; R. H. Charles, *Revelation,* II, 218; R. H. Mounce, *Revelation,* p. 396), while others insist that the speaker is John, not Jesus (H. Kraft, *Die Offenbarung des Johannes,* p. 282).

40. K. Berger, "Zu den sogenannten Sätzen heiligen Rechts," pp. 10-40; idem, "Die sog. Sätze heiligen Rechts' im N.T.: Ihre funktion und ihr Sitz im Leben," pp. 305-330.

41. The four types are: (1) *hos (gar) ean,* or *hos 'an,* introducing the protasis, (2) those beginning with *pas ho* with the present participle in the apodosis, or *pas hos (tis)* with a verb in the future tense in the apodosis, (3) *hotan* with the imperative or a demand in the apodosis, and (4) *ean* in the protasis with a command in the apodosis (K. Berger, "Zu den sogenannten Sätzen heiligen Rechts," pp. 16-18).

42. Ibid., pp. 19ff.

43. Ibid., p. 24.

44. K. Berger, "Die sog. 'Sätze heiligen Rechts' im N.T.: Ihre Funktion und ihr Sitz im Leben," pp. 305-330.

45. The discontinuity between oral and written tradition and the necessity of considering multiple settings for both have been emphasized by E. Güttgemanns, *Offene Fragen zur Formgeschichte,* pp. 70ff., 167ff. Perhaps the Germanic *Ordnungsliebe* (love of order) is partially responsible for the immense heuristic value placed on the careful analysis of oral and literary forms. J. Panagopoulos, "Die urchristliche Prophetie," p. 4, has rightly warned against forcibly fitting the forms of early Christian prophetic speech into the procrustean bed of existing form-critical categories. In my judgment U. B. Müller has done just that in his analysis of the prophetic speeches of Rev. 2-3 in his book *Prophetie und Predigt.*

46. See below, pp. 294-96, for an analysis of a closely related literary form, the "statements of reciprocity" of Ignatius of Antioch. M. E. Boring identifies the original form of Mark 3:28 as a pronouncement of sacral law, yet admits that there never was a form of the saying in which future judgment corresponded to present sin; he rightly observes that early Christian prophets were not slaves to formal patterns of speech ("The Unforgivable Sin Logion," p. 272 n. 26).

47. See the remarks of E. Schweizer, "Observance of the Law," pp. 226-27 n. 3.

48. See above, pp. 60-61.

49. I owe the suggestion that this speech fits the pattern of Käsemann's pronouncements of sacral law, complete with a chiastic pattern, to T. W. Gillespie, "A Pattern of Prophetic Speech," p. 79. The quotation is from Origen *Contra Celsum* vii.9 (trans. H. C. Chadwick).

50. Translation by the author. The connection between these two statements was suggested by R. M. Grant, *Early Christianity and Society,* p. 41. For an extended discussion of statements of reciprocity in the letters of Ignatius, see below, pp. 294-96.

51. N. Perrin, *Rediscovering the Teaching of Jesus,* p. 185, has commented on the presence of the pattern of pronouncements of sacral law in Rev. 3:5.

52. See below, p. 300.

53. See below, p. 304.

54. See J. M. Robinson, "The Formal Structure of Jesus' Message," pp. 91-110; the two-part structure analyzed by Robinson is discussed above, p. 166.

55. The basic arguments of Boring's 1970 Vanderbilt University dissertation, "Christian Prophets and the Gospel of Mark," were developed and incorporated into two articles, "Oracles of Christian Prophets," pp. 501-521, and "The Unforgivable Sin Logion," pp. 258-279. In basic agreement with Boring, G. F. Hawthorne, "Christian Prophecy and the Sayings of Jesus," pp. 105-129, sought to present an even more comprehensive case for the possibility that dominical sayings attributed to the pre-Easter Jesus arose in the post-Easter period through the activity of Christian prophets.

56. M. E. Boring, "Oracles of Christian Prophets," pp. 501ff.

57. Ibid., pp. 503ff.

58. Ibid., pp. 504ff.

59. Ibid., pp. 509-510.

60. M. E. Boring, "The Unforgivable Sin Logion," pp. 258-279.

61. Ibid., pp. 276-77. The elements which Boring claims are foreign to Jesus, all found in the second part of the reconstructed saying, are: the exaltation of the Spirit, the denial of forgiveness on theological grounds, and the use of the form pronouncements of sacral law. Boring's objections to each of these three elements are apparently based on the criterion of dissimilarity (see above, n. 2); i.e. each of these elements is a demonstrable characteristic of early Christianity and so cannot be characteristic of Jesus. Further, the denial of the first and second points to Jesus can also be based on a negative use of the criterion of multiple attestation, i.e. these emphases are found only here in synoptic tradition. I must confess a certain skepticism regarding the use of such criteria as reliable guides for determining the historicity of the various sayings of Jesus.

62. See the extended discussion above, pp. 164-65, as well as the brief rebuttal of the thesis of V. Hasler, *Amen* (who holds that virtually all occurrences of the formula originated in the speech of early Christian prophets), by K. Berger, *Die Amen-Worte Jesu*, pp. 153-163. Boring is correct in stating that *amēn* twice precedes the statement to which it is attached in Rev. 7:12 and 19:4 ("Oracles of Christian Prophets," p. 512), yet the *amēn* in both verses functions as a *response* to a previous utterance (K.-P. Jörns, *Das hymnische Evangelium*, pp. 85, 88).

63. Such blessing and curse formulas may have been integral to particular moments in early Christian worship (G. Bornkamm, "Das Anathema in der urchristlichen Abendmahlsliturgie," *Das Ende des Gesetzes*, I, 123-132), yet the attribution of such pronouncements to Christian prophets is sheer speculation.

64. See below, pp. 339-346.

65. P. Schäfer, *Die Vorstellung vom heiligen Geist*, pp. 21-26; J. Levy, *Wörterbuch*, III, 323-25; Strack-Billerbeck, III, 27ff.; E. Sjöberg, *TDNT*, VI, 381-82.

66. It is possible that the rabbinic view of the cessation of the Spirit from Israel was formulated as a polemic against early Christians who claimed to possess the Spirit (E. E. Urbach, "*Mty pśqh hnbw'h*," *Tarbiz*, 17 [1945-46], 1-11).

67. E. Schweizer, *TDNT*, VI, 397.

68. The antimagic apologetic in Mark, also found in Matthew and Luke, has not been seriously considered in recent gospel studies, with a few exceptions (cf. R. P. Martin, *Mark*, pp. 175-76, 214ff.). Surprisingly, it is not so much as mentioned in J. M. Hull, *Hellenistic Magic and the Synoptic Tradition*, pp. 73-86 (the brief section on Mark). Two important recent studies are J. Z. Smith, "Good News is No News: Aretalogy and Gospel," pp. 21-38, and M. Smith, *Jesus the Magician*, pp. 21-44. Among the more important earlier studies are P. Samain, "L'accusation de magie," pp. 449-490, A. Fridrichsen, "The Conflict of Jesus with the Unclean Spirits," pp. 122-135; idem, *The Problem of Miracle in Primitive Christianity*, pp. 85-118; and O. Bauernfeind, *Die Worte der Dämonen im Markusevangelium*. For further bibliography see D. E. Aune, "Magic in Early Christianity," pp. 1507-57.

69. Many such magical procedures are prescribed in the Greek and Demotic magical papyri from the first three centuries of the present era; see F. L. Griffith and H. Thompson, *The Demotic Magical Papyrus*; K. Preisendanz, *PGM,* papyri I-IV; cf. *PGM,* I, 1-2: "Ritual procedure: an assistant daimon will come who shall reveal everything to you clearly. . . ." The spirits or daimons of those who had died violent deaths were thought particularly susceptible to control by magical practitioners (Lucian *Philops.* 29; Tertullian *Apol.* 23.1).

70. A. Fridrichsen, *The Problem of Miracle,* pp. 85-118.

71. A number of other attempts to ascertain whether certain synoptic sayings of Jesus should be regarded as oracles of Christian prophets have either failed to demonstrate the prophetic origin of such sayings or have concluded that there is little reason to go beyond the hypothesis of the creativity of Christian scribes and teachers. In the Seminar on Early Christian Prophecy of the Society of Biblical Literature, active from 1973-77, first under the chairmanship of Prof. Boring and then the present author, a number of such test exegeses were attempted by members of the Seminar: M. E. Boring, "Christian Prophecy and Matthew 10:23," pp. 127-134; J. R. Michaels, "Christian Prophecy and Matthew 23:8-10," pp. 305-310; P. B. Mather, "Christian Prophecy and Matthew 28:16-20," pp. 103-116; M. E. Boring, "Christian Prophecy and Matthew 23:34-36," pp. 117-126; A. M. Hutchinson, Jr., "Christian Prophecy and Matthew 12:38-42," pp. 379-386; R. A. Guelich, "Early Christian Prophecy and the Sayings of Jesus in the Sermon on the Mount" (unpublished).

72. This general way of stating the case avoids the criticisms which have been leveled against two Scandinavian scholars who have proposed that Jesus taught his disciples, in rabbinic fashion, to memorize and accurately transmit his teachings. Among early Christian leaders, according to this theory, were specialists in the receiving and transmitting of tradition, including Paul, in a manner dependent upon rabbinic modes of teaching and transmission. See H. Riesenfeld, "The Gospel Tradition and Its Beginnings," pp. 1-29; B. Gerhardsson, *Memory and Manuscript*; idem, *Tradition and Transmission*; idem, *Die Anfänge der Evangelien Tradition.* This thesis, particularly as presented by B. Gerhardsson, has been criticized for projecting later rabbinic practices into the pre—A.D. 70 period by M. Smith, "Early Rabbinic Tradition," pp. 169-176. K. Stendahl, associated by some with this theory, has expressed the judgment that he finds the Riesenfeld-Gerhardsson theory difficult to project back into the ministry of Jesus (*The School of St. Matthew,* p. ix). D. Dungan thinks that Paul's manner of using the sayings of Jesus reinforces the Riesenfeld-Gerhardsson theory (*The Sayings of Jesus,* pp. 139-150). While the Riesenfeld-Gerhardsson theory is an attempt to emphasize the accuracy and authenticity of the synoptic tradition in opposition to the form-critical view of the creativity of the early church in the transmission process, our concern is simply the description of that process, of which memorization was certainly an important part.

73. D. Dungan, *The Sayings of Jesus,* pp. xvii-xxix, provides a brief review of the literature on this subject.

74. F. V. Filson, "The Christian Teacher," pp. 326-27; K. Stendahl, *The School of St. Matthew,* pp. 20-35.

75. M. Dibelius, *Formgeschichte,* pp. 8-34; V. Taylor, *Formation of the Gospel Tradition,* pp. 168-175. K. Stendahl, *The School of St. Matthew,* p. 19, is critical of this view and judges that "it is difficult to assume the Sitz im Leben of gospel material within the form of sermons in the primitive church and there are clearly great problems involved in the common view emanating from the statement 'In Anfang war die Predigt.'"

76. L. Gaston, *No Stone on Another,* p. 446; M. E. Boring, "Christian Prophets," p. 88.

77. G. Theissen, "Wanderradikalismus," pp. 245-271; the following summary is based on Theissen's views as expressed in this article. He has placed his theory into a broader context in *Sociology of Early Palestinian Christianity.*

78. On this subject see S. Fichter, *A Southern Parish,* p. 260, where the author presents a helpful distinction between "complete ideology," "practical ideology," and "actual behavior." The first, though unattainable, is what is striven for; the last is actual behavior, while the second is a compromise between the first and third.

79. The prophets of the Matthean community, according to E. Schweizer, *Matthäus und*

seine Gemeinde, pp. 140-48, 163-64, are similarly characterized as itinerant charismatics, though independently of Theissen.

80. The most detailed study of this subject is that of L. A. Vos, *The Synoptic Traditions in the Apocalypse.* While all the possible uses of the sayings of Jesus in the Apocalypse must be classified as allusions rather than quotations, Vos contends (quite rightly) that some uses of sayings of Jesus are more direct than others. He regards the following verses of the Apocalypse as reflecting this more direct use of sayings of Jesus: 1:3a (Luke 11:28); 1:7 (Matt. 24:30; both Rev. 1:7 and Matt. 24:30 reflect a conflation of Dan. 7:13 and Zech. 12:10); 2:7, 11, 17, 29; 3:6, 13, 22; cf. 13:9 (Matt. 11:15; 13:9; Mark 4:9; Luke 8:8; Matt. 13:43; Mark 4:23; Luke 14:35); 3:2-3; 16:15 (Matt. 24:42-43; Luke 12:39-40); 3:5c (Matt. 10:32; Luke 12:8); 3:20 (Mark 13:29; Matt. 24:33; cf. Luke 12:35ff.); 3:21 (Luke 22:28-30; Matt. 19:28); 13:10b (Matt. 26:52b). Vos observes that there is no evidence that John knew or used a written gospel, and that the more direct use of sayings of Jesus cluster in the first three chapters of the Apocalypse (p. 111). It is precisely here, of course, where most of the oracular material within the Apocalypse is concentrated. Later in his study Vos expresses the opinion that the sayings of Jesus were not increased in volume by prophetic activity, but that the prophet John used and adapted "the current sayings of Jesus as a mediatory means for the expression of his prophecy" (p. 224). Perhaps the longest list of possible allusions to sayings of Jesus in the Apocalypse is found in R. H. Charles, *Revelation,* I, lxxxiii-lxxxvi. H. B. Swete, *Apocalypse,* pp. clvi-clvii, records only those synoptic parallels which he regards as certain allusions: the phrase "the one who has ears, let him hear" (seven times in Rev. 2-3); 3:3 (Matt. 24:43); 3:5 (Matt. 10:32); 13:10 (Matt. 26:52); 21:6; 22:17 (John 4:10; 7:37). One of the more balanced discussions of this subject is by M. E. Boring, "The Apocalypse as Christian Prophecy," pp. 51ff. Boring compares the lists of Vos and Charles and concludes that only Rev. 1:3; 2:7, etc. (seven times); 3:3 (16:15); 3:5 represent sayings of Jesus used by John (p. 52).

81. See R. M. Grant, *Formation of the New Testament,* pp. 72ff.; G. F. Snyder, *The Shepherd of Hermas,* pp. 14-15 (Snyder has a list of references to words and phrases resembling those in the gospels on pp. 162-63). According to H. Köster, *Synoptische Überlieferungen,* Hermas probably knew the gospels, but there is no evidence that he used them.

82. See below, pp. 253-56.

83. C. Maurer, *Ignatius von Antiochien und das Johannesevangelium.*

84. R. M. Grant, *Formation of the New Testament,* pp. 99ff. Grant concludes that Ignatius knew Matthew and probably Luke, but that he did not regard them as "scripture" (p. 102). H. von Campenhausen, *Formation,* p. 118 n. 47, observes that Ignatius makes almost no use at all of the tradition of sayings of the Lord.

85. M. E. Boring, "Oracles of Christian Prophets," p. 503; idem, "Christian Prophets," p. 82 n. 3.

86. M. E. Boring, "The Paucity of Sayings in Mark," pp. 371-77.

87. In support of his position, Boring would have to argue (though he does not) that the prophet John was an atypical early Christian prophet, or that early Christian prophecy underwent profound changes ca. A.D. 70. D. Hill, "Prophecy and Prophets," pp. 401-418, argues that John is not representative of early Christian prophecy as it is known in the rest of the NT. For a refutation of this view, see above, pp. 206-208.

88. The fall of Jerusalem to the Romans in A.D. 70 is supposed to have been a major crisis in early Christianity, though Boring has selected that date because it coincides with the appearance of the Gospel of Mark. The problem with the thesis that the fall of Jerusalem radically affected early Christianity (popularly stated in N. Perrin, *The New Testament,* pp. 40-41) is that the event is hardly mentioned in early Christian literature (see J. A. T. Robinson, *Redating the New Testament,* pp. 13-30).

89. Evidence for an early dating of the Apocalypse (ca. A.D. 68-70) has been assembled by J. A. T. Robinson, *Redating the New Testament,* pp. 221-253.

90. J. Lindblom, *Prophecy in Ancient Israel,* pp. 239-279; see also above, p. 101.

91. H.-W. Kuhn, *Ältere Sammlungen im Markusevangelium*; J. Jeremias, *Eucharistic Words,*

pp. 90ff.; P. J. Achtemeier, "Toward the Isolation of pre-Markan Miracle Catenae," pp. 265-291; idem, "Origin and Function of the pre-Markan Miracle Catenae," pp. 198-221; E. Best, "An Early Sayings Collection," pp. 1-16; J. M. Robinson, "Logoi Sophon," pp. 71-113; R. Bultmann, *Geschichte*, pp. 347-355 (see bibliography in the *Ergänzungsheft*, p. 113).

92. If Christian prophets *always* prophesied using the first person of the risen Lord, then such hypothetical collections of oracles would *always* appear to be composed of sayings of Jesus. However, such prophets also delivered oracles in the name of the Holy Spirit, God, angelic beings, and in their own name using the third person singular.

93. See below, pp. 247-315.

94. On ancient Greco-Roman educational methods see H. I. Marrou, *A History of Education in Antiquity*; M. Nilsson, *Die hellenistische Schule*; F. C. Grant, *Roman Hellenism*, pp. 32ff. For Jewish and early Christian methods see B. Gerhardsson, *Memory and Manuscript*; idem, *The Origins of the Gospel Traditions*, pp. 19-24. The subject of education in early Christianity appears to be a neglected area.

95. J. Reiling, *Hermas and Christian Prophecy*, pp. 155-56; G. Dautzenberg, *Urchristliche Prophetie*, p. 302.

Chapter 10

1. See above, pp. 233-245.

2. N. A. Dahl, *Das Volk Gottes*, p. 270; E. Lohmeyer, *Grundlagen paulinischer Theologie*, pp. 200-208; M. Albertz, *Botschaft*, I/2, 121-24; L. Gaston, *No Stone on Another*, p. 445. In an article entitled "Is Paul also among the Prophets?" J. M. Myers and E. D. Freed list seven points in support of the view that Paul was a prophet: (1) He exhibits a relationship to OT prophets: (a) he has a fondness for them and frequently quotes them, (b) OT prophets are called "servants of the Lord," and Paul calls himself a "servant of Christ," (c) he speaks favorably of the phenomenon of Christian prophecy, and (d) much of his language has a poetic quality. (2) His call is analogous to OT prophetic calls. (3) He experienced a "wilderness period." (4) He was a visionary. (5) He was an intimate at the council of the Lord. (6) He functioned as an extension of the personality of Christ. (7) His discordant attitude toward ecclesiastical authorities parallels the anticultic attitude of some OT prophets. Not all these arguments have equal force, of course, and some of them are noticeably weak. The difficulty with this kind of argumentation (which we noticed above, p. 160, as applied to the prophetic status of Jesus) is that the image of the OT prophet formulated by modern scholarship is made the standard against which figures such as Paul are compared.

3. See above, pp. 202-203.

4. See above, Chapter 8, nn. 73-76.

5. On this subject see E. Benz, *Paulus als Visionär*, and G. P. Wetter, "Die Damascus-vision," pp. 80-92. Both treatments exaggerate somewhat, but on the whole the evidence is assembled and the implications nicely stated. For a refutation of the general position espoused by Benz and Wetter see D. Lührmann, *Das Offenbarungsverständnis bei Paulus*. Lührmann's discussion is seriously flawed, however, by a consistent distortion of the meaning of Pauline texts. See the review by E. Güttgemanns, *Theologische Literaturzeitung*, 93 (1968), 510-15.

6. This view is rejected, unconvincingly, by D. Lührmann, *Das Offenbarungsverständnis bei Paulus*, pp. 39-44, 73.

7. W. Bousset, *Himmelsreise*, p. 13; G. Dautzenberg, "Botschaft und Bedeutung," pp. 141, 154.

8. E. Benz, *Paulus als Visionär*, p. 21; G. P. Wetter, "Die Damaskusvision," p. 89.

9. E. Benz, *Paulus als Visionär*, pp. 12-15.

10. One can appeal to a number of other passages in the Pauline letters in order to demonstrate the frequency of Paul's revelatory experiences. In 2 Cor. 5:1ff. W. Bousset has suggested that Paul knows about the heavenly dwellings from his experience of ascent (*Himmelsreise*, p. 13). The frequency of Paul's trance experiences are reflected in 2 Cor. 5:13, according to E. Benz, *Paulus als Visionär*, p. 20.

11. The phrase *arrēta rhēmata* is derived from mystery religions according to H. Bietenhard,

Die himmlische Welt, pp. 166-67, followed by D. Lührmann, *Das Offenbarungsverständnis bei Paulus*, pp. 57-58. This is hardly surprising, however, in view of the close relationship between oracular injunctions to silence or oracular silence and the cultic silence enjoined by mystery cults. I intend to discuss this subject more fully in connection with Rev. 10:4 in a forthcoming commentary on the Revelation of John.

12. D. Deden, "Le 'mystère' Paulinien," pp. 416-17, has suggested three categories of revelation received by Paul: (1) doctrinal revelations (1 Thess. 4:15; 1 Cor. 15:51; Rom. 11:25); (2) precepts received by revelation (1 Cor. 9:14; 14:37); (3) personal revelations (2 Cor. 12:7-9; Gal. 2:1-2). In a very interesting parallel Asclepius reportedly appeared to Aelius Aristides, who grasped his head with his hands and asked him three times to save his friend Zosimus. Twice the god refused; the third time he gave Aristides the formula necessary to secure his friend's recovery (Aelius Aristides *Or.* 47.71).

13. J. Lindblom, *Gesichte und Offenbarungen*, p. 133.

14. E. Benz, *Paulus als Visionär*, p. 37, objects to the view that Paul had a simple inner awareness of the will of God.

15. According to G. P. Wetter, "Die Damascusvision," p. 86, "die Herrenworte (erhalten) die äussere Form der Orakelantwort." H. D. Betz, "Eine Christus-Aretalogie," pp. 294-303, has argued convincingly that 2 Cor. 12:9 exhibits the formal structure of the Hellenistic *Heilungsorakel*, and he furnishes a number of illustrative examples of this form of oracle. One of these examples is from Philostratus *Vita Apoll.* iv.34:

> Be of good courage,
> for the sea has given birth and brought forth land.

Two examples not cited by Betz occur in the *Sortes Astrampsychi* (G. M. Brown, *The Papyri of the Sortes Astrampsychi*, pp. 32ff.):

> You have been poisoned/ Help yourself.
> Your property is not to be sold at auction/ Do not fear.

16. On the form of the *Heilsorakel*, see above, pp. 94-95.

17. On the expository oracle, see above, pp. 59-60.

18. See above, pp. 91-92.

19. In Chap. 3 of *Der Apostel Paulus* H. D. Betz has attempted to demonstrate that 2 Cor. 12:1-10 is a parody on Hellenistic revelatory experience, and consequently of little value autobiographically for our knowledge of Paul's visionary and revelatory experiences. See the critique of Betz's thesis by A. Henrichs, *JBL*, 94 (1975), 310-14. Betz's formal analysis of the oracular form of 2 Cor. 12:9 is as convincing as his more speculative view of 2 Cor. 10-13 is not. Simply because Paul uses what appears to be personal experience for rhetorical purposes does not mean that such experiences were entirely concocted for literary reasons.

20. Here is a sample of scholars who hold this view: A. Schweitzer, *Mysticism of Paul*, pp. 172ff.; A. B. MacDonald, *Christian Worship*, pp. 21-22; D. Deden, "Le 'mystère' Paulinien," p. 410; P. Vielhauer, *New Testament Apocrypha*, II, 605; idem, "Propheten," *RGG*, V, 634-35; H. Greeven, "Propheten, Lehrer, Vorsteher," p. 11; F. Hahn, "Sendschreiben," p. 359; U. B. Müller, *Prophetie und Predigt*, pp. 224-25; M. E. Boring, "Christian Prophets," p. 56.

21. The most comprehensive study available is P. Fiedler, *Die Formel 'Und Siehe'.*

22. Ibid., p. 83.

23. Two good general studies on the concept "mystery" in the ancient world are G. Bornkamm, *TDNT*, IV, 802-828 (with an extensive bibliography on p. 802), and R. E. Brown, *The Semitic Background of the Term 'Mystery'*, with an extensive bibliography in the notes. In the OT, divine revelation in the form of enigmatical dreams constitutes an insoluble mystery (*raz*), until the proper interpretation (*pesher*) is revealed (cf. Dan. 2:30; 4:9). Similarly, at Qumran, members of the sect regarded themselves as living in the last days and they approached the biblical text as if it were filled with secret or mystical significance. On the charismatic exegesis operative within the Qumran community see O. Betz, *Offenbarung und Schriftforschung*, and F. F. Bruce, *Biblical Exegesis in the Qumran Texts*. On the transference of the type of dream interpretation found in Daniel to the *midrash pesher* exegesis of biblical texts

found at Qumran, see A. Finkel, "The Pesher of Dreams and Scripture," pp. 357-370; L. H. Silberman, "Unriddling the Riddle," pp. 323-364; K. Elliger, *Studien zum Habakuk-Kommentar,* pp. 154-57. Qumran texts referring to the prophetic mysteries in the OT that are regarded as fully understood by the sect include 1QpHab 2:1-2; 7:1-5, 8, 13-14; 1QS 11:3-4, 5-8. The phrase "I know a mystery" is used three times as a preface to the unfolding of a schema of future events in 1 Enoch (103:1; 104:10, 12; cf. U. B. Müller, *Prophetie und Predigt,* p. 131). In the NT the motif of the "mystery of God hidden for ages but now revealed" has been labeled the *revelation schema;* cf. 1 Cor. 2:7; Rom. 16:25-26; Eph. 3:5, 9-10; Col. 1:26-27; 2 Tim. 1:9-10; Tit. 1:2-3; 1 Pet. 1:20 (D. Lührmann, *Die Offenbarungsverständnis bei Paulus,* pp. 113-17; N. A. Dahl, "Formgeschichtliche Beobachtungen," pp. 3-9). Similar use of the term "mystery" in a prophetic context is found in Rev. 10:7: "the mystery of God, as he announced to his servants the prophets, should be fulfilled."

24. In Corpus Hermeticum i.16 Poimandres says: "This is the mystery hidden [*to kekrymmenon mystērion*] until this day" (author's trans.); cf. R. Reitzenstein, *Hellenistic Mystery-Religions,* p. 10.

25. The interest of the apocalyptic writers in cosmological matters can be at least partly accounted for in this way.

26. The parallelism of the first two lines of the oracle in 1 Cor. 15:51-52 is forced in a way not immediately evident in a translation. The probable Greek texts for those two lines is: *pantes ou koimēthēsomethai / pantes de allagēsometha.* Since in Greek the negative always precedes what is negated, by *pantes ou* Paul means (and should have written) *ou pantes* (N. Turner, *Syntax,* III, 286-87; cf. J. Weiss, *Der erste Korintherbrief,* p. 378). In order to maintain the parallelism of position between the two occurrences of *pantes,* Paul appears to have sacrificed syntactical propriety.

27. Note the number of tristichs in the salvation-judgment speech in 1 Enoch 1:3-9 (see above, pp. 119-120). The prophecy of Joshua ben Ananiah consists of two strophes of three lines each; the three lines in each strophe exhibit synonymous parallelism (Josephus *Bell.* vi.301; see above, pp. 135-37). See also the brief prophetic speech attributed to Maximilla the Montanist prophetess in Epiphanius *Haer.* xlviii.13.1: "The Lord of this work and covenant and promise sent me as its elector and revealer and interpreter as one who had been compelled willingly or unwillingly to learn the knowledge of God."

28. Note the title of the third part of U. B. Müller's study *Prophetie und Predigt:* "Prophetische Mahn-, Gerichts- und Heilspredigt in der Gestalt eigener Rede des Propheten."

29. P. Vielhauer in Hennecke-Schneemelcher, *New Testament Apocrypha,* II, 605; H. Greeven, "Propheten, Lehrer, Vorsteher," p. 11; U. B. Müller, *Prophetie und Predigt,* pp. 225-232; O. Michel, *Römer,* pp. 280-81; G. Delling, *Worship,* p. 30; M. E. Boring, "Christian Prophets," p. 56; K. Prümm, "Mysteres," p. 223; F. Hahn, "Sendschreiben," p. 359; B. Noack, "Romans," pp. 165-66; N. Hyldahl, "*Kai houtōs* i Rom 11,26," p. 233; *idem,* "Jesus og jøderne," pp. 249-250; somewhat critical is K. Drejergaard, "Jødernes fortrin," pp. 98, 101; W. Sanday and A. C. Headlam, *Romans,* p. 336. E. Käsemann, *Romans,* p. 312, describes Rom. 11:25-26 as "a particularly instructive example of a violent reshaping of Jewish and Jewish-Christian tradition." Yet he goes on to say (p. 313): "The reshaping of the tradition characterizes him as a prophet."

30. On this passage see E. E. Ellis, *Paul's Use of the Old Testament,* p. 123 n. 5, p. 140. O. Michel, *Paulus und Seine Bibel,* p. 281, suggests that Paul may have unconsciously blended the two OT passages, a not unlikely suggestion. While the MT of Isa. 59:20-21 contains the expression *leṣion* ("to Zion"), the LXX slightly alters this through the use of the more ambiguous preposition *heneken* ("for, because of"). This is of no great consequence, however, since it retains the sense of the original (C. H. Toy, *Quotations in the New Testament,* p. 158). There is a possibility that Paul has derived the expression *ek Siōn* from the LXX version of Ps. 13:7 (MT 14:7), but this would be mere speculation.

31. E. E. Ellis, *Paul's Use of the Old Testament,* pp. 139ff.

32. This division of the oracle into three stichoi follows the analysis of O. Michel, *Römer*, pp. 280-81.

33. B. Noack, "Romans," pp. 165-66; he is followed, so far as I can tell, only by N. Hyldahl, "Jesus og jøderne," pp. 249-250.

34. Cf. 4 Ezra 13:57-58; 2 Bar. 75:1-8; 1 Enoch 90:40; Dan. 2:20-23; 2 Chr. 20:18-19; Matt. 11:25; Corpus Hermeticum i.31; Josephus *Bell.* iii.351ff.

35. This idea is discussed in E. P. Sanders, *Paul and Palestinian Judaism*, pp. 244-257.

36. E. Käsemann, *Romans*, pp. 311ff.

37. One of the best surveys of the various theories on the possible sources of 1 Thess. 4:15ff. is found in B. Henneken, *Verkündigung und Prophetie*, pp. 73-98.

38. This position is espoused, in varying ways, by B. Weiss, *Biblical Theology*, II, 312; L. Cerfaux, *Christ*, p. 38; H. Holtzmann, *Erklärung des I. Thessalonicherbriefes*, p. 130. An important objection to this theory is that the term *logos* in 1 Thess. 4:15 should probably be understood as referring to actual speech (G. Kittel, *TDNT*, IV, 102; B. Henneken, *Verkündigung und Prophetie*, p. 85).

39. This view is particularly favored by J. Lindblom, *Gesichte und Offenbarungen*, pp. 132-33. On p. 133 he refers to "Christuskoinonia als Offenbarungsmedium."

40. This view is supported by B. Rigaux, *Thessaloniciens*, pp. 539-551 (a particularly excellent discussion), and K. Wegenast, *Das Verständnis der Tradition bei Paulus*, p. 109. The possible gospel parallels were exhaustively (and imaginatively) examined by A. Resch, *Paulinismus*, pp. 38, 459-460, 468, in support of his eccentric theory that both the gospels and Paul were dependent on a common "logia" source. More recently P. Nepper-Christensen, "Das verborgene Herrnwort," pp. 136-154, has regarded 1 Thess. 4:15ff. as a modified version of the saying also found in John 11:25-26. E. Peterson, "Einholung," pp. 699-700, suggested a close connection between 1 Thess. 4:15ff. and the parable of the ten virgins (Matt. 25:1ff.) who go out to meet *(hypantēsin)* their lord. In a different vein L. Hartman, *Prophecy Interpreted*, pp. 181-190, regards the passage as a Pauline interpretation and supplementation of one form of the eschatological discourse of Jesus in Mark 13 and parallels, which Hartman regards as a *midrash* on Daniel.

41. R. Steck, "Das Herrenwort 1 Thess. 4, 15," pp. 509-523, thought that 1 Thess. 4:15ff. was derived from 4 Ezra 5:41-42, a view which has been universally rejected. More recently the older theory that the passage has been derived from a Jewish apocalyptic writing no longer extant has been suggested by H. Koester, "Die ausserkanonische Herrenworte," p. 234, and P. Hoffmann, *Die Toten in Christus*, p. 219. Two very divergent reconstructions of the saying follow it back through a pre-Pauline Christian version to a Jewish apocalyptic version: W. Marxsen, "Auslegung von 1 Thess. 4,13-18," pp. 22-37, and W. Harnisch, *Eschatologische Existenz*, pp. 39-46. Harnisch thinks that a Jewish apocalyptic saying concerning the eschatological descent of the Son of man was reformulated by an early Christian prophet (pp. 40ff.), thereby combining this theory with the one which regards 1 Thess. 4:15ff. to be a prophetic utterance. Recent theories which emphasize OT allusions in 1 Thess. 4:15ff. include those of A. Strobel, "In dieser Nacht," p. 24, where impressive parallels between Exod. 19:17 (LXX) and 1 Thess. 4:14ff. are pointed out, and C. F. D. Moule, *Christology*, p. 42, who suggests that the passage alludes to the LXX version of Ps. 46:6 (MT 47:5): *anebē ho theos en alalagmō/ kyrios enphōnē salpingos*. In view of the sometimes intimate relationship between oracular speech and OT allusions in early Christian prophecy (cf. Rom. 11:25ff. above, pp. 252-53), the views of Strobel and Moule are not inconsistent with the oracular character of 1 Thess. 4:15ff.

42. This view has considerable scholarly support: T. Zahn, *Introduction*, I, 223-24; J. E. Frame, *Thessalonians*, p. 172; J. H. Ropes, *Die Sprüche Jesu*, p. 153; H.-A. Wilcke, *Das Problem eines messianischen Zwischenreichs*, pp. 131-32; M. Goguel, *Jesus the Nazarene*, p. 103; L. Morris, *Thessalonians*, p. 141; O. Cullmann, *Early Church*, p. 65; P. Schmidt, *Thessalonicherbrief*, p. 62;

J. Jeremias, *Unknown Sayings,* pp. 80-83; idem, *New Testament Apocrypha,* I, 88.

43. This is perhaps the most widely held view of the origin of 1 Thess. 4:15ff., and is held by W. Bornemann, *Die Thessalonicherbriefe,* p. 203; G. Lünemann, *Thessalonians,* p. 532; G. Milligan, *Thessalonians,* p. 58; A. Schlatter, *Die Briefe an die Thessalonicher,* p. 24; H. B. Swete, *Apocalypse,* p. 187; M. H. Bolkestein, *De Brieven aan de Tessalonicenzen,* pp. 119-120; O. Linton, *Pauli Mindre Brev,* p. 305; G. P. Wetter, "Damascusvision," pp. 86-87; E. Benz, *Paulus als Visionär,* p. 38; M Albertz, *Botschaft,* I/2, 124; W. Kramer, *Christ,* pp. 159-160; J. G. Davies, "Parousia," pp. 104-107; A. Schweitzer, *The Mysticism of Paul,* pp. 172ff.; B. Henneken, *Verkündigung und Prophetie,* pp. 88ff.; W. Neil, *Thessalonians,* p. 98; J. Baumgarten, *Paulus und die Apokalyptik,* p. 94; C. Masson, *Thessaloniciens,* p. 63; D. E. H. Whiteley, *Thessalonians,* pp. 70-71; C. J. Ellicott, *Thessalonians,* p. 75; L. Gaston, *No Stone on Another,* p. 448.

44. This view, which is essentially a refinement of that just mentioned, has been recently proposed by a number of scholars: E. Best, *Thessalonians,* pp. 193-94; U. Luz, *Geschichtsverständnis des Paulus,* pp. 326-331 (a very important contribution to the discussion); W. Harnisch, *Eschatologische Existenz,* pp. 39-46 (closely following Luz); U. Müller, *Prophetie und Predigt,* p. 224; F. Hahn, "Sendschreiben," p. 359; P. Siber, *Mit Christus Leben,* pp. 42-43.

45. J. H. Ropes, *Die Sprüche Jesu,* p. 153; J. Jeremias, *Unknown Sayings,* pp. 80-81; M. Dibelius, *Thessalonicher,* pp. 25-26; P. Nepper-Christensen, "Das verborgene Herrnwort," pp. 141-42; W. Harnisch, *Eschatologische Existenz,* pp. 41-42; E. Peterson, "Einholung," p. 682; J. Baumgarten, *Paulus und die Apokalyptik,* p. 94; U. Luz, *Geschichtsverständnis des Paulus,* pp. 326-331; P. Siber, *Mit Christus Leben,* p. 38. H.-A. Wilcke, *Das Problem eines messianischen Zwischenreichs,* p. 132, limits the quoted saying to 1 Thess. 4:15b on the basis of the *hoti,* which often introduces quoted material in the NT letters.

46. A variety of reconstructions of the saying are suggested by scholars: E. Best, *Thessalonians,* p. 194; W. Marxsen, "Auslegung von 1 Thess. 4,13-18," pp. 22-37; J. Jeremias, *Unknown Sayings,* p. 81; U. Luz, *Geschichtsverständnis des Paulus,* pp. 328-29; W. Harnisch, *Eschatologische Existenz,* pp. 41ff. (building on Luz); J. Baumgarten, *Paulus und die Apokalyptik,* p. 94 (accepting the reconstruction of Luz); P. Nepper-Christensen, "Das verborgene Herrnwort," pp. 142-43; G. Kegel, *Auferstehung Jesu,* pp. 35-36.

47. U. Luz, *Geschichtsverständnis des Paulus,* p. 329, correctly observes that the first-person plural is inappropriate in prophetic sayings; see our reconstruction of Rom. 11:25ff. above in that regard.

48. U. Luz, *Geschichtsverständnis des Paulus,* p. 329, referring to Rev. 14:13, substitutes "in the Lord" for "in Christ." While such a change is not impossible, it appears unnecessary. Luz is followed here by J. Baumgarten, *Paulus und die Apokalyptic,* p. 94.

49. Here I follow P. Nepper-Christensen, "Das verborgene Herrnwort," p. 147, and E. Best, *Thessalonians,* p. 194. Against U. Luz, *Geschichtsverständnis des Paulus,* p. 328.

50. Here I follow G. Kegel, *Auferstehung Jesu,* p. 35. H. Grass, *Ostergeschehen,* p. 151, claims that the "first"-"then" sequence is not temporal, but here I think he is quite wrong.

51. P. Siber, *Mit Christus Leben,* p. 38.

52. J. Jeremias, *Unknown Sayings,* p. 81, and W. Harnisch, *Eschatologische Existenz,* pp. 43ff., suggest substituting "Son of man" for "the Lord himself." Paul uses the phrase *autos ho* nine times, though in 1 Thess. 3:11 and 5:23 the phrase "God himself" begins sentences whose main verbs are in the optative mood in wish-prayers which are phrased in traditional liturgical language (so G. Wiles, *Paul's Intercessory Prayers,* pp. 30-31). Similarly, in 2 Thess. 2:16; 3:16, the phrase "the Lord himself" with aorist optatives in liturgical language occurs (cf. 1 Cor. 15:28; 2 Cor. 8:19).

53. W. Kramer, *Christ,* pp. 159-160, regards 1 Cor. 7:10 and 9:14 as well as 1 Thess. 4:15 as references to the *risen* Lord, and each of the connected sayings as utterances of Christian prophets. However, D. Dungan has convincingly demonstrated that, as freely as Paul quotes traditional sayings of Jesus, it is clear that the sayings in 1 Cor. 7:10 and 9:14 are drawn from gospel tradition (*Sayings of Jesus;* cf. D. E. Aune, *CBQ,* 34 [1972], 355-57). In contrast to Kramer, K. Wegenast, *Das Verständnis der Tradition bei Paulus,* p. 109, goes to the

opposite extreme of claiming that "the word of the Lord" in Paul *always* refers to traditional sayings of the historical Jesus.

54. H.-A. Wilcke, *Das Problem eines messianischen Zwischenreichs,* pp. 130-31. Such revelations, Wilcke correctly claims, are referred to by Paul as *apokalypsis* (Gal. 1:12; 2:2; 2 Cor. 12:1, 7; 1 Cor. 14:7; Eph. 3:3), *optasia* (2 Cor. 12:1), *arrēta rhēmata* (2 Cor. 12:4), or a *mystērion* (1 Cor. 15:51; Eph. 3:3), but never as *logos.*

55. The view of H.-A. Wilcke (see preceding note) is refuted in part by the following considerations: (1) We are arguing that 1 Thess. 4:16-17a is an oracle not originating with Paul but borrowed from another prophet. (2) Wilcke neglects to mention 1 Cor. 14:37, where Paul refers to a revelation given through him as an *entolē kyriou* (how different is this from a *logos kyriou?*), while in 1 Cor. 7:25 he can claim to have no *epitagēn kyriou,* where he presumably means specific traditions from the sayings of Jesus. (3) In 2 Cor. 12:8ff. Paul repeats a personal revelation by saying that *"kai eirēken (ho kyrios) moi."* It can hardly be denied that Paul would have thought of the logion in 2 Cor. 12:9 as a *logos kyriou.* (4) Personal revelations that Paul received and also mentioned in his letters are so infrequent and varied in terminology that Wilcke's argument loses its force.

56. J. G. Davies, "Imminent Parousia," pp. 105-106.

57. See especially the careful work of E. Peterson, "Die Einholung des Kyrios," pp. 682-702.

58. U. Luz, *Geschichtsverständnis des Paulus,* pp. 330-31.

59. Ibid., p. 355.

60. V. Neufeld, *Earliest Christian Confessions,* p. 44.

61. Ibid.

62. Origen *Contra Celsum* vi.28; cf. C. Jenkins, "Origen on 1 Corinthians," p. 30.

63. N. Brox, "ANATHEMA IESOUS," pp. 103-111, following W. Schmithals, *Gnosticism in Corinth,* pp. 123-130, and arguing against K. Maly, "1 Kor 12,1-3," pp. 82-95, who contends that the expression "Jesus is accursed!" is a literary rhetorical expression current in conservative Jewish circles. B. Pearson, "Did the Gnostics Curse Jesus?" pp. 301-305, has demonstrated that the gnostics did *not* curse Jesus, thus calling into serious question the interpretation of 1 Cor. 12:3 by both Schmithals and Brox.

64. This interpretation is supported by H.-D. Wendland, *Die Briefe an die Korinther,* p. 92; J. Weiss, *Der erste Korintherbrief,* p. 294; J. Alizon, *Étude sur le prophétisme Chrétien,* pp. 9-10; E. Schweizer, *TDNT,* VI, 423 n. 603; D. Lührmann, *Das Offenbarungsverständnis bei Paulus,* p. 29; H. Conzelmann, *1 Corinthians,* pp. 205-206.

65. Adapted from the marginal variant translation of the New English Bible; cf. H. Conzelmann, *1 Corinthians,* pp. 205-206.

66. See above, pp. 68-72.

67. See above, pp. 86, 140-41.

68. See below, pp. 270-74.

69. This is the view of G. P. Wetter, "Damascusvision," p. 87. J. Lindblom, *Gesichte und Offenbarungen,* p. 143, suggests that Paul is writing from the standpoint of his "Christus-koinonia," and that the preceding advice he has imparted was an articulation of his *revelatio interna* ("interior revelation"); he cites parallels in 2 Cor. 12:19; 13:3; Phil. 2:1.

70. Many scholars have solved the discrepancy by regarding 1 Cor. 14:33b-36 as a post-Pauline interpolation (G. Fitzer, *Das Weibe Schweige in der Gemeinde;* H. Conzelmann, *1 Corinthians,* p. 246; G. Dautzenberg, *Urchristliche Prophetie,* pp. 257-273. G. Dautzenberg goes further than the other scholars mentioned in that he regards 1 Cor. 14:37 as integrally related to vv. 33b-36, the whole of which he regards as a gloss (H. Conzelmann, *1 Corinthians,* p. 246, also sees a close relationship between v. 37 and the gloss in vv. 33b-36).

71. G. Dautzenberg, *Urchristliche Prophetie,* pp. 297-98, argues that the singular noun *entolē* (1 Cor. 14:37) cannot refer to a plurality of commands; i.e. it is not a collective singular. In fact, Paul and other NT authors use *entolē* as a collective singular referring to OT commands (Rom. 7:8ff.; 1 Tim. 6:14; 2 Pet. 3:2).

72. H. Kraft, "Die altkirchliche Prophetie," pp. 254-55; U. B. Müller, *Prophetie und Predigt*, p. 180; E. Käsemann, *New Testament Questions*, pp. 68ff.; H. Conzelmann, *I Corinthians*, p. 246; cf. p. 78.

73. See above, pp. 166-68.

74. D. Hill, "Prophecy and Prophets," p. 415 (Hill changed his mind in "Christian Prophets," p. 118 n. 32); H. Greeven, "Propheten, Lehrer, Vorsteher," p. 11.

75. E. D. Burton, *Galatians*, p. 311; H. Schlier, *Der Brief an die Galater*, p. 255 n. 4. In 1 Clem. 34:3 a composite citation from Isa. 40:10 and Prov. 24:12 is introduced by the phrase *prolegei gar hēmin* ("for he predicts for us"); all of Clement's introductory quotation formulas are tabulated by D. Hagner, *Clement of Rome*, pp. 26ff. Similary, *proeipon* is used in 1 Clem. 58:1 to refer to threats predicted by Wisdom against the disobedient. In the NT and early Christian literature, as well as in Greco-Roman authors, *proeipon* is frequently used in the sense of foretelling the future through a prophetic speech: Rom. 9:29 (followed by a quotation of Isa. 1:9); 2 Cor. 13:2; Acts 1:16; Mark 13:23 (Matt. 24:25). The verb *proeipon* is used to introduce another distinctively Christian prophecy in Jude 17 (cf. 2 Pet. 3:2); see below, pp. 288-290. For other references see W. Bauer, *Lexicon*, p. 711.

76. N. Turner, *Style*, pp. 87-88.

77. For the two-part structure of many of Jesus' prophetic sayings see above, pp. 166-69, (including pronouncements of sacral law and the eschatological correlative).

78. J. E. Frame, *Thessalonians*, pp. 128-29; H. Greeven, "Propheten, Lehrer, Vorsteher," p. 11.

79. E. E. Ellis, "The Role of the Prophet in Acts," p. 56 n. 4 (= *Prophecy and Hermeneutic*, p. 131 n. 8), suggests that *martyreō* seems to be a *terminus technicus* for an utterance of the Spirit (he refers to the following passages: Acts 2:40; 1 Thess. 2:12; Acts 10:42-43; 18:5; 20:21ff.; Eph. 4:17). The problem is that only Acts 20:21ff. (and possibly Acts 2:40) can be regarded as a prophetic use of this term.

80. For the oracular use of the oath formula in early Judaism and Greco-Roman paganism see above, pp. 115-16. In early Christian prophecy see the technical use of the oath formula in Rev. 1:2; 22:18, 20.

81. Although Paul frequently used the expression "through Jesus Christ," it is used with various verbs of speaking only three times: thanksgiving (Rom. 1:8), boasting (Rom. 5:11), and giving instructions (1 Thess. 4:2); only in the last case is it possible that oracular speech is involved. Elsewhere Paul uses the verb *parakaleō* ("request, implore") in such phrases as "I implore you, brothers, through the mercies of God" (Rom. 12:1); "I implore you, brothers, through our Lord" (Rom. 15:30); "I implore you, brothers, through the name of our Lord" (1 Cor. 1:10); "I Paul implore you through the meekness and gentleness of Christ" (2 Cor. 10:1); cf. Rom. 16:17; 1 Thess. 4:1. Using a different meaning of the same verb, Paul can say: "we command in the Lord Jesus" (2 Thess. 3:12); cf. 2 Thess. 3:6. U. B. Müller, *Prophetie und Predigt*, pp. 117ff., has argued that Paul used a stereotyped form of parenetic introduction consisting of the verb *parakaleō* (also *erōtaō*) and a prepositional phrase such as "in the Lord Jesus" (1 Thess. 4:1) or "through our Lord Jesus Christ" (Rom. 15:30; 1 Cor. 1:10), with the prepositional phrase functioning as a legitimation formula, just as the OT prophetic messenger formula legitimated prophetic speech (p. 118). Müller claims that "Paul has therefore preferred the form 'I admonish you through the Lord Jesus Christ' to the other prophetic introductory formula 'I say to you through the Spirit' " (Müller, p. 126). However, Müller's arguments are vitiated in the light of C. J. Bjerkelund's study *Parakalō: Form und Sinn der Parakalō-Sätze in den paulinischen Briefen* (Oslo, 1967), which carefully and convincingly demonstrates that Paul's *parakaleō* clauses are a stereotyped epistolary formula, not part of a parenesis form.

82. C. Roetzel, "Judgment Form in Paul's Letters," pp. 305-312; idem, *Judgment in the Community*, pp. 91-94.

83. See above, p. 97. We have designated this prophetic speech form as a "judicial

speech" *(Gerichtsrede).*

84. U. B. Müller, *Prophetie und Predigt,* pp. 117-130.

85. Ibid., p. 129.

86. Ibid., pp. 132ff.

87. Ibid., pp. 138ff.

88. Ibid., p. 139.

89. Ibid., pp. 140-174.

90. Ibid., pp. 175-214.

91. Ibid., pp. 214-233.

92. See our discussion of apocalyptic literature above, pp. 114-121.

93. Only at the very end of his study does Müller (vainly) attempt to distinguish the synagogue homily from the prophetic sermon *(Prophetie und Predigt,* p. 239).

94. See above, pp. 129-132, 154-56.

95. H. Patsch, "Die Prophetie des Agabus," pp. 228ff.; F. Schnider, *Jesus der Prophet,* p. 59.

96. See the discussion above, pp. 161-63, of the prophetic actions of Jesus. In Did. 11:11 the prophetic performance of a "cosmic mystery of the church" is regarded by a majority of commentators, following A. Harnack, as the enactment of a "spiritual marriage" by the prophets (H. Weinel, *Die Wirkungen des Geistes,* pp. 131-38; J. Lindblom, *Gesichte und Offenbarungen,* pp. 191-92 n. 51). John performs the symbolic acts of eating a scroll (Rev. 10:8-11; cf. Ezek. 2:8-3:3) and measuring the temple and the altar, an act symbolizing their protection (cf. Zech. 2:1-5). In Rev. 18:21-24 an angel performs a symbolic act and then interprets it in a manner reminiscent of Jer. 51:63-64. See above, Chapter 8, n. 214. For the gnostic prophet Markus and his followers sexual intercourse ("sacred marriage") symbolized the reception of the Spirit (Ireneus *Adv. haer.* i.13-21 is the sole source for the similar reports on the activity of Markus in Hippolytus *Ref. omn. haer.* vi.39-55 and Epiphanius *Haer.* xxxiv; see J. Reiling, "Marcus Gnosticus," pp. 161-179).

97. The extraordinary freedom allowed prophets is emphasized in Did. 10:7; 11:7, 9, 11.

98. On OT symbolic actions of prophets see above, pp. 100-101. The adverb *houtōs* is equivalent to the Hebrew terms, *kakah* or *ka'asher-ken,* both used to interpret OT prophetic actions (G. Fohrer, "Die Gattung der Berichte über symbolische Handlungen der Propheten," p. 107; idem, *Die symbolischen Handlungen der Propheten,* pp. 99ff.).

99. The pronoun *hode* was obsolete in Koine Greek, so that the introductory formula *tade legei* (Acts 21:11; Rev. 2:1, 8, 12, 18; 3:1, 7, 14), though found more than 250 times in the LXX, would have sounded archaic (G. Mussies, *Morphology,* p. 180; G. Thieme, *Inschriften,* p. 23; H. St. J. Thackeray, *Grammar,* p. 11; G. Rudberg, *Eranos,* 11 [1911], 177-78; E. Mayser, *Grammatik,* II/1, 74).

100. See H. Patsch, "Die Prophetie des Agabus," p. 230, and the references cited there.

101. Here, however, the formula is a literary imitation of OT usage, similar to the Christian additions to 4 Ezra 1-2.

102. See also Rev. 2:11, 17, 29; 3:6, 13, 22. In Rev. 14:13 we read: "Yes, says the Spirit"; cf. Ign. Philad. 7:2. The concluding formulas in the letters to seven churches in Rev. 2-3 are certainly modeled after the OT messenger formula (F. Hahn, "Sendschreiben," p. 366).

103. Early Christian prophetic formulas which mention the Spirit of God are discussed in detail by K. Berger, *Amen-Worte Jesu,* pp. 117-124.

104. See above, p. 56.

105. See above, pp. 60-61.

106. See above, p. 142. The Greco-Roman conditional oracle was often like a timebomb waiting to be activated. When particular events occur or when particular actions are taken, the prediction of the oracle becomes a reality. In ancient Israel, on the other hand, prophecies which operate so mechanically are unknown. Generally the prediction of OT prophets

(whether in terms of a threat or promise) is inevitably determined by God. At times, however (especially in Jeremiah), future threats may be avoided if those to whom the prophecy is directed change their behavior.

107. Here I have turned the indirect discourse of the text into direct discourse.

108. See above, pp. 217-222.

109. References to this famine during the reign of Claudius have been collected by J. Jeremias, *Jerusalem in the Time of Jesus,* pp. 141ff.; G. Vermes and F. Millar, *History of the Jewish People,* p. 457 n. 8.

110. E. Haenchen, *Acts,* pp. 62-63; J. Jeremias, *Jerusalem in the Time of Jesus,* pp. 142-43.

111. J. Jeremias has established the probability that 47/48 was a sabbatical year in "Sabbatjahr und neutestamentliche Chronologie," pp. 98-103; idem, *Jerusalem in the Time of Jesus,* p. 143, where he observes: "The famine must, therefore, have run the following course: Summer 47, the harvest failed; the sabbatical year 47-48 aggravated the famine, and prolonged it until the next harvest of spring 49." This is significant since B. Z. Wacholder, "Chrono-messianism," pp. 201-218, has theorized that eschatological movements in Palestine were consciously coordinated with sabbath years. While Wacholder certainly errs in describing Agabus as the leader of a messianic movement (pp. 213, 216), his theory would account for the association between a local famine and universal eschatological famine predicted by Agabus at precisely that time.

112. Famines were frequently predicted by OT prophets (Isa. 8:21; 14:30; Jer. 15:2; Ezek. 5:17; 14:13), and in early Jewish apocalyptic famine is part of the coming tribulation (1 Enoch 80:2; 2 Bar. 27:6; 70:8; 4 Ezra 6:22; Jub. 23:18; Sib. Or. iii.540-42), just as in early Christian apocalyptic (Matt. 24:7; Mark 13:8; Luke 21:11; Rev. 6:8; 18:8).

113. Rather than one universal famine, there appear to have been famines in various places at various times during the reign of Claudius. K. S. Gadd, "The Universal Famine Under Claudius," pp. 258-265, argues that on this basis the phrase "universal famine" in Acts 11:28 is justified.

114. E. Peterson, "La *leitourgia* des prophètes," p. 579; H. Kraft, "Die altkirchliche Prophetie," pp. 251-52; idem, "Vom Ende der urchristlichen Prophetie," p. 175.

115. H. Greeven, "Propheten, Lehrer, Vorsteher," p. 29.

116. So N. Bonwetsch, "Die Prophetie im apostolischen und nachapostolischen Zeit-alter," p. 420; J. Baumgarten, *Paulus und die Apokalyptik,* p. 51; E. Haenchen, *Acts,* p. 395; K. Lake and H. J. Cadbury, *Beginnings,* IV, 141-42.

117. E. Haenchen, *Acts,* p. 396; F. F. Bruce, *Acts,* p. 253; J. Lindblom, *Gesichte und Offen-barungen,* p. 183; referring to this passage and Gal. 2:2 ("I went up by revelation") are D. Lührmann, *Das Offenbarungsverständnis bei Paulus,* p. 42; J. D. G. Dunn, *Jesus and the Spirit,* p. 217.

118. Josephus is at least partially motivated by the desire to avoid the inference that God and man can have direct contact.

119. J. Lindblom, *Gesichte und Offenbarungen,* p. 186.

120. F. F. Bruce, *Acts,* p. 311. E. Haenchen, however, suggests such revelatory media as "inner voices, visions and dreams" (*Acts,* p. 485).

121. E. Haenchen, *Acts,* p. 379, thinks that prophets going about in bands is a literary creation of Luke based on OT models. Against Haenchen, the evidence suggests that early Christian prophets often functioned in groups for a variety of reasons and in a variety of settings (see above, pp. 198-200).

122. Acts 9:11-12; 10:10ff.; Hermas *Vis.* ii.2.1; iii.1.2; iii.10.6-7.

123. Cf. E. Peterson, "La *leitourgia* des Prophètes," pp. 577-79.

124. E. Dekkers, "*Prophēteia-Praefatio,*" pp. 190-95, argues that *prophēteia* in 1 Tim. 4:14 refers to the prayer *(praefatio)* accompanying the laying on of hands (cf. Acts 6:6; 13:3; 14:23). This interpretation, which is essentially anachronistic, is effectively refuted by N. Brox, "*Prophēteia* im ersten Timotheusbrief," pp. 229-232.

125. W. Lock, *The Pastoral Epistles,* p. 18.

126. C. Spicq, *Les Épîtres Pastorales*, p. 48, where both possibilities are suggested.

127. J. Lindblom, *Gesichte und Offenbarungen*, p. 184.

128. See above, pp. 57-58.

129. See above, pp. 68-70, 140-41.

130. See above, pp. 94-95, 117-18, 143-44.

131. See above, pp. 59-60; H. D. Betz, "Eine Christus-Aretalogie," pp. 288-305. Here is a further example of an incubation oracle with the basic features of the *oracle of assurance* (Philostratus *Vita Apoll.* iv.10): "Take courage [*tharsei*], for [*gar*] I will today put a stop to the course of the disease." The speaker is Asklepios.

132. Against H. Conzelmann, *Die Apostelgeschichte*, p. 106.

133. The phrase *epistas autō* (and synonyms; cf. 27:23-24) is a technical element in the narration of revelatory dream experiences (E. R. Dodds, *Irrational*, pp. 105-106). This device, found in both Israelite-Jewish and Greco-Roman traditions, is apparently based on the image of someone standing beside the bed or pallet of a sleeping figure (cf. Plutarch *Lucullus* xii.1-2; xxiii.3-4; *Lysander* xx.4-6; Pausanias i.21.2; Josephus *Vita* 42). J. Lindblom, *Gesichte und Offenbarungen*, p. 29, also suggests that Acts 23:11 reflects a dream experience.

134. See n. 133, and J. Lindblom, *Gesichte und Offenbarungen*, pp. 28-29.

135. See above, pp. 94-95.

136. On the significance of uttering oracles with a loud voice see F. J. Dölger, *"THEOU PHŌNE,"* pp. 218-223, and the discussion below, p. 292, on Ign. Philad. 7:1-2.

137. See above, pp. 68-70.

138. See above, p. 70.

139. See above, pp. 61-62.

140. L. Brun, *Segen und Fluch im Urchristentum* (Oslo, 1933), pp. 78ff. Punitive miracles are extremely rare in the NT. The gospels preserve no naratives of punitive miracles performed by Jesus with the single exception of the episode of the cursing of the fig tree (Mark 11:12-14, 20-25; Matt. 21:18-22). In early Christian apocryphal literature, however, the incidence of punitive miracles increases markedly (ibid., pp. 81ff.; W. Bauer, *Das Leben Jesu im Zeitalter der neutestamentlichen Apokryphen* [Tübingen, 1909], pp. 360-68).

141. See above, p. 92.

142. See above, pp. 148-152.

143. See above, pp. 148-152.

144. See above, p. 86.

145. See above, pp. 140-41.

146. E. Bevan, *Sibyls and Seers*, pp. 99-106. I feel somewhat uneasy about Bevan's judgment, however. My own impression is that during the Hellenistic and Roman periods stories regarding the occurrence of voices with a supernatural origin were on the increase.

147. See above, pp. 59-60.

148. This has been demonstrated by O. Bauernfeind, *Die Worte der Dämonen im Markusevangelium* (Stuttgart, 1927). Bauernfeind accepts the essential historicity of the demonic utterances preserved in Mark (p. 94).

149. J. Lindblom, *Gesichte und Offenbarungen*, p. 212; W. C. van Unnik, "A Formula Describing Prophecy," p. 94; D. Hill, "Prophecy and Prophets," pp. 401-418. All these scholars argue for the prophetic (as distinguished from the apocalyptic) character of both the author and his composition. One of the more recent commentaries on the Apocalypse, *Die Offenbarung des Johannes* (1974) by H. Kraft, views John in continuity with the tradition of OT prophecy, while his connections with Jewish apocalyptic are allowed to recede in significance.

150. J. Lindblom, *Gesichte und Offenbarungen*, p. 217.

151. Ibid., pp. 216-17; J. J. Collins, "Genre of the Revelation of John," pp. 329-343.

152. C. Schneider, *Die Erlebnisechtheit der Apokalypse des Johannes*; E. C. Selwyn, *The Christian Prophets*, p. 48.

153. J. Lindblom, *Gesichte und Offenbarungen*, pp. 206-239, has attempted on the basis of his interest in the psychology of revelatory experience to isolate the genuine visions from

those which are strictly literary creations.

154. G. R. Beasley-Murray, *Revelation,* p. 22.

155. H. Kraft, "Die altkirchliche Prophetie," p. 254; see above, pp. 114-121.

156. H. Weinel, *Die Wirkungen des Geistes,* p. 85, suggested that Rev. 14:13; 22:7, 16-17 were oracles. R. Bultmann, *Geschichte der synoptische Tradition,* pp. 134, 176, points to Rev. 3:20 and 16:15 as sayings of Christian prophets. J. Jeremias, *New Testament Theology,* I, 2, sees Rev. 1:17-20 as the utterance of a Christian prophet. This is just a sample of similar opinions, many of which will be referred to in the notes below.

157. P. Minear, *I Saw a New Earth,* p. 5; this analysis of the Apocalypse cannot be recommended too highly. It is written with the student in mind, and represents an exceptionally lucid and knowledgeable approach to the Apocalypse.

158. F. Hahn, "Sendschreiben," p. 363; A. Y. Collins, *Combat Myth,* pp. 5-8; W. M. Ramsay, *Letters to the Seven Churches,* pp. 35ff.

159. E. Lohmeyer, *Die Offenbarung des Johannes,* p. 40. Arguments for and against the "letters" as seven originally independent epistles later redacted when inserted into their present settings are summarized by W. Bousset, *Die Offenbarung Johannis,* pp. 234ff. The view that the letters were originally separate letters actually sent to their respective destinations is represented by R. H. Charles, *Revelation,* I, 37-47.

160. U. B. Müller, *Prophetie und Predigt,* p. 48.

161. F. Hahn, "Sendschreiben," p. 391; U. B. Müller, *Prophetie und Predigt,* pp. 101ff.; A. Feuillet, *Apocalypse,* pp. 48-49.

162. In many respects this analysis is dependent on the excellent study of F. Hahn, "Sendschreiben," pp. 357-394, though a number of modifications have been introduced. The strength of Hahn's analysis is that it is derived from the letters themselves and is not based on the imposition of external models (e.g. OT prophetic forms).

163. The messenger formula and the commissioning formula, which are closely interrelated, are discussed above, pp. 89-90.

164. On the kinds of commissions associated with early Christian prophets see below, pp. 330-31. For an excellent general study of NT commission forms see T. Y. Mullins, "New Testament Commission Forms," pp. 603-614.

165. For a discussion of this *Botenformel* (though too narrowly conceived), together with the various christological predications, see F. Hahn, "Sendschreiben," pp. 366-370. R. Mounce, *Revelation,* p. 83, notes that virtually all of the descriptions and epithets of the speaker (the risen and exalted Jesus) are derived from the vision in chap. 1.

166. See above, p. 90.

167. U. B. Müller, *Prophetie und Predigt,* pp. 93ff.

168. Ibid., pp. 62ff.

169. Ibid., pp. 57-75. Müller's work contains a great number of stimulating observations and suggestions, all of which cannot be reviewed here.

170. There he finds instances in which a warning is followed by a conditional proclamation of salvation or judgment; cf. U. B. Müller, *Prophetie und Predigt,* pp. 90ff.

171. Ibid., p. 103.

172. M. Smith, "Palestinian Judaism in the First Century," pp. 67-81; M. Hengel, *Judaism and Hellenism,* I, 252, 311-12; D. Flusser, "Paganism in Palestine," pp. 1065-1100; this last article should be supplemented with M. Smith, "On the Wine God in Palestine," pp. 815-829; I. H. Marshall, "Palestinian and Hellenistic Christianity: Some Critical Comments," *NTS,* 19 (1972-73), 271-287.

173. F. Hahn, "Sendschreiben," pp. 357-394.

174. See above, p. 73.

175. This formula is discussed comprehensively, though in a basically unsatisfactory way, by L. A. Vos, *The Synoptic Traditions in the Apocalypse,* pp. 71-75. Its secondary nature in the gospels is emphasized by J. Jeremias, *Parables of Jesus,* p. 110.

176. V. Taylor, *The Gospel According to St. Mark,* p. 254.

177. See above, p. 90.

178. The following considerations confirm the appropriateness of this code name: (1) The original Jezebel was a pagan Sidonian whom Jeroboam married (1 Kgs. 16:31), and who killed the prophets of Yahweh (1 Kgs. 18:13). (2) The phrase "her [i.e. Jezebel's] children" (Rev. 2:23a) may be interpreted as a prophetic guild under the direction of "Jezebel" (cf. 1 Kgs. 18:19); see above, p. 207. (3) Just as the original Jezebel was responsible for introducing pagan practices and opposed the true prophets of God, so John the seer finds himself (as a latter-day Elijah) opposed by the false prophetess of Thyatira.

179. On the OT self-disclosure oracle see above, pp. 95-96, and these OT examples: Exod. 7:5; 16:12b; 29:46a; Isa. 9:9; 41:20; 49:26b; 60:16; Ezek. 6:10, 14b; 7:27b; 12:15a, 16b; 24:27b; 25:11b, 17b; 34:30; 37:28.

180. See above, pp. 166-68, for a fuller discussion.

181. While E. Käsemann made only one reference to the Apocalypse in his seminal essay on the pronouncements of sacral law (to Rev. 22:18-19), N. Perrin, *Rediscovering the Teachings of Jesus,* pp. 185-191, suggested that Rev. 3:5b confirmed the prophetic origin of the kind of pronouncements of sacral law found in the synoptic gospels and attributed to Jesus. Perrin did not notice (nor, I think, has anyone else) that the *deny* element of the confess/deny motif is found within a prophetic speech in Hermas *Vis.* ii.2.7-8: "Blessed are you, as many as endure the great persecution which is coming, and as many as shall not deny [*arnēsomai*] their life. For the Lord has sworn by his Son that those who have denied their Christ have been rejected from their life, that is, those who shall now deny him in the days to come." One of the more detailed discussions of Rev. 3:5b and its relationship to the synoptic tradition is found in L. A. Vos, *The Synoptic Traditions in the Apocalypse,* pp. 85-94. Vos holds that both Rev. 3:5b and the synoptic parallels represent independent witnesses to a primitive tradition of the sayings of Jesus.

182. F. Hahn, "Sendschreiben," p. 362; cf. W. Bieder, "Die Sieben Seligpreisungen in der Offenbarung Johannes," pp. 13-30.

183. P. Minear, *I Saw a New Earth,* p. 17.

184. Rev. 1:7 is often regarded as a prophetic saying (H. Kraft, *Die Offenbarung des Johannes,* p. 34; A. Y. Collins, *Combat Myth,* p. 5; E. Lohmeyer, *Die Offenbarung des Johannes,* pp. 12-13). Rev. 1:7 is certainly based on a very old Christian interpretative conflation of Dan. 7:13 and Zech. 12:10 (see the very careful discussion in N. Perrin, *A Modern Pilgrimage,* pp. 10-22), but should it be regarded as a prophetic saying? Although it is predictive, it is not attributed to a supernatural being, but appears to be a pronouncement of John himself, though it obviously has roots in earlier Christian tradition. That John's oracles are characteristically the utterances of the risen Jesus, God, or angels would argue against the oracular nature of the saying, yet because of its predictive character, it can be regarded as of oracular origin. The saying is introduced with the demonstrative particle "behold" *(idou),* which is used in many OT and early Christian oracles (cf. 1 Cor. 15:51; Rev. 2:10, 22; 3:8, 9, 20), but is not an infallible indicator of prophetic speech.

185. See above, pp. 64-66, and especially the notes, where many of the parallels to early Christian literature are mentioned.

186. See above, pp. 95-96.

187. *PGM* III.211; IV.1040; V.468; VII.285, 605, 760; XIII.1020, 1047; XXIIa.24; LXXI.3.

188. G. Mussies, *Morphology,* pp. 93-94.

189. In the LXX *ho ōn* is used of God in Exod. 3:14 and in variant readings found in Jer. 1:6; 14:13; 39[32]:17. The phrase occurs frequently in Philo (cf. *De Abrahamo* 121; *Quod Deus sit immutabiles* 69), and several times in Josephus; cf. *Ant.* viii.350. In Exodus Rabbah 3:14, the Palestinian Targum to Ex. 3:14, and the Jerusalem Targum to Deut. 32:39, M. McNamara finds the phrase "I am he who is and who was and I am he who will be" (M. McNamara, *New Testament and Palestinian Targum,* p. 105).

190. The many parallels are listed and discussed by W. C. van Unnik, "A Formula Describing Prophecy," pp. 86-94.

191. Pausanias x.12.10 (author's trans.); this oracle is briefly discussed by H. W. Parke,

Oracles of Zeus, pp. 159-161.

192. M. McNamara, *New Testament and Palestinian Targum,* pp. 101ff., claims that the divine name in Rev. 1:4 and 1:8 is not Hellenistic. Yet the Jewish sources which he used (primarily the Targums) are very late and may themselves reflect Hellenistic influence.

193. A Byzantine lexicon called *The Suida* (late tenth century A.D.) specifically states that the prophetess of Dodona began her oracular speeches with the introductory phrase "thus says Zeus" *(tade legei Zeus);* see A. Adler (ed.), *Suidae Lexicon,* II, s.v. *Dōdōnē.* In Plato *Alc.* ii.149b an oracle of Zeus-Ammon is uttered by the *prophētēs* of the god with the introductory formula "thus says Ammon" *(tade legei Ammōn).* In J. Lindblom's excellent study of the general use of the messenger formula in the ancient world (*Die literarische Gattung,* pp. 102-108), he mentions neither of these references.

194. The sense of this line is misconstrued by both the RSV ("If any one is to be taken captive, to captivity he goes") and the NEB in contrast to the AV. The author is probably alluding to the LXX text of Jer. 15:2, which accurately reflects the meaning of the MT and must be translated as we have done here; see H. B. Swete, *Apocalypse,* pp. 167-68; R. H. Charles, *Revelation,* I, 355ff. (for a discussion of the textual difficulties).

195. H. Kraft, *Die Offenbarung des Johannes,* pp. 177-78.

196. See above, p. 90 (on the proclamation formula) and p. 97 (on the introductory use of the proclamation formula in judicial speeches). For a proclamation formula used as an introduction to an oracle spoken by Zeus see *Iliad* xix.101ff.

197. G. R. Beasley-Murray, *Revelation,* pp. 22, 221.

198. In the OT the "angel of the Lord" is often a surrogate for the revelations and self-manifestations of God. In the Shepherd of Hermas there is a hazy distinction between angels, the Spirit, and Christ (*Mand.* xii.4.5-7; xii.6.1-3; *Sim.* vi.1.4; ix.23.5; ix.24.4; ix.28.5-8; ix.31.1-32.5; ix.33.1).

199. See below, p. 292, on Ign. Philad. 7:1-2; cf. F. J. Dölger, *"THEOU PHŌNĒ,"* pp. 218-223. In the Apocalypse the loud voice is only infrequently used to introduce oracular speech (18:2; 21:3).

200. This is the meaning of the loud voice in Rev. 1:10; 5:2, 12; 6:10; 7:2, 10; 8:13; 10:3; 11:12, 15; 12:10; 14:2, 15, 18; 16:1, 17; 19:1, 17.

201. H. Weinel, *Die Wirkungen des Heiligen Geistes,* p. 85; T. Zahn, *Die Offenbarung des Johannes,* p. 522; H. Kraft, *Die Offenbarung des Johannes,* p. 195.

202. R. H. Charles, *Revelation,* II, 18, has unnecessarily "restored" Rev. 14:12-13 to their "original position" after 13:15.

203. Unidentified voices abound in the Apocalypse; they come from the midst of the four beasts (6:6), from heaven (10:4, 8; 11:12; 12:10; 14:2; 18:4), from the temple in heaven (16:1, 17), and from the throne (19:5; 21:3).

204. For the tendency in early Judaism to use the term "voice" for "voice of *God,*" or as a surrogate for the name of God, see above, pp. 136-37.

205. On Greco-Roman oracular beatitudes see above, p. 64; on the expository oracle, see pp. 59-60.

206. J. H. Ropes, *Die Sprüche Jesu,* p. 143; Ropes cites Matt. 24:43 and 22:11-14, neither of which is particularly impressive. G. B. Caird, *Revelation,* p. 207, sees possible allusions to Matt. 24:43 par. Luke 12:39. J. Jeremias, *Unknown Sayings,* p. 5, sees no reason for regarding Rev. 16:15 as an allusion to a traditional saying of Jesus.

207. R. Bultmann, *Geschichte der synoptischen Tradition,* pp. 134-35; J. Jeremias, *Unknown Sayings,* p. 15; idem, *New Testament Theology,* p. 2.

208. R. H. Charles, *Revelation,* II, 49, recognizes this, but tries to relocate the saying at a more appropriate juncture (between Rev. 3:3a and 3b).

209. J. Jeremias, *Parables of Jesus,* p. 50.

210. The use of a past tense (here the aorist: *epesen epesen*) to describe a future event as if it had already occurred is found in the OT not infrequently and has been labeled by grammarians the *perfectum propheticum* (E. Kautzsch, *Hebrew Grammar,* pp. 312-13). This pro-

phetic perfect is also reproduced in the LXX, as one very early biblical exegete, Justin Martyr, had observed: "Now when the prophetic Spirit speaks of things to come as already having happened. . . . Things he fully knows are to happen he speaks of in advance as if they had already occurred" (1 Apol. 42.1).

211. For the technical use of the adverb *houtōs* (and the Hebrew terms which it translated) see above, n. 98.

212. E. Lohmeyer, *Die Offenbarung des Johannes,* p. 153, refers to this phenomenon by noting that vv. 22-23 are a "Lied im Liede."

213. See also Mic. 2:1-3; Isa. 10:1-4; 30:1-5; G. M. Ramsey, "Speech-Forms in Hebrew Law," pp. 53-57.

214. See above, pp. 74-75.

215. W. Bousset, *Die Offenbarung Johannis,* p. 429; J. M. Ford, *Revelation,* p. 311.

216. E. Lohmeyer, *Die Offenbarung des Johannes,* p. 156; H. Kraft, *Die Offenbarung des Johannes,* p. 245.

217. See above, pp. 92-93.

218. See above, pp. 74-77.

219. Two different speakers are indicated by the sequence *kai eipen . . . kai legei . . . kai eipen* (H. B. Swete, *Apocalypse,* p. 279).

220. See above, pp. 90-91.

221. See above, pp. 115-16.

222. See above, pp. 166-68.

223. T. Fornberg, *An Early Church in a Pluralistic Society,* chap. 2.

224. There is no evidence to support K. Donfried's view that the "prophetic word" in 2 Clem. 11:2 is directed against "spirit-filled prophets" (*The Setting of Second Clement,* p. 151), a view which he also regards as conjectural (p. 152).

225. This has been the subject of a special investigation by H.-J. Michel, *Die Abschiedsrede des Paulus* (1973), pp. 50-51, who discusses the genre of the farewell discourse at great length. He thinks that the prediction of Acts 20:29-30 could not simply be interpreted as a formal motif (pp. 82-83).

226. *Iliad* xvi.851ff. (Scholium ad Il. xvi.854); xxii.358; Sophocles *Oed. Col.* 1370ff.; Xenophon *Cyrop.* viii.7.21; Plato *Apol.* 39C; Diodorus Siculus xviii.1; Cicero *De div.* i.63; Plutarch *De def. orac.* 40; Vergil *Aeneid* iv.6.4; x.739; Plotinus iv.3.27; Cyprian *De mortal.* 19; Lactantius *Div. inst.* vii.12.27ff.

227. M. E. Boring, "Christian Prophets," p. 124, has described this as a "pseudo-oracle," though on what basis I am not sure.

228. R. H. Charles, *Revelation,* I, cix.

229. The phrase "in those days" is found in Jer. 33:6; 50:4, 20; Joel 2:29; 1 Enoch 92:8; 97:5; 99:3, 4, 5, 10; 100:1, 4; 102:1; 105:1; Mark 13:17; Matt. 24:19; Luke 21:23. "In the latter days" is found in Dan. 2:28; 10:14; Hos. 3:5; Ezek. 38:16.

Chapter 11

1. This is one of several references to "prophets" in early Christian literature in which it is difficult to determine whether OT or early Christian prophets are referred to. That this reference is to OT prophets is maintained by C. K. Barrett, *The Gospel of John and Judaism* (Philadelphia, 1975), pp. 52-53.

2. Ignatius as a *pneumatikos* is discussed at some length by H. Schlier, *Religionsgeschichtliche Untersuchungen,* pp. 140-152.

3. This translation and the following are those of the author.

4. H. Weinel, *Die Wirkungen des Heiligen Geistes,* p. 89.

5. T. Zahn, *Ignatius von Antiochien,* p. 268; H. Schlier, *Religionsgeschichtliche Untersuchungen,* pp. 140ff.; F. J. Dölger, *"THEOU PHŌNE,"* pp. 218-223. The phenomenon of the loud voice with which an oracle can be uttered can be interpreted by the speaker and his audience as a sign of possession. In the NT demons are described as uttering loud cries through their

victims (Mark 1:26; 5:7; Luke 4:33; 8:28; Acts 8:7; 16:17). H. Leisegang, *PNEUMA HAGION*, pp. 23-24 n. 4, compares Jesus' loud cries in John 7:28, 37; 12:44 with the cries of the Hellenistic prophet or oracle giver. Hippolytus *Ref. omn. haer.* iv.28.3 criticizes the magician who utters a loud harsh cry which is unintelligible to all *(mega kai apēches kekrage kai pasin asyneton)*. The loud cries of Jesus in John are also compared to the technique of ancient magicians by C. Bonner, "Traces of Thaumaturgic Technique in the Miracles," *HTR*, 20 (1927), 171-181. The phenomenon of the loud cry, however, can be used in such varied settings that no firm conclusions can be drawn unless the cry is part of a constellation of elements which recur in a pattern.

6. See above, pp. 250-51.

7. H. Thyen, *Der Stil der jüdisch-hellenistischen Homilie,* p. 85; M. Dibelius, *Geschichte,* II, 65.

8. This possibility was first considered by T. Zahn, *Der Hirt des Hermas,* p. 109 n. 2, but has been rejected (without good reason, I think) by others.

9. O. Michel, *Prophet und Märtyrer,* p. 59.

10. W. Bauer, "Die Briefe des Ignatius," p. 252, and H. Schlier, *Religionsgeschichtliche Untersuchungen,* pp. 146ff., interpret "water" in Rom. 7:2 as a reference to baptism. R. Bultmann, *Das Evangelium des Johannes,* p. 135 n. 7, and H. Lewy, *Sobria Ebrietas,* p. 84, see it as a reference to the Spirit.

11. R. M. Grant, *An Introduction,* pp. 50-51; idem, *Ignatius,* pp. 134-35.

12. R. M. Grant, *Early Christianity and Society,* p. 41, emphasizes the close relationship between the injunction in Polyc. 6:1 and the prophetic saying in Philad. 7:1. See D. E. Aune, *Cultic Setting,* pp. 123-24, 155, where the similarities between Ignatian statements of reciprocity and Käsemann's pronouncements of sacral law are discussed.

13. A short introduction to the Odes together with an extensive bibliography is found in J. H. Charlesworth, *The Pseudepigrapha and Modern Research,* pp. 189-194.

14. This subject is discussed in greater detail in D. E. Aune, "The Odes of Solomon and Early Christian Prophecy," pp. 435-460.

15. Many early Christian hymns have been inserted into various literary settings in the NT, however; but little is known of their original setting and use. Some of the hymnic fragments more commonly identified include John 1:1-18; Phil. 2:5-11; Col. 1:15-20; 1 Tim. 3:16; Heb. 1:1-4.

16. Recent research on the hymns of the Apocalypse suggests that, in spite of traditional elements within them (on this see J. O'Rourke, "The Hymns of the Apocalypse," pp. 399-409), they are primarily literary compositions fashioned for their present context by the author and not borrowed by him from Christian liturgy (G. Delling, "Zum gottesdienstlichen Stil," pp. 134-35; R. Deichgräber, *Gotteshymnus und Christushymnus,* pp. 178-79; and particularly K.-P. Jörns, *Das hymnische Evangelium*). H. Kraft, however (*Die Offenbarung des Johannes,* p. 102), has suggested that John used "prophetic freedom" in reformulating and transforming Christian liturgical traditions.

17. German scholarship has tended to categorize the Odes as "gnostic" (cf. most recently by H. Koester, *Einführung in das Neue Testament,* pp. 656-57), while Anglo-American scholarship has tended to regard the Odes as nongnostic (J. H. Charlesworth, "The Odes of Solomon — Not Gnostic," pp. 357-369; H. Chadwick, "Some Reflections on the Character and Theology of the Odes of Solomon," pp. 266-270). Neither category appears fully appropriate, however.

18. D. Hill, *New Testament Prophecy,* pp. 161-64.

19. The versification is that of J. H. Charlesworth, *The Odes of Solomon,* as are the quotations which follow (unless otherwise specified).

20. R. Bultmann, *Geschichte der synoptischen Tradition,* p. 135 n. 1.

21. Translation by J. R. Harris, *The Odes and Psalms of Solomon,* pp. 102-103.

22. D. E. Aune, "The Odes of Solomon," pp. 445-453.

23. D. E. Aune, *The Cultic Setting of Realized Eschatology.*

24. Vv. 16, 16a-f (vv. 16a-f are found only in the Greek version, but according to Charlesworth, *Odes,* pp. 56-57 n. 31, they appear to be authentic).

25. The hymns (or hymnlike compositions) of the Apocalypse include 4:8c; 4:11; 5:9b-10; 5:12b; 5:13b; 7:10b; 7:12; 11:15b; 11:17-18; 12:10b-12; 15:3b-4; 16:5b-7; 19:1b-2; 19:3b; 19:5b; 19:6b-9.

26. K.-P. Jörns, *Das hymnische Evangelium,* p. 159.

27. L. L. Thompson, "Cult and Eschatology in the Apocalypse of John," *JR,* 49 (1969), 348-49.

28. See below, p. 325.

29. J. H. Charlesworth, "Paronomasia and Assonance," pp. 12-26.

30. J. Reiling, *Hermas and Christian Prophecy,* pp. 166ff. Since Reiling's book is primarily a commentary on *Mand.* xi, a detailed analysis of the prophetic oracles in the Shepherd is not his intention. Nevertheless he does discuss four reconstructed oracles in moderate detail: (1) *Vis.* iv.2.5-6; (2) *Vis.* ii.2.6-8; (3) *Vis.* v.6-7; (4) *Mand.* xii.1.5-6.3. Other passages are mentioned but not discussed: *Vis.* iii.9.1-10; iii.11.1-12.3; iv.3.1-6; *Sim.* i; v.1.2-3; ix.23.5; ix.24.4; ix.28.5; ix.29.3; ix.31.3-33.1; x.4.4. This list is basically acceptable with a few modifications. Reiling has omitted the oracle in *Vis.* ii.3.4, and *Vis.* v.6-7 is not an oracle but rather a literary summary of Hermas' revelatory message that functions both as a conclusion to the *Visions* and as an introduction to the *Mandates* and *Similitudes.* Further, *Sim.* v.1.2-3 does not appear to be an oracle according to the criteria which we have adopted, nor does *Vis.* iii.9.11-13.

31. The only exception to this is the shift to second-person singular in the oracle to Maximus in *Vis.* ii.3.4. Methodologically, the switch to second-person plural alone is not a sufficiently strong indicator of oracular speech (this phenomenon is not unknown to the NT, cf. John 3:11), since a nonprophetic homiletic form or epistolary form could exhibit the same features.

32. The quotations which follow have been modified by the author from the K. Lake translation in the LCL series.

33. See above, p. 90.

34. See above, pp. 203, 275-76.

35. See above, p. 90.

36. The general features of this speech form have been analyzed by H. Thyen, *Der Stil der jüdisch-hellenistischen Homilie.*

37. The most systematic discussion of the style of the Cynic-Stoic diatribe, that of R. Bultmann, *Der Stil der paulinischen Predigt und die kynisch-stoische Diatribe,* must now be supplemented by S. K. Stowers, *Diatribe.*

38. This has been emphasized by L. Pernveden, *Shepherd of Hermas,* p. 68, and R. Bauckham, "The Great Tribulation," pp. 27-40. Many scholars unnecessarily deny the eschatological element in the thought of Hermas.

39. The probable allusion in *Vis.* ii.2.6-8 to these synoptic passages is, surprisingly, not noted by H. Koester, *Synoptische Überlieferungen.*

40. See above, pp. 90-91.

41. See above, p. 115.

42. See above, p. 288.

43. On OT oracles of assurance see above, pp. 94-95; on early Jewish oracles of assurance see above, pp. 143-44; on early Christian oracles of assurance see above, pp. 266-68.

44. See above, pp. 143-44, 266-68.

45. See above, pp. 117-18, and Rev. 2:10.

46. L. Pernveden, *Shepherd of Hermas,* pp. 38-71.

47. M. Dibelius, *Hirt des Hermas,* pp. 572-76; H. Moxnes, "God and His Angel," p. 50.

48. I have used this argument elsewhere in a similar connection: D. E. Aune, "The Presence of God in the Community," pp. 454-55.

49. E. Bevan, *Sibyls and Seers,* p. 175 n. 1.

50. In *PGM* I.97-132 the benefits of revelatory magic are listed, including the acquisition of gold, silver, and bronze (line 100).

51. *Hist. eccl.* iii.5.3 (LCL translation modified by author).

51a. Rev. 12:6 (?); Clem. *Rec.* 1.39; Asc. Isa. 4:13; *Anabathmoi Jakobou* 2; Eusebius *Hist. eccl.* iii.5.3; Epiphanius *Haer.* xxix.7; xxx.2; *De mens. et pond.* xv.

52. E. Meyer, *Ursprung und Anfänge des Christentums*, III, 584-85; H. J. Schoeps, *Studien zur Unbekannten Religions- und Geistesgeschichte*, pp. 69-70; V. Taylor, *Mark*, p. 512; B. Reicke, "Synoptic Prophecies," p. 125; J. Weiss, *Earliest Christianity*, II, 714; W. Lane, *Mark*, pp. 467-68; C. H. Dodd, *Parables*, pp. 46-47.

53. R. Pesch, *Das Markusevangelium*, II, 266.

54. H. J. Lawlor argues, I think unsuccessfully, that Hegesippus is the source of both Eusebius and Epiphanius (*Eusebiana*, pp. 27-34). On the other hand, G. Lüdemann proposes that Epiphanius is dependent on Eusebius and that neither follows Hegesippus; following A. Schlatter he proposes that the source used by Eusebius was Ariso of Pella ("The Successors of Pre-70 Jerusalem Christianity," pp. 165-66). Lüdemann assumes too readily that Epiphanius *De mens. et pond.* xv is also based on Eusebius.

55. Those favoring the historicity of the Pella tradition (in addition to those mentioned in n. 34 above) include M. Simon, "La migration à Pella: legende ou réalité?", pp. 34-54; B. C. Gray, "The Movements of the Jerusalem Church," pp. 1-7; J. J. Gunther, "The Fate of the Jerusalem Church," pp. 81-94; H. Lietzmann, *A History of the Early Church*, I, 178; M. Hengel, *Die Zeloten*, pp. 306-307; H. J. Schoeps, *Judenchristentums*, p. 47 nn. 1-2, p. 267; idem, *Jewish Christianity*, pp. 21ff. The chief opponents of the historicity of the Pella tradition include S. G. F. Brandon, *The Fall of Jerusalem*, pp. 168-173, 263-64; idem, *Jesus and the Zealots*, pp. 208-217; W. Farmer, *Maccabees, Zealots and Josephus*, p. 125 n. 2; G. Strecker, *Das Judenchristentum*, pp. 229ff.; J. Munck, "Jewish Christianity in Post-Apostolic Times," 103-104. Brandon's arguments have been effectively refuted by S. Stowers, "The Circumstances and Recollection of the Pella Flight," pp. 305-320.

56. G. Lüdemann, "The Successors of Pre-70 Jerusalem Christianity," pp. 161-173.

56a. R. Bach, *Aufforderungen zur Flucht*, pp. 15-50 (the announcement of an *Unheilsankündigung* after the summons to flight is disscussed by Bach on p. 21); D. L. Christensen, *War Oracle*, pp. 47-48.

57. H. J. Schoeps, *Jewish Christianity*, p. 21. In a statement interpolated into the text of Josephus, referred to in Eusebius *Hist. eccl.* ii.23.20, and Origen *Contra Celsum* i.47, the destruction of Jerusalem is regarded as a punishment for the martyrdom of James. That is also the view of Eusebius himself (*Hist. eccl.* iii.5.1-7). Josephus reports that many people fled Jerusalem during the years 64-66 (*Ant.* xx.256), and J. A. T. Robinson, *Redating the New Testament*, p. 16 n. 15, regards this period as the most appropriate time for placing the flight to Pella. Prior to the Roman siege of Jerusalem, from A.D. 66-68, many more fled from Jerusalem and its environs (Josephus *Bell.* ii.538, 556; iv.378). By early 68, however, such flight had become difficult if not impossible (Josephus *Bell.* iv.377ff.; 410ff.).

58. E. Schürer, *A History of the Jewish People*, I, 498.

59. See Jer. 16:16; Ezek. 7:14-16; Zech. 14:5; and F. Busch, *Zum Verständnis der synoptischen Eschatologie*, pp. 94-95.

60. On Montanism see the excellent article by K. Aland, "Bemerkungen zum Montanismus und zur frühchristlichen Eschatologie," pp. 105-148. Most recently the subject has been completely reviewed by F. C. Klawiter, "The New Prophecy in Early Christianity" (1975).

61. Lucian *Alex.* 13-14. Lucian depicts Alexander as prophesying under divine influence and as uttering incomprehensible words, and finally as blessing (*emakarizen*) the city. These three elements are found in the same order in the quotation of the Anonymous by Eusebius in *Hist. eccl.* v.16.6-9.

62. E. Fascher, *PROPHĒTĒS*, pp. 222-23; J. Lindblom, *Gesichte und Offenbarungen*, pp. 204-205.

63. K. Aland, "Bemerkungen zum Montanismus," p. 137. W. Schepelern, *Der Montan-*

ismus und die phrygischen Kulte (Tübingen, 1929), emphasized that the prophecy of Montanus owed very little if anything to pagan cults of Phrygia.

64. H. Kraft, "Die altkirchliche Prophetie," p. 249, suggested that the self-designation of Montanism was "The Prophecy," and that the church added the pejorative adjective "new." The "New Prophecy," however, appears to have been the original self-designation of the Montanists; see W. Schepelern, *Der Montanismus,* pp. 10-11, and F. C. Klawiter, "The New Prophecy in Early Christianity," p. 69.

65. Eusebius *Hist. Eccl.* v.17.2-4; W. M. Calder, "Philadelphia and Montanism," pp. 329-330.

66. See above, pp. 121-22, 126-29.

67. This is emphasized, I think correctly, by F. C. Klawiter, "The New Prophecy in Early Christianity," pp. 97-99.

68. For a more detailed discussion see K. Aland, "Bemerkungen zum Montanismus," pp. 105ff.

69. In dependence upon such earlier scholars as Labriolle, Hilgenfeld, and Bonwetsch, K. Aland has prepared a new edition of the oracles, which he has arranged in three categories: genuine oracles, oracles of doubtful authenticity, and remnants of the contents of oracles; "Bemerkungen zum Montanismus," pp. 143-48.

70. The numbering of the oracles which follow is dependent on Aland (who supplies cross references to the editions of Labriolle, Hilgenfeld, and Bonwetsch), while the translations are generally dependent (with modifications) on E. Hennecke and W. Schneemelcher, *New Testament Apocrypha,* II, 686-87. In this translation, however, only fifteen oracles are presented. Aland's second oracle is not reproduced in Hennecke-Schneemelcher, with the result that the numbering of his collection, beginning with the third oracle, is one number ahead of the enumeration of Hennecke-Scheemelcher.

71. K. Aland, "Bemerkungen zum Montanismus," p. 112, quoting A. Hilgenfeld.

72. See above, pp. 70-72.

73. See above, p. 203.

Chapter 12

1. Because of the interpretative problems, not to mention the extent of the texts, ten examples of prophetic speeches from the Odes of Solomon have been included. All but Ode 7:16b-20 are speeches *ex ore Christi.*

2. Mark 5:7 is perhaps the clearest example of Mark's attribution of conventional magical procedures to loquacious demons (see O. Bauernfeind, *Die Worte der Dämonen im Markusevangelium*). Mark 5:7 therefore appears to be a strictly literary production modeled after the rhetoric of magical procedures rather than after popular conceptions of the form and content of oracles.

3. This subject is now treated in detail with copious references to specialized studies of various aspects of the matter by J. R. Fears, *Princeps A Diis Electus.*

4. This is an almost totally neglected subject which requires careful treatment in itself. See above, pp. 32-34, on the tendentious ancient penchant for describing the hysterical behavior of the Pythia, and pp. 147-152 for Philo's use of literary conventions in describing prophetic behavior and speech.

5. See above, pp. 148-152.

6. Cf. the discussion above, pp. 263-64.

7. Oracles of assurance are discussed above, pp. 94-95, 117-18, 143-44, 266-68.

8. D. Schroeder, "Lists, Ethical," pp. 546-47; idem, "Parenesis," p. 643 (both articles provide a good basic orientation and bibliographies). See also M. Dibelius, *Fresh Approach,* pp. 217-237.

9. G. Bornkamm, "Formen und Gattungen," col. 1003.

10. Ibid., col. 1004.

11. F. Bömer, *Untersuchungen über die Religion der Sklaven,* III, 207-208.

12. On this issue see H. W. Pleket, "The 'Believer' as Servant of the Deity in the Greek

World," pp. 152-192.

13. See below, p. 327.

14. See above, pp. 92-93.

15. See above, pp. 93, 118-121.

16. See above, pp. 74-77.

17. R. Pesch, *Markusevangelium*, II, 298-99; M. Hengel, *Die Zeloten*, pp. 238, 306-307.

18. The literature on this subject is enormous. See particularly R. Brown, *The Gospel According to John*, I, 533-38.

19. See above, pp. 64-66.

20. W. C. van Unnik, "A Formula Describing Prophecy," pp. 86-94.

21. D. E. Aune, "The Odes of Solomon," pp. 450-53.

22. H. Kraft, *Die Offenbarung des Johannes*, p. 37.

23. See above, pp. 219-222, on "The Evaluation of Prophecy in Paul."

24. A. Adler, *Suidae*, II, s.v. *Dōdōnē*.

25. Plato *Alc.* ii.149b.

26. E. Mayser, *Grammatik der griechischen Papyri*, II/1, pp. 73-74; G. Thieme, *Inschriften*, pp. 23-24.

27. D. E. Aune, "The Presence of God," pp. 451-59.

28. See above, p. 309.

29. See above, p. 90.

30. Frequent references occur in Greco-Roman literature to those ordered to write books while they are asleep: Plato *Phaedo* iv.60e-61b; Callimachus *Aetia* i.21-22; Propertius iii.3; Cicero *Academica Priora* ii.16.51 (Ennius *Annales* 5); Pliny *Ep.* iii.5.4; Pausanias 1.21.2. The priest of Sarapis named Apollonius was commanded to write an aretalogy of the god (H. Engelmann, *The Delian Aretalogy of Sarapis*, p. 7, lines 1-2; a convenient translation and commentary are available in F. Danker, *Benefactor*, pp. 186-191). Aelius Aristides was commanded to write down his dreams (*Or.* 48.2).

31. See above, p. 90.

32. F. Baumgärtel, "Die Formel *nᵉ'um jahwe*," pp. 277-290; H. W. Wolff, *Joel and Amos*, pp. 143-44.

33. D. E. Aune, "The Odes of Solomon," pp. 438-39.

34. Translation of J. H. Charlesworth, *The Odes of Solomon*.

35. See above, pp. 90-91.

36. A comprehensive discussion of the oath formula in Jewish apocalyptic is found in K. Berger, *Die Amen-Worte Jesus*, pp. 20-27; cf. also G. W. E. Nickelsburg, "The Apocalyptic Message," pp. 309-328. Berger lists the following passages where the oath formula occurs: 1 Enoch 98:1, 4, 6; 99:6; 103:1; 104:1; 2 Enoch 49:1; Asc. Isa. 1:8; 3:18; Apoc. Mos. 18; 3 Bar. 1:7; Test. Sol. 1:13; Rev. 10:6; 1 Clem. 58:2.

37. See above, pp. 250-51 and nn. 23, 24, 25.

38. Cf. G. Dautzenberg, "Botschaft und Bedeutung," pp. 131-161.

39. D. Lührmann, *Die Offenbarungsverständnis bei Paulus*, pp. 113-17.

40. U. B. Müller, *Prophetie und Predigt*, p. 131. See also the brief discussion of these passages in C. C. Caragounis, *The Ephesian 'Mysterion'*, pp. 24-26. 1 Enoch 103:1 and 104:12 and extant in a Greek text (cf. M. Black, *Apocalypsis Henochi Graece*).

41. U. B. Müller, *Prophetie und Predigt*, Part 3, in which the author discusses "Prophetische-, Mahn-, Gerichts- und Heilspredigt in der Gestalt eigener Rede des Propheten." Müller is the only scholar, to my knowledge, who discusses this subject in any detail.

42. See the discussion of the work of U. B. Müller and C. Roetzel, above, pp. 261-62.

43. J. Fontenrose, *The Delphic Oracle*, p. 207. Fontenrose tends to regard such oracles as inauthentic (p. 427), yet on this see G. Wolff, *Porphyrii de Philosophica*, p. 173; R. van den Broek, *Apollo in Asia*, p. 20 n. 2.

44. This problem is discussed by I. P. Seierstad, *Die Offenbarungserlebnisse der Propheten*, pp. 237-245 ("Die persönliche Aneignung des Offenbarungswortes"); idem, "Forholdet Mellom Apenbaringsopplevelsen og Utformingen av Budskapet hos Skriftprofetene," pp. 41-55.

45. H. Weinel, *Die Wirkungen des Heiligen Geist*, p. 89.

46. D. Hill, *NT Prophecy*, p. 123.

47. Oracles of one line: Mark 3:11 and par.; 13:6 and par.; John 1:36; Mark 13:21a, 21b; Acts 11:28; 13:2; 21:4; 1 Cor. 12:3; 2 Thess. 3:10; Rev. 14:13a; Did. 11:12a, 12b; Ignatius Rom. 7:2; Ignatius Philad. 7:2a, 2b, 2c, 2d, 2e; Montanist oracles 1, 2, 3, 10. Oracles of two lines: Matt. 16:16; Mark 1:11 and par.; 5:7 and par.; 9:7 and par.; John 1:29; Acts 7:55-56; 16:17; 19:15; 21:11; 2 Cor. 12:9; Gal. 5:21; 2 Thess. 3:6, 12; Rev. 1:8; 14:13b; 19:9; 21:5; Eusebius *Hist. eccl.* iii.53 (and par.); Montanist oracles 4, 13, 14. Oracles of three lines: Acts 18:9; 23:11; 27:23-24; 1 Thess. 3:4; Rev. 16:15; Ignatius Philad. 7:1; Montanist oracles 6, 7, 16. Oracles of four lines: Acts 13:9-11; 20:29-30; Rom. 11:25-26; 1 Cor. 14:37-38; Rev. 13:9-10; 22:16; Hermas *Sim.* ix.24.4; Montanist oracles 5, 11, 12. Oracles of five lines: 1 Tim. 4:1-3; Rev. 1:7, 17-20; Hermas *Vis.* ii.3.4; *Sim.* ix.23.5; Montanist oracles 9 and 15. Oracles of six lines: 1 Thess. 4:2-6, 16-17; Rev. 22:6-7; Odes Sol. 41:8-10; Montanist oracle 8. Oracles of seven lines: 1 Cor. 15:51-52. Oracles of eight lines: Rev. 21:3-4; 22:18-20; Hermas *Vis.* ii.2.6-8; *Sim.* vi.1.4. Oracles of ten lines: Rev. 18:21-24; 21:5-8; Odes Sol. 10:4-6. Oracles of twelve lines: Rev. 22:12-15; Hermas *Sim.* ix.33.1; *Mand.* xii.4.5-7. Oracles of thirteen lines: Hermas *Vis.* iv.2.5-6. Oracles of fifteen lines: Rev. 2:8-11; Odes Sol. 36:3-8. Oracles of eighteen lines: Hermas *Mand.* xii.6.1-3; *Sim.* ix.31.3-5; Odes Sol. 31:6-13. Oracles of twenty-two lines: Rev. 2:1-7; 3:1-6; Oracles of twenty-four lines: Odes Sol. 17:6-16. Oracles of twenty-six lines: Odes Sol. 28:9-20. Oracles of twenty-five lines: Rev. 2:18-29. Oracles of twenty-seven lines: Rev. 2:12-17. Oracles of twenty-eight lines: Odes Sol. 8:8-19. Oracles of twenty-nine lines: Odes Sol. 22:1-12. Oracles of thirty lines: Rev. 3:7-13. Oracles of thirty-one lines: Rev. 3:14-22. Oracles of thirty-five lines: Rev. 2:18-29. Oracles of forty-four lines: Odes Sol. 42:3-20.

48. D. E. Aune, "The Odes of Solomon," pp. 435-460.

49. For ancient Israelite prophecy, see p. 91; for Greco-Roman oracles, see pp. 58-62; for the rhetoric of Jesus, see p. 166.

50. See above, pp. 61-62.

51. See above, pp. 166-68, 237-240, 294-96.

52. See Berger's two instructive essays, "Zu den sogenannten Sätzen heiligen Rechts," pp. 10-40, and "Die sogenannte 'Sätze heiligen Rechts'," pp. 305-330.

53. P. Fiedler, *Die Formel 'Und Siehe'*.

54. D. E. Aune, "Magic in Early Christianity."

55. Cf. M. E. Boring, "The Apocalypse as Christian Prophecy," pp. 43-62; D. Hill, *New Testament Prophecy*, pp. 75ff.

56. This is the procedure used by M. E. Boring in several articles: "The Unforgivable Sin Logion," pp. 258-279; "How May We Identify Oracles," pp. 501-521; "Christian Prophecy and Matthew 10:23," pp. 127-136; "Christian Prophecy and Matthew 23:34-36," pp. 117-126.

57. I am in perfect agreement with the statement of D. Hill, *New Testament Prophecy*, p. 191 (quoted above, p. 14).

Appendix

1. W. H. Brownlee, "Biblical Interpretation," p. 61 n. 4. I owe this reference to a dissertation advisee, Winfield S. Hall (at the Lutheran School of Theology at Chicago), who recently completed (June, 1982) a Th.D. dissertation entitled "Paul's Role as a Christian Prophet in His Interpretation of the Old Testament in Romans 9-11."

2. M. Hengel, *Die Zeloten*, pp. 240-41; R. Meyer, *TDNT*, VI, 817-18. Josephus himself (see above, pp. 138-143) exhibits the phenomenon of "charismatic exegesis" (*Bell.* iii.352; *Ant.* x.195-96).

3. Cicero *De divinatione* i.6.12 (probably dependent on Posidonius of Apamea); Plato *Ion* 534c; Plutarch *De gen. Socr.* 593c-d.

4. Recently G. Dautzenberg, *Urchristliche Prophetie*, pp. 43-121, has sought to demonstrate the interpretative role of prophecy in early Judaism and to use the interpretative-exegetical model of prophecy to understand early Christian prophecy (pp. 122-148).

5. A. Finkel, "The Pesher of Dreams and Scripture," pp. 357-370; L. H. Silberman,

"Unriddling the Riddle," pp. 323-364; K. Elliger, *Studien zum Habakuk-Kommentar*, pp. 154-57.

6. This generally recognized fact is emphasized with admirable clarity by S. Sandmel, *Judaism and Christian Beginnings*, pp. 9-18. Sandmel has coined the phrase "synagogue Judaism" to refer to the Jewish thought and practice outside of the official temple cult (p. 16).

7. Ibid., p. 18; G. Vermes, *Scripture and Tradition*, pp. 7-8; R. Bloch, "Midrash," p. 1266; D. Patte, *Early Jewish Hermeneutic*, pp. 76-81, 118-127.

8. A. Wright, *Midrash*, p. 43.

9. Ibid., pp. 52-59; P. Weimar, "Formen frühjüdischer Literatur," pp. 135-155 (with detailed bibliographical references).

10. R. Bauckham, "Rise of Apocalyptic," p. 18.

11. 1 Enoch 91:1; 93:1; Vita Adae 29; 2 Enoch 22:4-13; Jub. 1; 4 Ezra 14; 2 Bar. 6:3; 10:1-3; 59; Sib. Or. iii.162, 306, 395-96, 489-491, 809-811; Mart. Isa. 1:7; 5:14; cf. M. E. Stone, "Apocalyptic—Vision or Hallucination," pp. 47-56; D. S. Russell, *Apocalyptic*, pp. 82, 158-177.

12. The literature on this subject has been reviewed recently by F. Dexinger, *Apokalyptikforschung*, pp. 45-57 (on p. 51 he comes to much the same conclusion as we have expressed). Cf. also J. Bloch, *Apocalyptic*, 130-143.

13. H.-P. Müller, "Mantische Weisheit," pp. 283-85. According to Müller mantic wisdom was one of the primary antecedents of Jewish apocalyptic.

14. F. F. Bruce, *Biblical Exegesis*, pp. 7-17.

15. J. J. Collins, *Daniel*, p. 75.

16. See above, n. 5.

17. Translated by A. Dupont-Sommer, *Essene Writings*, p. 262.

18. F. F. Bruce, "Josephus and Daniel," p. 159; idem, *Second Thoughts*, p. 93.

19. Translated by A. Dupont-Sommer, *Essene Writings*, p. 259.

20. O. Betz, *Offenbarung und Schriftforschung*, pp. 61-68, 88-99; A. Dupont-Sommer, *Essene Writings*, pp. 360-64; G. Jeremias, *Der Lehrer der Gerechtigkeit*, pp. 268-307; N. Wieder, "The 'Law Interpreter'," p. 171; A. S. van der Woude, *Die messianischen Vorstellungen*, pp. 75-89.

21. H. Braun, *Qumran und das Neue Testament*, II, 252: "The new element in the pneumatology of Qumran in comparison with ordinary Judaism is the *complete presence of the Spirit.*" See also M. Hengel, *Die Zeloten*, p. 241. This has been carefully demonstrated through a detailed exegesis of the relevant Qumran texts by H.-W. Kuhn, *Enderwartung und gegenwärtiges Heil*, pp. 117-139.

22. J. Levy, *Wörterbuch*, III, 323-25; P. Schäfer, *Die Vorstellung vom heiligen Geist*, pp. 21-26.

23. H. Ringgren, *Qumran*, pp. 87-90.

24. O. Betz, *Offenbarung und Schriftforschung*, pp. 99-109.

25. Ibid., pp. 98-99; K. Elliger, *Habakuk-Kommentar*, pp. 155ff.

26. Perhaps the most influential study in this regard has been C. H. Dodd, *According to the Scriptures*. More recently see K. Stendahl, *The School of St. Matthew*; E. E. Ellis, *Paul's Use of the Old Testament*; B. Lindars, *New Testament Apologetic*. An important article which both surveys the subject and reviews the literature is E. E. Ellis, "How the New Testament Uses the Old," in *Prophecy and Hermeneutic*, pp. 147-172. See also R. Longenecker, *Biblical Exegesis in the Apostolic Period*.

27. H. Conzelmann, *1 Corinthians*, p. 58 (with references to the discussion of the "revelation schema" form).

28. Particularly E. E. Ellis in *Paul and the Old Testament*, pp. 107-113, and in a number of articles, most of which have been collected in E. E. Ellis, *Prophecy and Hermeneutic*, where nine articles are gathered in Part 2 under the rubric "Prophecy as Exegesis: Early Christian Hermeneutic." See also E. C. Selwyn, *Oracles*, pp. 401-402; E. G. Selwyn, *1 Peter*, p. 134; and É. Cothenet, "Les prophètes chrétiens comme exégètes charismatiques de l'Écriture," pp. 77-107. Many other scholars have been content just to indicate that the Christian prophet was, among other things, a charismatic exegete without offering any specific lines of argumentation. So M. E. Boring, "Christian Prophets," pp. 90-99; L. Gaston, *No Stone on Another*, pp. 55-56 and *passim*; C. F. D. Moule, *Birth of the New Testament*, pp. 58, 85.

29. 1 Cor. 12:7; 14:3, 31; Acts 4:36; 9:27; 13:15; 15:32. Cf. the paracletic function of the

Spirit in John 14:16, 26; 15:16; 16:7.

30. This line of argumentation is pursued by É. Cothenet, "Les prophètes chrétiens comme exégètes charismatiques de l'Écriture," pp. 79-81. Cf. E. E. Ellis, *Prophecy and Hermeneutic*, pp. 131-32, where similar word-games are found.

31. E. E. Ellis, *Prophecy and Hermeneutic*, pp. 182-87 (an article reproduced from his earlier book, *Paul's Use of the Old Testament*, pp. 107-112). The nine OT quotations are found in Rom. 12:19; 14:11; 1 Cor. 14:21; 2 Cor. 6:16ff.; 10:16-17; 10:30; Acts 7:49; 15:16-17; Heb. 8:8-12.

32. E. E. Ellis, *Paul's Use of the Old Testament*, pp. 110-11; idem, *Prophecy and Hermeneutic*, p. 186.

33. The only real parallel cited by Ellis is Rev. 1:8: " 'I am the Alpha and the Omega,' says the Lord God [*legei kyrios ho theos*], 'who is and who was and who is to come.' " See below, n. 37.

34. The phrase is used in 2 Clement four times in connection with quotations or allusions to the sayings of Jesus (5:2; 6:1; 8:5; 15:4), and once this way in Barn. 6:13. The phrase "says God" (*legei ho theos*) is similarly used once in 2 Clem. 13:4. These occurrences are not counted in the tabulation mentioned above.

35. The texts cited by Barnabas in which *legei kyrios* occurs in an OT text include Barn. 2:5 (Isa. 1:11); 6:8 (Exod. 33:1, 3; here the original context was God speaking to Moses, while the quotation is phrased as if Moses were addressing the people: "Thus says the Lord . . ."); 9:2 (Jer. 7:2-3); 9:5 (Jer. 4:3-4); 14:8 (Isa. 49:6-7). Additions of the formula *legei kyrios* to the OT text are found in Barn. 3:1 (twice, Isa. 58:4-5); 3:3 (Isa. 58:6); 6:14 (Ezek. 11:19; 36:26); 9:1 (twice; Ps. 18:45 [Eng. 44]; Jer. 4:4).

36. Barnabas is one of the sources for model homilies for H. Thyen, *Der Stil der jüdisch-hellenistischen Homilie* (1956).

37. In early Christian literature the attribution of prophetic speech to God is found only in Rev. 1:8 and 21:5-8. Montanus, about the middle of the second century, is reported to have pronounced three oracles of God in the first-person singular (Epiphanius *Haer.* xlviii.11.1; xlviii.11.9; Didymus of Alexandria *De trinitate* iii.41.1; see Hennecke-Schneemelcher, *New Testament Apocrypha*, II, 686. These texts are discussed in some detail by P. Labriolle, *La crise Montaniste*, pp. 37-43. The phrase "Lord God almighty" in the first oracle of Montanus is the same phrase found in Rev. 1:8; 4:8; 11:17, and was perhaps derived by him from that source, either consciously or unconsciously. The paucity of the evidence for prophetic speech attributed to God or the Lord indicates that "says the Lord" in early Christianity was not a prophetic formula.

38. The formula "thus says the (Holy) Spirit" (and variations) is clearly a prophetic speech formula in early Christianity (Acts 21:11; Rev. 2:7, 11, 17, 29; 3:6, 13, 22; Ign. Philad. 7:2); cf. K. Berger, *Amen-Worte Jesu*, pp. 117-124.

39. At the conclusion of his article on the *legei kyrios* quotations, Ellis observes: "There is now ample evidence that it [i.e. Christian prophecy] also included the elaboration, interpretation, and application of O.T. Scriptures" (*Prophecy and Hermeneutic*, p. 187). Ellis slides imperceptibly from possibility to probability without marshalling convincing proofs for his case.

40. Elsewhere Ellis hypothesizes that the "in order that it might be fulfilled" (*hina plērōthē*) formulas introducing OT quotations in Matthew (1:22; 2:15, 17, 23; 4:14; 8:17; 12:17; 13:35; 21:4; 26:56; 27:9), and the "faithful is the saying" formulas of the Pastoral letters (1 Tim. 1:15; 4:9; 2 Tim. 2:11), might have originated in Christian prophetic circles (*Prophecy and Hermeneutic*, p. 149); cf. L. Gaston, *No Stone on Another*, pp. 445-46. No evidence to substantiate this proposal is presented, however.

41. P. Borgen, *Bread from Heaven*, found that homiletic patterns in Philo also characterized certain portions of the NT: Rom. 4:1-22; Gal. 3:6-29 (pp. 46-50). The focus of his monograph was the demonstration that such a homiletic pattern underlay much of John 6. See also J. W. Doeve, *Jewish Hermeneutics in the Synoptic Gospels and Acts*; W. Wuellner, "Haggadic Homily Genre in 1 Corinthians 1-3," pp. 199-204. E. E. Ellis, *Prophecy and Hermeneutic*,

pp. 247-253, presents the evidence for regarding 1 Cor. 1:18-31; 2:6-16 (pp. 213-17), Rom. 1:17-4:25; 9-11 (pp. 217-19), and the short letter of Jude (pp. 221-26) as exegetical products structured according to midrashic homily patterns. See also R. Scroggs, "Paul as Rhetorician: Two Homilies in Romans 1-11," pp. 271-298. For a short discussion of Jewish haggadic homily patterns in Paul see N. Turner, *Style,* pp. 86ff. (Interestingly, Turner does not refer to Borgen's work in connection with Johannine style.)

42. J. Panagopoulos, "Die urchristliche Prophetie," p. 13.

43. B. Lindars, *New Testament Apologetic,* pp. 36ff.

44. J. Panagopoulos, "Die urchristliche Prophetie," p. 13, claims that the prophetic sermon functions in this way for Luke, and on p. 17 he makes the general claim that it functioned this way for early Christianity generally. On p. 18, however, he admits that there is little direct evidence to substantiate this claim. The more generally accepted view is that recently articulated by G. Dautzenberg, "Botschaft und Bedeutung der urchristlichen Prophetie," pp. 157ff., who sees the message of prophecy and the kerygma as complementary, yet not completely identical.

45. U. B. Müller, *Prophetie und Predigt* (1975).

46. É. Cothenet, "Les prophètes chrétiens comme exégètes," pp. 91-94; E. E. Ellis, *Prophecy and Hermeneutic,* pp. 132ff. In his article "Midrashic Features in the Speeches of Acts" in *Prophecy and Hermeneutic,* pp. 198-208, Ellis does not mention the possibility of the prophetic origin of Acts 13:16-41 or any other of the speeches which he discusses.

47. O. Glombitz, "Acta XIII, 15-41," pp. 306-317; M. Dumais, *Le langage de l'evangelisation,* p. 87. Earlier, J. W. Bowker, "The Speeches in Acts," pp. 101-104, had suggested that Acts 13:16-41 conformed to the structure of a Jewish "proem" homily. Essentially the same opinion is held by J. W. Doeve, *Jewish Hermeneutics,* pp. 172-76, who argues for the historicity of the speech on that basis.

48. The prophetic character of Acts 13:16-41, as proposed by both Cothenet and Ellis, has been challenged by D. Hill, "Christian Prophets," pp. 125ff., and I find myself in complete agreement with Hill's skepticism regarding the prophetic origin of such homilies. On p. 127 n. 66, Hill observes: "At the heart of the disagreement [between himself and Ellis] lies my uncertainty about the correctness of attributing the exposition of Scripture to prophets in the Christian community: the interpretation of the Old Testament with reference to the Christ-event may more correctly be attributed to inspired teachers."

49. E. E. Ellis, *Prophecy and Hermeneutic,* pp. 131-32.

50. See above, n. 26.

Bibliography

Abramowski, R. "Der Christus der Salomooden," *ZNW,* 25 (1936), 44-69.

Achelis, H. "Katoptromantie bei Paulus," in *Theologische Festschrift für G. N. Bonwetsch.* Leipzig, 1918. Pp. 56-63.

Achtemeier, P. J. "Origin and Function of the Pre-Marcan Miracle Catenae," *JBL,* 91 (1972), 198-221.

————. "Toward the Isolation of Pre-Markan Miracle Catenae," *JBL,* 89 (1970), 265-291.

Adler, A. *Suidae Lexicon.* 5 vols. Leipzig, 1928-38.

Ahlström, G. W., "Prophecy," *Encyclopedia Britannica,* 15th ed., *Macropedia,* XV, 62-68.

Aland, K. "Bemerkungen zum Montanismus und zur frühchristlichen Eschatologie," in *Kirchengeschichtliche Entwürfe.* Gütersloh, 1960. Pp. 105-148.

————. "The Problem of Anonymity and Pseudonymity in Christian Literature of the First Two Centuries," *JTS,* 12 (1961), 39-49.

Albertz, M. *Die Botschaft des Neuen Testaments.* Zollikon-Zürich, 1952-54.

Albright, W. F. *From the Stone Age to Christianity.* 2nd ed. Garden City, New York, 1957.

Alexandre, C. *Excursus ad Sibyllina.* Paris, 1856.

Alföldi, A. " 'Redeunt Saturnia regna' IV: Apollo und die Sibylie in der Epoche der Bürgerkriege," *Chiron,* 5 (1975), 165-192.

Alizon, J. *Étude sur le prophétisme chrétien depuis les origines jusqu' à l'an 150.* Paris, 1911.

Althaus, P. *Der Brief an die Römer.* 6. Aufl. Göttingen, 1966.

Amandry, P. "La divination en Grece: état actuel de quelques problemes," in *La divination en Mésopotamie ancienne et dans les regions voisines.* Paris, 1966.

————. *La Mantique Apollinienne à Delphes.* Paris, 1950.

Andresen, C. *Die Kirchen der alten Christenheit.* Stuttgart, 1971.

Applebaum, S. "Economic Life in Palestine," in *Compendia Rerum Judaicarum ad Novum Testamentum.* Sec. I, vol. 2. Ed. S. Saffrai, M. Stern, and M. de Jonge. Philadelphia, 1976. Pp. 631-700.

Arenhoevel, D. *Die Theokratie nach dem 1. und 2. Makkabäerbuch.* Mainz, 1967.

Arens, E. *The Ēlthon-Sayings in the Synoptic Tradition.* Freiburg, 1976.

Arvedson, T. *Das Mysterium Christi: Eine Studie zu Mt. 11.25-30.* Uppsala, 1937.

Ash, J. L. "Decline of Ecstatic Prophecy in the Early Church," *TS,* 37 (1976), 227-252.

Athanassakis, A. N. *The Orphic Hymns: Text, Translation and Notes.* Missoula, 1977.

Audet, J. P. *La Didaché, Instructions des Apôtres.* Paris, 1958.

Aune, D. E. *The Cultic Setting of Realized Eschatology in Early Christianity.* Leiden, 1972.

————. "Divination," *The International Standard Bible Encyclopedia.* Rev. ed. Vol. I. Grand Rapids, 1979. Pp. 971-74.

————. "Herm. Man. 11.2: Christian False Prophets Who Say What People Wish to Hear," *JBL,* 97 (1978), 103-104.

————. "The Odes of Solomon and Early Christian Prophecy," *NTS,* 28 (1982), 435-460.

————. "The Presence of God in the Community: The Eucharist in Its Early Christian Cultic Context," *SJT,* 29 (1976), 451-59.

446 • Bibliography

—————. "Septem Sapientium Convivium (Moralia 146B-164D)," in *Plutarch's Ethical Writings and Early Christian Literature*. Ed. H. D. Betz. Leiden, 1978. Pp. 51-105.

—————. "The Significance of the Delay of the Parousia for Early Christianity," in *Current Issues in Biblical and Patristic Interpretation*. Ed. G. F. Hawthorne. Grand Rapids, 1975. Pp. 87-109.

—————. "The Use of *PROPHĒTĒS* in Josephus," *JBL*, 101 (1982), 419-421.

—————. "Magic in Early Christianity," in *Aufstieg und Niedergang der römischen Weit*. Ed. H. Temporini und W. Haase. Berlin and New York, 1980. II/26.2. Pp. 1507-57.

—————. "The Social Matrix of the Apocalypse of John," *BR*, 26 (1981), 16-32.

—————. "An Index to Synoptic Pericopae Ostensibly Influenced by Early Christian Prophets," in *SBL Seminar Papers for 1975*. 2 vols. Missoula, 1975. Vol. II, pp. 131-141.

—————. "The Problem of the Messianic Secret," *NovT*, 11 (1969), 1-31.

Bach, R. *Die Aufforderungen zur Flucht und zum Kampf im alttestamentlichen Prophetenspruch*. Neukirchen, 1962.

Bächli, E. *Die künstlerische Funktion von Orakelsprüchen, Weissagungen, Träumen usw. in der griechischen Tragödie*. Winterthur, 1954.

Bacht, H. "Die prophetische Inspiration in der kirchlichen Reflexion der vormontanistischen Zeit," *Scholastik*, 19 (1944), 1-18.

—————. "Religionsgeschichtliches zum Inspirationsproblem. Die Pythischen Dialoge Plutarchs von Chäronea," *Scholastik*, 17 (1942), 50-69.

—————. "Wahres und falsches Prophetentum," *Biblica*, 32 (1951), 237-262.

Baltzer, K. "Considerations Regarding the Office and Calling of the Prophet," *HTR*, 61 (1968), 567-581.

Bammel, E. "*ARCHIEREUS PROPHĒTEUŌN*," *TLZ*, 79 (1954), 351-56.

Barnard, L. W. "Hermas, the Church and Judaism," in *Studies in the Apostolic Fathers and Their Background*. Oxford, 1966. Pp. 151-163.

—————. "The Shepherd of Hermas in Recent Study," *HJT*, 9 (1968), 29-36.

Barnett, H. G. *Indian Shakers: A Messianic Cult of the Pacific Northwest*. Carbondale, Illinois, 1957.

Barnett, P. W. "The Jewish Sign Prophets — A.D. 40-70 — Their Intentions and Origin," *NTS*, 27 (1981), 679-697.

Baron, S. W. *A Social and Religious History of the Jews*, I. New York, 1952.

Barrett, C. K. *The Gospel of John and Judaism*. Philadelphia, 1975.

—————. *A Commentary on the First Epistle to the Corinthians*. New York, 1968.

Barth, G. "Matthew's Understanding of the Law," in Bornkamm, G., Barth, G., and Held, H. J., *Tradition and Interpretation in Matthew*. Philadelphia, 1963.

Bartsch, H. W. "Die 'Verfluchung' des Feigenbaums," *ZNW*, 53 (1962), 256-260.

Bauckham, R. J. "The Great Tribulation in the Shepherd of Hermas," *JTS*, 28 (1974), 27-40.

—————. "The Martyrdom of Enoch and Elijah: Jewish or Christian?" *JBL*, 95 (1976), 447-458.

—————. "The Rise of Apocalyptic," *Themelios*, 3 (1978), 10-23.

Bauer, W. *Orthodoxy and Heresy in Earliest Christianity*. Trans. and ed. R. A. Kraft, G. Krodel et al. Philadelphia, 1971.

—————. *Die Briefe des Ignatius von Antiochia und der Polykarpbrief*. Handbuch zum Neuen Testament, Ergänzungsband II: Die apostolischen Väter. Tübingen, 1920.

—————. *A Greek-English Lexicon of the New Testament and Other Early Christian Literature*. Ed. and trans. W. F. Arndt and F. W. Gingrich. 2nd ed. Rev. F. W. Gingrich and F. W. Danker. Chicago, 1979.

—————. *Das Leben Jesu in Zeitalter der neutestamentlichen Apokryphen*. Tübingen, 1909.

Bauernfeind, O. *Die Worte der Dämonen im Markusevangelium*. Stuttgart, 1927.

Baumgärtel, F. "Die Formel n^e'um jahwe," *ZAW*, 73 (1961), 277-290.

Baumgarten, J. *Paulus und die Apokalyptik*. Neukirchen-Vluyn, 1975.

Beasley-Murray, G. R. *The Book of Revelation*. London, 1974.

—————. *Jesus and the Future: An Examination of the Criticism of the Eschatological Discourse, Mark 13, with Special Reference to the Little Apocalypse Theory*. London, 1954.

—————. "Jesus and the Spirit," in *Mélanges bibliques en hommage au R. P. Béda Rigaux*. Ed. A. Descamps and A. de Halleux. Gembloux, 1970. Pp. 463-478.

—————. "The Two Messiahs in the Testaments of the Twelve Patriarchs," *JTS*, 48 (1947), 1-12.

—————. *A Commentary on Mark Thirteen*. New York, 1957.

Becker, H. *Die Reden des Johannesevangeliums und der Stil der gnostischen Offenbarungsrede*. Göttingen, 1956.

Becker, J. *Johannes der Täufer und Jesus von Nazareth*. Neukirchen-Vluyn, 1972.

Begrich, J. "Das priesterliche Heilsorakel," *ZAW*, 52 (1934), 81-92.

Behr, C. A. *Aelius Aristides and the Sacred Tales*. Amsterdam, 1968.

Bénazech, J. *Le prophétisme chrétien depuis les origines jusq'au Pasteur d'Hermas*. Cahors, 1901.

Bentzen, A. *Introduction to the Old Testament*. 2 vols. 7th ed. Copenhagen, 1957.

—————. *King and Messiah*. London, 1955.

Benz, E. *Paulus als Visionär*. Wiesbaden, 1952.

Berger, K. *Die Amen-Worte Jesu. Eine Untersuchung zum Problem der Legitimation in apokalyptischer Rede*. Berlin, 1970.

—————. *Die Auferstehung des Propheten und die Erhöhung des Menschensohnes: Traditionsgeschichtliche Untersuchung zur Deutung des Geschichtes Jesu in frühchristlichen Texten*. Göttingen, 1976.

—————. "Die sog. 'Sätze heiligen' Rechts im N.T.: Ihre Funktion und Ihr Sitz im Leben," *TZ*, 28 (1972), 305-330.

—————. "Zu den sogenannten Sätzen heiligen Rechts," *NTS*, 17 (1970-71), 10-40.

—————. "Zum traditionsgeschichtlichen Hintergrund christologischer Hoheitstitel," *NTS*, 17 (1971), 391-425.

—————. "Zur Frage des traditionsgeschichtlicher Wertes apokryphen Gleichnisse," *NovT*, 17 (1975), 58-76.

Berridge, J. M. *Prophet, People, and the Word of Yahweh: An Examination of Form and Content in the Proclamation of the Prophet Jeremiah*. Zürich, 1970.

Best. E. *A Commentary on the First and Second Epistles to the Thessalonians*. New York, 1972.

—————. "An Early Sayings Collection," *NovT*, 18 (1976), 1-16.

—————. "Spirit-Baptism," *NovT*, 4 (1960), 236-243.

Betz, H. D. "Eine Christus-Aretalogie bei Paulus (2 Kor 12,7-10)," *ZTK*, 66 (1969), 288-305.

—————. *Galatians*. Philadelphia, 1979.

—————. *Lukian von Samosata und das Neue Testament*. Berlin, 1961.

—————. "On the Problem of the Religion-Historical Understanding of Apocalypticism," *JTC*, 6 (1969), 134-156.

Betz, O. "The Dichotomized Servant and the End of Judas Iscariot," *RQ*, 5 (1964), 43-58.

—————. "Die Vision des Paulus im Tempel von Jerusalem — Apg 22, 17-21 als Beitrag zur Deutung des Damaskuserlebnisses," in *Verborum Veritas: Festschrift für G. Stählin*. Ed. O. Böcher and K. Haacker. Wuppertal, 1970. Pp. 113-123.

—————. *What Do We Know About Jesus?* Trans. M. Kohl. Philadelphia, 1968.

—————. "Die Frage nach dem messianischen Bewusstsein Jesu," *NovT*, 6 (1963), 24-37.

—————. *Offenbarung und Schriftforschung in der Qumransekte*. Tübingen, 1960.

Bevan, E. *Sibyls and Seers: A Survey of Some Ancient Theories of Revelation and Inspiration*. London, 1928.

Beyer, K. *Semitische Syntax in Neuen Testament. Band I: Satzlehre*. Göttingen, 1962.

Beyerlin, W. (ed.). *Near Eastern Religious Texts Relating to the Old Testament*. Trans. J. Bowden. Philadelphia, 1978.

Bianchi, U. *La Religione Greca*. Torino, 1975.

Bieder, W. "Die Sieben Seligpreisungen in der Offenbarung Johannes," *TZBas*, 10 (1954), 13-30.

448 • Bibliography

Bieler, L. *Theios Anēr. Das Bild des "göttlichen Menschen" in Spätantike und Frühchristentum.* 2 vols. Darmstadt, 1967.

Bietenhard, H. *Die himmlische Welt im Urchristentum und Spätjudentum.* Tübingen, 1951.

Bihler, J. *Die Stephanusgeschichte im Zusammenhang der Apostelgeschichte.* München, 1963.

Bjerkelund, J. *Parakalō: Form und Sinn der Parakalō-Sätze in den paulinischen Briefen.* Oslo, 1967.

Björk, G. *"Onar idein:* De la perception de la rêve chez les anciens," *Eranos,* 44 (1946), 306-314.

————. "Heidnische und christliche Orakel mit fortigen Antworten," *SO,* 19 (1939), 86-98.

Black, M. *An Aramaic Approach to the Gospels and Acts.* 3rd ed. Oxford, 1967.

————. "The Eschatology of the Similitudes of Enoch," *JTS,* 3 (1952), 1-10.

————. "The Throne-Theophany, Prophetic Commission and the 'Son of Man': A Study in Tradition-History," in *Jews, Greeks and Christians: Religious Cultures in Late Antiquity.* Ed. R. Hamerton-Kelly and R. Scroggs. Leiden, 1976. Pp. 57-63.

————. *Apocalypsis Henochi Graece.* Leiden, 1970.

Blass, F., Debrunner, A., and Funk, R. *A Grammar of the New Testament and Other Early Christian Literature.* Chicago, 1961.

Blau, L. "Bat Ḳol," *Jewish Encyclopedia,* II, 588-592.

Blenkinsopp, J. "The Oracle of Judah and the Messianic Entry," *JBL,* 80 (1961), 55-64.

————. *Prophecy and Canon: A Contribution to the Study of Jewish Origins.* Notre Dame, 1977.

————. "Prophecy and Priesthood in Josephus," *JJS,* 25 (1974), 239-262.

Bloch, J. *On the Apocalyptic in Judaism.* Philadelphia, 1952.

Bloch, R. *Les prodiges dans l'antiquité classique.* Paris, 1963.

Bluck, R. S. *Plato's Meno.* Cambridge, 1961.

Blumer, H. "Collective Behavior," in *New Outline of the Principles of Sociology.* Ed. A. M. Lee. New York, 1951.

Boas, F. *The Religion of the Kwatkiutl.* 2 vols. New York, 1930.

Böcher, O. "Wölfe in Schafspelzen: Zum religionsgeschichtlichen Hintergrund von Matth. 7, 15," *TZ,* 24 (1968), 405-426.

Böckh, A. *Corpus Inscriptionum Graecarum.* 4 vols. Berlin, 1828-77.

————. *Pindari Opera.* 2 vols. Leipzig, 1811-19.

Boecker, H. J. *Redeformen des Rechtsleben im Alten Testament.* 2. Aufl. Neukirchen, 1970.

Boisacq, E. *Dictionnaire étymologique de la langue Grecque.* 4th ed. Heidelberg, 1950.

Boismard, M. E. "Rapproachements littéraires entre l'évangile de Luc et l'Apocalypse," in *Synoptische Studien.* Ed. J. Schmid and A. Vögtle. Münich, 1953, Pp. 53-63.

Bolkestein, M. H. *De Brieven aan de Tessalonicenzen.* Nijkerk, 1970.

Boll, F. *Aus der Offenbarung Johannis: Hellenistische Studien zum Weltbild der Apokalypse.* Berlin, 1914.

Bömer, F. *Untersuchungen über die Religion der Sklaven in Griechenland und Rom.* 4 vols. Wiesbaden, 1957-63.

Bonner, C. "Some Phases of Religious Feeling in Later Paganism," *HTR,* 30 (1937), 119-140.

————. "Traces of Thaumaturgic Technique in the Miracles," *HTR,* 20 (1927), 171-181.

Bonwetsch, N. "Die Prophetie im apostolischen und nachapostolischen Zeitalter," *Zeitschrift für kirchliche Wissenschaft und kirchliches Leben,* 5 (1884), 408-424, 460-477.

Borgen, P. *Bread from Heaven.* Leiden, 1965.

Boring, M. E. "The Apocalypse as Christian Prophecy: A Discussion of the Issues Raised by the Book of Revelation for the Study of Early Christian Prophecy," in *SBL Seminar Papers for 1974.* 2 vols. Missoula, 1974. Vol. II, pp. 43-62.

————. "Christian Prophecy and Matthew 10:23: A Test Exegesis," in *SBL Seminar Papers for 1976.* Missoula, 1976. Pp. 127-136.

————. "Christian Prophecy and Matthew 23:34-36: A Test Exegesis," in *SBL Seminar Papers for 1977.* Missoula, 1977. Pp. 117-126.

————. "Christian Prophets and the Gospel of Mark." Ph.D. dissertation, Vanderbilt, 1970.

_____. "How May We Identify Oracles of Christian Prophets in the Synoptic Tradition? Mark 3:28-29 as a Test Case," *JBL*, 91 (1972), 501-521.

_____. "The Paucity of Sayings in Mark: A Hypothesis," in *SBL Seminar Papers for 1977*. Missoula, 1977. Pp. 371-77.

_____. "The Unforgivable Sin Logion Mark III 28-29 (Matt. XII 31-32/Luke XII 10): Formal Analysis and History of the Tradition," *NovT*, 18 (1976), 258-279.

Bornemann, W. *Die Thessalonicherbriefe*. Göttingen, 1894.

Bornkamm, G. *Early Christian Experience*. New York, 1969.

_____. "Formen und Gattungen im NT," *RGG*. 3. Aufl. II, 999-1005.

_____. "Das Anathema in der urchristlichen Abendmahlsliturgie," in *Das Ende des Gesetzes: Paulusstudien*. 5. Aufl. Müchen, 1966.

Bouché-Leclercq, A. *Histoire de la divination dans l'antiquité*. 4 vols. Paris, 1879-82.

Bourguignon, Erika. *Possession*. San Francisco, 1976.

_____. *Religion, Altered States of Consciousness, and Social Change*. Columbus, 1973.

Bousset, W. *Die Himmelsreise der Seele*. Darmstadt, 1960. Originally printed in *ARW*, 4 (1901), 136-169, 229-273.

_____. *Die Offenbarung Johannis*. 6. Aufl. Göttingen, 1906.

Bousset, W. and Gressmann, H. *Die Religion des Judentums im späthellenistischen Zeitalter*. 3. Aufl. Tübingen, 1966.

Bowker, J. W. "The Speeches in Acts: A Study in Proem and Yelammedanu Form," *NTS*, 14 (1967-68), 76-111.

Bowman, J. "Prophets and Prophecy in Talmud and Midrash," *EQ*, 22 (1950), 107-114, 205-220, 255-275.

Bowra, C. M. *Pindar*. Oxford, 1964.

Brandon, S. G. F. *The Fall of Jerusalem*. 2nd ed. London, 1977.

_____. *Jesus and the Zealots*. Manchester, 1967.

Brandt, W. *Die jüdischen Baptismen*. Giessen, 1910.

Braun, H. *Qumran und das Neue Testament*. 2 vols. Tübingen, 1966.

Brenk, F. E. *In Mist Apparelled: Religious Themes in Plutarch's Moralia and Lives*. Leiden, 1977.

Brinsmead, B. H. *Galatians — Dialogical Response to Opponents*. Chico, 1982.

Brock, S. P. "BARNABAS: HUIUS PARAKLĒSEŌS," *JTS*, 25 (1974), 93-98.

Broek, R. van den. "The Sarapis Oracle in Macrobius *Sat.* I, 20, 16-17," in *Hommages à Maarten J. Vermaseren*. Ed M. B. de Boer and T. A. Edridge. Leiden, 1978. Vol. I, pp. 123-141.

_____. *Apollo in Asia: De orakels van Clarus en Didyma in de tweede en derde eeuw na Chr.* Leiden, 1981.

Brosch, J. *Charismen und Ämter in der Urkirche*. Bonn, 1951.

Brown, P. "Sorcery, Demons, and the Rise of Christianity," *Witchcraft: Confessions and Accusations*. Ed. M. Douglas. London, 1970. Pp. 17-45.

Brown, R. E. *The Birth of the Messiah: A Commentary on the Infancy Narratives in Matthew and Luke*. New York, 1977.

_____. "The Messianism of Qumran," *CBQ*, 19 (1957), 53-82.

_____. *The Semitic Background of the Term "Mystery" in the New Testament*. Philadelphia, 1968.

_____. *The Gospel According to John*. 2 vols. Garden City, New York, 1966-70.

Browne, G. M. "The Composition of the *Sortes Astrampsychi*," *University of London Institute of Classical Studies Bulletin*, 17 (1970), 95-100.

_____. *The Papyri of the Sortes Astrampsychi*. Meisenheim am Glan, 1974.

Brownlee, W. H. "The Background of Biblical Interpretation at Qumran," in *Qumrân: Sa piété, sa théologie et son milieu*. Ed. M. Delcor. Paris and Louvain, 1978. Pp. 183-193.

_____. "John the Baptist in the New Light of Ancient Scrolls," in *The Scrolls and the New Testament*. Ed. K. Stendahl. New York, 1957. Pp. 33-53.

_____. "Messianic Motives of Qumran and the New Testament," *NTS*, 2 (1956), 12-30.

Brox, F. "ANATHEMA IESOUS (1 Kor 12,3)," *BZ*, 12 (1968), 103-111.

_____. "*Prophēteia* im ersten Timotheusbrief," *BZ*, 20 (1976), 229-232.

————. *Pseudepigraphie in der heidnischen und jüdisch-christlichen Antike.* Darmstadt, 1977.
Bruce, F. F. *Biblical Exegesis in the Qumran Texts.* Grand Rapids, 1959.
————. "The Book of Daniel and the Qumran Community," in *Neotestamentica et Semitica: Studies in Honour of Matthew Black.* Ed. E. E. Ellis and M. Wilcox. Edinburgh, 1969. Pp. 221-235.
————. *The Book of Acts.* London, 1954.
————. "Josephus and Daniel," *ASTI,* 4 (1965), 148-162.
Brun, L. *Segen und Fluch in Urchristentum.* Oslo, 1933.
Brunt, P. A. (trans.). *Arrian.* Vol. 1. Cambridge, 1976.
Buchanan, G. W. "The Word of God and the Apocalyptic Vision," in *SBL Seminar Papers for 1978.* Missoula, 1978. Pp. 183-192.
Bultmann, R. *Die Geschichte der synoptischen Tradition.* 8. Aufl. Göttingen, 1970. With the *Ergänzungsheft.* 4. Aufl. Ed. G. Theissen and P. Vielhauer. Göttingen, 1971.
————. *The Gospel of John: A Commentary.* Trans. G. R. Beasley-Murray et al. Philadelphia, 1971.
————. *Der Stil der paulinischen Predigt und die kynisch-stoische Diatribe.* Göttingen, 1910.
————. *Die Erforschung der synoptischen Evangelien.* 5. Aufl. Berlin, 1966.
————. *Commentary on the Johannine Epistles.* Trans. R. P. O'Hara et al. Ed. R. Funk. Philadelphia, 1973.
————. *Das Johannesevangelium.* 16. Aufl. Göttingen, 1959.
————. *The Theology of the New Testament.* 2 vols. Trans. K. Grobel. New York, 1951-55.
Bultmann, R. and Kundsin, K. *Form Criticism: Two Essays on New Testament Research.* Trans. F. C. Grant. New York, 1934.
Burchard, C. *Der dreizehnte Zeuge: Traditions- und Kompositionsgeschichtliche Untersuchungen zu Lukas' Darstellung der Frühzeit des Paulus.* Göttingen, 1970.
Buresch, K. *Klaros: Untersuchungen zum Orakelwesen des späteren Altertums.* Leipzig, 1889.
Burkert, W. *Griechische Religion der archäischen und klassischen Epoche.* Stuttgart, 1977.
Burney, C. F. *The Poetry of Our Lord: An Examination of the Formal Elements of Hebrew Poetry in the Discourses of Jesus Christ.* Oxford, 1925.
Burrows, M. "Prophecy and the Prophets at Qumran," in *Israel's Prophetic Heritage: Essays in Honor of James Muilenburg.* Ed. B. W. Anderson and W. Harrelson. New York, 1962. Pp. 223-232.
Burton, E. D. *A Critical and Exegetical Commentary on the Epistle to the Galatians.* Edinburgh, 1921.
Busch, F. *Zum Verständnis der synoptischen Eschatologie, Markus 13 neu untersucht.* Gütersloh, 1938.

Caird, G. B. *A Commentary on the Revelation of St. John the Divine.* New York, 1966.
Calder, W. M. "Philadelphia and Montanism," *BJRL,* 7 (1922-23), 309-354.
————. "Two Phrygian Epitaphs," *CR,* 50 (1936), 214-15.
Calvert, D. G. A. "An Examination of the Criteria for Distinguishing the Authentic Words of Jesus," *NTS,* 18 (1971-72), 209-218.
Campenhausen, H. von. *Ecclesiastical Authority and Spiritual Power in the Church of the First Three Centuries.* London, 1969.
————. *Kirchliches Amt und geistliche Vollmacht.* Tübingen, 1953.
Caragounis, C. C. *The Ephesian Mysterion: Meaning and Content.* Lund, 1977.
Casson, L. *Travel in the Ancient World.* Toronto, 1974.
Caster, M. *Études sur Alexandre ou le faux prophète.* Paris, 1938.
————. *Lucien et la Pensée Religieuse de son temps.* Paris, 1937.
Cavallin, H. C. C. "The False Teachers of 2 Pt as Pseudo-Prophets," *NovT,* 21 (1979), 263-270.
Cerfaux, L. *Christ in the Theology of St. Paul.* New York, 1959.
Chadwick, H. "Some Reflections on the Character and Theology of the Odes of Solomon," in *Kyriakon: Festschrift Johannes Quasten.* Ed. P. Granfield and J. A. Jungmann. 2 vols. Vol. I, pp. 266-270.
Chadwick, N. K. *Poetry and Prophecy.* Cambridge, 1942.

Charles, R. H. (ed.). *The Apocrypha and Pseudepigrapha of the Old Testament.* 2 vols. Oxford, 1913.
_____. *A Critical and Exegetical Commentary on the Revelation of St. John.* Edinburgh, 1920.
Charlesworth, J. H. *The Pseudepigrapha and Modern Research.* Missoula, 1976.
_____. *The Odes of Solomon: The Syriac Texts.* Corrected ed. Missoula, 1977.
_____. "Paranomasia and Assonance in the Syriac Text of the Odes of Solomon," *Semitics,* 1 (1970), 12-26.
Charlot, J. *New Testament Disunity: Its Significance for Christianity Today.* New York, 1970.
Chevallier, M.-A. *Esprit de Dieu, paroles d'hommes: Le rôle de l'esprit dans les ministères de la parole selon l'apôtre Paul.* Neuchatel, 1966.
Christ, F. *Jesus Sophia: Die Sophia-Christologie bei den Synoptikern.* Zürich, 1970.
Christensen, D. L. *Transformations of the War Oracle in Old Testament Prophecy.* Missoula, 1975.
Clark, R. J. "Trophonios: The Manner of His Revelation," *Proceedings of the American Philological Association,* 99 (1968), 63-75.
Clark, W. M. "Law," in *Old Testament Form Criticism.* Ed. J. H. Hayes. San Antonio, 1974. Pp. 99-139.
Clements, R. E. *Prophecy and Covenant.* Naperville, 1965.
Clifford, R. J. "The Use of HÔY in the Prophets," *CBQ,* 28 (1966), 458-464.
Cohn, N. *The Pursuit of the Millennium.* Rev. ed. Oxford, 1970.
Coleborne, W. "The Shepherd of Hermas," *Studia Patristica,* 10/1 (1970), 65-70.
Collin, M. F. "Hidden Vessels in Samaritan Traditions," *JSJ,* 3 (1972), 97-116.
Collins, A. Y. *The Combat Myth in the Book of Revelation.* Missoula, 1976.
_____. "The History-of-Religions Approach to Apocalypticism and the 'Angel of the Waters' (Rev. 16:4-7)," *CBQ,* 39 (1977), 367-381.
Collins, J. J. "Apocalypse: Towards the Morphology of a Genre," in *SBL Seminar Papers for 1977.* Missoula, 1977. Pp. 359-370.
_____. "Persian Apocalypses," *Semeia,* 14 (1979), 207-217.
_____. "Apocalyptic Eschatology as the Transcendence of Death," *CBQ,* 36 (1974), 21-43.
_____. *The Apocalyptic Vision of the Book of Daniel.* Missoula, 1977.
_____. "The Court-Tales in Daniel and the Development of Apocalyptic," *JBL,* 94 (1975), 218-234.
_____. "Jewish Apocalyptic Against Its Hellenistic Near Eastern Environment," *BASOR,* 220 (1975), 27-36.
_____. "Pseudonymity, Historical Reviews and the Genre of the Revelation of John," *CBQ,* 39 (1977), 329-343.
_____. *The Sibylline Oracles of Egyptian Judaism.* Missoula, 1974.
Conzelmann, H. *1 Corinthians.* Philadelphia, 1975.
_____. *Die Apostelgeschichte.* Tübingen, 1963.
Cordes, Jr., H. H. "The Religious Use of Oracles in Attic Tragedy." Ph.D. dissertation, University of Chicago, 1961.
Corssen, P. "Die Zeugnisse des Tacitus und Pseudo-Josephus über Christus," *ZNW,* 15 (1914), 114-140.
Cothenet, É. "Les prophètes chrétiens comme exégètes charismatiques de l'Écriture," in *Prophetic Vocation in the New Testament and Today.* Ed. J. Panagopoulos. Leiden, 1977. Pp. 77-107.
_____. "Les Prophètes chrétiens dans l'Évangile selon saint Matthieu," in *L'Évangile selon Matthieu. Rédaction et Théologie.* Ed. M. Didier. Gembloux, 1972. Pp. 281-308.
_____. "Prophétisme dans le Nouveau Testament," *DBSupp,* VIII, 1222-1337.
Coughenour, R. A. "The Woe-Oracles in Ethiopic Enoch," *JST,* 9 (1978), 192-97.
Crahay, R. "La bouche de la vérité," in *Divination et Rationalité.* Ed. J. P. Vernant et al. Paris, 1974. Pp. 201-219.
_____. *La littérature oraculaire chez Hérodote.* Paris, 1956.
Crenshaw, J. L. *Prophetic Conflict.* Berlin, 1971.
Crone, T. M. *Early Christian Prophecy: A Study of Its Origin and Function.* Baltimore, 1973.

Cross, Jr., F. M. *Canaanite Myth and Hebrew Epic: Essays in the History of the Religion of Israel.* Cambridge, Massachusetts, 1973.

————. "The Council of Yahweh in Second Isaiah," *JNES,* 12 (1953), 274-77.

————. "The Early History of the Qumran Community," *McCormick Quarterly,* 21 (1968), 249-264.

————. "New Directions in the Study of Apocalyptic," *JTC,* 6 (1969), 157-165.

Cullmann, O. *Early Christian Worship.* Trans. A. S. Todd and J. B. Torrance. London, 1953.

————. *Jesus and the Revolutionaries.* Trans. G. Putnam. New York, 1970.

————. *Christology of the New Testament.* Rev. ed. Trans. S. C. Guthrie and C. A. M. Hall. Philadelphia, 1963.

Cutten, G. B. *Speaking with Tongues.* New Haven, 1927.

Dahl, N. A. *Das Volk Gottes: Eine Untersuchung zum Kirchenbewusstsein des Urchristentums.* Reprint, Darmstadt, 1963.

Daniel, C. "Faux prophètes: surnom des Esséniens dans le sermon sur la montagne," *RQ,* 7 (1969), 45-79.

Danker, F. W. *Benefactor: Epigraphic Study of a Graeco-Roman and New Testament Semantic Field.* St. Louis, 1982.

Daube, D. " Public Retort and Private Explanation," in *The New Testament and Rabbinic Judaism.* London, 1956. Pp. 141-150.

————. "Rabbinic Methods of Interpretation and Hellenistic Rhetoric," *HUCA,* 32 (1949), 239-264.

Dautzenberg, G. "Zum religionsgeschichtlichen Hintergrund der *diakrisis pneumatikōn* (1 Kor 12:10)," *BZ,* 15 (1971), 93-104.

————. *Urchristliche Prophetie: Ihre Erforschung, ihre Voraussetzungen im Judentum und ihre Struktur im ersten Korintherbrief.* Stuttgart, 1975.

————. "Botschaft und Bedeutung der urchristlichen Prophetie nach dem ersten Korintherbrief (2:6-16; 12-14)," in *Prophetic Vocation in the New Testament and Today.* Ed. J. Panagopoulos. Leiden, 1977. Pp. 131-161.

Davies, J. G. "The Genesis of Belief in an Imminent Parousia," *JTS,* 14 (1963), 104-107.

Davies, Paul E. "Did Jesus Die as a Martyr-Prophet," *BR,* 19 (1974), 37-47.

————. "Jesus and the Role of the Prophet," *JBL,* 64 (1945), 241-254.

Davies, W. D. *The Setting of the Sermon on the Mount.* Cambridge, 1964.

————. "Reflections on Tradition: The Aboth Revisited," in *Christian History and Interpretation: Studies Presented to John Knox.* Ed. W. R. Farmer, C. F. D. Moule, and R. R. Niebuhr. London, 1967. Pp. 127-159.

Deden, D. "Le 'mystère' Paulinien," *ETL,* 13 (1936), 405-442.

Dégh, L. and Vázsonyi, A. "Legend and Belief," *Genre,* 4 (1971), 281-304.

Deichgräber, R. *Gotteshymnus und Christushymnus in der frühen Christenheit: Untersuchungen zu Form, Sprache und Stil der frühchristlichen Hymnen.* Göttingen, 1967.

de Jonge, M. *Jesus: Stranger from Heaven and Son of God.* Missoula, 1977.

————. "Josephus und die Zukunftserwartungen seines Volkes," in *Josephus-Studien.* Göttingen, 1974. Pp. 205-219.

Dekkers, E. *"Prophèteia-Praefatio,"* in *Mélanges offerts à Mademoiselle Christine Mohrmann.* Utrecht, 1963. Pp. 190-95.

Delatte, A. *Les conceptions de l'enthousiasme.* Paris, 1934.

Delcor, M. "The Selloi of the Oracle of Dodona and the Oracular Priests of the Semitic Religions," in *Religion d'Israël et proche orient ancien.* Leiden, 1976. Pp. 116-123.

Delling, G. "Die biblische Prophetie bei Josephus," in *Josephus-Studien.* Ed. O. Betz, K. Haacker, and M. Hengel. Göttingen, 1974. Pp. 109-121.

————. "Zum gottesdienstlichen Stil der Johannesapokalypse," *NovT,* 3 (1959), 107-137.

DeVries, S. J. *Prophet against Prophet: The Role of the Micaiah Narrative (I Kings 22) in the Development of Early Prophetic Tradition.* Grand Rapids, 1978.

Dexinger, F. *Henochs Zehnwochenapokalypse und offene Probleme der Apokalyptikforschung.* Leiden, 1977.

Dibelius, M. *Die Formgeschichte des Evangeliums.* Ed. G. Bornkamm. 6. Aufl. Tübingen, 1971.

_____. *Geschichte der urchristlichen Literatur.* 2 vols. Berlin, 1926.

_____. *Der Hirt des Hermas.* Tübingen, 1923.

_____. *An die Thessalonicher I.II. An die Philipper.* 2. Aufl. Tübingen, 1925.

_____. *A Fresh Approach to the New Testament and Early Christian Literature.* New York, 1936.

Diels, H. *Die Fragmente der Vorsokratiker.* 3. Aufl. Berlin, 1912.

Dietrich, E. L. "Das religiös-emphatische Ich-Wort bei den jüdischen Apokalyptikern, Weisheitslehrern und Rabbinen," *ZRGG,* 4 (1952), 289-311.

Dietzel, A. "Beten im Geist," *TZ,* 13 (1957), 12ff.

Dittenberger, W. *Sylloge Inscriptionum Graecarum.* 3. Aufl. 4 vols. Leipzig, 1915-24.

Dodd, C. H. *According to the Scriptures: The Substructure of New Testament Theology.* London, 1952.

_____. "The Beatitudes: A Form-Critical Study," in *More New Testament Studies.* Grand Rapids, 1968. Pp. 1-10.

_____. *The Bible and the Greeks.* London, 1935.

_____. *Historical Tradition in the Fourth Gospel.* Cambridge, 1965.

_____. *The Interpretation of the Fourth Gospel.* Cambridge, 1953.

_____. "Jesus as Teacher and Prophet," in *Mysterium Christi.* Ed. G. K. A. Bell and A. Deissmann. New York, 1930. Pp. 53-66.

_____. *The Parables of the Kingdom.* New York, 1961.

_____. "The 'Primitive Catechism' and the Sayings of Jesus," in *More New Testament Studies.* Grand Rapids, 1968. Pp. 11-19.

_____. "The Prophecy of Caiaphas (John XI, 47-53)," in *Neotestamentica et Patristica.* Leiden, 1962. Pp. 134-143.

Dodds, E. R. "Maendaism in the Bacchae," *HTR,* 33 (1940), 155-176.

_____. "New Light on the 'Chaldaean Oracles'," *HTR,* 54 (1961), 263-273.

_____. *The Greeks and the Irrational.* Berkeley and Los Angeles, 1951.

_____. *Pagan and Christian in an Age of Anxiety.* Cambridge, 1965.

_____. "Plato and the Irrational," in *The Ancient Concept of Progress and Other Essays on Greek Literature and Belief.* Oxford, 1973. Pp. 106-125.

_____. "The Religion of the Ordinary Man in Greece," in *The Ancient Concept of Progress.* Oxford, 1973. Pp. 140-155.

_____. "Supernormal Phenomena in Classical Antiquity," in *The Ancient Concept of Progress.* Oxford, 1973. Pp. 156-210.

Doeve, J. W. "The Flight of Rabban Yohanan be Zakkai from Jerusalem — When and Why?" in *Übersetzung und Deutung: Studien zu dem Alten Testament und seiner Umwelt.* Nijkerk, 1977. Pp. 50-65.

_____. *Jewish Hermeneutics in the Synoptic Gospels and Acts.* Assen, 1954.

Dölger, F. J. "THEOU PHŌNĒ," *Antike und Christentum,* 5 (1936), 218-223.

Donfried, K. *The Setting of Second Clement in Early Christianity.* Leiden, 1974.

Dornseiff, F. *Das Alphabet in Mystik und Magie.* Leipzig, 1922.

Dörrie, H. and Dörries, H. "Erotapokriseis," *RAC,* 6 (1966), 342-370.

Douglas, M. *Purity and Danger: An Analysis of Concepts of Pollution and Taboo.* New York, 1966.

_____. *Natural Symbols.* New York, 1973.

Drejergaard, K. "Jødernes fortrin," *DTT,* 35 (1973), 81-101.

Dübner, F. *Scholia Graeca in Aristophanem.* Reprint, Hildesheim, 1969.

Dungan, D. *The Sayings of Jesus in the Churches of Paul.* Philadelphia, 1971.

Dunn, J. D. G. *Jesus and the Spirit.* Philadelphia, 1975.

_____. *Baptism in the Holy Spirit.* Philadelphia, 1970.

_____. "New Wine in Old Wine Skins. VI. Prophet," *ExpTim,* 85 (1973), 4-8.

_____. "Prophetic 'I'-Sayings and the Jesus Tradition: The Importance of Testing Prophetic Utterances within Early Christianity," *NTS,* 24 (1977-78), 175-198.

————. "Spirit-and-Fire Baptism," *NovT,* 14 (1972), 81-92.

————. *Unity and Diversity in the New Testament: An Inquiry into the Character of Earliest Christianity.* Philadelphia, 1977.

Dupont, J. *Gnosis: La connaissance religieuse dans les épitres de saint Paul.* Paris, 1949.

Dupont-Sommer, A. *The Essene Writings from Qumran.* Trans. G. Vermes. Oxford, 1961.

Eddy, S. K. *The King is Dead: Studies in the Near Eastern Resistance to Hellenism 334-31 B.C.* Lincoln, 1961.

Edelstein, E. J. and Edelstein, L. *Asclepius: A Collection and Interpretation of the Testimonies.* Baltimore, 1945.

Edwards, R. A. "An Approach to a Theology of Q," *JR,* 51 (1971), 247-269.

————. "Christian Prophecy and the Q Tradition," in *SBL Seminar Papers for 1976.* Missoula, 1976. Pp. 119-126.

————. "The Eschatological Correlative as a *Gattung* in the New Testament," *ZNW,* 60 (1969), 9-20.

————. *The Sign of Jonah in the Theology of the Evangelists and Q.* Naperville, Illinois, n.d.

————. *A Theology of Q: Eschatology, Prophecy, and Wisdom.* Philadelphia, 1976.

Ehrlich, E. L. *Der Traum im Alten Testament.* Berlin, 1953.

————. "Der Traum in Talmud," *ZNW,* 47 (1956), 133ff.

Eichrodt, W. *Theology of the Old Testament.* 2 vols. Trans. J. A. Baker. Vol. I. Philadelphia, 1961.

Eissfeldt, O. *Einleitung in das Alte Testament.* 3. Aufl. Tübingen, 1964.

————. *The Old Testament: An Introduction.* Trans. P. R. Ackroyd. New York and Evanston, 1965.

Eitrem, S. *Orakel und Mysterien am Ausgang der Antike.* Zürich, 1947.

Eliade, M. *Patterns in Comparative Religion.* New York, 1958.

————. *The Quest. History and Meaning in Religion.* Chicago, 1969.

————. *The Sacred and the Profane.* New York, 1959.

————. *Shamanism: Archaic Techniques of Ecstasy.* New York, 1964.

Ellermeier, F. *Prophetie in Mari und Israel.* Herzberg, 1968.

Ellicott, C. J. *A Critical and Grammatical Commentary on St. Paul's Epistles to the Thessalonians.* Andover, 1864.

Elliger, K. *Studien zum Habakuk-Kommentar vom Toten Meer.* Tübingen, 1953.

Elliott-Binns, L. E. *Galilean Christianity.* London, 1956.

Ellis, E. E. "Luke 11.49-51: An Oracle of a Christian Prophet?" *ExpTim,* 74 (1963), 157-58.

————. "Midrash, Targum and New Testament Quotations," in *Neotestamentica et Semitica.* Ed. E. E. Ellis and M. Wilcox. Edinburgh, 1969. Pp. 61-69.

————. *Paul's Use of the Old Testament.* Grand Rapids, 1957.

————. *Prophecy and Hermeneutic in Early Christianity: New Testament Essays.* Grand Rapids, 1978.

————. "Prophecy in the New Testament Church — and Today," in *Prophetic Vocation in the New Testament and Today.* Ed. J. Panagopoulos. Leiden, 1977. Pp. 46-57.

————. "The Role of the Christian Prophet in Acts," in *Apostolic History and the Gospel.* Ed. W. W. Gasque and R. P. Martin. Grand Rapids, 1970. Pp. 55-67.

————. " 'Wisdom' and 'Knowledge' in 1 Corinthians," *Tyndale Bulletin,* 25 (1974), 82-98.

Engelsen, N. J. "Glossolalia and Other Forms of Inspired Speech according to I Corinthians 12–14." Ph. D. dissertation, Yale University, 1970.

Englemann, H. *The Delian Aretalogy of Sarapis.* Leiden, 1975.

Erbse, H. *Scholia Graeca in Homeri Iliadem (Scholia Vetera).* Vols. 3 and 4. Berlin, 1974-75.

Erichsen, W. *Demotische Orakelfragen.* Copenhagen, 1942.

Eustathius. *Commentarii ad Homeri Iliadem.* 2 vols. Leipzig, 1829.

Eynde, D. van den. *Les Normes de l'Enseignment chrétien dans la littérature patristique des trois premiers siècles.* Gembloux and Paris, 1933.

Farmer, W. *Maccabees, Zealots and Josephus.* New York, 1956.

Farnell, L. R. *Greek Hero Cults and Ideas of Immortality.* Oxford, 1921.

Fascher, E. *PROPHĒTĒS. Eine sprach- und religionsgeschichtliche Untersuchung.* Giessen, 1927.

Fears, J. R. *Princeps A Diis Electus: The Divine Election of the Emperor as a Political Concept at Rome.* Rome, 1977.

Ferguson, J. *The Religions of the Roman Empire.* Ithaca, New York, 1970.

——————. *Utopias of the Classical World.* London, 1975.

Festugière, A.-J. *Personal Religion among the Greeks.* Berkeley and Los Angeles, 1954.

——————. *La révélation d'Hermès Trismégiste.* 2nd ed. Vol. 1. Paris, 1950.

Feuillet, A. "Les vingt-quatre vieillards de l'Apocalypse," *RB,* 65 (1958), 5-32.

——————. *The Apocalypse.* Trans. T. E. Crane. Staten Island, 1965.

Fichter, S. *A Southern Parish.* Chicago, 1951.

Fiedler, P. *Die Formel "Und Siehe" im Neuen Testament.* München, 1969.

Filson, F. V. "The Christian Teacher in the First Century," *JBL,* 60 (1941), 317-328.

Finkel, A. "The Pesher of Dreams and Scripture," *RQ,* 4 (1960), 357-370.

Finkelstein, L. *Akiba.* Philadelphia, 1936.

Fischel, H. A. "Martyr and Prophet," *JQR,* 37 (1946-47), 265-280, 363-386.

Fischer, J. A. "Pauline Literary Forms and Thought Patterns," *CBQ,* 39 (1977), 209-223.

Fitzer, G. *Das Weibe Schweige in der Gemeinde.* München, 1963.

Flaceliere, R. *Greek Oracles.* Trans. D. Garman. London, 1965.

——————. *Plutarque sur la disparition des oracles.* Paris, 1947.

——————. *Plutarque sur l'E de Delphes.* Paris, 1941.

Flückiger, F. "Die Redaktion der Zukunftsrede in Markus 13," *TZ,* 26 (1970), 395-409.

Flusser, D. "Paganism in Palestine," in *Compendia Rerum Iudaicarum ad Novum Testamentum* Sec. I, vol. 1. Ed. S. Saffrai, M. Stern, and M. de Jonge. Philadelphia, 1976. Pp. 1065-1100

Foerster, W. "Der heilige Geist im Spätjudentum," *NTS,* 8 (1961-62), 117-134.

Fohrer, G. "Die Gattung der Berichte über symbolische Handlungen der Propheten," *ZAW,* 64 (1952), 101-120.

——————. *Die Propheten des Alten Testaments.* 7 vols. Gütersloh, 1974-77.

——————. "Prophetie und Magie," *ZAW,* 78 (1966), 25-47.

——————. *Die symbolischen Handlungen der Propheten.* Zürich, 1953.

Fontenrose, J. *The Delphic Oracle: Its Responses and Operations.* Berkeley and Los Angeles, 1978.

Fornberg, T. *An Early Church in a Pluralistic Society: A Study of 2 Peter.* Lund, 1977.

Fox, R. L. *Alexander the Great.* New York, 1974.

Frame, J. E. *A Critical and Exegetical Commentary on the Epistles of St. Paul to the Thessalonians.* Edinburgh, 1912.

Franklin, E. *Christ the Lord: A Study in the Purpose and Theology of Luke-Acts.* Philadelphia, 1975.

Freedman, D. N. "The Old Testament at Qumran," *McCormick Quarterly,* 21 (1967-68), 299-306.

Fridrichsen, A. "The Conflict of Jesus with the Unclean Spirits," *Theology,* 22 (1931), 122-135.

——————. *The Problem of Miracle in Primitive Christianity.* Trans. R. A. Harrisville and J. S. Hanson. Minneapolis, 1972.

Friedrich, G. "Geist und Amt," *Wort und Dienst,* 3 (1952), 61-85.

Frisk, H. *Griechisches etymologisches Wörterbuch.* 3 vols. Heidelberg, 1960-72.

Fuller, R. H. "The 'Thou Art Peter' Pericope and the Easter Appearances," *McCormick Quarterly,* 20 (1967), 309-315.

——————. *The Foundations of New Testament Christology.* New York, 1965.

Gager, J. G. *Kingdom and Community: The Social World of Early Christianity.* Englewood Cliffs, New Jersey, 1975.

Garrod, H. W. "Note on the Messianic Character of the Fourth Eclogue," *CR,* 9 (1905), 37-38.

Gärtner, B. *The Temple and the Community.* Cambridge, 1965.

Gaster, M. "The Logos Ebraikos in the Magical Papyrus of Paris and the Book of Enoch," *Journal of the Royal Asiatic Society,* 33 (1901), 109-117.

Gaston, L. *No Stone on Another: Studies in the Significance of the Fall of Jerusalem in the Synoptic Gospels.* Leiden, 1970.

Georgi, D. *Die Gegner des Paulus im 2. Korintherbrief: Studien zur religiösen Propaganda in der Spätantike.* Neukirchen-Vluyn, 1964.

Gerhardsson, B. *Die Anfänge der Evangelien Tradition.* Wuppertal, 1977.

—————. *Memory and Manuscript: Oral Tradition and Written Transmission in Rabbinic Judaism and Early Christianity.* 2nd ed. Uppsala and Lund, 1964.

—————. *Tradition and Transmission in Early Christianity.* Lund and Copenhagen, 1964.

Gerstenberger, E. "The Woe-Oracles of the Prophets," *JBL,* 81 (1962), 249-263.

Giblet, J. "Prophétisme et attente d'un messie prophète dans l'ancien Judaisme," in *L'Attente du Messie.* Ed. L. Cerfaux et al. Bruges, 1954. Pp. 85-130.

Giessen, H. "Der verdorrte Feigenbaum — Eine symbolische Aussage? Zu Mk. 11, 12-14, 20f.," *BZ,* 20 (1976), 95-111.

Giet, S. *Hermas et les Pasteurs. Les trois auteurs du Pasteur d'Hermas.* Paris, 1963.

Gillespie, T. W. "A Pattern of Prophetic Speech in First Corinthians," *JBL,* 97 (1978), 74-95.

Gils, F. *Jésus Prophète d'après les Évangiles synoptiques.* Louvain, 1957.

Ginzberg, L. *The Legends of the Jews.* 7 vols. Philadelphia, 1909-28.

Glasson, T. F. *Moses in the Fourth Gospel.* London, 1963.

Glover, R. "The Didache's Quotation and the Synoptic Gospels," *NTS,* 5 (1958-59), 22ff.

Goffman, I. *The Presentation of the Self in Everyday Life.* New York, 1955.

Goguel, M. *Jesus the Nazarene —Myth or History?* Trans. F. Stephens. London, 1926.

—————. *The Life of Jesus.* Trans. O. Wyon. London, 1933.

—————. "Pneumatisme of eschatologie," *Revue de l'histoire des religions,* 132 (1947), 124-169.

Goodenough, E. R. *By Light, Light: The Mystic Gospel of Hellenistic Judaism.* Reprint, Amsterdam, 1969.

Gotthold, Z. W. "A Supplementary Note," *Christian News from Israel,* 25 (1975), 48-50.

Gow, A. S. F. and Scholfield, A. F. *Nicander: The Poems and Poetical Fragments.* Cambridge, 1953.

Grabner-Haider, A. *Paraklese und Eschatologie bei Paulus.* Münster, 1968.

Graetz, H. *Kohelet oder der salomonische Prediger.* Leipzig, 1871.

Grant, F. C. *Roman Hellenism and the New Testament.* New York, 1962.

Grant, R. M. *The Apostolic Fathers: A Translation and Commentary.* Vol. I: *An Introduction.* New York, 1965.

—————. *The Apostolic Fathers: A Translation and Commentary.* Vol. II: *Ignatius.* New York, 1966.

—————. *Early Christianity and Society.* New York, 1977.

—————. *The Formation of the New Testament.* New York, 1965.

Grass, H. *Ostergeschehen und Osterberichte.* Göttingen, 1956.

Grässer, E. *Das Problem der Parusieverzögerung in den synoptischen Evangelien und in der Apostelgeschichte.* 3. Aufl. Berlin, 1978.

Gray, B. C. "The Movements of the Jerusalem Church during the First Jewish War," *JEH,* 24 (1973), 1-7.

Greene, G. C. *Scholia Platonica.* Haverford, 1938.

Greeven, H. "Propheten, Lehrer, Vorsteher bei Paulus: zur Frage der 'Amten' im Urchristentum," *ZNW,* 44 (1952-53), 1-43.

—————. " 'Wer unter euch...?' " *Wort und Dienst,* 3 (1952), 86-101.

—————. "Die Geistesgaben bei Paulus," *Wort und Dienst,* 6 (1959), 111-120.

Grenfell, B. P., Hunt, A. S., and Hogarth, D. G. *Fayûm Towns and Their Papyri.* London, 1900.

Gressmann, H. *Der Messias.* Göttingen, 1929.

Griffith, F. L., and Thompson, H. *The Leyden Papyrus: An Egyptian Magical Book.* Reprint, New York, 1974.

Grudem, W. A. *The Gift of Prophecy in 1 Corinthians.* Washington, D.C., 1982.

—————. "A Response to Gerhard Dautzenberg on 1 Cor. 12.10," *BZ,* 22 (1978), 253-270.

Gry, L. *Les dires prophétiques d'Esdras.* 2 vols. Paris, 1938.

Guillaume, A. *Prophecy and Divination among the Hebrews and Other Semites.* New York, 1938.

Guillon, P. *Les trépieds du Ptoion.* 2 vols. Paris, 1943.

Gunkel, H. "The Israelite Prophecy from the Time of Amos," in *Twentieth Century Theology in the Making.* Ed. J. Pelikan. New York, 1969. Pp. 48-75.

_____. *Die Wirkungen des heiligen Geistes nach den populären Anschauungen der apostolischen Zeit und der Lehre des Apostels Paulus.* 3. Aufl. Göttingen, 1909.

Gunther, J. J. "The Fate of the Jerusalem Church," *TZ,* 29 (1973), 81-94.

Günther, W. *Das Orakel von Didyma in hellenistischer Zeit.* Tübingen, 1971.

Güttgemanns, E. *Offene Fragen zur Formgeschichte des Evangeliums.* 2. Aufl. München, 1971.

Guy, H. A. *New Testament Prophecy: Its Origin and Significance.* London, 1947.

Habel, N. "The Form and Significance of the Call Narrative," *ZAW,* 77 (1965), 297-323.

Haenchen, E. *The Acts of the Apostles: A Commentary.* Trans. B. Noble et al. Ed. R. McL. Wilson. Philadelphia, 1971.

Hagner, D. A. *The Use of the Old and New Testaments in Clement of Rome.* Leiden, 1973.

Hahn, F. *The Titles of Jesus in Christology.* Trans. H. Knight and G. Ogg. New York and Cleveland, 1969.

_____. "Die Sendschreiben der Johannesapokalypse: Ein Beitrag zur Bestimmung prophetischer Redeformen," in *Tradition und Glaube.* Ed. G. Jeremias, H.-W. Kuhn, and H. Stegemann. Göttingen, 1971. Pp. 357-394.

_____. *The Worship of the Early Church.* Trans. D. E. Green. Ed. J. Reumann. Philadelphia, 1973.

Hahn, I. "Josephus und die Eschatologie von Qumran," in *Qumran-Probleme.* Ed. H. Bardtke. Berlin, 1963. Pp. 167-191.

Halliday, W. R. *Greek Divination: A Study of Its Methods and Principles.* Reprint, Chicago, 1967.

_____. *Greek Questions.* Oxford, 1928.

Hammershaimb, E. *Some Aspects of Old Testament Prophecy from Isaiah to Malachi.* Copenhagen, 1966.

Hammond, N. G. L. *Epirus.* Oxford, 1967.

Hanson, P. D. "Apocalypse, Genre," *The Interpreter's Dictionary of the Bible, Supplementary Volume.* Nashville, 1976. Pp. 27-28.

_____. "Apocalypticism," *The Interpreter's Dictionary of the Bible, Supplementary Volume.* Nashville, 1976. Pp. 28-34.

_____. "Jewish Apocalyptic Against Its Near Eastern Background," *RB,* 68 (1971), 31-58.

_____. "Old Testament Apocalyptic Reexamined," *Interpretation,* 25 (1971), 454-479.

_____. "Zechariah 9 and the Recapitulation of an Ancient Ritual Pattern," *JBL,* 92 (1973), 37-59.

_____. *The Dawn of Apocalyptic.* Philadelphia, 1975.

Haran, M. "From Early to Classical Prophecy: Continuity and Change," *VT,* 27 (1977), 385-397.

Hare, D. R. A. *The Theme of Jewish Persecution of Christians in the Gospel according to St. Matthew.* Cambridge, 1967.

Harnack, A. *Die Chronologie der altchristlichen Literatur bis Eusebius.* Leipzig, 1897.

_____. *The Constitution and Law of the Church in the First Two Centuries.* Trans. F. L. Pogson. Ed. H. D. A. Major. London, 1910.

_____. "Die Lehre der Zwölf Apostel," *TU,* 2 (1884).

_____. *Die Mission und Ausbreitung des Christentums in den ersten drei Jahrhunderten.* 4. Aufl. Leipzig, 1924.

_____. "Über Zwei von Grenfell und Hunt entdeckte und publicirte altchristliche Fragmente," *SBA,* 17 (1898), 516-520.

Harner, M. J. (ed.). *Hallucinogens and Shamanism.* New York and London, 1973.

Harner, P. B. "The Salvation Oracle in Second Isaiah," *JBL,* 88 (1969), 418-434.

Harnisch, W. *Eschatologische Existenz: Ein exegetischer Beitrag zum Sachanliegen von 1. Thessalonicher 4,13-5,11.* Göttingen, 1973.

Harrington, D. J. *Hebrew Fragments of Pseudo-Philo's Liber Antiquitatem Biblicarum.* Missoula, 1974.

Harris, J. R. *The Odes and Psalms of Solomon.* Cambridge, 1909.

Hartman, L. *Prophecy Interpreted: The Formation of Some Jewish Apocalyptic Texts and of the Eschatological Discourse Mark 13 par.* Lund, 1966.

Hasler, V. *Amen. Redaktionsgeschichtliche Untersuchung zur Einführungsformel der Herrenworte "Wahrlich ich sage euch."* Zürich, 1969.

Hausman, R. A. "The Function of Elijah as a Model in Luke-Acts." Ph.D. dissertation, University of Chicago, 1975.

Hawthorne, G. F. "Christian Prophecy and the Sayings of Jesus: Evidence of and Criteria for," in *SBL Seminar Papers for 1975.* 2 vols. Missoula, 1975. Vol. II, pp. 105-179.

Hay, D. M. *Glory at the Right Hand: Psalm 110 in Early Christianity.* Nashville, 1973.

Hayes, J. H. "The History of the Form-Critical Study of Prophecy," in *SBL Seminar Papers for 1973.* Cambridge, Mass., 1973. Pp. 60-99.

—————. "The Oracles against the Nations in the Old Testament: Their Usage and Theological Significance." Th.D. dissertation, Princeton Theological Seminary, 1964.

—————. "The Resurrection as Enthronement and the Earliest Church Christology," *Interpretation,* 22 (1968), 333-345.

Heinevetter, F. *Würfel — und Buchstaben — Orakel in Griechenland und Kleinasien.* Breslau, 1912.

Hendess, R. *Oracula Graeca.* Halis Saxonum, 1877.

Hengel, M. "Ist der Osterglaube noch zu retten?" *TQ,* 153 (1973), 252-269.

—————. *Judaism and Hellenism.* 2 vols. Trans. J. Bowden. Philadelphia, 1974.

—————. *Victory over Violence.* Trans. D. E. Green. Philadelphia, 1975.

—————. *Was Jesus a Revolutionist?* Trans. W. Klassen. Philadelphia, 1971.

—————. *Die Zeloten. Untersuchungen zur jüdischen Freiheitsbewegung in der Zeit von Herodes I.* Leiden, 1961.

Hennecke, E. *New Testament Apocrypha.* 2 vols. Ger. ed. W. Schneemelcher. Trans. A. J. B. Higgins et al. Eng. ed. R. McL. Wilson. Philadelphia, 1963-65.

Henneken, B. *Verkündigung und Prophetie im 1. Thessalonicherbrief.* Stuttgart, 1969.

Henrichs, A. "Zwei Orakelfragen," *Zeitschrift für Papyrologie und Epigraphik,* 11 (1973), 115-19.

Herr, M. D. "The Historical Significance of the Dialogues between Jewish Sages and Roman Dignitaries," *Scripta Hierosolymitana,* 22 (1971).

Herrmann, P. "Athena Polias in Milet," *Chiron,* 1 (1971), 291-98.

Herrmann, S. *Die prophetische Heilserwartungen im Alten Testament.* Stuttgart, 1966.

Heschel, A. J. "Prophetic Inspiration: An Analysis of Prophetic Consciousness," *Judaism,* 11 (1962), 3-13.

Hiers, R. *The Historical Jesus and the Kingdom of God.* Gainesville, 1973.

—————. *The Kingdom of God in the Synoptic Tradition.* Gainesville, 1970.

Higgins, A. J. B. *Jesus and the Son of Man.* Philadelphia, 1964.

—————. *The Son of Man in the Teaching of Jesus.* Cambridge, 1980.

Hill, D. "Christian Prophets as Teachers or Instructors in the Church," in *Prophetic Vocation in the New Testament and Today.* Ed. J. Panagopoulos. Leiden, 1977. Pp. 108-130.

—————. "False Prophets and Charismatics: Structure and Interpretation in Matthew 7, 15-23," *Biblica,* 57 (1976), 327-348.

—————. *New Testament Prophecy.* Richmond, 1979.

—————. "On the Evidence for the Creative Role of Christian Prophets," *NTS,* 20 (1974), 262-274.

—————. "Prophecy and Prophets in the Revelation of St. John," *NTS,* 18 (1971-72), 401-418.

Hillers, D. R. "A Convention in Hebrew Literature: The Reaction to Bad News," *ZAW,* 77 (1965), 86-90.

—————. *Treaty-Curses and the Old Testament Prophets.* Rome, 1964.

Hinnels, J. R. "The Zoroastrian Doctrine of Salvation in the Roman World," in *Man and His Salvation.* Ed. E. J. Sharpe and J. R. Hinnels. Manchester, 1973. Pp. 125-148.

Hirzel, R. *Der Dialog.* 2 vols. Leipzig, 1895.

Hock, R. F. *The Social Context of Paul's Ministry: Tentmaking and Apostleship.* Fortress, 1980.
Hoffmann, P. *Die Toten in Christus.* Münster, 1966.
_____. *Studien zur Theologie der Logienquelle.* Münster, 1972.
Holladay, C. H. *Theios Aner in Hellenistic Judaism: A Critique of This Category in New Testament Christology.* Missoula, 1977.
Holland, L. B. "The Mantic Mechanism at Delphi," *AJA,* 37 (1933), 201-214.
Hölscher, G. *Die Profeten.* Leipzig, 1914.
Holtz, T. "Zum Selbstverständnis des Apostels Paulus," *TLZ,* 91 (1966), 321-330.
Holtzmann, H. *Praktische Erklärung des I. Thessalonicherbriefes.* Ed. E. Simons. Tübingen, 1911.
Hommel, H. "Das Versorakel des gryneischen Apollon," *Philologus,* 102 (1958), 84-92.
_____. "Das Versorakel des Apollon von Didyma," in *Akte des IV. Internationalen Kongresses für griechische und lateinische Epigraphik.* 1964.
Hooker, M. D. "Christology and Methodology," *NTS,* 17 (1970-71), 480-88.
Hopfner, T. "Traumdeutung," *PW,* 2.VI. 2233-45.
_____. *Griechisch-ägyptischer Offenbarungszauber.* 2 vols. Leipzig, 1921-24.
Horst, F. "Die Visionsschilderungen der alttestamentlichen Propheten," *EvTh,* 20 (1960), 193ff.
Horstmann, M. *Studien zur markinischen Christologie.* Münster, 1969.
How, W. W. and Wells, J. *A Commentary on Herodotus.* 2 vols. Oxford, 1912.
Hubbard, B. J. "Commissioning Stories in Luke-Acts: A Study of Their Antecedents, Form and Content," *Semeia,* 8 (1977), 103-126.
Hughes, J. H. "John the Baptist: The Forerunner of God Himself," *NovT,* 14 (1972), 191-218.
Hull, J. M. *Hellenistic Magic and the Synoptic Tradition.* London, 1974.
Hummel, R. *Die Auseinandersetzung zwischen Kirche und Judentum in Matthäusevangelium.* München, 1963.
Hundt, J. *Der Traumglaube bei Homer.* Greifswald, 1935.
Hutchinson, Jr., A. M. "Christian Prophecy and Matthew 12:38-42, a Text Exegesis," in *SBL Seminar Papers for 1977.* Missoula, 1977. Pp. 379-386.
Hyldahl, N. "Jesus og jøderne ifolge 1 Tess 2,14-16," *SEA,* 27-28 (1972-73), 238-254.
_____. "Kai houtōs i Rom 11,26," *DTT,* 37 (1974), 231-34.

Isaacs, M. E. *The Concept of the Spirit: A Study of Pneuma in Hellenistic Judaism and Its Bearing on the New Testament.* London, 1976.
Isbell, C. D. "Glossolalia and Propheteialalia: A Study of 1 Corinthians 14," *Wesley Theological Journal,* 10 (1975), 15-22.
Isenberg, S. R. "Millenarianism in Greco-Roman Palestine," *Religion,* 4 (1914), 26-46.
_____. "Power through Temple and Torah in Greco-Roman Palestine," in *Christianity, Judaism and Other Greco-Roman Cults: Studies for Morton Smith at Sixty.* Ed. J. Neusner. Vol. 2. Leiden, 1975. Pp. 24-52.

Jacobi, W. *Die Ekstase der alttestamentlichen Propheten.* München und Wiesbaden, 1920.
Jacoby, F. *Die Fragmente der griechischen Historiker.* Vol. II, part B. Berlin, 1929.
Jaeger, W. *Aristotle: Fundamentals of the History of His Development.* Trans. R. Robinson. London, 1948.
James, M. R. *The Biblical Antiquities of Philo.* London, 1917.
Jansen, H. L. *Die Henochgestalt. Eine vergleichende religionsgeschichtliche Untersuchung.* Oslo, 1939.
Janssen, E. *Das Gottesvolk und Seine Geschichte: Geschichtsbild und Selbstverständnis im palästinensischen Schrifttum von Jesus Sirach bis Jehuda ha-Nasi.* Neukirchen-Vluyn, 1971.
Janzen, W. *Mourning Cry and Woe Oracle.* Berlin, 1972.
Jeanmaire, H. *Dionysos: Histoire du Culte de Bacchus.* Paris, 1951.
Jenkins, C. "Origen on 1 Corinthians," *JTS,* 10 (1909), 30ff.
Jepsen, A. *Nabi: Soziologische Studien zur alttestamentlichen Literatur und Religionsgeschichte.* Munich, 1934.

Jeremias, G. *Der Lehrer der Gerechtigkeit*. Göttingen, 1963.
Jeremias, J. *Jerusalem in the Time of Jesus*. Trans. F. H. and C. H. Cave. Philadelphia, 1969.
————. *New Testament Theology: The Proclamation of Jesus*. Trans. J. Bowden. New York, 1971.
————. *The Parables of Jesus*. Rev. ed. Trans. S. H. Hooke. New York, 1963.
————. *The Prayers of Jesus*. Trans. J. Bowden et al. Philadelphia, 1978.
————. "Sabbatjahr und neutestamentliche Chronologie," *ZNW,* 27 (1928), 98-103.
————. *Unknown Sayings of Jesus*. Trans. R. H. Fuller. 2nd ed. London, 1964.
Jeremias, Jörg. *Kultprophetie und Gerichtsverkündigung in der späten Königszeit Israels*. Neukirchen-Vluyn, 1970.
————. *Theophanie: Die Geschichte einer alttestamentliche Gattung*. Neukirchen-Vluyn, 1965.
Jervell, J. "Den oppstandnes aand," *NTT,* 77 (1976), 19-32.
Johnson, A. R. *The Cultic Prophet and Israel's Psalmody*. Cardiff, 1979.
Johnston, G. *The Spirit-Paraclete in the Gospel of John*. London, 1970.
Jones, B. W. "More about the Apocalypse as Apocalyptic," *JBL,* 87 (1968), 325-27.
Jörns, K.-P. *Das hymnische Evangelium: Untersuchungen zu Aufbau, Funktion und Herkunft der hymnischen Stücke in der Johannesoffenbarung*. Gütersloh, 1971.
Judge, E. A. "The Early Christians as a Scholastic Community," *JRH,* 1 (1960-61), 4-15, 125-137.
————. *The Social Pattern of Christian Groups in the First Century*. London, 1960.
Juel, D. *Messiah and Temple: The Trial of Jesus in the Gospel of Mark*. Missoula, 1977.
Junker, H. *Prophet und Seher in Israel*. Trier, 1927.
Juster, J. *Les Juifs dans l'Empire Romain*. 2 vols. Paris, 1914.

Kahn, C. H. *The Art and Thought of Heraclitus: An Edition of the Fragments with Translation and Commentary*. Cambridge, 1979.
Kaibel, G. *Epigrammata Graeca*. Berlin, 1878.
Kalias, J. "The Apocalypse — An Apocalyptic Book?" *JBL,* 86 (1967), 69-80.
Karpp, H. "'Prophet' oder 'Dolmetscher'?" in *Festschrift für Günther Dehn*. Ed. W. Schneemelcher. Neukirchen-Vluyn, 1957. Pp. 103-117.
Käsemann, E. *Commentary on Romans*. Trans. and ed. G. W. Bromiley. Grand Rapids, 1980.
————. "The Beginnings of Christian Theology," in *New Testament Questions of Today*. Philadelphia, 1969. Pp. 82-107.
————. "The Cry for Liberty in the Worship of the Church," in *Perspectives on Paul*. Philadelphia, 1971. Pp. 122-137.
————. "The Problem of the Historical Jesus," *Essays on New Testament Themes*. Naperville, 1964. Pp. 15-47.
————. "Sentences of Holy Law in the New Testament," in *New Testament Questions of Today*. Philadelphia, 1969. Pp. 66-81.
Käser, W. "Exegetische und theologische Erwägungen zur Seligpreisung der Kinderlosen, Lc 23,29b," *ZNW,* 54 (1963), 240-254.
Kee, H. C. *Community of the New Age: Studies in Mark's Gospel*. Philadelphia, 1977.
Kegel, G. *Auferstehung Jesu — Auferstehung der Toten*. Gütersloh, 1970.
Kelber, W. H. *The Kingdom in Mark: A New Place and a New Time*. Philadelphia, 1974.
Kern, O. *Die Religion der Griechen*. 3 vols. Berlin, 1935-38.
Kertelge, K. "Apokalypsis Jesou Christou (Gal. 1,12)," in *Neues Testament und Kirche*. Ed. J. Gnilka. Freiburg, 1974. Pp. 266-281.
Kingsbury, E. C. "The Prophets and the Council of Yahweh," *JBL,* 83 (1964), 279-287.
Kingsbury, J. D. *Matthew: Structure, Christology, Kingdom*. Philadelphia, 1975.
————. "The Verb *Akolouthein* ('to follow') as an Index of Matthew's View of His Community," *JBL,* 97 (1978), 56-73.
Kisch, G. *Pseudo-Philo's Liber Antiquitatum Biblicarum*. Notre Dame, 1949.
Klausner, J. *The Messianic Idea in Israel*. Trans. W. F. Stinespring. New York, 1955.
Klawiter, F. C. "The New Prophecy in Early Christianity: The Origin, Nature, and Development of Montanism, A.D. 165-200." Ph.D. dissertation, University of Chicago, 1975.

Bibliography • 461

Klees, H. *Die Eigenart des griechischen Glaubens an Orakel und Seher.* Stuttgart, 1962.

Klein, G. "Apokalyptische Naherwartung bei Paulus," in *Neues Testament und Christliche Existenz.* Ed. H. D. Betz and L. Schottroff. Tübingen, 1973. Pp. 241-262.

—————. *Die zwölf Apostel.* Göttingen, 1961.

Klotsche, E. H. *The Supernatural in the Tragedies of Euripides as Illustrated in Prayers, Curses, Oaths, Oracles, Prophecies, Dreams, and Visions.* Lincoln, 1918.

Koch, K. *The Growth of Biblical Tradition.* Trans. S. M. Cupitt. New York, 1969.

—————. "Pseudonymous Writing," *The Interpreter's Dictionary of the Bible, Supplementary Volume.* Nashville, 1976. Pp. 712-14.

—————. *The Rediscovery of Apocalyptic.* Naperville, Illinois, n.d.

Koenen, L. "The Prophecies of a Potter: A Prophecy of World Renewal Becomes an Apocalypse," in *Proceedings of the Twelfth International Congress of Papyrology.* Ed. D. H. Samuel. Toronto, 1970. Pp. 249-254.

—————. "Die Prophezeiungen des 'Töpfers'," *Zeitschrift für Papyrologie und Epigraphik,* 2 (1968), 178-209.

Koester, H. *Synoptische Überlieferungen bei den apostolischen Vätern.* Berlin, 1957.

—————. *Einführung in das Neue Testament.* Berlin and New York, 1980.

—————. "Die ausserkanonischen Herrenworte als Produkte der christlichen Gemeinde," *ZNW,* 48 (1957), 220-237.

Kolf, M. C. van der. "Prophetes und Prophetis," *PW,* 23/1 (1957), 797-816.

Kornfeld, W. *Religion und Offenbarung in der Geschichte Israels.* Innsbruck, 1970.

Koster, W. J. W. *Scholia in Aristophanem.* Groningen and Amsterdam, n.d.

Kötting, B. *Peregrinatio Religiosa. Wallfahrten in der Antike und das Pilgerwesen in der alten Kirche.* Münster, 1950.

Kraeling, C. H. *John the Baptist.* New York, 1951.

—————. "Was Jesus Accused of Necromancy?" *JBL,* 59 (1940), 147-157.

Kraft, H. "Die altkirchliche Prophetie und die Entstehung des Montanismus," *TZ,* 11 (1955), 249-271.

—————. "Die Anfänge des geistlichen Amts," *TLZ,* 100 (1975), 81-98.

—————. *Die Offenbarung des Johannes.* Tübingen, 1974.

—————. "Vom Ende der urchristlichen Prophetie," in *Prophetic Vocation in the New Testament and Today.* Ed. J. Panagopoulos. Leiden, 1977. Pp. 162-185.

Krämer, M. "Hütet euch vor den falschen Propheten. Eine überlieferungsgeschichtliche Untersuchung zu Mt. 7,15-23/Lk 6,43-46/Mt. 12,33-37," *Biblica,* 57 (1976), 349-377.

Kramer, W. *Christ, Lord, Son of God.* Naperville, Illinois, 1966.

Kraus, H.-J. *Worship in Israel: A Cultic History of the Old Testament.* Trans. G. Buswell. Richmond, 1966.

Kredel, E. M. "Der Apostelbegriff in der neueren Exegese," *ZKT,* 78 (1956), 169-193.

Kretschmar, G. "Ein Beitrag zur Frage nach dem Ursprung frühchristlicher Askese," *ZTK,* 61 (1964), 27-67.

Kroeber, A. L. *The Nature of Culture.* Chicago, 1952.

Kroll, W. *De oracula Chaldaicis.* Breslau, 1894.

Kuhn, H.-W. *Ältere Sammlungen im Markusevangelium.* Göttingen, 1971.

—————. *Enderwartung und gegenwärtiges Heil.* Göttingen, 1966.

Kuhn, K. G. "The Two Messiahs of Aaron and Israel," in *The Scrolls and the New Testament.* Ed. K. Stendahl. New York, 1957. Pp. 54-64.

Kühnert, W. "Der antimontanistische Anonymus des Eusebius," *TZ,* 5 (1949), 436-446.

Kümmel, W. G. "Die Naherwartung in der Verkündigung Jesu," in *Heilsgeschehen und Geschichte. Gesammelte Aufsätze 1933-1964.* Ed. E. Grässer et al. Marburg, 1965. Pp. 457-470.

—————. *Promise and Fulfilment: The Eschatological Message of Jesus.* Trans. D. M. Barton. 2nd ed. London, 1961.

Kutsch, E. "Gideons Berufung und Alterbau Jdc 6,11-24," *TL,* 81 (1956), 79-82.

Labriolle, P. de. *La crise Montaniste.* Paris, 1913.

Lacocque, A. *Le Livre de Daniel*. Neuchatel-Paris, 1976.

Ladd, G. E. *Jesus and the Kingdom: The Eschatology of Biblical Realism*. New York, 1964.

Laeuchli, S. *The Language of Faith*. Nashville, 1962.

Lake, K. "Did Paul Use the Logia?" *AJT*, 10 (1906), 104-111.

Lambert, W. G. "The Fifth Tablet of the Era Epic," *Iraq*, 24 (1962), 119-124.

Lambrecht, J. *Die Redaktion der Markus-Apokalypse: Literarische Analyse und Strukturuntersuchung*. Rome, 1967.

Lampe, G. W. H. "The Holy Spirit in the Writings of St. Luke," in *Studies in the Gospels*. Ed. D. E. Nineham. Oxford, 1957. Pp. 159-200.

—————. *A Patristic Greek Lexicon*. Oxford, 1961.

Lanczkowski, G. "Ägyptischer Prophetismus im Lichte des alttestamentlichen," *ZAW*, 70 (1958), 31-38.

—————. *Altägyptischer Prophetismus*. Wiesbaden, 1960.

—————. "Eschatology in Ancient Egyptian Religion," in *Proceedings of the IXth International Congress for the History of Religions*. Tokyo, 1960. Pp. 129-134.

Lane, W. *A Commentary on the Gospel of Mark*. Grand Rapids, 1973.

Latte, K. *Hesychii Alexandrini Lexicon*. 2 vols. Copenhagen, 1953-66.

—————. "The Coming of the Pythia," *HTR*, 33 (1940), 9-18.

Lattimore, R. "Portents and Prophecies in Connection with the Emperor Vespasian," *CJ*, 29 (1933-34), 441-49.

—————. *Themes in Greek and Latin Epitaphs*. Urbana, Illinois, 1963.

Lawlor, J. *Eusebiana*. Oxford, 1912.

Le Déaut, R. "Apropos a Definition of Midrash," *Interpretation*, 25 (1971), 259-282.

Leiman, S. Z. *The Canonization of Hebrew Scripture: The Talmudic and Midrashic Evidence*. Hamden, Connecticut, 1976.

Leipoldt, J. and Morenz, S. *Heilige Schriften: Betrachtungen zur Religionsgeschichte der antiken Mittelmeerwelt*. Leipzig, 1953.

Leisegang, H. *Pneuma Hagion: Der Ursprung des Geistbegriffs der synoptischen Evangelien aus der griechischen Mystik*. Leipzig, 1922.

Lévi-Strauss, C. *Structural Anthropology*. Trans. C. Jacobson and G. B. Schoepf. Garden City, New York, 1967.

Levy, J. *Wörterbuch über die Talmudim und Midraschim*. 4 vols. Darmstadt, 1963.

Lewis, I. M. *Ecstatic Religion: An Anthropological Study of Spirit Possession and Shamanism*. Baltimore, 1971.

Lewy, H. *Chaldaean Oracles and Theurgy*. Cairo, 1956.

—————. *Sobria Ebrietas: Untersuchungen zur Geschichte der antiken Mystik*. Giessen, 1929.

Lichtenberg, N. "The Literary Use of Oracles in Aristophanes." Master's thesis, University of Chicago, 1932.

Liddell, H. G. and Scott, R. *A Greek-English Lexicon*. Rev. H. S. Jones and R. McKenzie. 9th ed. with Supplement. Oxford, 1968.

Lieberman, S. *Hellenism in Jewish Palestine*. New York, 1950.

Liechtenhan, R. *Die Offenbarung in Gnosticismus*. Göttingen, 1901.

Lietzmann, H. *An die Römer*. 4. Aufl. Tübingen, 1933.

Limburg, J. "The Prophets in Recent Study: 1967-77," *Interpretation*, 32 (1978), 56-68.

Lindars, B. *New Testament Apologetic: The Doctrinal Significance of the Old Testament Quotations*. London, 1961.

Lindblom, J. *Gesichte und Offenbarungen: Vorstellungen von göttlichen Weisungen und übernatürlichen Erscheinungen im ältesten Christentum*. Lund, 1968.

—————. *Die literarische Gattung der prophetischen Literatur: Eine literargeschichtliche Untersuchung zum Alten Testament*. Uppsala, 1924.

—————. "Lotcasting in the Old Testament," *VT*, 12 (1962), 164-178.

—————. *Prophecy in Ancient Israel*. London, 1962.

—————. "Theophanies in Holy Places in Hebrew Religion," *HUCA*, 32 (1964), 91-106.

_____. "Die Vorstellung vom Sprechen Yahwes zu den Menschen im Alten Testament," *ZNW*, 75 (1963), 263ff.

Lindner, H. *Die Geschichtsauffassung des Flavius Josephus im Bellum Judaicum.* Leiden, 1972.

Lindsey, R. L. " 'Verily' or 'Amen' — What did Jesus say?" *Christian News from Israel*, 25 (1975), 144-48.

Linforth, I. M. *The Arts of Orpheus.* Berkeley and Los Angeles, 1941.

_____. "The Corybantic Rites in Plato," *University of California Publications in Classical Philology*, 13. Berkeley and Los Angeles, 1946. Pp. 121-162.

_____. "Telestic Madness in Plato, Phaedrus 244DE," *University of California Publications in Classical Philology*, 13. Berkeley and Los Angeles, 1946. Pp. 163-172.

Linton, O. *Das Problem der Urkirche in der neueren Forschung: Eine kritische Darstellung.* Uppsala, 1932.

_____. *Pauli Mindre Brev.* Stockholm, 1964.

Ljungdahl, A. *Profetrörelser: deras orsaker, innebörd och förutsättningar.* Stockholm, 1969.

Lods, A. "Le rôle des oracles dans la nomination des rois, des prêtres et des magistrats, chez les Israélites, les Égyptiens et les Grecs," in *Mélanges Maspero.* Vol. 1. Cairo, 1934. Pp. 91-100.

_____. "Une tablette inédite de Mari, intéressante pour l'histoire ancienne du prophétisme sémitique," in *Studies in Old Testament Prophecy.* Ed. H. H. Rowley. Edinburgh, 1950. Pp. 103-110.

Loftus, F. "The Anti-Roman Revolts of the Jews and the Galileans," *JQR*, 68 (1977), 78-98.

Lohmeyer, E. *Das Evangelium des Markus.* 10. Aufl. Göttingen, 1937.

_____. *Grundlagen paulinischer Theologie.* Tübingen, 1929.

_____. *Die Offenbarung des Johannes.* Tübingen, 1953.

Lohse, E. "Die alttestamentliche Sprache des Sehers Johannis," in *Die Einheit des Neuen Testaments.* Göttingen, 1973. Pp. 329-333.

_____. "Ich aber sage euch," in *Die Einheit des Neuen Testaments.* Göttingen, 1973. Pp. 73-87.

Long, B. O. "The Effect of Divination upon Israelite Literature," *JBL*, 92 (1973), 489-497.

_____. "Reports of Visions Among the Prophets," *JBL*, 95 (1976), 353-365.

_____. "Two Question and Answer Schemata in the Prophets," *JBL*, 90 (1971), 129-139.

Longenecker, R. *Biblical Exegesis in the Apostolic Period.* Grand Rapids, 1975.

Lövestam, E. "Wunder und Symbolhandlung," *KuD*, 8 (1962), 124-135.

Luckmann, T. *The Sociology of Language.* Indianapolis, 1975.

Lüdemann, G. "The Successors of Pre-70 Jerusalem Christianity: A Critical Evaluation of the Pella-Tradition," in *Jewish and Christian Self-Definition.* Ed. E. P. Sanders. Vol. 1. Philadelphia, 1980. Pp. 161-173.

Lührmann, D. "Jesus und Seine Propheten: Gesprächsbeitrag," in *Prophetic Vocation in the New Testament and Today.* Ed. J. Panagopoulos. Leiden, 1977. Pp. 210-17.

_____. *Das Offenbarungsverständnis bei Paulus und in den paulinischen Gemeinden.* Neukirchen-Vluyn, 1965.

Lundström, G. *The Kingdom of God in the Teaching of Jesus: A History of Interpretation from the Last Decades of the Nineteenth Century to the Present Day.* Edinburgh and London, 1963.

Lünemann, G. *Critical and Exegetical Handbook to the Epistles to the Thessalonians.* Trans. P. J. Gloag, New York, 1889.

Luz, U. *Das Geschichtsverständnis des Paulus.* München, 1968.

Maas, P. *Greek Metre.* trans. H. Lloyd-Jones. Oxford, 1962.

McCown, C. C. "Hebrew and Egyptian Apocalyptic Literature," *HTR*, 18 (1925), 357-411.

MacDermot, V. *The Cult of the Seer in the Ancient Middle East.* Berkeley and Los Angeles, 1971.

MacDonald, A. B. *Christian Worship in the Primitive Church.* Edinburgh, 1934.

McDonald, J. I. H. *Kerygma and Didache.* Cambridge, 1980.

McKelvey, R. J. *The New Temple: The Church in the New Testament.* Oxford, 1969.

McLeon, W. E. "Oracle Bards at Delphi," *Transactions and Proceedings of the American Philological Association*, 92 (1961), 317-325.

464 • Bibliography

MacMullen, R. *Enemies of the Roman Order: Treason, Unrest and Alienation in the Empire.* Cambridge, Mass., 1966.

—————. *Roman Social Relations: 50 B.C. to A.D. 284.* New Haven, 1974.

McNamara, M. *The New Testament and the Palestinian Targum to the Pentateuch.* Rome, 1966.

Malherbe, A. J. "The Inhospitality of Diotrephes," in *God's Christ and His People: Studies in Honour of Nils Alstrup Dahl.* Ed. J. Jervell and W. A. Meeks. Oslo, 1976. Pp. 222-232.

—————. *Social Aspects of Early Christianity.* Baton Rouge, 1977.

Maly, K. "1 Kor 12,1-3, eine Regel zur Unterscheidung der Geister?" *BZ,* 10 (1966), 82-95.

—————. *Mündige Gemeinde: Untersuchungen zur pastoralen Führung des Apostels Paulus im 1. Korintherbrief.* Stuttgart, 1967.

Manson, T. W. *The Teachings of Jesus: Studies in Its Form and Content.* 2nd ed. Cambridge, 1935.

March, W. E. "Prophecy," in *Old Testament Form Criticism.* Ed. J. H. Hayes. San Antonio, 1974. Pp. 141-177.

Marrou, H. I. *A History of Education in Antiquity.* New York, 1964.

Marshall, I. H. *The Epistles of John.* Grand Rapids, 1976.

—————. *I Believe in the Historical Jesus.* Grand Rapids, 1977.

—————. "Palestinian and Hellenistic Christianity: Some Critical Comments," *NTS,* 19 (1972-73), 271-287.

Martin, R. and Metzger, H. *La religion grecque.* Paris, 1976.

Martin, R. P. *Mark: Evangelist and Theologian.* Exeter, 1972.

Martyn, J. L. *History and Theology in the Fourth Gospel.* New York and Evanston, 1968.

—————. "We Have Found Elijah," in *Jews, Greeks and Christians: Religious Cultures in Late Antiquity.* Ed. R. Hamerton-Kelly and R. Scroggs. Leiden, 1976. Pp. 181-219.

Marxsen, W. "Auslegung von 1 Thess 4,13-18," *ZTK,* 66 (1969), 22-37.

—————. *Mark the Evangelist: Studies on the Redaction History of the Gospel.* Trans. R. A. Harrisville. Nashville, 1969.

Masson, C. *Les deux Épitres de Saint Paul aux Thessaloniciens.* Neuchatel, 1957.

Mather, P. B. "Christian Prophecy and Matthew 28:16-20: A Test Exegesis," in *SBL Seminar Papers for 1977.* Missoula, 1977. Pp. 103-116.

Maurer, C. *Ignatius von Antiochien und das Johannesevangelium.* Zürich, 1949.

Mayer, R. and Möller, C. "Josephus — Politiker und Prophet," in *Josephus-Studien.* Ed. O. Betz, K. Haacker, and M. Hengel. Göttingen, 1974. Pp. 271-284.

Mayser, E. *Grammatik der griechischen Papyri aus der Ptolemaerzeit.* Vol. 2, part 1. Berlin and Leipzig, 1926.

Meeks, W. A. *The Prophet-King. Moses Traditions and the Johannine Christology.* Leiden, 1967.

Meek, T. J. *Hebrew Origins.* 3rd ed. New York, 1960.

Meinhold, P. "Geschehen und Deutung im Ersten Clemensbrief," *ZKG,* 58 (1939), 82-129.

Meltzer, H. "Der Fetisch im Heiligtum des Zeus Ammon," *Philologus,* 63 (1904), 186-223.

Merkelbach, R. "Ein didymaeisches Orakel," *Zeitschrift für Papyrologie und Epigraphik,* 8 (1971), 93-95.

—————. "Ein Orakel des gryneischen Apollo," *Zeitschrift für Papyrologie und Epigraphik,* 5 (1970), 48.

Mettinger, T. N. D. *King and Messiah. The Civil and Social Legitimation of the Israelite Kings.* Lund, 1976.

Metzger, B. M. "Literary Forgeries and Canonical Pseudepigrapha," *JBL,* 91 (1972), 3-24.

Meyer, E. *Ursprung und Anfänge des Christentums.* 3 vols. Stuttgart, 1925.

Meyer, R. "Bemerkungen zum literargeschichtlichen Hintergrund der Kanontheorie des Josephus," in *Josephus-Studien.* Göttingen, 1974. Pp. 285-299.

—————. *Der Prophet aus Galiläa.* 2. Aufl. Darmstadt, 1970.

Michaels, J. R. "Christian Prophecy and Matthew 23:8-12: A Test Exegesis," in *SBL Seminar Papers for 1976.* Missoula, 1976. Pp. 305-310.

—————. "The Johannine Words of Jesus and Christian Prophecy," in *SBL Seminar Papers for 1975.* 2 vols. Missoula, 1975. Vol. II, 233-264.

Michel, H.-J. *Die Abschiedsrede des Paulus an die Kirche Apg 20,17-38: Motivgeschichte und theologische Bedeutung.* München, 1973.

Michel, O. "Fragen zu 1 Thessalonicher 2,14-16: Antijüdische Polemik bei Paulus," in *Antijudaismus in Neuen Testament? Exegetische und systematische Beiträge.* Ed. W. Eckert et al. München, 1967. Pp. 50-59.

_____. " 'Ich Komme' (Jos. Bell. III. 400)," *TZ,* 24 (1968), 123-24.

_____. *Prophet und Märtyrer.* Gütersloh, 1932.

_____. *Der Brief an die Römer.* 13. Aufl. Göttingen, 1966.

_____. *Paulus und seine Bibel.* Gütersloh, 1929.

_____. "Spätjüdisches Prophetentum," in *Neutestamentliche Studien für Rudolf Bultmann.* Ed. W. Eltester. Göttingen, 1954. Pp. 60-66.

Michel, O. and Bauernfeind, O. *Flavius Josephus, De Bello Judaico.* 3 vols. München, 1959-69.

Milik, J. T. *The Books of Enoch: Aramaic Fragments of Qumrân Cave 4.* Oxford, 1976.

_____. "Problèmes de la Littérature Hénochique à la Lumière des Fragments Araméens de Qumran," *HTR,* 64 (1971), 333-378.

Miller, P. D. *The Divine Warrior in Early Israel.* Cambridge, Mass., 1973.

Milligan, G. *St. Paul's Epistles to the Thessalonians.* London, 1908.

Minear, P. S. "False Prophecy and Hypocrisy in the Gospel of Matthew," *Neues Testament und Kirche.* Ed. J. Gnilka. Freiburg, 1974.

_____. *I Saw a New Earth.* Washington, 1968.

_____. "Luke's Use of the Birth Stories," *Studies in Luke-Acts.* Ed. L. E. Keck and J. L. Martyn. New York, 1966. Pp. 111-130.

_____. *To Heal and to Reveal: The Prophetic Vocation According to Luke.* New York, 1976.

Miranda, J. P. *Der Vater, der mich gesandt hat. Religionsgeschichtliche Untersuchungen zu den johanneischen Sendungsformeln; zugleich ein Beitrag zur johanneischen Christologie und Ekklesiologie.* Bern and Frankfurt am Main, 1972.

Moffatt, J. *The First Epistle of Paul to the Corinthians.* New York, 1938.

Moke, D. F. "Eroticism in the Greek Magical Papyri." Ph.D. dissertation, University of Minnesota, Minneapolis, 1975.

Momigliano, A. "Popular Religious Beliefs and the Late Roman Historians," in *Popular Belief and Practice.* Ed. G. J. Cuming and D. Baker. Cambridge, 1972. Pp. 1-18.

Montgomery, J. A. *The Samaritans: The Earliest Jewish Sect, Their History, Theology and Literature.* New York, 1907.

Mooney, J. *The Ghost-Dance Religion and the Sioux Outbreak of 1890.* Chicago, 1965.

Moore, C. H. "Prophecy in the Ancient Epic," *Harvard Studies in Classical Philology,* 32 (1921), 99-175.

Moore, G. F. *Judaism in the First Centuries of the Christian Era: The Age of the Tannaim.* 3 vols. Cambridge, Mass., 1927-30.

Morris, L. *The First and Second Epistles to the Thessalonians.* Grand Rapids, 1959.

Mosiman, E. *Das Zungenreden geschichtlich und psychologisch untersucht.* Tübingen, 1911.

Moule, C. F. D. *The Origin of Christology.* Cambridge, 1977.

Mounce, R. H. *The Book of Revelation.* Grand Rapids, 1977.

Mowinckel, S. *He That Cometh.* Trans. G. W. Anderson. Nashville, 1954.

_____. *The Psalms in Israel's Worship.* 2 vols. Trans D. R. Ap-Thomas. Nashville, 1962.

Moxnes, H. "God and His Angel in the Shepherd of Hermas." *ST,* 28 (1974), 49-56.

Muilenburg, J. "Form Criticism and Beyond," *JBL,* 88 (1969), 1-18.

Müller, H.-P. "Mantische Weisheit und Apokalyptik," in *Congress Volume, Uppsala 1971.* VT Supp. 22. Leiden, 1972. Pp. 268-293.

Müller, K. *Fragmenta Historicorum Graecorum.* 5 vols. Paris, 1851-85.

Müller, U. B. *Prophetie und Predigt im Neuen Testament. Formgeschichtliche Untersuchungen zur urchristlichen Prophetie.* Gütersloh, 1975.

_____. "Vision und Botschaft: Erwägungen zur prophetischen Struktur der Verkündigung Jesu," *ZTK,* 74 (1977), 416-448.

——————. *Zur Frühchristlichen Theologiegeschichte: Judenchristentum und Paulinismus in Kleinasien an der Wende vom ersten zum Zweiten Jahrhundert n. Chr.* Gütersloh, 1976.

——————. *Messias und Menschensohn in jüdischen Apokalypsen und in der Offenbarung des Johannes.* Gütersloh, 1972.

Mullins, T. Y. "New Testament Commission Forms, Especially in Luke-Acts," *JBL,* 95 (1976), 602-614.

Munck, J. "Discours d'adieu dans le Nouveau Testament et dans la littérature biblique," in *Aux sources de la tradition chrétienne: Mélanges offerts à M. Maurice Goguel.* Neuchâtel, 1950. Pp. 155-170.

——————. "Jewish Christianity in Post-Apostolic Times," *NTS,* 6 (1959), 103-116.

——————. "La vocation de l'Apôtre Paul," *ST,* 1 (1947), 131-145.

Murray, G. *Five Stages of Greek Religion.* 3rd ed. Garden City, New York, 1951.

Myers, J. M. *I and II Esdras: Introduction, Translation and Commentary.* Garden City, New York, 1974.

Myers, J. M. and Freed, E. D. "Is Paul also among the Prophets?" *Interpretation,* 20 (1966), 40-53.

Nauck, A. *Tragicorum Graecorum Fragmenta.* 2nd ed. Leipzig, 1889.

Nauck, W. "Freude im Leiden: Zum Problem einer urchristlichen Verfolgungstradition," *ZNW,* 46 (1955), 68-80.

Neal, M. A. "How Prophecy Lives," *Social Analysis,* 33 (1972), 125-141.

Neil, W. *The Epistle of Paul to the Thessalonians.* New York, 1950.

Nepper-Christensen, P. "Das verborgene Herrnwort. Eine Untersuchung über 1 Thess. 4,13-18," *ST,* 19 (1965), 136-154.

Neufeld, V. *The Earliest Christian Confessions.* Grand Rapids, 1963.

Newsome, J. D. "Toward a New Understanding of the Chronicler and His Purposes," *JBL,* 94 (1975), 201-217.

Nicholson, E. W. *Deuteronomy and Tradition.* Philadelphia, 1967.

Nickelsburg, G. W. E. "The Apocalyptic Message of *I Enoch* 92-105," *CBQ,* 39 (1977), 309-328.

Nicol, D. M. "The Oracle of Dodona," *Greece and Rome,* 5 (1958), 128-143.

Nicoll, W. *The Sēmeia in the Fourth Gospel.* Leiden, 1972.

Nikiprowetzky, V. *La Troisième Sibylle.* Paris, 1970.

Nilsson, M. P. *Cults, Myths, Oracles, and Politics in Ancient Greece.* Lund, 1951.

——————. *Greek Popular Religion.* New York, 1940.

——————. *Geschichte der Griechischen Religion.* 3. Aufl. 2 vols. München, 1967.

——————. "Das delphische Orakel in der neuesten Literatur," *Historia,* 7 (1958), 237-250.

——————. *Die hellenistische Schule.* München, 1955.

——————. Review of J. H. Oliver, *The Athenian Expounder of the Sacred and Ancestral Law, AJP,* 71 (1950), 420-25.

——————. "Universal Religion," *Opuscula Selecta.* 3 vols. Lund, 1960.

Nineham, D. E. *The Gospel of St. Mark.* New York, 1963.

Noack, B. "Current and Backwater in the Epistle to the Romans," *ST,* 19 (1965), 155-166.

Nock, A. D. "Alexander of Abonuteichos," *Classical Quarterly,* 22 (1928), 160-62.

——————. *Conversion: The Old and the New in Religion from Alexander the Great to Augustine of Hippo.* Oxford, 1933.

——————. "Oracles Théologiques," in *Essays on Religion and the Ancient World.* Ed. Z. Stewart. 2 vols. Oxford, 1972.

Nock, A. D. and Festugière, A. J. *Hermes Trismégiste.* 4 vols. Paris, 1949-52.

Norden, E. "Josephus und Tacitus über Jesus Christus und eine messianische Prophetie," *Neue Jahrbücher für das klassische Altertum,* 16 (1913), 637-666.

——————. *Agnostos Theos.* Leipzig, 1913.

——————. *Kleine Schriften zum klassischen Altertum.* Berlin, 1966.

North, R. "Prophecy to Apocalyptic via Zechariah," in *Congress Volume, Uppsala 1971.* VT Supp. 22. Leiden, 1972. Pp. 47-71.

Nützel, J. M. "Zum Schicksal der eschatologischen Propheten," *BZ,* 20 (1976), 59-94.

Oesterreich, T. K. *Possession: Demoniacal and Other.* London, 1930.
O'Hagen, A. P. "The Great Tribulation to Come in the Pastor of Hermas," in *Studia Patristica,* 4. *TU,* 79 (1961), 305-311.
Ohlert, K. *Rätsel und Rätselspiele der alten Griechen.* 2. Aufl. Berlin, 1912.
Oliver, J. H. *The Athenian Expounders of the Sacred and Ancestral Law.* Baltimore, 1950.
O'Neill, J. C. "The Six Amen Sayings in Luke," *JTS,* 10 (1959), 1-9.
Opitz, H. *Ursprünge frühkatholischen Pneumatologie.* Berlin, 1960.
Oppenheimer, A. *The 'Am Ha-Aretz: A Study in the Social History of the Jewish People in the Hellenistic-Roman Period.* Leiden, 1977.
O'Rourke, J. "The Hymns of the Apocalypse," *CBQ,* 30 (1968), 399-409.
Orr, W. F. and Walther, J. A. *1 Corinthians: A New Translation. Introduction with a Study of the Life of Paul, Notes, and Commentary.* Garden City, New York, 1976.
Osten-Sacken, P. von der. *Die Apokalyptik in ihrem Verhältnis zu Prophetie und Weisheit.* München, 1969.
Otte, K. *Das Sprachverständnis bei Philo von Alexandrien.* Tübingen, 1968.

Palmer, R. E. A. *Roman Religion and Roman Empire: Five Essays.* Philadelphia, 1974.
Panagopoulos, J. "Die urchristliche Prophetie: Ihr Charakter und ihre Funktion," in *Prophetic Vocation in the New Testament and Today.* Ed. J. Panagopoulos. Leiden, 1977. Pp. 1-32.
Panitz, H. *Mythos und Orakel bei Herodot.* Greifswald, 1935.
Pardee, D. "An Overview of Ancient Hebrew Epistolography," *JBL,* 97 (1978), 321-346.
Parke, H. W. *Greek Oracles.* London, 1967.
——————. "The Newly Discovered Delphic Responses from Paros," *CQ,* 8 (1958), 90-94.
——————. *The Oracles of Zeus: Dodona, Olympia, Ammon.* Oxford, 1967.
——————. "Three Enquiries from Dodona," *JHS,* 87 (1967), 132-33.
——————. "The Use of Other than Hexameter Verse in Delphic Oracles," *Hermathena,* 65 (1945), 58-66.
Parke, H. W. and Wormell, D. E. W. "A Neglected Delphic Oracle," *Hermathena,* 117 (1974), 18-20.
——————. *The Delphic Oracle.* 2 vols. Oxford, 1956.
Parker, S. B. "Possession Trance and Prophecy in Pre-Exilic Israel," *VT,* 28 (1978), 271-285.
Patsch, H. "Die Prophetie des Agabus," *TZ,* 28 (1972), 228-232.
Paulsen, H. "Papyrus Oxyrhynchus I. 5 und die DIADOCHĒ TŌN PROPHĒTŌN," *NTS,* 25 (1979), 443-453.
Pearson, A. C. *The Fragments of Sophocles.* 2 vols. Cambridge, 1917.
Pearson, B. A. "Did the Gnostics Curse Jesus?" *JBL,* 86 (1967), 301-305.
Pedersen, J. *Israel: Its Life and Culture.* 4 vols. 2nd ed. London, 1926-59.
Perkins, P. *The Gnostic Dialogue: The Early Church and the Crisis of Gnosticism.* New York, 1980.
Pernveden, L. *The Concept of the Church in the Shepherd of Hermas.* Lund, 1966.
Perrin, N. *A Modern Pilgrimage in New Testament Christology.* Philadelphia, 1974.
——————. *The New Testament: An Introduction.* New York, 1974.
——————. *Rediscovering the Teaching of Jesus.* New York and Evanston, 1967.
——————. "Towards an Interpretation of the Gospel of Mark," in *Christology and a Modern Pilgrimage: A Discussion with Norman Perrin.* Claremont, 1971. Pp. 1-78.
Perrot, C. "Prophètes et prophétisme dans le Nouveau Testament," *Lumière et Vie,* 22 (1973), 25-39.
Pesch, R. *Naherwartungen: Tradition und Redaktion in Mk 13.* Düsseldorf, 1968.
——————. "Stellungnahme zu den Diskussionsbeiträgen," *TQ,* 153 (1973), 270-283.
——————. *Die Vision des Stephanus. Apg. 7,55-56 im Rahmen der Apostelgeschichte.* Stuttgart, 1966.
——————. "Zur Entstehung des Glaubens an die Auferstehung Jesu," *Tübinger Theologische Quartalschrift,* 153 (1973), 201-228.

_____. *Das Markusevangelium.* 2 vols. Freiburg, Basel, and Wien, 1977.

Petersen, D. L. *Late Israelite Prophecy: Studies in Deutero-Prophetic Literature and in Chronicles.* Missoula, 1977.

Peterson, E. *EIS THEOS.* Göttingen, 1926.

_____. "La *Leitourgia* des Prophètes et des Didascales à Antioche," *RSR,* 36 (1949), 577-79.

_____. "Die Einholung des Kyrios," *ZST,* 7 (1930), 682-702.

_____. *Frühkirche, Judentum und Gnosis.* Rome, Freiburg, and Vienna, 1959.

Pfeffer, F. *Studien zur Mantik in der Philosophie der Antike.* Meisenheim am Glan, 1976.

Pfister, F. "Ekstasis," *Pisicule: Studien zur Religion und Kultur des Altertums.* Ed. T. Klauser and A. Rücker. Münster, 1939. Pp. 178-191.

Phillips, A. "The Ecstatics' Father," in *Words and Meanings: Essays Presented to David Winton Thomas.* Ed. P. R. Ackroyd and B. Lindars. Cambridge, 1968. Pp. 183-194.

Places, E. des. *Oracles Chaldaïques avec un choix de commentaires anciens.* Paris, 1971.

Plath, M. "Der neutestamentliche weheruf über Jerusalem (Lk 13, 34-35 = Matth 23, 37-39)," *Theologische Studien und Kritiken,* 78 (1905), 455-460.

Pleket, H. W. "Religious History as the History of Mentality: The 'Believer' as Servant of the Deity in the Greek World," in *Faith, Hope and Worship: Aspects of Religious Mentality in the Ancient World.* Ed. H. S. Versnel. Leiden, 1981. Pp. 152-192.

Plöger, O. "Prophetisches Erbe in den Sekten des frühen Judentums," *TL,* 79 (1954), 291-96.

_____. *Theocracy and Eschatology.* Trans. S. Rudman. Richmond, 1968.

Pollard, J. *Seers, Shrines and Sirens.* London, 1965.

Powell, J. E. *A Lexicon to Herodotus.* Cambridge, 1938.

Preisendanz, K. *Papyri Graecae Magicae: Die griechischen Zauberpapyri.* 2. Aufl. 2 vols. Ed. A. Henrichs. Stuttgart, 1973-74.

Preisigke, D. et al. (eds.). *Samuelbuch griechischer Urkunden aus Ägypten.* Strassburg, 1915ff.

Pridie, J. R. *The Spiritual Gifts.* London, 1921.

Prigent, P. "L'hérésie asiate et l'église confessante de l'Apocalypse à Ignace," *VC,* 31 (1977), 1-22.

Pritchard, J. B. *Ancient Near Eastern Texts Relating to the Old Testament.* 3rd ed. with Supplement. Princeton, 1969.

Pritchett, W. K. *The Greek State at War.* 3 vols. Berkeley and Los Angeles, 1971-79.

Prümm, K. "Mystères," *DBSupp,* VI (1960), 1-225.

_____. *Religionsgeschichtliches Handbuch f. d. Raum der altchristlichen Umwelt.* Rome, 1954.

Quell, G. *Wahre und falsche Propheten.* Gütersloh, 1952.

Rad, G. von. "Die falschen Propheten," *ZAW,* 51 (1933), 109-120.

_____. "The Levitical Sermon in *I* and *II* Chronicles," in *The Problem of the Hexateuch and Other Essays.* Trans. E. W. Trueman Dicken. Edinburgh and London, 1966. Pp. 267-280.

_____. *Old Testament Theology.* 2 vols. Trans. D. M. G. Stalker. New York, 1965.

_____. *Wisdom in Israel.* Trans. J. D. Martin. Nashville, 1972.

Rahnenführer, D. "Das Testament des Hiob und das Neue Testament," *ZNW,* 62 (1971), 68-93.

Raitt, T. "The Prophetic Summons to Repentance," *ZAW,* 83 (1971), 30-49.

Ramsay, W. M. *The Cities and Bishoprics of Phrygia.* 2 vols. Oxford, 1897.

_____. *The Letters to the Seven Churches of Asia.* New York, 1904.

_____. "Roads and Travel (in the New Testament)," *Hastings Dictionary of the Bible,* V, 375-402.

Ramsey, G. M. "Speech-Forms in Hebrew Law and Prophetic Oracles," *JBL,* 96 (1977), 45-58.

Reicke, B. "A Synopsis of Early Christian Preaching," in *The Root of the Vine: Essays in Biblical Theology.* London, 1953. Pp. 128-160.

Reiling, J. *Hermas and Christian Prophecy: A Study of the Eleventh Mandate.* Leiden, 1973.

_____. "Marcus Gnosticus and the New Testament: Eucharist and Prophecy," in *Miscel-*

lanea Neotestamentica. Ed. T. Baarda, A. F. J. Klijn, and W. C. van Unnik. Leiden, 1978. Pp. 161-179.

—————. "Prophecy, the Spirit and the Church," in *Prophetic Vocation in the New Testament and Today.* Ed. J. Panagopoulos. Leiden, 1977. Pp. 58-76.

—————. "The Use of *PSEUDOPROPHĒTĒS* in the Septuagint, Philo and Josephus," *NovT,* 13 (1971), 147-156.

Reitzenstein, R. *Die hellenistischen Mysterienreligionen nach ihren Grundgedanken und Wirkungen.* 2. Aufl. Berlin, 1920.

—————. *Poimandres: Studien zur griechisch-ägyptischen und frühchristlichen Literatur.* Leipzig, 1904.

—————. *Hellenistic Mystery-Religions.* Pittsburgh, 1979.

Reitzenstein, R. and Schaeder, H. H. *Studien zum antiken Synkretismus aus Iran und Griechenland.* Leipzig, 1926.

Rengstorf, K. H. *Das Evangelium nach Lukas.* Göttingen, 1968.

Resch, A. *Agrapha: Aussercanonische Schriftfragmenta.* Reprint, Darmstadt, 1967.

—————. *Der Traum im Heilsplan Gottes: Deutung und Bedeutung des Traums im Alten Testament.* Freiburg, 1964.

—————. *Der Paulinismus und die Logia Jesu.* Leipzig, 1904.

Reventlow, H. G. *Liturgie und prophetisches Ich bei Jeremia.* Gütersloh, 1963.

Rhoads, D. M. *Israel in Revolution: 6-74 C.E. A Political History Based on the Writings of Josephus.* Philadelphia, 1976.

Richter, W. "Traum und Traumdeutung im AT: Ihre Form und Verwendung," *BZ,* 7 (1963), 202ff.

Riesenfeld, H. *The Gospel Tradition and Its Beginnings: A Study in the Limits of Formgeschichte.* London, 1957.

Ringgren, H. *The Faith of Qumran.* Trans. E. T. Sander. Philadelphia, 1963.

—————. *Israelite Religion.* Trans. D. E. Green. Philadelphia, 1966.

—————. "The Impact of the Ancient Near East on Israelite Tradition," in *Tradition and Theology in the Old Testament.* Ed. D. Knight. Philadelphia, 1977. Pp. 31-46.

—————. "Jüdische Apokalyptik," *RGG.* 3. Aufl., I, 464-66.

Rissi, M. *The Future of the World: An Exegetical Study of Revelation 19:11 – 22:15.* Naperville, Illinois, n.d.

Robert, L. *Études anatoliennes.* Paris, 1937.

Roberts, B. J. "The Dead Sea Scrolls and the Old Testament Scriptures," *BJRL,* 36 (1953-54), 75-96.

Robertson, A. and Plummer, A. *A Critical and Exegetical Commentary on the First Epistle of St. Paul to the Corinthians.* Edinburgh, 1914.

Robertson, E. "The 'Urim and Tummim'," *VT,* 14 (1964), 67-74.

Robinson, H. W. *Inspiration and Revelation in the Old Testament.* Oxford, 1946.

Robinson, J. A. T. *Redating the New Testament.* Philadelphia, 1976.

Robinson, J. M. "The Formal Structure of Jesus' Message," in *Current Issues in New Testament Interpretation.* Ed. W. Klassen and G. F. Snyder. New York, 1962. Pp. 91-110.

—————. "LOGOI SOPHON: On the Gattung of Q," in *Trajectories through Early Christianity.* Philadelphia, 1971. Pp. 71-113.

—————. *The Nag Hammadi Documents.* New York and San Francisco, 1978.

Robinson, T. H. "The Council of Yahweh," *JTS,* 45 (1945), 151-57.

—————. "The Prophet in Israel and in Greece," in *Studies in Honour of Gilbert Norwood.* Ed. M. E. White. Toronto, 1952. Pp. 229-238.

Roetzel, C. "The Judgment Form in Paul's Letters," *JBL,* 88 (1969), 305-312.

—————. *Judgment in the Community: A Study of the Relationship between Eschatology and Ecclesiology in Paul.* Leiden, 1972.

Rohde, E. *Psyche, Seelenkult und Unsterblichkeitsglaube der Griechen.* 2 vols. 3. Aufl. Tübingen and Leipzig, 1903.

Roloff, J. *Apostolat — Verkündigung — Kirche.* Gütersloh, 1965.

——————. Das Kerygma und der irdische Jesus: Historische Motive in den Jesus-Erzählungen der Evangelien. Göttingen, 1970.

Ropes, J. H. Die Sprüche Jesu die in den kanonischen Evangelien nicht überliefert sind. Leipzig, 1896.

Roth, C. "The Cleansing of the Temple and Zechariah 14.21," NovT, 4 (1960), 174-181.

Rousseau, F. L'Apocalypse et le milieu prophétique du Nouveau Testament. Paris, 1971.

Rowley, H. H. "Ritual and the Hebrew Prophets," JSS, 1 (1956), 338-360.

Russell, D. S. The Method and Message of Jewish Apocalyptic. Philadelphia, 1964.

Rutherford, W. G. Scholia Aristophania. 3 vols. London, 1896.

Ryle, H. E. The Canon of the Old Testament. London, 1892.

Rzach, A. Oracula Sibyllina. Leipzig, 1891.

Sagnard, F. M. M. La Gnose valentinienne et le témoignage de Saint Irénée. Paris, 1947.

Samain, P. "L'accusation de magie contre le Christ dans les Évangiles," ETL, 15 (1938), 449-490.

Sand, A. Das Gesetz und die Propheten: Untersuchungen zur Theologie des Evangeliums nach Matthäus. Regensburg, 1974.

Sanday, W. and Headlam, A. C. A Critical and Exegetical Commentary on the Epistle of Paul to the Romans. 5th ed. Edinburgh, 1925.

Sanders, J. A. "From Isaiah 61 to Luke 4," in Christianity, Judaism and Other Greco-Roman Cults. Ed. J. Neusner. Vol. 1. Leiden, 1975. Pp. 75-106.

Sanders, J. P. Paul and Palestinian Judaism. Philadelphia, 1977.

Sandmel, S. Judaism and Christian Beginnings. New York, 1978.

Sass, G. Apostelamt und Kirche. München, 1939.

Satake, A. Die Gemeindeordnung in der Johannesapokalypse. Neukirchen, 1966.

Schachter, A. "A Boeotian Cult Type," University of London Institute of Classical Studies Bulletin, 14 (1967), 1-16.

Schäfer, P. Die Vorstellung vom heiligen Geist in der rabbinischen Literatur. München, 1972.

Schalit, A. "Die Erhebung Vespasians nach Flavius Josephus, Talmud und Midrasch. Zur beschichte einer messianischen Prophetie," Aufstieg und Niedergang der römischen Welt. Ed. H. Temporini and W. Haase. Vol. II, part 2. Berlin, 1975. Pp. 208-327.

Schelke, K. H. "Jesus — Lehrer und Prophet," in Orientierung an Jesus: Zur Theologie der Synoptiker. Ed. P. Hoffman et al. Freiburg, 1973. Pp. 300-308.

Schell, H. Religion und Offenbarung. 2. Aufl. Paderborn, 1902.

Schepelern, W. Der Montanismus und die phrygischen Kulte. Tübingen, 1929.

Schille, G. "Das Recht der Propheten und Apostel — gemeinderechtliche Beobachtungen zu Didache Kapitel 11-13," in Theologische Versuche. Ed. P. Wätzel and G. Schille. Berlin, 1966. Pp. 84-103.

——————. Das vorsynoptische Judenchristentum. Stuttgart, 1970.

Schlatter, A. Das Alte Testament in der johanneischen Apokalypse. Gütersloh, 1912.

——————. Die Briefe an die Thessalonicher, Philipper, Timotheus und Titus. Stuttgart, 1950.

——————. The Church in the New Testament Period. Trans. P. P. Levertoff. London, 1955.

Schlier, H. Religionsgeschichtliche Untersuchungen zu den Ignatiusbriefen. Giessen, 1929.

——————. Der Apostel und seine Gemeinde: Auslegung des ersten Briefes an die Thessalonicher. 2. Aufl. Freiburg, 1972.

——————. Der Brief an die Galater. 13. Aufl. Göttingen, 1965.

Schmeichel, W. "Christian Prophecy in Lukan Thought: Luke 4:16-30 as a Point of Departure," in SBL Seminar Papers for 1976. Missoula, 1976. Pp. 293-304.

Schmidt, D. "The LXX Gattung 'Prophetic Correlative'," JBL, 96 (1977), 517-522.

Schmidt, J. M. Die jüdische Apokalyptik: Die Geschichte ihrer Erforschung von den Anfängen bis zu den Textfunden von Qumran. Neukirchen-Vluyn, 1963.

Schmidt, K. L. Der Rahmen der Geschichte Jesu: Literarkritische Untersuchungen zur ältesten Jesusüberlieferung. Reprint, Darmstadt, 1963.

Schmidt, P. Der erste Thessalonicherbrief. Berlin, 1885.

Schmiedel, P. W. Thessalonicher, Korinth. 2. Aufl. Tübingen, 1892.

Schmithals, W. *Paul and the Gnostics.* Trans. J. E. Steely. Nashville, 1972.

──────. *Gnosticism in Corinth: An Investigation of the Letters to the Corinthians.* Trans. J. E. Steely. Nashville and New York, 1971.

Schnackenburg, R. "Die Erwartung des Propheten nach dem Neuen Testament und den Qumrantexten," *TU,* 73 (1959), 622-639.

──────. *Die Johannesbriefe.* 2. Aufl. Freiburg, Basel, and Wien, 1963.

──────. *Das Johannesevangelium.* 2 vols. Freiburg, Basel, and Wien, 1971-72.

Schneider, C. *Die Erlebnisechtheit der Apokalypse des Johannes.* Leipzig, 1930.

Schneider, O. *Nicandrea.* Leipzig, 1856.

Schnider, F. *Jesus der Prophet.* Fribourg, 1973.

Schoeps, H. J. "Die jüdischen Prophetenmorde," in *Aus frühchristlichen Zeit: Religionsgeschichtliche Untersuchungen.* Tübingen, 1950. Pp. 126-143.

──────. *Studien zur unbekannten Religions- und Geistesgeschichte.* Göttingen, 1963.

Scholem, G. *Major Trends in Jewish Mysticism.* 3rd ed. New York, 1961.

Schrage, W. *Die konkreten Einzelgebote in der paulinischen Paränese.* Gütersloh, 1961.

Schreiner, J. "Die apokalyptische Bewegung," in *Literatur und Religion des Frühjudentums.* Würzburg and Gütersloh, 1973. Pp. 214-253.

──────. "Interpretation innerhalb der schriftlichen Überlieferung," in *Literatur und Religion des Frühjudentums.* Würzburg and Gütersloh, 1973. Pp. 19-30.

Schroeder, D. "Lists, Ethical," *The Interpreter's Dictionary of the Bible, Supplementary Volume.* Nashville, 1976. Pp. 546-47.

──────. "Parenesis," *The Interpreter's Dictionary of the Bible, Supplementary Volume.* Nashville, 1976. P. 643.

Schubart, W. "Orakelfragen," *Zeitschrift für ägyptische Sprache und Altertumsurkunde,* 67 (1931), 110-15.

Schulz, S. *Q: Die Spruchquelle der Evangelisten.* Zürich, 1972.

Schulz, W. *Rätsel aus dem hellenischen Kulturkreise.* Vol. I. Leipzig, 1909.

Schürer, E. *The History of the Jewish People in the Age of Jesus Christ.* Rev. ed. G. Vermes and F. Millar. Vol. I. Edinburgh, 1973.

──────. "Die Prophetin Isabel in Thyatira: Offenb. Johan. 2.20," *Theologische Abhandlungen.* Freiburg, i. B., 1892. Pp. 37-58.

Schürmann, H. "Die Symbolhandlungen Jesu als eschatologische Erfüllungszeichen," *BLit,* 11 (1970), 29-41, 73-78.

──────. *Traditionsgeschichtliche Untersuchungen zu den synoptischen Evangelien.* Düsseldorf, 1968.

Schütz, J. H. *Paul and the Anatomy of Apostolic Authority.* London, 1975.

Schweitzer, A. *The Mysticism of Paul the Apostle.* Trans. W. Montgomery. New York, 1931.

──────. *The Quest of the Historical Jesus.* Trans. W. Montgomery. London, 1910.

Schweizer, E. *The Good News According to Mark.* Trans. D. H. Madvig. Richmond, 1970.

──────. *Church Order in the New Testament.* Trans. F. Clarke. London, 1961.

──────. *Matthäus und seine Gemeinde.* Stuttgart, 1974.

──────. "The Service of Worship," in *Neotestamentica.* Zürich, 1963.

──────. "Observance of the Law and the Charismatic Activity in Matthew," *NTS,* 16 (1970-71), 213-230.

Schwenn, F. "Pindaros," *PW,* 20 (1950), 1606-97.

Scobie, C. H. H. *John the Baptist.* Philadelphia, 1964.

Scroggs, R. "Paul as Rhetorician: Two Homilies in Romans 1-11," in *Jews, Greeks and Christians: Religious Cultures in Late Antiquity.* Ed. R. Hamerton-Kelly and R. Scroggs. Leiden, 1976. Pp. 271-298.

Seierstad, I. P. *Die Offenbarungserlebnisse der Propheten Amos, Jesaja und Jeremia.* 2. Aufl. Oslo, 1965.

──────. "Forholdet mellom Åpenbaringsopplevelsen og Utformingen av Budskapet hos Skriftprofetene," in *Budskapet: Et utvalg av gammeltestamentlige artikler.* Oslo, 1971. Pp. 41-55.

Sellin, E. and Fohrer, G. *Einleitung in das Alte Testament.* 10 Aufl. Heidelberg, 1965.

_____. *Introduction to the Old Testament.* Trans. D. E. Green. Nashville, 1968.

Selwyn, E. C. *The Christian Prophets and the Prophetic Apocalypse.* London, 1900.

_____. *The Oracles in the New Testament.* London, 1912.

Selwyn, E. G. *The First Epistle of St. Peter.* London, 1946.

Sethe, K. "Die Berufung eines Hohenpriesters des Amon unter Ramses II," *Zeitschrift für ägyptische Sprach und Altertumsurkunde,* 44 (1907-8), 30-35.

Siber, P. *Mit Christus Leben: Eine Studie zur paulinischen Auferstehungshoffnung.* Zürich, 1971.

Silberman, L. H. "Unriddling the Riddle: A Study in the Structure and Language of the Habakkuk Pesher," *RQ,* 3 (1961), 323-364.

Simon, M. "La migration à Pella: legende ou réalité?" *RSR,* 60 (1972), 37-54.

Sint, J. A. *Pseudonymität im Altertum, ihre Formen und ihre Gründe.* Innsbruck, 1960.

Sjöberg, E. *Der verborgene Menschensohn in den Evangelien.* Lund, 1955.

Skard, E. "Zum temporalem Gebrauch von *houtōs,*" *SO,* 37 (1961), 151-52.

Skeat, T. C. and Turner, E. G. "An Oracle of Hermes Trismegistos at Saqqâra," *Journal of Egyptian Archaeology,* 54 (1968), 199-208.

Slater, D. A. "Was the Fourth Eclogue Written to Celebrate the Marriage of Octavia to Mark Antony? — A Literary Parallel," *CR,* 26 (1912), 114-19.

Smallwood, E. M. *Philonis Alexandrini Legatio ad Gaium.* 2nd ed. Leiden, 1970.

Smelser, N. J. *Theory of Collective Behavior.* New York, 1962.

Smith, J. Z. "Good News is No News: Aretalogy and Gospel," in *Christianity, Judaism and Other Greco-Roman Cults.* Ed. J. Neusner. Vol. I. Leiden, 1975. Pp. 21-38.

_____. "Native Cults in the Hellenistic Period," *History of Religions,* 11 (1971-72), 236-249.

_____. "Wisdom and Apocalyptic," in *Religious Syncretism in Antiquity: Essays in Conversation with Geo Widengren.* Ed. B. A. Pearson. Missoula, 1975. Pp. 131-156.

Smith, M. *Jesus the Magician.* New York, 1978.

_____. "Zealots and Sicarii, Their Origins and Relation," *HTR,* 64 (1971), 1-19.

_____. "A Comparison of Early Christian and Early Rabbinic Tradition," *JBL,* 82 (1963), 169-176.

_____. "Palestinian Judaism in the First Century," in *Israel: Its Role in Civilization.* Ed. M. Davis. New York, 1966.

_____. "Prolegomena to a Discussion of Aretalogies, Divine Men, the Gospels and Jesus," *JBL,* 90 (1971), 74-99.

_____. "On the Wine God in Palestine," in *Salo Wittmayer Baron Jubilee Volume.* 3 vols. Ed. S. Lieberman. Jerusalem, 1975. Vol. II, pp. 815-829.

_____. *Tannaitic Parallels to the Gospels.* Philadelphia, 1951.

Smith, W. D. "The So-Called Possession in Pre-Christian Greece," *Transactions and Proceedings of the American Philological Association,* 96 (1965), 403-436.

Smyth, H. W. *Greek Grammar.* Rev. G. M. Messing. Cambridge, 1956.

Snell, B. (ed.). *Pindarus.* 3. Aufl. 2 vols. Leipzig, 1959 and 1964.

Snyder, G. *The Shepherd of Hermas.* Vol. 6 of *The Apostolic Fathers: A New Translation and Commentary.* Ed. R. M. Grant. London, 1968.

Soden, W. von. "Verkündigung des Gotteswillens durch prophetisches Wort in den altbabylonischen Briefen aus Mâri," *Die Welt des Orients,* 1 (1947-52), 397-403.

Souček, J. B. "La prophétie dans le Nouveau Testament," *CommViat,* 4 (1961), 221-231.

Speyer, W. *Die literarische Fälschung im heidnischen und christlichen Altertum.* München, 1971.

Spicq, C. *Les épitres Pastorales.* 4th ed. 2 vols. Paris, 1969.

Spinoza, B. *Spinoza Opera: Im Auftrag der Heidelberger Akademie der Wissenschaften.* Vol. 3. Heidelberg, 1925.

Stachowiak, L. R. "Paraenesis Paulina et Instructio de duobus spiritibus in 'Regula' Qumranensi," *Verbum Dominum,* 51 (1963), 245-250.

Staehlin, R. *Das Motiv der Mantik im antiken Drama.* Giessen, 1912.

Stanford, W. G. *The Odyssey, Edited with General and Grammatical Introduction, Commentary, and Indexes.* 2 vols. London, 1947-48.

Stauffer, E. "Der Methurgeman des Petrus," in *Neutestamentliche Aufsätze*. Ed. J. Blinzler, O. Kuss, and F. Mussner. Regensburg, 1963. Pp. 283-293.

Steck, O. H. *Israel und das gewaltsame Geschick der Propheten*. Neukirchen, 1967.

_____. *Israel und das gewaltsame Geschick der Propheten*. Heidelberg, 1965.

_____. "Formgeschichtliche Bemerkungen zur Darstellung des Damaskusgeschehens in der Apostelgeschichte," *ZNW*, 67 (1976), 20-28.

Steck, R. "Das Herrenwort 1. Thess. 4,15," *Jahrbücher für protestantische Theologie*, 13 (1883), 509-523.

Stendahl, K. *The School of St. Matthew and Its Use of the Old Testament*. 2nd ed. Philadelphia, 1967.

Stone, M. E. "Apocalyptic — Vision or Hallucination," *Milla wa-Milla*, 14 (1974), 47-56.

Stowers, S. K. *The Diatribe and Paul's Letter to the Romans*. Chico, 1981.

Strack, H. L. and Billerbeck, P. *Kommentar zum Neuen Testament aus Talmud und Midrasch*. 5 vols. München, 1922-61.

Strecker, G. *Das Judenchristentum in den Pseudoklementinen*. Berlin, 1958.

_____. *Der Weg der Gerechtigkeit*. 3. Aufl. Göttingen, 1971.

Streeter, B. H. *The Primitive Church*. New York, 1929.

Strobel, A. "In dieser Nacht (Luk 17,34)," *ZTK*, 58 (1961), 16-29.

Strugnell, J. " 'Amen, I Say Unto You' in the Sayings of Jesus and in Early Christian Literature," *HTR*, 67 (1974), 177-182.

Suggs, M. J. *Wisdom, Christology, and Law in Matthew's Gospel*. Cambridge, Mass., 1970.

Suter, D. W. "Apocalyptic Patterns in the Similitudes of Enoch," in *SBL Seminar Papers for 1978*. Missoula, 1978. Vol. I, pp. 1-13.

_____. "Tradition and Composition in the Parables of Enoch." Ph.D. dissertation, University of Chicago, 1977.

Swete, H. B. *The Apocalypse of St. John*. Grand Rapids, n.d.

_____. *The Holy Spirit in the New Testament*. London, 1909.

Szörényi, A. "Das Buch Daniel, ein kanonisierter *pescher?*" *Volume du Congrès, Genève 1965*. VT Supp. 15. Leiden, 1966. Pp. 278-294.

Tarn, W. W. *Alexander the Great*. 2 vols. Cambridge, 1948.

_____. "Alexander Helios and the Golden Age," *JRS*, 2 (1932), 135-160.

Tarn, W. W. and Charlesworth, M. P. "The War of the East Against the West," in *The Cambridge Ancient History*, vol. 10: *The Augustan Empire 44 B.C. — A.D. 70*. Cambridge, 1934. Pp. 66-111.

Tatum, W. B. "The Epoch of Israel: Luke I-II and the Theological Plan of Luke-Acts," *NTS*, 13 (1966-67), 184-195.

Taylor, A. E. *A Commentary on Plato's Timaeus*. Oxford, 1928.

Taylor, V. *The Formation of the Gospel Tradition*. London, 1953.

_____. *The Gospel According to St. Mark*. 2nd ed. London, 1966.

_____. *The Passion Narrative of St. Luke: A Critical and Historical Investigation*. Cambridge, 1972.

_____. *The Person of Christ in New Testament Teaching*. London, 1950.

Tcherikover, V. A. *Hellenistic Civilization and the Jews*. Trans. J. S. Applebaum. Philadelphia, 1959.

Tcherikover, V. A., Fuks, A. and Stern, M. (eds.). *Corpus Papyrorum Judaicarum*. 3 vols. Cambridge, Mass., 1957-64.

Teeple, H. M. *The Mosaic Eschatological Prophet*. Philadelphia, 1957.

Theissen, G. "Legitimation und Lebensunterhalt: Ein Beitrag zur Soziologie urchristlicher Missionare," *NTS*, 21 (1975), 192-221.

_____. *Sociology of Early Palestinian Christianity*. Trans. J. Bowden. Philadelphia, 1978.

_____. "Soziale Schichtung in der korinthischen Gemeinde; ein Beitrag zur Soziologie der hellenistischen Urchristentums," *ZNW*, 65 (1974), 232-272.

_____. "Die soziologische Auswertung religiöser Überlieferungen: ihre methodologischen Probleme am Beispiel des Urchristentums," *Kairos*, 17 (1975), 284-299.

————. "Die Tempelweissagung Jesu. Prophetie in Spannungsfeld von Stadt und Land," *TZ,* 32 (1976), 144-158.

————. "Wanderradikalismus: Literatursoziologische Aspekte der Überlieferung von Worten Jesu im Urchristentum," *ZTK,* 70 (1973), 245-271.

Therrien, G. *Le discernment dans les écrits pauliniens.* Paris, 1973.

Thieme, G. *Die Inschriften von Magnesia am Mäander und das Neue Testament.* Borna-Lepizig, 1905.

Thomas, J. *Le movement baptiste en Palestine et Syrie (150 av. J.-C. — 300 ap. J.-C.).* Gembloux, 1935.

Thompson, L. L. "Cult and Eschatology in the Apocalypse of John," *JR,* 49 (1969), 330-350.

Thrämer, E. "Health and Gods of Healing (Greek)," *Encyclopedia of Religion and Ethics,* VI, 540-553.

Thrupp, S. (ed.). *Millennial Dreams in Action: Studies in Revolutionary Religious Movements.* New York, 1970.

Thyen, H. *Der Stil der jüdisch-hellenistischen Homilie.* Göttingen, 1956.

Tödt, H. E. *The Son of Man in the Synoptic Tradition.* Trans. D. M. Barton. Philadelphia, 1965.

Torrey, C. C. *Documents of the Primitive Church.* New York, 1941.

————. *The Lives of the Prophets: Greek Texts and Translation.* Philadelphia, 1946.

Toy, C. H. *Quotations in the New Testament.* New York, 1884.

Trilling, W. "Amt und Amtsverständnis bei Matthäus," in *Mélanges bibliques en hommage au R. P. Béda Rigaux.* Ed. A. Descamps and A. de Halleux. Gembloux, 1970. Pp. 29-44.

Tucker, G. M. *Form Criticism of the Old Testament.* Philadelphia, 1971.

————. "Prophetic Speech," *Interpretation,*, 32 (1978), 31-45.

Turner, N. *Style.* Vol. 4 of *Grammar of New Testament Greek.* Ed. J. H. Moulton. Edinburgh, 1976.

Turner, V. *The Ritual Process: Structure and Anti-Structure.* Baltimore, 1974.

Unnik, W. C. van. "A Formula Describing Prophecy," *NTS,* 9 (1963), 86-94.

————. " 'Den Geist löschet nicht aus' (1 Thessalonicher V 19)," *NovT,* 10 (1968), 255-269.

————. "A Greek Characteristic of Prophecy in the Fourth Gospel," in *Text and Interpretation.* Ed. E. Best and R. McL. Wilson. Cambridge, 1979. Pp. 211-229.

————. "Die Prophetie bei Josephus," in *Flavius Josephus als historischer Schriftsteller.* Heidelberg, 1978. Pp. 41-45.

Urbach, E. E. "When Did Prophecy Disappear" (Hebrew), *Tarbiz,* 17 (1945-46), 1-11.

Vaux, R. de. *Ancient Israel.* 2 vols. Trans. J. McHugh. New York, 1965.

Vermes, G. *Scripture and Tradition in Judaism: Haggadic Studies.* 2nd ed. Leiden, 1973.

Vermeylen, J. *Du prophète Isaie à l'apocalyptique.* 2 vols. Paris, 1977-78.

Vidman, S. *Sylloge Inscriptionum Religionis Isiacae et Sarapiacae.* Berlin, 1969.

Veilhauer, P. "Gottesreich und Menschensohn," in *Festschrift für Günther Dehn.* Ed. W. Schneemelcher. Neukirchen, 1957. Pp. 51-79.

Vögtle, A. "Exegetische Erwägungen über das Wissen und Selbstbewusstsein Jesu," in *Gott in Welt: Festgabe für K. Rahner.* 2 vols. Ed. J. B. Metz et al. Freiburg, 1964. Vol. I, pp. 608-667.

Vollgraff, W. *Bulletin de Correspondence Hellénique,* 33 (1909), 450-55 (no. 22).

Volz, P. *Jüdische Eschatologie von Daniel bis Akiba.* 2. Aufl. Tübingen, 1934.

Vos, L. A. *The Synoptic Traditions in the Apocalypse.* Kampen, 1965.

Wacholder, B. Z. "Chronomessianism: The Timing of Messianic Movements and the Calendar of Sabbatical Cycles," *HUCA,* 46 (1975), 201-218.

Wackernagel, J. *Vorlesungen über Syntax mit besonderer Berücksichtigung von Griechisch, Lateinisch und Deutsch.* 2. Reihe. Basel, 1924.

Warmuth, G. *Das Mahnwort: Seine Bedeutung für die Verkündigung der vorexilischen Propheten Amos, Hosea, Micha, Jesaja und Jeremia.* Frankfurt a. M., 1976.

Waszink, J. H. "Die sogenannte Fünfteilung der Träume bei Chalcidius und Ihre Quellen," *Mnemosyne,* 9 (1941), 65-85.

_____. *Tertullian: De Anima.* Amsterdam, 1947.

Weber, W. *Josephus und Vespasian: Untersuchungen zu dem jüdischen Krieg des Flavius Josephus.* Stuttgart, 1921.

_____. *Der Prophet und sein Gott: Eine Studie zur vierten Ekloge Vergils.* Leipzig, 1925.

Wegenast, K. *Das Verständnis der Tradition bei Paulus und in den Deuteropaulinen.* Neukirchen, 1962.

Weimar, P. "Formen frühjüdischer Literatur: Ein Skizze," in *Literatur und Religion des Frühjudentums.* Ed. J. Maier and J. Schreiner. Würzburg, 1973.

Weinel, H. *Die Wirkungen des Geistes und der Geister im nachapostolischen Zeitalter bis auf Irenäus.* Freiburg, 1899.

_____. *Die Wirkungen des Heiligen Geistes nach den populären Anschauungen der apostolischen Zeit und den Lehre des Apostels Paulus.* Göttingen, 1909.

Weinfeld, M. "Ancient Near Eastern Patterns in Prophetic Literature," *VT,* 27 (1977), 178-195.

_____. *Deuteronomy and the Deuteronomic School.* Oxford, 1972.

Weinrich, O. "Alexandros der Lügenprophet und seine Stellung in der Religiosität des 2. Jahrhunderts n. Chr.," *Neue Jahrbücher für das klassische Altertum,* 47 (1921), 129-151.

_____. "Antike Himmelsbriefe," in *Ausgewählte Schriften.* Ed. G. Wille. Vol. 1. Amsterdam, 1969. Pp. 5-6.

_____. *Ausgewählte Schriften.* Ed. G. Wille. Vol. 1. Amsterdam, 1969.

_____. "Menekrates Zeus und Salmoneus," in *Religionsgeschichtliche Studien.* .Darmstadt, 1968. Pp. 299-434.

_____. "Türöffnung im Wunder-, Prodigien- und Zauberglauben der Antike, des Judentums und Christentums," in *Genethliakon Wilhelm Schmid.* Stuttgart, 1929. Pp. 200-464.

_____. "Typisches und Individuelles in der Religiosität des Älius Aristides," *Neue Jahrbücher für das klassische Altertum,* 33 (1914), 597-606.

Weiser, A. *Einleitung in das Alte Testament.* 5. Aufl. Göttingen, 1963.

_____. *The Old Testament: Its Formation and Development.* Trans. D. M. Barton. New York, 1961.

Weiss, B. *Biblical Theology of the New Testament.* 2 vols. Trans. D. Eaton. Edinburgh, 1888.

Weiss, J. *Der erste Korintherbrief.* 10. Aufl. Göttingen, 1925.

_____. *Earliest Christianity: A History of the Period A.D. 30-150.* 2 vols. Trans. F. C. Grant et al. New York, 1959.

_____. *Jesus' Proclamation of the Kingdom of God.* Trans. and ed. R. H. Hiers and D. L. Holland. Philadelphia, 1971.

Wellhausen, J. *Analyse der Offenbarung Johannis.* Berlin, 1907.

_____. *Das Evangelium Marci.* Berlin, 1903.

Wendland, H.-D. *Die Briefe an die Korinther.* 10. Aufl. Göttingen, 1964.

Werblowsky, R. J. Z. "Prophet," *Encyclopedia Britannica* (1973), XVIII, 633-35.

_____. "Le prophétisme dans le judaïsme contemporain," *Lumière et Vie,* 22 (1973), 40-47.

West, M. L. "Oracles of Apollo Kareios: A Revised Text," *Zeitschrift für Papyrologie und Epigraphik,* 1 (1967), 183-87.

Westermann, C. *Basic Forms of Prophetic Speech.* Trans. H. C. White. Philadelphia, 1967.

_____. "Die Begriffe für Fragen und Suchen im Alten Testament," *Kerygma und Dogma,* 6 (1960), 2-30.

_____. "Das Heilswort bei Deuterojesaja," *ET,* 24 (1964), 355-373.

_____. *Isaiah 40—66: A Commentary.* Trans. D. M. G. Stalker. Philadelphia, 1969.

_____. "Sprache und Struktur der Prophetie Deuterojesajas," in *Forschung am Alten Testament.* München, 1964. Pp. 92-170.

Wetter, G. P. "Die Damascusvision und das paulinische Evangelium," in *Festgabe für A. Jülicher.* Tübingen, 1927. Pp. 80-92.

White, J. L. *The Form and Structure of the Official Petition: A Study in Greek Epistolography.* Missoula, 1972.

White, J. L. and Kensinger, K. A. "Categories of Greek Papyrus Letters," in *SBL Seminar Papers for 1976.* Missoula, 1976. Pp. 79-91.

White, R. J. (ed.). *Artemidorus, The Interpretation of Dreams (Oneirocritica).* Park Ridge, New Jersey, 1975.

Whiteley, D. E. H. *Thessalonians.* London, 1969.

Wieder, N. "The 'Law-Interpreter' of the Sect of the Dead Sea Scrolls: The Second Moses," *JJS,* 4 (1953), 158-175.

Wiegand, T. *Didyma.* 2. Teil: *Die Inschriften.* Ed. A. Rehm and R. Harder. Berlin, 1958.

Wikenhauser, A. "Doppelträume," *Biblica,* 29 (1958), 100-111.

————. "Die Traumgesichte des Neuen Testaments in religionsgeschichtliche Sicht," in *Piscicule: Studien zur Religion und Kultur des Altertums.* Ed. T. Klauser and A. Rücker. Münster, 1939. Pp. 320-333.

Wilamowitz-Moellendorff, U. von. *Der Glaube der Hellenen.* 2 vols. Berlin, 1931-32.

————. *Pindaros.* Berlin, 1922.

Wilcke, H.-A. *Das Problem eines messianischen Zwischenreichs bei Paulus.* Zürich, 1967.

Wilcken, U. *Alexander der Gross.* Leipzig, 1931.

Wiles, G. *Paul's Intercessory Prayers.* Cambridge, 1974.

Williams, C. G. "Ecstaticism in Hebrew Prophecy and Christian Glossolalia," *SR,* 3 (1973-74), 320-338.

Williams, J. G. "The Prophetic 'Father': A Brief Explanation of the Term 'Sons of the Prophets'," *JBL,* 85 (1966), 344-48.

Wilson, B. R. *Magic and the Millennium: A Sociological Study of Religious Movements of Protest among Tribal and Third-World Peoples.* New York, 1973.

Wilson, R. R. "Early Israelite Prophecy," *Interpretation,* 32 (1978), 3-16.

————. "Form-Critical Investigation of the Prophetic Literature: The Present Situation," in *SBL Seminar Papers for 1973.* 2 vols. Cambridge, Mass., 1973. Vol. I, pp. 100-127.

————. "Prophecy and Ecstasy: A Reexamination," *JBL,* 98 (1979), 321-337.

————. *Prophecy and Society in Ancient Israel.* Philadelphia, 1980.

————. "Prophecy and Society in Ancient Israel: The Present State of the Inquiry," in *SBL Seminar Papers for 1977.* Missoula, 1977. Pp. 341-358.

Wilson, W. J. "The Career of the Prophet Hermas," *HTR,* 20 (1927), 21-62.

Winandy, J. "La prophétie de Syméon (Lc ii, 34-35)," *RB,* 72 (1965), 321-351.

Windisch, H. "Jesus und der Geist," in *Studies in Early Christianity.* Ed. S. J. Case. New York and London, 1928. Pp. 206-236.

————. *Die Orakel des Hystaspes.* Amsterdam, 1929.

————. *Paulus und Christus.* Leipzig, 1934.

Wink, W. *John the Baptist in the Gospel Tradition.* Cambridge, 1968.

Winnington-Ingram, R. P. "The Role of Apollo in the Oresteia," *CR,* 47 (1933), 97-104.

Winter, M. *Pneumatiker und Psychicker in Korinth.* Marburg, 1975.

Witt, R. E. *Isis in the Graeco-Roman World.* Ithaca, 1971.

Wolff, C. *Jeremia im Früjudentum und Urchristentum.* Berlin, 1976.

Wolff, G. *Porphrii de Philosophia ex Oraculis Haurienda.* Berlin, 1856.

Wolff, H. W. "Die Begründungen der prophetischen Heils- und Unheilssprüche," *ZNW,* 11 (1934), 1-22.

————. *Hosea.* Trans. G. Stansell. Ed. P. Hanson. Philadelphia, 1974.

————. *Joel and Amos.* Trans. W. Janzen et al. Ed. S. D. McBride. Philadelphia, 1977.

————. "Prophecy from the Eighth through the Fifth Century," *Interpretation,* 32 (1978), 17-30.

Wolfson, H. A. *Philo: Foundations of Religious Philosophy in Judaism, Christianity, and Islam.* 2 vols. Cambridge, Mass., 1947.

Worsley, P. *The Trumpet Shall Sound: A Study of 'Cargo' Cults in Melanesia.* 2nd ed. New York, 1968.

Woude, A. S. van der. *Die messianischen Vorstellungen der Gemeinde von Qumran.* Assen, 1957.

Wrege, H.-T. *Die Überlieferungsgeschichte der Bergpredigt.* Tübingen, 1968.

Wuellner, W. "Haggadic Homily Genre in I Corinthians 1-3," *JBL,* 89 (1970), 199-204.

_____. "The Sociological Implications of I Corinthians 1:26-28 Reconsidered," *TU,* 112 (1973), 666-672.

Young, F. W. "Jesus the Prophet: A Re-Examination," *JBL,* 68 (1949), 285-299.

Zahn, T. *Der Hirt des Hermas.* Gotha, 1868.

_____. *Ignatius von Antiochien.* Gotha, 1873.

_____. *Introduction to the New Testament.* 3 vols. Trans. J. M. Trout et al. Edinburgh, 1909.

_____. *Die Offenbarung des Johannes.* 2 vols. Leipzig and Erlangen, 1924-26.

Zeitlin, S. "Dreams and Their Interpretation from the Biblical Period to the Tannaitic Time: An Historical Study," *JQR,* 66 (1975), 1-18.

Ziegler, K. *Plutarchos von Chaironeia.* 2nd ed. Stuttgart, 1964.

Zimmerli, W. *Ezekiel 1.* Trans. R. E. Clements. Ed. F. M. Cross et al. Philadelphia, 1979.

_____. "Das Wort des göttlichen Selbsterweises (Erweiswort), eine prophetische Gattung," in *Gottes Offenbarung: Gesammelte Aufsätze zum Alten Testament.* München, 1963. Pp. 120-132.

Zimmermann, H. "Das absolute *Egō eimi* als die neutestamentliche Offenbarungsformel," *BZ,* 4 (1960), 54-69, 226-276.

INDEXES

I. SUBJECTS

II. AUTHORS

III. FOREIGN WORDS AND PHRASES

A. GREEK

IV. PASSAGES

A. OLD TESTAMENT